ADO *and* ADO.NET
Programming

ADO *and* ADO.NET Programming

Mike Gunderloy

SYBEX

San Francisco · London

Associate Publisher: Richard Mills

Acquisitions and Developmental Editor: Denise Santoro Lincoln

Editor: Jim Gabbert

Production Editor: Liz Burke

Technical Editor: Acey J. Bunch

Graphic Illustrator: Tony Jonick

Electronic Publishing Specialist: Maureen Forys, Happenstance Type-O-Rama

Proofreaders: Nancy Riddiough, Yariv Rabinovitch, Nelson Kim, Nanette Duffy, Jennifer Campbell, Laurie O'Connell

Indexer: Ted Laux

CD Coordinator: Erica Yee

CD Technician: Kevin Ly

Cover Designer: Caryl Gorska, Gorska Design

Cover Illustrator/Photographer: Jon Morgan, Photo Japan

This one's for Di and Shelley—
always close despite the distance.

Foreword

No application gets very far without data access. Any project you take on will, at some point, need some way to read, modify, and manipulate data. If you're using Microsoft technology, you'll most likely use ADO or ADO.NET as your data-access API. If you're using VBA or VB 6, ADO is your best bet. If you're using the .NET platform, you'll probably use ADO.NET. In any case, it's imperative that you learn at least the basics of working with either or both of these APIs. But that's no simple task. Although Microsoft has done a lot of work to make both of these APIs as full-featured and functional as possible, the company hasn't focused on ease of use or ease of discovery. The documentation is acceptable, but you're not going to get far with only that information.

Therefore, you need this book. You're going to need help, and Mike Gunderloy can provide it. He has certainly helped me out over the years. I've known and worked with Mike since 1993, and honestly, I haven't run across anyone who can figure things out and explain them as well as Mike. He's been doing it for at least 15 years, and he's got the techniques wired.

Back in 1993, before we met personally, Mike and I had conversed online for months, providing support for Microsoft Access on the public CompuServe forums. I traveled to New York on business, and Mike and I agreed to meet, in 3D, in the lobby of a Manhattan hotel. We headed out to a nearby deli and chatted for several hours about data, technology, and Microsoft. I don't remember the exact details, but that conversation made it clear that Mike was someone I wanted to know. I'm sure you would feel the same way if you were to meet him. Since then, we've worked together on books, development projects, courseware, consulting projects, and conference talks. I've seen Mike explain everything from project management to concurrency issues in SQL Server.

In this book, Mike attempts to cover as much of ADO and ADO.NET as he can cram into a reasonably sized book. He has done the research, culling the important issues that you'll face right away, and has compiled it in this one volume. You may find more detail in the online help, but you won't find the perspective that you'll discover here. Mike has added his own unique point of view, incorporating tips to help you make the best use of these complex technologies without requiring you to wade through the mountains of documentation. And that's the point, right? Start here, get the ideas about what ADO and ADO.NET can do, and then begin working. Use the online help as necessary, but I'd guess that you'll find yourself coming back to Mike's book frequently for more suggestions, help, and information about ADO and ADO.NET.

I must confess that when Mike and I first discussed this book, I was a bit surprised that he would write a book covering both ADO and ADO.NET. I tried to talk him out of it. Why would anyone want a book about both? He was committed to the project, however, and continued with the original plan. What has become clear now, as ADO.NET has come under scrutiny, is that many developers will continue to use both ADO and ADO.NET, supporting legacy applications and writing new applications concurrently. It's important to take both APIs into account at the same time, comparing and contrasting their behaviors. Mike has taken on this task, and I think he's done an admirable job.

I have a copy of every book Mike has worked on during the past 10 years (including several we've coauthored, making it clear that I'm not totally unbiased here), and I haven't found another technical author more capable of digging in, explaining, and clarifying complex technical topics. I hope you will agree, after reading this book. I've found a number of new ADO.NET issues here that I had missed in my own research. I'm sure you will, too.

Ken Getz
Senior Consultant, MCW Technologies, LLC
Coauthor of *Access 2002 Desktop* and
Enterprise Developer's Handbooks

Acknowledgments

As always, my thanks go to the editorial team who helped turn this book from a vague idea into a finished volume: Richard Mills, Denise Santoro Lincoln, Christine McGeever, Liz Burke, Jim Gabbert, and Acey Bunch. Thanks also to the production team who took care of much of the hard work: Maureen Forys, Tony Jonick, Nancy Riddiough, Yariv Rabinovitch, Nelson Kim, Nanette Duffy, Jennifer Campbell, Laurie O'Connell, Erica Yee, and Kevin Ly.

In addition to writing the foreword, Ken Getz was always available to help me sort out knotty programming issues. Andy Baron, Mary Chipman, and Brian Randell have also contributed much to my understanding of data access over the years. Of course, any remaining misunderstandings are due to my own pigheadedness.

The readers of "Smart Access Extra" and the contributors to the AccessD mailing list provoked me to dig into various odd corners of the ADO world. Thanks for the inspiration.

Tim Sneath, Joe Jorden, Mary Chipman, Ken Getz, and other coauthors all worked with me on previous books that helped contribute to the knowledge that shaped this one. I appreciate my coauthors even more after writing this one by myself.

And, as always, deep and eternal thanks to Dana Jones for helping raise babies, vegetables, and farm animals, and for generally keeping me sane. Special thanks to Adam for his smile and hugs. Books are always easier to write when life is good.

Contents at a Glance

Contents

Introduction

The first database I ever used on a PC was PC-File. Oh, you've probably never heard of it, but in its day, this product of Buttonware (the company founded by Jim Button, who is sometimes known as "the father of shareware") was terribly advanced. PC-File was a flat-file database that you could actually configure yourself, and in the mid- to late 1980s, I used it extensively to manage mailing lists and other information.

But all the information I had in PC-File is long gone, a victim of changing magnetic media sizes and an obsolete file format. Generalized APIs for PC database access hadn't been invented yet. If you put your data in PC-File, it stayed there.

In the early 1990s, after a brief stint of programming Q&A (a horrid integrated program about which the less said, the better), I moved over to Microsoft Access for my database needs. Windows brought a burst of innovative programming to the PC scene (although for a while, no one was quite sure whether Windows or OS/2 was going to be the more widely adopted platform), and Access was part of that burst. Not only could that desktop database do things that PC-File and Q&A never dreamed of, it could actually read data that was stored in other file formats. You could use Access to steal data right out from under a dBASE programmer if you wanted to. And there was also the first of the Microsoft data-access object models, DAO, to puzzle over. I can still remember reporting as a bug the fact that Users had a Groups collection and Groups had a Users collection—a feature, of course, that was completely intentional.

There were a few fits and starts on the Microsoft data-access front after that, but in 1996, the first version of ADO came out, and a new acronym, UDA—universal data access—started showing up in Microsoft literature. I personally tend to think of UDA as plumbing. There are standard pipe sizes that you can hook up to one another. Tighten all the joints, turn the valve, and data flows from one end of your application to the other. There are joints and couplers for hooking different sizes of pipe together, so that everything can be connected, no matter where it comes from. With ADO, you can learn the patterns of data-access coding and use them over and over and over again, regardless of the user interface at one end or the data source at the other.

And now, in 2002, we have ADO.NET. Based just on my own history, I'd guess that this is the API that I'll use for the majority of data-access code in my own applications for the next five years. In some ways, ADO.NET is a refinement of ADO; in others, it's a whole new way to look at the world. The most significant new capabilities are in the area of disconnected data and XML compatibility. ADO made it possible to use any data source with any application; ADO.NET enhances this capability by removing the necessity to stay connected to the data source. You can grab the data that you want to work with, ship it around the world via HTTP, edit it tomorrow, send it back later, and still have the updates succeed.

ADO.NET in particular and the .NET Framework in general are poised to have a huge effect on the way developers write and deploy applications (for the desktop as well as for the Web). By removing most of the differences between desktop programming and distributed programming, the .NET Framework makes it possible to learn a single (albeit vastly complex) set of metaphors for data access and to use them everywhere. The .NET Framework makes it possible to write code in a full-featured IDE and still have the results work properly in almost any web browser, without making the developer write a single line of HTML code. Microsoft's decades of experience in data-access and framework development will pay off now for those who adapt to this new environment.

On the other hand, older code isn't going to stop working just because newer code is available. ADO will remain a viable data-access API for the next few years, and in some cases, it's still clearly superior to ADO.NET. Some OLE DB providers, for example, are tested and supported with ADO but not yet supported for use with ADO.NET. If you need to use one of those providers, you'll want to stick with ADO.

What's clear is that data access is a part of almost any serious application today, and that the demise of the closed, non-interoperable file format (remember PC-File?) has made life quite a bit easier for the developer working with data. But there are still a lot of different techniques to learn within the broad boundaries of ADO and ADO.NET. From simple data retrieval and editing, through schema modification and multidimensional aggregation, to synchronizing relational data with an XML representation, these APIs have many uses. In this book, I'll present you with a broad survey of both ADO and ADO.NET. I won't go into every possible technique in detail; areas like OLAP or SQL Server development are broad enough to demand entire books of their own. But you should be able to use this as a first reference for all of your data-access needs.

How This Book Is Organized

There are six parts to this book, plus some appendixes.

Part I (Chapters 1–2) provides an overview of the data-access landscape. In these chapters, I'll introduce the software that I'll be using in the rest of the book, briefly review the earlier Microsoft data-access APIs, and then discuss the overall architecture of ADO and ADO.NET.

Part II (Chapters 3–10) covers "classic" COM-based ADO. In these chapters, you'll learn the basics of retrieving and altering data, as well as see more advanced techniques, such as the use of hierarchical Recordsets, disconnected data, and ADO events.

Part III (Chapters 11–13) provides an introduction to the .NET Framework. Some of this material isn't focused strictly on data access, but I expect that this will be the first time that many readers have had the chance to look seriously at .NET. This part of the book also covers the use of COM-based ADO from .NET applications.

Part IV (Chapters 14–19) covers the details of ADO.NET. This part of the book starts with simple data retrieval and editing and then progresses to more advanced areas, such as XML synchronization and the use of ASP.NET with ADO.NET.

Part V (Chapters 20–23) focuses on some of the provider-specific areas of ADO. Although ADO does allow you to use data from diverse sources as though all the data were the same, it also allows you to take advantage of the special capabilities of individual data sources. This part of the book covers SQL Server, Oracle, and Jet data, as well as several other, less common providers.

Part VI (Chapters 24–27) looks at the other end of the equation with some client-specific topics. These chapters discuss the use of ADO and ADO.NET from Visual Basic, Access, Excel, and Visual Basic .NET.

Finally, a set of appendixes cover the major object models used in the book, as well as some useful utilities and introductions to the SQL and MDX query languages.

NOTE　　"ADO" in this book refers to the ADO 2.7 library of COM objects unless otherwise indicated. Any time I'm referring to the newer .NET version, I'll call it ADO.NET specifically.

About the Sample Code

The companion CD contains all the sample code from the book. There are a few things you should keep in mind when working with this code:

- In most cases, there is one sample project per chapter. The samples follow a simple naming scheme: ADOChapter3, for example, is the sample project that contains all the code from Chapter 3.

- The ADO samples are usually written in Visual Basic 6, and the ADO.NET samples in Visual Basic .NET. Some of the samples from Part VI of the book are written for Access 2002 and Excel 2002.

- Most of the samples initially display a menu form with a set of buttons that run the individual sections of code shown in the chapter. It should be obvious which button runs which section of code.

- All the forms use the form name as the form caption. That way, if you see a screen shot showing a form that's captioned "frmHierarchy," you can quickly find the corresponding form in the sample project.

- Much of the code is of demonstration quality rather than production quality. In particular, the error trapping is primitive (generally limited to displaying errors on the user interface) or even nonexistent in most of the samples. To use this code in your own applications, you may need to make some changes.

Keeping Up to Date

This book was written in 2001 using the then-current versions of the software it discusses:

- SQL Server 2000 with Service Pack 1
- Visual Basic 6 with Service Pack 5
- Windows 2000 with Service Pack 2
- Office XP
- Oracle8i Release 3 (8.1.7)
- Visual Studio .NET Beta 2

I've chosen to provide sample code in Visual Basic and Visual Basic .NET because these are widely used languages that can use all the APIs and objects that I discuss in the book. These languages also tend to be easy for developers to read, even developers who don't specialize in Visual Basic.

Inevitably, the software I've written about will be updated. Sharp-eyed readers will let Sybex and me know when they find bugs. If I have any major changes to the samples, we'll make copies available on the Sybex website, `www.sybex.com`. (Enter this book's ISBN code, **2994**, in the Search box on the Sybex home page to locate the page for the book.) In particular, when Visual Studio .NET is released, I'll post updated copies of the .NET samples for downloading.

If you do find any problems with the samples or have any questions or suggestions, I'll be happy to hear from you via e-mail. You can write to me at `MikeG1@larkfarm.com`. Of course, I can't guarantee an answer to every question, but I'll do my best.

About the CD

The companion CD contains the following:

- All of the sample code and applications from the book
- Appendix E, "ADO and ADO.NET Utilities"
- Appendix F, "SQL and MDX Language Primer"
- The open-source MySQL database
- George Poulouse's ADO Query Tool

- SmithVoice's Database Code Creator
- PEYO's ADO Explorer
- LockwoodTech Software's Query-Blaster and Proc-Blaster
- Joseph Albahari's ADO.NET Query Express
- Blueshell Data Guy

To use the CD content, just insert the disc into your CD-ROM drive. The CD's installation program should launch automatically. If you've turned off AutoPlay, you can open the file `readme.htm` in the root directory of the CD to get started.

PART I

Understanding Data Access

An Overview of ADO and ADO.NET

- A brief history of ADO

- Moving forward with ADO.NET

- Getting ADO or ADO.NET

During the past five years, ActiveX Data Objects (ADO) has solidified its position as one of the most important of Microsoft's technology initiatives. ADO offers one-stop programming for access to data sources of all types—not just traditional databases, but file systems, e-mail stores, and even data on the Internet. In this book, I'll survey a wide range of ADO techniques, from simple data access to more complex techniques. I'll also introduce you to the new ADO.NET technology that was in beta while I was writing. Part of the broader .NET Framework, ADO.NET will force you to learn some new development skills while it preserves the goal of universal data access.

In this chapter, I'll introduce ADO and ADO.NET and discuss how you can make sure that you're working with the latest versions.

A Brief History of ADO

Despite the fact that the version numbers of ADO used in this book—2.6 and 2.7—are relatively low, ADO has, in fact, been through a number of major versions. On the one hand, this is a good thing, since it shows how actively Microsoft has been working on this library. But on the other hand, it leads to the disease of "versionitis," where it's hard to be entirely sure just what software is installed on a particular machine. Hence, it's worth taking a quick look at the history of ADO, to give some hints of which versions have shipped where.

ADO 1.0 was released as an object library wrapper for OLE DB (a function that the current release still fulfills) in 1996, as a part of Microsoft Internet Information Server (IIS) 3.0. You'll learn a bit more about OLE DB, the collection of COM (Component Object Model) interfaces for retrieving data, in Chapter 2, "Understanding Data Access Architectures." This version included the first version of the Advanced Data Connector (ADC), which was superseded by the Remote Data Service (RDS) in later releases. I'll look at RDS in Chapter 8, "Working with Disconnected Recordsets."

ADO 1.0 was also included in Visual Studio 97, as a part of both Visual Interdev and the OLE DB SDK (Software Development Kit). At that time, there was no single unified installation for ADO and OLE DB, resulting in version conflicts even among individual products within Visual Studio 97.

ADO 1.5 was released in 1997 as part of MDAC 1.5. MDAC stands for Microsoft Data Access Components, a single setup that was designed to bring more coordination to all the various bits of data access technology that Microsoft was shipping. MDAC 1.5 includes ADO 1.5, OLE DB 1.5, RDS 1.5, and ODBC (Open Database Connectivity) 3.5. Although OLE DB is replacing ODBC, it's doing so slowly, and the older ODBC drivers are still necessary to retrieve data from sources for which no OLE DB providers exist.

MDAC 1.5 was available for free download from the Internet, as have been all subsequent versions. Microsoft has been investing heavily in making data access a part of the operating system by offering it for free (well, for free if you have a free download connection). MDAC 1.5 went through a series of bug-fix releases culminating in version 1.5d, which was included with Internet Explorer 4.01 Service Pack 1.

ADO 2.0 was shipped in MDAC 2.0, again as a free Web download, in 1997. In addition to ADO 2.0, MDAC 2.0 includes OLE DB 2.0 and RDS 2.0. ODBC has remained at version 3.5, because development on that component has practically ceased. ADO 2.0 added asynchronous operations and hierarchical Recordsets to the basic ADO model. This version also introduced ADO MD, a set of multidimensional extensions for ADO that I'll cover in Chapter 10, "Analyzing Multidimensional Data with ADO MD."

In early 1999, Microsoft released ADO 2.1 as a part of MDAC 2.1. A version of ADO 2.1 shipped with Microsoft SQL Server 7.0, but the final version wasn't available until the shipment of Office 2000. Referred to as MDAC 2.1.1.3711.11 (GA), this version (sometimes called MDAC 2.1 SP1) introduced the Seek method and the Index property, as well as the ability to save a Recordset as XML. A revised version, 2.1.2.4202.3 (GA), otherwise known as MDAC 2.1 SP2, was released in July 1999. This version didn't introduce any new features.

NOTE All versions of MDAC starting with MDAC 2.1 (up to the most recent released version) are available for download from the Microsoft Universal Data Access website, www .microsoft.com/data/download.htm.

ADO 2.5 was shipped as part of MDAC 2.5 with Windows 2000 in February 2000. This version is the first in which ADO is installed as a system component. It also introduced the Record and Stream objects, allowed the use of URLs as connection strings, and let providers create heterogeneous Recordsets in which not all rows of the Recordset have the same structure. This was the first MDAC release to include the OLE DB Provider for Microsoft Active Directory Service and the OLE DB Provider for Internet Publishing. I'll discuss the new features of ADO 2.5 in more detail later in this chapter. There have been two service pack releases for MDAC 2.5. MDAC 2.5 SP1, released in August 2000, matches the components from Windows 2000 SP1. MDAC 2.5 SP2, released in May 2001, matches the components from Windows 2000 SP2. Neither of these service packs includes any new features.

ADO 2.6 was shipped with SQL Server 2000 in September 2000 and as part of the independent MDAC 2.6 release. This version includes changes to the Command object to support SQL Server 2000's XML integration, enhanced ADO error reporting, and an improved setup. Starting with MDAC 2.6, the MDAC setup no longer installs the Microsoft Jet engine components. There's a separate Jet 4.0 Service Pack 3 release that you can download to install those components. I'll give you more detail on the new ADO 2.6 features later in this chapter. MDAC 2.6 SP1 was released in June 2001 and includes no new features.

ADO 2.7 is currently in beta as I write this chapter, poised to ship with the Microsoft .NET Framework in early 2002 and (presumably) with an independent MDAC 2.7 release. The only major new feature in ADO 2.7 is support for 64-bit Windows. But the big news is that several components are now officially deprecated, and slated for removal in future releases. I'll discuss these changes later in the chapter.

So, what does all this mean for the developer of ADO-using applications? In practice, it's fairly simple:

- For legacy applications that don't use any of the new features in ADO 2.5 or later releases, you'll want to download MDAC 2.1 SP2 from the Internet, and use that to make sure client computers are running the most recent available version of ADO 2.1. Of course, if those computers have more recent versions of MDAC installed, older applications should continue to function just fine.

- For new applications on Windows 95, Windows 98, Windows Me, or Windows NT 4, you'll need to obtain and install MDAC 2.5 or later. For most applications, the differences between MDAC 2.5, 2.6, and 2.7 are insignificant. Whether to use the most recent version or a version that has been tested in your organization is up to you.

- For new applications on Windows 2000 or Windows XP, ADO 2.5 is a part of the operating system. You should ensure that you have the most recent Windows 2000 service pack installed. If your application needs ADO 2.6 or 2.7 features, you can upgrade the operating system with the latest MDAC downloads.

What's New in ADO 2.5

Of the versions released since ADO 2.1, ADO 2.5 contains the most significant changes for most developers. In this section, I'll briefly introduce you to the new features in ADO 2.5:

- ADO as a system component
- Record and Stream objects
- URLs as connection strings
- Provider-supplied fields
- New OLE DB providers

If you're not already familiar with ADO, you might want to skip over this section, because I won't explain the individual features in depth. Don't worry, though—all these features are covered in their proper context later in the book.

ADO as a System Component

Starting with Windows 2000, ADO is a standard part of the Windows operating system. What this means is that ADO 2.5 is automatically installed as a part of the Windows 2000 installation. If you're writing applications that use ADO and intend to deploy them only on computers using the Windows 2000 or Windows XP operating system, you don't have to worry about installing a data access library, because it's already there. The exception to this, of course, is applications that require the new features of ADO 2.6 or ADO 2.7.

Windows 2000 system components, including ADO 2.5, are subject to more stringent controls than past components have been. Specifically, they can be installed or updated only by the Microsoft Installer, and only as a part of an operating system service pack. This is all part of Microsoft's broad strategy to make Windows a more robust operating system and to eliminate the library version conflicts (commonly known as "DLL hell") that have made debugging client-side installations a time-consuming and difficult activity. The various MDAC installers include special code to enable them to update these components on Windows 2000.

Record and Stream Objects

ADO 2.5 introduced two new objects to the ADO hierarchy: the Record object and the Stream object. These objects are designed to help extend ADO to a wider understanding of what a "data source" can be.

A Record object can represent a single record within a Recordset object, but more typically, it provides an object-oriented view of more heterogeneous data. For example, you might use a Record object to represent a file or folder in a file system, a message in an e-mail store, or a storage or stream within a COM compound file.

Record objects are also designed to represent hierarchically organized data. A Record object can represent either a node or a leaf within a tree of data. Properties of the Record object tell you whether any particular Record object represents a leaf or a non-leaf node. (A leaf node, of course, is one that doesn't have any child nodes of its own.)

A Stream object represents binary data associated with a particular Record object. If you have a Record object representing a file, for example, its associated Stream object contains the binary data for that file.

Record and Stream objects are discussed in more detail in Chapter 3, "Using the ADO Objects to Retrieve Data."

URLs as Connection Strings

ADO 2.5 allows the use of Uniform Resource Locators (URLs) to specify the data source for a particular ADO Connection object. These URLs are then passed to an underlying OLE

DB provider that can interpret them. For example, you can now use these URLs as valid locations to open a connection (with the appropriate OLE DB provider):

```
file://MyServer/CDrive/SomeFile.txt
http://www.myserver.com/data.html
```

Using URLs as connection strings allows better integration with Web-based applications and simplifies the process of retrieving data from arbitrary files using ADO.

Provider-Supplied Fields

ADO 2.5 introduced the concept of a heterogeneous Recordset. In previous versions of ADO, every record in a Recordset contained exactly the same fields. In a heterogeneous Recordset, depending on the underlying OLE DB provider, this need not be the case.

For example, a provider that retrieves data from an electronic mail store might insert To, From, and Subject fields in every record. However, only records representing e-mail messages with attachments would have an Attachment field.

This new capability lets a custom provider represent almost anything as an ADO Recordset. You could build a provider that represented a file system, for example, and set a Parent-Application field only on records representing documents. In general, this capability lets records in a Recordset be as different from one another as is necessary for the current programming task.

In addition, a special class of providers known as Document Source Providers are devoted to managing documents—for example, in a file system. In this case, the properties of each record are not the documents themselves, but a set of values that describe the document. There are constants in ADO 2.5 that allow you to easily retrieve two special fields: one representing the Stream object with the actual contents of the document, and one holding the URL that describes the document's contents.

New OLE DB Providers

In addition to the changes to ADO itself, MDAC 2.5 also introduced several new OLE DB providers. These providers help extend the reach of ADO to new types of data:

- The Microsoft OLE DB Provider for Microsoft Active Directory Service allows ADO to connect to heterogeneous directory services. In addition to full access to the Active Directory Service in Windows 2000, this provider supplies read-only access to Windows NT 4 Directory Services, Novell Directory Services, and any LDAP-compliant directory services provider (where LDAP translates as Lightweight Directory Access Protocol).

- The Microsoft OLE DB Provider for Internet Publishing gives you access to Web resources under the control of Microsoft FrontPage and Microsoft Internet Information Server.

What's New in ADO 2.6

ADO 2.6 included a small number of new features, many of which were designed expressly for use with SQL Server 2000:

- Use of Stream objects with Command objects and results
- Field Status values
- Single-row result sets in Record objects

In addition to those changes, there are minor improvements in ADO 2.6, including a CubeDef.GetSchemaObject method in ADO MD, provider-specific properties on ADOX Group and User objects, and a NamedParameters property to indicate that Command objects should use named parameters.

NOTE ADOX is the library that contains the ActiveX Data Objects for DDL and Security, a set of objects that allow you to manipulate the design of databases. You'll learn more about ADOX in Chapter 9, "Using ADOX for Data Definition and Security Operations."

Use of Streams with Commands and Results

The most significant improvement in ADO 2.6 is the use of Stream objects for input and output with Command objects. You can now initialize a Command object with one Stream, and retrieve the results from the Command into a second Stream. This functionality provides an essential link between ADO and XML.

In particular, Microsoft has defined an XML namespace to represent SQL Server queries. Within this namespace, you can construct XML documents such as this one:

```
<root xmlns:sql='urn:schemas-microsoft-com:xml-sql'>
    <sql:query> SELECT * FROM Customers ORDER BY Country
        FOR XML AUTO </sql:query>
</root>
```

By using that string as an input Stream to a Command object, you can tell the Command to run using the SQL that's encapsulated within the XML document. The results can be retrieved as a new Stream, which itself will contain XML (as dictated by the FOR XML AUTO clause in the encapsulated SQL). Or, if you're executing code within an ASP page, you can pipe the results directly into the ASP Response object for display on the generated HTML page.

I'll cover the use of the Stream and Command objects in Chapter 6, "Using Records and Streams."

Field Status Values

ADO's error-reporting capabilities have been enhanced to report detailed error information in the case of failed schema changes. The mechanism for this is the Status property of the Field object. For example, if you try to use ADOX to delete a field from a table, that deletion can fail for a variety of reasons. With ADO 2.6, you can inspect the Status property of the affected field to learn the reason; for example, the deletion would violate referential integrity, or the user doesn't have sufficient permissions to perform the operation.

Single-Row Result Sets in Record Objects

With ADO 2.6, you can use a Record object to hold any result set that has only a single row, making the Record a sort of lightweight Recordset. For example, you could use the following code to retrieve a Record representing a single customer from the SQL Server Northwind database:

```
Dim cnn As ADODB.Connection
Dim rec As ADODB.Record
Dim fld As ADODB.Field

On Error GoTo HandleErr

Set cnn = New ADODB.Connection
cnn.Open "Provider=SQLOLEDB;Data Source=(local);" & _
    "Initial Catalog=Northwind;Integrated Security=SSPI"

Set rec = New ADODB.Record
rec.Open "SELECT * FROM Customers WHERE CustomerID = 'ALFKI'", _
    cnn, adModeReadWrite, , adOpenExecuteCommand
```

Figure 1.1 shows the frmGetRecord form from the ADOChapter1 sample project, which uses this code to populate a listbox on the user interface. (The sample projects are described in this book's introduction.)

WARNING   If you attempt to open a result set containing more than one row as a Record object, the Record will contain the first row of the result set, and a runtime error will be triggered.

What's New in ADO 2.7

ADO 2.7 adds 64-bit support to the existing ADO components. More importantly, though, it clearly signals Microsoft's future directions by deprecating some MDAC components.

Using a Record object
to retrieve a single
row from a database

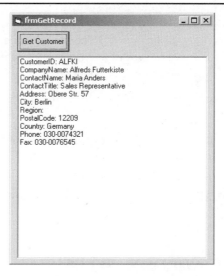

64-Bit Support

With the release of Intel's Itanium processor, Microsoft is now shipping its first 64-bit version of Windows: Windows Advanced Server, Limited Edition. By the time you read this, Windows XP 64-bit edition may be shipping as well. Of course, these new versions of Windows need 64-bit versions of system components, and ADO is no exception. On the 64-bit platform, ADO is a 64-bit component. As a practical matter, though, this should be completely transparent to your ADO development. Your ADO 2.7 code should work regardless of which current version of Windows it's run on.

Deprecated Components

MDAC 2.7 officially lists several components as "deprecated." What this means is that, although the components are still included in this release, Microsoft considers them obsolete, will do no further development on them, and may remove them from future releases. Not all of these components are involved with ADO code, but for completeness, here's the entire list of deprecated components in this release:

Microsoft OLE DB Provider for ODBC Data Sources   The end is in sight for the venerable ODBC standard for data access, at least as far as Microsoft is concerned. You should make every effort to move to data sources for which a native OLE DB provider is available.

Remote Data Service   Not surprisingly, RDS is becoming obsolete, thanks to the release of many new Internet data access components as a part of Microsoft .NET. Microsoft recommends that you replace RDS code with calls to the Simple Object Access Protocol (SOAP). I'll cover the use of SOAP to retrieve data over the Internet in Chapter 16, "Working with Disconnected DataSets."

Jet and Replication objects   With the Jet engine officially no longer being enhanced, MDAC is dropping support for this optional component.

AppleTalk and Banyan Vines SQL network libraries   These methods of SQL Server connectivity are no longer being enhanced. You should migrate to the TCP/IP library instead.

16-bit ODBC support   Native 16-bit ODBC support, as implemented in Windows 3.1 and Windows for Workgroups, is finally on the way out.

Moving Forward with ADO.NET

Looking at the list of changes for ADO 2.6 and 2.7, you can tell that ADO is a mature library that doesn't need a lot of further development. But that doesn't mean that the data access developers at Microsoft have been taking it easy. On the contrary, they've been developing a whole new set of data access components known as ADO.NET. ADO.NET is in wide beta use as I write this (as part of the Microsoft .NET Framework and of Visual Studio .NET), and should be released in early 2002.

I'll introduce you to some of the details of ADO.NET in Chapter 2. Later on, in Chapters 11 through 19, I'll discuss ADO.NET in detail. But to get you started thinking about this new development, here's a brief introduction.

Microsoft has been evangelizing ADO.NET by calling it "as similar as possible to ADO" and suggesting that "current ADO developers do not have to start from the beginning in learning a brand-new data access technology." Despite these hopeful words, I (and other ADO developers with whom I've spoken) view ADO.NET as a revolution rather than an evolution. You won't find any of the familiar ADO objects in ADO.NET, and the new ADO.NET objects don't have direct analogs in ADO. Expect to spend a lot of time understanding the new design patterns that you'll need to use in order to make efficient use of the ADO.NET objects.

TIP   You don't need to master ADO.NET to begin using databases from the .NET languages. You can use the existing ADO libraries or ADO components from your new .NET applications. I'll cover this in Chapter 13, "Using ADO from .NET."

The key design points in ADO.NET revolve around the use of the .NET Framework to develop distributed applications. In particular, disconnected sets of data (now represented by the new DataSet object) are the rule rather than the exception in ADO.NET. The designers did a great deal of work to let you move disconnected DataSets between components and to have everything work the way you'd expect. Another key piece of the ADO.NET puzzle is tight XML integration. The ADO.NET classes and the .NET Framework classes to deal with XML are designed for easy interoperation, and XML is the default format for moving ADO.NET data from place to place.

If you're designing a new application, you'll need to decide whether to use ADO or ADO.NET for data access. Here are some points to consider:

- ADO.NET (and .NET generally) is supported on Windows NT 4 with Service Pack 6a, Windows 2000, Windows XP, Windows 98, and Windows Me. For older versions of Windows, you'll need to stick with ADO.

- ADO.NET excels when you're creating distributed applications. If your application is designed to work over the Internet or an intranet, or to integrate with XML, using ADO.NET will make your life easier.

- In its initial release, ADO.NET includes providers for SQL Server, Oracle, Jet, and ODBC data sources. For other data sources, you may need to stick with ADO.

- If you have existing ADO code, you'll find it easier to continue using ADO rather than to migrate to ADO.NET. You should consider whether it makes sense to integrate ADO data access code with other .NET code in a single application.

Overall, ADO.NET (and the .NET Framework generally) represents the most significant upgrade to development in a Windows environment to come along in years. Over time, I expect most new applications to be written in the .NET universe. So the sooner you learn about ADO.NET, the sooner you'll be able to take advantage of this trend.

Getting ADO or ADO.NET

Although ADO 2.5 is a system component in Windows 2000, there are still multiple options for getting copies of the most recent ADO code. You should know about these, from the simple MDAC redistributable to the complex MDAC SDK. There are also several ways to get ADO.NET. I'll discuss these various avenues in this section.

MDAC

In versions of ADO before 2.5, MDAC was the only way to get ADO onto any system. Now, it's still the sole way to install ADO on a pre–Windows 2000 system. Even products that include ADO (such as Visual Studio) handle the installation by running the MDAC program.

Usually, the install program is called `mdac_typ.exe`. This self-extracting setup program contains all the components needed to support ADO code on a client computer, and it doesn't require the user to make choices.

You should distribute the latest `mdac_typ.exe` program along with any program that makes use of ADO. Although products such as Visual Basic include a version of this program, your best bet is to download the most current version from the Microsoft Universal Data Access website (`www.microsoft.com/data`). That way, you're guaranteed the latest bug fixes and the most recent versions of all ADO components.

> **WARNING**   You may find references in some books to a minimum version, `mdac_min.exe`. Starting with ADO 2.1, there's no longer such a version. The only ADO to install is the full version.

MDAC SDK

If you're serious about database work, you should get a copy of the MDAC SDK (Software Development Kit). This kit contains not only ADO but all the other data-related technologies that Microsoft is supporting as a part of Windows, along with sample code, tools, and more. Here are some of the components in the MDAC SDK:

- Conformance tests for OLE DB drivers
- OLE DB
- OLE DB for OLAP
- Current ODBC drivers
- The OLE DB Simple Provider Toolkit
- ADO
- RDS
- ADO MD
- ADOX
- Jet and Replication objects
- Various OLE DB providers
- Complete OLE DB documentation

Many parts of this SDK are written for C++ programmers rather than for Visual Basic programmers. Nevertheless, you'll find its documentation of ADO (and the ADO extensions such as ADOX and ADO MD) useful for Visual Basic programs.

You can download the MDAC SDK from the Microsoft Universal Data Access website at www.microsoft.com/data. The download is around 15 megabytes, so it may take a while. But it's worth it, even if you're only working with ADO, to get the enhanced ADO documentation and help files. If you're a serious Windows developer, you should take a look at the Microsoft Developer Network (MSDN) program. This annual subscription program will deliver the entire Windows SDK, including the MDAC SDK, straight to your door four times a year. You can find out more at http://msdn.microsoft.com/subscriptions.

.NET Framework SDK

The .NET Framework Software SDK supplies all of the infrastructure that .NET applications depend on, including ADO.NET. You can access the .NET Framework SDK via the MSDN website; you'll find the SDK at http://msdn.microsoft.com/library/default .asp?url=/nhp/Default.asp?contentid=28000451. This site includes a good variety of articles on .NET, as well as a download link that will get you the entire SDK. As of beta 2, the download is 127 megabytes, which makes this a practical way to get ADO.NET only if you have a broadband connection to the Internet.

Visual Studio .NET

ADO.NET is also included in Visual Studio .NET, the next iteration of Microsoft's integrated design environment for Windows and Web applications. The Visual Studio .NET home page is at http://msdn.microsoft.com/vstudio/nextgen/default.asp. You can download beta 2 of Visual Studio .NET as I write this chapter, although that will change by the time this book is published. The home page should have information on obtaining the release version when it's available. Visual Studio .NET will go to MSDN Universal subscribers as part of their subscription, and will also be available as a packaged product.

MDAC.NET?

It's possible that Microsoft will make a separate version of MDAC available for installing the .NET data access components on computers where you're deploying .NET applications. No information about such a release is available yet, but the place to watch for one is www.microsoft.com/data.

Summary

In this chapter, you've learned about the various versions of ADO and ADO.NET that you may encounter as you work with development tools and versions of Windows that are currently (or soon to be) in circulation. This chapter should guide you in choosing the appropriate version of the software to deploy with your application. With that background information in hand, it's time to look at the actual software in more depth. In the next chapter, I'll discuss the overall architectural design of ADO and ADO.NET so that you can see in more detail how all the pieces fit together.

CHAPTER 2

Understanding Data Access Architectures

- ADO and OLE DB

- ADO.NET

- Earlier data access libraries

- Choosing a data access library

Now that you've got the broad overview of ActiveX Data Objects (ADO) and ADO.NET, it's time to drill down into a bit more detail. Although the basic idea of the ADO technologies is simple—to use one method of programming to retrieve any data, anywhere—the implementation is complex. In this chapter, you'll learn about the basic architecture of ADO and OLE DB, and see how they work together to bring heterogeneous data to your applications. Then you'll see how ADO.NET brings new ideas to bear on data programming, while still interacting with the existing ADO architecture. I'll also briefly review the older data access strategies of Data Access Objects (DAO), Remote Data Objects (RDO), and Open Database Connectivity (ODBC), since you'll still run across these libraries in many applications. Finally, I'll give some pointers on choosing the appropriate data access library for particular circumstances.

ADO and OLE DB

ADO and OLE DB are really two faces of the same technology. OLE DB provides low-level connections to data via COM interfaces, while ADO provides an object model that simplifies the process of using OLE DB in your applications to retrieve data. OLE DB itself is implemented as a series of COM interfaces. The goal of ADO is to collect those interfaces into objects that make sense as abstract entities. For example, the ADO Recordset object can be thought of as a set of records together with a pointer to a current record.

In this section, I'll take a brief look at the overall architecture of OLE DB, and then look at what ADO adds to the picture. In the ADO portions of this book, I'll be concerned exclusively with the high-level ADO syntax, but it's important to realize that there's an entire layer beneath ADO that gets invoked implicitly every time an application uses ADO to retrieve data.

OLE DB Architecture

OLE DB is a set of interfaces that deal directly with data. OLE DB is built on top of COM (the Component Object Model), Microsoft's overall method of enabling communication between different data-processing components. OLE DB, in fact, is nothing more than a set of COM interfaces designed for data access.

The low-level details of using OLE DB are beyond the scope of this book, but it's worthwhile to understand the high-level architecture that OLE DB uses. By understanding OLE DB on this overview level, you can more easily conceptualize how your data is being retrieved, as well as troubleshoot any problems that may occur.

NOTE   The gory details of OLE DB are covered in the Microsoft Data Access Components (MDAC) Software Development Kit (SDK). This SDK is included in the Microsoft Developer Network (MSDN) Platform SDK and is also available for downloading separately from www.microsoft.com/data.

OLE DB defines three types of data access components:

- *Data providers* expose data to other components. Data providers are not strictly part of OLE DB; they are external programs such as databases or e-mail systems.
- *Data consumers* use the data contained in data providers.
- *Service components* process and transport data.

For example, if you were to use OLE DB to retrieve SQL Server data and display it on a dedicated interface built in C++, SQL Server would be the data provider, your interface application would be the data consumer, and the cursor engine that maintained a set of records would be a service component.

When using Visual Basic and ADO to retrieve data, ADO itself is the OLE DB data consumer. All the samples in this book use ADO (or ADO.NET) as the OLE DB data consumer. Using ADO as the data consumer hides all the messy details of the COM interfaces that underlie OLE DB.

Most of the functionality of OLE DB is contained in the data providers and service components that retrieve and manipulate the data your application uses. However, there are a number of core components that are contained in the OLE DB libraries:

The **Data Conversion Library** supports converting from one datatype to another across a wide variety of standard datatypes.

The **Row Position object** keeps track of the current row in a Recordset. This allows a variety of other components to agree on what data they're currently working with.

The **Root Enumerator** can search the registry for known OLE DB data providers.

The **IDataInitialize interface** contains functionality to allow working with data sources.

The **IDBPromptInitialize interface** contains functionality to let applications work with the Data Link Properties dialog box.

When working with ADO and ADO.NET, you won't be using any of these components directly. However, they're all being invoked as needed by OLE DB when you work with data through ADO.

What ADO Brings to OLE DB

In a word, ADO brings simplicity into the OLE DB picture. OLE DB is a call-oriented API (application programming interface). To perform operations using OLE DB directly, you may need to make many different API calls in a specific sequence. Although there's nothing to prevent your learning and using this API directly, it's complex and you won't often need the full power and flexibility of OLE DB.

ADO adds another layer on top of OLE DB. The ADO layer is an object-oriented API. Rather than call functions in the OLE DB API directly, you manipulate the methods and properties of a few simple objects. Figure 2.1 shows the overall ADO object model. Chapter 3, "Using the ADO Objects to Retrieve Data," and Appendix A, "The ADO Object Model," cover this object model in depth. For now, the most important thing to understand is that you can manipulate nine objects instead of learning hundreds of API calls.

FIGURE 2.1:

The ADO object model

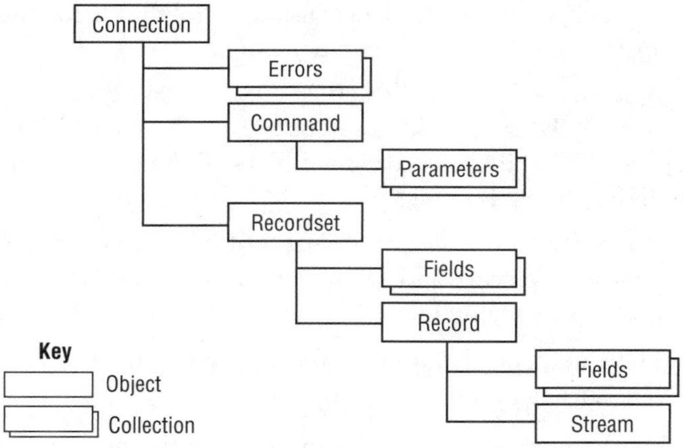

The ADO object model includes these objects, which can be used to abstract almost any data access operation:

The **Connection** object represents a persistent connection to a data source.

The **Error** object represents a single error during the data access process.

The **Command** object represents a stored procedure or other data access object that can return data. The Command object can also be used to execute stored procedures that don't return data.

The **Parameter** object represents a runtime parameter used to specify the data desired from a Command object.

The **Recordset** object represents a set of records retrieved from a data source, together with a current record pointer.

The **Field** object represents a single field of data within a Recordset.

The **Record** object represents a single record within a Recordset. It's also possible to have stand-alone Record objects based on a data source that allows retrieving individual nodes from a hierarchy.

The **Stream** object represents a binary stream of data contained within a Record object.

The **Property** object defines a characteristic of an object. It is not shown on Figure 2.1, because each of the other objects has its own collection of Properties. The Properties collection is extensible with custom properties, which lets individual providers customize the core ADO objects.

In addition to the core ADO objects mentioned above, ADO defines a second set of objects that are part of the Remote Data Service (RDS). RDS defines a separate object model and programming sequence that can be used to retrieve data in a three-tier system, typically with RDS running on a client that communicates with an intermediary such as Microsoft Internet Information Server (IIS), which in turn uses ADO to retrieve data from the ultimate data source. The goal of RDS is to hide all the complexity of this model and to make three-tier development as easy as two-tier development (in which your client program talks directly to the data source). RDS is most often used for retrieving data over the Internet or from a database server on a corporate intranet.

I'll cover RDS in more detail in Chapter 8, "Working with Disconnected Recordsets." The basic steps for using RDS, and objects that it provides, are as follows:

1. Create an RDS.DataSpace object to connect to a specific server.

2. Use the RDS.DataFactory object to create a Recordset on the server.

3. Pass the Recordset to the client.

4. Pass changes back to the RDS.DataFactory object to write back to the data source.

RDS also defines the RDS.DataControl object. This object provides a bindable source of data that can be used directly on client interfaces such as web pages, and is designed to encapsulate as many of the details of data access as possible without custom programming.

Available OLE DB Components

Many OLE DB components are already available, and the number is growing every day as new companies add OLE DB functionality to their products. In this section, I'll review the components that ship as part of the Microsoft Data Access Components (MDAC). You can generally expect this set of components to be available on any computer where ADO and OLE DB have been installed. ADO and OLE DB components can be installed from their own dedicated setup programs or as part of another product. Currently, ADO and OLE DB are shipped in a variety of Microsoft products, including Microsoft Office XP, Microsoft SQL Server 2000, and Windows 2000.

WARNING   Unfortunately, the mere fact that MDAC has been installed on a computer doesn't mean that all the components listed in this section will be available on that computer. This list is based on the version of MDAC 2.7 included with the Release Candidate version of Visual Studio .NET, the most recent version as of this writing. But there have been such frequent releases of MDAC in recent years that you may find a mix of MDAC 2.0, 2.1, 2.5, 2.6, and 2.7 in a single organization. Microsoft has a tool called the Component Checker available to determine the version of MDAC components on any computer. You can download the most recent release of the Component Checker from `www.microsoft.com/data/download.htm`.

Data Providers

Data providers connect to data sources and supply data, either directly to client applications or to service providers. Microsoft currently supplies these data providers as part of various versions of MDAC:

- Microsoft OLE DB Provider for ODBC
- Microsoft OLE DB Provider for Microsoft Indexing Service
- Microsoft OLE DB Provider for Microsoft Active Directory Service
- Microsoft OLE DB Provider for Microsoft Jet
- Microsoft OLE DB Provider for SQL Server
- Microsoft OLE DB Provider for Oracle
- Microsoft OLE DB Provider for Internet Publishing

In addition, other OLE DB providers are shipped as part of other Microsoft products. For example, SQL Server installs the Microsoft OLE DB Provider for DTS Packages.

Microsoft OLE DB Provider for ODBC

The Microsoft OLE DB Provider for ODBC allows ADO to use any ODBC driver to retrieve data. (ODBC was the previous Microsoft standard for connecting to heterogeneous data sources and is discussed later in this chapter.) In other words, this is a way to use OLE DB to get data from data sources that don't have an OLE DB provider available, as long as they have an ODBC driver. If you omit the Provider keyword from an OLE DB connection string, this is the default provider that OLE DB will try to use to retrieve data.

Currently, this is a very important driver, since there still exist many data sources for which there is no native OLE DB driver. However, you need to be aware of several problems when using this provider. First, because the data goes through additional processing layers, using this provider is necessarily slower than using a native provider. Second, because OLE DB calls don't map perfectly to ODBC calls, some OLE DB functionality isn't available through this driver.

Microsoft OLE DB Provider for Microsoft Indexing Service

The Microsoft OLE DB Provider for Microsoft Indexing Service supplies read-only access to the information maintained by the Microsoft Indexing Service (formerly Microsoft Index Server). The Indexing Service, a component of IIS and Windows 2000, maintains both full-text and property indexes of files and web pages on a specific server. For example, you might have a set of web pages describing all the components offered for sale by an electrical supply company. By using the Indexing Service on the computer containing the web pages, you can run queries via ADO and this provider in order to retrieve the names of, say, all web pages containing information on circuit breakers.

Microsoft OLE DB Provider for Microsoft Active Directory Service

The Microsoft OLE DB Provider for Microsoft Active Directory Service can retrieve read-only information from Windows 2000 (or later) Active Directory, Windows NT 4 Directory Services, Novell Directory Services, and any other LDAP-compliant directories. (LDAP—the Lightweight Directory Access Protocol—is an industry standard describing the format in which directory information should be supplied.) Using this provider lets you explore the various directories of computers, users, and other resources maintained by directory servers within your organization.

Microsoft OLE DB Provider for Microsoft Jet

The OLE DB Provider for Microsoft Jet is used to retrieve information directly from Microsoft Jet databases. These can be Microsoft Access databases or other databases created directly with the Jet database engine—for example, from a Visual Basic program. In addition, this driver can use the Jet IISAM (Installable Indexed Sequential Access Method) drivers to retrieve data from other client-side database formats including Paradox, FoxPro, dBASE, text, and Excel files. I'll use this provider in many of the examples in this book.

The Jet provider doesn't support dynamic cursors; if you request a dynamic cursor, you'll get a keyset cursor instead. You'll learn more about cursors later in this section, and I'll discuss ADO cursor types in detail in Chapter 3.

Microsoft OLE DB Provider for SQL Server

The Microsoft OLE DB Provider for SQL Server is a native provider designed to retrieve information directly from Microsoft SQL Server databases. Many of the examples in this book use this provider.

Microsoft OLE DB Provider for Oracle

The Microsoft OLE DB Provider for Oracle is a native provider for data in Oracle databases (although the provider was developed by Microsoft). Some of the examples in this book use this provider to retrieve data from Oracle databases. Currently, this provider supports Oracle 7.3 and Oracle 8, but not Oracle 9, databases.

Microsoft OLE DB Provider for Internet Publishing

The Microsoft OLE DB Provider for Internet Publishing uses OLE DB to communicate with Microsoft FrontPage Server Extensions or Microsoft Internet Information Server. It's designed to retrieve or create files on a website or another server that's accessible over the Internet or an intranet.

Enumerating Data Providers

In most cases, you'll know which data provider you need to use when you're writing your application. Sometimes, though, it's useful to allow the user to pick a provider. For example, you might be writing a tool that retrieves a list of tables from a data source chosen by the user.

The easiest way to handle this is to display the standard Data Link Properties dialog box, as shown in Figure 2.2. By using the OLE DB core components, you can display this dialog box and automatically create an ADO Connection object based on the user's choice.

FIGURE 2.2:

The Data Link Properties dialog box

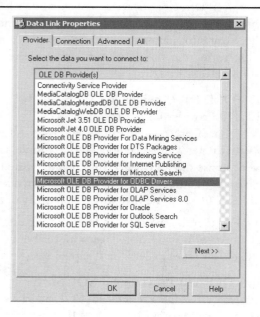

I've provided a sample of the code to display this dialog box in the ADOChapter2 sample project. The project includes a reference to the Microsoft OLE DB Service Component 1.0 Type Library. This type library is installed by OLE DB, so any computer where ADO is available should have this type library installed. Here's the code to display the Data Link Properties dialog box and to return the result to the user interface:

```
Private Sub cbdShowDialog_Click()

    Dim dlk As MSDASC.DataLinks
    Dim cnn As ADODB.Connection

    txtConnectionString.Text = ""

    Set dlk = New MSDASC.DataLinks
    ' Make the dialog box a child of the VB form
    dlk.hWnd = Me.hWnd
    ' Create the Connection by prompting the user
    Set cnn = dlk.PromptNew

    If Not cnn Is Nothing Then
        txtConnectionString.Text = cnn.ConnectionString
    End If

    Set cnn = Nothing
    Set dlk = Nothing

End Sub
```

Service Providers

Service providers consume data from data providers and modify it. The modified data can be made available directly to client applications or to other service providers. Figure 2.3 shows schematically how service providers fit into the OLE DB architecture.

Microsoft currently supplies these service providers as part of MDAC:

- Microsoft Data Shaping Service for OLE DB
- Microsoft OLE DB Persistence Provider
- Microsoft OLE DB Remoting Provider
- Microsoft Cursor Service for OLE DB

Microsoft Data Shaping Service for OLE DB

The Microsoft Data Shaping Service for OLE DB supports the construction of "shaped" (hierarchical) Recordsets. When using this service provider, you specify an OLE DB data provider that will supply the actual data from the underlying data source. After the data is retrieved by the data provider, the Data Shaping Service turns it into a hierarchical Recordset. You'll learn more about data shaping in Chapter 7, "Data Shaping."

FIGURE 2.3:

Data providers and
service providers

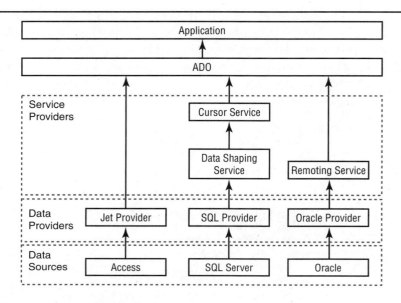

Microsoft OLE DB Persistence Provider

The Microsoft OLE DB Persistence Provider is used to save an ADO Recordset to a file, and to later retrieve the Recordset from the file. You can use the Save method of any Recordset object to create such a file, and then use the Persistence Provider at a later date to open the saved file:

```
Dim cnn As New ADODB.Connection
Dim rst As New ADODB.Recordset
cnn.Open "Provider=MSPersist"
Set rst = cnn.Execute("c:\SavedRecordset.adtg")
```

The saved file includes information on where the data originally came from, and ADO operations can transparently span the saving and restoring operations. For example, you can create a Recordset, edit some records, save the Recordset, and, at a later date, open the persisted Recordset, reconnect it to the original data source, and commit the changes.

The Persistence Provider supports two data formats. One, the ADTG (Advanced Data Table-Gram) format, is a proprietary Microsoft format that's designed to minimize storage and transmission requirements. Starting in ADO 2.5, this provider also supports Extensible Markup Language (XML). XML is a W3C standard for storing heterogeneous data across a variety of products. (You'll learn more about XML in Chapter 6, "Using Records and Streams," and in Part IV, "Understanding ADO.NET.") In addition to persisting data to a file, the Persistence Provider can store data in an ADO Stream object. You'll learn more about using the Persistence Provider in Chapter 8, "Working with Disconnected Recordsets."

NOTE   You can learn more about XML at the W3C website, www.w3.org/XML/.

Microsoft OLE DB Remoting Provider

The Microsoft OLE DB Remoting Provider supports using data sources on remote computers (for example, servers connected to the Internet) as though you were logged on locally. For the most part, you won't need to deal directly with this provider. It's automatically invoked if you use RDS to retrieve data from a remote server. For more details on RDS, see Chapter 8.

Microsoft Cursor Service for OLE DB

The Microsoft Cursor Service for OLE DB enhances the cursor support built into many providers. A cursor is simply a pointer to a particular row in a Recordset that might move backward and forward. When you use the MoveNext method of the Recordset object, for example, you're manipulating a cursor. Although many products support cursors, they vary in terms of which operations their cursors are capable of performing. The effect of the Microsoft Cursor Service is to hide this unevenness. Invoking the cursor service doesn't require modifying the OLE DB connection string; rather, it's automatically used any time you specify a client-side cursor. You can specify client-side cursors by setting the Cursor-Location property of either the Connection object or the Recordset object:

```
Dim cnn As New ADODB.Connection
Dim rst As New ADODB.Recordset
cnn.CursorLocation = adUseClient
rst.CursorLocation = adUseClient
```

ADO Extensibility

One of the key features of ADO is that it's extensible. That is, although the basic object model of ADO is quite sparse, it's designed so that other libraries may add additional objects that interact with the core ADO objects. Two sets of these extensions are shipped with ADO: the Microsoft ADO Extensions for DDL and Security and the Microsoft ADO (Multidimensional) extensions.

ADO Extensions for DDL and Security

The ADO Extensions for DDL and Security (ADOX) include objects for manipulating the schema of your database and for controlling the security of objects within the database. (DDL stands for Data Definition Language, a standard set of SQL keywords for defining objects.) ADOX adds the following objects to the standard ADO objects:

The **Catalog** object represents the entire schema of a database.

The **Table** object represents design information on a single table.

The **Column** object represents design information on a single column (field) within a table, index, or key.

The **Index** object represents design information on a single index within a table.

The **Key** object represents design information on a primary key or foreign key.

The **Group** object represents a group of users with uniform security.

The **User** object represents an individual database user.

The **Procedure** object represents a stored procedure within a database.

The **View** object represents a view within a database.

We'll examine ADOX and show how you can use it in your own applications in Chapter 9, "Using ADOX for Data Definition and Security Operations."

ADO (Multidimensional) Extensions

The ADO (Multidimensional) extensions (ADO MD) provide additional objects to allow you to work with multidimensional data from an ADO client application. Multidimensional data is typically supplied by an Online Analytical Processing (OLAP) server such as Microsoft Analysis Services, which ships with SQL Server 2000. OLAP servers are designed to summarize large amounts of data and make totals and other statistics available for querying. For example, if you had individual sales data on five million sales, you could use an OLAP server to quickly provide information on the number of sales in Massachusetts during April, without having to run a slow, expensive query directly on the original data.

The ADO MD library adds these objects to the standard ADO objects:

The **Catalog** object represents schema information for a single OLAP database.

The **CubeDef** object represents a cube from an OLAP server. A cube contains data summarized in many different ways.

The **Dimension** object represents a dimension within a cube. A dimension is a single way of summarizing data—for example, by geographic location.

The **Hierarchy** object represents a way in which a dimension can be summarized, or "rolled up."

The **Level** object represents a single part of a hierarchy—for example, the city information in a geographic level.

The **Cellset** object represents the results of a single multidimensional query. It's analogous to a Recordset object in regular ADO.

The **Cell** object represents one piece of information from a single multidimensional query. It's analogous to a Field object in regular ADO.

The **Axis** object represents filtering information for a Cellset object.

The **Position** object provides additional information about the location of a Cell or Axis object.

The **Member** object represents the basic unit of information that's summarized in a particular data cube.

You'll learn about the basics of using ADO MD to retrieve multidimensional data in Chapter 10, "Analyzing Multidimensional Data with ADO MD."

The Big Picture

Figure 2.4 is an attempt to give you an overview of how all these components fit together. Depending on your application, there can be many layers of components between the user interface and the data.

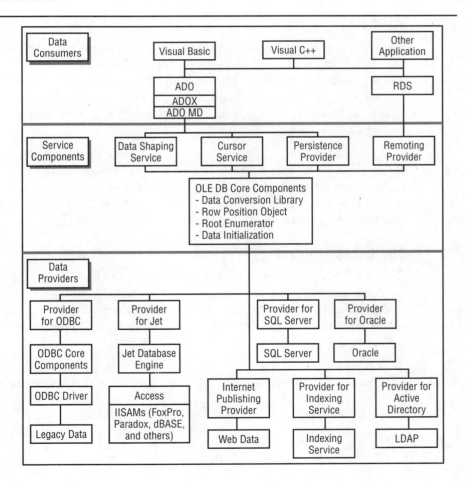

FIGURE 2.4:

ADO and OLE DB components

The good news is that you don't have to comprehend this picture as one seamless entity. The ADO programming model is designed so that you can concentrate on two simple tasks to do most of the work you want to do with data:

- Connecting to the desired data source
- Retrieving the desired data

The first task revolves around building OLE DB connection strings, while the second centers on creating and manipulating Recordsets. In later chapters, you'll learn how to do both of these operations, with examples in Visual Basic 6 code. You'll also learn how to perform the analogous operations with .NET objects, using examples in Visual Basic .NET.

ADO.NET

As far as most people knew when Windows 2000 was released, ADO was going to be Microsoft's data access solution forever. But the wheels were already turning in Redmond, and in June 2000, Microsoft announced the .NET initiative. .NET is poised, as we write this, to change the way that many applications are written. Microsoft says that .NET is their "platform for XML web services," and they appear to have focused much of their corporate energy on that platform.

.NET is an extremely large topic, and in this book, I'm only going to dig into the data access portion of it in any depth. That data access portion is ADO.NET, which is presented as an incremental update of ADO so that it makes more sense in a world of distributed services. In this section, I'll give you an overview of ADO.NET. Later in the book, I'll dig into this technology in detail.

The DataSet Object

The key .NET object for representing data is the DataSet. The DataSet is sort of a beefed-up Recordset object that represents an entire schema of relational data rather than a single table. As Figure 2.5 shows, the DataSet is the top level of a hierarchy of objects. Although the DataSet gets populated by .NET code in a single operation, you can actually drill down into its constituent objects.

The DataSet object itself has a wide selection of methods and properties for working with data. Some of the important methods of the DataSet object are listed in Table 2.1.

FIGURE 2.5:

ADO.NET DataSet
classes

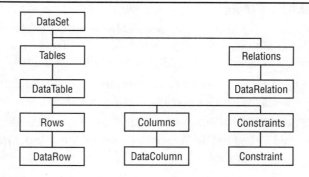

TABLE 2.1: DataSet Methods

Method Name	Description
AcceptChanges	Commits all changes made to the DataSet since it was loaded, or since AcceptChanges was last called.
Clear	Discards all data in the DataSet.
Copy	Clones both the structure and the data of the DataSet.
GetXml	Returns an XML stream representing the entire DataSet.
Merge	Merges two DataSets.
ReadXml	Loads a DataSet from an XML stream.

NOTE   I'll cover the use of DataSet objects in more detail in Chapter 15, "Editing Data with ADO.NET."

The DataSet object is explicitly designed for use in disconnected scenarios. It's easy to load the DataSet with data and then disconnect it from the original data source. Saving changes later requires only a few lines of code.

When you're using XML to move data between components, you can choose to move all the data, or only data that has been changed since the last time the AcceptChanges method was executed. If you choose to move only the changes, ADO.NET constructs a *DiffGram*. A DiffGram is a specially formatted XML message that contains information on the original data of a row, information on the new data, and a unique identifier to allow the receiving DataSet to know which row has been changed. Using DiffGrams to move changes helps reduce the amount of network traffic and makes your application more responsive.

ADO.NET Providers

ADO.NET connects to data sources by using sets of classes called .NET data providers. Unlike traditional OLE DB providers, .NET data providers are implemented as a series of classes. The beta version .NET Framework includes two data providers:

- The *.NET SQL Data Provider* (implemented in the System.Data.SqlClient namespace) includes the SqlConnection, SqlCommand, SqlDataReader, and SqlDataAdapter classes.

- The *.NET OLE DB Data Provider* (implemented in the System.Data.OleDb namespace) includes the OleDbConnection, OleDbCommand, OleDbDataReader, and OleDb-DataAdapter classes.

Note the close mapping between the classes of the two data providers. In the .NET documentation, you will find the data access classes referred to as simply Connection, Command, DataReader, and DataAdapter, even though, strictly speaking, there are no such classes.

The SQL Data Provider can retrieve data from Microsoft SQL Server version 7 or later. It uses low-level SQL Server APIs to communicate directly with the SQL Server database engine, without going through the overhead of a universal data access library such as OLE DB or ODBC. On the one hand, this speeds up SQL Server data access. But it's also a step backward from universal interoperability.

The OLE DB Data Provider can retrieve data from OLE DB data sources. However, it can use only a small number of OLE DB providers. In particular, the OLE DB Data Provider can retrieve data using these OLE DB providers:

- The SQLOLEDB provider, for Microsoft SQL Server data sources

- The MSDAORA provider, for Oracle data sources

- The Microsoft.Jet.OLEDB.4.0 provider, for Microsoft Jet data sources

WARNING   If you need to connect to databases other than SQL Server, Oracle, or Jet databases, you'll need to use the older ADO objects via .NET/COM interop. I'll cover this technique in Chapter 13, "Using ADO from .NET."

The ADO.NET Process

I'll be digging into ADO.NET extensively in Part IV of this book. But to give you a taste of how ADO.NET works, I'll show you a bit of sample code here, using the OLE DB Data Provider. These samples are written in Visual Basic .NET.

ADO.NET uses the Connection object (SqlConnection or OleDbConnection) to represent a connection to a particular data source. When you instantiate a Connection object, you can supply a connection string to specify the data source, just as in ADO. For example, you might create and hook up a Connection object for a Jet database like this:

```
Private cnn As OleDbConnection
cnn = New OleDbConnection("Provider=" & _
  "Microsoft.Jet.OLEDB.4.0;Data Source=" & _
  "C:\NWIND.MDB")
```

After you've established a connection to a data source, you can create a Command object (SqlCommand or OleDbCommand) that executes SQL against that data source and, possibly, returns data. The easiest way to do this is to use the CreateCommand method of the Connection object, and then set the CommandText property of the new Command object:

```
Private cmdCustomers As OleDbCommand
cmdCustomers = cnn.CreateCommand()
cmdCustomers.CommandText = "SELECT CustomerID, " & _
  "CompanyName, ContactName FROM Customers"
```

The Command object doesn't directly return a DataSet object. Rather, you can use the DataAdapter object (SqlDataAdapter or OleDbDataAdapter) to populate a DataSet object with the results of a command. In particular, if a Command object represents a SELECT statement, you can use the DataAdapter to connect it to a DataSet this way:

```
Private daCustomers As OleDbDataAdapter
Private dsCustomers As DataSet
daCustomers = New OleDbDataAdapter()
daCustomers.SelectCommand = cmdCustomers
```

TIP Note that there is only one DataSet class, whether you're using the Sql or OleDb classes to retrieve data. Once you reach the DataSet, you've reached a level where the details of the underlying data source have been abstracted away.

By setting the SelectCommand property of the DataAdapter object, you're telling the adapter that it should execute the specified Command object whenever data needs to be retrieved from the underlying data source. The DataAdapter also has InsertCommand, UpdateCommand, and DeleteCommand properties. Setting these properties allows the DataAdapter to modify data by executing the appropriate Command object.

If the data in a DataSet is based on a single table, you can use the CommandBuilder object (SqlCommandBuilder or OleDbCommandBuilder) to avoid the tedium of constructing individual insert, update, and delete commands. After you have set the SelectCommand property of a DataAdapter object, you can pass that object to a CommandBuilder object:

```
Private ocbCustomers As OleDbCommandBuilder
ocbCustomers = New OleDbCommandBuilder(daCustomers)
```

The CommandBuilder object handles all the details of setting up the insert, update, and delete commands to work with the underlying data source.

ADO.NET allows you to construct all of the scaffolding for retrieving and updating data without actually connecting to the data source. Once you're ready to work with data, only a few lines of code are needed to populate the DataSet:

```
Private dsCustomers As DataSet
cnn.Open()
dsCustomers = New DataSet()
daCustomers.Fill(dsCustomers, "Customers")
cnn.Close()
```

> **TIP**   Note that there's no need to maintain a persistent connection to a data source in ADO.NET. When you call the Fill method of the DataSet, it retrieves all the data from the data source into the DataSet and its subsidiary objects. At that point, you should close the Connection object to free resources.

As an alternative to using the DataAdapter and DataSet objects, you can use a DataReader object. The DataReader object can be created by calling the ExecuteReader method of the Command object. For example:

```
Private drCustomers As OleDbDataReader
DrCustomers = cmdCustomers.ExecuteReader()
Do While (drCustomers.Read())
    ' Do something with the data here
Loop
```

The stream of data provided by the DataReader is always forward-only and read-only. This is very similar to the "firehose" cursor provided by ADO when you open a forward-only, read-only Recordset.

The Big Picture

Figure 2.6 gives a schematic view of the different ADO.NET components and how they fit together. Note that as of this writing, ADO.NET is considerably simpler than ADO for data access. That's partly because it's a new technology and no third-party data providers are available yet.

It's clear that ADO.NET is meant to supplement, rather than supplant, ADO. Microsoft apparently has no intention of extending ADO.NET as a truly universal data access method, preferring instead to concentrate on optimizing ADO.NET for a few particular situations. Because .NET applications can use existing COM components, I expect to see a mix of ADO and ADO.NET data access in most .NET applications.

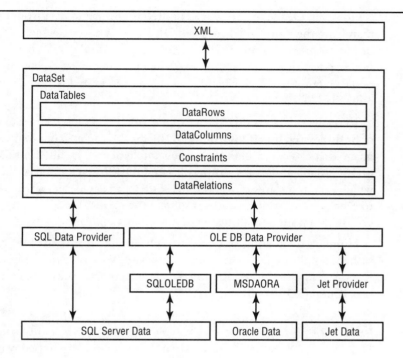

Earlier Data Access Libraries

ADO and ADO.NET are tools for retrieving data, but (despite the universal data access scheme) they are not the only such tools. Although ADO or ADO.NET should be your first choice for new applications, you're likely to find a variety of other data access libraries used in older applications. Three of these libraries, in particular, are common enough that you should be familiar with them:

- Open Database Connectivity (ODBC)
- Data Access Objects (DAO)
- Remote Data Objects (RDO)

ODBC

In many ways, ODBC is the father of OLE DB. ODBC is an earlier attempt at universal data access; like OLE DB, it was designed largely by Microsoft with some industry participation. Also like OLE DB, ODBC depends on data source–specific driver software being written to actually retrieve data.

However, ODBC is pretty well limited to retrieving data from relational databases, rather than from the more widely defined OLE DB data sources such as e-mail and HTML pages or files, because the core ODBC software expects all data to be retrieved with SQL queries. Ultimately, this proved to be enough of a limiting factor to convince Microsoft to design a replacement, OLE DB, which is also better integrated with the core Windows operating systems than ODBC ever was.

To retrieve data via ODBC, an application first converts its request into a standard dialect of SQL defined by ODBC. This ODBC SQL is an attempt to create a universal SQL language that can cover all the variations implemented by different database providers. The ODBC Manager locates an appropriate ODBC driver and passes the request to the driver, which then translates it from ODBC SQL into database-specific SQL. This SQL is then fed to the database, which returns results to the driver. These results are passed back to the ODBC Manager and ultimately to the client application.

Although it's possible to write an application that uses the ODBC API directly, this is rather complicated. To tame this complexity, Microsoft introduced a pair of object models, Data Access Objects and Remote Data Objects, that allow object-oriented access through the procedural ODBC API.

DAO

Data Access Objects (DAO) is the native object model shipped with Microsoft Access. It can use the Jet engine directly to retrieve data from Access databases, but it's also capable of using ODBC to retrieve data from any database for which you have an ODBC driver.

Figure 2.7 shows a portion of the DAO object model. As you can see, it's similar to the ADO object model.

Because it has been distributed with every copy of Microsoft Access or Visual Basic, there may be more applications using DAO for data access than any other data access library. However, DAO has certain weaknesses. First, it was designed for local data access, and its ability to handle client-server data access via ODBC was added later. This resulted in some performance compromises for using server-based data. Second, DAO isn't extensible. Rather, it tries to encompass all possible data operations within one large object model, including DDL and security operations. This has resulted in a very complex object model that takes a long time to learn and uses up a lot of computer resources.

DAO also suffers from a strictly hierarchical approach to objects. To use DAO, you always need to start with the top-level DBEngine object and work your way down the hierarchy to the objects you're interested in. ADO, by contrast, allows you to create a Recordset object directly and retrieve data immediately.

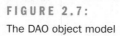

FIGURE 2.7:

The DAO object model

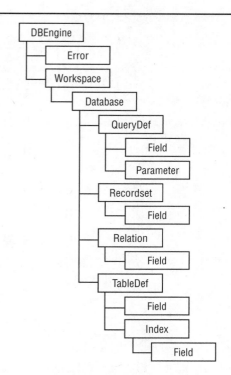

DAO also has no notion of disconnected Recordsets. Data in DAO is either connected or nonexistent.

RDO

Remote Data Objects (RDO) provides yet another data access library layered on top of ODBC. First shipped with Visual Basic 4.0, RDO has been a feature of Visual Basic ever since. Figure 2.4 shows the RDO object model.

RDO was a conscious attempt to correct some of the problems of DAO, especially with regard to client-server data. The RDO object model is simpler than the DAO model (although not as simple as the ADO model) and correspondingly faster. However, RDO keeps the SQL orientation and the hierarchical approach of DAO, as well as the orientation toward always-connected data. The idiosyncratic naming of objects and exclusivity to Visual Basic also put off many developers. Although RDO represents a distinct advance over DAO, especially with regard to raw speed, it's not as optimized for general-purpose data access as ADO.

FIGURE 2.8:

The RDO object model

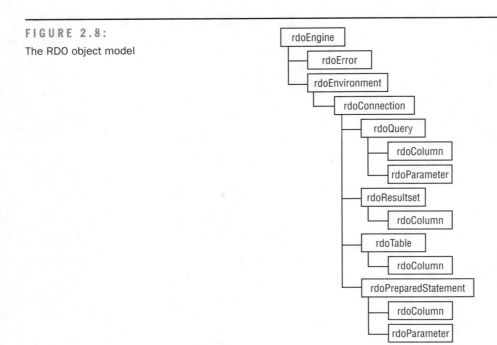

Choosing a Data Access Library

Given the variety of choices for moving data from a database to a client application, how do you decide which data access library to use? The easy answer is to just go for the latest model, ADO or ADO.NET. But this might not be the correct answer in all circumstances. Here are a few things to think about when you're deciding how to retrieve data:

- If you need a feature that's available only in ADO, such as the ability to use the Stream object to retrieve binary data from a file considered a record in a set of records supplied by a directory service provider, you've got no choice but to use ADO.

- Similarly, if you need a feature that's available only in ADO.NET, such as transmission of disconnected data via XML, your choice is easy.

- For multitiered applications, particularly those that use the Internet to move data between tiers, you should consider either ADO or ADO.NET. Microsoft, of course, is heavily promoting ADO.NET for this purpose. But you need to balance that against the possibility that .NET might not, after all, be a success.

- If you're writing an application from scratch, evaluate ADO and ADO.NET for your data access code. When making your decision, you should consider the learning curve for your developers, compatibility with existing applications, and the availability of appropriate providers.

- If you require the absolutely fastest data access and if development costs are of little concern, you should think about using OLE DB directly by writing a custom data consumer. You should be aware, though, that this will take *much* longer than using ADO, and result in, at best, a modest performance gain.

- If you need data from nontraditional data sources such as e-mail storage or file systems, and there's an OLE DB provider for the data you're interested in, you should seriously consider using ADO.

- If you need portability to older 16-bit (Windows 3.1 or Windows for Workgroups) platforms and don't want to maintain multiple code bases, you need to use one of the older data access interfaces. Both DAO and ODBC are available in 16-bit versions, making it easier to maintain one code base for both old and new platforms.

- If you're updating an existing application that uses one of the older methods (such as DAO), you've got a tough problem. Staying with the current data access library will likely result in the fastest development cycle, but at the cost of not being able to use the latest features. If there are substantial problems with your existing application, you might find it worthwhile to upgrade to ADO while you're fixing the other problems and to take all the development hit in a single cycle.

Ultimately, most new applications in the foreseeable future (say, two to four years) will probably benefit from using ADO.NET as the data access library. Now that Microsoft has committed its substantial resources to ADO.NET, you can expect other vendors to join the parade and release .NET data providers. Microsoft has announced that they are standardizing on ADO.NET in their own applications, but you should take this with a grain of salt. Many of the applications that Microsoft is shipping still use older data access methods. And, as always, it will be easier to get technical support on new interfaces than on old ones.

Summary

In this chapter, I've tried to give you the grand overview of Microsoft's current and past data access libraries: ADO, ADO.NET, ODBC, DAO, and RDO. Now it's time to learn some of the details of working with the ADO and ADO.NET libraries. In Part II of this book, I'll turn our attention to ADO; following that, Part III will focus on the changes coming in .NET, and Part IV will deal with ADO.NET in depth.

PART II

Understanding ADO

CHAPTER 3

Using the ADO Objects to Retrieve Data

- Introducing the ADO object model

- Connecting to data sources

- Opening Recordsets

- Using stored procedures to retrieve data

- Finding and sorting data

In this chapter, I'm going to begin looking at ADO in more detail. I'll start with a brief tour of the ADO object model, and then look at the most basic of all data operations: connecting to a data source and retrieving data for use by your own applications.

NOTE "ADO" in this book refers to the ADO 2.7 library of COM objects unless otherwise indicated. Whenever I refer to the newer .NET version, I'll call it ADO.NET specifically.

Introducing the ADO Object Model

COM components such as ADO expose their functionality through objects, which can have methods, properties, and events. ADO is no exception to this rule. Like many other COM components, the ADO objects are arranged in a hierarchy, where objects contain collections of other objects. Figure 3.1 shows the entire ADO hierarchy. For an object model with so few objects, ADO provides a lot of functionality.

In this section, I'll briefly introduce the objects that make up the ADO object model. Rather than provide an exhaustive list of the methods, properties, and events of these objects, I'll give you a general sense of their uses. You'll learn more about the details of these objects as we dig into sample code that makes use of them.

TIP For more details on the ADO objects, see Appendix A, "The ADO Object Model." You can also find complete documentation in the MDAC SDK, available from www.microsoft.com/data.

FIGURE 3.1:

The ADO object model

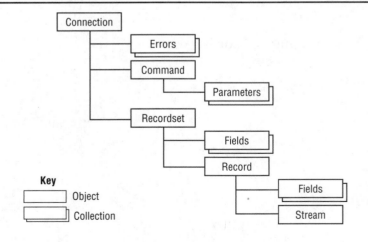

The Connection Object

A Connection object represents a single connection to an OLE DB data source. ADO Connection objects can be either explicit or implicit. To use an explicit Connection object, you declare and instantiate it like any other object, and then pass it to other ADO objects:

```
Dim cnn As ADODB.Connection
    Dim rst As ADODB.Recordset

    Set cnn = New ADODB.Connection
    cnn.Open ("Provider=SQLOLEDB;Data Source=(local);" & _
     "Initial Catalog=pubs;Integrated Security=SSPI")
    Set rst = New ADODB.Recordset
    Set rst.ActiveConnection = cnn
    rst.Open "authors"
```

NOTE   The string "Provider=SQLOLEDB;Data Source=(local);Initial Catalog=pubs;Integrated Security=SSPI" is an ADO *connection string*. A connection string tells ADO what data source to use for its operations. You'll learn more about connection strings later in the chapter. This particular connection string provides a connection to a SQL Server database.

Implicit Connection objects, on the other hand, don't need to be declared. ADO creates them as necessary as you work with other ADO objects:

```
Dim rst As ADODB.Recordset

    Set rst = New ADODB.Recordset
    rst.Open "authors", "Provider=SQLOLEDB;Data Source=(local);" & _
     "Initial Catalog=pubs;Integrated Security=SSPI"
```

In this case, there's no Connection object in the code. Instead, the code supplies a connection string to open the Recordset object. ADO will create a Connection object behind the scenes and assign it the supplied connection string.

In general, you should use explicit Connection objects any time you need to perform multiple operations with the same data source. That's because they can be reused, while implicit Connection objects need to be recreated with each use. This leads to a performance problem, because your code continually connects to and disconnects from the data source.

The Command Object

A Command object represents a single instruction to an OLE DB data source to produce data. Depending on the back end, this might be a SQL query, a stored procedure, or something else entirely. Command objects have two major uses:

- To execute code such as SQL statements directly against an OLE DB data source
- To retrieve a Recordset from an OLE DB data source, based on the results of a SQL statement or a stored procedure

The Parameter Object

A Parameter object represents a single parameter for a Command object. This might be a runtime parameter in a SQL query or an input or output parameter in a stored procedure. More generally, parameters are used with any type of parameterized commands, where an action is defined once but can have different results depending on the values that have been assigned to the defined parameters.

The Recordset Object

A Recordset object represents a set of records retrieved from an OLE DB data provider. Because this is the object that allows you to retrieve and modify data, it's indispensable to most ADO processing. ADO allows you to open a Recordset object directly or to create one from a Connection or Command object.

In database terms, a Recordset object represents a *cursor*. A cursor is a set of results (normally arranged in rows and columns, or, in ADO terminology, records and fields), together with a pointer to a current record. ADO Recordset objects support four types of cursors:

- A *dynamic cursor* lets you see changes to the data made by other users, and it supports all types of cursor movement that don't rely on bookmarks. It may allow bookmarks if the data provider supports them.

- A *keyset cursor* is dynamic but doesn't let you see records added or deleted by other users. (It does allow you to see changes to the data made by other users.) Keyset cursors support bookmarks and all other kinds of movement through the Recordset.

- A *static cursor* provides a frozen copy of the data at the time the Recordset was opened. Additions, changes, and deletions by other users have no impact on the Recordset, because it's never refreshed after it's created. Static cursors support bookmarks and all other kinds of movement through the Recordset.

- A *forward-only cursor* is a static cursor that allows you only to move forward through the Recordset. This is ADO's default cursor. A forward-only cursor is similar to a static cursor in that it also gives you a snapshot of the data at the time the cursor was opened.

ADO Recordset objects support a number of advanced data manipulation methods, including immediate and batch updating, as well as optimistic batch updating via disconnected Recordsets. You'll learn more about these techniques in Chapter 4, "Editing Data with ADO."

WARNING   Although ADO supports four types of cursors, OLE DB providers are not required to supply all four types. Later in the chapter, I'll discuss cursor degradation and show you how to check which type of cursor you've actually opened.

The Field Object

A Field object represents a single column of data from a Recordset object. Once you've retrieved a Recordset, you'll usually work with the Fields collection to read the data in the Recordset. Because the Fields collection is the default property of the Recordset object, you usually won't need to specify it in your code. In addition, the Value property of the Field object, which contains the actual data, is the default property of the Field object. So the following four lines of code all refer to the same value:

```
rst.Fields(0).Value
rst.Fields (0)
rst(0).Value
rst(0)
```

The Record Object

The ADO Record object is designed to represent a row in a Recordset when the underlying OLE DB provider naturally supports a hierarchical data store rather than rows and columns. For example, Record objects can be used with providers that supply information from file systems, web servers, or e-mail storage. They generally cannot be used with providers that supply information from standard relational databases (even if there's a hierarchy within the database).

WARNING   There's no easy way to tell whether an arbitrary OLE DB provider supports the Record object. Perhaps the best way is to attempt to open a Record object using the provider. If the provider can't supply one, it will generally return error 3251, Operation Not Supported.

The Stream Object

The Stream object represents binary data. Most often, you'll want to open a Stream object to retrieve the data associated with a Record object. You can also create your own stand-alone Stream objects and use them as handy spots to store binary data. The Record, Stream, and Recordset objects work together to help you navigate through hierarchical storage:

- You can open a Record object at the root level of a hierarchical storage system.

- Using the Record's GetChildren method, you can open a Recordset object containing all the children of a node. You can in turn set a Record object equal to one of these children.

- Using the Record's associated Stream object, you can retrieve the actual binary data from within the record. You can think of Records as directory entries and Streams as the data contained within the files referred to by those entries.

The Error Object

An Error object represents a single error from a data provider or an error that's internal to ADO. Because one data access operation can generate multiple errors, Error objects are contained in an Errors collection. If the most recent ADO operation succeeded, this collection will be empty. Otherwise, you can use the For Each operator to examine each Error in turn.

WARNING   If there is no valid Connection object, you will have to use the Visual Basic Err object instead of the Errors collection. This is the case if you've directly opened a Recordset using a connection string, for example; you can't access the implicit Connection object's Errors collection.

Connecting to Data Sources

Not surprisingly, you use the Connection object to connect to a data source. After all, that's what a Connection object represents: a connection to a single data source. All data operations in ADO involve instantiating a Connection object, either explicitly or implicitly. When you create a Connection object and later associate that object with a Recordset object, you're using an explicit connection. When you simply open a Recordset object, supplying a connection string when you do so, you're using an implicit connection. ADO creates a Connection object in the latter case, but it's strictly internal to ADO's own workings.

You can control the behavior of the Connection object to some extent by setting properties before you call the object's Open method (these properties cannot be changed for a connection that's already open). The properties of interest are as follows:

- ConnectionString
- ConnectionTimeout
- Mode
- CursorLocation
- DefaultDatabase
- IsolationLevel
- Provider

The *ConnectionString* property can be used to specify a data source or to supply other information making up an ADO connection string. I'll discuss the format used for connection strings in the next section of this chapter. Although you can specify the ConnectionString property before calling the Open method, it's usually just as convenient to supply it as an argument to that method.

The *ConnectionTimeout* property tells ADO how many seconds it should wait for a data source to respond. By default, this is set to 15. If you're connecting across a busy network, or the Internet, you may need to increase this timeout value. You can also set this property to the special value *0* to have no timeout, in which case your code will wait forever for the data source to respond.

You can use the *Mode* property to ask for particular permissions when you open a connection. If the requested permissions can't be set, you'll get an error when you call the Open method. By default, the Mode of a Connection object is adModeUnknown. Table 3.1 shows the possible values for the Mode property.

TABLE 3.1: Mode Property Values

Value	Meaning
adModeRead	Read-only.
adModeReadWrite	Read-write.
adModeWrite	Write-only.
adModeShareDenyRead	Prohibit other applications from opening a connection with read permissions.
adModeShareDenyWrite	Prohibit other applications from opening a connection with write permissions.
adModeShareDenyNone	Allow other applications to open a connection with any permissions.
adModeShareExclusive	Prohibit other applications from opening a connection at all.
adModeRecursive	Propagates sharing restrictions to all subrecords of the current record.

The *CursorLocation* property can be set to adUseServer to use the cursors supplied by the OLE DB provider for the connection, or set to adUseClient to use the client-side cursor library. For advanced functionality (such as disconnected Recordsets), you may need to use the client-side library, although this will add additional overhead to some operations.

You can use the *DefaultDatabase* property to specify which database on a server a particular Connection object should use for data operations. Alternatively, you can specify this as a part of the connection string. For example, if you're using the SQL Server provider, you can either set the DefaultDatabase property or put the name of the default database in as the Initial Catalog argument in the connection string. The advantage of using the DefaultDatabase property is that it's provider-independent. Any objects that use this Connection object will inherit its default database.

The *IsolationLevel* property controls the effect that one transaction has on other transactions from different connections. Table 3.2 shows the possible settings for this property.

TABLE 3.2: IsolationLevel Property Values

Constant	Effect
adXactUnspecified	Value is returned when the provider is unable to determine the current isolation level.
adXactChaos	Prohibits overwriting changes that are pending from more highly isolated transactions. This is the default setting.
adXactBrowse	Allows you to view, but not change, uncommitted changes from other transactions.
adXactReadUncommitted	Same as adXactBrowse.
adXactCursorStability	Allows you to view changes from other transactions only after they've been committed.
adXactReadCommitted	Same as adXactCursorStability.
adXactRepeatableRead	Allows requerying a Recordset to include changes pending from other transactions.
adXactIsolated	Forces all transactions to be isolated from other transactions. Choose this value for the strictest transactional processing.
adXactSerializable	Same as adXactIsolated.

The *Provider* property allows you to specify an OLE DB provider before opening the connection. It's usually more convenient to include this as the Provider argument in the connection string.

Connection strings are used with the Connection object's Open method. The syntax of this method is as follows:

```
Connection.Open [ConnectionString][, UserID][, Password][, Options]
```

Depending on how you write your code, you might supply all, some, or none of the four arguments to the method. One way or another, you must supply a connection string, either by filling in the ConnectionString argument in the Open method or by setting the connection's ConnectionString property before calling the Open method.

Usually, you'll supply the UserID and Password as part of the connection string. However, in cases where that information is supplied by the user, you might find it more convenient to use the arguments to the Open method. For example, you'll find the following code (to open a SQL Server connection with a supplied user ID and password) in frmCodeSamples in the ADOChapter3 sample project:

```
Private Sub cmdConnect1_Click()
    ' Connect using ID and password supplied
    ' by the user interface
    Dim cnn As ADODB.Connection

    On Error GoTo HandleErr

    Set cnn = New ADODB.Connection
    cnn.Open "Provider=SQLOLEDB.1;" & _
     "Server=(local);Initial Catalog=pubs", _
     txtUserID, txtPassword

    MsgBox "Connection Succeeded"
    cnn.Close
    Set cnn = Nothing

ExitHere:
    Exit Sub

HandleErr:
    MsgBox "Error " & Err.Number & ": " & _
     Err.Description, , "cmdConnect1_Click"
    Resume ExitHere
    Resume

End Sub
```

As you can see, by using the UserID and Password arguments, you can avoid either hard-coding security information or editing the connection string to insert these values.

TIP   If you specify UserID and Password both in the connection string and as separate arguments, the arguments override any values set in the connection string.

The last argument to the Open method specifies whether the connection should be opened synchronously. You can use the constant adConnectUnspecified for a synchronous connection (the default, so you needn't bother to specify a value at all in this case) or the constant adAsyncConnect for an asynchronous connection. I'll demonstrate code for asynchronous connections in Chapter 5, "Managing Activity with ADO Events."

You should also be familiar with the Close method of the Connection object. This method disconnects the Connection object from the data source without destroying the object itself. While the object is in this state, you can change the connection string or other properties and then execute the Open method again to reconnect with new information. When you're completely done with a Connection object, you can either set it equal to Nothing or just let it go out of scope to reclaim the memory it's using. Most developers feel that it's better practice to explicitly set the variable to Nothing, to indicate that you're done with it.

Connection Strings

To manage ADO connections effectively, you need to know the details of constructing connection strings. An OLE DB connection string has this format:

```
Provider=value;File Name=value;Remote Provider=value;
➥ Remote Server=value;URL=value;
```

The format includes these five arguments:

- The *Provider* argument specifies the name of the OLE DB provider to use. Table 3.3 shows the possible values this argument can have for some of the OLE DB providers that are available from Microsoft.

- The *File Name* value specifies a file containing connection information—for example, an ODBC file data source. If you use the File Name argument, you must omit the Provider argument.

- The *Remote Provider* value specifies the name of a provider to use on the server when opening a client-side connection. This option applies to Remote Data Service (RDS) connections only. See Chapter 8, "Working with Disconnected Recordsets," for more information on RDS.

- The *Remote Server* value specifies the name of a server to retrieve data from when using RDS.

- The *URL* value specifies the connection string as a URL rather than as an ODBC-style string.

All these arguments are optional (although you must supply one of the Provider, File Name, or URL arguments). You can include additional arguments in the ConnectionString property, in which case they are passed to the OLE DB provider without any alteration by ADO. Each provider has its own list of additional arguments it can interpret.

NOTE   You can specify a provider by a name with or without a version number. For example, SQLOLEDB.1 refers to a particular release of the SQL Server provider, while SQLOLEDB refers to the most recent release of the driver installed on the computer where the code is running. If you use versioned names, you don't have to worry about retesting your code when a provider is updated (although you also can't take advantage of any of the new features of the provider).

TABLE 3.3: OLE DB Providers

Provider Name	Argument	Description
Microsoft Jet 3.51 OLE DB Provider	Microsoft.Jet.OLEDB.3.51	Allows access to Jet 3.51 data sources.
Microsoft Jet 4.0 OLE DB Provider	Microsoft.Jet.OLEDB.4.0	Allows access to Jet 4.0 data sources.
Microsoft OLE DB Provider for Internet Publishing	MSDAIPP.DSO	Used for record and stream access to data on web servers.
Microsoft OLE DB Provider for ODBC Drivers	MSDASQL	Allows access to any data for which you have an ODBC driver.
Microsoft OLE DB Provider for OLAP Services	MSOLAP	Allows access to data in Microsoft Analysis Services databases.
Microsoft OLE DB Provider for Oracle	MSDAORA	Allows access to Oracle 7.3 and 8 databases.
Microsoft OLE DB Provider for SQL Server	SQLOLEDB	Allows access to data in Microsoft SQL Server databases.
MS OLE DB Remoting Provider	MS Remote	Allows retrieving data from remote data sources as if they were local.
Microsoft Data Shaping Service for OLE DB	MSDataShape	Allows the creation of hierarchical Recordsets.
Microsoft OLE DB Provider for Microsoft Indexing Services	MSIDX	Used to retrieve data from Microsoft Indexing Service.
Microsoft OLE DB Provider for Microsoft Directory Services	ADSDSOObject	Used to retrieve data from Microsoft Active Directory.
Microsoft OLE DB Persistence Provider	MSPersist	Stores data from any provider to a local disk file.
Microsoft OLE DB Provider for Data Mining Services	MSDMine	Allows access to data warehouses through the OLE DB for Data Mining interfaces.

One way to create a connection string is to use the Data Link Properties dialog box. You'll see this dialog box, shown in Figure 3.2, frequently as you work with applications that use ADO. But you can also use it directly from Windows Explorer as a way to explore OLE DB providers. To create and examine a connection string with the Data Link Properties dialog box, follow these steps:

1. Right-click in any Explorer window and choose New ➢ Text Document.

2. Save the document with the file extension `.udl`. You'll get a warning from Windows that changing a file extension is a bad thing to do; tell it yes, you want to do this.

3. Double-click the UDL file. This will open the Data Link Properties dialog box.

4. Click the Provider tab of the Data Link Properties dialog box. Choose an OLE DB provider.

5. Fill in the rest of the tabs with appropriate information for the provider and data you want to use.

6. Click OK to save the file.

7. Use Windows Notepad (or the text editor of your choice) to open the UDL file. It will contain an OLE DB connection string.

Although you normally can connect to a data source using just the provider name, user ID, and password, if you examine connection strings that were built using the Data Link Properties dialog box, you'll find that they're usually much more complex than that. This is because any argument that's not understood by ADO itself is automatically passed to the underlying OLE DB driver for interpretation, and most OLE DB drivers understand a wide variety of arguments.

FIGURE 3.2:

The Data Link Properties dialog box

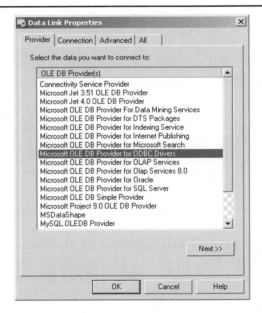

For an exhaustive listing of the arguments understood by any given provider, you'll need to consult that provider's documentation. You'll find documentation for the Microsoft-supplied providers in the Platform SDK, which is part of the Microsoft Developer Network Library (available by subscription or online at http://msdn.microsoft.com/library/default.asp). Table 3.4 lists some of the available arguments for the Jet, SQL Server, and Oracle providers that are used in the examples in this book.

TABLE 3.4: Connection String Arguments

Provider	Argument	Description
Jet	Data Source	Name of the Jet database to connect to
Jet	Jet OLEDB:System Database	Name of the system database to use when verifying the username and password
Jet	Jet OLEDB:Database Password	Database password (for simple security only)
Jet	Jet OLEDB:Lock Retry	Number of times to repeat an attempt to read a locked page
Jet	Jet OLEDB:Lock Delay	Number of milliseconds to wait between lock retries
Jet	Jet OLEDB:Max Locks Per File	Maximum number of locks to use in a single database (default is 9,500)
Jet	Jet OLEDB:Registry Path	Path to the registry key that contains the Jet engine tuning and security parameters
SQL Server	Integrated Security	Set to the literal value "SSPI" to use Windows NT login security
SQL Server	Data Source	Name of the SQL Server to connect to
SQL Server	Server	Name of the SQL Server to connect to
SQL Server	Initial Catalog	Name of the SQL Server database to use
SQL Server	Database	Name of the SQL Server database to use
SQL Server	User ID	Username for SQL Server authentication
SQL Server	Uid	Username for SQL Server authentication
SQL Server	Password	Password for SQL Server authentication
SQL Server	Pwd	Password for SQL Server authentication
SQL Server	Trusted_Connection	Set to "yes" to use Windows NT authentication; "no" to use SQL Server authentication
SQL Server	Use Procedure For Prepare	Set to "yes" to create temporary stored procedures when a command is prepared
Oracle	Data Source	Name of the Oracle server to connect to
Oracle	User ID	Username for authentication
Oracle	Password	Password for authentication

Sample Connection Strings

In this book, I'll use (for the most part) Microsoft SQL Server, Microsoft Access, and Oracle databases for the examples. Most of the examples use Microsoft SQL Server, but I'll use Access and Oracle when necessary to demonstrate differences in the way their providers handle ADO code. In this section, I'll explain sample connection strings for these three providers.

Here's a typical SQL Server connection string using a user ID and password:

```
Provider=SQLOLEDB.1;Server=SQL01;Initial Catalog=pubs;UserID=sa;pwd=;
```

That connects to the database pubs on the SQL Server SQL01, logging on as the sa user with no password. If the code is running on the same computer as the server, you can use the special keyword (local) (including the parentheses) instead of the server name:

```
Provider=SQLOLEDB.1;Server=(local);Initial Catalog=pubs;UserID=sa;pwd=;
```

SQL Server also supports (depending on the choices made during server installation) Windows integrated authentication. If you're using Windows integrated authentication, you don't have to supply a user ID and password to the server. Rather, it will use the user ID and password of your Windows account to log in to SQL Server. You can specify Windows integrated authentication with the Integrated Security=SSPI property:

```
Provider=SQLOLEDB.1;Server=SQL01;Initial Catalog=pubs;
➡ Integrated Security=SSPI;
```

For Microsoft Access connection strings, you need to specify a file location rather than a server name. That's because Access is a file-based database rather than a client-server database:

```
Provider=Microsoft.Jet.OLEDB.4.0;Data Source=C:\Program Files\
➡ Microsoft Office\Office\Samples\Northwind.mdb; Persist Security Info=False
```

The Persist Security Info=False setting tells ADO that there is no stored user or password information for this connection string. The Jet OLEDB provider will first try opening the specified database as the Admin user with no password. If that fails, it will prompt the user for a user ID and password combination. You can also specify the login information in the connection string:

```
Provider=Microsoft.Jet.OLEDB.4.0;Password=tribbles;User ID=Joe;
➡ Data Source=C:\Program Files\Microsoft Office\Office\Samples\
➡ Northwind.mdb;Persist Security Info=True
```

| TIP | The order of information in an OLE DB connection string isn't critical. By convention, I put the provider first, but the rest of the settings can be rearranged without affecting the functionality of the connection string. |

Connection strings for Oracle databases specify a data source and user information:

```
Provider=MSDAORA.1;Password=TIGER;User ID=SCOTT;
➥ Data Source=PEACOCK;Persist Security Info=True
```

Note that for Oracle, the Data Source property is not a server name or a database name, but a database alias. You can use the Oracle client tools (such as SQL*Net or Net8) to set up a database alias that points to a specific database on a specific server.

Internet Connections

ADO also has the ability to connect to a data source over the Internet, using any OLE DB provider that's installed on the web server. The ADO component that enables this is called the Remote Data Service, or RDS. RDS is a proxy that translates ADO calls to HTTP requests. These requests are then sent to a web server, where a server-side component (installed by default with IIS 4 or 5) translates them back to ADO. The results return to the client via HTTP and are then translated back to an ADO Recordset by RDS.

RDS is an example of an OLE DB *service provider*. Rather than connecting directly to a database, RDS is used to manipulate requests to a normal OLE DB *data provider*, which does the actual database access.

> **WARNING** Generally, RDS is *not safe* on an IIS server connected to the Internet! I'll discuss safe ways to use RDS in Chapter 8.

Opening Recordsets

To retrieve data in ADO, you will usually use the Recordset object. You can also retrieve data with the Record and Stream objects, but only in some situations. We'll discuss those objects in Chapter 6, "Using Records and Streams." The Command object can also return information in output parameters; you'll see that technique later in this chapter.

A Recordset object can be initialized to contain data by calling its Open method:

```
Recordset.Open Source, ActiveConnection, CursorType, LockType, Options
```

All these arguments are optional in the call to the Open method, because they can all be supplied by setting properties of the Recordset object before calling the Open method. For example, you can omit the LockType argument here if you have already set the LockType property of the Recordset object, or if you're happy with the default value of the property.

> **NOTE** Although the arguments are optional in the Open method, you must supply at least the Source and ActiveConnection before opening a Recordset, either as property settings or in the Open method.

Recordset Properties

The Source argument specifies the location where ADO should obtain the data for the Recordset. Because OLE DB providers are so flexible, there are a lot of possibilities for the Source argument. Depending on the provider, this argument can be any of the following:

- A Command object that returns records
- An SQL statement
- A table name
- A stored procedure name
- The name of a file containing a persisted Recordset
- The name of a Stream object containing a persisted Recordset
- A URL that specifies a file or other location with data

The ActiveConnection argument specifies the ADO connection to use. This can be either a Connection object that you've already opened or a connection string. In the latter case, ADO creates an implicit Connection object specifically for this Recordset to use.

The CursorType argument specifies some of the behavior of the Recordset object. You can specify one of four constants here:

- To open a dynamic Recordset, use *adOpenDynamic*. A dynamic Recordset allows all types of movement through the Recordset and keeps your copy of the data updated with any changes made by other users.

- To open a keyset Recordset, use *adOpenKeyset*. A keyset Recordset functions like a dynamic Recordset, except that you won't see new records added by other users; nor will records deleted by other users be removed.

- To open a static cursor, use *adOpenStatic*. A static Recordset doesn't show you any changes made by other users while the Recordset is open, and is therefore most useful for reporting or other applications that don't need to be kept completely up to date. This cursor type must be used for disconnected Recordsets.

- Finally, to open a forward-only cursor, use *adOpenForwardOnly*. A forward-only cursor is identical to a static cursor, except that you can only move forward in the Recordset to go to a different record. This offers the fastest performance of any of the cursor types, at the expense of flexibility.

Note that the forward-only Recordset is more flexible than you might think at first. In addition to using the MoveNext method, you can also use the Move method to skip intervening records, as long as you're moving forward. A forward-only Recordset also supports the MoveFirst method, although this seems contradictory. Be aware, though, that this may be an expensive operation, as it might force the provider to close and reopen the Recordset.

In general, if you stick with a cursor type that has no more functionality than you need in your application, you'll get the best possible performance. If you don't specify a cursor type, ADO defaults to the fastest (and least functional) type, which is a forward-only Recordset.

The Lock Type argument specifies the record-locking behavior that will be used for editing operations within this Recordset. Here again you have four choices:

- *adLockReadOnly*, for Recordsets that cannot be edited

- *adLockPessimistic*, for pessimistic locking (record locks are taken for the duration of all editing operations)

- *adLockOptimistic*, for optimistic locking (record locks are taken only while data is being updated)

- *adLockBatchOptimistic*, for Recordsets that will use the UpdateBatch method to update multiple records in a single operation

If you don't specify a lock type, ADO defaults to the fastest type, which is a read-only Recordset.

TIP   I'll cover updating Recordsets, including batch updating, in Chapter 4.

The Options argument supplies additional information to the provider. Generally, you can omit this argument, but some providers may be able to open a Recordset more quickly if you supply the appropriate options. Valid constants for this argument include the following:

- *adCmdUnknown*, which is the default and supplies no additional information to the provider

- *adCmdText*, which tells the provider that the CommandText property is a textual definition of a stored procedure

- *adCmdTable*, which tells the provider that the CommandText property is the name of a table

- *adCmdStoredProc*, which tells the provider that the CommandText property is the name of a stored procedure

- *adCmdFile*, which tells the provider that the CommandText property is the name of a file

- *adCmdTableDirect*, which tells the provider that the CommandText property is the name of a table that should be opened using low-level calls. (Most providers don't support this. You can use only the Seek method, covered later in this chapter, on Recordsets opened with the adCmdTableDirect option. The adCmdTableDirect constant is also used with the Microsoft OLE DB Provider for Internet Publishing to indicate that the data source is a URL.)

- *adAsyncExecute*, which tells the provider that the command should be executed asynchronously
- *adAsyncFetch*, which tells the provider that the cache should be filled synchronously, and then additional rows fetched asynchronously
- *adAsyncFetchNonBlocking*, which tells the provider to fetch records asynchronously if it can be done without blocking the main thread of execution

You can use the And operator to supply more than one value for the Options argument. For example, for asynchronous execution of a stored procedure, you could use this code:

```
rst.Options = adCmdStoredProc And adAsyncExecute
```

> **NOTE**   You'll find references in some ADO literature to another constant, adCmdURLBind. Starting with ADO 2.5, this constant is deprecated and has been replaced by adCmdTableDirect.

In addition to the properties that you can specify as arguments to the Open method, three other properties affect the behavior of the Recordset object:

- CacheSize
- CursorLocation
- MaxRecords

These properties should be set before calling the Open method.

The *CacheSize* property specifies the number of records that ADO will retrieve at once and cache locally. By caching records locally, you can speed up navigation between nearby records, at the cost of longer initial load times. The default value of CacheSize is 1, which results in only a single record being retrieved at a time.

> **WARNING**   If you set CacheSize greater than 1, records in the cache will not reflect changes made by other users, even if the cursor type of the Recordset is adOpenKeyset or adOpenDynamic. To force the cache to reflect changes made by other users, call the Recordset's Resync method.

Some OLE DB providers limit the cache size because of server resource constraints. You can check this limit for a particular Recordset by retrieving the Maximum Open Rows property from the Recordset object:

```
lngMax = rst.Properties("Maximum Open Rows")
```

If the Maximum Open Rows property is zero, the provider doesn't enforce a limit on the CacheSize property.

The *CursorLocation* property can be set to either adUseServer, for server-side cursors, or adUseClient, for client-side cursors. Remember, a cursor is a set of records in memory, and, of course, some software has to be responsible for keeping track of this set of records. Server-side cursors are maintained by the actual data source from which the records are retrieved. Client-side cursors are maintained by the Microsoft Cursor Service for OLE DB, which attempts to level the playing field by supplying capabilities that some servers lack. The default CursorLocation is adUseServer.

> **WARNING** The default Recordset in ADO uses a server-side, forward-only, read-only cursor. If you want to move through records at random, or edit records, you must specify the cursor type and lock type to use!

Some functionality is available only in client-side cursors—for example, re-sorting Recordsets or using an index to find records. If you need these capabilities, you should use client-side cursors. Otherwise, you may find that server-side cursors provide better performance. General-purpose code that can connect to many different data sources will generally benefit from client-side cursors, which will hide, as far as possible, the differences between providers.

The *MaxRecords* property limits the number of records that will potentially be returned when you open a Recordset. If you are worried about trying to retrieve a very large amount of data over a slow connection, you may want to set this property to a reasonable value. The default is zero, which doesn't set a limit to the number of records that will be returned.

Example Code

Perhaps the simplest way to open a Recordset is to just supply the name of a table in the data source as the source of the Recordset. The ADOChapter3 sample project contains code that allows you to try this method on SQL Server, Access, or Oracle data:

```
Private Sub cmdOpenDefault_Click()
    ' Open a Recordset using table name & default
    Dim strConn As String
    Dim strTableName As String
    Dim rst As ADODB.Recordset

    If optSQLServer Then
        strConn = "Provider=SQLOLEDB.1;Server=(local);" & _
        "Initial Catalog=Northwind;Integrated Security=SSPI"
        strTableName = "Customers"
    ElseIf optAccess Then
        strConn = "Provider=Microsoft.Jet.OLEDB.4.0;" & _
        "Data Source=C:\Program Files\Microsoft Office\" & _
```

```
                "Office10\Samples\Northwind.mdb;"
            strTableName = "Customers"
        Else ' Oracle
            strConn = "Provider=MSDAORA.1;Password=TIGER;User ID=SCOTT;" & _
            "Data Source=PEACOCK"
            strTableName = "DEMO.CUSTOMER"
        End If

        Set rst = New ADODB.Recordset

        rst.Open strTableName, strConn

        frmRecordsetProperties.Show
        frmRecordsetProperties.CollectProperties rst

        rst.Close
        Set rst = Nothing

    End Sub
```

This procedure, and some of the others in the project, use frmRecordsetProperties to display the properties of the resulting Recordset object. This form has a single public method named CollectProperties that accepts a Recordset as an argument, and then decodes the properties of that Recordset to its user interface. Figure 3.3 shows this form in action.

FIGURE 3.3:

Using frmRecordset-
Properties

The problem with using the name of a table as the source for a Recordset is that you may well retrieve all the data in that table from the server to your client. If you're using ADO to retrieve data in a client-server or three-tier setting, this probably isn't the best thing to do. A general rule of client-server processing is to retrieve only the data you actually need at the moment. You can do this by supplying a SQL statement to be resolved by the data source. In this case, only the requested records will be returned. Here's an example, again with a choice of data sources:

```
Private Sub cmdOpenSQLStatement_Click()
    ' Open a Recordset using a SQL statement
    Dim strConn As String
    Dim strSQLStatement As String
    Dim rst As ADODB.Recordset

    If optSQLServer Then
        strConn = "Provider=SQLOLEDB.1;Server=(local);" & _
        "Initial Catalog=Northwind;Integrated Security=SSPI"
        strSQLStatement = "SELECT * FROM Customers " & _
        "WHERE CustomerID LIKE 'A%'"
    ElseIf optAccess Then
        strConn = "Provider=Microsoft.Jet.OLEDB.4.0;" & _
        "Data Source=C:\Program Files\Microsoft Office\" & _
        "Office10\Samples\Northwind.mdb;"
        strSQLStatement = "SELECT * FROM Customers " & _
        "WHERE CustomerID LIKE 'A*'"
    Else ' Oracle
        strConn = "Provider=MSDAORA.1;Password=TIGER;User ID=SCOTT;" & _
        "Data Source=PEACOCK"
        strSQLStatement = "SELECT * FROM DEMO.CUSTOMER " & _
        "WHERE CUSTOMER_ID = 100"
    End If

    Set rst = New ADODB.Recordset

    rst.Open strSQLStatement, strConn

    frmRecordsetProperties.Show
    frmRecordsetProperties.CollectProperties rst

    rst.Close
    Set rst = Nothing

End Sub
```

Alternatively, you can open a Recordset by specifying the name of a view that already exists on the server instead of a table. This allows you to define a persistent set of joins and restrictions directly on the server:

```
Private Sub cmdView_Click()
    ' Open a Recordset using a view name
    Dim strConn As String
    Dim strViewName As String
```

```
Dim rst As ADODB.Recordset

If optSQLServer Then
    strConn = "Provider=SQLOLEDB.1;Server=(local);" & _
      "Initial Catalog=Northwind;Integrated Security=SSPI"
    strViewName = "Invoices"
ElseIf optAccess Then
    strConn = "Provider=Microsoft.Jet.OLEDB.4.0;" & _
      "Data Source=C:\Program Files\Microsoft Office\" & _
      "Office10\Samples\Northwind.mdb;"
    strViewName = "Invoices"
Else ' Oracle
    strConn = "Provider=MSDAORA.1;Password=DEMO;User ID=DEMO;" & _
      "Data Source=PEACOCK"
    strViewName = "SALES"
End If

Set rst = New ADODB.Recordset

rst.Open strViewName, strConn

frmRecordsetProperties.Show
frmRecordsetProperties.CollectProperties rst

rst.Close
Set rst = Nothing

End Sub
```

Counting Records

If you've checked the properties of any of the Recordsets in the samples earlier in this chapter, you may have noticed that the record count is showing up as –1. That's because the RecordCount property isn't always accurate. You'll find that:

- If the provider doesn't support counting records, the RecordCount property will be equal to –1.

- If the provider supports approximate positioning or bookmarks, the RecordCount property will be accurate.

- If the provider (or cursor type) doesn't support approximate positioning or bookmarks, the RecordCount property won't be accurate until you've retrieved every record in the Recordset.

- Forward-only cursors will always return –1 for the RecordCount property, even after all the records have been retrieved.

WARNING You should exercise some caution when retrieving the RecordCount property of a Recordset object. With some OLE DB providers, calculating this property will require retrieving and counting every record one by one, which can take a long time for large Recordsets.

Moving Around in Recordsets

Once you've retrieved data into a Recordset, you'll most likely want to view the data. There are two ways to move around in a Recordset. First, there are methods of the Recordset object that allow you to position the current record pointer within the cursor that has been retrieved. Second, there are Field objects that represent individual columns of data within the Recordset.

There are five methods of the Recordset object that can be used to position the current record pointer:

- *MoveFirst* sets the record pointer to the first record in the Recordset.
- *MoveNext* moves the record pointer one record closer to the end of the Recordset.
- *MovePrevious* moves the record pointer one record closer to the start of the Recordset.
- *MoveLast* moves the record pointer to the last record in the Recordset.
- *Move n* moves the record pointer *n* records from the current record.

In conjunction with these methods, you'll find two Boolean properties of the Recordset object useful. The BOF property is True when you've moved backward one record from the start of the Recordset, and the EOF property is True when you've moved forward one record past the end of the Recordset.

A typical use of these methods and properties is to visit each record in a Recordset. For example, you can use the following code to move from the start to the end of a Recordset:

```
rst.MoveFirst
Do Until rst.EOF
    ' Do something with each record here
    rst.MoveNext
Loop
```

Another use is to check for an empty Recordset. If a Recordset contains no records, both the EOF and BOF properties will be True simultaneously:

```
If rst.EOF And rst.BOF Then
    ' The Recordset is empty
End If
```

To work with the data contained in a Recordset, you use the Field object. The most important properties of the Field object are the Name property, which holds the name of the field or column in the original data source, and the Value property, which holds the value of that field for the current record in the Recordset. A Recordset object contains a Fields collection, which holds one Field object for each column of data in the Recordset. This chapter's sample project contains a procedure that uses Field objects to dump the contents of an arbitrary Recordset to a listbox:

```
Private Sub DisplayRecordset(rst As ADODB.Recordset)
    ' Dump the contents of a Recordset to a listbox
    Dim fld As ADODB.Field
    Dim strTemp As String

    lstResults.Clear
    Do Until rst.EOF
        strTemp = ""
        For Each fld In rst.Fields
            strTemp = strTemp & fld.Value & " "
        Next fld
        lstResults.AddItem strTemp
        rst.MoveNext
    Loop

    Set fld = Nothing

End Sub
```

If you're working with a Field whose name you know, you can also retrieve its value directly:

```
Debug.Print rst.Fields("CustomerID").Value
```

Because the Fields collection is the default property of the Recordset, and the Value property is the default property of the Field, the preceding line of code can be simplified like this:

```
Debug.Print rst("CustomerID")
```

Recordset Degradation

Just to make things more interesting, what you ask for isn't always what you get. Not every provider supports every possible combination of cursor location, cursor type, and lock type parameters. In fact, no provider that I know of supports all the combinations perfectly. In almost every case, though, you'll get something close to what you asked for. But, for example, if you try to open a client-side, static, pessimistic Recordset on a SQL Server data source, what you actually get is a client-side, static, batch optimistic Recordset. This is sometimes called "graceful degradation," but if you're not expecting it to happen, it might strike you more as "nasty surprise."

If you aren't sure what you're getting, you need to check the values of the CursorType, CursorLocation, and LockType properties of the Recordset object after calling its Open method to see what ADO delivered. It's also worth being aware that Recordset performance can be affected drastically by the options you choose. For example, a forward-only Recordset can generally be opened much more quickly than a dynamic Recordset. So you should choose the simplest Recordset type that will do the job you have in mind, and then test to see what you got.

Table 3.4 shows the effects of graceful degradation with the Microsoft SQL Server, Access, and Oracle OLE DB providers.

TABLE 3.4: Graceful Degradation of Recordsets

Requested Recordset Type	Delivered Recordset Type
Server-Side SQL Server	
Forward-only read-only	Same as requested
Forward-only pessimistic	Same as requested
Forward-only optimistic	Same as requested
Forward-only batch optimistic	Same as requested
Keyset read-only	Same as requested
Keyset pessimistic	Same as requested
Keyset optimistic	Same as requested
Keyset batch optimistic	Same as requested
Dynamic read-only	Same as requested
Dynamic pessimistic	Same as requested
Dynamic optimistic	Same as requested
Dynamic batch optimistic	Same as requested
Static read-only	Same as requested
Static pessimistic	Server-side keyset pessimistic
Static optimistic	Server-side keyset optimistic
Static batch optimistic	Server-side keyset batch optimistic
Server-Side Access	
Forward-only read-only	Same as requested
Forward-only pessimistic	Server-side keyset pessimistic
Forward-only optimistic	Server-side keyset optimistic
Forward-only batch optimistic	Server-side keyset batch optimistic
Keyset read-only	Same as requested
Keyset pessimistic	Same as requested

continued on next page

TABLE 3.4 CONTINUED: Graceful Degradation of Recordsets

Requested Recordset Type	Delivered Recordset Type
Server-Side Access	
Keyset optimistic	Same as requested
Keyset batch optimistic	Same as requested
Dynamic read-only	Server-side static read-only
Dynamic pessimistic	Server-side keyset pessimistic
Dynamic optimistic	Server-side keyset optimistic
Dynamic batch optimistic	Server-side keyset batch optimistic
Static read-only	Same as requested
Static pessimistic	Server-side keyset pessimistic
Static optimistic	Server-side keyset optimistic
Static batch optimistic	Server-side keyset batch optimistic
Server-Side Oracle	
Forward-only read-only	Same as requested
Forward-only pessimistic	Server-side forward-only read-only
Forward-only optimistic	Server-side forward-only read-only
Forward-only batch optimistic	Server-side forward-only read-only
Keyset read-only	Server-side static read-only
Keyset pessimistic	Server-side static read-only
Keyset optimistic	Server-side static read-only
Keyset batch optimistic	Server-side static read-only
Dynamic read-only	Server-side static read-only
Dynamic pessimistic	Server-side static read-only
Dynamic optimistic	Server-side static read-only
Dynamic batch optimistic	Server-side static read-only
Static read-only	Same as requested
Static pessimistic	Server-side static read-only
Static optimistic	Server-side static read-only
Static batch optimistic	Server-side static read-only
Client-Side SQL Server	
Forward-only read-only	Client-side static read-only
Forward-only pessimistic	Client-side static batch optimistic
Forward-only optimistic	Client-side static optimistic
Forward-only batch optimistic	Client-side static batch optimistic
Keyset read-only	Client-side static read-only

continued on next page

TABLE 3.4 CONTINUED: Graceful Degradation of Recordsets

Requested Recordset Type	Delivered Recordset Type
Client-Side SQL Server	
Keyset pessimistic	Client-side static batch optimistic
Keyset optimistic	Client-side static optimistic
Keyset batch optimistic	Client-side static batch optimistic
Dynamic read-only	Client-side static read-only
Dynamic pessimistic	Client-side static batch optimistic
Dynamic optimistic	Client-side static optimistic
Dynamic batch optimistic	Client-side static batch optimistic
Static read-only	Same as requested
Static pessimistic	Client-side static batch optimistic
Static optimistic	Same as requested
Static batch optimistic	Same as requested
Client-Side Access	
Forward-only read-only	Client-side static read-only
Forward-only pessimistic	Client-side static batch optimistic
Forward-only optimistic	Client-side static optimistic
Forward-only batch optimistic	Client-side static batch optimistic
Keyset read-only	Client-side static read-only
Keyset pessimistic	Client-side static batch optimistic
Keyset optimistic	Client-side static optimistic
Keyset batch optimistic	Client-side static batch optimistic
Dynamic read-only	Client-side static read-only
Dynamic pessimistic	Client-side static batch optimistic
Dynamic optimistic	Client-side static optimistic
Dynamic batch optimistic	Client-side static batch optimistic
Static read-only	Same as requested
Static pessimistic	Client-side static batch optimistic
Static optimistic	Same as requested
Static batch optimistic	Same as requested
Client-Side Oracle	
Forward-only read-only	Client-side static read-only
Forward-only pessimistic	Client-side static batch optimistic
Forward-only optimistic	Client-side static optimistic
Forward-only batch optimistic	Client-side static batch optimistic

continued on next page

TABLE 3.4 CONTINUED: Graceful Degradation of Recordsets

Requested Recordset Type	Delivered Recordset Type
Client-Side Oracle	
Keyset read-only	Client-side static read-only
Keyset pessimistic	Client-side static batch optimistic
Keyset optimistic	Client-side static optimistic
Keyset batch optimistic	Client-side static batch optimistic
Dynamic read-only	Client-side static read-only
Dynamic pessimistic	Client-side static batch optimistic
Dynamic optimistic	Client-side static optimistic
Dynamic batch optimistic	Client-side static batch optimistic
Static read-only	Same as requested
Static pessimistic	Client-side static batch optimistic
Static optimistic	Same as requested
Static batch optimistic	Same as requested

NOTE   The values in Table 3.4 were obtained from the cmdInvestigateCursors procedure in the ADOChapter3 sample project. Other factors, including server and driver version, the presence or absence of keys and indexes, and the exact Recordset source, can affect these results. So make sure you test with your own values before assuming that you'll see the same results as those in the table.

Using Stored Procedures to Retrieve Data

Opening a Recordset by using a table name or a SQL string in your code works, but it may not be the most efficient way to retrieve a set of records. In many cases, you'll be better off creating a *stored procedure* (a SQL statement or collection of SQL statements saved as a persistent object) on the database server and using that stored procedure to determine which records to return. By moving this piece of logic from the client to the server, you can both increase performance and make sure that particular business rules are enforced. Some databases precompile statements saved as stored procedures so that they will execute more quickly. In addition, you may find it easier to maintain the logic of your application by using stored procedures, which provide a central point for modification.

In this section, I'll demonstrate the use of a Command object to return a Recordset based on a stored procedure.

Returning Recordsets

Let's start by considering a simple stored procedure from the Northwind sample database that ships with SQL Server. It's named "Ten Most Expensive Products" and defined with this SQL code:

```
CREATE PROCEDURE "Ten Most Expensive Products" AS
SET ROWCOUNT 10
SELECT Products.ProductName AS TenMostExpensiveProducts,
 Products.UnitPrice
FROM Products
ORDER BY Products.UnitPrice DESC
```

As you can probably guess from the name, this stored procedure returns a Recordset consisting of the 10 most expensive products stored in the Products table.

There are two ways that you can open a Recordset based on a stored procedure such as this one. First, you can specify the stored procedure as the Source in the call to the Recordset.Open method:

```
Private Sub cmdWithoutParameters1_Click()
    ' Open a Recordset using a stored procedure name
    Dim strConn As String
    Dim rst As ADODB.Recordset

    strConn = "Provider=SQLOLEDB.1;Server=(local);" & _
     "Initial Catalog=Northwind;Integrated Security=SSPI"

    Set rst = New ADODB.Recordset

    rst.Open "[Ten Most Expensive Products]", strConn

    DisplayRecordset rst

    rst.Close
    Set rst = Nothing

End Sub
```

The alternative way to retrieve the same data is to use an ADO Command object to represent the stored procedure:

```
Private Sub cmdWithoutParameters2_Click()
    ' Open a Recordset using a stored procedure name
    Dim strConn As String
    Dim rst As ADODB.Recordset
    Dim cmd As ADODB.Command

    strConn = "Provider=SQLOLEDB.1;Server=(local);" & _
```

```
        "Initial Catalog=Northwind;Integrated Security=SSPI"

    Set cmd = New ADODB.Command
    cmd.ActiveConnection = strConn
    cmd.CommandText = "[Ten Most Expensive Products]"

    Set rst = cmd.Execute

    DisplayRecordset rst

    rst.Close
    Set rst = Nothing
    Set cmd = Nothing

End Sub
```

In this case, the connection to the database is made via the Command object. The most important properties of the Command object are the ActiveConnection property, which holds either a Connection object or a connection string, and the CommandText property, which holds the name of the object to be executed by the command. Calling the Command object's Execute method tells the database to execute the stored procedure, and returns a Recordset with any results.

In this particular case, using the Command object offers no advantage over opening the Recordset directly from the stored procedure. However, in general, you'll find the Command object useful and necessary. That's because you can work with input and output parameters to a stored procedure only through a Command object, as shown in the next section.

Handling Parameters

Stored procedures can take input parameters and return output parameters. For example, in the Northwind SQL Server database, there's a stored procedure named SalesByCategory. Here's the SQL that creates that stored procedure:

```
CREATE PROCEDURE SalesByCategory
    @CategoryName nvarchar(15),
    @OrdYear nvarchar(4) = '1998'
AS
IF @OrdYear != '1996'
 AND @OrdYear != '1997'
 AND @OrdYear != '1998'
BEGIN
    SELECT @OrdYear = '1998'
END
SELECT ProductName,
    TotalPurchase=ROUND(SUM(CONVERT(decimal(14,2),
    OD.Quantity * (1-OD.Discount) * OD.UnitPrice)), 0)
```

```
FROM [Order Details] OD, Orders O, Products P, Categories C
WHERE OD.OrderID = O.OrderID
   AND OD.ProductID = P.ProductID
   AND P.CategoryID = C.CategoryID
   AND C.CategoryName = @CategoryName
   AND SUBSTRING(CONVERT(
     nvarchar(22), O.OrderDate, 111), 1, 4) = @OrdYear
GROUP BY ProductName
ORDER BY ProductName
```

Here, `@CategoryName` and `@OrdYear` are a pair of input parameters to the stored procedure, both defined as being of the nvarchar datatype. The stored procedure uses these parameters to filter a Recordset of order information. The Recordset becomes the return value of the stored procedure.

Retrieving a Recordset from a stored procedure with input parameters is a three-step process:

1. Create a Command object and connect it to a data source.

2. Supply values for the input parameters.

3. Use the Command object's Execute method to retrieve the data to a Recordset object.

As an example, consider this code from this chapter's sample project:

```
Private Sub cmdWithParameters_Click()
    Dim cnn As New ADODB.Connection
    Dim cmd As New ADODB.Command
    Dim prm As ADODB.Parameter
    Dim rst As ADODB.Recordset
    Dim fld As ADODB.Field

    Dim strTemp As String

    ' Connect to the data source and the SP
    cnn.Open "Provider=SQLOLEDB.1;" & _
      "Data Source=(local);Initial Catalog=" & _
      "Northwind;Integrated Security=SSPI"
    With cmd
        .ActiveConnection = cnn
        .CommandText = "SalesByCategory"
        .CommandType = adCmdStoredProc
        .Parameters.Refresh
    End With

    ' Now walk through the Parameters, filling
    ' in the input parameters
    For Each prm In cmd.Parameters
        If (prm.Direction = adParamInput) Or _
        (prm.Direction = adParamInputOutput) Then
```

```
        prm.Value = InputBox(prm.Name, _
          "Enter parameter value")
      End If
   Next prm

   ' Retrieve and display the records
   Set rst = cmd.Execute
   DisplayRecordset rst

   rst.Close
   cnn.Close
   Set rst = Nothing
   Set cnn = Nothing
   Set cmd = Nothing
   Set prm = Nothing
   Set fld = Nothing

End Sub
```

| **TIP** | To test this code, try Beverages for the category name and 1996 for the order year. |

This code starts by connecting to the Northwind database on the local SQL Server, using Windows NT security. (As always, if your environment is different, you may have to modify the connection string.) Then it creates a Command object and loads it with the SalesByCategory stored procedure. Setting the CommandType property of the Command object to adCmdStoredProc tells ADO that this Command object will represent a stored procedure (commands may also be used to open SQL statements or tables, among other alternatives).

The call to the Refresh method of the Command object's Parameters collection tells ADO to query the data source and find out what parameters are required by this stored procedure. Once the Parameters collection is populated, the code walks through it one Parameter at a time, and prompts the user for values for all input Parameters.

Finally, the Execute method of the Command object is used to send the Parameter values to the data source and to fill in the Recordset with the returned data.

Although this method works, it's not the most efficient way to execute a stored procedure. The bottleneck is the Refresh method of the Parameters collection. To do its job, this method can require multiple round-trips of information between the client and the server. If you already know the details of the stored procedure, you can avoid using the Refresh method by creating your own parameters. This method is also demonstrated in this chapter's sample project:

```
Private Sub cmdWithParameters2_Click()
   Dim cnn As New ADODB.Connection
   Dim cmd As New ADODB.Command
```

```
    Dim prm As ADODB.Parameter
    Dim rst As ADODB.Recordset
    Dim fld As ADODB.Field
    Dim strCategoryName As String
    Dim strOrdYear As String

' Connect to the data source and the SP
    cnn.Open "Provider=SQLOLEDB.1;" & _
      "Data Source=(local);Initial Catalog=" & _
      "Northwind;Integrated Security=SSPI"
    With cmd
        .ActiveConnection = cnn
        .CommandText = "SalesByCategory"
        .CommandType = adCmdStoredProc
    End With

    ' Create the necessary parameters, using
    ' the values supplied by the user
    strCategoryName = InputBox("Enter Category Name")
    strOrdYear = InputBox("Enter Order Year")
    Set prm = cmd.CreateParameter( _
      "@CategoryName", _
      adVarWChar, adParamInput, 15, _
      strCategoryName)
    cmd.Parameters.Append prm
    Set prm = cmd.CreateParameter( _
      "@OrdYear", _
      adVarWChar, adParamInput, 4, _
      strOrdYear)
    cmd.Parameters.Append prm

    ' Retrieve and display the records
    Set rst = cmd.Execute
    DisplayRecordset rst

    rst.Close
    cnn.Close
    Set rst = Nothing
    Set cnn = Nothing
    Set cmd = Nothing
    Set prm = Nothing
    Set fld = Nothing

End Sub
```

The difference between this procedure and the previous one is in the method used to populate the Parameters collection of the Command object. This procedure uses the CreateParameter method of the Command object:

```
Command.CreateParameter Name, Type, Direction, Size, Value
```

You can use each of these optional arguments as follows:

- The *Name* argument must match exactly the name that the underlying data source is expecting for the parameter.

- The *Type* argument specifies a datatype for the parameter. These datatypes are expressed by constants supplied by ADO. Because ADO uses a single set of constants for all data sources, you might have trouble determining the appropriate constant to use in some cases. The simplest solution to this problem is to first use the Parameters.Refresh method to get the parameter from the server and then examine the Type property of the returned parameter. Once you know what this type is, you can create your own matching parameter in the future.

- The *Direction* argument is a constant that tells ADO whether this is an input or output parameter (or both).

- The *Size* argument specifies the size of the parameter. You don't need to specify a size for fixed-length datatypes such as integer or datetime. On the other hand, with some datatypes, you might need to set additional properties. For floating-point parameters, for example, you need to explicitly set the Precision and NumericScale properties.

- The *Value* argument specifies the actual value to use for the parameter. Make sure to specify Null for the value if there's a chance you won't be passing a value to the stored procedure; otherwise, the stored procedure will think there's no data for the parameter and raise an error.

You can create parameters and then set the properties afterwards if you prefer not to do the entire operation in one line of code.

WARNING Note that by default, newly created Parameter objects are not appended to the Parameters collection! You must remember to call the Command object's Parameters collection's Append method, or else your newly created Parameter object won't be attached to the Command. ADO is deliberately designed this way to allow you to create additional provider-specific properties before appending the Parameter object, if that's ever necessary.

In general, if you're writing code that will always call the same stored procedure, it's worth your while to explicitly code the parameters using the CreateParameter method. You should save the Parameters.Refresh method for situations where you don't know in advance what the Parameters collection should contain.

Finding and Sorting Data

Given a set of records, there are some common tasks. For example, you might want to find a particular record, or the first record meeting some criterion. Or you might want to sort the Recordset. In this section, I'll review the basics of finding and sorting data in ADO Recordsets.

Finding Data

How you find a record depends on the type of Recordset. A few OLE DB providers (notably the Microsoft Jet Provider) support a special type of Recordset, the direct table Recordset. Such Recordsets (opened with the adCmdTableDirect option) can use an indexed search via the Seek method to find data. Other Recordsets must use a slower sequential search via the Find method.

TIP   For a programmatic way of determining whether a particular Recordset supports the Seek method, see the section on the Supports method in Chapter 4.

Finding Data in a Direct Table Recordset

If you've created a direct table Recordset object, some providers allow you to use the fast Seek method to locate specific rows. (Attempting to use the Seek method with any other Recordset results in a runtime error.) You must take two specific steps to use the Seek method to find data:

1. Set the Recordset's Index property to the name of an index on the underlying table. This tells ADO which index you'd like it to search through. If you want to use the primary key for searching, you must know the name of the primary key. (For Microsoft Access, this is usually PrimaryKey, unless your application has changed it.)

2. Use the Seek method to find the value you want. The Seek method works from a search operator and one or more values to search for. The search operator must be one of the intrinsic constants shown in Table 3.5. If the index is on a single column, you supply a value to search for in that column. If the index is on multiple columns, you should supply one search value for each column, using the Visual Basic Array() function to create an array from those values.

WARNING   Currently, the only provider shipped as part of MDAC that supports Index and Seek is the Jet provider.

TABLE 3.5: Seek Options

Seek Option	Meaning
adSeekAfterEQ	Seek the key equal to the value supplied, or, if there is no such key, the first key after the point where the match would have occurred.
adSeekAfter	Seek the first key after the point where a match occurs or would occur.
adSeekBeforeEQ	Seek the key equal to the value supplied, or, if there is no such key, the first key before the point where the match would have occurred.
adSeekBefore	Seek the first key before the point where a match occurs or would occur.
adSeekFirstEQ	Seek the first key equal to the value supplied.
adSeekAfterEQ	Seek the last key equal to the value supplied.

You'll find an example of using the Seek method in this chapter's sample project:

```
Private Sub cmdSeek_Click()
    ' Find a record using the Seek method
    ' This requires a direct table Recordset
    Dim rst As New ADODB.Recordset
    Dim strSeek As String

    rst.Open "Customers", _
     "Provider=Microsoft.Jet.OLEDB.4.0;" & _
     "Data Source=C:\Program Files\Microsoft Office\" & _
     "Office10\Samples\Northwind.mdb;", _
     adOpenDynamic, adLockOptimistic, _
     adCmdTableDirect

    ' Now set the index we want to seek on
    rst.Index = "PrimaryKey"
    ' Get a value to seek for
    strSeek = InputBox("Customer ID to Find:", _
     "Seek input", "FOLKO")

    ' Seek the record and report results
    rst.Seek strSeek, adSeekAfterEQ
    If rst.EOF Then
        MsgBox "No matching record found"
    Else
        MsgBox "Found customer " & _
         rst("CompanyName")
    End If

    rst.Close
    Set rst = Nothing

End Sub
```

Note that the procedure checks the EOF property of the Recordset after invoking the Seek method. If the Seek fails, EOF will be set to True. This is the only way to tell whether the Seek method found a matching record.

With the Jet 4.0 OLE DB provider, the Seek method works only on Recordsets created from Jet 4.0 databases (for example, databases created with Access 2000 or Access 2002).

Finding Data Using the Find Method

Most Recordsets cannot use the Seek method for finding data. Fortunately, ADO provides a second method for finding records that's universally supported. This is the Find method of the Recordset, which is implemented with a great deal of flexibility. It allows you to optimize the search such that it will look through the smallest number of rows to find the data it needs.

Because you can also use Find to continue searching with the next record, you won't need to start back at the beginning of the Recordset to find subsequent matches. In addition, you can use loops to walk your way through the records, because you can restart the search without going back to the first row. The biggest disadvantage of the Find method is that you can search on only a single criterion.

The syntax for the Find method is as follows:

```
Recordset.Find Criteria, SkipRows, SearchDirection, Start
```

All the parameters except the first one are optional.

- *Criteria* is a WHERE clause formatted as though in a SQL expression, without the word *WHERE*.

- *SkipRows* specifies the offset from the current row where the search should begin. It defaults to starting with the current row.

- *SearchDirection* can be adSearchForward (the default) or adSearchBackward.

- *Start* is an optional bookmark indicating where the search should begin. The default is to begin with the current row. I'll discuss bookmarks in the next section.

Here's an example of the Find method from this chapter's sample project:

```
Private Sub cmdFind_Click()
    ' Use the Find method to locate records
    Dim rst As New ADODB.Recordset
    Dim strCriteria As String

    rst.Open "SELECT * FROM authors", _
      "Provider=SQLOLEDB.1;Server=(local);" & _
      "Initial Catalog=pubs;Integrated Security=SSPI", _
      adOpenStatic, adLockPessimistic
```

```
' Find all the authors in California
strCriteria = "State = 'CA'"
With rst
    .Find strCriteria
    Do While Not .EOF
        Debug.Print rst("au_lname")
        ' Continue with the next record
        .Find strCriteria, 1
    Loop
End With

rst.Close
Set rst = Nothing

End Sub
```

Just as with the Seek method, you must follow every call to a Find method with a check of the Recordset's EOF property (or BOF property if SearchDirection is adSearchBackward). If that property is True, there is no current row, and the Find method failed to find any matching records.

Note also the use of the SkipRows argument in the second call to the Find method in the sample code. By skipping a single row with each call, you can continue to find records starting at the point where the last search left off.

> **WARNING** Find criteria treat Null values differently from the way that some database engines (such as Jet) do. Because the ADO Find method doesn't understand the IsNull() or similar functions, the correct way to search for a Null using the Find method is with an expression such as "FieldName = Null" or "FieldName <> Null."

Bookmarks

The Bookmark property of a Recordset functions just like a bookmark in a book: as the way to remember a position within the Recordset. The Bookmark property returns a variant that's different for every record in the Recordset. To record the current position in a Recordset, you need to save this property to a variable:

```
Dim varBookmark As Variant
varBookmark = rst.Bookmark
```

Later in the same procedure, you can return to the bookmarked record by setting the property equal to the saved value:

```
rst.Bookmark = varBookmark
```

Sorting Data

Unless you specify a sorting order for a Recordset, the rows for that Recordset might show up in any order. The order could depend on data from more than one table, and on the OLE DB provider that's supplying the original data. In any case, if you need a specific ordering, you must set up that ordering yourself. You can do this either within a SQL statement that is the Source for a Recordset, or with the Recordset object's Sort property.

Using a SQL ORDER BY Clause

You can create a Recordset object using a SQL statement that includes an ORDER BY clause. To do so, specify the SQL expression as the row source for the Recordset's Open method. For example, you could use this code fragment to create a Recordset based on the Customers table, ordered by Company Name:

```
Dim rst As New ADODB.Recordset
rst.Open "SELECT * FROM Customers " & _
  "ORDER BY CompanyName", _
  "Provider=Microsoft.Jet.OLEDB.4.0;" & _
  "Data Source=C:\Program Files\" & _
  "Microsoft Visual Studio\VB98\Nwind.mdb", _
  adOpenKeyset, adLockOptimistic
```

Using the Sort Property

You can also set the Sort property of a Recordset to change its sort order. The Sort property must be a string, in the same style as the ORDER BY clause of a SQL expression (that is, it's a comma-separated list of field names, optionally with ASC or DESC to indicate ascending or descending sorts).

Some OLE DB providers don't implement the necessary interfaces to allow sorting. If you're using a Recordset from such a provider, you can still use the Sort method, but only if you've created a client-side cursor.

For example, this code from this chapter's sample project demonstrates how to change the sort order of a Recordset from the Jet provider, even though the Jet provider itself doesn't support sorting:

```
Private Sub cmdSort_Click()
    ' Sort a Recordset using the Sort property
    Dim rst As New ADODB.Recordset

    ' Fetch a Recordset in native order
    rst.CursorLocation = adUseClient
    rst.Open "Customers", _
     "Provider=Microsoft.Jet.OLEDB.4.0;" & _
     "Data Source=C:\Program Files\Microsoft Office\" & _
```

```
        "Office10\Samples\Northwind.mdb;", _
        adOpenKeyset, adLockOptimistic

    Do Until rst.EOF
        Debug.Print rst.Fields("CompanyName")
        rst.MoveNext
    Loop

    ' Now sort it on the CompanyName field
    MsgBox "Click OK to sort descending"
    rst.Sort = "CompanyName DESC"
    rst.MoveFirst
    Do Until rst.EOF
        Debug.Print rst.Fields("CompanyName")
        rst.MoveNext
    Loop

    rst.Close
    Set rst = Nothing

End Sub
```

Note the use of the SQL DESC keyword to force a descending sort. The new sort takes effect as soon as the Sort property is set. In some cases, you may find that it's faster to simply open a new Recordset based on a SQL statement with an ORDER BY clause than it is to use the Sort property.

Summary

In this chapter, I covered some of the basics of using ADO to retrieve data, including:

- Connecting to data sources
- Opening Recordsets
- Moving through Recordsets
- Using stored procedures with and without parameters
- Finding and sorting data

So far, I've been treating the data in Recordsets as static. ADO allows a full range of editing options for this data. In the next chapter, you'll see how to add new records, delete existing records, and modify the contents of records within an ADO Recordset.

CHAPTER 4

Editing Data with ADO

- Updating data

- Adding data

- Deleting data

- Using the Supports method to determine capabilities

- Using transactions

n Chapter 3, you learned how to use ADO to view existing data in your applications. But for most database applications, access to existing data is only one of the requirements. You'll frequently need to update existing data, add new data, or delete data that is no longer needed. Fortunately, ADO offers methods to perform all of those operations. In this chapter, I'll discuss the details of editing data with ADO. I'll also show you the Supports method, which will help you determine which operations you can perform with any given data source.

Updating Data

There are two ways you can update data with ADO. First, you can work directly within a Recordset that contains the data that you want to change. Second, you can use a Command object to perform the updates directly on the data source, without any need to open a Recordset or otherwise retrieve the data to the local computer. In this section, I'll explore both of these alternatives.

Working Directly in Recordsets

Within a Recordset, you can perform updates by calling the Recordset's Update method. If you have exclusive access to the data, it's that simple. Often, however, you'll be using ADO to work with data that is simultaneously being accessed by other users. In that case, you'll need to worry about write conflicts or other inconsistencies in the data caused by simultaneous changes by two or more users.

Immediate Updating

Changing data in a Recordset is a three-step process:

1. Move to the row of the Recordset containing the data.

2. Set new values for the fields that you want to change.

3. Use the Recordset object's Update method to save the new values.

If you don't explicitly call the Update method, ADO calls it automatically when you move off a row, and saves any pending changes to the record. You can also explicitly discard changes by calling the Recordset's CancelUpdate method. If you close or destroy a Recordset while there are pending changes, those changes are simply discarded.

The Update method also accepts two optional parameters, as illustrated here:

```
rst.Update Fields, Values
```

These parameters allow you to supply the data for the update directly in the call to the Update method. The Fields parameter can be either the name of a field or an array of field names; the Values parameter is correspondingly a new value or an array of new values to be committed to the record.

The ADOChapter4 sample project contains code to demonstrate these methods of updating with Access, SQL Server, or Oracle data. Listing 4.1 shows the sample code for updating an Access database; the other two versions are similar.

Listing 4.1:   **Immediate Updates to an Access Database**

```
Private Sub cmdImmediateAccess_Click()

    Dim cnn As ADODB.Connection
    Dim rst As ADODB.Recordset

    On Error GoTo HandleErr

    lboResults.Clear
    lboResults.AddItem "Immediate updates with Access"

    ' Open a Recordset
    Set cnn = New ADODB.Connection
    cnn.Open "Provider=Microsoft.Jet.OLEDB.4.0;" & _
     "Data Source=C:\Program Files\Microsoft Office\" & _
     "Office10\Samples\Northwind.mdb;"
    Set rst = New ADODB.Recordset
    rst.Open "SELECT * FROM Customers", cnn, adOpenDynamic, adLockOptimistic

    ' Show the city for the first customer
    lboResults.AddItem "Initial Value = " & rst.Fields("City").Value

    ' Perform an edit and show the results
    rst.Fields("City") = "Munich"
    rst.Update
    lboResults.AddItem "After Update = " & rst.Fields("City").Value

    ' Commit an edit implicitly by leaving the record
    rst.Fields("City") = "Stuttgart"
    rst.MoveNext
    rst.MovePrevious
    lboResults.AddItem "Implicit Update = " & rst.Fields("City").Value

    ' Supply information directly in the Update method
    rst.Update "City", "Berlin"
    lboResults.AddItem "Direct Update = " & rst.Fields("City").Value

    ' Cancel an update
    rst.Fields("City") = "Nuremburg"
    rst.CancelUpdate
    lboResults.AddItem "Cancelled Update = " & rst.Fields("City").Value

    ' Clean up
    rst.Close
    Set rst = Nothing
```

```
    cnn.Close
    Set cnn = Nothing

ExitHere:
    Exit Sub

HandleErr:
    MsgBox "Error " & Err.Number & ": " & Err.Description, _
      vbOKOnly, "cmdImmediateAccess"
    Resume ExitHere
    Resume

End Sub
```

Write Conflicts

Because ADO allows multiple users to work with the same data simultaneously, it must make provision for write conflicts—cases where two users change (or attempt to change) the same data at more or less the same time. The LockType property of the Recordset object controls ADO's behavior in this regard. If you're used to other products (such as Microsoft Access), though, you may find ADO's behavior counterintuitive. The basic rules ADO follows are as follows:

- With pessimistic locking, ADO does what it needs to do to make the edit succeed. This means that if two users edit the same record, both edits will succeed, even if the editing and the Update methods are interleaved.

- With optimistic locking, ADO doesn't do anything special to make the edit succeed. This means that if two users edit the same record, the second edit will likely fail, because the data provider will realize that the user is trying to edit stale data.

Listing 4.2 shows code that demonstrates these rules with Access data.

Listing 4.2:   **Write Conflicts with Optimistic and Pessimistic Locking**

```
Private Sub cmdWriteConflict_Click()

    Dim cnn1 As ADODB.Connection
    Dim rst1 As ADODB.Recordset
    Dim cnn2 As ADODB.Connection
    Dim rst2 As ADODB.Recordset

    On Error GoTo HandleErr

    lboResults.Clear
    lboResults.AddItem "Write conflict"
```

```
' Open two Recordsets on independent connections.
' Use pessimistic locking
lboResults.AddItem "Pessimistic"
Set cnn1 = New ADODB.Connection
cnn1.Open "Provider=Microsoft.Jet.OLEDB.4.0;" & _
 "Data Source=C:\Program Files\Microsoft Office\" & _
 "Office10\Samples\Northwind.mdb;"
Set rst1 = New ADODB.Recordset
rst1.Open "SELECT * FROM Customers", cnn1, adOpenStatic, adLockPessimistic
Set cnn2 = New ADODB.Connection
cnn2.Open "Provider=Microsoft.Jet.OLEDB.4.0;" & _
 "Data Source=C:\Program Files\Microsoft Office\" & _
 "Office10\Samples\Northwind.mdb;"
Set rst2 = New ADODB.Recordset
rst2.Open "SELECT * FROM Customers", cnn1, adOpenStatic, _
 adLockPessimistic

' Show the city for the first customer
lboResults.AddItem "Initial Value 1 = " & rst1.Fields("City").Value
lboResults.AddItem "Initial Value 2 = " & rst2.Fields("City").Value

' Edit both copies and show the results
rst1.Fields("City") = "Munich"
rst2.Fields("City") = "Nuremburg"
lboResults.AddItem "Edited Value 1 = " & rst1.Fields("City").Value
lboResults.AddItem "Edited Value 2 = " & rst2.Fields("City").Value

' Commit the edits and show the results
rst1.Update
rst2.Update
lboResults.AddItem "Updated Value 1 = " & rst1.Fields("City").Value
lboResults.AddItem "Updated Value 2 = " & rst2.Fields("City").Value

' Now try with optimistic locking
rst1.Close
Set rst1 = Nothing
rst2.Close
Set rst2 = Nothing
lboResults.AddItem "Optimistic"
Set cnn1 = New ADODB.Connection
cnn1.Open "Provider=Microsoft.Jet.OLEDB.4.0;" & _
 "Data Source=C:\Program Files\Microsoft Office\" & _
 "Office10\Samples\Northwind.mdb;"
Set rst1 = New ADODB.Recordset
rst1.Open "SELECT * FROM Customers", cnn1, adOpenStatic, adLockOptimistic
Set cnn2 = New ADODB.Connection
cnn2.Open "Provider=Microsoft.Jet.OLEDB.4.0;" & _
 "Data Source=C:\Program Files\Microsoft Office\" & _
 "Office10\Samples\Northwind.mdb;"
Set rst2 = New ADODB.Recordset
rst2.Open "SELECT * FROM Customers", cnn1, adOpenStatic, adLockOptimistic
```

```
' Show the city for the first customer
lboResults.AddItem "Initial Value 1 = " & rst1.Fields("City").Value
lboResults.AddItem "Initial Value 2 = " & rst2.Fields("City").Value

' Edit both copies and show the results
rst1.Fields("City") = "Munich"
rst2.Fields("City") = "Nuremburg"
lboResults.AddItem "Edited Value 1 = " & rst1.Fields("City").Value
lboResults.AddItem "Edited Value 2 = " & rst2.Fields("City").Value

' Commit the edits and show the results
rst1.Update
rst2.Update
lboResults.AddItem "Updated Value 1 = " & rst1.Fields("City").Value
' Next line will result in a runtime error
lboResults.AddItem "Updated Value 2 = " & rst2.Fields("City").Value

' Clean up
rst1.Close
Set rst1 = Nothing
rst2.Close
Set rst2 = Nothing
cnn1.Close
Set cnn1 = Nothing
cnn2.Close
Set cnn2 = Nothing

ExitHere:
    Exit Sub

HandleErr:
    MsgBox "Error " & Err.Number & ": " & Err.Description, _
      vbOKOnly, "cmdWriteConflict"
    Resume ExitHere
    Resume

End Sub
```

Batch Updating

If you use the client-side cursor library with a keyset or static cursor, you can also take advantage of ADO's ability to perform batch updates. Batch updating allows you to edit multiple records in a Recordset, and then send all the updates to the underlying OLE DB provider to be stored in a single operation.

To use batch updates, simply open a Recordset with the adLockBatchOptimistic lock type, change as many records as you please, and then call the UpdateBatch method. If you've used a client-side cursor, your changes will be cached on the client until you call the UpdateBatch method. At that time, all the changes will be sent to the server as a single operation.

If any of your changes can't be saved (for example, because another user has deleted the record), a runtime error occurs. In this case, you can use the Filter property with the adFilterAffectedRecords constant to filter the Recordset down to only those records that had problems.

Batch updating, like most other programming techniques, has its good side and its bad side. On the good side, you can cache multiple changes on the client until you're ready to submit them to the server, and thus cut down on potentially slow and expensive client-server round-trips. On the bad side, in a multiuser environment (which most multitiered environments are), the longer you cache changes, the greater the chance that someone else will have changed a record that you were both working with.

ADO provides two methods to deal with record conflicts during batch updating. You can use the Resync method of the Recordset object to investigate changes on the server before submitting your changes. Alternatively, you can use the Filter method to determine which (if any) changes failed after calling the BatchUpdate method. I'll work through both of these methods in this section.

Using Resync to Detect Potential Conflicts

As you might guess, the Resync method is used to resynchronize client and server Recordsets. The syntax is:

```
Recordset.Resync AffectRecords, ResyncValues
```

The AffectRecords argument takes one of four values:

- adAffectCurrent, to resynchronize only the current record
- adAffectGroup, to resynchronize all records matching the current Filter setting
- adAffectAll, to resynchronize the entire Recordset
- adAffectAllChapters, to resynchronize multiple Recordsets in a hierarchical Recordset. (For more information on hierarchical Recordsets, see Chapter 7, "Data Shaping.")

The ResyncValues argument can be either adResyncAllValues (the default) or adResyncUnderlyingValues. If you choose adResyncAllValues, the client Recordset is made to match the server Recordset, and any pending updates are cancelled. Of course, this isn't what you'd want to do when checking the potential for update conflicts. The alternative, adResyncUnderlyingValues, retrieves the most current data from the server but stores it in the UnderlyingValue property instead of the Value property.

Listing 4.3 shows code from this chapter's sample project that demonstrates the use of the Resync method.

Listing 4.3: **Using the Resync Method**

```
Private Sub cmdResync_Click()
    ' Open two Recordsets, change both, and
    ' demonstrate the Resync method
    Dim rst1 As New ADODB.Recordset
    Dim rst2 As New ADODB.Recordset

    On Error GoTo HandleErr

    lboResults.Clear

    ' Retrieve the records on one connection
    rst1.CursorLocation = adUseClient
    rst1.Open "Customers", _
     "Provider=SQLOLEDB.1;Server=(local);" & _
     "Initial Catalog=Northwind;Integrated Security=SSPI", _
     adOpenDynamic, adLockBatchOptimistic
    rst1.MoveFirst

    ' And on another connection
    rst2.CursorLocation = adUseClient
    rst2.Open "Customers", _
     "Provider=SQLOLEDB.1;Server=(local);" & _
     "Initial Catalog=Northwind;Integrated Security=SSPI", _
     adOpenDynamic, adLockBatchOptimistic
    rst2.MoveFirst

    ' Change and commit from the first Recordset
    rst1.Fields("ContactTitle") = "SalesRep"
    rst1.UpdateBatch
    lboResults.AddItem _
     "Title changed to SalesRep on server"

    ' Now change the second Recordset
    rst2.Fields("ContactTitle") = "Representative"
    lboResults.AddItem _
     "Title changed to Representative on client"

    ' Resync the changes
    rst2.Resync adAffectAll, _
     adResyncUnderlyingValues

    ' And show the results
    lboResults.AddItem _
     "Value = " & rst2.Fields("ContactTitle").Value
    lboResults.AddItem _
     "Original Value = " & _
     rst2.Fields("ContactTitle").OriginalValue
    lboResults.AddItem _
     "Underlying Value = " & _
     rst2.Fields("ContactTitle").UnderlyingValue
```

```
        rst1.Close
        Set rst1 = Nothing
        rst2.Close
        Set rst2 = Nothing

ExitHere:
    Exit Sub

HandleErr:
    MsgBox "Error " & Err.Number & ": " & Err.Description, _
     vbOKOnly, "cmdResync"
    Resume ExitHere
    Resume

End Sub
```

This procedure starts by opening two Recordsets containing the same data. Because these Recordsets are using implicit connections, each gets its own connection to the database, and it's possible to make independent changes on each Recordset. Both Recordsets are opened on the client with optimistic batch locking, to enable batch updating.

First, the code makes a change to the first record in rst1 and uses the UpdateBatch method to save this change back to the server. Then it makes a conflicting change to the same record in rst2. Rather than call the UpdateBatch method, though, the code calls the Resync method to investigate the properties of this field. If you run the code, you'll see results similar to these:

```
Value = Representative
Original Value = Sales Representative
Underlying Value = SalesRep
```

This tells you that, although the original value on the server was "Sales Representative," it's now "SalesRep," indicating that another user changed the record during the course of your edits. How you'd respond to this in code, of course, depends on the business logic that you're trying to implement. You might want to save your updates anyway, or you might want to warn the user that there had been a change and to perform a full Resync operation to reset to the values currently on the server.

Using Filter to Detect Actual Conflicts

As an alternative, you might just go ahead and call the UpdateBatch method after making whatever changes are necessary to your copy of the Recordset. In this case, if there are any conflicts (records that have already been changed by another user), ADO will ignore those records in your changes, although it will save all the other changes. ADO will also raise an error for your Visual Basic code to intercept.

But then what? The best answer is to use the Filter property of the Recordset object to see exactly which records failed to update. Listing 4.4 illustrates this technique.

Listing 4.4:   **Using the Filter Property to Locate Failed Updates**

```
Private Sub cmdFilter_Click()
    ' Open two Recordsets, change both, and
    ' demonstrate the Filter method
    Dim rst1 As New ADODB.Recordset
    Dim rst2 As New ADODB.Recordset

    Const conBadUpdate = -2147217864

    On Error GoTo HandleErr

    lboResults.Clear

    ' Retrieve the records on one connection
    rst1.CursorLocation = adUseClient
    rst1.Open "Customers", _
     "Provider=SQLOLEDB.1;Server=(local);" & _
     "Initial Catalog=Northwind;Integrated Security=SSPI", _
     adOpenDynamic, adLockBatchOptimistic
    rst1.MoveFirst

    ' And on another connection
    rst2.CursorLocation = adUseClient
    rst2.Open "Customers", _
     "Provider=SQLOLEDB.1;Server=(local);" & _
     "Initial Catalog=Northwind;Integrated Security=SSPI", _
     adOpenDynamic, adLockBatchOptimistic
    rst2.MoveFirst

    ' Change and commit from the first Recordset
    rst1.Fields("ContactTitle") = "SalesCritter"
    rst1.UpdateBatch
    lboResults.AddItem _
     "Title changed to SalesCritter on server"

    ' Now change the second Recordset
    rst2.Fields("ContactTitle") = "New Rep"
    lboResults.AddItem _
     "Title changed to New Rep on client"

    ' Update the changes to the server
    rst2.UpdateBatch

    ' Clean up
    rst1.Close
    Set rst1 = Nothing
    rst2.Close
    Set rst2 = Nothing

ExitHere:
    Exit Sub
```

```
HandleErr:
    If Err.Number = conBadUpdate Then
        rst2.Filter = adFilterConflictingRecords
        lboResults.AddItem _
        "In error handler, " & rst2.RecordCount & _
        " record(s) conflicting"
    Else
        MsgBox "Error " & Err.Number & ": " & Err.Description, _
            vbOKOnly, "cmdImmediateAccess"
    End If
    Resume ExitHere
    Resume

End Sub
```

This code performs the same operations as the previous example, up to the point where the second Recordset is changed. Then, instead of checking to see whether the changes can be saved, it simply calls the UpdateBatch method to try to save them. This will cause a run-time error, which will cause the processing to be thrown into the error-handling routine.

This routine sets the Filter property of the Recordset in question to adFilterConflicting-Records. This tells ADO to rework the Recordset, keeping only the records that didn't update successfully. You could then take necessary action, such as prompting the user or resyncing and then resaving changes.

The Filter property is designed for flexibility. It can filter Recordsets in a variety of ways, not just to hold update conflicts. Table 4.1 shows the possible values that you can set for this property.

TABLE 4.1: Filter Property Values

Value	Meaning
Criterion string (such as "LastName = 'Butler'")	Filters the Recordset to include only records matching the specified criterion.
Array of bookmarks	Filters the Recordset to include only records matching the supplied bookmarks.
"" (Zero-length string)	Removes any filters and returns all records to the Recordset.
adFilterNone	Removes any filters and returns all records to the Recordset.
adFilterPendingRecords	Filters the Recordset to hold only records with changes that have not yet been sent to the server.
adFilterAffectedRecords	Filters the Recordset to hold only records that were changed by the last call to the Delete, Resync, UpdateBatch, or CancelBatch method.
adFilterFetchedRecords	Filters the Recordset to hold only the most recent records placed in the record cache.
adFilterConflictingRecords	Filters the Recordset to hold only the records that failed to update in an UpdateBatch operation.

NOTE There is another variation of batch updating known as *optimistic batch updating*, in which you make updates to a disconnected Recordset. I'll discuss this in Chapter 8, "Working with Disconnected Recordsets."

Using Command Objects

You can also edit data without opening a Recordset by using a Command object. In many circumstances, this technique can be faster than editing in a Recordset, because it lets all the work be done on the server without the overhead of moving records to the client. To perform the edit, the Command object can use either a SQL statement contained directly in your code or a stored procedure located on the server.

There are several examples of this technique in this chapter's sample project. Listing 4.5 shows a procedure for changing a record in an Access database via a Command object.

Listing 4.5:   **Changing Access Data with a Command Object**

```
Private Sub cmdCommandUpdateAccess_Click()

    Dim cnn As ADODB.Connection
    Dim cmd As ADODB.Command
    Dim lngRecordsAffected As Long

    On Error GoTo HandleErr

    lboResults.Clear
    lboResults.AddItem "Command update with Access"

    ' Connect to the data source and create a command
    Set cnn = New ADODB.Connection
    cnn.Open "Provider=Microsoft.Jet.OLEDB.4.0;" & _
      "Data Source=C:\Program Files\Microsoft Office\" & _
      "Office10\Samples\Northwind.mdb;"

    Set cmd = New ADODB.Command
    cmd.CommandType = adCmdText
    Set cmd.ActiveConnection = cnn
    cmd.CommandText = "UPDATE Customers SET City = 'Berlin' " & _
      "WHERE CustomerID = 'ALFKI'"

    ' Execute the command
    cmd.Execute lngRecordsAffected
    lboResults.AddItem lngRecordsAffected & " records affected"

    ' Clean up
    Set cmd = Nothing
    cnn.Close
```

```
        Set cnn = Nothing

ExitHere:
        Exit Sub

HandleErr:
        MsgBox "Error " & Err.Number & ": " & Err.Description, _
         vbOKOnly, "cmdCommandUpdateAccess_Click"
        Resume ExitHere
        Resume

End Sub
```

To edit data using a Command object, follow these steps:

1. Create a Connection object and use it to open your data source.

2. Create a Command object and set its ActiveConnection, CommandType, and Command-Text properties. If the command text is a SQL statement, the CommandType should be set to adCmdText. If the command text is the name of a stored procedure on the server, the command type should be set to adCmdStoredProc.

3. Supply values for any parameters of the Command object.

4. Call the Command's Execute method. If you supply a variable for the RecordsAffected argument, ADO will set this variable equal to the number of records that are changed when the Command is executed.

Listing 4.5 demonstrates this process for a SQL statement that's embedded directly in the ADO code. Listing 4.6 shows the equivalent steps for a stored procedure as used in a SQL Server database.

Listing 4.6:   Changing SQL Server Data with a Command Object

```
Private Sub cmdCommandUpdateSQLServer_Click()

        Dim cnn As ADODB.Connection
        Dim cmd As ADODB.Command
        Dim lngRecordsAffected As Long

        Const conErrSPExists = -2147217900

        On Error GoTo HandleErr

        lboResults.Clear
        lboResults.AddItem "Command update with SQL Server"

        ' Connect to the data source and create a command
        Set cnn = New ADODB.Connection
```

```vb
cnn.Open "Provider=SQLOLEDB.1;Server=(local);" & _
  "Initial Catalog=Northwind;Integrated Security=SSPI"

Set cmd = New ADODB.Command
cmd.CommandType = adCmdText
Set cmd.ActiveConnection = cnn
cmd.CommandText = "CREATE PROCEDURE spUpdateCustomerCity " & _
  "@custID nchar(5), " & _
  "@city nvarchar(15) " & _
  "AS " & _
  "UPDATE Customers " & _
  "SET City = @city " & _
  "WHERE CustomerID = @custID"

' Execute the command to create a stored procedure on the server
cmd.Execute

'Now that the stored procedure exists, point the command at it
Set cmd = New ADODB.Command
cmd.CommandType = adCmdStoredProc
Set cmd.ActiveConnection = cnn
cmd.CommandText = "spUpdateCustomerCity"

' Supply the parameters
cmd.Parameters.Refresh
cmd.Parameters("@custID") = "ALFKI"
cmd.Parameters("@city") = "Munich"

' And execute the command
cmd.Execute lngRecordsAffected
lboResults.AddItem lngRecordsAffected & " records affected"

' Clean up
Set cmd = Nothing
cnn.Close
Set cnn = Nothing

ExitHere:
    Exit Sub

HandleErr:
    If Err.Number = conErrSPExists Then
        ' Stored proc already exists on the server
        Resume Next
    End If
    MsgBox "Error " & Err.Number & ": " & Err.Description, _
      vbOKOnly, "cmdCommandUpdateSQLServer_Click"
    Resume ExitHere
    Resume

End Sub
```

Before changing data, the code in Listing 4.6 uses a Command object to execute a SQL statement directly on the server. This SQL statement creates a stored procedure on the SQL Server. The second use of the Command object in this listing makes use of the new stored procedure to edit data on the server.

You can either use the `Parameters.Refresh` method to retrieve parameter information from the server or create new Parameter objects directly on the client. Both of these methods of dealing with Command object parameters are discussed in Chapter 3, "Using the ADO Objects to Retrieve Data."

Adding Data

Of course, you can also add new records to a data source using ADO. As with updating data, you can either do this directly in a Recordset (by calling the AddNew and Update methods) or use a Command object to execute SQL text or a stored procedure.

You can also use the Execute method of the Connection object to execute SQL statements directly. But because this isn't quite as flexible as using the Execute method of the Command object (for instance, you can't specify a CommandType property when using Connection.Execute), I generally prefer to use the Command object instead of the Connection object for this purpose.

Working Directly in Recordsets

Like updating data, adding new rows to a Recordset is a three-step process:

1. Call the AddNew method of the Recordset object to create a new row.

2. Fill in the Value property of any field that should contain a value other than Null or the field's default.

3. Call the Update method to save the new row to the data source.

If you move off the row without calling Update, ADO helpfully calls the Update method for you (unless you've opened the Recordset for batch updating). When you use the AddNew method, the new record becomes the current row as soon as you call the Update method.

When you call the Update method (or otherwise commit the new record), the values in the fields must be acceptable to the underlying OLE DB provider. ADO will initialize all the fields to the default value supplied by the provider or, if there is no default value, to Null. If there are non-nullable fields that don't have a default value, you must explicitly supply values for those fields before calling the Update method.

You can also commit a new record by moving off the record, or by calling the AddNew method a second time to start adding another record. In this case, the new record will *not* become the current record. Even if you execute a MoveNext to leave the record followed by a MovePrevious, you won't necessarily be viewing the record that you just added.

The AddNew method, like the Update method, can optionally take two arrays as arguments: an array of field names and an array of values. This syntax allows you to add a new record with a single line of code.

Like the Update method, the AddNew method can be cancelled by calling the Cancel-Update method.

WARNING   Some OLE DB providers, such as the Microsoft SQL Server provider, will leave the Recordset without a current row if you cancel an AddNew. In that case, trying to retrieve any information from the Recordset immediately after an AddNew/CancelUpdate pair will result in error 3021. If you call CancelUpdate in such a case, you should also call one of the Move methods to position the cursor on an existing record.

Listing 4.7 shows these various uses of the AddNew method with an Access database. Here's the output that results from running this procedure in this chapter's sample project, using an Access database:

```
AddNew with Access
Current Record = ALFKI
Current Record = XXXXX
Current Record = ALFKI
Current Record = ZZZZZ
Current Record = ZZZZZ
```

If you trace through the code, you'll see how this output includes explicit and implicit commits, as well as the effects of cancelling an AddNew. The project also contains similar procedures using SQL Server data and Oracle data.

Listing 4.7:   **Adding New Records to an Access Database**

```
Private Sub cmAddNewAccess_Click()

    Dim cnn As ADODB.Connection
    Dim rst As ADODB.Recordset

    On Error GoTo HandleErr

    lboResults.Clear
    lboResults.AddItem "AddNew with Access"

    ' Open a Recordset
    Set cnn = New ADODB.Connection
```

```
    cnn.Open "Provider=Microsoft.Jet.OLEDB.4.0;" & _
     "Data Source=C:\Program Files\Microsoft Office\" & _
     "Office10\Samples\Northwind.mdb;"
    Set rst = New ADODB.Recordset
    rst.Open "SELECT * FROM Customers", cnn, adOpenDynamic, adLockOptimistic

    ' Show the first customer
    lboResults.AddItem "Current Record = " & rst.Fields("CustomerID").Value

    ' Add a new record and show the current record
    rst.AddNew
        rst.Fields("CustomerID") = "XXXXX"
        rst.Fields("CompanyName") = "X-Ray Company"
    rst.Update
    lboResults.AddItem "Current Record = " & rst.Fields("CustomerID").Value

    ' Commit an update implicitly by leaving the record
    rst.AddNew
        rst.Fields("CustomerID") = "YYYYY"
        rst.Fields("CompanyName") = "Your Industries"
    rst.MoveNext
    rst.MovePrevious
    lboResults.AddItem "Current Record = " & rst.Fields("CustomerID").Value

    ' Supply information directly in the AddNew method
    rst.AddNew Array("CustomerID", "CompanyName"), _
     Array("ZZZZZ", "Zebra Inc.")
    lboResults.AddItem "Current Record = " & rst.Fields("CustomerID").Value

    ' Cancel an add
    rst.AddNew
        rst.Fields("CustomerID") = "AAAAA"
        rst.Fields("CompanyName") = "AardvarkWare"
    rst.CancelUpdate
    lboResults.AddItem "Current Record = " & rst.Fields("CustomerID").Value

    ' Clean up
    rst.Close
    Set rst = Nothing
    cnn.Close
    Set cnn = Nothing

ExitHere:
    Exit Sub

HandleErr:
    MsgBox "Error " & Err.Number & ": " & Err.Description, _
     vbOKOnly, "cmdAddNewAccess"
    Resume ExitHere
    Resume

End Sub
```

Using Command Objects

Just as you can use Command objects for updating data, you can use them to add new data. In fact, from the point of view of the Command object, the technique is exactly the same in the two cases. The only difference is that, if you'd like to add new records, the Command-Text property of the Command object should be an INSERT INTO SQL statement or the name of a stored procedure that performs an INSERT INTO.

In general, you can use an ADO Command object to execute any arbitrary SQL statement or stored procedure in a data source.

Deleting Data

The third major editing operation that any modern application needs to support is deleting existing data, and ADO is no exception. As with updating and adding data, you can delete data either by working directly in a Recordset or by executing an appropriate Command object.

Working Directly in Recordsets

Deleting a record from a Recordset is simple. You just move to the desired row and call the Delete method of the Recordset object.

You don't need to use the Update method when deleting a row, unlike the case of adding a row. Once you delete it, it's gone—unless, of course, you wrapped the entire thing in a transaction. In that case, you can roll back the transaction to retrieve the deleted row. You'll learn more about transactions later in this chapter.

After you delete a record, it is still the current record. The previous row is still the previous row, and the next row is still the next row. To reposition the cursor at a valid row after a deletion, you'll need to call one of the record navigation methods, such as Move, Seek, or Find.

The Delete method can also be used to delete a group of records in a single operation. There is an optional argument to the method to indicate this mode of operation:

```
Recordset.Delete AffectRecords
```

If you set the AffectRecords argument to the value adAffectGroup, all records matching the current Filter property of the Recordset will be deleted when the line of code is executed. The Filter property must be set to one of the symbolic constants listed in Table 4.1, or to an array of bookmarks. The delete operation will fail if the Filter property is set to a WHERE clause.

Listing 4.8 demonstrates both uses of the Delete method in a SQL Server database, with code from this chapter's sample project.

Listing 4.8:   **Deleting Records from a SQL Server Database**

```
Private Sub cmdDeleteSQLServer_Click()

    Dim cnn As ADODB.Connection
    Dim rst As ADODB.Recordset
    Dim varBookmark1 As Variant
    Dim varBookmark2 As Variant

    On Error GoTo HandleErr

    lboResults.Clear
    lboResults.AddItem "Delete with SQL Server"

    ' Open a Recordset
    Set cnn = New ADODB.Connection
    cnn.Open "Provider=SQLOLEDB.1;Server=(local);" & _
      "Initial Catalog=Northwind;Integrated Security=SSPI"
    Set rst = New ADODB.Recordset
    rst.Open "SELECT * FROM Customers", cnn, adOpenKeyset, adLockOptimistic

    ' Find a record we added
    rst.Find "CustomerID = 'XXXXX'"

    ' And delete it
    rst.Delete
    lboResults.AddItem "Deleted one record"

    ' Find and bookmark two records
    rst.MoveFirst
    rst.Find "CustomerID = 'YYYYY'"
    varBookmark1 = rst.Bookmark
    rst.Find "CustomerID = 'ZZZZZ'"
    varBookmark2 = rst.Bookmark

    ' Filter the Recordset to show only these records
    rst.Filter = Array(varBookmark1, varBookmark2)

    ' And delete all records matching the filter
    rst.Delete adAffectGroup
    lboResults.AddItem "Deleted group of records"

    ' Clean up
    rst.Close
    Set rst = Nothing
    cnn.Close
    Set cnn = Nothing

ExitHere:
    Exit Sub
```

```
HandleErr:
    MsgBox "Error " & Err.Number & ": " & Err.Description, _
      vbOKOnly, "cmdDeleteSQLServer"
    Resume ExitHere
    Resume

End Sub
```

Using Command Objects

Command objects can be used to delete data by setting their CommandText property to a SQL string that performs a DELETE or TRUNCATE TABLE operation, or by setting the property to the name of a stored procedure that performs such an operation. The technique is otherwise exactly the same as that for updating records via a Command object.

Using the Supports Method to Determine Capabilities

There are many different ways that you can open a Recordset. Consider the various permutations of the CursorLocation, CursorType, LockType, and Options properties, and the different potential OLE DB providers that can be supplying the data. With all this flexibility, it can be difficult to be sure just which methods will work on which Recordsets. Fortunately, ADO provides the Supports method, which allows you to query a Recordset as to the functionality that it supports.

The Supports method returns True or False for specific options:

```
fReturn = rst.Supports(CursorOptions)
```

The CursorOptions argument must be one of the intrinsic constants shown in Table 4.2.

TABLE 4.2: Constants for the Supports Method

CursorOption	Returns True if...
adAddNew	You can use the AddNew method to add records to this Recordset.
adApproxPosition	You can use the AbsolutePosition and AbsolutePage properties with this Recordset.
adBookmark	You can use the Bookmark property with this Recordset.
adDelete	You can use the Delete method to delete records from this Recordset.
adFind	You can use the Find method to find records in this Recordset.
adHoldRecords	You can change the Recordset position without committing changes to the current record. This is necessary for batch updates.

continued on next page

TABLE 4.2 CONTINUED: Constants for the Supports Method

CursorOption	Returns True if...
adIndex	You can use the Index property to set an index for this Recordset.
adMovePrevious	You can use MoveFirst and MovePrevious, or the Move method, to move backward in this Recordset.
adNotify	This Recordset supports events.
adResync	You can use the Resync method to resynchronize this Recordset with the underlying data.
adSeek	You can use the Seek method to find records in this Recordset.
adUpdate	You can use the Update method to modify records in this Recordset.
adUpdateBatch	You can use the UpdateBatch and CancelBatch methods on this Recordset.

Figure 4.1 shows frmSupports from the sample project, which demonstrates the use of the Supports method. This form allows you to choose options for a Recordset. After selecting the options, click the Open Recordset button, and the form will display the results.

FIGURE 4.1:

Using the Supports method to check the applicable methods for a Recordset

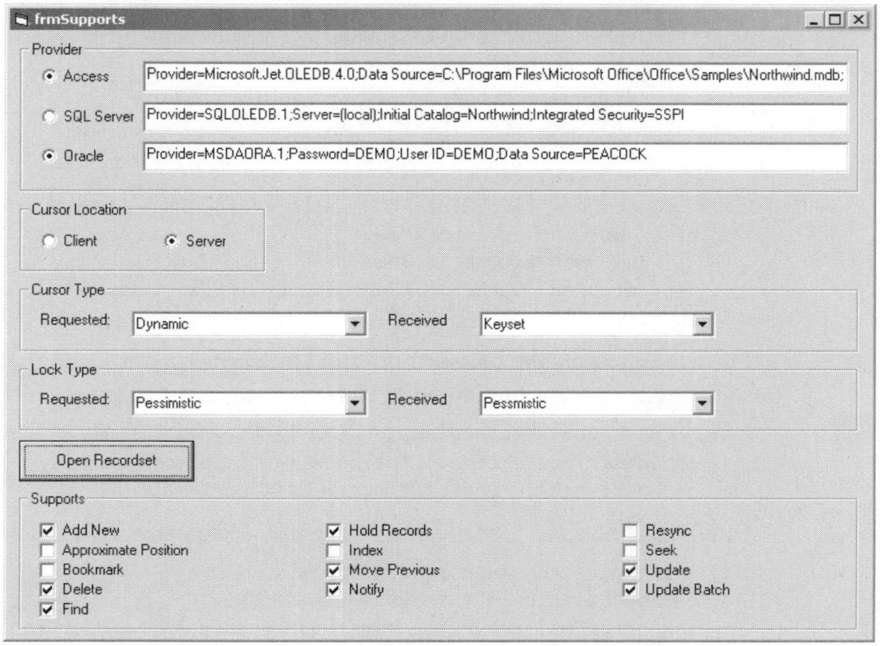

The form starts by initializing objects and setting options for the Recordset object:

```
Set cnn = New ADODB.Connection
Set rst = New ADODB.Recordset

' Set properties based on UI choices
If optClient Then
    rst.CursorLocation = adUseClient
Else
    rst.CursorLocation = adUseServer
End If

rst.CursorType = cboCursorTypeRequested.ListIndex
rst.LockType = cboLockTypeRequested.ListIndex + 1
```

The Cursor Type and Lock Type combo boxes are designed to hold the possible Cursor-Type and LockType constants in numerical order. Note that the ListIndex property of a combo box is zero-based, as is the CursorType property, while the LockType property is one-based.

Next, the code opens a Connection and a Recordset based on the user's choice of database:

```
' Open a Connection and a Recordset
If optAccess.Value = True Then
    cnn.Open txtAccess.Text
    rst.Open "SELECT * FROM Customers", cnn
ElseIf optSQLServer.Value = True Then
    Set cnn = New ADODB.Connection
    cnn.Open txtSQLServer.Text
    rst.Open "SELECT * FROM Customers", cnn
Else 'optOracle.Value=True
    cnn.Open txtOracle.Text
    rst.Open "SELECT * FROM DEMO.CUSTOMER", cnn
End If
```

The form inspects the CursorType and LockType properties of the Recordset after it has been opened. These values are used to set the corresponding user interface controls:

```
' Check the returned cursor and lock types
cboCursorTypeReceived.ListIndex = rst.CursorType
cboLockTypeReceived.ListIndex = rst.LockType - 1
```

And finally, the form calls the Supports method separately to set each check box on the form:

```
' Evaluate the supported actions
chkAddNew.Value = rst.Supports(adAddNew) * -1
chkApproxPosition.Value = rst.Supports(adApproxPosition) * -1
chkBookmark.Value = rst.Supports(adBookmark) * -1
chkDelete.Value = rst.Supports(adDelete) * -1
chkFind.Value = rst.Supports(adFind) * -1
```

```
chkHoldRecords.Value = rst.Supports(adHoldRecords) * -1
chkIndex.Value = rst.Supports(adIndex) * -1
chkMovePrevious.Value = rst.Supports(adMovePrevious) * -1
chkNotify.Value = rst.Supports(adNotify) * -1
chkResync.Value = rst.Supports(adResync) * -1
chkSeek.Value = rst.Supports(adSeek) * -1
chkUpdate.Value = rst.Supports(adUpdate) * -1
chkUpdateBatch.Value = rst.Supports(adUpdateBatch) * -1
```

Note that the Supports method returns True (–1) or False (0), while the valid values for a check box control are vbChecked (1) or vbUnchecked (0). This explains the multiplication by –1 in the code.

NOTE   Because the Recordset Source properties are hard-coded, this form still doesn't show all the possibilities. You'd need to allow setting the Source and Options properties to explore all the combinations.

Using Transactions

ADO also supports transactions. This support is provided through methods of the Connection object. In this section, I'll review the basic idea of transactions and then discuss how they are implemented in ADO.

What Is a Transaction?

The idea of a transaction is one of the core concepts of modern database theory. The simplest way to think of a transaction is as an indivisible unit of work. That is, all of the changes within a transaction succeed or fail as a unit. There's never a situation where one part of a transaction succeeds while another part fails.

Formally, we say that transactions are identified by the ACID properties. This is an acronym for four properties: atomicity, consistency, isolation, and durability.

Atomicity   Atomicity is a fancy way to refer to the concept of a transaction being a unit of work. When a transaction is over, either all of the work within the transaction has been performed in the database or none of it has been performed. You'll never find a database in a state where only part of a transaction has been performed.

Consistency   When a transaction is committed or rolled back, everything must be left in a consistent state. This means that none of the operations within the transaction can violate any of the constraints or rules of the database. If any part of the transaction would leave the database in an inconsistent state, the transaction cannot be committed.

Isolation   If two transactions are in progress at once (for example, two users at different computers might be modifying the same table), the transactions can't "see" each other. Each transaction is isolated from the other. When a transaction goes to read data from the database, the transaction will find everything either in the state that it was before other transactions were started or in the state that it becomes after the other transactions are committed. A transaction never sees an intermediate state in another transaction.

Because transactions are isolated from one another, you're guaranteed to get the same results if you start with a fresh copy of the database and execute all the operations over again in the same order as you did the first time. This is why a database can be restored from a backup and a transaction log.

Durability   Finally, once a transaction has been committed, it endures. The work performed by a transaction is saved permanently. If you commit a transaction, and the computer later crashes, the results of the transaction will still be present after a reboot.

Transactions in ADO

Transactions in ADO are implemented through three methods of the Connection object:

```
Connection.BeginTrans
Connection.CommitTrans
Connection.RollbackTrans
```

- When you call the *BeginTrans* method, the Connection's underlying OLE DB provider starts grouping all subsequent data changes into a transaction. This includes updates, additions, and deletions. None of these changes will be immediately written to the database.

- When you call the *CommitTrans* method, all data changes since the most recent Begin-Trans call are committed to the database. If you call CommitTrans without calling BeginTrans, you'll get an error.

- When you call the *RollbackTrans* method, all data changes since the most recent Begin-Trans call are discarded. If you call RollbackTrans without calling BeginTrans, you'll get an error.

Some providers support nested transactions—that is, you can begin a transaction while there's a transaction already open. In this case, the BeginTrans will return a value indicating the depth of the transaction nesting. In other words, the first time you call BeginTrans, you'll get a return value of 1; the second time you call BeginTrans (without either committing or rolling back the existing transaction), you'll get a return value of 2; and so on.

On the other hand, not all providers support transactions at all. If you looked for a Supports method of the Connection object, you'd be disappointed. Instead, you would need to check the open Connection to see whether it has a provider-defined property named "Transaction

DDL." The basGeneral module in the sample project includes a procedure that you can use to check whether a particular Connection supports transactions:

```
Public Function SupportsTransactions(cnn As ADODB.Connection) As Boolean
    ' Returns True if the connection supports transactions
    Dim prp As ADODB.Property
    On Error Resume Next
    Set prp = cnn.Properties("Transaction DDL")
    SupportsTransactions = (Err.Number = 0)
    Set prp = Nothing

End Function
```

This procedure works by trying to retrieve a property with the appropriate name from the Connection's Properties collection. If the property doesn't exist, then the (Err.Number = 0) test will return False, indicating that the Connection doesn't support transactions.

You can also exercise some control over transactions by setting the Connection object's Attributes property. If you set this property to adXactAbortRetaining, the provider will automatically begin a new transaction whenever you roll back an existing transaction. If you set this property to adXactCommitRetaining, the provider will automatically begin a new transaction whenever you commit an existing transaction. You can cause both commits and rollbacks to begin a new transaction by setting the Attributes property to the sum of these two constants.

Listing 4.9 demonstrates the use of the transaction methods. If you run this procedure in the sample project, you'll see that the final value in the City field depends on whether you choose to commit or roll back the transaction.

Listing 4.9:   **Using Transactions with an Access Database**

```
Private Sub cmdTransactions_Click()

    Dim cnn As ADODB.Connection
    Dim rst As ADODB.Recordset
    Dim intRet As Integer

    On Error GoTo HandleErr

    ' Open a Recordset
    Set cnn = New ADODB.Connection
    cnn.Open "Provider=Microsoft.Jet.OLEDB.4.0;" & _
      "Data Source=C:\Program Files\Microsoft Office\" & _
      "Office10\Samples\Northwind.mdb;"
    Set rst = New ADODB.Recordset
    rst.Open "SELECT * FROM Customers", cnn, adOpenDynamic, adLockOptimistic

    ' Begin a transaction
    cnn.BeginTrans
```

```
' Change the city for the first customer
lboResults.Clear
lboResults.AddItem "Initial value = " & rst.Fields("City")
rst.Fields("City") = "Potsdam"
rst.Update
lboResults.AddItem "Changed value = " & rst.Fields("City")

' Prompt the user
intRet = MsgBox("City has been changed. Commit change?", vbYesNo)

' Commit or rollback depending on user response
If intRet = vbYes Then
    cnn.CommitTrans
Else
    cnn.RollbackTrans
End If

lboResults.AddItem "Final value = " & rst.Fields("City")

' Clean up
rst.Close
Set rst = Nothing
cnn.Close
Set cnn = Nothing

ExitHere:
    Exit Sub

HandleErr:
    MsgBox "Error " & Err.Number & ": " & Err.Description, _
     vbOKOnly, "cmdTransactions"
    Resume ExitHere
    Resume

End Sub
```

Summary

In this chapter, you learned how to use ADO to edit data. In particular, you saw that you can update existing records, add new records, or delete records by manipulating either Recordset or Command objects. You also learned about some of the more advanced features of ADO, including Filters, the Supports method, and transactions.

Now that you've got a basic grounding in ADO objects, properties, and methods, it's time to take a look at the last part of the ADO object model: ADO events. I'll cover those in the next chapter.

CHAPTER 5

Managing Activity with ADO Events

- An event sample

- Connection events

- Recordset events

Most of the communication between your code and ADO is strictly one-way. Your code calls methods or changes properties of the ADO objects, and the objects react. However, two of the ADO objects have the ability to call back to portions of your code by raising events. The Connection and Recordset objects both support a set of events that allow them to trigger portions of your code when their internal state changes. In this chapter, I'll explore the ADO events, and you'll see the interactions that they enable.

An Event Sample

Later in the chapter, I'll systematically discuss the various events that the Connection and Recordset objects make available. But first, let's look at an example, to get a feel for how these events work. Open the ADOChapter5 sample project, run the project by pressing F5, and then click the Connect button on frmSamples. This will cause ADO to open a Connection to an Access database. (All the code in this chapter uses Access; the events work pretty much the same, regardless of which OLE DB provider you're using.)

The sample will print two lines to a listbox on the form:

```
--- cmdConnect ---
    mcnn WillConnect
```

After these two lines, you'll get a prompt similar to the one shown in Figure 5.1. The path in the prompt will depend on where you've installed the samples.

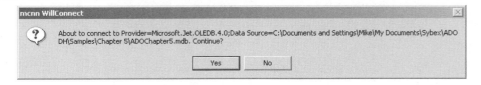

If you respond Yes to the prompt, the listbox will be completed with these lines:

```
--- Leaving cmdConnect ---
    mcnn ConnectComplete
```

On the other hand, if you click No, the listbox will be completed with this text:

```
    mcnn WillConnect cancelled
    mcnn ConnectComplete
    cmdConnect cancelled
--- Leaving cmdConnect ---
```

In these examples, mcnn is the name of an ADO Connection object, and WillConnect and ConnectComplete are events of that object. Even before you trace through the code, you can see that you have the ability to interact with the object while it's working, and to change what it's doing during an event.

The code for this example is entirely contained in frmSamples. It starts with a declaration of a module-level Command object:

```
Private WithEvents mcnn As ADODB.Connection
```

You may not have run across the Visual Basic WithEvents keyword before. This keyword tells Visual Basic that you'd like to trap events from this object. When you declare an object WithEvents, Visual Basic adds the object to the Object combo box in the code editor and adds the object's events to the Procedure combo box. You can declare an object WithEvents only in a class module (including a form's module—all form modules are class modules), and the object must have module scope.

Listing 5.1 shows the cmdConnect_Click procedure, which is responsible for instantiating the Connection object and opening the Connection to the ADOChapter5 Access sample database.

Listing 5.1:   **Code to Connect to a Jet Database**

```
Private Sub cmdConnect_Click()

    On Error GoTo HandleErr

    lboEvents.AddItem " --- cmdConnect ---"

    Set mcnn = New ADODB.Connection

    mcnn.Open "Provider=Microsoft.Jet.OLEDB.4.0;" & _
      "Data Source=" & App.Path & "\ADOChapter5.mdb", , , _
      adAsyncConnect

ExitHere:
    lboEvents.AddItem " --- Leaving cmdConnect ---"

    Exit Sub

HandleErr:
    Select Case Err.Number
        Case conErrConnectCancelled
            ' This is expected if the user cancelled the connection
            lboEvents.AddItem " cmdConnect cancelled"
        Case Else
            MsgBox "Error " & Err.Number & ": " & Err.Description, _
                vbOKOnly, "cmdConnect"
    End Select
    Resume ExitHere
    Resume

End Sub
```

You can see that the call to the Open method specifies an asynchronous Connection object. If you look at what gets printed when you click Yes in the message box, you'll find that this procedure exits before the Connection is actually open. Just before ADO opens the Connection, it will fire the Connection's WillConnect event. Listing 5.2 shows the code for that event.

Listing 5.2:   **Code to Handle the WillConnect Event**

```
Private Sub mcnn_WillConnect(ConnectionString As String, _
 UserID As String, Password As String, Options As Long, _
 adStatus As ADODB.EventStatusEnum, _
 ByVal pConnection As ADODB.Connection)

    Dim intRet As Integer

    On Error GoTo HandleErr

    lboEvents.AddItem "  mcnn WillConnect"

    If adStatus <> adStatusCantDeny Then
        intRet = MsgBox("About to connect to " & _
         pConnection.ConnectionString & ". Continue?", _
         vbQuestion + vbYesNo, "mcnn WillConnect")
        If intRet = vbNo Then
            adStatus = adStatusCancel
            lboEvents.AddItem "  mcnn WillConnect cancelled"
        End If
    End If

ExitHere:
    Exit Sub

HandleErr:
    MsgBox "Error " & Err.Number & ": " & Err.Description, _
     vbOKOnly, "mcnn_WillConnect"
    Resume ExitHere
    Resume

End Sub
```

You can see that this is the event that allows the user to cancel the Connection before it happens. The key is the adStatus argument to the event procedure. If this argument has any value other than adStatusCantDeny when the procedure is called, the event and its consequences can be cancelled by setting the adStatus argument to the value adStatusCancel. Note also that the arguments to the WillConnect event serve to characterize the particular Connection that's being attempted.

When ADO makes the Connection, or when it stops trying (because the Connection has been cancelled), it fires the Connection's ConnectComplete event. Once again, there's code in the sample to respond to this event; it's shown in Listing 5.3.

Listing 5.3:   **Code to Handle the ConnectionComplete Event**

```
Private Sub mcnn_ConnectComplete(ByVal pError As ADODB.Error, _
  adStatus As ADODB.EventStatusEnum, _
  ByVal pConnection As ADODB.Connection)

    On Error GoTo HandleErr

    lboEvents.AddItem "  mcnn ConnectComplete"

ExitHere:
    Exit Sub

HandleErr:
    MsgBox "Error " & Err.Number & ": " & Err.Description, _
      vbOKOnly, "mcnn_ConnectComplete"
    Resume ExitHere
    Resume

End Sub
```

And that's it for the code. In overview, here's what happens when you click the Connect button:

1. The cmdConnect_Click procedure adds the line `--- cmdConnect ---` to the listbox.
2. The WillConnect event happens synchronously (before cmdConnect_Click exits), even though the Open method is called asynchronously. This procedure adds the line `mcnn WillConnect` to the listbox and prompts the user.
3. If the user tells ADO to go ahead and connect, the cmdConnect_Click procedure exits, adding the line `--- Leaving cmdConnect ---` to the listbox. Some time later, the ConnectComplete event fires, adding the line `mcnn ConnectComplete` to the listbox.
4. On the other hand, if the user cancels the Connection, the WillConnect procedure adds the line `mcnn WillConnect cancelled` to the listbox. The ConnectComplete event still fires, although synchronously in this case, and adds the line `mcnn ConnectComplete` to the listbox. It then returns control to the cmdConnect_Click procedure by raising an error. The error trap in that procedure adds the line `cmdConnect cancelled` to the listbox. Then the cmdConnect_Click procedure exits, adding the line `--- Leaving cmdConnect ---` to the listbox.

TIP   You'll find this sequence of events less confusing if you put a breakpoint at the top of the cmdConnect_Click procedure and then single-step through the code.

Connection Events

The Connection object makes nine events available in these four categories:

- *Connection management* events notify you when a Connection is opened or closed.

- *Transaction management* events notify you when a transaction is started, committed, or rolled back.

- *Command management* events notify you when a Command is executed.

- *Informational* events notify you when ADO or the OLE DB provider has additional information available about the current operation.

Connection Management Events

The Command object provides three events that notify you of Connection activity:

- WillConnect

- ConnectComplete

- Disconnect

You've already seen two of these events, WillConnect and ConnectComplete. These two events exemplify a common pattern in ADO events, that of before-and-after notifications. Before a Connection is opened, the WillConnect event fires. This event passes all the pertinent information about the Connection attempt, and can be cancelled. After the Connection is opened, the ConnectComplete attempt fires. This event notifies you of something that has already happened, so it can't be cancelled. But ConnectComplete is a good place to take action if you need to respond to successful Connections.

Here's the event procedure definition for the WillConnect event:

```
Private Sub mcnn_WillConnect(ConnectionString As String, _
  UserID As String, Password As String, Options As Long, _
  adStatus As ADODB.EventStatusEnum, _
  ByVal pConnection As ADODB.Connection)
```

This event has six arguments, most of which are pretty obvious:

- The *ConnectionString* argument contains the full connection string that's being used to contact the OLE DB provider.

- The *UserID* argument contains the user ID being used, if any, or an empty string.

- The *Password* argument contains the password being used, if any, or an empty string.

- The *Options* argument contains the value of the Connection.Options property.

- The *adStatus* argument contains one of the values from Table 5.1.

- The *pConnection* argument is a pointer to the actual Connection object being opened.

TABLE 5.1: adStatus Values

Value	Meaning
adStatusOK	The operation that fired the event was successful.
adStatusErrorsOccurred	The operation that fired the event failed.
adStatusCantDeny	The event cannot be cancelled.
adStatusCancel	Cancel this event.
adStatusUnwantedEvent	Prevent firing this event.

You'll see that all the arguments are passed by reference. That means that you can actually edit them within the WillConnect event procedure. This can be a useful technique for redirecting Connections. For example, you can change the ConnectionString to use a different server than was specified when the event was invoked.

The adStatus argument lets you modify event processing. The adStatus value when an event procedure is invoked will always be adStatusOK, adStatusErrorsOccured, or adStatus-CantDeny. If it's any value other than adStatusCantDeny, you can set it to adStatusCancel within the event procedure. This has the effect of cancelling the event and its consequences (as you saw in the example of the WillConnect event at the start of the chapter). You can also set this argument to adStatusUnwantedEvent. This tells ADO not to bother firing this particular event in the future.

The ConnectComplete event fires when ADO is done making the Connection:

```
Private Sub mcnn_ConnectComplete(ByVal pError As ADODB.Error, _
  adStatus As ADODB.EventStatusEnum, _
  ByVal pConnection As ADODB.Connection)
```

This event has three arguments:

- The *pError* argument points to an ADO Error object if there was any error during the Connection attempt, or to Nothing if no error occurred.

- The *adStatus* argument contains one of the values from Table 5.1.

- The *pConnection* argument is a pointer to the actual Connection object that was opened.

It's important to realize that the ConnectComplete event is fired even if the WillConnect event is cancelled. In this case, the pError object will contain error 3712, "Operation has been cancelled by the user." Note that this will *not* raise an error during the event procedure itself; the error is raised in the original calling procedure.

When you disconnect from a data source, the Connection object raises a Disconnect event:

```
Private Sub mcnn_Disconnect(adStatus As ADODB.EventStatusEnum, _
  ByVal pConnection As ADODB.Connection)
```

You've already seen both of the arguments to the Disconnect event. The Disconnect event can be cancelled by setting the adStatus argument to adStatusCancel if you'd like to keep the Connection open. This event is fired when you explicitly call the Close method of the Connection object. It's *not* fired if you simply let the Connection go out of scope or set it to Nothing without closing it.

Transaction Management Events

The Connection object provides three events to let you monitor the status of transactions on the Connection:

- BeginTransComplete
- CommitTransComplete
- RollbackTransComplete

Because these three events fire after the transaction operations are completed, they cannot be cancelled.

TIP   For more information on transactions in ADO, see Chapter 4, "Editing Data with ADO."

The BeginTransComplete event procedure has four arguments, as illustrated in this statement:

```
Private Sub mcnn_BeginTransComplete(ByVal TransactionLevel As Long, _
  ByVal pError As ADODB.Error, _
  adStatus As ADODB.EventStatusEnum, _
  ByVal pConnection As ADODB.Connection)
```

You've seen the pError, adStatus, and pConnection arguments in other Connection events. The other argument, TransactionLevel, contains the nesting level of the transaction that triggered the event: 1 for an outer transaction, 2 for a first nested transaction, and so on.

Within the BeginTransComplete event, you could check the pError argument to see whether the OLE DB provider was able to begin a transaction, and to take appropriate action (perhaps a warning message to the user) if it was not able to do so.

The CommitTransComplete and RollbackTransComplete event procedures supply almost the same information that BeginTransComplete supplies:

```
Private Sub mcnn_CommitTransComplete(ByVal pError As ADODB.Error, _
  adStatus As ADODB.EventStatusEnum, _
  ByVal pConnection As ADODB.Connection)

Private Sub mcnn_RollbackTransComplete(ByVal pError As ADODB.Error, _
  adStatus As ADODB.EventStatusEnum, _
  ByVal pConnection As ADODB.Connection)
```

Again, monitoring the pError argument in these events gives you a handy way to make sure that transaction processing is being allowed by the OLE DB provider. These events are a good place to perform other activities after completion of a transaction. For example, you might want to requery a Recordset and update the user interface of your application every time you commit or roll back a transaction.

Command Management Events

The most detailed event information supplied by the Connection object comes from the two command management events:

- WillExecute

- ExecuteComplete

As with the WillConnect and ConnectComplete events, the first of these fires before a change in the data, and the second after the data has been changed.

The WillExecute event occurs whenever a Command is about to be executed. This may be caused by the Connection.Execute method, the Command.Execute method, or the Recordset.Open method:

```
Private Sub mcnn_WillExecute(Source As String, _
  CursorType As ADODB.CursorTypeEnum, _
  LockType As ADODB.LockTypeEnum, _
  Options As Long, _
  adStatus As ADODB.EventStatusEnum, _
  ByVal pCommand As ADODB.Command, _
  ByVal pRecordset As ADODB.Recordset, _
  ByVal pConnection As ADODB.Connection)
```

If the WillExecute event is in response to the Recordset.Open method, the Source, CursorType, LockType, Options, and pRecordset arguments characterize the Recordset object. You can modify any of these arguments within the WillExecute event to change the nature or behavior of the Recordset.

If the WillExecute event is in response to the Command.Execute method, the pCommand argument points to the Command being executed. In any case, the pConnection argument points to the Connection where the activity is happening.

The WillExecute event can be cancelled by setting the adStatus argument to adStatusCancel.

This event is a good place to adjust Recordset parameters when you're working with a Recordset. One thing you might like to do in some cases is evaluate the Source argument to see what's going on. For example, suppose you have an application that somehow allows the end user to enter a SQL string to evaluate as a Recordset. You can use the WillExecute event to look at the SQL string before it's sent to the OLE DB provider. You might want to cancel the event if the string has the form SELECT * FROM tablename, because that might attempt to retrieve too many records to handle.

After the command has been executed, you'll get an ExecuteComplete event from the ADO Connection object:

```
Private Sub mcnn_ExecuteComplete(ByVal RecordsAffected As Long, _
  ByVal pError As ADODB.Error, _
  adStatus As ADODB.EventStatusEnum, _
  ByVal pCommand As ADODB.Command, _
  ByVal pRecordset As ADODB.Recordset, _
  ByVal pConnection As ADODB.Connection)
```

Most of the arguments to ExecuteComplete are familiar by now. The exception is the RecordsAffected argument, which tells you how many records were affected by the command. One use for this event is saving audit trail information within an application; you could record every successful Command by looking at the pCommand.CommandText or pRecordset.Source properties, together with the number of records involved in the operation.

Informational Events

The last event supported by the Connection object is used to pass information back to your application from the OLE DB provider:

```
Private Sub mcnn_InfoMessage(ByVal pError As ADODB.Error, _
  adStatus As ADODB.EventStatusEnum, _
  ByVal pConnection As ADODB.Connection)
```

Any information that the provider chooses to make available to you will be contained in the pError object (which might represent, in this case, a warning or just a message rather than an actual error).

NOTE   Providers vary in their support for the InfoMessage event. Most providers I've worked with seldom use this event. The SQL Server provider occasionally supplies informational messages.

Recordset Events

The Recordset object makes eleven events available in these three categories:

- *Retrieval* events notify you when data is being fetched from the database.
- *Navigation* events notify you when the current record changes in the Recordset.
- *Change Management* events notify you when data is being updated.

Retrieval Events

The Recordset object supplies a pair of events that let you monitor the progress in retrieving data to the Recordset:

- FetchProgress
- FetchComplete

WARNING The FetchProgress and FetchComplete events will fire only if the Recordset is using a client-side cursor.

These two events are fired when you open a Recordset asynchronously (that is, when the Options argument to the Recordset.Open method includes the adAsyncExecute, adAsyncFetch, or adAsyncFetchNonBlocking flag). The FetchProgress event is fired periodically when the OLE DB cursor service wants to update you as to how many records have been retrieved:

```
Private Sub mrst_FetchProgress(ByVal Progress As Long, _
  ByVal MaxProgress As Long, _
  adStatus As ADODB.EventStatusEnum, _
  ByVal pRecordset As ADODB.Recordset)
```

The Progress argument contains the number of rows that have been fetched so far, and the MaxProgress argument contains ADO's best guess as to how many rows will be fetched to fill the Recordset. At any time, you can cancel further record retrieval by setting the adStatus argument to adStatusCancel.

The obvious use of the FetchProgress event is to update a progress meter or similar control on an application's user interface so that the user can keep track of the completion status of a lengthy Recordset operation.

When all the records in a Recordset have been fetched, ADO fires the FetchComplete event:

```
Private Sub mrst_FetchComplete(ByVal pError As ADODB.Error, _
  adStatus As ADODB.EventStatusEnum, _
  ByVal pRecordset As ADODB.Recordset)
```

This event is a good place to activate user interface controls that depend on having data present, or to otherwise indicate to the user that they can proceed with further Recordset operations.

Navigation Events

Three events let you monitor the movement of the current record pointer in a Recordset:

- WillMove

- MoveComplete
- EndOfRecordset

The WillMove and MoveComplete events make up another pair that flank every move in the Recordset. The WillMove event, of course, occurs just before the current record pointer is actually changed:

```
Private Sub mrst_WillMove(ByVal adReason As ADODB.EventReasonEnum, _
   adStatus As ADODB.EventStatusEnum, _
   ByVal pRecordset As ADODB.Recordset)
```

Table 5.2 shows the possible values for the adReason argument. Not all of these values will occur in WillMove events, but as you'll see later in the chapter, this enumeration is also used by some other Recordset events.

TABLE 5.2: adReason Values

Value	Explanation
adRsnAddNew	A new record was added to the Recordset.
adRsnDelete	A record was deleted from the Recordset.
adRsnUpdate	An existing record was updated.
adRsnUndoUpdate	An update was reversed.
adRsnUndoAddNew	A new record addition was reversed.
adRsnUndoDelete	A record deletion was reversed.
adRsnRequery	The Recordset.Requery method was executed.
adRsnResynch	The Recordset was resynchronized with the database.
adRsnClose	The Recordset was closed.
adRsnMove	The current record pointer was moved to an arbitrary location.
adRsnFirstChange	The record was changed (edited but not yet saved).
adRsnMoveFirst	The current record pointer was moved to the first row.
adRsnMoveNext	The current record pointer was moved to the next row.
adRsnMovePrevious	The current record pointer was moved to the previous row.
adRsnMoveLast	The current record pointer was moved to the last row.

When you set the adStatus argument to adStatusUnwantedEvent to cancel further event firing, the cancellation is specific to that particular reason. That is, if adReason is adRsn-MoveFirst and you set adStatus to adStatusUnwantedEvent, you'll still see the event for all other reasons, such as adRsnMoveLast.

Of course, you can cancel the current record pointer movement entirely by setting adStatus to adStatusCancel. If you don't do this, the MoveComplete event will be fired immediately after the current record pointer is moved:

```
Private Sub mrst_MoveComplete(ByVal adReason As ADODB.EventReasonEnum,_
  ByVal pError As ADODB.Error, _
  adStatus As ADODB.EventStatusEnum, _
  ByVal pRecordset As ADODB.Recordset)
```

The WillMove and MoveComplete methods can be triggered by a variety of operations, including these:

The Recordset.Open method

The Recordset.Move method

The Recordset.MoveFirst method

The Recordset.MoveLast method

The Recordset.MoveNext method

The Recordset.MovePrevious method

The Recordset.AddNew method

The Recordset.Requery method

Setting the Recordset.Filter property

Setting the Recordset.Index property

Setting the Recordset.Bookmark property

Setting the Recordset.AbsolutePage property

Setting the Recordset.AbsolutePosition property

The third navigational event, the EndOfRecordset event, is fired when you attempt to move the cursor past the end of the Recordset (there is no corresponding StartOfRecordset event):

```
Private Sub mrst_EndOfRecordset(fMoreData As Boolean, _
  adStatus As ADODB.EventStatusEnum, _
  ByVal pRecordset As ADODB.Recordset)
```

Within the EndOfRecordset event, you can actually add more data to the Recordset. If you do this, you should set the fMoreData argument to True, which will tell the Recordset object that it's not actually past the end of the Recordset after all.

Change Management Events

Finally, the Recordset object provides six change management events:

- WillChangeField
- FieldChangeComplete
- WillChangeRecord
- RecordChangeComplete
- WillChangeRecordset
- RecordsetChangeComplete

These events can be grouped in three pairs. The first pair, WillChangeField and Field-ChangeComplete, brackets any change to the value of a field:

```
Private Sub mrst_WillChangeField(ByVal cFields As Long, _
  ByVal Fields As Variant, _
  adStatus As ADODB.EventStatusEnum, _
  ByVal pRecordset As ADODB.Recordset)

Private Sub mrst_FieldChangeComplete(ByVal cFields As Long, _
  ByVal Fields As Variant, _
  ByVal pError As ADODB.Error, _
  adStatus As ADODB.EventStatusEnum, _
  ByVal pRecordset As ADODB.Recordset)
```

Ordinarily, these events will be called for a change to a single field. But remember that some ADO methods can change multiple fields in a single operation. For instance, the Update method can update an entire array of fields at once. As a result, the first two arguments to these events contains field information:

- *cFields* is the number of fields that are being changed.
- *Fields* is a variant array containing ADO Field objects.

The next pair of events monitors for changes in entire records. These events can be triggered by the Update, Delete, CancelUpdate, AddNew, UpdateBatch, or CancelBatch methods of the Recordset object:

```
Private Sub mrst_WillChangeRecord(ByVal adReason As ADODB.EventReasonEnum, _
  ByVal cRecords As Long, _
  adStatus As ADODB.EventStatusEnum, _
  ByVal pRecordset As ADODB.Recordset)

Private Sub mrst_RecordChangeComplete( _
  ByVal adReason As ADODB.EventReasonEnum, _
  ByVal cRecords As Long, _
```

```
    ByVal pError As ADODB.Error, _
    adStatus As ADODB.EventStatusEnum, _
    ByVal pRecordset As ADODB.Recordset)
```

The cRecords argument is set to the number of records changing. This might be more than one if these events are called as the result of a batch update. The adReason argument will be one of the values listed in Table 5.2.

During the WillChangeRecord event, ADO will set the Filter property of the Recordset to adFilterAffectedRecords. As a result, the pRecordset argument will contain only the records that are being changed. You can't change the Filter property within this event.

The final pair of change management events occurs when there is a change that affects the entire Recordset:

```
Private Sub mrst_WillChangeRecordset( _
  ByVal adReason As ADODB.EventReasonEnum, _
  adStatus As ADODB.EventStatusEnum, _
  ByVal pRecordset As ADODB.Recordset)

Private Sub mrst_RecordsetChangeComplete( _
  ByVal adReason As ADODB.EventReasonEnum, _
  ByVal pError As ADODB.Error, _
  adStatus As ADODB.EventStatusEnum, _
  ByVal pRecordset As ADODB.Recordset)
```

These events don't fire for data changes; that's the job of the WillChangeRecord and RecordChangeComplete events. Rather, they fire when a method changes the overall Recordset. In particular, these events occur for these methods:

Recordset.Open

Recordset.Close

Recordset.Requery

Recordset.Resync

Of course, you can tell which of these methods is involved during a particular call to the event procedures by inspecting the value of the adReason argument.

Another Example

This chapter's sample project contains a form named frmRecordset, which you can open by clicking the Recordset button on the main form in the sample. This form, shown in Figure 5.2, is designed to let you see the order of events when you interact with the records in a database.

FIGURE 5.2:

Investigating events
with frmRecordset

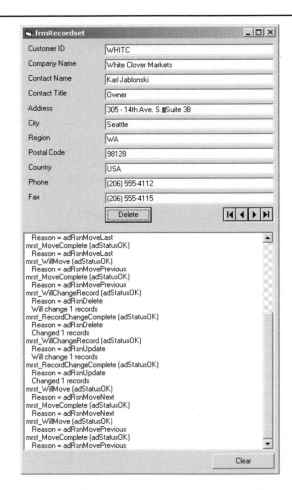

The form includes two module-level ADO variables, a Connection and a Recordset. These two variables are automatically initialized when the form is loaded. Listing 5.4 shows the code that does this.

Listing 5.4:   **Initializing a Recordset**

```
Private WithEvents mcnn As ADODB.Connection
Private WithEvents mrst As ADODB.Recordset

Private Sub Form_Load()

    On Error GoTo HandleErr
```

```
    Set mcnn = New ADODB.Connection

    mcnn.Open "Provider=Microsoft.Jet.OLEDB.4.0;" & _
      "Data Source=" & App.Path & "\ADOChapter5.mdb"

    Set mrst = New ADODB.Recordset
    mrst.CursorLocation = adUseClient
    mrst.Open "SELECT * FROM Customers", mcnn, _
      adOpenKeyset, adLockOptimistic

    Set Adodc1.Recordset = mrst

ExitHere:
    Exit Sub

HandleErr:
    MsgBox "Error " & Err.Number & ": " & Err.Description, _
      vbOKOnly, "Form_Load"
    Resume ExitHere
    Resume

End Sub
```

You can see that after the Recordset has been opened, it is assigned to the Recordset property of an ADO Data Control. This technique allows you to use bound controls to display data (which is what this form does) while still receiving events from the Recordset involved.

The form has a pair of helper functions whose job is to convert adStatus and adReason values into human-readable strings. Listing 5.5 shows these functions.

Listing 5.5:   Helper Functions to Translate Event Arguments

```
Private Function TranslateStatus(lngStatus As Long) As String
    Select Case lngStatus
        Case adStatusOK
            TranslateStatus = "adStatusOK"
        Case adStatusErrorsOccurred
            TranslateStatus = "adStatusErrorsOccurred"
        Case adStatusCantDeny
            TranslateStatus = "adStatusCantDeny"
    End Select
End Function

Private Function TranslateReason(lngReason As Long) As String
    Select Case lngReason
        Case adRsnAddNew
            TranslateReason = "adRsnAddNew"
        Case adRsnDelete
            TranslateReason = "adRsnDelete"
```

```
              Case adRsnUpdate
                  TranslateReason = "adRsnUpdate"
              Case adRsnUndoUpdate
                  TranslateReason = "adRsnUndoUpdate"
              Case adRsnUndoAddNew
                  TranslateReason = "adRsnUndoAddNew"
              Case adRsnUndoDelete
                  TranslateReason = "adRsnUndoDelete"
              Case adRsnRequery
                  TranslateReason = "adRsnRequery"
              Case adRsnResynch
                  TranslateReason = "adRsnResynch"
              Case adRsnClose
                  TranslateReason = "adRsnClose"
              Case adRsnMove
                  TranslateReason = "adRsnMove"
              Case adRsnFirstChange
                  TranslateReason = "adRsnFirstChange"
              Case adRsnMoveFirst
                  TranslateReason = "adRsnMoveFirst"
              Case adRsnMoveNext
                  TranslateReason = "adRsnMoveNext"
              Case adRsnMovePrevious
                  TranslateReason = "adRsnMovePrevious"
              Case adRsnMoveLast
                  TranslateReason = "adRsnMoveLast"
          End Select
      End Function
```

The rest of the code for this form is in the event procedures. Every event procedure of the Connection and Recordset objects has been modified to write a notice out to the listbox on the form when it is called. This allows you to follow the events as they happen, and to see how they interact. This portion of the code is shown in Listing 5.6.

Listing 5.6:   **Event Procedures for frmRecordset**

```
Private Sub mcnn_BeginTransComplete(ByVal TransactionLevel As Long, _
  ByVal pError As ADODB.Error, _
  adStatus As ADODB.EventStatusEnum, _
  ByVal pConnection As ADODB.Connection)
    lboEvents.AddItem "mcnn_BeginTransComplete (" & _
    TranslateStatus(adStatus) & ")"
End Sub

Private Sub mcnn_CommitTransComplete(ByVal pError As ADODB.Error, _
  adStatus As ADODB.EventStatusEnum, _
  ByVal pConnection As ADODB.Connection)
    lboEvents.AddItem "mcnn_CommitTransComplete (" & _
    TranslateStatus(adStatus) & ")"
End Sub
```

```
Private Sub mcnn_ConnectComplete(ByVal pError As ADODB.Error, _
 adStatus As ADODB.EventStatusEnum, _
 ByVal pConnection As ADODB.Connection)
    lboEvents.AddItem "mcnn_ConnectComplete (" & _
      TranslateStatus(adStatus) & ")"
End Sub

Private Sub mcnn_Disconnect(adStatus As ADODB.EventStatusEnum, _
 ByVal pConnection As ADODB.Connection)
    lboEvents.AddItem "mcnn_DisConnect (" & _
      TranslateStatus(adStatus) & ")"
End Sub

Private Sub mcnn_ExecuteComplete(ByVal RecordsAffected As Long, _
 ByVal pError As ADODB.Error, _
 adStatus As ADODB.EventStatusEnum, _
 ByVal pCommand As ADODB.Command, _
 ByVal pRecordset As ADODB.Recordset, _
 ByVal pConnection As ADODB.Connection)
    lboEvents.AddItem "mcnn_ExecuteComplete (" & _
      TranslateStatus(adStatus) & ")"
    lboEvents.AddItem "    " & CStr(RecordsAffected) & " records affected"
End Sub

Private Sub mcnn_InfoMessage(ByVal pError As ADODB.Error, _
 adStatus As ADODB.EventStatusEnum, _
 ByVal pConnection As ADODB.Connection)
    lboEvents.AddItem "mcnn_InfoMessage (" & _
      TranslateStatus(adStatus) & ")"
    lboEvents.AddItem "    " & pError.Description
End Sub

Private Sub mcnn_RollbackTransComplete(ByVal pError As ADODB.Error, _
 adStatus As ADODB.EventStatusEnum, _
 ByVal pConnection As ADODB.Connection)
    lboEvents.AddItem "mcnn_RollbackTransComplete (" & _
      TranslateStatus(adStatus) & ")"
End Sub

Private Sub mcnn_WillConnect(ConnectionString As String, _
 UserID As String, Password As String, Options As Long, _
 adStatus As ADODB.EventStatusEnum, _
 ByVal pConnection As ADODB.Connection)
    lboEvents.AddItem "mcnn_WillConnect (" & _
      TranslateStatus(adStatus) & ")"
End Sub

Private Sub mcnn_WillExecute(Source As String, _
 CursorType As ADODB.CursorTypeEnum, _
 LockType As ADODB.LockTypeEnum, _
 Options As Long, _
```

```
    adStatus As ADODB.EventStatusEnum, _
    ByVal pCommand As ADODB.Command, _
    ByVal pRecordset As ADODB.Recordset, _
    ByVal pConnection As ADODB.Connection)
        lboEvents.AddItem "mcnn_WillExecute (" & _
          TranslateStatus(adStatus) & ")"
        lboEvents.AddItem "    Source = " & Source
End Sub

Private Sub mrst_EndOfRecordset(fMoreData As Boolean, _
 adStatus As ADODB.EventStatusEnum, _
 ByVal pRecordset As ADODB.Recordset)
        lboEvents.AddItem "mrst_EndOfRecordset (" & _
          TranslateStatus(adStatus) & ")"
End Sub

Private Sub mrst_FetchComplete(ByVal pError As ADODB.Error, _
 adStatus As ADODB.EventStatusEnum, _
 ByVal pRecordset As ADODB.Recordset)
        lboEvents.AddItem "mrst_FetchComplete (" & _
          TranslateStatus(adStatus) & ")"
End Sub

Private Sub mrst_FetchProgress(ByVal Progress As Long, _
 ByVal MaxProgress As Long, _
 adStatus As ADODB.EventStatusEnum, _
 ByVal pRecordset As ADODB.Recordset)
        lboEvents.AddItem "mrst_FetchProgress (" & _
          TranslateStatus(adStatus) & ")"
        lboEvents.AddItem "    Fetched " & CStr(Progress) & _
          " of " & CStr(MaxProgress)
End Sub

Private Sub mrst_FieldChangeComplete(ByVal cFields As Long, _
 ByVal Fields As Variant, _
 ByVal pError As ADODB.Error, _
 adStatus As ADODB.EventStatusEnum, _
 ByVal pRecordset As ADODB.Recordset)
        Dim inti As Integer
        lboEvents.AddItem "mrst_FieldChangeComplete (" & _
          TranslateStatus(adStatus) & ")"
        For inti = 0 To cFields - 1
            lboEvents.AddItem "    Changed " & Fields(inti).Name
        Next inti
End Sub

Private Sub mrst_MoveComplete(ByVal adReason As ADODB.EventReasonEnum, _
 ByVal pError As ADODB.Error, _
 adStatus As ADODB.EventStatusEnum, _
 ByVal pRecordset As ADODB.Recordset)
        lboEvents.AddItem "mrst_MoveComplete (" & _
```

```
        TranslateStatus(adStatus) & ")"
      lboEvents.AddItem "   Reason = " & TranslateReason(adReason)
End Sub

Private Sub mrst_RecordChangeComplete( _
 ByVal adReason As ADODB.EventReasonEnum, _
 ByVal cRecords As Long, _
 ByVal pError As ADODB.Error, _
 adStatus As ADODB.EventStatusEnum, _
 ByVal pRecordset As ADODB.Recordset)
      lboEvents.AddItem "mrst_RecordChangeComplete (" & _
       TranslateStatus(adStatus) & ")"
      lboEvents.AddItem "   Reason = " & TranslateReason(adReason)
      lboEvents.AddItem "   Changed " & CStr(cRecords) & " records"
End Sub

Private Sub mrst_RecordsetChangeComplete( _
 ByVal adReason As ADODB.EventReasonEnum, _
 ByVal pError As ADODB.Error, _
 adStatus As ADODB.EventStatusEnum, _
 ByVal pRecordset As ADODB.Recordset)
      lboEvents.AddItem "mrst_RecordsetChangeComplete (" & _
       TranslateStatus(adStatus) & ")"
      lboEvents.AddItem "   Reason = " & TranslateReason(adReason)
End Sub

Private Sub mrst_WillChangeField(ByVal cFields As Long, _
 ByVal Fields As Variant, _
 adStatus As ADODB.EventStatusEnum, _
 ByVal pRecordset As ADODB.Recordset)
      Dim inti As Integer
      lboEvents.AddItem "mrst_WillChangeField (" & _
       TranslateStatus(adStatus) & ")"
      For inti = 0 To cFields - 1
          lboEvents.AddItem "   Will change " & Fields(inti).Name
      Next inti
End Sub

Private Sub mrst_WillChangeRecord(ByVal adReason As ADODB.EventReasonEnum, _
 ByVal cRecords As Long, _
 adStatus As ADODB.EventStatusEnum, _
 ByVal pRecordset As ADODB.Recordset)
      lboEvents.AddItem "mrst_WillChangeRecord (" & _
       TranslateStatus(adStatus) & ")"
      lboEvents.AddItem "   Reason = " & TranslateReason(adReason)
      lboEvents.AddItem "   Will change " & CStr(cRecords) & " records"
End Sub

Private Sub mrst_WillChangeRecordset( _
 ByVal adReason As ADODB.EventReasonEnum, _
 adStatus As ADODB.EventStatusEnum, _
```

```
ByVal pRecordset As ADODB.Recordset)
    lboEvents.AddItem "mrst_WillChangeRecordset (" & _
    TranslateStatus(adStatus) & ")"
    lboEvents.AddItem "    Reason = " & TranslateReason(adReason)
End Sub

Private Sub mrst_WillMove(ByVal adReason As ADODB.EventReasonEnum, _
  adStatus As ADODB.EventStatusEnum, _
  ByVal pRecordset As ADODB.Recordset)
    lboEvents.AddItem "mrst_WillMove (" & _
    TranslateStatus(adStatus) & ")"
    lboEvents.AddItem "    Reason = " & TranslateReason(adReason)
End Sub
```

Only some of these event procedures will be called by the controls on the form in the sample project. For example, because there's no transaction processing hooked up to the user interface, the BeginTransComplete, CommitTransComplete, and RollbackTransComplete events will never be fired.

You should also be aware that the sequence of events that you discover via this form (or similar code in your own applications) is not necessarily fixed. In cases where a single operation triggers multiple events, the ADO documentation says that the order of events is undefined. This is most easily seen in the Recordset change-management events. If you change data in a record, four events will be triggered:

- WillChangeField
- WillChangeRecord
- FieldChangeComplete
- RecordChangeComplete

The two Will events will fire before the two Complete events, but within each group, the order may vary. For example, you might see the events in this order:

1. WillChangeField
2. WillChangeRecord
3. RecordChangeComplete
4. FieldChangeComplete

More interesting is the case in which one of the Will events is cancelled by setting its adStatus argument to adStatusCancel. If you cancel the first event, the corresponding Complete event will fire immediately with its adStatus argument set to adStatusErrorsOccurred:

1. WillChangeField (cancelled)
2. FieldChangeComplete

On the other hand, if you cancel the second Will event, both Complete events will fire:

1. WillChangeField
2. WillChangeRecord (cancelled)
3. FieldChangeComplete
4. RecordChangeComplete

Summary

In this chapter, you learned about ADO events. The Connection and Recordset objects in ADO expose a fairly rich event model. These events allow you to monitor such activities as connecting to a data source, changing data in a Recordset, or manipulating database transactions.

In the next chapter, I'll discuss two recent additions to the ADO object model, the Record and Stream objects. You'll see how these objects can be used to work with a variety of data sources other than simple fields stored in relational databases.

CHAPTER 6

Using Records and Streams

- Using ADO with nonrelational data

- Working with BLOBs in Recordsets

- Using Command and result Streams

O ne of the big advances of ADO over previous data access models such as DAO or RDO is that ADO has been explicitly extended to deal with nonrelational data. By implementing a pair of specialized objects (Record and Stream), Microsoft has made it possible to treat data sources as diverse as web sites and Exchange servers in ADO code. The Record and Stream objects are also used to integrate ADO with XML. In this chapter, you'll learn how to use these objects for a variety of data access tasks.

Using ADO with Nonrelational Data

ADO was designed from the start to handle nonrelational data in a database-like manner. For example, many types of data are better represented as a hierarchy than as a relational database:

- Folders and messages in an e-mail system
- Folders and files on a hard drive
- Directories and files on an FTP server

The Record, Stream, and Recordset objects work together to help you navigate through hierarchical storage:

- You can open a Record object at the root level of a storage.
- Using the Record's GetChildren method, you can open a Recordset object containing all the children of a node. You can, in turn, set a Record object equal to one of these children.
- Using the Record's associated Stream object, you can retrieve the actual binary data from within the Record. You can think of Records as directory entries and Streams as the data contained within the files that those entries refer to.

WARNING   There's no easy way to tell whether an arbitrary OLE DB provider supports the Record object. Perhaps the best way is to attempt to open a Record object using the provider. If the provider can't supply one, it will generally return error 3251, Operation Not Supported.

Using the Record Object

A Record object represents one row of data, or, more abstractly, one item returned by an OLE DB provider. Although a Record object resembles a single-row Recordset, the Record object has fewer methods and properties than the Recordset and requires less application overhead to open and manipulate. Table 6.1 shows some of the methods and properties of the Record object.

TABLE 6.1: Selected Details about the Record Object

Name	Type	Explanation
ActiveConnection	Property	The OLE DB connection from which this Record object was retrieved.
Close	Method	Removes the connection between this object and the original data source.
DeleteRecord	Method	Deletes the contents of the Record object.
Fields	Collection	Field objects contained within this Record.
GetChildren	Method	Opens a Recordset containing the Records (for example, subdirectories and files) in a hierarchical data structure directly below this Record.
Open	Method	Associates the Record with a data source.
RecordType	Property	Indicates the type of data represented by this object. This can be adCollectionRecord (a Record that contains child nodes), adSimpleRecord (a Record without child nodes), adStructDoc (a COM structured document), or adRecordUnknown (an unknown or uninitialized Record).
Source	Property	Contains the URL or Recordset from which this Record was derived.

TIP   For complete details on the Record and Stream objects, refer to Appendix A, "The ADO Object Model."

Figure 6.1 shows the frmWeb form in the ADOChapter6 sample project. This form illustrates the use of the Record object in conjunction with the Recordset object to retrieve the structure of a website, by using the Microsoft OLE DB Provider for Internet Publishing.

The code in this example is mildly complex. Most of the complexity comes from managing two sets of objects: the Record and Recordset objects that represent the structure of the chosen web server, and the Node objects that map that structure back to the TreeView control on the form. Listing 6.1 shows the code that runs after the user enters a URL and clicks the Load button.

WARNING   You must have administrative privileges over the web server in order to retrieve data via the OLE DB Provider for Internet Publishing. Otherwise, you'll get Error -2147467259, which shows up as "unspecified error."

FIGURE 6.1:

A website as displayed via ADO

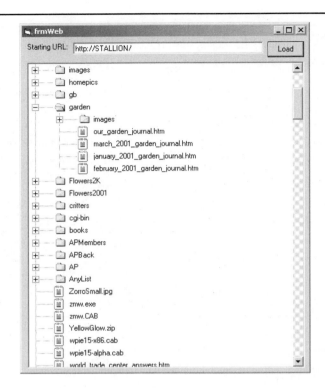

Listing 6.1:   **cmdLoad_Click Procedure**

```
Private Sub cmdLoad_Click()

    Dim rec As ADODB.Record
    Dim rstChildren As ADODB.Recordset
    Dim nodRoot As Node
    Dim nod As Node
    Dim strURL As String
    Dim strPath As String

    On Error GoTo HandleErr

    ' Clear the treeview
    tvwWeb.Nodes.Clear

    ' Open the indicated URL
    Set rec = New ADODB.Record
    rec.Open "", "URL=" & txtURL.Text
```

```
        ' Add this as the root of the treeview
        Select Case rec.RecordType
            Case adSimpleRecord
                Set nodRoot = tvwWeb.Nodes.Add( , , _
                URLtoKey(txtURL.Text), txtURL.Text, conImageDocument)
                ' No child nodes, we're done
            Case adCollectionRecord
                Set nodRoot = tvwWeb.Nodes.Add( , , _
                URLtoKey(txtURL.Text), txtURL.Text, conImageFolderClosed)
                ' Open a Recordset containing this record's children.
                Set rstChildren = rec.GetChildren
                Do Until rstChildren.EOF
                    strURL = rstChildren.Fields("RESOURCE_PARSENAME")
                    strPath = rstChildren.Fields("RESOURCE_ABSOLUTEPARSENAME")
                    rec.Close
                    rec.Open rstChildren
                    Select Case rec.RecordType
                        Case adSimpleRecord
                            Set nod = tvwWeb.Nodes.Add(nodRoot, tvwChild, _
                            URLtoKey(strPath), strURL, conImageDocument)
                        Case adCollectionRecord
                            Set nod = tvwWeb.Nodes.Add(nodRoot, tvwChild, _
                            URLtoKey(strPath), strURL, conImageFolderClosed)
                            ' Keep track of where we are
                            nod.Tag = strPath
                            ' Add a dummy child to get expandability
                            Set nod = tvwWeb.Nodes.Add(nod, tvwChild, _
                            "D" & nod.Key, "DUMMY")
                    End Select
                    rstChildren.MoveNext
                Loop
        End Select

        ' Cleanup
        If Not rstChildren Is Nothing Then
            rstChildren.Close
            Set rstChildren = Nothing
        End If
        rec.Close
        Set rec = Nothing

ExitHere:
        Exit Sub

HandleErr:
        MsgBox "Error " & Err.Number & ": " & Err.Description, _
        vbOKOnly, "cmdLoad"
        Resume ExitHere
        Resume

End Sub
```

The cmdLoad procedure opens with a call to the Open method of the Record object. This particular procedure uses a specialized syntax:

```
rec.Open "", "URL=" & txtURL.Text
```

When you omit source information and supply a URL as the connection string for the Record object, it automatically uses the Microsoft OLE DB Provider for Internet Publishing to open that URL. However, you're free to use other OLE DB providers with the Record object.

Here's the full syntax of the Record.Open method:

```
Record.Open Source, ActiveConnection, Mode,
➡ CreateOptions, Options, UserName, Password
```

This method has several arguments:

- The *Source* may be a URL, a Command object (in which case the Record object will hold the first row of the Recordset returned by the Command object), a SQL statement, or a table name.

- The *ActiveConnection* can be a connection string or an open Connection object.

- The *Mode* argument can be any of the constants that are used with the Connection object to specify a locking mode.

- The *CreateOptions* argument specifies whether a new Record object should be created or an existing Record opened.

- The *Options* argument allows fine-tuning of some of the Record object's opening behavior. For example, you can use adOpenOutput to retrieve the results of an ASP page instead of the source of the page.

- The *UserName* and *Password* arguments supply security information.

TIP   For additional information on the constants for Mode, CreateOptions, and Options, refer to the ADO API Reference in the MDAC SDK.

The code then checks the RecordType of the retrieved Record to determine whether the supplied URL points to a folder or a document. If the RecordType is adSimpleRecord, the URL will indicate a document, and there won't be any child documents. In this case, the code just needs to add a single node to the TreeView, and the job is done:

```
Set nodRoot = tvwWeb.Nodes.Add(, , _
    URLtoKey(txtURL.Text), txtURL.Text, conImageDocument)
```

TIP   The URLtoKey procedure removes illegal characters to turn an arbitrary URL into a string that can be used as a Node.Key property.

More commonly, though, the opening URL will be a folder (in Figure 6.1, it's the root of a web server named STALLION on my local network). The code can detect this by noting that the RecordType of the Record object will be adCollectionRecord. In that case, after adding the root node (which, in this case, uses the closed folder image rather than the document image), the code calls the GetChildren method of the Record. This method returns a Recordset that contains one member for each of the children of the Record. The code iterates through this Recordset and adds child nodes for each member of the Recordset.

The code at this point uses a dodge to avoid having to retrieve the structure of the entire web server at once. The TreeView control will show the + sign to indicate node expandability only if there is a child node. In this case, if a node has the RecordType of adCollection-Record, the code adds a dummy node directly beneath it so that the + sign will be displayed:

```
Set nod = tvwWeb.Nodes.Add(nod, tvwChild, _
    "D" & nod.Key, "DUMMY")
```

When the user expands a node, the code in Listing 6.2 runs to handle the necessary display changes.

Listing 6.2:   tvwWebExpand

```
Private Sub tvwWeb_Expand(ByVal Node As MSComctlLib.Node)
    ' Called when the user expands a node. This will always
    ' be a folder in this case
    Dim rec As ADODB.Record
    Dim rstChildren As ADODB.Recordset
    Dim nod As Node
    Dim strURL As String
    Dim strPath As String

    On Error GoTo HandleErr

    ' First, switch to the Open Folder image
    If Node.Image = conImageFolderClosed Then
        Node.Image = conImageFolderOpen
    End If

    ' Check to see if the first child is a dummy node
    If Node.Child.Text = "DUMMY" Then
        ' If so, we need to delete the dummy node and
        ' get the real children
        tvwWeb.Nodes.Remove (Node.Child.Index)
        Set rec = New ADODB.Record
        rec.Open "", "URL=" & Node.Tag
        Set rstChildren = rec.GetChildren
        Do Until rstChildren.EOF
            strURL = rstChildren.Fields("RESOURCE_PARSENAME")
            strPath = rstChildren.Fields("RESOURCE_ABSOLUTEPARSENAME")
            rec.Close
```

```
            rec.Open rstChildren
            Select Case rec.RecordType
                Case adSimpleRecord
                    Set nod = tvwWeb.Nodes.Add(Node, tvwChild, _
                    URLtoKey(strPath), strURL, conImageDocument)
                Case adCollectionRecord
                    Set nod = tvwWeb.Nodes.Add(Node, tvwChild, _
                    URLtoKey(strPath), strURL, conImageFolderClosed)
                    ' Keep track of where we are
                    nod.Tag = strPath
                    ' Add a dummy child to get expandability
                    Set nod = tvwWeb.Nodes.Add(nod, tvwChild, _
                    "D" & nod.Key, "DUMMY")
            End Select
            rstChildren.MoveNext
        Loop
    End If

    ' Cleanup
    If Not rstChildren Is Nothing Then
        rstChildren.Close
        Set rstChildren = Nothing
    End If
    If Not rec Is Nothing Then
        rec.Close
        Set rec = Nothing
    End If

ExitHere:
    Exit Sub

HandleErr:
    MsgBox "Error " & Err.Number & ": " & Err.Description, _
    vbOKOnly, "tvwWeb_Expand"
    Resume ExitHere
    Resume

End Sub
```

You can see in Listing 6.2 how the rest of the delayed information retrieval works. If the first child of the node being expanded is a dummy node, the code deletes that node and then opens a Recordset populated with the actual children. By using this technique, the time to load the information is spread out instead of being concentrated at the initial load. Even better, if a node is never displayed, no time is wasted on creating that node.

Resource Recordsets

The Recordset returned by the Record.GetChildren method isn't simply a collection of Record objects representing child documents. Rather, it's an example of what's called a *resource Recordset*. A resource Recordset is a collection of fields that describe the child documents, without containing the child documents themselves.

Resource Recordsets are created by a class of OLE DB providers known as *document source providers*. The Microsoft OLE DB Provider for Internet Publishing is one such provider. The fields of the resource Recordset are dictated by the provider. Table 6.2 lists the fields in the resource Recordset from the OLE DB Provider for Internet Publishing. Two of these fields (RESOURCE_PARSENAME and RESOURCE_ABSOLUTEPARSENAME) are used in the code in Listings 6.1 and 6.2.

TABLE 6.2: Resource Recordset Fields from the Internet Publishing Provider

Field	Meaning
RESOURCE_PARSENAME	URL of the resource
RESOURCE_PARENTNAME	URL of the parent record
RESOURCE_ABSOLUTEPARSENAME	URL, including the path of the resource
RESOURCE_ISHIDDEN	True if the resource is hidden
RESOURCE_ISREADONLY	True if the resource is read-only
RESOURCE_CONTENTTYPE	MIME type of the document
RESOURCE_CONTENTCLASS	Usually empty, but with an Office document, contains the template used to create the document
RESOURCE_CONTENTLANGUAGE	Language of the content
RESOURCE_CREATIONTIME	Date and time the resource was created
RESOURCE_LASTACCESSTIME	Date and time the resource was last read
RESOURCE_LASTWRITETIME	Date and time the resource was last modified
RESOURCE_STREAMSIZE	Size in bytes of the resource's default stream
RESOURCE_ISCOLLECTION	True if the resource is a directory or other collection
RESOURCE_ISSTRUCTUREDDOCUMENT	True if the resource is a structured document
DEFAULT_DOCUMENT	True if the resource is the default document of the parent folder
RESOURCE_DISPLAYNAME	Friendly name, if any, of the resource
RESOURCE_ISROOT	True if the resource is the root of a tree
RESOURCE_ISMARKEDFOROFFLINE	True if the resource is set to allow offline use

Using the Stream Object

The Stream object represents binary data. Most often, you'll want to open a Stream object to retrieve the data associated with a Record object. You can also create your own stand-alone Stream objects and use them as handy spots to store binary data. Later in the chapter, you'll see that Stream objects also integrate well with XML data.

Table 6.3 lists some of the details of the Stream object.

TABLE 6.3: Selected Details about the Stream Object

Name	Type	Explanation
Charset	Property	Character set to be used when storing this Stream object.
Close	Method	Disassociates this object from its data source.
LoadFromFile	Method	Loads the contents of a local disk file into an open Stream.
Open	Method	Retrieves data into the Stream.
Read	Method	Reads data from a binary Stream.
ReadText	Method	Reads data from a text Stream.
SaveToFile	Method	Writes the contents of the Stream to a local disk file.
Size	Property	Number of bytes in the Stream.
Type	Property	Specifies whether the Stream is binary (adTypeBinary) or textual (adTypeText) information.
Write	Method	Writes data to a binary Stream.
WriteText	Method	Writes data to a text Stream.

One good use of Stream objects is retrieving the binary data (if any) associated with a Record object. The web example that I've been using in this chapter makes use of this functionality to display the contents of web pages.

To run the following code, you can right-click any document in the TreeView and select View Contents from the pop-up menu:

```
Private Sub mnuShortcutViewContents_Click()

    Dim rec As ADODB.Record
    Dim stm As ADODB.Stream

    On Error GoTo HandleErr

    ' If this node represents a document, it will have
    ' no children. In that case, retrieve the stream.
    If tvwWeb.SelectedItem.Children = 0 Then
        Set rec = New ADODB.Record
        rec.Open "", "URL=" & tvwWeb.SelectedItem.Tag
        Set stm = New ADODB.Stream
        stm.Open rec, adModeRead, adOpenStreamFromRecord
        Load frmStream
        If stm.Type = adTypeBinary Then
            frmStream.txtStream.Text = stm.Read(adReadAll)
        Else ' stm.type=adTypeText
```

```
            stm.Charset = "ascii"
            frmStream.txtStream.Text = stm.ReadText(adReadAll)
        End If
        frmStream.Show vbModal
    End If

    'Clean up
    rec.Close
    Set rec = Nothing
    stm.Close
    Set stm = Nothing

ExitHere:
    Exit Sub

HandleErr:
    MsgBox "Error " & Err.Number & ": " & Err.Description, _
     vbOKOnly, "tvwWeb_DblClick"
    Resume ExitHere
    Resume

End Sub
```

The code first uses the information stored in the TreeView to open a Record variable referring to the selected document. It then calls the Open method of the Stream object to grab the binary or text data of the Record. Given the Stream object, you call either the Read or the ReadText method to obtain the actual data, depending on whether the Stream is binary or text, which you can determine from the Stream object's Type property.

Note the use of the Charset property of the Stream object. The data in the Stream is always stored in Unicode. However, it's a fact of life that you probably want a non-Unicode character set for display. The ASCII character set, as shown in this example, is usually a safe bet. If you'd like to know what other options are available on your computer, check the Registry under `HKEY_CLASSES_ROOT\Mime\Database\Charset`.

Here's the full syntax of the Stream object's Open method:

```
Stream.Open Source, Mode, OpenOptions, UserName, Password
```

As you see, the method has five arguments:

- The *Source* argument specifies the source of the data to be stored in the Stream object. This can be a Record object (as in the example above) or a URL. The Source argument is optional; if you don't specify a source, an empty Stream object is opened.

- The *Mode* argument specifies the connection mode for the Stream. This argument uses the same constants that are used with the Mode property of the Connection object.

- The *OpenOptions* argument allows you to specify that the Stream will be opened from a Record, or that it should be opened asynchronously.

- The *UserName* and *Password* arguments are used to set the security context of the Open operation.

Using Streams for Arbitrary Data

You can also create your own Stream objects and use them as general-purpose receptacles to hold any type of data that you care to store. One use for this technique is integrated directly into ADO. You can persist the contents of a Recordset to a Stream, or take a Stream that has such contents and reload it into a Recordset. You can also store the contents of a Stream to a disk file, or load a Stream from a disk file.

Figure 6.2 shows frmStreamPersist from this chapter's sample project. This form lets you move data from a database to a Recordset to a Stream to a disk file and back again.

FIGURE 6.2:

Experimenting with Streams

Let's trace the code for these data transformations step by step. First, the code for loading data from a database to a Recordset uses the familiar Recordset.Open method:

```
Private Sub cmdOpenRecordsetFromDatabase_Click()
    mrst.Open "Customers", _
    "Provider=Microsoft.Jet.OLEDB.4.0;" & _
    "Data Source=" & App.Path & "\ADODHChapter6.mdb", _
    adOpenKeyset, adLockOptimistic
    lblRecordset.BackColor = &H8000000C
End Sub
```

NOTE   The BackColor property changes in this example provide a visual cue as to which objects contain data at any given time.

To move the data from a Recordset to a Stream, you call the Recordset's Save method:

```
Private Sub cmdOpenStream_Click()
    mrst.Save mstm, adPersistXML
    lblStream.BackColor = &H8000000C
End Sub
```

The second argument to the Save method specifies the storage format for the data. This can be either adPersistXML (to use industry-standard XML) or the default adPersistADTG (to use the proprietary Microsoft Advanced Data Tablegram format). If your OLE DB provider supplies its own format for saving Recordsets, you can also specify adPersist-ProviderSpecific to use this format.

TIP   To save a Recordset directly to a disk file, specify the name of the disk file as the first argument to the Save method.

WARNING   Although most Recordsets can be saved to XML, hierarchical Recordsets with pending updates or parameterized hierarchical Recordsets can be saved in ADTG format only. You'll learn more about hierarchical Recordsets in Chapter 7, "Data Shaping."

Given a Stream that contains data, you can save the data to a disk file by calling the Stream's SaveToFile method:

```
Private Sub cmdSave_Click()
    mstm.SaveToFile App.Path & "\Customers.xml", adSaveCreateOverWrite
    lblDiskFile.BackColor = &H8000000C
End Sub
```

The second argument in this case tells the Stream that it's okay to overwrite the file if it already exists. If the file does not exist, the Save method will create it.

Moving data in the other direction, you can open a Stream from a disk file by calling the Stream's LoadFromFile method:

```
Private Sub cmdLoad_Click()
    mstm.LoadFromFile App.Path & "\Customers.xml"
    lblStream.BackColor = &H8000000C
End Sub
```

The LoadFromFile method overwrites any data that the Stream object might already contain. This method can be used with any file, not just a file that was created from a Stream object.

Finally, to move data from a Stream back to a Recordset, you can use the Recordset's Open method:

```
Private Sub cmdOpenRecordsetFromStream_Click()
    mrst.Open mstm
    lblRecordset.BackColor = &H8000000C
End Sub
```

TIP   The Open method will fail if the Stream doesn't contain data in a format that ADO recognizes as being a Recordset.

Using Stream objects and disk files in this manner can provide your applications with a great deal of flexibility. For example, you can open a Recordset when you're connected to a network that contains a database server, and then save that Recordset into a disk file (either directly or via an intermediate Stream object). If you later disconnect from the network, you can still reconstitute the Recordset from the disk file, even if the server is no longer available. You can even save a Recordset with pending updates, open it later when you're connected to the server, and commit the updates at that time.

Working with BLOBs in Recordsets

Streams also provide a handy way to work with binary large objects (BLOBs) in Recordsets. Before the Stream object was added to ADO, the only way to manipulate data in a BLOB field was by using the GetChunk and AppendChunk methods of the Field object. Now, however, you can use a Stream object to easily retrieve data from or save data to a BLOB field.

Here's an example using the SQL Server OLE DB provider:

```
Private Sub cmdBlob_Click()

    Dim cnn As ADODB.Connection
    Dim rst As ADODB.Recordset
    Dim stm As ADODB.Stream

    On Error GoTo HandleErr

    Set cnn = New ADODB.Connection
    cnn.Open "Provider=SQLOLEDB.1;Server=(local);" & _
      "Initial Catalog=pubs;Integrated Security=SSPI"

    Set rst = New ADODB.Recordset
    rst.Open "pub_info", cnn, adOpenKeyset, adLockOptimistic

    Set stm = New ADODB.Stream
    stm.Type = adTypeBinary
    stm.Open
    stm.Write rst.Fields("logo").Value
    stm.SaveToFile "c:\temp\test.gif", adSaveCreateOverWrite

    Image1.Picture = LoadPicture("c:\temp\test.gif")

    'Clean up
    stm.Close
    Set stm = Nothing
    rst.Close
    Set rst = Nothing
```

```
        cnn.Close
        Set cnn = Nothing

    ExitHere:
        Exit Sub

    HandleErr:
        MsgBox "Error " & Err.Number & ": " & Err.Description, _
          vbOKOnly, "cmdBLOB"
        Resume ExitHere
        Resume

    End Sub
```

WARNING   This code depends on the existence of a C:\temp folder on the system where it's run. If there is no such folder, you'll get an error message when the Stream attempts to write to a file in that folder.

After using the Connection and Recordset objects to open a table of data that includes a SQL Server image column, this procedure instantiates a Stream object and sets its data type to binary. It then calls the Stream's Open method with no arguments. This makes the Stream object available to hold data, without actually placing any data in the Stream. Calling the Stream's Write method then moves data from the method's argument (in this case, the raw data contained in the logo field in the table) to the Stream. Once the data is in the Stream, it can be treated just like any other Stream data. For example, it can be saved to a disk file, as in this particular example.

To move data in the other direction—from a Stream to a BLOB field—you call the Stream's Read method. In the preceding example, to move data back from the Stream to the field in the Recordset, you could use this line of code:

```
    rst.Fields("logo").Value = stm.Read
```

Figure 6.3 shows the result. A graphic that was stored in the database is now visible on the frmMenu form.

FIGURE 6.3:

Loading a graphic from a Stream

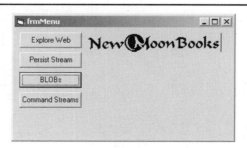

> **TIP**
> The Read and Write methods of the Stream object refer to what is being done to the Stream, not to actions the Stream takes. That is, the Write method puts data into the Stream, and the Read method retrieves data from the Stream. This is reversed from the usual sense of these verbs, and can thus be a source of confusion.

Using Command and Result Streams

The ADO Command object also has a connection to the Stream object. Streams can be used for both the definition of the Command and the results returned by executing the Command. I'll demonstrate the syntax of these Stream objects within a Visual Basic application; then I'll show how these objects make it easier to use ADO to manage XML data within a web page when using an appropriate provider, such as that for Microsoft SQL Server 2000.

Figure 6.4 shows a sample form (frmCommandStreams) in this chapter's sample project that demonstrates the use of Command and result Streams. In this case, I've retrieved the Customers table from a SQL Server database and displayed the results as XML.

> **TIP**
> In order to use Streams with the Command object, you must be using an OLE DB provider that supports the necessary interfaces. Currently, this limits the use of this feature to Microsoft SQL Server 2000.

The code for this example starts by defining a Command Stream as XML:

```
strCommand = "<root xmlns:sql='urn:schemas-microsoft-com:xml-sql'>" & _
    vbCrLf & _
    "<sql:query> SELECT * FROM Customers ORDER BY Country " & _
    "FOR XML AUTO </sql:query>" & vbCrLf & _
    "</root>"
```

FIGURE 6.4:

Retrieving information as an XML Stream

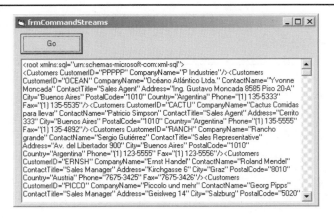

If you take away the Visual Basic syntax that quotes this string and spread it over several program lines, the generated XML is as follows:

```
<root xmlns:sql='urn:schemas-microsoft-com:xml-sql'>
  <sql:query> SELECT * FROM Customers ORDER BY Country
FOR XML AUTO </sql:query>
</root>
```

This particular piece of XML is called an *XML template query*. There are two essential pieces to this query:

- The root tag includes a reference to the XML namespace defined by Microsoft for XML queries to SQL Server.

- The sql:query tag contains the text of a SELECT query to be executed by SQL Server. In this particular case, the query uses the FOR XML AUTO tag to return the results as XML.

Once the XML template query has been defined, the code places it into a Stream object:

```
Set stmCommand = New ADODB.Stream
stmCommand.Open
stmCommand.WriteText strCommand, adWriteChar
stmCommand.Position = 0
```

The Open method makes the Stream object ready to receive text, and the WriteText method actually places the text into the Stream. The Position property is used to make sure that the next reading of the text starts at the beginning of the text rather than the end.

The next step in this example is to create a Command object that's associated with a connection to a SQL Server:

```
Const DBGUID_MSSQLXML = "{5D531CB2-E6Ed-11D2-B252-00C04F681B71}"

Set cnn = New ADODB.Connection
cnn.Open "Provider=SQLOLEDB.1;Server=(local);" & _
  "Initial Catalog=Northwind;Integrated Security=SSPI"

Set cmd = New ADODB.Command
Set cmd.ActiveConnection = cnn
Set cmd.CommandStream = stmCommand
cmd.Dialect = DBGUID_MSSQLXML
```

There are a couple of features of this Command object that you haven't seen in previous examples. First, rather than setting the CommandText property, this code sets the Command-Stream property. Note that because CommandStream actually holds a Stream object, you must use the Set keyword when setting it. The CommandText and CommandStream properties are mutually exclusive. If you set the CommandText property, ADO will automatically set the CommandStream property to Nothing. If you set the CommandStream property, ADO will automatically set the CommandText property to an empty string, losing any text that was previously in that property.

Second, this code uses the Dialect property of the Command object. The Dialect property is a globally unique identifier (GUID) that tells the OLE DB provider how to interpret the CommandStream. The possible values for this property are supplied by the OLE DB provider. In this case, I've used a GUID that SQL Server specifies to indicate that the Command-Stream contains an XML template query.

If you don't set the Dialect property, ADO will set it to the default value of {C8B521FB-5CF3-11CE-ADE5-00AA0044773D}, which tells the OLE DB provider to make its best guess as to how to interpret the CommandStream.

In addition to the value used in this example, the SQL Server OLE DB provider supports two other special values for the Dialect property. You can use {C8B522D7-5CF3-11CE-ADE5-00AA0044773D} to indicate that the CommandStream contains a Transact-SQL query, or {EC2A4293-E898-11D2-B1B7-00C04F680C56}, to indicate that the Command-Stream contains an XPath query.

The remaining code in this example uses the Command object to retrieve the results to a second Stream object:

```
Set stmResponse = New ADODB.Stream
stmResponse.Open
cmd.Properties("Output Stream") = stmResponse

cmd.Execute , , adExecuteStream

txtXML.Text = stmResponse.ReadText()
```

This code first creates and opens the stmResponse Stream, so that it can be used to contain data. It then sets the provider-supplied Output Stream property of the Command object to the name of this Stream. Calling the Execute method of the Command object with the adExecuteStream constant tells ADO to pass the CommandStream and Dialect to the underlying OLE DB provider, and to return the results to the text of the second Stream object. Finally, the code uses the ReadText method of the second Stream object to place the text on the form's user interface.

Although this code demonstrates the basic technique of using Command and response Streams, the real value of this method of retrieving data lies not in Visual Basic but in code to be run on the Internet. Using Streams with a Command provides an ideal way to create a web page with an XML representation of the results of a query.

Figure 6.5 shows an XML document constructed with this technique and displayed in Internet Explorer 5.0. Beginning with this version, Internet Explorer has the ability to display XML documents directly, using a built-in XSLT stylesheet. This simplifies the task of preparing an XML document for display.

NOTE   For more information on XSLT stylesheets, see Chapter 18, "Synchronizing DataSets with XML."

FIGURE 6.5:

XML query results in Internet Explorer 5.0

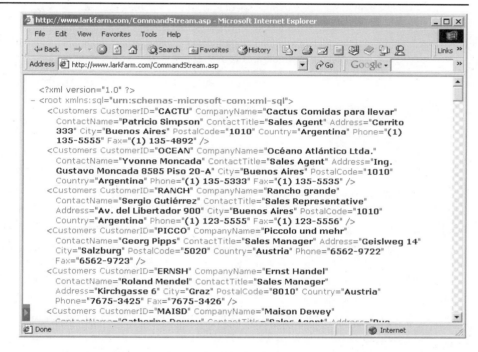

Listing 6.3 shows the code for the ASP page that produced Figure 6.5.

Listing 6.3:   CommandStream.asp

```
<% Response.ContentType = "text/xml" %>
<!-- #include file="adovbs.inc" -->
<% Dim cnn
   Dim cmd
   Dim stmCommand
   Dim strCommand

   strCommand = "<root xmlns:sql='urn:schemas-microsoft-com:xml-sql'>" & _
     "<sql:query> SELECT * FROM Customers ORDER BY Country " & _
     "FOR XML AUTO </sql:query></root>"

   Set stmCommand = Server.CreateObject("ADODB.Stream")
   stmCommand.Open
```

```
stmCommand.WriteText strCommand, adWriteChar
stmCommand.Position = 0

Set cnn = Server.CreateObject("ADODB.Connection")
cnn.CursorLocation = adUseClient
cnn.Open "Provider=SQLOLEDB;Server=(local);" & _
  "Initial Catalog=Northwind;Integrated Security=SSPI"

Set cmd = Server.CreateObject("ADODB.Command")
Set cmd.ActiveConnection = cnn
Set cmd.CommandStream = stmCommand
cmd.Dialect = "{5D531CB2-E6Ed-11D2-B252-00C04F681B71}"

Response.Write("<?xml version=""1.0"" ?>")
cmd.Properties("Output Stream") = Response

cmd.Execute , , adExecuteStream
%>
```

If you compare the ASP code in Listing 6.3 with the Visual Basic code I've already reviewed in this section, you'll see that the skeleton of the code is the same. But there are some changes that I had to make to get the same code to function in a browser context:

- The ContentType property of the ASP Response object has to be set to tell Internet Explorer that the returned bytes should be treated as an XML file, even though the extension of the page is .asp. To be effective, this property must be set as the very first operation in the ASP file.

- The adovbs.inc file needs to be included to make the ADO constants (such as adExecuteStream) available to the ASP interpreter. This file is shipped as a part of ADO, but you'll need to copy it to your web server before you can use it.

- The ASP code uses Server.CreateObject to create objects, rather than the New keyword as used in Visual Basic.

- Instead of using a separate Stream object to hold the query results, the ASP code uses the built-in ASP Response object. This is possible because the Response object implements the IStream interface.

- Before sending the query results to the Response object, the code uses Response.Write to send a standard XML header.

Although I've chosen in this case to display the results in a web browser, in an actual business setting, you'd more likely use this XML file as the input to some other business process. With XML becoming the standard language of many business interchange applications, it's useful to know how to generate XML results from SQL Server data, as shown here.

Summary

In this chapter, you learned about the ADO Record and Stream objects. You saw how these objects extend the reach of ADO from traditional relational databases to other sorts of data, including hierarchical data, BLOB data, and XML Streams.

In the next chapter, I'll explore another extension that ADO offers to the relational model: data shaping. With data shaping, you can create a hierarchical Recordset that combines data from several tables into one multilevel, browsable structure.

CHAPTER 7

Data Shaping

- What is data shaping?

- Types of hierarchical Recordsets

- The SHAPE statement

- Examples of the SHAPE statement

- Synchronizing Recordsets

- Reshaping

- Fabricated Recordsets

For the most part, the SQL statements you execute through ADO are executed by the underlying OLE DB provider that delivers data to the active Connection object. There are some exceptions to this rule, though. One of these is the SHAPE statement, which is a Microsoft-defined extension to ANSI SQL. The SHAPE statement is interpreted by the Data Shaping Service, a component of the Microsoft Data Access Components. In this chapter, I'll discuss the Data Shaping Service and the shaped Recordsets that it can deliver to your applications.

What Is Data Shaping?

Data shaping is the process of defining a shaped Recordset. Okay, so what's a *shaped Recordset*? Well, a shaped Recordset is one that may contain more than just data. In particular, the columns of a shaped Recordset can contain:

- Data (just like the columns in any other Recordset)
- Pointers to another Recordset
- Calculated values based on other columns in the Recordset
- Values derived from calculations such as the sum of all values in a column in a related Recordset
- Empty, fabricated columns that aren't part of the original data source

Obviously, shaped Recordsets are more flexible than regular Recordsets. In this chapter, I'll explore the uses of these flexible Recordsets. You'll see how shaped Recordsets can make it easier to work with hierarchical data within your applications.

Hierarchical Recordsets

The most common use for a shaped Recordset is allowing one Recordset to contain a column that is a pointer to a second Recordset. By allowing a Recordset to contain a pointer to another Recordset, a shaped Recordset is an ideal way to represent a hierarchy of information.

In traditional SQL, you handle a hierarchy by joining tables. This results in redundant information in the resulting Recordset. For example, suppose you were interested in information regarding customers and orders. With traditional SQL, you would create a Recordset based on a SQL statement such as this:

```
SELECT Customers.CustomerID, Customers.CompanyName,
Orders.CustomerID, Orders.OrderDate
FROM Customers INNER JOIN Orders
ON Customers.CustomerID = Orders.CustomerID
```

Executing this statement returns a Recordset that contains repeated information from the Customers table. The CustomerID and CompanyName fields are repeated once for each order the customer has placed.

By contrast, with data shaping, you could base a Recordset containing the same basic information on a SQL statement such as this:

```
SHAPE {SELECT CustomerID, CompanyName FROM Customers}
APPEND ({SELECT * FROM Orders}
RELATE CustomerID to CustomerID)
```

By using a shaped Recordset to hold the information, you would get a Recordset where each customer's information is repeated only once. This means less data to pass around and, ultimately, better performance.

Figure 7.1 shows a visual comparison of the two types of Recordsets. In this example (which you can find in the ADOChapter7 sample project), I've opened Recordsets using the two SQL statements that you've just seen. The Recordsets are bound to two instances of the Microsoft Hierarchical FlexGrid control. This control, which ships as a part of Visual Basic, has the ability to bind to either a standard, unshaped Recordset or to a shaped Recordset. When you use it to display a shaped Recordset, the Hierarchical FlexGrid automatically displays small Plus (+) and Minus (–) signs to allow you to expand or collapse the hierarchy. Listing 7.1 shows the code that's used to open the Recordsets.

FIGURE 7.1:

Unshaped and shaped Recordsets

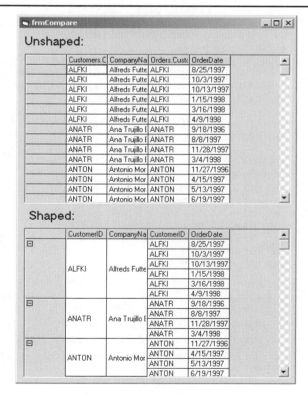

Listing 7.1:   **frmCompare**

```
Private Sub Form_Load()

    Dim cnnUnshaped As ADODB.Connection
    Dim cnnShaped As ADODB.Connection
    Dim rstUnshaped As ADODB.Recordset
    Dim rstShaped As ADODB.Recordset

    Set cnnUnshaped = New ADODB.Connection
    cnnUnshaped.Open "Provider=Microsoft.Jet.OLEDB.4.0;" & _
      "Data Source=" & App.Path & "\ADOChapter7.mdb"
    Set rstUnshaped = New ADODB.Recordset
    rstUnshaped.Open _
      "SELECT Customers.CustomerID, Customers.CompanyName, " & _
      "Orders.CustomerID, Orders.OrderDate " & _
      "FROM Customers INNER JOIN Orders " & _
      "ON Customers.CustomerID = Orders.CustomerID", cnnUnshaped, _
      adOpenKeyset, adLockOptimistic

    Set cnnShaped = New ADODB.Connection
    cnnShaped.Open "Provider=MSDataShape; " & _
      "Data Provider=Microsoft.Jet.OLEDB.4.0;" & _
      "Data Source=" & App.Path & "\ADOChapter7.mdb"
    Set rstShaped = New ADODB.Recordset
    rstShaped.Open _
      "SHAPE {SELECT CustomerID, CompanyName FROM Customers} " & _
      "APPEND ({SELECT CustomerID, OrderDate FROM Orders} " & _
      "RELATE CustomerID to CustomerID)", cnnShaped, _
      adOpenKeyset, adLockOptimistic

    Set hfgUnshaped.Recordset = rstUnshaped
    Set hfgShaped.Recordset = rstShaped

    ' Clean up
    rstShaped.Close
    Set rstShaped = Nothing
    rstUnshaped.Close
    Set rstUnshaped = Nothing
    cnnShaped.Close
    Set cnnShaped = Nothing
    cnnUnshaped.Close
    Set cnnUnshaped = Nothing

End Sub
```

When you create a hierarchical Recordset, the top-level Recordset contains a field that points to a second Recordset. When you retrieve the value of this field, you get a child Recordset that is filtered to include only records that are related to the current row of the parent Recordset. This filtered subset of the child Recordset is called a *chapter*. Here's how you might list the fields in both the parent and child Recordsets:

```
Debug.Print "Fields in parent Recordset"
For Each fld In rstShaped.Fields
    Debug.Print "   " & fld.Name
Next fld
Set rstChild = rstShaped.Fields("Chapter1").Value
Debug.Print "Fields in child Recordset"
For Each fld In rstChild.Fields
    Debug.Print "   " & fld.Name
Next fld
```

If you execute this code, you'll see these results:

```
Fields in parent Recordset
  CustomerID
  CompanyName
  Chapter1
Fields in child Recordset
  CustomerID
  OrderDate
```

TIP   Note the use of the Value property in retrieving the child Recordset. Although Value is the default property of the Field object, the explicit use of the property is *not* optional in this particular case.

Of course, if you like, you can include an alias in the SHAPE statement to give the child Recordset a name other than Chapter1. For example, the following SHAPE statement would name the child Recordset CustOrders:

```
SHAPE {SELECT CustomerID, CompanyName FROM Customers}
APPEND ({SELECT * FROM Orders}
RELATE CustomerID to CustomerID) AS CustOrders
```

Hierarchical Recordsets can be nested. That is, a child Recordset itself can contain a pointer to yet another child Recordset, a grandchild of the original Recordset. For example, a Recordset might contain customer, order, and line item information at three different levels of nesting.

The Data Shaping Service

The OLE DB standard allows for two types of OLE DB providers: data providers and service providers. A *data provider* is a provider that connects directly to a data source. A *service provider* is a provider that receives its information from a data provider, and then changes that information. ADO can retrieve data from either data providers or service providers. Figure 7.2 shows this in schematic form.

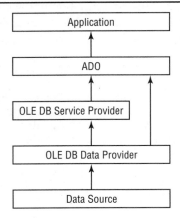

Data shaping is implemented in a service provider, the Data Shaping Service for OLE DB. Connection strings for connections that will use data shaping must specify both the Data Shaping Service as the provider and another OLE DB provider as the data provider. For example, a connection string to provide shaped data from a SQL Server database might look like this:

```
Provider=MSDataShape;
Data Provider=SQLOLEDB.1;
Server=(local);
User ID=sa;
Initial Catalog=Northwind
```

NOTE   Other service providers include the OLE DB Persistence Provider (used for saving Record-sets to a disk file) and the OLE DB Remoting Provider (used to connect to data on a computer across the Internet).

You can create a connection string for data shaping out of any existing connection string just by making two changes:

1. Change the Provider keyword in the existing connection string to Data Provider.

2. Add Provider=MSDataShape to the connection string.

You can also set the two different providers as properties of the Connection object, as in this snippet of code:

```
cnnShaped.Provider = "MSDataShape"
cnnShaped.Properties("Data Provider") = "Microsoft.Jet.OLEDB.4.0"
cnnShaped.Open "Data Source=" & App.Path & "\ADOChapter7.mdb"
```

The Data Provider property is a dynamic property that is added to the Connection object's Properties collection by the MSDataShape provider.

For data shaping to work properly, you must be using client-side cursors. Setting the provider to be the Data Shaping Service will automatically set the cursor for any Recordset using that connection to be client-side.

Types of Hierarchical Recordsets

The SHAPE statement is able to produce three types of hierarchical Recordsets:

- A *relation hierarchy* represents a set of parent records and associated child records. The example you saw earlier in the chapter was of a relation hierarchy.

- A *parameterized hierarchy* also represents parent records and associated child records, but fetches child records on demand.

- A *grouping hierarchy* represents child records plus a parent Recordset composed of aggregate functions.

You'll see each of these types of hierarchical Recordsets later in this chapter. In this section, I'll describe their general properties.

Relation Hierarchies

A relation hierarchy represents a set of parent records and associated child records. This Recordset is similar to the Recordset you can create with a SQL JOIN statement, but it doesn't have the redundancy of a Recordset based on a JOIN.

With a relation hierarchy, all the records involved are read into the local cache before the SHAPE statement is processed. This can result in substantial overhead if your Recordset is based on a large number of records. However, once the original Recordset has been constructed, subsequent fetches are quick because all the data is already cached locally. You can continue to work with records in a relation hierarchy even after closing the connection on which the Recordset is based.

Parameterized Hierarchies

A parameterized hierarchy also represents parent records and associated child records, but fetches child records on demand. Just like a relation hierarchy, it contains the same information as a Recordset based on a JOIN, but without the redundant rows.

When you open a parameterized hierarchy, all the records in the parent Recordset are retrieved. However, child records aren't retrieved until you explicitly open a Recordset based on a chapter field. This means that opening a parameterized hierarchy can be much faster than opening the corresponding relation hierarchy. However, each time you open a child Recordset in a parameterized hierarchy, ADO must go back to the data source for more records; thus, moving through the Recordset may be slower than with a relation hierarchy. You must also remain connected to the data source for as long as you want to work with records in a parameterized hierarchy.

Grouping Hierarchies

A grouping hierarchy represents child records plus a parent Recordset composed of aggregate functions. This is equivalent to joining a detail SQL statement with an aggregate SQL statement based on the same columns. Because the summary and calculated columns might be based on more than one record, those columns are always non-updatable in a grouping hierarchy.

Like relation hierarchies, all records that are required to create a grouping hierarchy are read as soon as you open a Recordset on the SHAPE statement.

The SHAPE Statement

As you've seen, hierarchical Recordsets are generated by the SHAPE statement. In this section, I'll review the syntax of that statement. There are actually two different varieties of the SHAPE statement. SHAPE...APPEND is used to create relation and parameterized hierarchies, while SHAPE...COMPUTE is used to create grouping hierarchies. Either of these statements can contain aggregate functions or calculated expressions.

SHAPE...APPEND

The general syntax of the SHAPE...APPEND statement is as follows:

```
SHAPE {parent_command} AS parent_alias
APPEND ({child_command} AS child_alias
RELATE parent_column TO child_column) AS chapter_alias
```

As an example of a SHAPE...APPEND statement, take another look at one of the statements you saw earlier in this chapter:

```
SHAPE {SELECT CustomerID, CompanyName FROM Customers}
APPEND ({SELECT * FROM Orders}
RELATE CustomerID to CustomerID) AS CustOrders
```

In that statement:

- The *parent_command* is SELECT CustomerID, CompanyName FROM Customers.
- The *child_command* is SELECT * FROM Orders.
- The *parent_column* for the relation between the two commands is the CustomerID field from the Customers table.

- The *child_column* for the relation is the `CustomerID` column from the Orders table.
- The *chapter_alias* for the child Recordset is `CustOrders`.
- I did not supply a *parent_alias* or *child_alias*.

There's no need to qualify the *parent_column* or *child_column* variables with the names of their respective tables. The parent column is always supplied first.

The parent and child commands must be two row-returning entities. They can be any of the following:

- SQL statements that return records. Because the SQL statement is passed through to the underlying data provider, it must use syntax that is understood by that provider.
- Nested SHAPE statements.
- The TABLE keyword, followed by the name of a table in the data source.

A SHAPE…APPEND statement may contain multiple APPEND clauses. This has the effect of creating a parent Recordset with multiple chapter columns, each of which refers to a subsidiary Recordset. You can relate the parent and child commands by specifying a pair of fields, or by specifying a group of pairs of fields. For example, this would be a valid RELATE clause:

```
RELATE OrderID TO OrderID, OrderDate TO OrderDetailDate
```

For a parameterized hierarchy, the syntax of the SHAPE…APPEND command is slightly different:

```
SHAPE {parent_command} AS parent_alias
APPEND ({parameterized_child_command} AS child_alias
RELATE parent_column TO PARAMETER parameter_number) AS chapter_alias
```

A parameterized child command is a SQL statement in which a variable in the WHERE clause is indicated by a question mark character. This variable will be filled in by the SHAPE provider at runtime from the current value of the parent column. In the RELATE clause, the parameter is indicated by the PARAMETER keyword plus a number, starting at zero. For example, this SHAPE…APPEND command would generate a parameterized hierarchy:

```
SHAPE {SELECT CustomerID, CompanyName FROM Customers}
APPEND ({SELECT * FROM Orders WHERE CustomerID = ?}
RELATE CustomerID TO PARAMETER 0)
```

Here, the question mark within the definition of the child command indicates the column that should be parameterized at runtime, and the PARAMETER 0 in the RELATE clause shows how this parameter relates to the parent command. The effect is that each time the parent command moves to a new row and you request the chapter Recordset, the child SQL is issued, with the question mark replaced by the current value of CustomerID from the parent command.

A parameterized hierarchy can also contain multiple parameters, in which case you will need to indicate the multiple parameters in the RELATE clause with sequential numbers:

```
SHAPE {SELECT CustomerID, CompanyName, BranchID FROM Customers}
APPEND ({SELECT * FROM Orders WHERE CustomerID = ? And BranchID = ?}
RELATE CustomerID TO PARAMETER 0, BranchID TO PARAMETER 1)
```

SHAPE...COMPUTE

Grouping hierarchies are produced by the SHAPE...COMPUTE statement. Its general syntax is as follows:

```
SHAPE {child_command} AS child_alias
COMPUTE child_alias, appended_column_list
BY group_field_list
```

The curly braces are required, just as they are in SHAPE...APPEND. The *child_command* can be one of these row-returning entities:

- A SQL statement that returns a child Recordset. Because the SQL statement is passed through to the underlying data provider, it must use syntax that is understood by that provider.

- Another SHAPE statement (so these commands can be nested).

- The TABLE keyword followed by the name of a table.

In the case of SHAPE...COMPUTE, you *must* supply an alias for the child command. This alias must be repeated in the column list in the COMPUTE clause; it defines the relation between the child Recordset and the calculated parent Recordset.

The *appended_column_list* is optional. If you supply a list here, it can be composed of aggregate functions on the child Recordset, new fabricated columns, and calculated columns. Each member of the appended column list defines a column in the generated parent Recordset.

The *group_field_list* is also optional. If you supply a list of columns here, the parent Recordset is constructed so that each row has unique values in those columns, and the child Recordset is filtered to match. Any columns you list here will become columns in the parent Recordset.

If you omit the *group_field_list*, there will be only one row in the parent Recordset, and any aggregate it contains will refer to the entire child Recordset. If you do supply this list in a BY clause, the parent Recordset will contain multiple rows, with the specified grouping.

Here's an example of the SHAPE...COMPUTE statement:

```
SHAPE {SELECT OrderID, OrderDate FROM Orders} AS OrdDates
COMPUTE OrdDates, COUNT(OrdDates.OrderID)
BY OrderDate
```

The result of executing this statement will be a parent Recordset with three columns:

- `COUNT(OrdDates.OrderID)` contains the count of orders for a particular date.

- `OrdDates` is a chapter column with a pointer to a child Recordset. The child Recordset will contain the `OrderID` and `OrderDate` for each record that went into the aggregation in the parent Recordset.

- `OrderDate` contains the order date from which the data for this particular row is aggregated.

Aggregate Functions

An aggregate function performs some calculation across all rows of a child (or other descendant) Recordset. All aggregate functions accept *fully qualified names* for columns. A fully qualified name is simply one that specifies the entire path to a column. For example, if you have a hierarchical Recordset in which the top level contains Customers information plus a chapter named Orders, which in turn is a Recordset that contains a chapter named OrderDetails, which in turn contains a column named Quantity, the fully qualified name of this column would be:

```
Customers.Orders.OrderDetails.Quantity
```

Table 7.1 shows the aggregate functions that are available in the SHAPE syntax.

TABLE 7.1: Aggregate Functions Supported in SHAPE

Function	Description
SUM(column)	Calculates the sum of all values in the specified column.
AVG(column)	Calculates the average of all values in the specified column.
MAX(column)	Retrieves the maximum value from the column.
MIN(column)	Retrieves the minimum value from the column.
COUNT(chapter) or COUNT(column)	Counts the number of rows in the chapter or in the column. If you specify a column name, only rows for which that column contains a non-Null value are included in the count.
STDEV(column)	Calculates the standard deviation of the column.
ANY(column)	Picks a value from the column. (It appears that this generally returns the first value, in cases where the column isn't uniform. However, this behavior is not documented and therefore is not guaranteed.)

Calculated Expressions

A calculated column can use an arbitrary expression to produce a result, but it can operate only on values in the row of the Recordset containing the CALC expression. CALC understands a variety of Visual Basic for Applications (VBA) functions. These are listed in Table 7.2.

TABLE 7.2: VBA Functions Available to CALC

Function Type	Function
Conversion	Asc, CBool, CByte, CCur, CDate, CDbl, CInt, CLng, CSng, CStr, CVar, CVDate, CVErr, Format, Format$, Hex, Hex$, Oct, Oct$, Val
Date and Time	Date, Date$, DateAdd, DateDiff, DatePart, DateSerial, DateValue, Day, Hour, Minute, Month, Now, Second, Time, Time$, Timer, TimeSerial, TimeValue, Weekday, Year
Financial	DDB, FV, IPmt, IRR, MIRR, NPer, NPV, Pmt, PPmt, PV, Rate, SLN, SYD
Mathematical	Abs, Atn, Cos, Exp, Fix, Int, Log, Rnd, Sgn, Sin, Sqr, Tan
Miscellaneous	Error, Error$, IIF, IsDate, IsEmpty, IsError, IsNull, IsNumeric, IsObject, QBColor, RGB, TypeName, VarType
String	Chr, ChrB, ChrW, Chr$, ChrB$, InStr$, LCase, LCase$, Left, LeftB, Left$, LeftB$, Len, LTrim, LTrim$, Mid, Mid$, Right, RightB, Right$, RightB$, RTrim, RTrim$, Space, Space$, Str, Str$, StrComp, StrConv, String, String$, Trim, Trim$, UCase, UCase$

Calculated expressions are created with the CALC keyword. For example, to calculate the year in which an order was placed, you could use the expression CALC(Year(OrderDate)).

Fabricated Columns

You can also create new columns in a SHAPE...COMPUTE statement. These columns are introduced by the NEW keyword along with a datatype. The datatype can be specified by either an OLE DB constant or an ADO constant. Table 7.3 shows the constants that can be used with the NEW keyword.

TABLE 7.3: NEW Datatypes for SHAPE...COMPUTE

OLE DB Datatype	ADO Datatype
DBTYPE_BSTR	adBSTR
DBTYPE_BOOL	adBoolean
DBTYPE_DECIMAL	adDecimal
DBTYPE_UI1	adUnsignedTinyInt
DBTYPE_I1	adTinyInt
DBTYPE_UI2	adUnsignedSmallInt
DBTYPE_UI4	adUnsignedInt
DBTYPE_I8	adBigInt
DBTYPE_UI8	adUnsignedBigInt
DBTYPE_GUID	adGuid

continued on next page

TABLE 7.3 CONTINUED: NEW Datatypes for SHAPE...COMPUTE

OLE DB Datatype	ADO Datatype
DBTYPE_BYTES	adBinary, AdVarBinary, adLongVarBinary
DBTYPE_STR	adChar, adVarChar, adLongVarChar
DBTYPE_WSTR	adWChar, adVarWChar, adLongVarWChar
DBTYPE_NUMERIC	adNumeric
DBTYPE_DBDATE	adDBDate
DBTYPE_DBTIME	adDBTime
DBTYPE_DBTIMESTAMP	adDBTimeStamp
DBTYPE_VARNUMERIC	adVarNumeric
DBTYPE_FILETIME	adFileTime
DBTYPE_ERROR	adError

Some datatypes may need to be specified with other options, such as field size or precision. For example, the following datatypes are valid for fabricated columns:

- NEW DBTYPE_DECIMAL(12,2) for a decimal column with 12-digit precision and 2-digit scale

- NEW adVarChar(50) for a character column that can hold up to 50 non-Unicode characters

- NEW adBoolean for a Boolean column

Fabricated columns are initially empty when a shaped Recordset is opened. You can update them just as you would any other column.

Examples of the SHAPE Statement

Let's take a look at some examples of SHAPE statements. All of these examples are available through frmExamples in the ADOChapter7 sample project. This form contains a set of command buttons, one for each example. When you click a button, the corresponding example is bound to a Hierarchical FlexGrid control. This lets you quickly see the Recordsets returned by each example.

TIP   The frmExamples form also lets you experiment with SHAPE commands on your own, using the tables in the ADOChapter7 database. You can either edit the SQL from one of the built-in commands or type your own SQL in the text box on the form, and then click the Refresh button to see the corresponding Recordset.

Single-Level Relation Hierarchy

A single-level relation hierarchy relates two Recordsets—in this case, Customers and Orders:

```
SHAPE {SELECT CustomerID, CompanyName, ContactName FROM Customers}
APPEND ({SELECT * FROM Orders}
RELATE CustomerID TO CustomerID)
```

Figure 7.3 shows the Recordset retrieved by this command. Note that both the parent and child Recordsets are sorted by the data provider as it chooses (in this case, they're both in primary key order). If you want to impose a sort on either Recordset, you can use an ORDER BY clause in either the parent or child command clause.

FIGURE 7.3:

A single-level relation hierarchy Recordset

	CustomerID	CompanyNa	ContactNam	OrderID	CustomerID	EmployeeID	OrderDate	RequiredDa
ALFKI	ALFKI	Alfreds Futte	Maria Ander	10643	ALFKI	6	8/25/1997	9/22/1997
				10692	ALFKI	4	10/3/1997	10/31/1997
				10702	ALFKI	4	10/13/1997	11/24/1997
				10835	ALFKI	1	1/15/1998	2/12/1998
				10952	ALFKI	1	3/16/1998	4/27/1998
				11011	ALFKI	3	4/9/1998	5/7/1998
ANATR	ANATR	Ana Trujillo E	Ana Trujillo	10308	ANATR	7	9/18/1996	10/16/1996
				10625	ANATR	3	8/8/1997	9/5/1997
				10759	ANATR	3	11/28/1997	12/26/1997
				10926	ANATR	4	3/4/1998	4/1/1998
ANTON	ANTON	Antonio Mor	Antonio Mor	10365	ANTON	3	11/27/1996	12/25/1996
				10507	ANTON	7	4/15/1997	5/13/1997
				10535	ANTON	4	5/13/1997	6/10/1997
				10573	ANTON	7	6/19/1997	7/17/1997
				10677	ANTON	1	9/22/1997	10/20/1997
				10682	ANTON	3	9/25/1997	10/23/1997
				10856	ANTON	3	1/28/1998	2/25/1998
AROUT	AROUT	Around the H	Thomas Har	10355	AROUT	6	11/15/1996	12/13/1996
				10383	AROUT	8	12/16/1996	1/13/1997
				10453	AROUT	1	2/21/1997	3/21/1997
				10558	AROUT	1	6/4/1997	7/2/1997

One pitfall that you need to watch out for with relation hierarchies is that you may retrieve more data from the server than you really need. For example, consider this statement (the same as the previous example, but with a WHERE clause on the first SELECT statement):

```
SHAPE {SELECT CustomerID, CompanyName, ContactName FROM Customers
  WHERE CustomerID = "ALFKI"}
APPEND ({SELECT * FROM Orders}
RELATE CustomerID TO CustomerID)
```

This statement will work, in the sense that the child Recordset retrieved from the chapter field in the parent Recordset will contain only related records, thanks to the RELATE clause. But when you execute this SHAPE statement, you'll actually retrieve every single record in the Orders table, even though you can tell by inspection that you need only the records for orders placed by the customer whose CustomerID is ALFKI. That's because the Data Shaping Service makes no attempt to parse the SQL statements that it executes to create Recordsets; it simply passes them on to the data provider. Thus, the Data Shaping Service has no way of knowing that the WHERE clause in the parent Recordset in this case should apply also to the child Recordset.

One way to avoid this problem is to convert the SHAPE statement to a parameterized statement:

```
SHAPE {SELECT CustomerID, CompanyName, ContactName FROM Customers
  WHERE CustomerID = "ALFKI"}
APPEND ({SELECT * FROM Orders WHERE CustomerID = ?}
RELATE CustomerID TO PARAMETER 0)
```

Making this change will cause the Data Shaping Service to ask for child records only as they are needed, with the result that it will never ask for too many records.

The other possible solution is to use appropriate SQL to restrict the child Recordset. For example:

```
SHAPE {SELECT CustomerID, CompanyName, ContactName FROM Customers
  WHERE CustomerID = "ALFKI"}
APPEND ({SELECT * FROM Orders WHERE CustomerID = "ALFKI"}
RELATE CustomerID TO CustomerID)
```

This will have the same effect of retrieving only the required records. In this case, because the restriction in the parent Recordset is on the linking field, you could just copy the same restriction to the child Recordset. In the more general case, it may be necessary to base the child Recordset on a SQL statement that joins the parent and child tables and applies the restriction to the parent table.

TIP   The fact that the data shaping provider passes commands through to the underlying data provider means that you can issue arbitrary commands to the underlying provider without creating a separate connection to that provider. For example, SHAPE {DROP TABLE TempTable} is a perfectly valid command to the data shaping provider, and causes it to issue the DROP TABLE TempTable command to the underlying data provider.

Multiple-Level Relation Hierarchy

The next step up in complexity is the nesting of two or more SHAPE...APPEND commands to create a Recordset with multiple levels in the hierarchy. For example, the following nested command creates a Recordset based on the Customers, Orders, and Order Details tables:

```
SHAPE {SELECT CustomerID, CompanyName FROM Customers}
APPEND ((SHAPE {SELECT CustomerID, OrderID, OrderDate FROM Orders}
        APPEND ({SELECT * FROM [Order Details]}
        AS rstOrderDetails
        RELATE OrderID TO OrderID))
RELATE CustomerID TO CustomerID)
```

Figure 7.4 shows the Recordset that results from this command.

A multiple-level
relation hierarchy
Recordset

CustomerID	CompanyNa	CustomerID	OrderID	OrderDate	OrderID	ProductID	UnitPrice
					10643	28	45.6
		ALFKI	10643	8/25/1997	10643	39	18
					10643	46	12
		ALFKI	10692	10/3/1997	10692	63	43.9
		ALFKI	10702	10/13/1997	10702	3	10
					10702	76	18
ALFKI	Alfreds Futte	ALFKI	10835	1/15/1998	10835	59	55
					10835	77	13
		ALFKI	10952	3/16/1998	10952	6	25
					10952	28	45.6
		ALFKI	11011	4/9/1998	11011	58	13.25
					11011	71	21.5
		ANATR	10308	9/18/1996	10308	69	28.8
					10308	70	12
		ANATR	10625	8/8/1997	10625	14	23.25
					10625	42	14
ANATR	Ana Trujillo				10625	60	34
		ANATR	10759	11/28/1997	10759	32	32
		ANATR	10926	3/4/1998	10926	11	21
					10926	13	6
					10926	19	9.2

Parameterized Hierarchy

There's no difference in the overall Recordset retrieved by a parameterized hierarchy and that retrieved by the equivalent relation hierarchy. Here's the parameterized equivalent of the first, single-level example:

```
SHAPE {SELECT CustomerID, CompanyName, ContactName FROM Customers}
APPEND ({SELECT * FROM Orders WHERE CustomerID = ?}
RELATE CustomerID TO PARAMETER 0)
```

Although this Recordset will initially open faster than the equivalent relation hierarchy, you won't see a performance difference between the two on the frmExamples form. That's because the Hierarchical FlexGrid control has to move through all the rows in the Recordset to populate itself, removing any performance difference between the two versions of the command.

Multiple Relation Hierarchy

By using more than one set of clauses in the APPEND part of the SHAPE statement, you can create a Recordset with more than one chapter field, and thus more than one child Recordset. For example, this statement relates one parent Recordset to two child Recordsets:

```
SHAPE {SELECT OrderID, CustomerID, EmployeeID FROM Orders}
APPEND({SELECT OrderID, Quantity, UnitPrice FROM [Order Details]}
        RELATE OrderID to OrderID),
      ({SELECT * FROM Employees}
        RELATE EmployeeID TO EmployeeID)
```

Figure 7.5 shows the result of this statement. Note that the Hierarchical FlexGrid control displays each child Recordset with its own set of rows. There isn't any relation between the two child Recordsets that can put them into a single set of rows.

FIGURE 7.5:

A multiple relation hierarchy Recordset

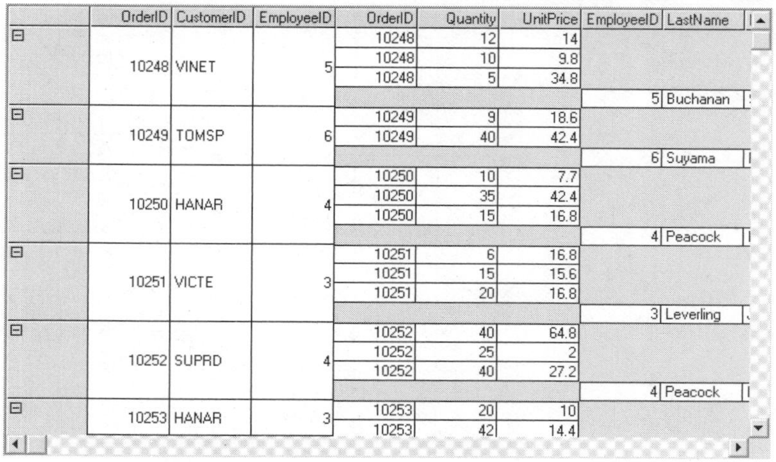

You can also use this technique to divide a single child Recordset into multiple groups of records, perhaps to limit the number of records that you need to work with at any one time. For example, this statement divides the Order Details table into two groups of records depending on whether or not the value of the Quantity field is greater than 10:

```
SHAPE {SELECT OrderID, CustomerID, EmployeeID FROM Orders}
APPEND({SELECT OrderID, Quantity, UnitPrice FROM [Order Details]
        WHERE Quantity <= 10}
        RELATE OrderID to OrderID),
    ({SELECT OrderID, Quantity, UnitPrice FROM [Order Details]
        WHERE Quantity > 10}
        RELATE OrderID to OrderID)
```

Relation Hierarchy with Aggregate

Although I discussed aggregate columns earlier in the chapter in the context of grouping hierarchies, you can also choose to include aggregate columns within a relation hierarchy, as in this example:

```
SHAPE {SELECT CustomerID, CompanyName FROM Customers}
APPEND ({SELECT CustomerID, OrderID, ShippedDate FROM Orders}
        RELATE CustomerID TO CustomerID),
MIN(Chapter1.ShippedDate) As FirstShip
```

This creates a Recordset with customer and order information, plus an additional aggregate column that contains the smallest value from any record in the ShippedDate column for each customer. Figure 7.6 shows the resulting Recordset.

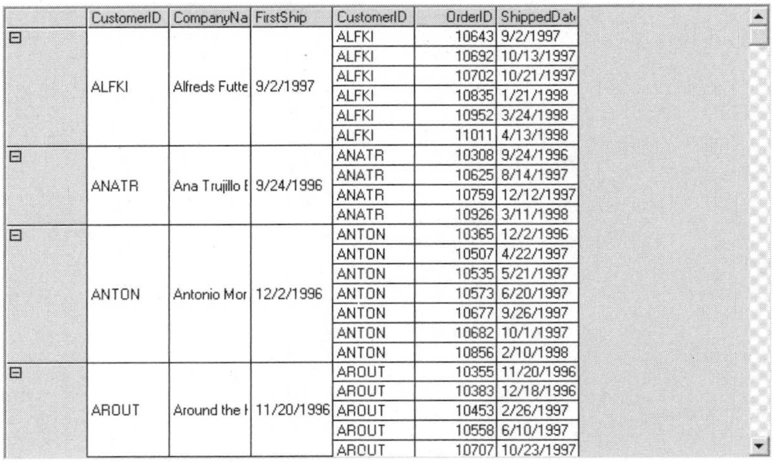

CustomerID	CompanyNa	FirstShip	CustomerID	OrderID	ShippedDat
ALFKI	Alfreds Futte	9/2/1997	ALFKI	10643	9/2/1997
			ALFKI	10692	10/13/1997
			ALFKI	10702	10/21/1997
			ALFKI	10835	1/21/1998
			ALFKI	10952	3/24/1998
			ALFKI	11011	4/13/1998
ANATR	Ana Trujillo E	9/24/1996	ANATR	10308	9/24/1996
			ANATR	10625	8/14/1997
			ANATR	10759	12/12/1997
			ANATR	10926	3/11/1998
ANTON	Antonio Mor	12/2/1996	ANTON	10365	12/2/1996
			ANTON	10507	4/22/1997
			ANTON	10535	5/21/1997
			ANTON	10573	6/20/1997
			ANTON	10677	9/26/1997
			ANTON	10682	10/1/1997
			ANTON	10856	2/10/1998
AROUT	Around the H	11/20/1996	AROUT	10355	11/20/1996
			AROUT	10383	12/18/1996
			AROUT	10453	2/26/1997
			AROUT	10558	6/10/1997
			AROUT	10707	10/23/1997

FIGURE 7.6: A relation hierarchy with an aggregate Recordset

Grouping Hierarchy

A grouping hierarchy still shows detailed and aggregated information, but the parent Recordset is created by aggregating columns from the child Recordset:

```
SHAPE {SELECT OrderID, OrderDate FROM Orders} AS OrdDates
COMPUTE OrdDates, COUNT(OrdDates.OrderID)
BY OrderDate
```

If you run this example, you'll see that the OrderDate field is repeated in both parent and child Recordsets. Figure 7.7 shows this Recordset.

Grand Total

If you omit the BY clause from a grouping hierarchy, you'll get a parent Recordset that consists of a single row that totals any aggregates across the entire child Recordset. For example, you could modify the example that you just saw by removing the BY clause:

```
SHAPE {SELECT OrderID, OrderDate FROM Orders} AS OrdDates
COMPUTE OrdDates, COUNT(OrdDates.OrderID)
```

Figure 7.8 shows the effect of this change. The value in the first column is now a count of all the orders in the child Recordset.

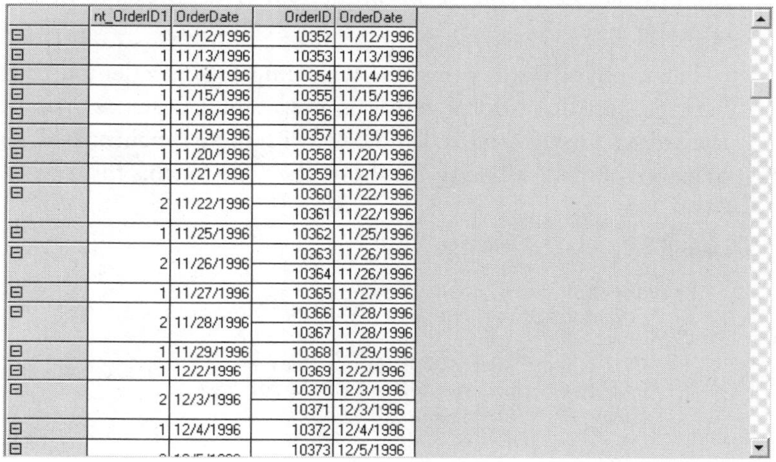

FIGURE 7.7:

A grouping hierarchy
Recordset

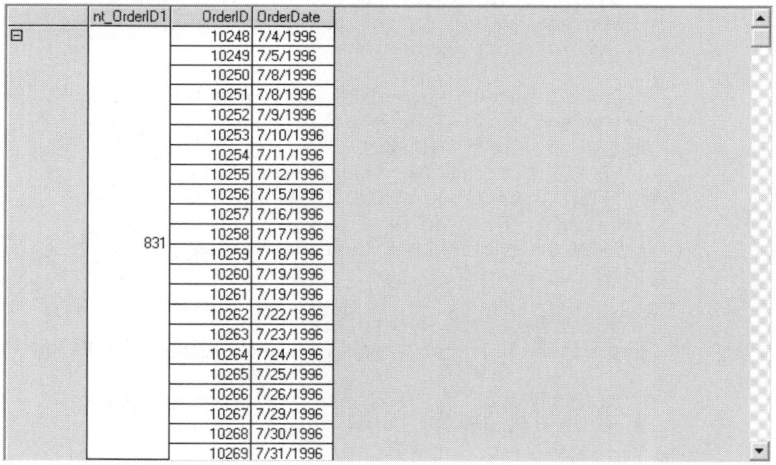

nt_OrderID1	OrderDate	OrderID	OrderDate
1	11/12/1996	10352	11/12/1996
1	11/13/1996	10353	11/13/1996
1	11/14/1996	10354	11/14/1996
1	11/15/1996	10355	11/15/1996
1	11/18/1996	10356	11/18/1996
1	11/19/1996	10357	11/19/1996
1	11/20/1996	10358	11/20/1996
1	11/21/1996	10359	11/21/1996
2	11/22/1996	10360	11/22/1996
		10361	11/22/1996
1	11/25/1996	10362	11/25/1996
2	11/26/1996	10363	11/26/1996
		10364	11/26/1996
1	11/27/1996	10365	11/27/1996
2	11/28/1996	10366	11/28/1996
		10367	11/28/1996
1	11/29/1996	10368	11/29/1996
1	12/2/1996	10369	12/2/1996
2	12/3/1996	10370	12/3/1996
		10371	12/3/1996
1	12/4/1996	10372	12/4/1996
		10373	12/5/1996

FIGURE 7.8:

A grand total
Recordset

nt_OrderID1	OrderID	OrderDate
	10248	7/4/1996
	10249	7/5/1996
	10250	7/8/1996
	10251	7/8/1996
	10252	7/9/1996
	10253	7/10/1996
	10254	7/11/1996
	10255	7/12/1996
	10256	7/15/1996
	10257	7/16/1996
	10258	7/17/1996
831	10259	7/18/1996
	10260	7/19/1996
	10261	7/19/1996
	10262	7/22/1996
	10263	7/23/1996
	10264	7/24/1996
	10265	7/25/1996
	10266	7/26/1996
	10267	7/29/1996
	10268	7/30/1996
	10269	7/31/1996

Synchronizing Recordsets

When you're moving through a Recordset that contains a chapter field, you can control whether a child Recordset based on that field remains synchronized to the parent Recordset by setting the parent Recordset's StayInSync property appropriately. If you set this property to False, moving the cursor in the parent Recordset will have no effect on the contents of the child Recordset. If you set this property to True, the child Recordset will be refetched whenever you move the cursor in the parent Recordset.

The frmSync form in this chapter's sample project demonstrates the effects of the StayInSync property. This form performs a series of data access operations twice—once with the Recordsets unsynchronized and once with them synchronized. Results are printed to a pair of listbox controls. Listing 7.2 shows the code for this form.

Listing 7.2:   **frmSync**

```
Private Sub Form_Load()
    ' Demonstrate the use of StayInSync

    Dim cnn As New ADODB.Connection
    Dim rstParent As New ADODB.Recordset
    Dim rstChild As New ADODB.Recordset

    ' Open a connection
    cnn.Open "Provider=MSDataShape;" & _
     "Data Provider=SQLOLEDB.1;" & _
     "Server=(local);Integrated Security=SSPI;" & _
     "Initial Catalog=Northwind"

    ' Open a parent Recordset, unsynchronized
    rstParent.StayInSync = False
    rstParent.Open "SHAPE {" & _
     "SELECT CustomerID, CompanyName " & _
     "FROM Customers} APPEND ({SELECT " & _
     "CustomerID, OrderDate " & _
     "FROM Orders} RELATE CustomerID " & _
     "TO CustomerID)", cnn

    ' Open the child Recordset
    Set rstChild = rstParent.Fields("Chapter1").Value

    ' Step through records and demonstrate results
    With lboNoSync
        .AddItem "Not synchronized"
        .AddItem " Parent Recordset:"
        .AddItem "   " & _
         rstParent.Fields("CustomerID")
        .AddItem " Child Recordset"
        .AddItem rstChild.Fields("CustomerID")
        .AddItem "Executing MoveNext"
        rstParent.MoveNext
        .AddItem " Parent Recordset:"
        .AddItem "   " & _
         rstParent.Fields("CustomerID")
        .AddItem " Child Recordset"
```

```
            .AddItem rstChild.Fields("CustomerID")
    End With

    ' Close the Recordsets and reopen, synchronized
    rstChild.Close
    rstParent.Close
    rstParent.StayInSync = True
    rstParent.Open "SHAPE {" & _
     "SELECT CustomerID, CompanyName " & _
     "FROM Customers} APPEND ({SELECT " & _
     "CustomerID, OrderDate " & _
     "FROM Orders} RELATE CustomerID " & _
     "TO CustomerID)", cnn

    ' Open the child Recordset
    Set rstChild = rstParent.Fields("Chapter1").Value

    ' Step through records and demonstrate results
    With lboSync
        .AddItem "Synchronized"
        .AddItem " Parent Recordset:"
        .AddItem "   " & _
         rstParent.Fields("CustomerID")
        .AddItem " Child Recordset"
        .AddItem rstChild.Fields("CustomerID")
        .AddItem "Executing MoveNext"
        rstParent.MoveNext
        .AddItem " Parent Recordset:"
        .AddItem "   " & _
         rstParent.Fields("CustomerID")
        .AddItem " Child Recordset"
        .AddItem rstChild.Fields("CustomerID")
    End With

    ' Clean up
    rstChild.Close
    Set rstChild = Nothing
    rstParent.Close
    Set rstParent = Nothing
    cnn.Close
    Set cnn = Nothing

End Sub
```

Figure 7.9 shows the results of running this procedure.

TIP
The default setting for the StayInSync property is True. This helps ensure that you are working with consistent data when you're using both the parent and the child Recordsets in your code.

FIGURE 7.9:

Synchronized and
unsynchronized
Recordsets

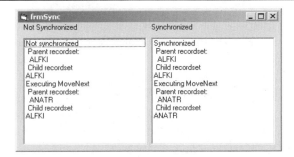

Reshaping

Data shaping is a client-side technology. In particular, when you open a relation hierarchy without using a parameter, the Data Shaping Service reads all the records from the server and uses them on the client to construct the hierarchical Recordset. As long as it has the records cached locally, the Data Shaping Service is free to reuse them in other relations, a process referred to as *reshaping*. In particular, there are three common uses for reshaping:

- Reusing a child Recordset with a new parent Recordset

- Calculating new aggregations from a child Recordset

- Flattening a chaptered Recordset into a single Recordset

I'll look at each of these techniques in the following sections. The code for these examples is included with frmReshape in this chapter's sample project. Figure 7.10 shows this form in action.

Reusing a Child Recordset with a New Parent Recordset

Suppose you have an application that requires Recordsets representing two different parent–child relations:

- Customers with the Orders that they placed

- Employees with the Orders that they took

You might use code like this to place these two hierarchical Recordsets into Hierarchical FlexGrid controls:

```
cnn.Open "Provider=MSDataShape;" & _
  "Data Provider=SQLOLEDB.1;" & _
  "Server=(local);Integrated Security=SSPI;" & _
  "Initial Catalog=Northwind"
```

FIGURE 7.10:

Reshaping a
Recordset

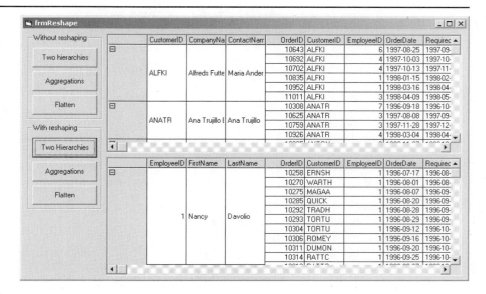

```
rstCustomerOrders.Open _
  "SHAPE {SELECT CustomerID, CompanyName, ContactName " & _
  "FROM Customers} " & vbCrLf & _
  "APPEND ({SELECT * FROM Orders} " & vbCrLf & _
  "RELATE CustomerID TO CustomerID)", _
  cnn, adOpenKeyset, adLockOptimistic
Set hfg1.Recordset = rstCustomerOrders

rstEmployeeOrders.Open _
  "SHAPE {SELECT EmployeeID, FirstName, LastName " & _
  "FROM Employees} " & vbCrLf & _
  "APPEND ({SELECT * FROM Orders} " & vbCrLf & _
  "RELATE EmployeeID TO EmployeeID)", _
  cnn, adOpenKeyset, adLockOptimistic
Set hfg2.Recordset = rstEmployeeOrders
```

There's a serious redundancy built into this approach, though. By opening two separate hierarchical Recordsets, each of which includes the entire contents of the Orders table as a child Recordset, you're forcing the Data Shaping Service to fetch the contents of that table twice from the data source.

The solution is to use reshaping. Here is code to open the same two Recordsets, but using reshaping to reuse the child Recordset:

```
cnn.Open "Provider=MSDataShape;" & _
  "Data Provider=SQLOLEDB.1;" & _
```

```
 "Server=(local);Integrated Security=SSPI;" & _
 "Initial Catalog=Northwind"

rstCustomerOrders.Open _
 "SHAPE {SELECT CustomerID, CompanyName, ContactName " & _
 "FROM Customers} " & vbCrLf & _
 "APPEND ({SELECT * FROM Orders} AS rstOrders " & vbCrLf & _
 "RELATE CustomerID TO CustomerID)", _
 cnn, adOpenKeyset, adLockOptimistic
Set hfg1.Recordset = rstCustomerOrders

rstEmployeeOrders.Open _
 "SHAPE {SELECT EmployeeID, FirstName, LastName " & _
 "FROM Employees} " & vbCrLf & _
 "APPEND (rstOrders " & vbCrLf & _
 "RELATE EmployeeID TO EmployeeID)", _
 cnn, adOpenKeyset, adLockOptimistic
Set hfg2.Recordset = rstEmployeeOrders
```

There are two key differences in this second approach:

- The child Recordset is assigned an alias (rstOrders) in the initial Shape statement.
- That alias is used to refer to the child Recordset in the second Shape statement.

Note that when you use an alias as a child command in this way, you don't use the curly braces that would ordinarily surround the child command. In fact, you'll get a syntax error if you try to do so.

You are not required to assign your own alias to reuse the child Recordset. The Data Shaping Service will assign a name to any Recordset that it opens. You can retrieve that name by retrieving the Reshape Name dynamic property of the Recordset. But it's usually easier to assign your own alias name for reuse.

WARNING The reshaped Recordset must use the same connection as the original Recordset, and the original Recordset must still be open at the time that the reshaping is performed.

Calculating New Aggregations from a Child Recordset

In cases where you'd like to calculate aggregations based on an existing Recordset, you can pass that Recordset into a SHAPE...COMPUTE statement. For example, suppose you have a hierarchical Recordset containing customers with their orders and you'd like to know the total number of orders that were taken by each of your employees. Without reshaping, you could use these two SHAPE statements:

```
SHAPE {SELECT CustomerID, CompanyName, ContactName FROM Customers}
```

```
APPEND ({SELECT * FROM Orders}
RELATE CustomerID TO CustomerID)

SHAPE {SELECT OrderID, EmployeeID FROM Orders} AS rstOrders
COMPUTE rstOrders, Count(rstOrders.OrderID)
BY EmployeeID
```

As with the preceding example, this strategy would result in fetching information from the Orders table twice. As long as the first Recordset is open when you want to create the second Recordset, you can use reshaping instead:

```
SHAPE {SELECT CustomerID, CompanyName, ContactName FROM Customers}
APPEND ({SELECT * FROM Orders} AS rstOrders
RELATE CustomerID TO CustomerID)

SHAPE rstOrders
COMPUTE rstOrders, Count(rstOrders.OrderID)
BY EmployeeID
```

Once again, the aliased child Recordset name is used as the data source for the second SHAPE statement.

Flattening a Chaptered Recordset into a Single Recordset

Finally, you can use reshaping to remove the hierarchical information in a Recordset. For instance, you might want a hierarchical Recordset containing both customers and orders, and another (nonhierarchical) Recordset with only order information that includes orders for all customers. Here's the code to do that without reshaping:

```
cnn.Open "Provider=MSDataShape;" & _
  "Data Provider=SQLOLEDB.1;" & _
  "Server=(local);Integrated Security=SSPI;" & _
  "Initial Catalog=Northwind"

rstCustomerOrders.Open _
  "SHAPE {SELECT CustomerID, CompanyName, ContactName " & _
  "FROM Customers} " & vbCrLf & _
  "APPEND ({SELECT * FROM Orders} " & vbCrLf & _
  "RELATE CustomerID TO CustomerID)", _
  cnn, adOpenKeyset, adLockOptimistic
Set hfg1.Recordset = rstCustomerOrders

rstOrders.Open _
  "SELECT * FROM Orders", _
  cnn, adOpenKeyset, adLockOptimistic
Set hfg2.Recordset = rstOrders
```

TIP   As this example demonstrates, the Hierarchical FlexGrid has no trouble displaying a non-hierarchical Recordset.

And here's the code to do the same thing using reshaping, without opening a second copy of the Orders Recordset:

```
cnn.Open "Provider=MSDataShape;" & _
  "Data Provider=SQLOLEDB.1;" & _
  "Server=(local);Integrated Security=SSPI;" & _
  "Initial Catalog=Northwind"

rstCustomerOrders.Open _
  "SHAPE {SELECT CustomerID, CompanyName, ContactName " & _
  "FROM Customers} " & vbCrLf & _
  "APPEND ({SELECT * FROM Orders} AS rstOrders" & vbCrLf & _
  "RELATE CustomerID TO CustomerID)", _
  cnn, adOpenKeyset, adLockOptimistic
Set hfg1.Recordset = rstCustomerOrders

rstOrders.Open _
  "SHAPE rstOrders", _
  cnn, adOpenKeyset, adLockOptimistic
Set hfg2.Recordset = rstOrders
```

This technique is especially useful if you're using batch updates. If you've made changes to a number of child records but have not yet sent the batch back to the server, it can be tedious to find all the changed records. But because reshaping reuses exactly the same records, you can reshape the child records into one big Recordset and then apply a filter with the adFilterPendingRecords constant to see only the changed records.

TIP   See Chapter 3, "Using the ADO Objects to Retrieve Data," for more information on the Recordset.Filter property.

Fabricated Recordsets

Although the Data Shaping Service is an OLE DB service provider, it's a rather peculiar service provider in that it's able to operate without any underlying data provider at all. You can use the Data Shaping Service to create arbitrary hierarchical Recordsets that you can then populate at runtime with data, all without a data source. These Recordsets are referred to as *fabricated Recordsets*.

One intriguing use of this technology is to convert any hierarchical data you have available in your application to XML, using Microsoft's standard XML schema for rowsets. Figure 7.11

shows the frmFabricate form from this chapter's sample application. The code behind this
form creates a fabricated Recordset, populates it with some data, displays it in a Hierarchical
FlexGrid control, saves it to XML, and then displays the created XML.

FIGURE 7.11:

Working with a fabri-
cated Recordset

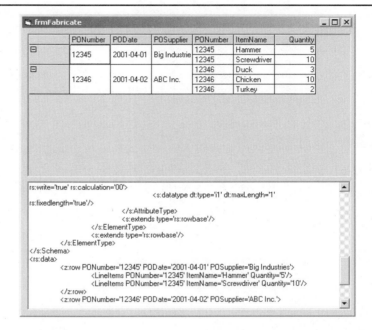

Listing 7.3 shows the code that carries out the operations on frmFabricate.

Listing 7.3:   frmFabricate

```
Private Sub Form_Load()

    Dim rstPurchaseOrder As ADODB.Recordset
    Dim rstLineItems As ADODB.Recordset
    Dim intFile As Integer
    Dim strLine As String
    Dim strTemp As String

    On Error GoTo HandleErr

    ' Create a Recordset directly on the Shape provider
    Set rstPurchaseOrder = New ADODB.Recordset
    rstPurchaseOrder.ActiveConnection = _
      "Provider=MSDataShape;Data Provider=None"

    ' Open the Recordset to create its shape
    rstPurchaseOrder.Open _
```

```
"SHAPE APPEND NEW adChar(5) AS PONumber, " & _
" NEW adDBDate AS PODate, " & _
" NEW adVarChar(50) AS POSupplier, " & _
" ((SHAPE APPEND NEW adChar(5) AS PONumber, " & _
"   NEW adVarChar(50) AS ItemName, " & _
"   NEW adTinyInt AS Quantity) " & _
"   RELATE PONumber TO PONumber) AS LineItems", _
, adOpenStatic, adLockOptimistic

' Add a record to the parent Recordset
rstPurchaseOrder.AddNew Array("PONumber", "PODate", "POSupplier"), _
 Array("12345", "4/1/01", "Big Industries")
rstPurchaseOrder.Update

' Add two records to the child Recordset
Set rstLineItems = rstPurchaseOrder("LineItems").Value
rstLineItems.AddNew Array("ItemName", "Quantity"), _
 Array("Hammer", 5)
rstLineItems.Update
rstLineItems.AddNew Array("ItemName", "Quantity"), _
 Array("Screwdriver", 10)
rstLineItems.Update

' Add a record to the parent Recordset
rstPurchaseOrder.AddNew Array("PONumber", "PODate", "POSupplier"), _
 Array("12346", "4/2/01", "ABC Inc.")
rstPurchaseOrder.Update

' Add three records to the child Recordset. Note that
' this automatically synchronizes with the parent Recordset
rstLineItems.AddNew Array("ItemName", "Quantity"), _
 Array("Duck", 3)
rstLineItems.Update
rstLineItems.AddNew Array("ItemName", "Quantity"), _
 Array("Chicken", 10)
rstLineItems.Update
rstLineItems.AddNew Array("ItemName", "Quantity"), _
 Array("Turkey", 2)
rstLineItems.Update

' Display the Recordset
Set hfgMain.Recordset = rstPurchaseOrder

' Destroy any existing disk file
On Error Resume Next
Kill App.Path & "\po.xml"
On Error GoTo HandleErr

' Persist the Recordset as XML
rstPurchaseOrder.Save App.Path & "\po.xml", adPersistXML

' Open the file and show the contents
intFile = FreeFile
```

```
    Open App.Path & "\po.xml" For Input As #intFile
    Do Until EOF(intFile)
        Line Input #intFile, strLine
        strTemp = strTemp & strLine & vbCrLf
    Loop
    Close #intFile
    txtXML.Text = strTemp

    ' Cleanup
    rstLineItems.Close
    Set rstLineItems = Nothing
    rstPurchaseOrder.Close
    Set rstPurchaseOrder = Nothing

ExitHere:
    Exit Sub

HandleErr:
    MsgBox "Error " & Err.Number & ": " & Err.Description, _
     vbOKOnly, "Form_Load"
    Resume ExitHere
    Resume

End Sub
```

After declaring variables and setting an error handler, the code instantiates an ADO Recordset object and sets its connection string. The connection string uses the special keyword None for the data provider:

```
rstPurchaseOrder.ActiveConnection = _
 "Provider=MSDataShape;Data Provider=None"
```

Using `Data Provider=None` tells the Data Shaping Service that you're going to be working with no data source, and that all of the data it will be managing will be supplied directly by the application.

The code next uses the Open method of the Recordset with a SHAPE command. When the Data Shaping Service receives this command, it will create the indicated Recordset in memory. Here, stripped of the Visual Basic syntax, is the SHAPE command used by this example:

```
SHAPE APPEND NEW adChar(5) AS PONumber,
  NEW adDBDate AS PODate,
  NEW adVarChar(50) AS POSupplier,
  ((SHAPE APPEND NEW adChar(5) AS PONumber,
    NEW adVarChar(50) AS ItemName,
    NEW adTinyInt AS Quantity)
    RELATE PONumber TO PONumber) AS LineItems
```

Each of the two SHAPE APPEND commands here creates a Recordset. The inner Recordset, aliased to the name LineItems, includes fields named PONumber, ItemName, and Quantity.

The outer Recordset includes fields named PONumber, PODate, and POSupplier. Nesting the two commands and including the RELATE clause causes the outer Recordset to include a chapter column containing the inner Recordset.

If you're used to creating tables with the SQL CREATE TABLE statement, watch out! The SHAPE APPEND command declares columns with *datatype* AS *fieldname*, which is precisely backward from the way it's done in CREATE TABLE.

Once the Recordset has been opened, you can add as many records as you like using the AddNew and Update methods of the Recordset object. This code makes use of the streamlined dual-array method of adding records, which I discussed in Chapter 4:

```
rstPurchaseOrder.AddNew Array("PONumber", "PODate", "POSupplier"), _
    Array("12345", "4/1/01", "Big Industries")
```

After the first record has been added to the outer Recordset, the code sets a Recordset variable to the inner Recordset. Note the use of the required Value property, as well as the alias that was assigned in the SHAPE APPEND statement:

```
Set rstLineItems = rstPurchaseOrder("LineItems").Value
```

With pointers to both the outer and inner Recordsets, the code proceeds to add several more records. It then uses the Recordset property of the Hierarchical FlexGrid control to display the data on-screen.

The final step is to persist the data to an XML file and then display the persisted file. Persisting the data is done by calling the Recordset's Save method:

```
rstPurchaseOrder.Save App.Path & "\po.xml", adPersistXML
```

ADO automatically takes care of the details of converting both the inner and outer Recordsets to XML. The rest of the code is simple Visual Basic file I/O code that just reads the disk file as text and displays it in a text box.

Summary

In this chapter, you learned about the Data Shaping Service and its ability to create and work with hierarchical Recordsets. You saw the different types of shaped Recordsets as well as some examples of the SHAPE commands that create them. You also learned how to synchronize a pair of Recordsets, how to use reshaping to avoid excess communication with the data source, and how to create a fabricated Recordset.

In the next chapter, I'll introduce you to disconnected Recordsets. You'll see how you can use optimistic batch updating to save changes that were made while your application wasn't connected to a data source, and how to use the Remote Data Service to connect to data over the Internet.

CHAPTER 8

Working with Disconnected Recordsets

- Optimistic batch updating

- Creating synthetic Recordsets

- Remote Data Service

- Using ADO in multitiered applications

In previous chapters, you have worked directly with data in a data source. Normally, when you open a Recordset, ADO maintains communication with the data source that provided the records. However, ADO is also capable of working with *disconnected* Recordsets. A disconnected Recordset is one that doesn't have an open Connection to a data source. In this chapter, I'll discuss creating and updating such disconnected Recordsets as well as the Remote Data Service that allows ADO to send Recordsets across an Internet or intranet connection.

Optimistic Batch Updating

Like any other programming object, a Recordset has two different representations. So far, I've been discussing Recordsets at the level of abstraction, where a Recordset is defined as a set of records plus a current record pointer. But you can also view Recordsets at the level of implementation. At this level, a Recordset is simply information in your computer's memory that was originally drawn from a data source.

When you think about things at the implementation level, it becomes clear that continuous communication with a data source isn't an essential part of a Recordset. Suppose you opened a Recordset based on a table on a SQL Server across your network. The records for that table were read into memory for your later use. Then suppose that immediately after this memory was set up, the SQL Server computer melted down into a smoking pile of rubble. At that moment, the Recordset would still contain perfectly valid, usable data.

That's how disconnected Recordsets work, although without the smoking pile of rubble. After you've opened a Recordset, you can disconnect it from its data source by setting the ActiveConnection property of the Recordset to Nothing. You can do this only if you're using the Microsoft Cursor Service for OLE DB, which is the component that implements disconnected Recordsets. You're using this service any time that you set the CursorLocation property of a Recordset to adUseClient.

The Cursor Service provides much more than the ability to continue using a Recordset after it has been disconnected. In particular, you can actually edit a disconnected Recordset, and later reconnect that Recordset and save changes back to the original data source. Figure 8.1 shows the frmBatchUpdates form from the ADOChapter8 sample project, which allows you to experiment with these capabilities.

FIGURE 8.1:

Editing disconnected
Recordsets

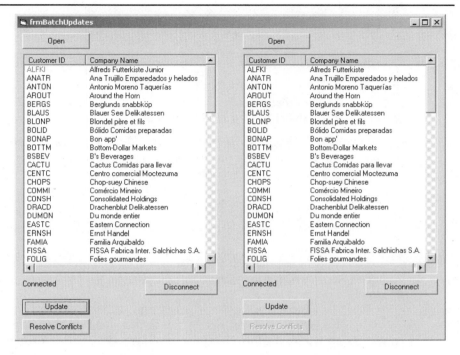

This form is set up to allow you to edit two different Recordsets based on the same underlying table. This provides an easy way to explore what happens when two users make conflicting edits. To see this process in action, follow these steps:

1. Run the sample project and open frmBatchUpdates by clicking the Batch Updates button on frmMenu.

2. Click each of the two Open buttons. This will open two copies of the same Recordset, using two independent Connection objects. The CustomerID and CompanyName fields will be displayed for both Recordsets.

3. Click each of the two Disconnect buttons. This will disconnect both Recordsets from the data source.

4. Double-click one of the records in the left-hand ListView. This will open a dialog box that lets you change the company name for that record. Make a change to that record and then click OK.

5. Now double-click the same record in the right-hand ListView. Make a different change to that record and then click OK. At this point, you have made inconsistent changes in the two disconnected Recordsets.

6. Double-click another record in the left-hand ListView and edit its company name. The edited records will show with the CustomerID in green. Note that the Recordset may contain multiple edited records at the same time.

7. Click each of the two Connect buttons to reconnect the Recordsets to the data source.

8. Click the left-hand Update button. This will save the changes from the Recordset on the left to the underlying data source, and reload the ListView. Both edited records will be saved (this is the "batch" part of batch updating).

9. Click the right-hand Update button. The CustomerID for the edited record will turn red, to indicate that ADO met a conflict when trying to save the record (because the row in the database didn't contain the same value that the row in the Recordset originally contained).

10. Click the right-hand Resolve Conflicts button. This will allow you to choose whether to overwrite the value in the data source with the new value from the Recordset.

TIP You can actually use optimistic batch updating with any Recordset, not just with a disconnected Recordset. But the technique is most useful when changes cannot be sent immediately to the data source.

Let's take a look at the code used by this form to manage the data involved. The easiest place to start is with the form-level declarations and the form's Load procedure:

```
Dim mcnn1 As ADODB.Connection
Dim mcnn2 As ADODB.Connection
Dim mrst1 As ADODB.Recordset
Dim mrst2 As ADODB.Recordset

Private Sub Form_Load()
    Set mcnn1 = New ADODB.Connection
    Set mcnn2 = New ADODB.Connection
    Set mrst1 = New ADODB.Recordset
    Set mrst2 = New ADODB.Recordset
    mrst1.CursorLocation = adUseClient
    mrst2.CursorLocation = adUseClient
    mcnn1.Open "Provider=Microsoft.Jet.OLEDB.4.0;" & _
      "Data Source=" & App.Path & "\ADOChapter8.mdb"
    mcnn2.Open "Provider=Microsoft.Jet.OLEDB.4.0;" & _
      "Data Source=" & App.Path & "\ADOChapter8.mdb"
End Sub
```

This block of code sets up persistent variables to hold two Connections to a database and two Recordsets. Note that the CursorLocation property of each Recordset is set to adUseClient, so that the Recordset can be disconnected. Both of the Connection objects are initialized to point to the same Access database. By using two Connection objects in this way, the code simulates two independent users who might (in a real-world situation) be working on different computers.

When you click either Open button, the form opens a Recordset and then transfers information from the Recordset to the user interface. Listing 8.1 shows the code that handles this transfer.

Listing 8.1: **Opening a Recordset**

```
Private Sub cmdOpen1_Click()

    Dim li As ListItem

    On Error GoTo HandleErr

    lvw1.ListItems.Clear

        mrst1.Open "Customers", mcnn1, adOpenStatic, adLockBatchOptimistic

    Do Until mrst1.EOF
        Set li = lvw1.ListItems.Add(, mrst1.Fields("CustomerID"), _
      mrst1.Fields("CustomerID"))
        li.SubItems(1) = mrst1.Fields("CompanyName")
        mrst1.MoveNext
    Loop

    lblStatus1.Caption = "Connected"
    cmdConnect1.Enabled = True

ExitHere:
    Exit Sub

HandleErr:
    MsgBox "Error " & Err.Number & ": " & Err.Description, _
      vbOKOnly, "cmdOpen1"
    Resume ExitHere
    Resume

End Sub
```

NOTE   I'm showing the code for only half of the form here. The code for the other half is identical except for control and variable names.

The lvw1 control on the form is a ListView control, from the Microsoft Windows Common Controls library. The Add method for a ListView control looks like this:

```
ListView.Add ([Index], [Key], [Text], [Icon], [SmallIcon]) As ListItem
```

The arguments to this method, all of which are optional, are as follows:

Index   Position in the ListItems collection for the new item

Key   Unique key for the new item

Text   Text to display on the user interface for the new item

Icon   Index into an ImageList control for the icon to display with this item in Large Icons view

SmallIcon   Index into an ImageList control for the icon to display with this item in Small Icons view

In this case, I'm using the value from the CustomerID field of the database record as both the key and the text of the item. I know from the database design that this is a unique key, so it works well as the key for the ListView as well. When you're displaying a ListView in multiple columns, as in this example, the text is used as the value for the first column.

The Add method returns a ListItem object. Each row in a ListView is represented by a ListItem object. This object has a collection of SubItems, each of which has as its default property the text of one column of the ListView. In this code, I assign the CompanyName field from the Recordset to the text of the first SubItem of each ListItem.

As you can see, the Open button sets up a mapping between the rows in the Recordset and the rows in the corresponding ListView. This pattern continues throughout the sample: Operations in the ListView are mapped back to the Recordset, and vice versa.

After the Recordset is opened, you can use the Disconnect button to sever its Connection with the data source. Listing 8.2 shows the code to sever the Connection.

Listing 8.2:   **Changing a Recordset's Connection Status**

```
Private Sub cmdConnect1_Click()

    On Error GoTo HandleErr

    Select Case lblStatus1.Caption
        Case "Connected"
            Set mrst1.ActiveConnection = Nothing
            lblStatus1.Caption = "Disconnected"
            cmdUpdate1.Enabled = False
            cmdConnect1.Caption = "Connect"
        Case "Disconnected"
            Set mrst1.ActiveConnection = mcnn1
            lblStatus1.Caption = "Connected"
            cmdUpdate1.Enabled = True
            cmdConnect1.Caption = "Disconnect"
    End Select
```

```
ExitHere:
    Exit Sub

HandleErr:
    MsgBox "Error " & Err.Number & ": " & Err.Description, _
     vbOKOnly, "cmdConnect1"
    Resume ExitHere
    Resume

End Sub
```

The form uses the same button to both connect and disconnect the Recordset. Depending on the caption of the button, it either sets the ActiveConnection property of the Recordset to Nothing or sets the property to the open Connection object, and adjusts the user interface accordingly.

When you double-click an item in the ListView, the code takes care of editing the corresponding row in the Recordset:

```
Private Sub lvw1_DblClick()

    Dim strInput As String

    On Error GoTo HandleErr

    strInput = InputBox("Edit company name:", , lvw1.SelectedItem.SubItems(1))

    If strInput <> lvw1.SelectedItem.SubItems(1) Then
        lvw1.SelectedItem.SubItems(1) = strInput
        lvw1.SelectedItem.ForeColor = &HFF00&
        mrst1.MoveFirst
        mrst1.Find "CustomerID = '" & lvw1.SelectedItem.Text & "'"
        mrst1.Fields("CompanyName") = strInput
    End If

ExitHere:
    Exit Sub

HandleErr:
    MsgBox "Error " & Err.Number & ": " & Err.Description, _
     vbOKOnly, "lvw1_DblClick"
    Resume ExitHere
    Resume

End Sub
```

The lvw1_DblClick procedure uses the text of the selected item in the ListView to find the corresponding row in the Recordset and change it according to the user's input. Note that there's no call to the Recordset's Update method after the edit. As long as the Recordset was opened with the adLockBatchOptimistic locking constant, you can make as many changes as you like without saving updates.

When you click the Update button, the form uses the UpdateBatch method to try to save all the updates that are pending in the Recordset. Listing 8.3 demonstrates the update process.

Listing 8.3:   **Updating a Disconnected Recordset**

```
Private Sub cmdUpdate1_Click()

    Dim li As ListItem

    On Error Resume Next

    mrst1.UpdateBatch

    If mrst1.ActiveConnection.Errors.Count > 0 Then
        For Each li In lvw1.ListItems
            li.ForeColor = 0
        Next li
        mrst1.Filter = adFilterConflictingRecords
        Do Until mrst1.EOF
            lvw1.ListItems(CStr(mrst1.Fields("CustomerID"))).ForeColor = _
              &HFF&
            mrst1.MoveNext
        Loop
        mrst1.Filter = adFilterNone
        cmdResolve1.Enabled = True
    Else
        lvw1.ListItems.Clear
        mrst1.Resync adAffectAllChapters, adResyncAllValues
        mrst1.MoveFirst
        Do Until mrst1.EOF
            Set li = lvw1.ListItems.Add(, mrst1.Fields("CustomerID"), _
              mrst1.Fields("CustomerID"))
            li.SubItems(1) = mrst1.Fields("CompanyName")
            mrst1.MoveNext
        Loop
    End If

End Sub
```

The UpdateBatch method raises an error if there are problems with saving any of the waiting changes. Generally, you'll get an error if the original record on the data source was changed by another user after the Recordset containing the update was opened. The code detects this condition by checking `mrst1.ActiveConnection.Errors.Count`. If there are any errors pending on the Connection, it knows that at least one update failed.

> **WARNING** You must check the Errors collection via the ActiveConnection property rather than through the underlying Connection object. This is where ADO will post any errors for a disconnected Recordset.

If there are any errors, the code sets the Filter property of the Recordset to adFilterConflictingRecords. This reduces the Recordset to only those records that couldn't be saved to the data source. The code then loops through the (now-reduced) Recordset and alters the user interface by changing the ForeColor of each affected record to red. The affected records are located in the ListView by using the CustomerID field as a key into the ListItems collection. The code also enables the Resolve Conflicts button at this point.

> **WARNING** You must use the CStr() function to explicitly convert key values to strings in order to use them for lookup in a ListView's ListItems collection. Otherwise, even if the values are from a string field, you'll get a type mismatch error.

On the other hand, if there are no errors, you know that all the changes were saved successfully. In this case, the code clears the ListView and calls the Recordset's Resync method to read all changes from the underlying data source (including any changes that were made by other users that didn't conflict with my own changes). The newly synchronized Recordset is then transferred back to the user interface.

Finally, in case of conflicts, you can click the Resolve Conflicts button to decide what to do on a record-by-record basis. Listing 8.4 shows an example of conflict resolution.

Listing 8.4:   **Resolving Conflicts in a Recordset**

```
Private Sub cmdResolve1_Click()

    Dim intRet As Integer
    Dim li As ListItem

    On Error GoTo HandleErr

    cmdResolve1.Enabled = False

    On Error Resume Next
    mrst1.UpdateBatch
    On Error GoTo HandleErr
    mrst1.Filter = adFilterConflictingRecords
    mrst1.Resync adAffectAll, adResyncUnderlyingValues
    mrst1.MoveFirst
```

```
       Do Until mrst1.EOF
           intRet = MsgBox("Customer ID " & mrst1.Fields("CustomerID") & _
               ". Original value was " & _
               mrst1.Fields("CompanyName").OriginalValue & _
               ". Value on server is " & _
               mrst1.Fields("CompanyName").UnderlyingValue & _
               ". You changed it to " & mrst1.Fields("CompanyName").Value & _
               ". Save your change?", vbQuestion + vbYesNo, "Record conflict")
           If intRet = vbNo Then
               mrst1.Fields("CompanyName").Value = _
                mrst1.Fields("CompanyName").UnderlyingValue
               mrst1.Update
           End If
           mrst1.MoveNext
       Loop
       mrst1.UpdateBatch
       mrst1.Filter = adFilterNone
       lvw1.ListItems.Clear
       mrst1.Resync adAffectAllChapters, adResyncAllValues
       mrst1.MoveFirst
       Do Until mrst1.EOF
           Set li = lvw1.ListItems.Add(, mrst1.Fields("CustomerID"), _
            mrst1.Fields("CustomerID"))
           li.SubItems(1) = mrst1.Fields("CompanyName")
           mrst1.MoveNext
       Loop

   ExitHere:
       Exit Sub

   HandleErr:
       MsgBox "Error " & Err.Number & ": " & Err.Description, _
        vbOKOnly, "cmdResolve1"
       Resume ExitHere
       Resume

 End Sub
```

This procedure also starts by filtering the Recordset to hold only conflicting records. It then calls the Resync method with the adResyncUnderlyingValues flag. This has the effect of retrieving information from the data source about the current value of the affected records. At this point, each record has three (potentially different) values, stored in three different properties:

OriginalValue   The value of the field in the data source when the Recordset was first opened

UnderlyingValue   The value of the field in the data source when the Recordset was resynchronized

Value   The value of the field in the Recordset

The code uses these three values to build a prompt for the user; an example is shown in Figure 8.2. Depending on the user's response, the value might be left as-is, or reset to the UnderlyingValue property. Either way, when all the records have been reviewed, the code calls the UpdateBatch method again to save the changes, and then resynchronizes the Recordset and rebuilds the user interface.

FIGURE 8.2:

Value information for a conflicting row

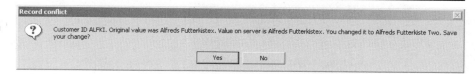

By combining client-side cursors, disconnected Recordsets, the UpdateBatch method, and the record-by-record error handling shown in this example, you have the freedom to treat a Recordset as a package that you can work on without constant reference to the underlying data source. If you throw in the techniques for persisting Recordsets that is discussed in Chapter 6, "Using Records and Streams," you gain even more flexibility. For example, you could design an application that used these steps to allow offsite editing:

1. Open a Recordset holding the data that you need to edit, using client-side cursors and optimistic batch locking.

2. Disconnect the Recordset and save it to a file.

3. E-mail the file to a remote location.

4. Open the file with an application designed to reconstitute a Recordset from the file.

5. Edit the Recordset, changing multiple rows if necessary.

6. Persist the Recordset back to a file.

7. E-mail the file to the original location.

8. Read the file back into a Recordset.

9. Connect the Recordset to the original data source.

10. Call the UpdateBatch method to save changes, and then resolve any conflicting records.

Creating Synthetic Recordsets

In Chapter 7, "Data Shaping," you saw the use of the Microsoft Data Shaping Service to create a completely synthetic hierarchical Recordset. The Microsoft Cursor Service supplies the same facility for regular, nonhierarchical Recordsets. To create a Recordset without any Connection at all to a data source, follow these steps:

1. Instantiate a Recordset variable.

2. Set the CursorLocation property of the Recordset to adUseClient.

3. Add fields to the Recordset by calling the Append method of the Recordset's Fields collection.

4. Call the Recordset's Open method.

A Synthetic Recordset Example

Why would you want to use this technique? One good reason is to allow a user to edit data with a familiar bound-control interface, even when the data isn't in a database. For example, consider this simple XML file (available on the companion CD as `Customers.xml`):

```
<Root_Element>
    <Customer>
        <CustomerName>KNG Consulting</CustomerName>
        <CustomerCity>Los Angeles</CustomerCity>
        <CustomerState>CA</CustomerState>
    </Customer>
    <Customer>
        <CustomerName>Lark Group, Inc.</CustomerName>
        <CustomerCity>Endicott</CustomerCity>
        <CustomerState>WA</CustomerState>
    </Customer>
    <Customer>
        <CustomerName>Litwin Consulting</CustomerName>
        <CustomerCity>Seattle</CustomerCity>
        <CustomerState>WA</CustomerState>
    </Customer>
    <Customer>
        <CustomerName>Key Data Systems</CustomerName>
        <CustomerCity>Singer Island</CustomerCity>
        <CustomerState>FL</CustomerState>
    </Customer>
    <Customer>
        <CustomerName>ElectricHead, Inc.</CustomerName>
        <CustomerCity>Upland</CustomerCity>
        <CustomerState>CA</CustomerState>
    </Customer>
  </Root_Element>
```

Although the structure of this file is easy for a human being to see, it's not in the form that can be directly loaded by a Recordset. However, by using a synthetic Recordset, I can edit this data on a bound form, such as that shown in Figure 8.3.

ADO Recordsets can load XML data directly if the XML is attribute-centric, but not if the XML is element-centric.

FIGURE 8.3:

Editing XML data

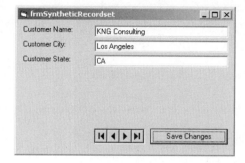

This form contains an ADO Data Control and a set of bound text box controls. When you open the form, it calls code to construct and initialize a Recordset. Listing 8.5 shows the code that constructs the Recordset.

Listing 8.5:   **Constructing a Recordset**

```
Private Sub Form_Load()

    On Error GoTo HandleErr

    ' First, create a synthetic Recordset
    Set mrst = New ADODB.Recordset
    mrst.CursorLocation = adUseClient

    mrst.Fields.Append "CustomerName", adVarChar, 50
    mrst.Fields.Append "CustomerCity", adVarChar, 50
    mrst.Fields.Append "CustomerState", adVarChar, 50

    mrst.Open , , adOpenStatic, adLockOptimistic

    ' Load the data and bind it to the user interface
    LoadCustomerData
    mrst.MoveFirst
    Set Adodc1.Recordset = mrst

ExitHere:
    Exit Sub

HandleErr:
    MsgBox "Error " & Err.Number & ": " & Err.Description, _
        vbOKOnly, "Form_Load"
```

```
        Resume ExitHere
        Resume

    End Sub
```

The LoadCustomerData procedure is used to read data from the XML file and transfer it to the Recordset. In this particular case, it simply uses Visual Basic string processing to do its job. Listing 8.6 shows this procedure.

Listing 8.6:   LoadCustomerData

```
Private Sub LoadCustomerData()
    ' Load data from the XML file to a Recordset

    Dim intFile As Integer
    Dim strTemp As String
    Dim strCustomerName As String
    Dim strCustomerCity As String
    Dim strCustomerState As String
    Dim fDone As Boolean

    On Error GoTo HandleErr

    intFile = FreeFile
    Open App.Path & "\Customers.xml" For Input As #intFile

    ' Throw away the opening root element
    Line Input #intFile, strTemp

    ' Now loop through all the customers
    Do Until fDone
        Line Input #intFile, strTemp
        strTemp = Trim(strTemp)
        ' At this point, strTemp is either <Customer> or </Root_Element>
        If strTemp = "<Customer>" Then
            ' Read in the data
            Line Input #intFile, strTemp
            strCustomerName = GetStringData(strTemp)
            Line Input #intFile, strTemp
            strCustomerCity = GetStringData(strTemp)
            Line Input #intFile, strTemp
            strCustomerState = GetStringData(strTemp)
            ' Add it to the Recordset
            mrst.AddNew _
             Array("CustomerName", "CustomerCity", "CustomerState"), _
             Array(strCustomerName, strCustomerCity, strCustomerState)
            ' And throw away the closing </Customer> tag
            Line Input #intFile, strTemp
        Else
```

```
                    fDone = True
            End If
        Loop

        Close #intFile

    ExitHere:
        Exit Sub

    HandleErr:
        MsgBox "Error " & Err.Number & ": " & Err.Description, _
          vbOKOnly, "LoadCustomerData"
        Resume ExitHere
        Resume

    End Sub

    Private Function GetStringData(strInput As String) As String
        ' Extract string data from a single-row XML tag

        Dim intStart As Integer
        Dim intEnd As Integer

        On Error GoTo HandleErr

        strInput = Trim(strInput)
        intStart = InStr(1, strInput, ">") + 1
        intEnd = InStr(intStart + 1, strInput, "<")

        GetStringData = Mid(strInput, intStart, intEnd - intStart)

    ExitHere:
        Exit Function

    HandleErr:
        MsgBox "Error " & Err.Number & ": " & Err.Description, _
          vbOKOnly, "GetStringData"
        Resume ExitHere
        Resume

    End Function
```

TIP

For a more complex XML file, it would be worthwhile to use the XML Document Object Model to parse the original data. You can find details on this technique in Kurt Cagle's *XML Developer's Handbook* (Sybex, 2000).

As you can see, this code splits the task of parsing the source data from that of displaying the data to the user and allowing the user to edit the data. If I wanted to use a different XML file, or even something like an Excel worksheet or a Visio drawing as the data source, I'd simply need to rewrite the LoadCustomerData function to parse the new data source. Once the data is loaded into a synthetic Recordset, it can be handled using the standard Recordset tools and techniques.

The final bit of code behind this form handles the job of taking the Recordset and rebuilding the XML file from it. Listing 8.7 shows this code.

Listing 8.7: **Saving Changes from a Recordset to XML**

```
Private Sub cmdSaveChanges_Click()

    Dim intFile As Integer

    On Error GoTo HandleErr

    ' Remove the old file
    Kill App.Path & "\Customers.xml"

    ' And open it anew
    intFile = FreeFile
    Open App.Path & "\Customers.xml" For Output As #intFile

    ' Write the root element
    Print #intFile, "<Root_Element>"

    ' Write out the customers
    mrst.MoveFirst
    Do Until mrst.EOF
        Print #intFile, "    <Customer>"
        Print #intFile, "        <CustomerName>" & _
         mrst.Fields("CustomerName") & "</CustomerName>"
        Print #intFile, "        <CustomerCity>" & _
         mrst.Fields("CustomerCity") & "</CustomerCity>"
        Print #intFile, "        <CustomerState>" & _
         mrst.Fields("CustomerState") & "</CustomerState>"
        Print #intFile, "    </Customer>"
        mrst.MoveNext
    Loop

    ' Finish things off
    mrst.MoveFirst
    Print #intFile, "</Root_Element>"
    Close #intFile

ExitHere:
    Exit Sub

HandleErr:
```

```
MsgBox "Error " & Err.Number & ": " & Err.Description, _
   vbOKOnly, "cmdSaveChanges"
Resume ExitHere
Resume

End Sub
```

Appending Fields

The key to building a synthetic Recordset is the Append method of the Fields collection:

```
Fields.Append Name, Type[, DefinedSize][, Attrib]
```

The Append method has up to four arguments:

Name   The name of the new field.

Type   The datatype of the new field. Table 8.1 shows the constants that can be used to designate field datatypes.

DefinedSize   The size, in characters or bytes, of the new field. ADO treats any field with a size over 255 as a variable-length field.

Attrib   Attributes for the new field. Table 8.2 shows the constants that can be used to designate field attributes.

> **TIP**
>
> If you look up the Append method in the Object Browser, you'll find a fifth argument, Field-Value. This argument is valid only for the Fields collection of a Record object.

TABLE 8.1: ADO Datatypes for Fields.Append Method

Constant	Description
adBigInt	8-byte signed integer
adBinary	Raw binary data
adBoolean	Boolean
adBSTR	Null-terminated Unicode character string
adChar	Character string
adCurrency	Currency, stored with 4 digits to the right of the decimal point
adDate	Date/time
adDBDate	Date only, with no time value
adDBTime	Time only, with no date value
adDBTimeStamp	Time stamp
adDecimal	Decimal with fixed precision and scale

continued on next page

TABLE 8.1 CONTINUED: ADO Datatypes for Fields.Append Method

Constant	Description
adDouble	Double-precision floating-point number
adError	32-bit error code
adFileTime	64-bit file time stamp
adGUID	Globally unique identifier
adInteger	4-byte signed integer
adNumeric	Decimal with fixed precision and scale
adSingle	Single-precision floating-point number
adSmallInt	2-byte signed integer
adTinyInt	1-byte signed integer
adUnsignedBigInt	8-byte unsigned integer
adUnsignedInt	4-byte unsigned integer
adUnsignedSmallInt	2-byte unsigned integer
adUnsignedTinyInt	1-byte unsigned integer
adUserDefined	User-defined data type (UDT)
adVarWChar	Null-terminated Unicode character string
adWChar	Null-terminated Unicode character string

TIP

There are other datatypes that cannot be used when defining fields in a synthetic Recordset. These include adArray, adChapter, adIDispatch, adEmpty, adIUnknown, adLongVarBinary, adLongVarChar, adLongVarWChar, adPropVariant, adVarBinary, adVarChar, adVariant, and adVarNumeric.

For decimal fields (defined with adDecimal or adNumeric), you should also set the NumericScale and Precision properties to indicate the number of digits to the right of the decimal point and the total number of digits that the field will hold.

TABLE 8.2: Field Attribute Constants

Constant	Description
adFldFixed	Field contains fixed-length data.
adFldIsNullable	Field can contain Null values.
adFldLong	Long binary field, accessible via GetChunk and AppendChunk methods.
adFldMayBeNull	Field can contain Null values.
adFldNegativeScale	Decimal field where the Scale value may be negative.
adFldUpdatable	Field can be updated (default).

TIP There are attribute constants that don't apply to fields in a synthetic Recordset. These include adFldCacheDeferred, adFldIsChapter, adFldIsCollection, adFldIsDefaultStream, adFldIsRowURL, adFldMayDefer, adFldRowID, adFldRowVersion, and adFldUnknownUpdatable.

You can append fields only to a Recordset that hasn't been opened and isn't connected to a data source.

Remote Data Service

The Remote Data Service (RDS) is another technology designed to allow you to work with data without having a direct Connection to the Recordset. When using RDS, your connection to the data is indirect, with a web server acting as a proxy to send requests and data in both directions. RDS is a mixed client-and-server technology. Some of the RDS components run on the client, while others must be installed on a web server that also hosts the database from which you're retrieving information.

There are a variety of ways in which you can use RDS, ranging from the simple use of a disconnected Recordset to complex scenarios involving custom server-side objects. In this section, I'll explore the use of RDS in a variety of scenarios.

WARNING Older versions of RDS interacted with older versions of Internet Information Server to produce a severe security hole. If you're running RDS with IIS 4, you need to read Microsoft Security Bulletin MS99-025, available at www.microsoft.com/technet/security/bulletin/MS99-025.asp.

Examining RDS

The basic idea of RDS is to enable the use of Hypertext Transfer Protocol (HTTP), one of the major transmission protocols of the Internet, between the client application and a middleware layer. In this case, the middleware layer consists of Microsoft Internet Information Server (IIS). IIS, in turn, uses server-side RDS components to query the database and return results to the client. Since HTTP is a *stateless* protocol (meaning that one HTTP message knows nothing about the messages that have come before), RDS is best suited for use with a disconnected Recordset. Typically, an RDS client program will retrieve results into a local Recordset, disconnect that Recordset from the server, and later reconnect the Recordset to send back updates (if necessary). Figure 8.4 shows the basic RDS process.

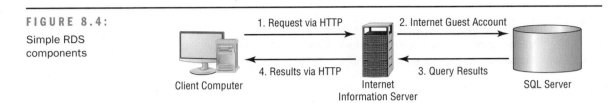

FIGURE 8.4:

Simple RDS components

1. Request via HTTP

4. Results via HTTP

Client Computer

2. Internet Guest Account

3. Query Results

Internet
Information Server

SQL Server

Because RDS involves components spread across multiple computers, it can be difficult to set up. The biggest configuration headache is probably security. You could embed a username and password in your client application, but often that's not an acceptable way to proceed, particularly if the application is going to be using a web page over the Internet to connect to your data. More likely, you'll want to handle security completely on the server. Assuming you're using the SQL Server OLE DB provider, here are some things to keep in mind:

- The SQL Server software and the IIS software must be installed and running on the same computer. The database, of course, can be elsewhere on your network (on any computer that the SQL Server can access).

- You need to enable anonymous access on the web server. To do this, follow these steps:

   1. Open the Internet Service Manager and select Properties for the website that will be used to access the data.

   2. Choose the Directory Security tab and click the Edit button in the Anonymous Access and Authentication Control section.

   3. Select the Allow Anonymous Access check box and click the Edit button for the account used.

   4. Select the Internet guest account, which will be an account starting with IUSR (for example, for the web server STALLION, this account is IUSR_STALLION). Check the Allow IIS to Control Password check box. This ensures that Windows will recognize the account as a valid domain account.

- You need to make sure your client computers can use the files in the MSADC folder on the web server. By default, these files are locked down so that they cannot be used from client computers. To do this, follow these steps:

   1. In the Internet Service Manager, select Properties for the MSADC virtual directory within your website.

   2. Navigate to the Directory Security tab. Click the Edit button for IP Address and Domain Name Restrictions.

   3. You can choose to grant access to all computers, or you can add the IP address of a specific computer or group of computers to the list of allowed computers.

- You also need to make sure the web account has the permission to log on locally, so that it can get to your SQL Server databases. You'll need to use the Local Security Policy application to check this if you're using Windows 2000; refer to the Windows 2000 documentation for details.

- You also need to tell SQL Server that this account should be allowed to retrieve data. Follow these steps:

    1. In SQL Enterprise Manager, expand the Security folder and click the Logins node.

    2. Right-click this node and choose New Login. Type in the domain and name of the Internet guest account (for example, for a server named STALLION in a domain named CANYON, enter CANYON\IUSR_STALLION), click the option button for Windows NT Authentication, choose your domain, and select the Grant Access option button.

    3. Select the default database from which you're going to retrieve data. Then select the Database Access tab and check all databases that you want to access over the Internet. SQL Server shows this as granting access for the login, but, of course, you know that this login will represent connections from the Internet.

- Finally, you need to specify that when you send the original RDS request, the server should use Windows NT Integrated Security rather than SQL Server security. This ensures that all the work you've done to set up the operating system account as a SQL Server user is worthwhile. To do this, include `Integrated Security=SSPI` in your OLE DB connection string.

> **NOTE**
>
> To test the sample code, I used Internet Information Services 5 and SQL Server 2000 running on Windows 2000 Advanced Server. Other combinations of IIS, SQL Server, and Windows will also work with RDS, although you may find that some of the user interface options are slightly different from those documented above.

Once everything is set up, the easiest way to check your work is to actually retrieve and change some data from the server. I'll show you three ways to do this, in order of increasing complexity:

- Using a disconnected Recordset
- Using the RDS.DataControl object
- Using a custom business object

Using RDS Handlers

Earlier versions of RDS had severe security problems, because they allowed users to execute arbitrary SQL statements against the database. By accepting SQL statements over HTTP,

RDS opened servers to a variety of attacks. As a trivial example, someone could locate a computer that accepted RDS connections and then send it a DROP TABLE statement to destroy a table on the SQL Server.

RDS 2.0 and later versions add the concept of *RDS handlers* to put an end to this vulnerability. RDS handlers allow clients across the Internet to execute only certain specified commands. They work by assigning keywords to represent connection strings and SQL statements, and then checking for those keywords in the RDS commands. Only SQL statements corresponding to the keywords set up by the system administrator will be executed; the server will reject any attempt to execute arbitrary SQL statements.

RDS handlers are specified by a file named msdfmap.ini, which you will find in your systemroot directory (usually, c:\winnt). Listing 8.8 shows the default msdfmap.ini file from a clean installation of Windows 2000 Advanced Server.

Listing 8.8: **msdfmap.ini**

```
;[connect name] will modify the connection if ADC.connect="name"
;[connect default] will modify the connection if name is not found
;[sql name] will modify the Sql if ADC.sql="name(args)"
;[sql default] will modify m Sql if name is not found
;Override strings: Connect, UserId, Password, Sql.
;Only the Sql strings support parameters using "?"
;The override strings must not equal "" or they are ignored
;A Sql entry must exist in each sql section or the section is ignored
;An Access entry must exist in each connect section or the section is ignored
;Access=NoAccess
;Access=ReadOnly
;Access=ReadWrite
;[userlist name] allows specific users to have special access
;The Access is computed as follows:
;   (1) First take the access of the connect section.
;   (2) If a user entry is found, it will override.

[connect default]

;If we want to disable unknown connect values, we set Access to NoAccess.
Access=NoAccess

[sql default]
;If we want to disable unknown sql values, we set Sql to an invalid query.
Sql=" "

[connect CustomerDatabase]
Access=ReadWrite
Connect="DSN=AdvWorks"
```

```
[sql CustomerById]
Sql="SELECT * FROM Customers WHERE CustomerID = ?"

[connect AuthorDatabase]
Access=ReadOnly
Connect="DSN=MyLibraryInfo;UID=MyUserID;PWD=MyPassword"

[userlist AuthorDatabase]
Administrator=ReadWrite

[sql AuthorById]
Sql="SELECT * FROM Authors WHERE au_id = ?"
```

As you can see, there are three types of entries in this file. Connect entries control which databases can be accessed via RDS. Userlist entries set security on a user-by-user basis. SQL entries provide aliases for SQL commands.

For example, to connect to the AdvWorks sample database via a Data Source Name (DSN)—which, being stored on the server, could contain username and password information—you'd use a connection string similar to this:

```
cnn.Open "Provider=MS Remote;" & _
  "Remote Server=http://STALLION;" & _
  "Handler=MSDFMAP.Handler;" & _
  "Data Source=CustomerDatabase"
```

When RDS receives this connection string, it will expand the Data Source parameter to the replacement value of "DSN=AdvWorks". Similarly, you could open a Recordset with information from the Customers table with this statement:

```
Rst.Open "CustomerById"
```

If you don't need the security provided by RDS handlers, you can edit the msdfmap.ini file to allow read/write access by default and to pass through all SQL statements. Just change the default sections of the file to the following:

```
[connect default]
;If we want to disable unknown connect values, we set Access to NoAccess.
Access=ReadWrite

[sql default]
;If we want to disable unknown sql values, we set Sql to an invalid query.
;Sql=" "
```

This is inherently unsafe and should be done only on a server that is solely used on an intranet, with no Internet connection at all.

Using a Disconnected Recordset

The frmMSRemote form in the ADOChapter8 sample project demonstrates the most basic way to use RDS:

1. Fetch a Recordset using the MSRemote OLE DB provider.

2. Disconnect the Recordset from its data source.

3. Reconnect the Recordset if changes are to be saved.

The MSRemote OLE DB provider doesn't connect directly to a data source itself. Instead, it takes the Internet name of another computer and a connection string that's valid on that computer (if you have disabled RDS handlers) or the keyword for a connect handler. MSRemote looks for IIS on the other computer, sends it the connection string, and lets IIS make the connection using OLE DB on its own computer. Thus, for this sample, the connection string is as follows:

```
"Provider=MS Remote;" & _
  "Remote Server=http://STALLION;" & _
  "Handler=MSDFMAP.Handler;" & _
  "Data Source=frmMSRemote"
```

To make this sample work, you'll need to change STALLION to the name of your test server. You'll also need to add two sections to the msdfmap.ini file on your server:

```
[connect frmMSRemote]
Access=ReadWrite
Connect="Provider=SQLOLEDB;Data Source=(local);
➥ Database=Northwind;Integrated Security=SSPI"

[sql frmMSRemote]
sql="SELECT * FROM Customers"
```

Here, the Remote Server option is the only thing that the MSRemote provider processes. The provider takes the rest of the OLE DB connection string and passes it off to the IIS server running at that address. The server-side RDS components then use the msdfmap.ini file to translate the handler name into an actual OLE DB connection string. You'll see that the result is a standard connection string for the SQL Server OLE DB provider. Note the use of the Integrated Security option, as discussed earlier in the chapter.

Listing 8.9 shows the code used for fetching the data.

Listing 8.9:   **Fetching Data via RDS**

```
Private mrstCustomers As New ADOR.Recordset
Private Sub Form_Load()
    Dim cnn As New ADODB.Connection
    ' Connect to the server
    cnn.Open "Provider=MS Remote;" & _
      "Remote Server=http://STALLION;" & _
```

```
        "Handler=MSDFMAP.Handler;" & _
        "Data Source=frmMSRemote"
        ' Set the Recordset options
        Set mrstCustomers.ActiveConnection = cnn
        mrstCustomers.Source = "frmMSRemote"
        mrstCustomers.CursorLocation = adUseClient
        mrstCustomers.CursorType = adOpenStatic
        mrstCustomers.LockType = adLockBatchOptimistic
        ' Open the Recordset
        mrstCustomers.Open
        ' Set the marshalling option
        mrstCustomers.MarshalOptions = _
         adMarshalModifiedOnly
        ' Disconnect the Recordset
        Set mrstCustomers.ActiveConnection = Nothing
        cnn.Close
        Set cnn = Nothing
        ' Load the data to the UI
        LoadData
        mfLoaded = True
End Sub

Private Sub LoadData()
        ' Move the current Recordset row to the form
        mfLoaded = False
        With mrstCustomers
            txtCustomerID = .Fields("CustomerID") & ""
            txtCompanyName = .Fields("CompanyName") & ""
            txtContactName = .Fields("ContactName") & ""
            txtContactTitle = .Fields("ContactTitle") & ""
            txtAddress = .Fields("Address") & ""
            txtCity = .Fields("City") & ""
            txtRegion = .Fields("Region") & ""
            txtPostalCode = .Fields("PostalCode") & ""
            txtCountry = .Fields("Country") & ""
            txtPhone = .Fields("Phone") & ""
            txtFax = .Fields("Fax") & ""
            ' And update the record counter
            txtRecord = .AbsolutePosition & " of " & _
              .RecordCount
        End With
        mfLoaded = True
End Sub
```

There are a few points of interest here. First, you'll notice that the Recordset object is declared as ADOR.Recordset instead of ADODB.Recordset. ADOR is the ProgID for the Microsoft ActiveX Data Objects Recordset library. This library matches the regular ADO library precisely for the Recordset object, but it contains no other objects. In a client program that doesn't need other ADO objects, this can save you a bit of overhead. (Of course, here it's used only for demonstration, since the Connection object comes from the regular ADO library.)

Next, you can see the steps necessary to create a disconnected Recordset:

1. Open a Connection to the data source (in this case, using the MS Remote OLE DB provider).

2. Set the ActiveConnection property of the Recordset to use this Connection.

3. Set the Source property of the Recordset to the name of an RDS SQL handler from the msdfmap.ini file.

4. Set other properties of the Recordset to control what type of cursor you'll get. Note that with a disconnected Recordset, even if you call for a dynamic or keyset cursor, you'll receive a static cursor, since there's no way for a disconnected Recordset to receive updates from other users. You must choose client-side cursors, since you're not going to remain connected to the server.

5. Be sure to set the lock type to adLockBatchOptimistic. If you neglect this step, even though the disconnected Recordset will cache multiple changes locally, it will save only a single change (at most) to the server and you won't get any error messages about the other changes being lost. If you don't specify a lock type, you won't be able to make any changes to the Recordset at all.

6. Open the Recordset.

7. Set the MarshalOptions property to adMarshalModifiedOnly. This tells ADO to send only changed records to the server when you reconnect, rather than every record, and will vastly speed up operations.

8. Set the ActiveConnection property to Nothing and close the Connection (this is what makes it a disconnected Recordset). Although you may think this step would invalidate the Recordset, what it does, in fact, is to keep the Recordset in client-side memory.

Once you've got such a Recordset, you can work with it just as you would with any other Recordset. For example, there are no surprises in the record navigation code, nor in the code that saves changes from the user interface back to the Recordset. You can see this code in Listing 8.10.

Listing 8.10:   Code for Navigation and Saving Data

```
Private Sub cmdFirst_Click()
    mrstCustomers.MoveFirst
    LoadData
End Sub

Private Sub cmdLast_Click()
    mrstCustomers.MoveLast
    LoadData
End Sub
```

```
Private Sub cmdNext_Click()
    If Not mrstCustomers.EOF Then
        mrstCustomers.MoveNext
        If mrstCustomers.EOF Then
            mrstCustomers.MoveLast
        End If
    End If
    LoadData
End Sub

Private Sub cmdPrevious_Click()
    If Not mrstCustomers.BOF Then
        mrstCustomers.MovePrevious
        If mrstCustomers.BOF Then
            mrstCustomers.MoveFirst
        End If
    End If
    LoadData
End Sub
Private Sub txtAddress_Change()
    ' Write changes to the Recordset
    If mfLoaded Then
        mrstCustomers.Fields("Address") = _
         txtAddress.Text & ""
        mfDirty = True
        cmdSaveChanges.Enabled = True
    End If
End Sub
' Code for other textbox change events is similar
```

Figure 8.5 shows the frmMSRemote form with data loaded.

FIGURE 8.5:

Editing a disconnected Recordset

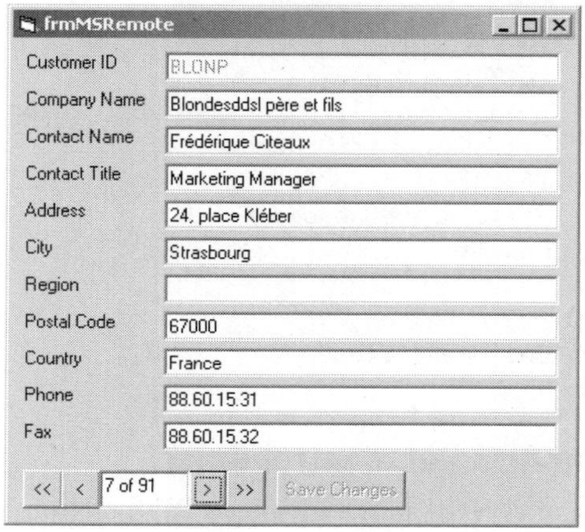

To save changes back to the server, you simply open a fresh Connection and assign the Recordset's ActiveConnection property back to that Connection:

```
Private Sub cmdSaveChanges_Click()
    Dim cnn As New ADODB.Connection
    mfLoaded = False
    ' Reconnect to the server
    cnn.Open "Provider=MS Remote;" & _
      "Remote Server=http://STALLION;" & _
      "Handler=MSDFMAP.Handler;" & _
      "Data Source=frmMSRemote"
    Set mrstCustomers.ActiveConnection = cnn
    mrstCustomers.UpdateBatch
    mfDirty = False
    cmdSaveChanges.Enabled = False
    ' Need to update the client Recordset
' before disconnecting again
    mrstCustomers.Resync
    LoadData
    Set mrstCustomers.ActiveConnection = Nothing
    cnn.Close
    Set cnn = Nothing
    mfLoaded = True
End Sub
```

Finally, the frmMSRemote form in this chapter's sample project implements a warning on the form's QueryUnload event, since it's possible for the user to attempt to close the form with multiple data changes pending:

```
Private Sub Form_QueryUnload(Cancel As Integer, _
  UnloadMode As Integer)
    Dim intRet As Integer
    If mfDirty Then
        intRet = MsgBox( _
          "Would you like to save your changes?", _
          vbYesNo, "frmMSRemote")
        If intRet = vbYes Then
            cmdSaveChanges_Click
        End If
    End If
    mfDirty = False
    mrstCustomers.Close
End Sub
```

Using the RDS.DataControl Object

To continue with the more advanced RDS techniques, you need to be sure that the Microsoft Remote Data Services library is loaded (under Project ➤ References, of course). This library provides two objects of interest. You'll learn about the RDS.DataSpace object in the next section of this chapter. Now, though, it's time to look at the RDS.DataControl object, which provides a bindable, remotable source of data. You can see this object in action on the frmRemoteDataControl form in this chapter's sample project.

This form uses the RDS.DataControl object (which, despite the name, is not a user interface control but an object that you manipulate in code) along with the Visual Basic BindingCollection object to open a Recordset and bind it to user interface controls. Listing 8.11 shows this code.

Listing 8.11: **Binding to an RDS.DataControl Object**

```
' Bindable source for the Recordset
Private mdc As RDS.DataControl
' Bindings for this source
Private mBindCol As BindingCollection

Private Sub Form_Load()
    ' Initialize the data control
    Set mdc = New RDS.DataControl
    With mdc
        .Connect = "Handler=MSDFMAP.Handler;" & _
    "Data Source=frmMSRemote"
        .Server = "http://STALLION"
        .SQL = "frmMSRemote"
        .ExecuteOptions = adcExecAsync
        .Refresh
        Do While .ReadyState = adcReadyStateLoaded
            DoEvents
        Loop
    End With
    ' And bind it to the UI
    Set mBindCol = New BindingCollection
    With mBindCol
        Set .DataSource = mdc
        .Add txtCustomerID, "Text", "CustomerID"
        .Add txtCompanyName, "Text", "CompanyName"
        .Add txtContactName, "Text", "ContactName"
        .Add txtContactTitle, "Text", "ContactTitle"
        .Add txtAddress, "Text", "Address"
        .Add txtCity, "Text", "City"
        .Add txtRegion, "Text", "Region"
        .Add txtPostalCode, "Text", "PostalCode"
        .Add txtCountry, "Text", "Country"
        .Add txtPhone, "Text", "Phone"
        .Add txtFax, "Text", "Fax"
    End With
    txtRecord = mdc.Recordset.AbsolutePosition & _
        " of " & mdc.Recordset.RecordCount
    mfLoaded = True
End Sub
```

As you can see, you need to set a few properties of this "control" (actually an object in memory, not something you can place directly on a form) before using it:

- The Connect property holds the handler information that will be used to connect to the database.

- The SQL property holds a SQL handler to be translated into a SQL statement on the server.

- The Server property holds the Internet address of the IIS server that will handle creating the Recordset.

- The ExecuteOptions property can be set (as it is here) for asynchronous operation, so that the user could proceed with another operation if the data took a long time to fetch.

Once you've called the DataControl's Refresh method, you're all set. You just create a new BindingCollection object and use it to bind form fields to Recordset fields, and you've automatically got a bound, updatable, disconnected Recordset. The DataControl disconnects the Recordset automatically because it has been fetched via the stateless HTTP protocol.

NOTE   The BindingCollection object provides a general-purpose method for connecting fields in a Recordset to properties of user interface controls. For more information on this object, see the Visual Basic online help files.

Record navigation is done by calling the standard methods of the DataControl's exposed Recordset object, as shown in Listing 8.12.

Listing 8.12:   **Navigating with the RDS.Datacontrol**

```
Private Sub cmdFirst_Click()
    mfLoaded = False
    mdc.Recordset.MoveFirst
    txtRecord = mdc.Recordset.AbsolutePosition & _
     " of " & mdc.Recordset.RecordCount
    mfLoaded = True
End Sub

Private Sub cmdLast_Click()
    mfLoaded = False
    mdc.Recordset.MoveLast
    txtRecord = mdc.Recordset.AbsolutePosition & _
     " of " & mdc.Recordset.RecordCount
    mfLoaded = True
End Sub

Private Sub cmdNext_Click()
    mfLoaded = False
```

```
        If Not mdc.Recordset.EOF Then
            mdc.Recordset.MoveNext
            If mdc.Recordset.EOF Then
                mdc.Recordset.MoveLast
            End If
        End If
        txtRecord = mdc.Recordset.AbsolutePosition & _
        " of " & mdc.Recordset.RecordCount
        mfLoaded = True
    End Sub

    Private Sub cmdPrevious_Click()
        mfLoaded = False
        If Not mdc.Recordset.BOF Then
            mdc.Recordset.MovePrevious
            If mdc.Recordset.BOF Then
                mdc.Recordset.MoveFirst
            End If
        End If
        txtRecord = mdc.Recordset.AbsolutePosition & _
        " of " & mdc.Recordset.RecordCount
        mfLoaded = True
    End Sub
```

Because this Recordset is disconnected, you must explicitly save any changes back to the server before destroying the Recordset. The DataControl object wraps the entire reconnect-and-save operation in a single method named SubmitChanges, so you don't have to handle the details yourself. Once again, the form includes code to help prevent the user from inadvertently losing changes by closing the form before saving the Recordset:

```
    Private Sub cmdSaveChanges_Click()
        mdc.SubmitChanges
        mfDirty = False
    End Sub
    Private Sub Form_QueryUnload(Cancel As Integer, _
      UnloadMode As Integer)
        Dim intRet As Integer
        If mfDirty Then
            intRet = MsgBox( _
              "Would you like to save your changes?", _
              vbYesNo, "frmMSRemote")
            If intRet = vbYes Then
                cmdSaveChanges_Click
            End If
        End If
        mfDirty = False
    End Sub
```

Invoking Business Objects on the Server

The DataControl does its work through a piece of server-side code called the DataFactory. This piece of code knows how to open Recordsets based on SQL strings. The most interesting (and advanced) use of RDS is for replacing the default DataFactory with your own object. This server-side business object can use whatever logic you wish to program in order to return data to the client via RDS.

To use a custom business object, you need to use the RDS DataSpace object. This object supports a CreateObject method:

```
DataSpace.CreateObject(ProgID, ServerName)
```

Look familiar? The syntax of DataSpace.CreateObject is similar to that of the intrinsic Visual Basic CreateObject function, with the addition of an argument to specify the server. By explicitly invoking the DataSpace object, you can create your own server-side business objects and use them to retrieve data into disconnected Recordsets via HTTP, employing the rest of the RDS services.

Here are a few points to keep in mind when using custom business objects:

- If you attempt to create an object on a server that doesn't exist or can't be reached, you'll get an error on the DataSpace.CreateObject method.

- If you attempt to create an unknown or unusable object, the DataSpace.CreateObject method will still proceed happily without error. But the first time you attempt to use a method of the object, you'll get an error.

- All objects created in this way are late-bound. Since you're connecting to the object over the Internet, the usual slight performance degradation to late-binding doesn't really matter. On the positive side, this means that you don't need the TypeLib for the custom object to be installed on the client.

- Because the remoting is done over the stateless HTTP protocol, there's no way to have persistent properties in a business object that's used by RDS. Each time you call a method from a custom business object, the object is recreated on the server.

In order for a custom business object to be usable from RDS, you have to tell IIS that the object is safe to launch. This requires creating a key in the Registry:

```
HKEY_LOCAL_MACHINE
 \SYSTEM
  \CurrentControlSet
   \Services
   \W3SVC
    \Parameters
    \ADCLaunch
    \MyServer.MyObject
```

Obviously, you replace *MyServer.MyObject* with the actual ProgID and ClsID of your custom business object.

For an example of this technique, look at frmCustomObject in this chapter's sample project. In order for this sample to work, you'll need to build the RDSServerDemo project on the computer that's running IIS and SQL Server (or build it on another computer and use the Visual Basic Package and Deploy Wizard to install it). You'll also need to run the RDSServerDemo.reg file to create the launch permissions key in the Registry.

WARNING If you're debugging a business object, you'll find that IIS doesn't release the DLL once it's loaded. In order to make changes and recompile, you'll need to use the Services administrative tool to stop and restart the World Wide Web publishing service.

The frmCustomObject sample form starts by creating an object of the appropriate custom class, and then calls its GetCountries method to retrieve a list of countries. It then lets the user select a country and retrieves the records from that country:

```
Private Sub Form_Load()
    ' Create a DataFactory object on the server
    Set mdf = mds.CreateObject("RDSServerDemo.DataFactory", _
     "http://STALLION")
    Set mrstCountries = mdf.GetCountries
    Do Until mrstCountries.EOF
        lboCountry.AddItem mrstCountries.Fields("Country")
        mrstCountries.MoveNext
    Loop
End Sub
Private Sub lboCountry_Click()
    Dim ctl As Control
    ' Use the DataFactory to grab a Recordset
    Set mrstCustomers = mdf.GetCustomers(lboCountry.Text)
    ' Initialize the data control
    Set mdc = New RDS.DataControl
    Set mdc.SourceRecordset = mrstCustomers
    ' And bind it to the UI
    Set mBindCol = New BindingCollection
    With mBindCol
        Set .DataSource = mdc
        .Add txtCustomerID, "Text", "CustomerID"
        .Add txtCompanyName, "Text", "CompanyName"
        .Add txtContactName, "Text", "ContactName"
        .Add txtContactTitle, "Text", "ContactTitle"
        .Add txtAddress, "Text", "Address"
        .Add txtCity, "Text", "City"
        .Add txtRegion, "Text", "Region"
```

```
        .Add txtPostalCode, "Text", "PostalCode"
        .Add txtCountry, "Text", "Country"
        .Add txtPhone, "Text", "Phone"
        .Add txtFax, "Text", "Fax"
    End With
    txtRecord = mdc.Recordset.AbsolutePosition & _
        " of " & mdc.Recordset.RecordCount
    mfLoaded = True
    For Each ctl In Me.Controls
        ctl.Enabled = True
    Next ctl
    txtCustomerID.Enabled = False
    cmdSaveChanges.Enabled = False
End Sub
```

Figure 8.6 shows this form with the customers from Brazil loaded.

FIGURE 8.6:

Retrieving data with
a custom business
object

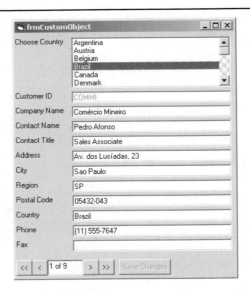

As you can see, once you've created a data factory object of any class, you can call its methods just as you call any other object method in Visual Basic. When there are changes to return, the client program just sends the entire changed Recordset back to the server. This is necessary, of course, because the business object is stateless.

```
Private Sub cmdSaveChanges_Click()
    mdf.SubmitChanges mrstCustomers
    mfDirty = False
End Sub
```

The business object itself is implemented in an ActiveX DLL with a single class. That class exposes four methods. First, there is one that's not used at all in the sample code:

```
Const conVersion = "1.00"

Public Function Version() As String
    ' Calling this method provides an easy way to
    ' test proper business object registration
    Version = conVersion
End Function
```

Providing a simple method like this in your custom business classes allows you to check quickly whether you've got the connection to the class set up and everything registered properly. You can use the DataSpace object's CreateObject method to create the class, then display its Version method. If you get the hard-coded string back, all is well. If not, something's not right (perhaps you forgot to give the object launch permissions?).

The GetCountries method returns a list of all the values of the Country field in the Customers table in the Northwind database on the local server:

```
Public Function GetCountries() As ADODB.Recordset
    ' Return all countries in the table
    Dim cn As New ADODB.Connection
    Dim rst As New ADODB.Recordset

    cn.CursorLocation = adUseClient
    cn.Open "Provider=SQLOLEDB;" & _
      "Data Source=(local);" & _
      "Initial Catalog=Northwind;" & _
      "Integrated Security=SSPI"

    rst.Open _
      "SELECT Country From Customers GROUP BY Country", _
      cn, adOpenKeyset, adLockBatchOptimistic

    Set GetCountries = rst
    Set rst.ActiveConnection = Nothing
End Function
```

Although the client program assigns the result of this function to an ADOR Recordset, the function itself uses an ADODB Recordset. That's because the business object has to have the entire ADO library loaded so that it can use the Connection object. Fortunately, there's no problem in assigning the two types of Recordsets back and forth.

You'll see that the function does the entire work of opening and connecting to the database itself. Obviously, you could use code here to specify a database user with higher privileges than you want to give to the Internet guest account.

Note also that although the Recordset is disconnected within the function, the Connection is left open. This is necessary, because if you closed the Connection, the Recordset would close, too! Everything gets cleaned up neatly at the end of the function.

When the client program calls GetCustomers with the name of a country, the server executes a query to retrieve just those customers:

```
Public Function GetCustomers(strCountry As String) _
  As ADODB.Recordset
    ' Return all customers in the specified country
    Dim cn As New ADODB.Connection
    Dim rst As New ADODB.Recordset

    cn.CursorLocation = adUseClient
    cn.Open "Provider=SQLOLEDB;" & _
      "Data Source=(local);" & _
      "Initial Catalog=Northwind;" & _
      "Integrated Security=SSPI"

    rst.Open "SELECT * From Customers WHERE Country = '" & _
      strCountry & "'", cn, adOpenKeyset, _
      adLockBatchOptimistic

    Set GetCustomers = rst
    Set rst.ActiveConnection = Nothing
End Function
```

Finally, the code used to submit changes is also simple:

```
Public Function SubmitChanges( _
  rstCustomers As ADODB.Recordset)

    Dim cn As New ADODB.Connection
    Dim rst As New ADODB.Recordset

    cn.CursorLocation = adUseClient
    cn.Open "Provider=SQLOLEDB;" & _
      "Data Source=(local);" & _
      "Initial Catalog=Northwind;" & _
      "Integrated Security=SSPI"

    rst.Open rstCustomers, cn
    rst.UpdateBatch
    rst.Close
    Set rst = Nothing
    cn.Close
    Set cn = Nothing
End Function
```

Opening a Recordset using an existing Recordset as the source and a specified Connection has the effect of reconnecting the disconnected Recordset that was shipped in from the client. Because the client is using changed records marshalling, this Recordset will contain only the updated records, rather than all the records that were originally sent out. If you needed to do some sort of custom conflict resolution between multiple users, this function would be the place for the code.

This example just scratches the surface of what you can do with a custom business object that's instantiated via RDS. As the name suggests, such objects are a good place to implement business rules for distributed applications. For example, if you used such an object to return a list of customers, you could check credit ratings when edited customers were returned and take action based on the ratings. Such rules would be enforced no matter what client created the objects.

Using ADO in Multitiered Applications

Disconnected Recordsets provide an ideal way to use ADO in multitiered applications. By shipping Recordsets between tiers, instead of simpler pieces of data, you can take advantage of bound controls, grids, and other user interface standards to present a rich editing experience without the overhead of a constant distributed Connection to a database server.

For example, consider a simple order-taking application with these requirements:

- Agents are presented with a list of all active customers.

- When agents select a customer, they receive all of that customer's past orders.

- Agents can edit past orders or enter new orders.

- Because customers have a single purchasing agent, it's unlikely that two agents will take orders from the same customer simultaneously.

This application could be implemented with a traditional three-tier division of the application into a database, a business object layer, and a user interface layer.

The database layer stores the customer and order information. It includes two stored procedures. The first one, spGetCustomers, returns a Recordset consisting of all customers. The second stored procedure, spGetOrders, takes a customer ID as an input parameter and returns all orders for that customer.

The business layer uses the spGetCustomers stored procedure to construct a Recordset of customer names. This Recordset can be disconnected immediately from the database, because there are no provisions for updating customers from within this application.

When the user interface layer is started, it first creates an object in the business layer and then retrieves the Recordset of customer names. Because this is a disconnected Recordset, it can be passed between the business and user interface layers by a number of means, including direct COM communication or as an XML file. When the agent selects a customer to work with, the user interface layer sets a property of an object in the business layer to that customer's customer ID.

The business layer can then use the spGetOrders stored procedure to retrieve the orders for the selected customer into a second disconnected Recordset. This Recordset of orders can be passed, in turn, to the user interface layer, where the agent can interact with the data that it contains. When the agent is ready to save changes, the user interface layer passes the Recordset back to the business layer, where it is reconnected to the database. At that point, the Recordset's UpdateBatch method can be used to save changes to existing orders and to persist new orders into the database.

Obviously, you can complicate this scenario as much as necessary. By using advanced technologies such as Microsoft Transaction Server (MTS), you could distribute the business layer across multiple servers. Note that it wouldn't even matter if a Recordset that was created on one business layer server were sent to a different business layer server to update; as long as both servers can see the same database, it doesn't matter where the Recordset is located when the updates are made. You could also use RDS with a web server between any pair of tiers in this model, thus potentially distributing the application across the entire Internet.

> **NOTE** The .NET Framework includes extensive support for disconnected data editing, but it doesn't use RDS as a part of this support. For new applications, you should consider using .NET instead of RDS. You'll find the details of the .NET way of handing disconnected data in Chapter 16, "Working with Disconnected DataSets."

Summary

In this chapter, you learned about the disconnected Recordset capabilities of ADO. You saw how optimistic batch updating makes it possible to queue up multiple edits on the client without loading up the server. You also learned how to use synthetic Recordsets to hold any data you want to work with, whether the data is in a traditional database or elsewhere. You also saw that the Remote Data Service, RDS, provides a flexible way to move disconnected Recordsets over Internet and intranet links.

So far, most of what you've done with ADO has been data manipulation: adding, editing, or deleting data. However, ADO also provides facilities for data definition—for example, adding or deleting columns in a table. These facilities are contained in the ADOX library, which is the subject of the next chapter.

CHAPTER 9

Using ADOX for Data Definition and Security Operations

- The ADOX object model

- The limitations of ADOX

- Creating new database objects

- Using the Procedure and View objects

- Manipulating database security

When Microsoft released ADO, the company made a deliberate break with past data access libraries such as DAO and RDO that tried to do everything. DAO, in particular, was marked by a proliferation of objects, properties, and methods that made the library very difficult to learn. With ADO, the basic data access library is stripped down to the essential objects needed to retrieve and manipulate data.

But there are times when you need functionality beyond that of the core ADO objects, and that's why the ADO developers came up with the notion of an extension library. An ADO extension library is a group of objects that act in concert with the core ADO objects to provide additional capabilities. By splitting functionality in this fashion, ADO can stay small and fast, while having the ability to grow for specific tasks.

In this chapter, I'll look at one of those extension libraries, the ADO Extensions for DDL and Security, more commonly called ADOX. (DDL stands for Data Definition Language, a standard set of SQL keywords for defining objects.) ADOX adds objects for manipulating the design of database objects, and for handling security issues, to the core ADO library.

The ADOX Object Model

Figure 9.1 shows the ADOX object model. Note that the Connection object isn't a part of the ADOX library. Rather, this is the standard ADO Connection object, which provides the hook by which ADOX integrates with ADO.

FIGURE 9.1:

The ADOX
object model

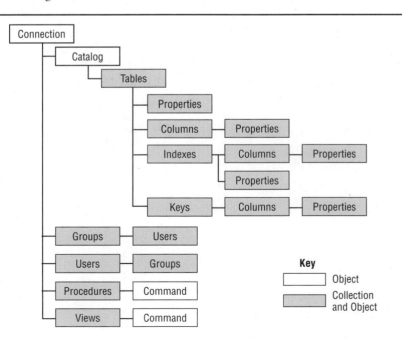

As you can see, ADOX has a more hierarchical orientation than ADO itself. Objects are arranged into collections, which are nested. For example, the Catalog object contains a collection named Tables, containing individual Table objects, each of which contains a collection named Columns, containing individual Column objects. Some of the objects in the ADOX hierarchy (Table, Index, and Column) have Properties collections containing the individual properties of the object. Other ADOX objects, such as the Catalog object, still have properties, but those properties are accessible only by name rather than through a collection.

In this section, I'll review the ADOX objects, along with some of their methods and properties. Because these objects are used for design work rather than interaction with data, they don't support any events.

Catalog

The Catalog object represents the schema (design information) of a data source. All your ADOX code will start by declaring and instantiating a Catalog object. You associate the Catalog object with an ADO Connection object by setting the Catalog's ActiveConnection property; this is what gives you access to the schema of a particular data source.

If you're working with Jet data, you can use the Catalog.Create method to create a new database. This method is not currently supported by any other OLE DB provider.

Table 9.1 shows some of the methods and properties of the Catalog object.

TABLE 9.1: Selected Methods and Properties of the Catalog Object

Name	Type	Description
ActiveConnection	Property	ADO Connection through which schema information is to be retrieved
Tables	Property	Pointer to the Tables collection
Views	Property	Pointer to the Views collection
Procedures	Property	Pointer to the Procedures collection
Users	Property	Pointer to the Users collection
Groups	Property	Pointer to the Groups collection
GetObjectOwner	Method	Determine the database user who owns a particular object
SetObjectOwner	Method	Specify the database user to own a particular object

The frmExplore form in the ADOChapter9 sample project uses module-level Connection and Catalog objects to establish a connection to a Jet data source. Listing 9.1 shows the code to do this.

Listing 9.1:   **Connecting with ADOX**

```
Dim mcat As ADOX.Catalog
Dim mcnn As ADODB.Connection

Private Sub cmdConnect_Click()

    Dim strConnect As String
    Dim tbl As ADOX.Table
    Dim prc As ADOX.Procedure
    Dim vw As ADOX.View

    On Error GoTo HandleErr

' Additional code omitted

    Set mcnn = New ADODB.Connection
    Set mcat = New ADOX.Catalog

    strConnect = "Provider=Microsoft.Jet.OLEDB.4.0;" & _
      "Data Source=" & txtDatabase.Text
    mcnn.Open strConnect
    Set mcat.ActiveConnection = mcnn

' Additional code omitted

ExitHere:
    Exit Sub

HandleErr:
    MsgBox "Error " & Err.Number & ": " & Err.Description, _
      vbOKOnly, "cmdConnect"
    Resume ExitHere
    Resume

End Sub
```

Table

As you might expect, the Table object represents a table in a database. Of course, things aren't quite that simple: A Table object might correspond to a system table, a temporary table, or something else entirely. In fact, the Jet provider even places queries without parameters into the Tables collection. The Type property of the Table object will return a string that tells you the general class of this particular object.

Table 9.2 shows some of the properties of the Table object. This object has no methods.

TABLE 9.2: Selected Properties of the Table Object

Name	Type	Description
DateCreated	Property	Original creation date and time of this Table
Columns	Property	Pointer to the Columns collection of the Table
Indexes	Property	Pointer to the Indexes collection of the Table
Keys	Property	Pointer to the Keys collection of the Table
ParentCatalog	Property	Pointer to the Catalog containing this Table
Type	Property	Type of the Table

On the frmExplore form, double-clicking the name of a table in the Tables listbox will open a form showing the properties of the Table object. The properties are retrieved and displayed with this code:

```
Private Sub lboTables_DblClick()

    Dim tbl As ADOX.Table
    Dim prp As ADOX.Property

    On Error GoTo HandleErr

    Load frmProperties
    frmProperties.lboProperties.Clear

    Set tbl = mcat.Tables(lboTables.Text)
    frmProperties.txtDateCreated = tbl.DateCreated
    frmProperties.txtDateModified = tbl.DateModified
    frmProperties.txtName = tbl.Name
    frmProperties.txtType = tbl.Type

    For Each prp In tbl.Properties
        frmProperties.lboProperties.AddItem prp.Name & ": " & prp.Value
    Next prp

    frmProperties.Show

    'Clean up
    Set tbl = Nothing
    Set prp = Nothing

ExitHere:
    Exit Sub

HandleErr:
```

```
MsgBox "Error " & Err.Number & ": " & Err.Description, _
  vbOKOnly, "lboTables_DblClick"
Resume ExitHere
Resume

End Sub
```

Figure 9.2 shows the results of running this code on one of the tables in the Northwind sample database.

FIGURE 9.2:

Retrieving the properties of a Jet table

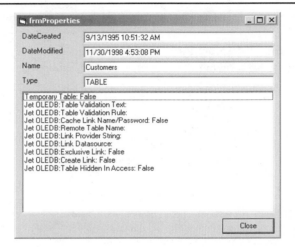

If you inspect the properties shown in Figure 9.2, you'll notice an odd thing: The default properties of a Table (DateCreated, DateModified, Name, and Type) do not show up in the Properties collection, even though the code in Listing 9.1 iterates through the entire collection. In fact, that's generally how ADOX works. Intrinsic properties that are provided by ADOX (such as Table.Name) must be retrieved by name. On the other hand, properties that are specific to an individual OLE DB provider must be retrieved from the Properties collection.

Column

The ADOX Column object represents a single column or field in a table, index, or key. Because of its general-purpose nature, not all Column properties apply to all instances of a Column object. For example, the RelatedColumn property is meaningful only for Columns that are part of Key objects.

Table 9.3 shows some of the properties of the Column object. This object has no methods.

TABLE 9.3: Selected Properties of the Column Object

Name	Type	Description
Name	Property	Name of this Column
Type	Property	Data type of the Column
Attributes	Property	Will return the value adColFixed for a fixed-length Column, adCol-Nullable if the Column can contain Null values, or the sum of these two constants for a fixed-length nullable Column
DefinedSize	Property	Maximum length of the Column
NumericScale	Property	Scale for a numeric Column
Precision	Property	Precision for a numeric Column

Figure 9.3 shows the properties of a Column from a table in a Jet database. Once again, you can see that the Properties collection contains only custom properties from the OLE DB provider (you can also see that the Jet provider doesn't use a consistent scheme for naming properties).

FIGURE 9.3:

Retrieving the properties of a Jet Column

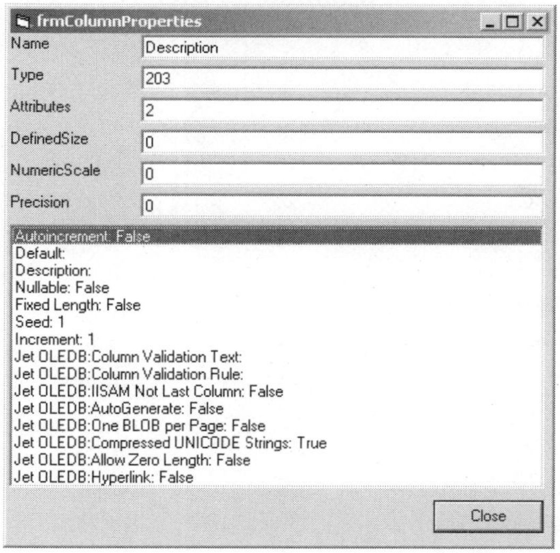

Table 9.4 shows the possible values for the Type property of a Column object.

TABLE 9.4: ADOX Datatypes for Column Objects

Constant	Value	Description
adBigInt	20	8-byte signed integer
adBinary	128	Raw binary data
adBoolean	11	Boolean
adBSTR	8	Null-terminated Unicode character string
adChar	129	Character string
adCurrency	6	Currency, stored with 4 digits to the right of the decimal point
adDate	7	Date/time
adDBDate	133	Date only, with no time value
adDBTime	134	Time only, with no date value
adDBTimeStamp	135	Time stamp
adDecimal	14	Decimal with fixed precision and scale
adDouble	5	Double-precision, floating-point number
adError	10	32-bit error code
adFileTime	64	64-bit file time stamp
adGUID	72	Globally unique identifier
adInteger	3	4-byte signed integer
adLongVarBinary	205	Long binary
adLongVarChar	201	Long string
adLongWVarChar	203	Long Unicode string
adNumeric	131	Decimal with fixed precision and scale
adSingle	4	Single-precision, floating-point number
adSmallInt	2	2-byte signed integer
adTinyInt	16	1-byte signed integer
adUnsignedBigInt	21	8-byte unsigned integer
adUnsignedInt	19	4-byte unsigned integer
adUnsignedSmallInt	18	2-byte unsigned integer
adUnsignedTinyInt	17	1-byte unsigned integer
adUserDefined	132	User-defined datatype (UDT)
adVarBinary	204	Binary
adVarChar	200	String
adVarNumeric	139	Numeric
adVarWChar	202	Null-terminated Unicode character string
adWChar	130	Null-terminated Unicode character string

Listing 9.2 shows a code sample demonstrating how frmExplore retrieves property values from a Column object.

Listing 9.2: **Retrieving the Properties of a Column**

```
Private Sub lboColumns_DblClick()

    Dim col As ADOX.Column
    Dim prp As ADOX.Property

    On Error GoTo HandleErr

    Load frmColumnProperties
    frmColumnProperties.lboProperties.Clear

    Set col = mcat.Tables(lboTables.Text).Columns(lboColumns.Text)

    frmColumnProperties.txtAttributes = col.Attributes
    frmColumnProperties.txtDefinedSize = col.DefinedSize
    frmColumnProperties.txtName = col.Name
    frmColumnProperties.txtType = col.Type
    frmColumnProperties.txtNumericScale = col.NumericScale
    frmColumnProperties.txtPrecision = col.Precision

    For Each prp In col.Properties
        frmColumnProperties.lboProperties.AddItem _
        prp.Name & ": " & prp.Value
    Next prp

    frmColumnProperties.Show

    'Clean up
    Set col = Nothing
    Set prp = Nothing

ExitHere:
    Exit Sub

HandleErr:
    MsgBox "Error " & Err.Number & ": " & Err.Description, _
    vbOKOnly, "lboColumns_DblClick"
    Resume ExitHere
    Resume

End Sub
```

Index

An ADOX Index object represents an index on a table. Like the Table and Column objects, the Index object has built-in ADOX properties as well as a collection of provider-supplied properties. Table 9.5 shows some of the properties of the Column object. This object has no methods.

TABLE 9.5: Selected Properties of the Index Object

Name	Type	Description
Name	Property	Name of this Index
Clustered	Property	True if this is a clustered Index
PrimaryKey	Property	True if this Index is the primary key of the Table
Unique	Property	True if values in this Index must be unique

Like the Table object, the Index object has a Columns collection. In addition to the properties you've already seen for Columns, Columns in an Index have a SortOrder property that indicates whether that portion of the index is sorted in ascending or descending order.

In this chapter's sample project, the frmExplore form uses code to retrieve the properties of a selected Index. You'll find this code in Listing 9.3.

Listing 9.3:   **Retrieving the Properties of an Index**

```
Private Sub lboIndexes_DblClick()

    Dim idx As ADOX.Index
    Dim prp As ADOX.Property

    On Error GoTo HandleErr

    Load frmIndexProperties
    frmIndexProperties.lboProperties.Clear

    Set idx = mcat.Tables(lboTables.Text).Indexes(lboIndexes.Text)

    frmIndexProperties.txtClustered = idx.Clustered
    frmIndexProperties.txtName = idx.Name
    frmIndexProperties.txtPrimaryKey = idx.PrimaryKey
    frmIndexProperties.txtUnique = idx.Unique

    For Each prp In idx.Properties
        frmIndexProperties.lboProperties.AddItem _
         prp.Name & ": " & prp.Value
    Next prp
```

```
    frmIndexProperties.Show

    'Clean up
    Set idx = Nothing
    Set prp = Nothing

ExitHere:
    Exit Sub

HandleErr:
    MsgBox "Error " & Err.Number & ": " & Err.Description, _
      vbOKOnly, "lboIndexes_DblClick"
    Resume ExitHere
    Resume

End Sub
```

NOTE   If you inspect the Properties collection of an Index in a Jet database, you'll discover some redundant properties. The Jet provider supplies properties named Clustered, Unique, and Primary Key (note the space), which are distinct from the built-in Clustered, Unique, and Primary-Key properties. Fortunately, the two sets of properties are always in sync.

Key

A Key object in ADOX represents a primary, foreign, or unique key on a table. Table 9.6 shows some of the properties of the Key object. This object has no methods.

TABLE 9.6: Selected Properties of the Key Object

Name	Type	Description
Name	Property	Name of this Key
Type	Property	A constant indicating whether this is a primary, foreign, or unique Key
RelatedTable	Property	Related table for a primary or foreign Key

Column objects within a Key object have a RelatedColumn property. This property is used in conjunction with the Key.RelatedTable property to specify the relationship between primary and foreign Keys.

Listing 9.4 shows the code that this chapter's sample project uses to retrieve properties of a Key.

Listing 9.4:　　　**Retrieving the Properties of a Key**

```
Private Sub lboKeys_DblClick()

    Dim key As ADOX.key
    Dim prp As ADOX.Property

    On Error GoTo HandleErr

    Load frmKeyProperties

    Set key = mcat.Tables(lboTables.Text).Keys(lboKeys.Text)

    frmKeyProperties.txtName = key.Name
    frmKeyProperties.txtRelatedTable = key.RelatedTable
    frmKeyProperties.txtType = key.Type

    frmKeyProperties.Show

    'Clean up
    Set key = Nothing
    Set prp = Nothing

ExitHere:
    Exit Sub

HandleErr:
    MsgBox "Error " & Err.Number & ": " & Err.Description, _
      vbOKOnly, "lboKeys_DblClick"
    Resume ExitHere
    Resume

End Sub
```

WARNING　　Key objects don't have a Properties collection. There is no way to set provider-defined properties on a Key.

Group

The ADOX Group object represents a single security group within a Jet database. Although the ADOX interface is designed to be general-purpose, only the Jet OLE DB provider, in fact, currently supports the Group (and User) objects. Later in this chapter, you'll see how to use the Group and User objects to manipulate security in a Jet database.

Table 9.7 shows the properties and methods of the Group object.

TABLE 9.7: Selected Properties and Methods of the Group Object

Name	Type	Description
Name	Property	Name of this Group
Users	Property	Pointer to a collection of Users in this Group
Properties	Property	Collection of provider-defined properties
GetPermissions	Method	Returns the current permissions of this Group on a database object
SetPermissions	Method	Sets the permissions of this Group on a database object

The frmSecure form in the sample project demonstrates the use of the User and Group objects. Figure 9.4 shows this form in action.

FIGURE 9.4:
Retrieving Jet users and groups

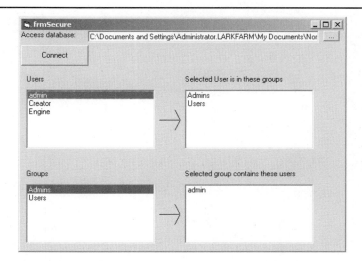

Listing 9.5 shows the code that this form uses to stock the initial User and Group listboxes when the user connects to a database.

Listing 9.5:   Retrieving Users and Groups

```
Dim mcat As ADOX.Catalog
Dim mcnn As ADODB.Connection
Private Sub cmdConnect_Click()

    Dim strConnect As String
    Dim usr As ADOX.User
```

```
Dim grp As ADOX.Group

On Error GoTo HandleErr

lboUsers.Clear
lboGroups.Clear

Set mcnn = New ADODB.Connection
Set mcat = New ADOX.Catalog

strConnect = "Provider=Microsoft.Jet.OLEDB.4.0;" & _
  "Data Source=" & txtDatabase.Text & _
  ";Jet OLEDB:System Database=" & _
  "c:\Program Files\Common Files\System\system.mdw"

mcnn.Open strConnect
Set mcat.ActiveConnection = mcnn

For Each usr In mcat.Users
    lboUsers.AddItem usr.Name
Next usr

For Each grp In mcat.Groups
    lboGroups.AddItem grp.Name
Next grp

'Clean up
Set usr = Nothing
Set grp = Nothing

ExitHere:
    Exit Sub

HandleErr:
    MsgBox "Error " & Err.Number & ": " & Err.Description, _
      vbOKOnly, "cmdConnect"
    Resume ExitHere
    Resume

End Sub
```

WARNING   This code uses the Jet OLE DB System Database property in the connection string to specify the location of the workgroup (MDW) file to use when retrieving security information. If you don't specify a workgroup file, you'll get error 3251 when trying to retrieve any information about Users or Groups via ADOX. The location of this file on your hard drive depends on which version of Access you have installed.

User

The ADOX User object represents a single user in a Jet database. Like the Group object, the User object is available only when you are using the Jet OLE DB provider.

Table 9.8 shows the properties and methods of the User object.

TABLE 9.8: Selected Properties and Methods of the User Object

Name	Type	Description
Name	Property	Name of this User
Groups	Property	Pointer to a collection of Groups containing this User
Properties	Property	Collection of provider-defined properties
ChangePassword	Method	Change the password of this User
GetPermissions	Method	Returns the current permissions of this User on a database object
SetPermissions	Method	Sets the permissions of this User on a database object

In the sample code for this chapter, selecting a user on the frmSecure form causes the code to use ADOX to enumerate the Groups of which that User is a member. Listing 9.6 shows this code.

Listing 9.6:   **Enumerating the Groups That Contain a User**

```
Private Sub lboUsers_Click()

    Dim usr As ADOX.User
    Dim grp As ADOX.Group

    On Error GoTo HandleErr

    lboUserGroups.Clear

    Set usr = mcat.Users(lboUsers.Text)
    For Each grp In usr.Groups
        lboUserGroups.AddItem grp.Name
    Next grp

    'Clean up
    Set usr = Nothing
    Set grp = Nothing

ExitHere:
    Exit Sub
```

```
HandleErr:
    MsgBox "Error " & Err.Number & ": " & Err.Description, _
        vbOKOnly, "lboUsers_Click"
    Resume ExitHere
    Resume

End Sub
```

NOTE   You may find it confusing that both the Users and Groups collections appear in two places in the object model. The Catalog.Users collection contains all Users in the entire database, and the Catalog.Groups collection contains all Groups in the entire database. By contrast, the Group.Users collection contains only the Users in a particular group, and the User.Groups collection contains all the Groups to which the particular User belongs.

Procedure

The Procedure object in ADOX represents a stored procedure. Depending on the provider, that may be an actual stored procedure, or something that resembles a stored procedure. For example, the Jet provider places queries with parameters in the Procedures collection.

Table 9.9 shows the properties of the Procedure object. This object has no methods.

TABLE 9.9: Properties of the Procedure Object

Name	Type	Description
Name	Property	Name of this Procedure
DateCreated	Property	Original creation date and time of this Procedure
DateModified	Property	Last change date and time of this Procedure
Command	Property	Pointer to an associated Command object

On the frmExplore form, the code uses a simple loop through the Procedures collection to list the Procedures in the selected database:

```
Dim prc As ADOX.Procedure
For Each prc In mcat.Procedures
    lboProcedures.AddItem prc.Name
Next prc
```

View

The View object in ADOX represents a view. Depending on the provider, that may be an actual view, or something that resembles a view. For example, the Jet provider places queries without parameters in the Views collection.

Table 9.10 shows the properties of the View object. This object has no methods.

TABLE 9.10: Properties of the View Object

Name	Type	Description
Name	Property	Name of this View
DateCreated	Property	Original creation date and time of this View
DateModified	Property	Last change date and time of this View
Command	Property	Pointer to an associated Command object

On the frmExplore form, the code uses a simple loop through the Views collection to list the views in the selected database:

```
Dim vw As ADOX.View
For Each vw In mcat.Views
    lboViews.AddItem vw.Name
Next vw
```

Command

If you look again at the ADOX object model diagram in Figure 9.1, you'll see that the Procedure and View objects have an associated Command object (retrieved via the Command property of the parent object). In fact, this is a standard ADO Command object. The ADOX library doesn't contain its own Command object. You can use the associated Command object for a Procedure or View object to retrieve detailed information about a particular Procedure or View, or even to execute the Procedure or View.

WARNING The Procedure.Command and View.Command properties are not supported by all OLE DB providers. See the next section of this chapter for details.

Later in this chapter, you'll see an example of using the associated Command objects from Procedure or View objects.

Limitations of ADOX

Support for ADOX isn't as widespread as support for ADO. That is, many OLE DB providers don't implement the interfaces that ADOX uses to do its work. In fact, I know of only four providers with ADOX support:

- Microsoft OLE DB Provider for Jet
- Microsoft OLE DB Provider for ODBC

- Microsoft OLE DB Provider for SQL Server
- Microsoft OLE DB Provider for Oracle

The Jet provider is the standard for ADOX functionality; all ADOX features work with this provider. The other three providers with support have limitations in the form of unimplemented features. In fact, the Jet provider is the only provider that implements the security-related features of ADOX.

The ODBC provider does not implement these ADOX features:

- The Catalog.Create method
- The Append and Delete methods of the Tables, Procedures, Indexes, and Keys collections
- The ability to modify properties of existing Table objects
- The Procedure.Command property
- The Users and Groups collections

The SQL Server provider does not implement these ADOX features:

- The Catalog.Create method
- The Append and Delete methods of the Procedures and Keys collections
- The ability to modify properties of existing Table objects
- The Procedure.Command property
- The Views, Users, and Groups collections

The Oracle provider does not implement these ADOX features:

- The Catalog.Create method
- The Append and Delete methods of the Tables, Views, Procedures, Indexes, and Keys collections
- The ability to modify properties of existing Table objects
- The Procedure.Command property
- The View.Command property
- The Users and Groups collections

TIP   If you're working with an OLE DB provider that doesn't include ADOX support, you can still use some ADOX functionality by using the OLE DB Provider for ODBC to open a second connection to the data source (assuming, that is, that you have available an ODBC driver for the data source).

TIP In some cases, you can get around the ADOX limitations by the creative use of ADO. For instance, although the SQL Server provider doesn't support the Catalog.Create method to create a new database, you can create a new database by using a regular ADO Command object to execute a CREATE DATABASE SQL statement.

Creating New Database Objects

The code samples you've seen in this chapter so far use ADOX to retrieve schema information about existing database objects (the samples use a Jet database, but they could be rewritten for other databases, subject to the limitations I covered in the preceding section). However, a more important use of ADOX in most applications is in creating new database objects. Depending on support from the underlying OLE DB provider, ADOX can generally create all the objects that it can examine. In this section, I'll show you how to use ADOX to create some common database objects:

- Databases
- Tables and Columns
- Indexes
- Relationships
- Views and Stored Procedures

Several types of application developers will find the ability to create new objects programmatically useful. First, of course, are those developers who are writing tools. For example, you might decide that the available interfaces for creating a SQL Server table are too complex for your users, and create a simple Table Wizard as a replacement. This tool could gather information via the user interface and then use ADOX to create the desired table.

ADOX can also be useful to developers who need to create objects temporarily. There are times, for example, when you will want to work with an arbitrary database chosen by the user, but still need application-specific tables. You can use ADOX to create these tables (and, if you like, to delete them when you're done with them).

Creating a Database

In the examples so far, you've been working with existing databases. As you've seen, instantiating an ADOX Catalog object to point to an existing database requires setting its Active-Connection property:

```
Set cnn = New ADODB.Connection
Set cat = New ADOX.Catalog
```

```
strConnect = "Provider=Microsoft.Jet.OLEDB.4.0;" & _
 "Data Source=" & txtDatabase.Text
mcnn.Open strConnect
Set cat.ActiveConnection = cnn
```

Creating a new database with ADOX is even simpler. All you need to do is instantiate a Catalog object and then call its Create method:

```
Set cat = New ADOX.Catalog
cat.Create "Provider=Microsoft.Jet.OLEDB.4.0;" & _
 "Data Source=" & App.Path & "\CreateObjects.mdb"
```

TIP You'll find this code, and the rest of the example code for this section, behind the Create Objects button on frmMenu in the ADOChapter9 sample project.

WARNING As of this writing, the Catalog.Create method is supported only by the Jet OLE DB provider. If you're working with a non-Jet database, you'll need to find a method other than ADOX to create new databases.

Creating a Table

Creating a Table object will be the first example of a common pattern in data definition using ADOX. Creating objects is a three-part operation:

1. Instantiate the appropriate ADOX object.

2. Set the properties of the ADOX object.

3. Append the object to the appropriate collection.

It's the third step, appending the object to a collection, that actually saves the object to the database. If you neglect that step, your code may run perfectly, except for the minor problem that no changes will actually be made to the database.

When you're creating a Table, you'll actually follow this pattern at multiple levels. First, you need to create the Table object and set its properties. Then you can create individual Column objects, set their properties, and append them to the Table's Columns collection. Finally, you can append the Table to the Catalog's Tables collection.

Listing 9.7 shows code to create two Tables, each with three Columns.

Listing 9.7: **Creating Tables with ADOX**

```
' Create a table
Set tbl = New ADOX.Table
tbl.Name = "Customers"
```

```
' Add some columns to the table
Set col = New ADOX.Column
col.Name = "CustomerID"
col.Type = adInteger      ' Jet Long Integer type
' Associate with the provider so we can set
' provider-specific properties
Set col.ParentCatalog = cat
col.Properties("Autoincrement") = True
col.Properties("Description") = "Unique Customer Number"
tbl.Columns.Append col

Set col = New ADOX.Column
col.Name = "CustomerName"
col.Type = adVarWChar
col.DefinedSize = 50
col.Attributes = 0   ' Not nullable
Set col.ParentCatalog = cat
col.Properties("Description") = "Customer Name"
tbl.Columns.Append col

Set col = New ADOX.Column
col.Name = "Customer City"
col.Type = adVarWChar
col.DefinedSize = 50
Set col.ParentCatalog = cat
col.Properties("Description") = "Customer City"
tbl.Columns.Append col

' And save the table
cat.Tables.Append tbl

' Create another table
Set tbl = New ADOX.Table
tbl.Name = "Orders"

' Add some columns to the table
Set col = New ADOX.Column
col.Name = "OrderID"
col.Type = adInteger
Set col.ParentCatalog = cat
col.Properties("Autoincrement") = True
col.Properties("Description") = "Unique Order Number"
tbl.Columns.Append col

Set col = New ADOX.Column
col.Name = "OrderDate"
col.Type = adDate
Set col.ParentCatalog = cat
col.Properties("Description") = "Date the order was placed"
tbl.Columns.Append col
```

```
Set col = New ADOX.Column
col.Name = "OrderComments"
col.Type = adVarWChar
col.DefinedSize = 50
Set col.ParentCatalog = cat
col.Properties("Description") = "Comments on the order"
tbl.Columns.Append col

' And save the table
cat.Tables.Append tbl
```

TIP   ADOX will create databases and the objects they contain in Access 2000 format, even if Access 2002 is installed on your computer.

Note the use of the ParentCatalog property of the Column objects. This property exists to get around a catch in ADOX programming: You can set provider-specific properties of only objects that are in a database, but you can't save the objects to the database until you set their properties. By setting the ParentCatalog property to a Catalog for a Jet database, you're telling ADOX that you intend for these Column objects to be columns in Jet tables. Once you've made that association, you're free to set provider-specific properties such as Auto-Increment and Description.

TIP   Remember, provider-specific properties can be accessed only through the Properties collection.

Creating an Index

Because an Index object is also made up of Columns, creating an Index is very similar in outline to creating a Table. First, you instantiate an Index object and set its properties. Then you append Column objects to the Index's Columns collection, representing the Columns in the Table that are indexed. Finally, you append the Index itself to the Table's Indexes collection.

Here's some code for creating two Indexes on a Table:

```
' Now create an index on the primary key field
Set idx = New ADOX.Index
idx.Name = "PrimaryKey"
idx.PrimaryKey = True
idx.Unique = True
' Specify the column for the index
idx.Columns.Append "CustomerID"
' And add the index to the table
tbl.Indexes.Append idx
```

```
' Create a second index on the City field
Set idx = New ADOX.Index
idx.Name = "CityIndex"
idx.Unique = False
idx.Columns.Append "CustomerCity"
tbl.Indexes.Append idx
```

Note the shortcut method that this code uses to append Columns to the Index objects. By calling the Indexes.Append method with a Column name, you both create the Column and append it to the Index in a single operation.

WARNING   One thing to watch out for is that Indexes must be created after the Columns that they index have been added to the Table. Otherwise, you'll get an error when you try to append the Index to the Table's Indexes collection.

Creating a Relationship

Creating a relationship between two Tables requires creating two Keys: a primary Key on one Table, and a foreign Key on the other. Like Tables and Indexes, Keys are made up of Columns, although, as this code sample illustrates, the Columns in a Key can have additional properties:

```
' Create a foreign key pointing at the Customer table
Set ky = New ADOX.key
ky.Name = "CustomerKey"
ky.Type = adKeyForeign
ky.RelatedTable = "Customers"
Set col = New ADOX.Column
col.Name = "CustomerID"
col.RelatedColumn = "CustomerID"
ky.Columns.Append col
tbl.Keys.Append ky
```

As you can see, when you're creating a foreign Key, the RelatedTable and RelatedColumn properties determine the Table and Column of the related primary Key.

WARNING   If you create an Index with the PrimaryKey property set to True, ADOX will automatically create a Key for that Column as well. You'll get a runtime error if you try to create both a PrimaryKey Index and a Key with the type adKeyPrimary in the same Table.

Listing 9.8 shows the full code from the Create Objects example. This code creates two Tables and a relationship between them. Figure 9.5 shows the created objects open in Microsoft Access 2002.

Listing 9.8: **cmdCreateObject_Click**

```vb
Private Sub cmdCreateObjects_Click()

    Dim cat As ADOX.Catalog
    Dim tbl As ADOX.Table
    Dim col As ADOX.Column
    Dim idx As ADOX.Index
    Dim ky As ADOX.key

    Screen.MousePointer = vbHourglass

    ' Delete the database if it exists
    On Error Resume Next
    Kill App.Path & "\CreateObjects.mdb"
    On Error GoTo HandleErr

    ' Create the database
    Set cat = New ADOX.Catalog
    cat.Create "Provider=Microsoft.Jet.OLEDB.4.0;" & _
      "Data Source=" & App.Path & "\CreateObjects.mdb"

    ' Create a table
    Set tbl = New ADOX.Table
    tbl.Name = "Customers"

    ' Add some columns to the table
    Set col = New ADOX.Column
    col.Name = "CustomerID"
    col.Type = adInteger      ' Jet Long Integer type
    ' Associate with the provider so we can set
    ' provider-specific properties
    Set col.ParentCatalog = cat
    col.Properties("Autoincrement") = True
    col.Properties("Description") = "Unique Customer Number"
    tbl.Columns.Append col

    Set col = New ADOX.Column
    col.Name = "CustomerName"
    col.Type = adVarWChar
    col.DefinedSize = 50
    col.Attributes = 0   ' Not nullable
    Set col.ParentCatalog = cat
    col.Properties("Description") = "Customer Name"
    tbl.Columns.Append col

    Set col = New ADOX.Column
    col.Name = "CustomerCity"
    col.Type = adVarWChar
    col.DefinedSize = 50
    Set col.ParentCatalog = cat
```

```
col.Properties("Description") = "Customer City"
tbl.Columns.Append col

' Now create an index on the primary key field
' As a side effect, this will create the
' primary key
Set idx = New ADOX.Index
idx.Name = "PrimaryKey"
idx.PrimaryKey = True
idx.Unique = True
' Specify the column for the index
idx.Columns.Append "CustomerID"
' And add the index to the table
tbl.Indexes.Append idx

' Create a second index on the City field
Set idx = New ADOX.Index
idx.Name = "CityIndex"
idx.Unique = False
idx.Columns.Append "CustomerCity"
tbl.Indexes.Append idx

' And save the table
cat.Tables.Append tbl

' Create another table
Set tbl = New ADOX.Table
tbl.Name = "Orders"

' Add some columns to the table
Set col = New ADOX.Column
col.Name = "OrderID"
col.Type = adInteger
Set col.ParentCatalog = cat
col.Properties("Autoincrement") = True
col.Properties("Description") = "Unique Order Number"
tbl.Columns.Append col

Set col = New ADOX.Column
col.Name = "CustomerID"
col.Type = adInteger
Set col.ParentCatalog = cat
col.Properties("Description") = "Customer Placing this Order"
tbl.Columns.Append col

Set col = New ADOX.Column
col.Name = "OrderDate"
col.Type = adDate
Set col.ParentCatalog = cat
col.Properties("Description") = "Date the order was placed"
tbl.Columns.Append col
```

```
    Set col = New ADOX.Column
    col.Name = "OrderComments"
    col.Type = adVarWChar
    col.DefinedSize = 50
    Set col.ParentCatalog = cat
    col.Properties("Description") = "Comments on the order"
    tbl.Columns.Append col

    ' Create an index on the primary key field
    Set idx = New ADOX.Index
    idx.Name = "PrimaryKey"
    idx.PrimaryKey = True
    idx.Unique = True
    ' Specify the column for the index
    idx.Columns.Append "OrderID"
    ' And add the index to the table
    tbl.Indexes.Append idx

    ' Create a foreign key pointing at the Customer table
    Set ky = New ADOX.key
    ky.Name = "CustomerKey"
    ky.Type = adKeyForeign
    ky.RelatedTable = "Customers"
    Set col = New ADOX.Column
    col.Name = "CustomerID"
    col.RelatedColumn = "CustomerID"
    ky.Columns.Append col
    tbl.Keys.Append ky

    ' And save the table
    cat.Tables.Append tbl

    ' Clean up
    Set cat = Nothing
    Set tbl = Nothing
    Set col = Nothing
    Set idx = Nothing
    Set ky = Nothing

ExitHere:
    Screen.MousePointer = vbDefault
    Exit Sub

HandleErr:
    MsgBox "Error " & Err.Number & ": " & Err.Description, _
    vbOKOnly, "cmdCreateObjects"
    Resume ExitHere
    Resume

End Sub
```

FIGURE 9.5:

Objects created
with ADOX

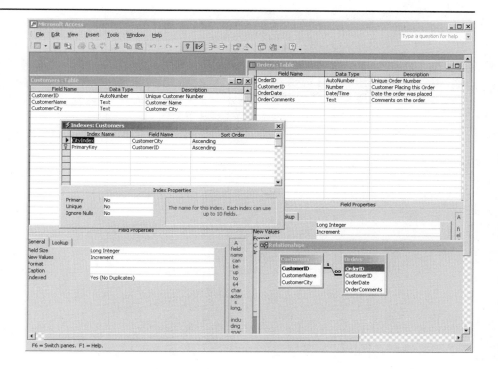

Creating Views and Stored Procedures

ADOX also allows you to create Views and Stored Procedures. I've written a separate chunk of code to demonstrate these, as the process is somewhat different. Unlike other objects, creating a View or Stored Procedure object requires you to interact with an ADO object: the Command object.

To create a View or a Stored Procedure, you need to follow these steps:

1. Create an ADO Command object.

2. Set its properties to represent the View or Stored Procedure, most notably its Command-Text property.

3. Use the Views.Append or Procedures.Append method to create the View or Stored Procedure based on this Command.

Listing 9.9 shows an example, from the Create View button on frmMenu.

Listing 9.9:   Creating a View

```
Private Sub cmdCreateView_Click()

    Dim cnn As ADODB.Connection
    Dim cat As ADOX.Catalog
    Dim cmd As ADODB.Command

    On Error GoTo HandleErr

    ' Connect to the database created by the
    ' Create Objects procedure
    Set cnn = New ADODB.Connection
    Set cat = New ADOX.Catalog
    cnn.Open "Provider=Microsoft.Jet.OLEDB.4.0;" & _
      "Data Source=" & App.Path & "\CreateObjects.mdb"
    Set cat.ActiveConnection = cnn

    ' Create a new Command object representing a view
    Set cmd = New ADODB.Command
    cmd.CommandText = "SELECT * FROM Customers"

    ' And save this as a view
    cat.Views.Append "vwAllCustomers", cmd

    ' Clean up
    cnn.Close
    Set cnn = Nothing
    Set cmd = Nothing
    Set cat = Nothing

ExitHere:
    Screen.MousePointer = vbDefault
    Exit Sub

HandleErr:
    MsgBox "Error " & Err.Number & ": " & Err.Description, _
      vbOKOnly, "cmdCreateObjects"
    Resume ExitHere
    Resume

End Sub
```

The code for creating a Procedure object is very similar. The main difference is that a Procedure uses different SQL in the Command. The Jet provider, in fact, is not at all fussy. If you append a Command to the Views collection that should have been saved as a Procedure, the provider will simply create a Stored Procedure instead of a View.

Using Procedure and View Objects

Because of their intimate link with the regular ADO object model, the Procedure and View objects allow you to move back from database design to data manipulation, even when you've started with ADOX rather than ADO. The key to doing this is to use the Procedure.Command or View.Command property to retrieve a Command object based on the Procedure or View, which can then be used like any other ADO Command object.

Figure 9.6 shows frmViews from this chapter's sample project. This form allows you to choose any Access database and retrieve a list of the Views and Procedures that it contains. You can then double-click any of these Views or Procedures to run them and retrieve their results to a grid control on the form.

The code to retrieve the list of Views and Stored Procedures is very similar to the code you've already seen from frmExplore. When you double-click one of these items, the application takes advantage of the ADO–ADOX association to build a Recordset based on the selected item. Listing 9.10 shows the code for this technique.

FIGURE 9.6:

Retrieving and running views

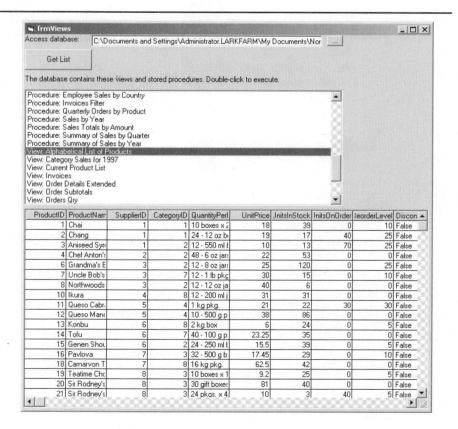

Listing 9.10:   **Opening a Recordset from a View or Stored Procedure**

```
If Left(lboViews.Text, 4) = "View" Then
    ' Retrieve the associated command
    Set cmd = mcat.Views(Mid(lboViews.Text, 7)).Command
    ' Use a separate Recordset so we can set its
    ' properties. Otherwise, we'd get a FO/RO Recordset,
    ' and the grid would show only one row
    Set rst = New ADODB.Recordset
    rst.CursorLocation = adUseClient
    rst.CursorType = adOpenStatic
    rst.LockType = adLockReadOnly
    ' Stock the Recordset with the command results
    rst.Open cmd
    ' And display it on the grid
    Set hfgMain.Recordset = rst
Else
    Set cmd = mcat.Procedures(Mid(lboViews.Text, 12)).Command
    Set rst = New ADODB.Recordset
    rst.CursorLocation = adUseClient
    rst.CursorType = adOpenStatic
    rst.LockType = adLockReadOnly
    ' For a procedure, need to retrieve and then fill
    ' in the parameters
    cmd.Parameters.Refresh
    For Each prm In cmd.Parameters
        If prm.Direction = adParamInput Or _
          prm.Direction = adParamInputOutput Then
            prm.Value = InputBox("Enter value for parameter " & prm.Name)
        End If
    Next prm
    rst.Open cmd
    Set hfgMain.Recordset = rst
End If
```

There are a few things to note about this code:

- The code to stock the listbox contains `"View"` or `"Procedure"` before each item. This code uses those prefixes to determine which type of object it's working with, and then uses the Mid() function to get the actual name of the View or Procedure.

- The code instantiates a separate Recordset object and then sets the grid's Recordset property to this object after opening the Recordset. You can't shortcut this process by opening the Command directly into the grid's Recordset property. If you do that, the Recordset will open as the forward-only, read-only default, and the grid will display only a single row of data.

- The difference between Views and Procedures is that Procedures have Parameters that must be filled in to retrieve data. This code uses a simple For Each loop to prompt the user for a value for each Parameter.

TIP   For more information on Parameters in ADO, refer to Chapter 3, "Using the ADO Objects to Retrieve Data."

Listing 9.11 shows the complete code from the frmViews form.

Listing 9.11:   **frmViews**

```
Dim mcat As ADOX.Catalog
Dim mcnn As ADODB.Connection

Private Sub cmdBrowse_Click()
    ' Browse for an Access database to open
    With dlgCommon
        .FileName = ""
        .Filter = "Access databases (*.mdb)|*.mdb|All Files (*.*)|*.*"
        .CancelError = False
        .ShowOpen
        txtDatabase.Text = .FileName
    End With
End Sub

Private Sub cmdGetList_Click()

    Dim strConnect As String
    Dim prc As ADOX.Procedure
    Dim vw As ADOX.View

    On Error GoTo HandleErr

    lboViews.Clear

    ' Instantiate and connect the Catalog
    Set mcnn = New ADODB.Connection
    Set mcat = New ADOX.Catalog

    strConnect = "Provider=Microsoft.Jet.OLEDB.4.0;" & _
     "Data Source=" & txtDatabase.Text
    mcnn.Open strConnect
    Set mcat.ActiveConnection = mcnn

    ' Retrieve all view and procedure names
    For Each prc In mcat.Procedures
        lboViews.AddItem "Procedure: " & prc.Name
    Next prc
```

```
     For Each vw In mcat.Views
          lboViews.AddItem "View: " & vw.Name
     Next vw

     ' Clean up
     Set prc = Nothing
     Set vw = Nothing

ExitHere:
     Exit Sub

HandleErr:
     MsgBox "Error " & Err.Number & ": " & Err.Description, _
       vbOKOnly, "cmdGetList"
     Resume ExitHere
     Resume

End Sub

Private Sub lboViews_DblClick()

     Dim cmd As ADODB.Command
     Dim rst As ADODB.Recordset
     Dim prm As ADODB.Parameter

     On Error GoTo HandleErr

     If Left(lboViews.Text, 4) = "View" Then
          ' Retrieve the associated command
          Set cmd = mcat.Views(Mid(lboViews.Text, 7)).Command
          ' Use a separate Recordset so we can set its
          ' properties. Otherwise, we'd get a FO/RO Recordset,
          ' and the grid would only show one row
          Set rst = New ADODB.Recordset
          rst.CursorLocation = adUseClient
          rst.CursorType = adOpenStatic
          rst.LockType = adLockReadOnly
          ' Stock the Recordset with the command results
          rst.Open cmd
          ' And display it on the grid
          Set hfgMain.Recordset = rst
     Else
          Set cmd = mcat.Procedures(Mid(lboViews.Text, 12)).Command
          Set rst = New ADODB.Recordset
          rst.CursorLocation = adUseClient
          rst.CursorType = adOpenStatic
          rst.LockType = adLockReadOnly
```

```
            ' For a procedure, need to retrieve and then fill
            ' in the parameters
            cmd.Parameters.Refresh
            For Each prm In cmd.Parameters
                If prm.Direction = adParamInput Or _
                  prm.Direction = adParamInputOutput Then
                    prm.Value = InputBox("Enter value for parameter " & prm.Name)
                End If
            Next prm
            rst.Open cmd
            Set hfgMain.Recordset = rst
        End If

        ' Clean up
        rst.Close
        Set rst = Nothing
        Set cmd = Nothing
        Set prm = Nothing

ExitHere:
    Exit Sub

HandleErr:
    MsgBox "Error " & Err.Number & ": " & Err.Description, _
      vbOKOnly, "lboViews_DblClick"
    Resume ExitHere
    Resume

End Sub
```

Manipulating Database Security

So far in this chapter, all the examples have been concerned with the schema of a database. That's the "Data Definition" part of the ADOX library name. ADOX also offers facilities for manipulating database security in databases that use a groups/users/permissions model of security. In particular, you can perform the following operations (subject, as always, to the limits of your OLE DB provider):

- Create a Group
- Create a User
- Change object ownership
- Set object permissions

In this section, I'll show you the basic code to perform these security operations.

Creating a New Group

To create a new security Group, you just give it a name and append it to the Groups collection of a catalog, as illustrated in Listing 9.12. (This code example, along with the others in this section, depends on the database created by the Create Objects sample earlier in the chapter.)

WARNING   The group and user examples will make changes to your Access workgroup if you run them. To reverse those changes, you can use the Cleanup button on frmMenu in this chapter's sample project. If you don't run the cleanup procedure, the changes to the Access workgroup will affect all of your Access applications.

Listing 9.12:   Creating a Group

```
Private Sub cmdCreateGroup_Click()

    Dim cnn As ADODB.Connection
    Dim cat As ADOX.Catalog
    Dim strConnect As String

    On Error GoTo HandleErr

    Set cnn = New ADODB.Connection
    Set cat = New ADOX.Catalog

    strConnect = "Provider=Microsoft.Jet.OLEDB.4.0;" & _
      "Data Source=" & App.Path & "\CreateObjects.mdb" & _
      ";Jet OLEDB:System Database=" & _
      "c:\Program Files\Common Files\System\system.mdw;" & _
      "User ID=Admin;Password="
    cnn.Open strConnect
    Set cat.ActiveConnection = cnn

    ' Add a group named Accounting
    cat.Groups.Append "Accounting"
    ' And put the Admin user in this group
    cat.Groups("Accounting").Users.Append "Admin"

    ' Clean up
    cnn.Close
    Set cnn = Nothing
    Set cat = Nothing
```

```
ExitHere:
    Exit Sub

HandleErr:
    MsgBox "Error " & Err.Number & ": " & Err.Description, _
        vbOKOnly, "cmdConnect"
    Resume ExitHere
    Resume

End Sub
```

> **NOTE**   The security examples depend on your default Access workgroup having a user named Admin in the Admins group, with no password. If you've changed the Admin password, or otherwise modified Access security on your computer, you'll need to update the connection string to match. You may also need to change the path to the system.mdw file to match its location on your system.

Note that any code that manipulates security in an Access database (which is the only type of database that ADOX security features are designed for) must specify a system database and also provide a username and password to use with that database. (You can omit the username and password if the default Admin user exists with a blank password.)

After you create a Group, you can add Users to the Group by appending them to the Group's Users collection. The Users must already exist in the Catalog's Users collection.

Creating a New User

The code for creating a new User, shown in Listing 9.13, is very similar to the code for creating a new Group.

Listing 9.13:   **Creating a User**

```
Private Sub cmdCreateUser_Click()

    Dim cnn As ADODB.Connection
    Dim cat As ADOX.Catalog
    Dim strConnect As String

    On Error GoTo HandleErr

    Set cnn = New ADODB.Connection
    Set cat = New ADOX.Catalog

    strConnect = "Provider=Microsoft.Jet.OLEDB.4.0;" & _
        "Data Source=" & App.Path & "\CreateObjects.mdb" & _
        ";Jet OLEDB:System Database=" & _
```

```
            "c:\Program Files\Common Files\System\system.mdw;" & _
            "User ID=Admin;Password="

        cnn.Open strConnect
        Set cat.ActiveConnection = cnn

        ' Add a User named Fred
        cat.Users.Append "Fred", "OriginalPW"
        ' And put them in the Accounting group
        cat.Users("Fred").Groups.Append "Accounting"

        ' Change Fred's password
        cat.Users("Fred").ChangePassword "OriginalPW", "Trout"

        ' Clean up
        cnn.Close
        Set cnn = Nothing
        Set cat = Nothing

ExitHere:
        Exit Sub

HandleErr:
        MsgBox "Error " & Err.Number & ": " & Err.Description, _
           vbOKOnly, "cmdConnect"
        Resume ExitHere
        Resume

End Sub
```

After you create a User, you can put the User in a Group by adding that Group to the User's Groups collection. The Group, of course, must already exist. Alternately, you can add the User to the Group's Users collection. The effect is exactly the same.

Listing 9.13 also shows how you can use the ChangePassword method to assign a new password to a user. You must know the old password for this method to succeed.

WARNING   Of course, in a real application, you wouldn't want to actually embed a password in source code! Typically, you'd prompt the user for that information at runtime.

Changing Object Ownership

Oddly enough, to change the ownership of an object, you don't use the Groups or Users collection at all. Instead, you can retrieve ownership information or assign ownership to a new User with methods of the Catalog object. Listing 9.14 shows this technique.

Listing 9.14:   **Changing Object Ownership**

```vb
Private Sub cmdChangeOwnership_Click()

    Dim cnn As ADODB.Connection
    Dim cat As ADOX.Catalog
    Dim strConnect As String
    Dim strOwner As String
    Dim intRet As Integer

    On Error GoTo HandleErr

    Set cnn = New ADODB.Connection
    Set cat = New ADOX.Catalog

    strConnect = "Provider=Microsoft.Jet.OLEDB.4.0;" & _
      "Data Source=" & App.Path & "\CreateObjects.mdb" & _
      ";Jet OLEDB:System Database=" & _
      "c:\Program Files\Common Files\System\system.mdw;" & _
      "User ID=Admin;Password="

    cnn.Open strConnect
    Set cat.ActiveConnection = cnn

    ' Display the current owner of the Customers table
    strOwner = cat.GetObjectOwner("Customers", adPermObjTable)
    intRet = MsgBox("Customers table is currently owned by " & _
      strOwner & ". Give ownership to Fred?", vbYesNo)
    If intRet = vbYes Then
        cat.SetObjectOwner "Customers", adPermObjTable, "Fred"
    End If

    ' Clean up
    cnn.Close
    Set cnn = Nothing
    Set cat = Nothing

ExitHere:
    Exit Sub

HandleErr:
    MsgBox "Error " & Err.Number & ": " & Err.Description, _
      vbOKOnly, "cmdConnect"
    Resume ExitHere
    Resume

End Sub
```

Both the GetObjectOwner method and the SetObjectOwner method take a parameter that indicates what sort of object you are working with. Table 9.11 shows the possible values for this parameter.

TABLE 9.11:   Object Types

Type	Object
adPermObjColumn	Column
adPermObjDatabase	Database
adPermObjProcedure	Stored Procedure
adPermObjTable	Table
adPermObjView	View
adPermObjProviderSpecific	Provider-specific object

If you specify adPermObjProviderSpecific, you must provide an additional parameter to the GetObjectOwner or SetObjectOwner method:

```
cat.GetObjectOwner ObjectName, ObjectType, ObjectTypeId
cat.SetObjectOwner ObjectName, ObjectType, UserName, ObjectTypeId
```

In this case, the ObjectTypeId will be a GUID defined by the particular OLE DB provider involved, to refer to an object that's not in the standard list. For example, the Jet OLE DB provider includes GUIDs for Access forms, reports, and macros, as shown in Table 9.12.

TABLE 9.12:   Jet Object Type IDs

Object	ID
Form	{C49C842E-9DCB-11D1-9F0A-00C04FC2C2E0}
Report	{C49C8430-9DCB-11D1-9F0A-00C04FC2C2E0}
Macro	{C49C842F-9DCB-11D1-9F0A-00C04FC2C2E0}

Setting Object Permissions

To set the permissions on an object, you call the SetPermissions method of either a User or a Group. Listing 9.15 shows an example.

Listing 9.15:   **Setting Permissions**

```
Private Sub cmdSetPermissions_Click()

    Dim cnn As ADODB.Connection
```

```
        Dim cat As ADOX.Catalog
        Dim strConnect As String

        On Error GoTo HandleErr

        Set cnn = New ADODB.Connection
        Set cat = New ADOX.Catalog

        strConnect = "Provider=Microsoft.Jet.OLEDB.4.0;" & _
         "Data Source=" & App.Path & "\CreateObjects.mdb" & _
         ";Jet OLEDB:System Database=" & _
         "c:\Program Files\Common Files\System\system.mdw;" & _
         "User ID=Admin;Password="

        cnn.Open strConnect
        Set cat.ActiveConnection = cnn

        ' Grant Fred permissions on the Customers table
        cat.Users("Fred").SetPermissions "Customers", adPermObjTable, _
         adAccessSet, adRightFull

        'Clean up
        cnn.Close
        Set cnn = Nothing
        Set cat = Nothing

ExitHere:
    Exit Sub

HandleErr:
    MsgBox "Error " & Err.Number & ": " & Err.Description, _
       vbOKOnly, "cmdSetPermissions"
    Resume ExitHere
    Resume

End Sub
```

The SetPermissions method has four required and two optional parameters:

- *Name* is the name of the object to manipulate.

- *ObjectType* is the type of the object. See Table 9.11 for the possible object types.

- *Action* is either adAccessDeny to remove the specified permissions, adAccessGrant to add the specified permissions to any already in place, adAccessRevoke to remove all permissions, or adAccessSet to set the exact permissions supplied.

- *Rights* is a constant indicating which permissions to grant. Table 9.13 shows the possible values for this constant.

- The optional *Inherit* parameter can be set to a constant to control whether objects contained within the specified object should inherit the specified permissions. You're unlikely to need this parameter.

- The optional *ObjectTypeId* is used when the ObjectType is set to adPermObjProvider-Specific, just as it is used with the ownership methods.

TABLE 9.13: Rights Constants

Constant	Meaning
adRightCreate	Permission to create new objects of the specified type
adRightDelete	Permission to delete data
adRightDrop	Permission to delete objects of the specified type
adRightExclusive	Permission to lock the object exclusively
adRightExecute	Permission to execute
adRightFull	All possible permissions on the object
adRightInsert	Permission to insert data
adRightMaximumAllowed	All possible permissions, including provider-specific permissions
adRightNone	No permissions on the object
adRightRead	Permission to read data
adRightReadDesign	Permission to retrieve schema information
adRightReadPermissions	Permission to retrieve permission information
adRightReference	Permission to reference
adRightUpdate	Permission to edit existing data
adRightWithGrant	Permission to grant permissions
adRightWriteDesign	Permission to modify the design of the object
adRightWriteOwner	Permission to change object ownership
adRightWritePermissions	Permission to change the specified permissions

Summary

In this chapter, you learned about ADOX, the first of the ADO extension libraries. In particular, you saw how to use the ADOX library for a variety of schema-related tasks, including retrieving the schema of a database, creating a variety of new database objects, executing Views and Procedures, and manipulating database security.

In the next chapter, I'll introduce the other important ADO extension library, the ADO (Multidimensional) extensions, usually known as ADO MD. This library helps you manipulate data from Microsoft Analysis Services or another OLAP provider within your applications.

CHAPTER 10

Analyzing Multidimensional Data with ADO MD

- Multidimensional data architecture

- Introduction to Microsoft Analysis Services

- Creating a cube

- The ADO MD object model

- Retrieving multidimensional data

The ADO (Multidimensional) library is another major extension to the ADO object model (in fact, it contains more objects than the core ADO library itself). This library, called ADO MD for short, is designed to retrieve schema information and data from multidimensional data sources, as typified by Microsoft Analysis Services (a component of Microsoft SQL Server 2000). In this chapter, I'll introduce the basic concepts of multidimensional data and demonstrate the use of ADO MD with multidimensional data sources.

Multidimensional Data Architecture

Before you can use ADO MD productively, you need to understand the basics about multidimensional data. The basic idea behind multidimensional data is to preprocess the data so that you can aggregate it quickly and easily in a variety of ways. The basic structure of multidimensional data is the cube, which consists of data plus aggregations. Figure 10.1 shows one view of a typical cube, in a tool known as the Cube Browser (this tool is supplied as part of Microsoft Analysis Services).

FIGURE 10.1:

Browsing a cube

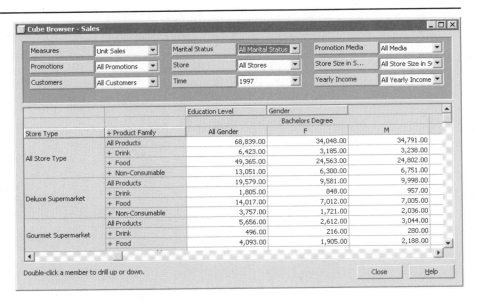

The data in Figure 10.1 comes from the Sales cube in the FoodMart 2000 sample database, which is installed as part of Analysis Services.

The reason this is called multidimensional data is that it is aggregated in many different ways. For example, Figure 10.1 shows sales data grouped by store type, product family, and education and gender of the buyer. Each of these ways of grouping the data is a dimension.

More generally, multidimensional data is a feature of OLAP products. OLAP stands for Online Analytical Processing and is distinguished from OLTP, or Online Transaction Processing. Typical relational databases (such as SQL Server or Access) are OLTP products. They are optimized for quickly editing or retrieving data from single records. But they're not very good at aggregating data quickly so that you can spot overall patterns. That's the job of OLAP products. In this chapter, I'll focus on Microsoft Analysis Services, the OLAP product that ships as a part of Microsoft SQL Server 2000. Figure 10.2 shows the major architectural components of a multidimensional solution based on Microsoft Analysis Services.

FIGURE 10.2:

Microsoft Analysis
Services architecture

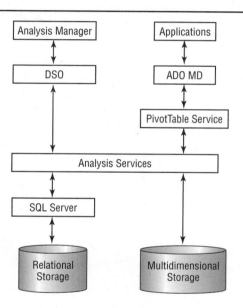

This diagram shows the major components of a multidimensional solution, from data sources (at the bottom of the diagram) through the user interface (at the top of the application). Although ADO MD is only one of these components, it's hard to understand ADO MD's value without looking at the overall picture. So let's look at each of these components in turn.

TIP   For a more in-depth treatment of Analysis Services than I can offer in this chapter, see *SQL Server Developer's Guide to OLAP with Analysis Services* by Mike Gunderloy and Tim Sneath (Sybex, 2001).

Analysis Manager

Analysis Manager (shown in Figure 10.3) provides the administrative interface for Microsoft Analysis Services. Analysis Manager is an MMC (Microsoft Management Console) application that is installed on the server where Analysis Services is being hosted.

FIGURE 10.3:

Analysis Manager

Analysis Manager is the best starting point if you'd like to learn about Analysis Services. Although, in this chapter, I'll concentrate on using code to interact with Analysis Services, you should keep in mind that Analysis Manager often offers a quick and easy interface for OLAP operations. It also includes an excellent set of tutorials and wizards that will enhance your understanding of OLAP database development.

NOTE   To run the code in this chapter, you'll need a computer on which Analysis Services and SQL Server 2000 are installed. Both the Enterprise Edition and the Developer Edition of SQL Server 2000 contain all of the Analysis Services components. The Standard Edition of SQL Server 2000 contains a subset of Analysis Services components that is adequate for use with the examples in this chapter.

Decision Support Objects

The Decision Support Objects (DSO) library provides an object-oriented interface for Analysis Manager administrative tasks. You can use objects within the DSO library to perform operations that are usually done with Analysis Manager, such as building a new cube or reprocessing a cube so that it reflects the latest source data.

Because the DSO library is not closely related to ADO, I won't be using DSO objects in this chapter.

ADO MD

ADO MD is a set of extensions to ADO that allow COM-based applications to operate against a multidimensional source via the OLE DB for OLAP interfaces. ADO MD uses some of the existing ADO objects and collections but extends them with some additional new objects that you can use to query specific elements of the multidimensional structures. This extension process is similar to the use of ADOX to add DDL and security capabilities to ADO. In both cases, the add-on library shares some objects with ADO and then provides additional functionality through additional objects.

Listing 10.1 shows a simple example (from the ADOChapter10 sample project) of the use of ADO MD. This code prints out the names of all the dimensions in a cube (you'll learn more about cubes and dimensions later in the chapter).

Listing 10.1:   **Listing the Dimensions in a Cube**

```
Private Sub cmdListDimensions_Click()

    Dim cnn As New ADODB.Connection
    Dim cat As New ADOMD.Catalog
    Dim cub As ADOMD.CubeDef
    Dim dmn As ADOMD.Dimension

    On Error GoTo HandleErr

    cnn.Open "Provider=MSOLAP;Data Source=localhost;" & _
      "Initial Catalog=FoodMart 2000"
    Set cat.ActiveConnection = cnn
    Set cub = cat.CubeDefs("Sales")

    For Each dmn In cub.Dimensions
        Debug.Print dmn.Name
    Next dmn

ExitHere:
    Exit Sub
```

```
HandleErr:
    MsgBox "Error " & Err.Number & ": " & Err.Description, _
    vbOKOnly, "cmdListDimensions"
    Resume ExitHere
    Resume

End Sub
```

NOTE To run this code, you'll need to set references to the Microsoft ActiveX Data Objects 2.6 Library and the Microsoft ActiveX Data Objects (Multidimensional) 2.5 Library within your Visual Basic project. The sample also assumes that you're running Visual Basic on the computer that also runs Analysis Services. If that's not the case, you'll need to change the name of the data source in the Open statement from localhost to the actual name of the computer that runs Analysis Services.

You can also use ADO MD to execute MDX statements against an Analysis Services database. MDX is a querying language that I'll discuss briefly later in the chapter; it's designed to retrieve information from a multidimensional data source. The ADO MD Cellset object is an n-dimensional structure used to hold data returned from an MDX query. Listing 10.2 shows code for doing this.

Listing 10.2:   **Printing Cellset Information**

```
Private Sub cmdCellset_Click()

    Dim cst As New ADOMD.Cellset
    Dim intI As Integer

    On Error GoTo HandleErr

    With cst
        .ActiveConnection = "Provider=MSOLAP;" & _
        "Data Source=localhost;" & _
        "Initial Catalog=FoodMart 2000"
        .Source = "SELECT {Product.Children} ON COLUMNS, " & _
        "{[Store Type].Children} ON ROWS " & _
        "FROM [Sales] " & _
        "WHERE ([Store].[All Stores].[USA])"
        .Open
    End With

    Debug.Print vbTab & cst.Axes(0).Positions(0).Members(0).Caption & _
    vbTab & cst.Axes(0).Positions(1).Members(0).Caption & _
    vbTab & cst.Axes(0).Positions(2).Members(0).Caption
    For intI = 0 To cst.Axes(1).Positions.Count - 1
```

```
            Debug.Print cst.Axes(1).Positions(intI).Members(0).Caption & _
               vbTab & cst(0, intI).Value & vbTab & cst(1, intI).Value & _
               vbTab & cst(2, intI).Value
        Next intI

        ' Clean up
        cst.Close
        Set cst = Nothing

    ExitHere:
        Exit Sub

    HandleErr:
        MsgBox "Error " & Err.Number & ": " & Err.Description, _
          vbOKOnly, "cmdCellset"
        Resume ExitHere
        Resume

    End Sub
```

This example opens a Cellset that includes the total sales for each product type for each store type in a cube named `Sales`. It then prints the results by iterating through the Cellset.

PivotTable Service

The PivotTable Service plays a dual role in Microsoft's OLAP architecture. It serves both as a pipeline from a client application to Analysis Services and as a client-side calculation engine. When used in conjunction with an Analysis Services server, the PivotTable Service caches data and attempts to answer queries without further trips to the server whenever possible.

In its second role as an OLAP calculation engine, the PivotTable Service delivers the ability to create, populate, and query *local cubes*. A local cube is the equivalent of an Analysis Services database kept in a disk file. By using the PivotTable Service, client applications such as Excel can perform multidimensional analyses on the contents of a local cube file—for example, by creating an Excel PivotTable based directly on the cube data.

Analysis Services

Analysis Services itself is a multidimensional database engine that is shipped with, and works in tandem with, SQL Server 2000. Analysis Services handles the data-crunching work of looking through large amounts of data and providing it in aggregated format to client applications by way of the PivotTable Service. Any client computer with a SQL Server Client Access License (CAL) can freely use Analysis Services. Analysis Services can be installed on the same computer as SQL Server itself or on a different computer elsewhere on the network.

SQL Server

Analysis Services is intimately connected with the SQL Server database engine. It uses SQL Server for two purposes. First, the source data (say, the individual sales for an OLAP sales database) can be stored in a SQL Server database. Second, Analysis Services can store its own aggregated data in a SQL Server database.

Relational Storage

In the Analysis Services world, *relational storage* refers to a database managed by SQL Server (or another relational database engine). Most often, relational storage is used for the source data that Analysis Services works with, but it can also be used for the data that Analysis Services creates.

Multidimensional Storage

In addition to relational storage, Analysis Services can manage its own efficient multidimensional storage databases. These databases don't hold transactional source data. Rather, they are optimized to store the aggregated, multidimensional results that Analysis Services calculates.

Analysis Services Concepts

Now that you've seen the way that Analysis Services fits into an overall OLAP architecture, let's look at some of the key concepts within Analysis Services itself. These include:

- Dimensions
- Measures
- Cubes
- MOLAP, ROLAP, and HOLAP storage

> **NOTE**   Although I'm using Microsoft Analysis Services to focus the discussion, these concepts are common to most OLAP products.

Dimensions

One of the key features of OLAP is the capability to aggregate data in a variety of ways. For example, suppose you have a database of sales across a store chain. For each sale, the database could contain a variety of data, including:

- The date of the sale
- The product purchased

- The purchase price
- The store where the sale took place

With Analysis Services, you could aggregate sales using any or all of these fields. You might look at sales by product, or by date, or by store, and so on. Each of the ways in which you can aggregate the data is called a *dimension*.

Dimensions alone aren't always sufficient to break down the information to a manageable or interesting form. For example, suppose that the sale date is recorded by time-stamping the cash register receipt for each sale. Grouping sales by date and time would result in a large number of groups, perhaps one for each second of the working day. Analysis Services allows you to group such information into larger "buckets." Perhaps you'd like to see the sales total by hours, by days, or by months. Many dimensions can naturally be organized into such a hierarchical structure. Each member of such a hierarchy within a dimension is called a *level*.

> **NOTE**   ADO MD allows a single dimension to contain multiple hierarchies. Analysis Services doesn't implement this additional level of complexity.

Figure 10.4 shows schematically some possible dimensions together with the levels that they might contain.

Measures

When you're using Analysis Services to group data, the actual data that is being grouped is referred to as a *measure*. For example, if you produce an analysis of total price of products sold by product and by store, then product price is a measure in that analysis (and, of course, product and store are dimensions).

FIGURE 10.4:

Organizing data into dimensions and levels

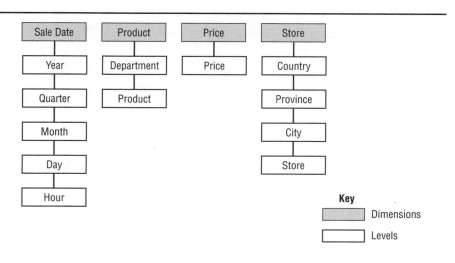

Key
Dimensions
Levels

It's not unusual for a database to contain more than one measure. For example, a database of sales could plausibly hold measures such as these:

- Retail price
- Wholesale price
- Quantity sold

Measures are generally numeric values that can be aggregated by adding multiple records together, although Analysis Services does allow for aggregation functions other than SUM().

TIP   In general, if you can describe your data in terms of "I need to see x, y, and z pieces of information broken down by a, by b, by c...," the x, y, and z will represent measures, and the a, b, and c will represent dimensions.

Cubes

In OLAP terms, the aggregated data used in an analysis is called a *cube*. A cube is a storage unit that combines a number of dimensions and measures into one whole.

NOTE   The term *cube* can sometimes be confusing, as it implies both a number of dimensions and, worse, an underlying structure for the data storage. But in OLAP databases, cubes can contain more or fewer than three dimensions.

Figure 10.5 shows an actual cube from the FoodMart 2000 sample application (which is installed when you install Analysis Services). In this example:

- Product and Education are dimensions.
- Product Family, Product Department, and Product Category are levels.
- The sales total for each combination (in the unshaded cells) is a measure.
- All of these together make up one view of a cube.

FIGURE 10.5:

Cubes, dimensions, levels, and measures

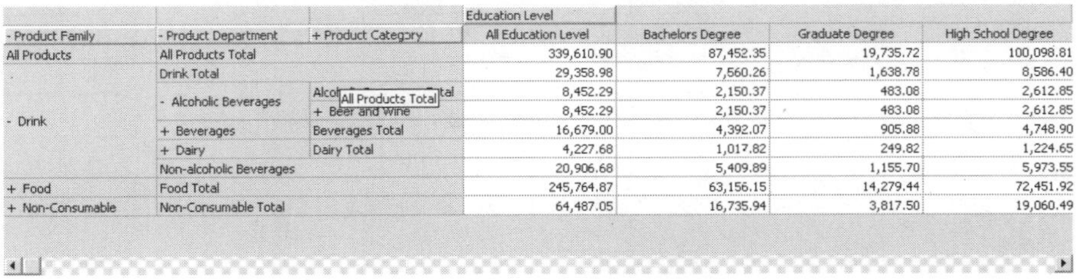

- Product Family	- Product Department	+ Product Category	Education Level All Education Level	Bachelors Degree	Graduate Degree	High School Degree
All Products	All Products Total		339,610.90	87,452.35	19,735.72	100,098.81
	Drink Total		29,358.98	7,560.26	1,638.78	8,586.40
- Drink	- Alcoholic Beverages	Alco All Products Total tal + Beer and wine	8,452.29 8,452.29	2,150.37 2,150.37	483.08 483.08	2,612.85 2,612.85
	+ Beverages	Beverages Total	16,679.00	4,392.07	905.88	4,748.90
	+ Dairy	Dairy Total	4,227.68	1,017.82	249.82	1,224.65
	Non-alcoholic Beverages		20,906.68	5,409.89	1,155.70	5,973.55
+ Food	Food Total		245,764.87	63,156.15	14,279.44	72,451.92
+ Non-Consumable	Non-Consumable Total		64,487.05	16,735.94	3,817.50	19,060.49

MOLAP, ROLAP, and HOLAP

As you saw in Figure 10.2, Analysis Services can actually use two different kinds of databases for storing its data. The first is a multidimensional database that is managed by Analysis Services itself. The second is a relational database that is managed by Microsoft SQL Server. These two storage formats offer three choices for cubes, referred to as MOLAP, ROLAP, and HOLAP storage.

MOLAP

The *M* in MOLAP stands for Multidimensional. In MOLAP, *both* the source data *and* the aggregations are stored in a multidimensional format. MOLAP is almost always the fastest option for data retrieval; however, it often requires the most disk space.

ROLAP

In the ROLAP (or Relational OLAP) approach, all data, including aggregations, is stored within the source relational database structure. ROLAP is always the slowest option for data retrieval. Whether an aggregation exists or not, a ROLAP database must access the database itself.

HOLAP

HOLAP (or Hybrid OLAP) is an attempt to get the best of both worlds. A HOLAP database stores the aggregations that exist within a multidimensional structure, leaving the cell-level data itself in a relational form. Where the data is preaggregated, HOLAP offers the performance of MOLAP; where the data must be fetched from tables, HOLAP is as slow as ROLAP.

Creating a Cube

OLAP and Analysis Services can be very confusing the first time you run across them. To help make sure you understand the concepts introduced in this chapter, this section will walk you through the process of creating a cube through the Analysis Manager interface.

In this example, you'll build a simple cube based on the sample data that's installed as part of Analysis Services. This particular sample data is in a Microsoft Access database. Analysis Services can base cubes on SQL Server, Access, or Oracle data, so you can use this database directly.

To build the sample cube, follow these steps:

1. Launch Analysis Manager by choosing Start ➤ Programs ➤ Microsoft SQL Server ➤ Analysis Services ➤ Analysis Manager.

2. Expand the Analysis Services node in the left-hand pane of the Analysis Manager interface. You should see the name of your server as a child of this node. If not, right-click the Analysis Services node, select Register Server, type the name of the computer where Analysis Services is running, and click OK.

3. Expand the server node. There will be a brief pause while Analysis Manager connects to the server, and then the treeview will show the names of the existing Analysis Services databases.

4. Right-click the server name and select New Database. Type **ADO** as the name of the database, and **ADO Programming Sample** as the description of the database. Then click OK to create the new Analysis Services database that will hold the definition of the cube.

5. Expand the node in the treeview for the new database. You'll see that it has five child nodes: data sources, cubes, shared dimensions, mining models, and database roles. Right-click the data sources node and select New Data Source. This will open the Data Link Properties dialog box.

6. You use the Data Link Properties dialog box to choose the source data for the new cube. On the Provider tab, choose the Microsoft Jet 4.0 OLE DB provider. On the Connection tab, use the browse button to locate the `foodmart 2000.mdb` sample database (by default, this is in `C:\Program Files\Microsoft Analysis Services\Samples\`). Select Admin for the username and check the Blank Password check box. Click OK to create the data source and return to Analysis Manager.

7. Right-click the Cubes node in Analysis Manager and select New Cube ➤ Wizard. This will launch the Cube Wizard, which starts with an introductory panel that explains the purpose of the wizard. Click Next.

8. On the Select Fact panel, choose the sales_fact_1998 table. Click Next.

9. The next panel allows you to select numeric columns to be the measures in your new cube. All the numeric fields in the chosen fact table are available here. Choose store_cost and store_sales as measures and then click Next.

10. The next panel is the Select Dimensions panel. Because you just created this Analysis Services database, there are no existing dimensions to choose. Click New Dimension to launch the Dimension Wizard.

11. The Dimension Wizard starts with an introductory panel that explains the purpose of the wizard. Click Next.

12. On the Dimension Type panel, choose Star Schema and then click Next.

13. On the Select Dimension Table panel, choose Store and then click Next.

14. On the Select Dimension Type panel, choose Standard Dimension and then click Next.

15. On the Select Levels panel, select store_country, store_city, and store_name. Then click Next.

16. On the Specify Member Key Columns panel, click Next.

17. On the Select Advanced Options panel, click Next.

18. On the Finish panel, name the new dimension **Store** and then click Finish.

19. You'll now be back in the Cube Wizard. Note that the Store dimension that you just created has been automatically selected for the cube.

20. Click New Dimension again to launch the Dimension Wizard.

21. The Dimension Wizard starts with an introductory panel that explains the purpose of the wizard. Click Next.

22. On the Dimension Type panel, choose Star Schema and then click Next.

23. On the Select Dimension Table panel, choose Customer and then click Next.

24. On the Select Dimension Type panel, choose Standard Dimension and then click Next.

25. On the Select Levels panel, select country, state_province, and city. Then click Next.

26. On the Specify Member Key Columns panel, click Next.

27. On the Select Advanced Options panel, click Next.

28. On the Finish panel, name the new dimension **Customer** and then click Finish.

29. You'll now be back in the Cube Wizard. Note that the Customer dimension that you just created has been automatically selected for the cube.

30. Click Next. You'll see the Fact Table Row Count warning shown in Figure 10.6. Click Yes.

FIGURE 10.6:

Fact Table Row Count warning

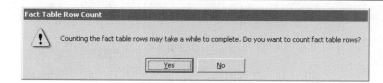

31. On the Finish panel of the Cube Wizard, name the new cube **Sales_1998** and then click Finish. The Cube Wizard will construct the new cube and open it in the Cube Editor.

32. Choose File ➢ Save and then File ➢ Exit. The editor will ask whether you'd like to design data storage options. Click Yes to launch the Storage Design Wizard.

33. The Storage Design Wizard starts with an introductory panel that explains the purpose of the wizard. Click Next.

34. Select MOLAP storage and then click Next.

35. Click Start and wait for the wizard to design storage aggregations. Then click Next.

36. Select Process Now and then click Finish. This will open the Process dialog box shown in Figure 10.7. Wait for the processing to finish and then click Close.

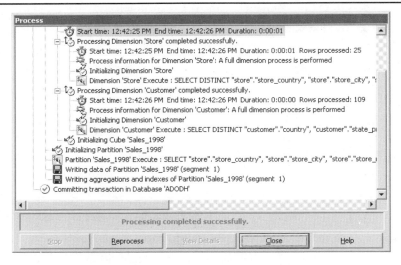

Your new cube will now be located in the Cubes folder in Analysis Manager. Expand this folder, right-click the cube name, and choose Browse Data. This will open the Cube Browser. Drag the Store dimension from the top of the Cube Browser and drop it on top of the Measures button above the grid. You can now double-click dimension cells (shown in gray on the Cube Browser interface) and view the corresponding aggregated measures in the grid area (shown in white). Figure 10.8 shows the sample cube open in the Cube Browser.

FIGURE 10.8:

Browsing the
new cube

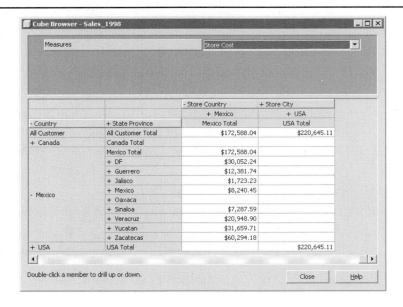

The ADO MD Object Model

Like the ADOX library that I discussed in Chapter 9, the ADO MD library contains its own object model. This object model hooks up with the ADO objects at some points. For instance, ADO MD reuses the standard ADO Connection object to connect to multidimensional data sources.

The ADO MD object model can be neatly divided into two sections. One group of objects deals with the schema of the OLAP database, allowing a program to navigate through the dimensions, levels, members, calculated measures, and so forth. The second group of objects provides access to the data returned from a query against an OLAP data source (these queries use a special language called Multidimensional Expressions, or MDX), supporting a multidimensional return set and the formatting of individual cells.

Figure 10.9 shows the ADO MD object model. In addition to the objects shown here, all ADO MD objects except the Position object have a Properties collection.

FIGURE 10.9:

The ADO MD object model

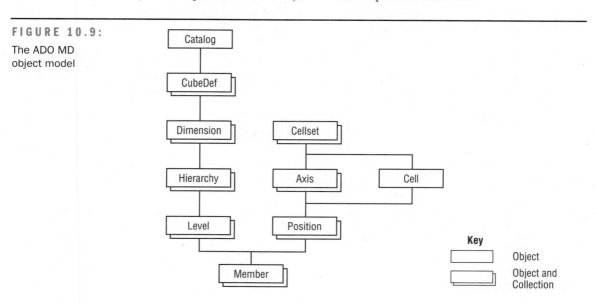

Table 10.1 lists all of the objects that are provided by the ADO MD library. You'll see each of these objects in more detail as you dig into ADO MD.

TABLE 10.1: Overview of the ADO MD Object Model

Object	Description
Catalog	This object represents an individual OLAP database connection and can be used to connect to a particular provider. The Catalog object is the highest-level object in the library and is the starting point for most ADO MD code. This object can be attached to a particular OLAP database by using an ADO Connection object.
CubeDefs	A collection of CubeDef objects.
CubeDef	Represents an individual OLAP cube and the properties associated with it.
Dimensions	A collection of Dimension objects.
Dimension	Represents a single dimension within a cube.
Hierarchies	A collection of Hierarchy objects.
Hierarchy	Represents a hierarchy within a cube. For most dimensions, there is only one Hierarchy object within the Hierarchies collection. Generally, you'll use this object only as a stepping-stone to the Level object.
Levels	A collection of Level objects.
Level	Represents a specific level within a dimension or hierarchy.
Members	A collection of Member objects.
Member	Represents an individual point within the cube, which might be an aggregation of a number of underlying members or an individual row descriptor from the fact table itself.
Cellset	The multidimensional equivalent of an ADO Recordset, a Cellset contains individual Cell objects representing the data returned from an MDX query. There is no collection of Cellsets.
Cell	Represents one discrete element of information (similar to the ADO Field object), together with properties including formatting information.
Axes	A collection of Axis objects.
Axis	Represents an individual axis within the returned Cellset (such as columns or rows). There may be multiple dimensions or levels within one axis.
Positions	A collection of Position objects.
Position	Represents a set of one or more members of different dimensions that define a particular point within a given axis.

Schema Objects

This section covers each of the ADO MD objects relating to the cube schema. These objects are the ADO MD equivalents of the ADOX objects. They're useful for retrieving information about cubes, but not for retrieving the data that the cube contains.

The Connection Object

The Connection object, although not formally a part of the ADO MD library, is essential to using ADO MD. Before you can execute a query or retrieve schema information with ADO

MD, you need to make a connection to the Analysis Services engine. You can either create an explicit ADO Connection object or use the ActiveConnection property of the Catalog object to implicitly create a Connection object. Either way, you need to create a connection string that makes sense to ADO MD.

Table 10.2 lists some of the parameters that are valid in a connection string that will be used with ADO MD.

TABLE 10.2: Connection String Values

Parameter	Value
Provider	The name of the OLE DB for OLAP provider that you are using to connect to the OLAP engine. For solutions using Analysis Services, this value is always MSOLAP2, the name of the Microsoft OLE DB Provider for OLAP Services 8.0.
Data Source	This should be the name of the server where Analysis Services is running. If your code is running on the same computer as Analysis Services, you can use the special name localhost.
Initial Catalog	The name of the OLAP database to which you want to connect.
Integrated Security	To use Windows-integrated security, include the string Integrated Security=SSPI in your connection string.
User ID	Username to use when connecting to the server.
Password	Password to use when connecting to the server.

NOTE You can also use Provider=MSOLAP instead of Provider=MSOLAP2. However, in some cases, this may prevent you from using new functionality introduced in the SQL Server 2000 version of Analysis Services.

The Catalog Object

Once your code has made a valid connection to the Analysis Services engine, you can start using the various objects that expose functionality within ADO MD. At the top of the schema objects hierarchy lies the Catalog object. This object is used to represent the concept of an OLAP database in its entirety, containing all the cubes and their underlying components.

Table 10.3 details the interface of the Catalog object.

NOTE In Table 10.3 and the tables following, the Type column indicates whether a particular item is a property (P), an object property (O), or a collection (C) of the parent object. The default member of the object is highlighted in italics.

TABLE 10.3: Catalog Object Details

Name	Type	Explanation
ActiveConnection	P	The connection string used to retrieve the Catalog object.
CubeDefs	*C*	*A collection containing a CubeDef object for each of the cubes within the OLAP database.*
Name	P	The name of the catalog (i.e., the name of the OLAP database).

The Catalog object doesn't actually do very much at all, apart from providing the facility to make a direct connection. Its function is purely to connect to an Analysis Services database or offline cube file and to provide access to the cubes contained within that store.

The CubeDef Object

The CubeDef object represents the definition of a particular OLAP cube and its underlying dimensions. Table 10.4 lists the interface details of the CubeDef object.

TABLE 10.4: CubeDef Object Details

Name	Type	Explanation
Description	P	Provides a brief description of the OLAP cube as set within OLAP Manager (read-only).
Dimensions	*C*	*A collection containing a Dimension object for every dimension within the cube (read-only).*
GetSchemaObject	M	Retrieves a Dimension, Hierarchy, Level, or Member object directly, without the need to navigate through the intervening levels of the object model.
Name	P	Contains the name of the cube, as used for referencing purposes (read-only).
Properties	C	A collection containing an object for each property relating to the cube that has been exposed by the data provider (read-only).

Note that the Properties collection of a CubeDef object contains properties from the OLE DB provider only, not properties from ADO MD. That's generally true of all the Properties collections within the ADO MD hierarchy. This means that you need to refer to properties in two different ways, depending on where they come from. ADO MD properties must be retrieved directly:

```
CubeDef.Description
```

But provider-specific properties must be retrieved from the Properties collection:

```
CubeDef.Properties("CREATED_ON")
```

Table 10.5 shows some of the properties available through the CubeDef Properties collection when the MSOLAP provider is used to access the cube.

TABLE 10.5: CubeDef Properties Collection

Name	Description
CATALOG_NAME	The name of the catalog (database) to which this cube belongs
SCHEMA_NAME	The name of the schema to which this cube belongs
CUBE_NAME	The name of the cube (this value is the same as CubeDef.Name)
CUBE_GUID	128-bit globally unique identifier (GUID) for the cube
CREATED_ON	The date/time when the cube was originally created
LAST_SCHEMA_UPDATE	The time stamp for the last update to the cube schema
SCHEMA_UPDATED_BY	The user context under which the cube schema was last modified
LAST_DATA_UPDATE	The time stamp for the last update to the cube data/aggregations
DATA_UPDATED_BY	The user context under which the cube data/aggregations were last modified
DESCRIPTION	The description of the cube (this value is the same as CubeDef.Description)

The Dimension Object

The Dimension object contains information about an individual dimension within a cube. It allows you to view the properties of a particular dimension and extract the hierarchies, levels, and members as collections from within a dimension. Table 10.6 shows the properties and collections available within the Dimension object.

TABLE 10.6: Dimension Object Details

Name	Type	Explanation
Description	P	Provides a description of the dimension as set within OLAP Manager (read-only).
Hierarchies	*C*	*A collection containing a Hierarchy object for every hierarchy within the dimension (read-only). (For dimensions not using hierarchies, this collection contains only a single hierarchy containing all the levels.)*
Name	P	Contains the name of the dimension, as used for referencing purposes (read-only).
Properties	C	A collection containing an object for each property relating to the dimension that has been exposed by the data provider (read-only).
UniqueName	P	A property containing the fully qualified name for a particular dimension, in the form [*dimension*] (read-only).

TIP   Because Analysis Services doesn't offer support for creating multiple hierarchies in a dimension through its user interface, you are unlikely to encounter multiple hierarchies in practice. The exception to this rule is in parent–child dimensions, which represent hierarchical information such as an organization chart.

Like the CubeDef's Properties collection, the Dimension's Properties collection is populated by the underlying OLE DB provider. Table 10.7 lists some of the properties that you'll find in this collection.

TABLE 10.7: Dimension Properties Collection

Name	Description
CATALOG_NAME	The name of the catalog from which the cube (and ultimately the dimension) is derived
SCHEMA_NAME	The name of the schema to which this dimension belongs
CUBE_NAME	The name of the cube to which this dimension belongs
DIMENSION_NAME	The name of the dimension (this is the same as Dimension.Name)
DIMENSION_UNIQUE_NAME	Fully qualified name for the dimension (this is the same as Dimension.UniqueName)
DIMENSION_GUID	128-bit globally unique identifier (GUID) for the dimension
DIMENSION_CAPTION	A label associated with the dimension
DIMENSION_ORDINAL	The index number for the dimension within the Dimensions collection
DIMENSION_CARDINALITY	The total number of members contained within the dimension
DESCRIPTION	A brief description of the dimension, if available

The Hierarchy Object

The Hierarchy object contains information for any hierarchies that are stored within the dimension. In Analysis Services, hierarchies are used within the context of parent–child dimensions for handling the relationship between parent and child. They can also be used for normal dimensions to allow a single dimension to be broken down in several different ways.

Table 10.8 lists the properties and collections available within the Hierarchy object.

For dimensions that don't contain hierarchies, this object is empty; however, it's still used as part of the object model for the purpose of navigation. If you know that a dimension falls into this category, you can reference the levels through the zeroth Hierarchy object (where cub is a CubeDef object):

```
cub.Dimensions("Projects").Hierarchies(0).Levels
```

TABLE 10.8: Hierarchy Object Details

Name	Type	Explanation
Description	P	Provides a description of the hierarchy as set within OLAP Manager or DSO (read-only).
Levels	*C*	*A collection containing a Level object for every level within the hierarchy (read-only).*
Name	P	Contains the name of the hierarchy, as used for referencing purposes (read-only).
Properties	C	A collection containing an object for each property relating to the hierarchy that has been exposed by the data provider (read-only).
UniqueName	P	A field containing the fully qualified name for a particular hierarchy, in the form [*dimension*].[*hierarchy*] (read-only).

Like the Dimension and CubeDef objects, the Hierarchy object also has a Properties collection, which can be used to access additional information about the hierarchy. Table 10.9 provides a list of some of the provider-supplied properties available for the Hierarchy object and their usage.

TABLE 10.9: Hierarchy Properties Collection

Name	Description
CATALOG_NAME	The name of the catalog from which the cube (and ultimately the hierarchy) is derived
SCHEMA_NAME	The name of the schema to which this hierarchy belongs
CUBE_NAME	The name of the cube to which this hierarchy belongs
DIMENSION_UNIQUE_NAME	The unique name of the dimension to which this hierarchy belongs
HIERARCHY_NAME	The name of the current Hierarchy object (same as Hierarchy.Name)
HIERARCHY_UNIQUE_NAME	The fully qualified name for the current Hierarchy object (same as Hierarchy.UniqueName)
HIERARCHY_GUID	The 128-bit globally unique identifier (GUID) for the Hierarchy
HIERARCHY_CAPTION	A display name for the hierarchy, if available
HIERARCHY_CARDINALITY	The total number of members contained within this particular hierarchy
DESCRIPTION	A description for the hierarchy, if available (same as Hierarchy.Description)

The Level Object

The Level object represents an individual level within a dimension. For example, if you have a Store dimension that is broken down by country, state, city, and store number, each of those would correspond to a Level within the Levels collection of the default hierarchy of the dimension. Table 10.10 shows the properties and collections available for this object.

TABLE 10.10: Level Object Details

Name	Type	Explanation
Caption	P	A display name for the level (read-only).
Depth	P	A value indicating the depth of the level or the number of levels between the current level and the parent hierarchy (read-only).
Description	P	Provides a description of the level as set within OLAP Manager or DSO (read-only).
Members	*C*	*A collection containing a Member object for every member within the level (read-only).*
Name	P	Contains the name of the level, as used for referencing purposes (read-only).
Properties	C	A collection containing an object for each property relating to the level that has been exposed by the data provider (read-only).
UniqueName	P	A field containing the fully qualified name for a particular level, in the form [*dimension*].[*level*] (read-only).

Table 10.11 lists some of the properties that are stored in the ADO Properties collection within the Level object and are supplied by the MSOLAP provider.

TABLE 10.11: Level Properties Collection

Name	Description
CATALOG_NAME	The name of the catalog from which the cube (and ultimately the level) is derived
SCHEMA_NAME	The name of the schema to which this level belongs
CUBE_NAME	The name of the cube to which this level belongs
DIMENSION_UNIQUE_NAME	The unique name of the dimension to which this level belongs
HIERARCHY_UNIQUE_NAME	The unique name of the current Hierarchy object to which the level belongs
LEVEL_NAME	The name of the level itself, presented as a string
LEVEL_UNIQUE_NAME	The fully qualified level name, including the parents of the level as required

continued on next page

TABLE 10.11 CONTINUED: Level Properties Collection

Name	Description
LEVEL_GUID	The 128-bit globally unique identifier (GUID) for the Level
LEVEL_CAPTION	A display name for the level, if available
LEVEL_NUMBER	A number indicating the level's position within the Levels collection stored in its parent Hierarchy object
LEVEL_CARDINALITY	The total number of members contained within this particular level
DESCRIPTION	A description for the level, if available (same as Level.Description)
LEVEL_NAME_SQL_COLUMN_NAME	The column in the underlying database containing the names for the level

The Member Object

The Member object is the bottom of the hierarchy of schema objects, containing actual information from the underlying database. For example, the Member objects within a Level named Country might be United States, France, Germany, and England. Table 10.12 shows the properties and collections available for the Member object.

TABLE 10.12: Member Object Details

Name	Type	Explanation
Caption	P	A display name for the member (read-only).
ChildCount	P	Returns an estimate of the number of children below this member (read-only).
Children	C	A collection of the member's children containing a Member object for each child (read-only).
Description	P	Provides a description of the member if set within OLAP Manager or DSO (read-only).
DrilledDown	P	A Boolean value indicating whether there are any child members of this object; this is faster than using ChildCount to return a number of children (read-only).
LevelDepth	P	Returns the number of levels between the member and the root member (read-only).
LevelName	P	Returns the name of the level to which the member belongs (read-only).
Name	P	Contains the name of the member, as used for referencing purposes (read-only).
Parent	O	Contains the parent member, if one exists (read-only).
ParentSameAsPrev	P	A Boolean value indicating whether the parent of the member is the same as the member immediately before it (read-only).
Properties	C	A collection containing an object for each property relating to the member that has been exposed by the data provider (read-only).

continued on next page

TABLE 10.12 CONTINUED: Member Object Details

Name	Type	Explanation
Type	P	A value representing the type of member (regular, measure, formula, or container), as described in the MemberTypeEnum enumeration (read-only).
UniqueName	P	A field containing the fully qualified name for a particular member, in the form [*dimension*].[*hierarchy*].[*level*].[*member*] (read-only).

WARNING Some of the properties and objects described in Table 10.12 are not available when accessing the Member objects from a Level.Members collection. They are valid only for Member objects in a Position.Members collection. I'll discuss the Position object later in the chapter.

The Member object, like those objects above it, contains a Properties collection. Table 10.13 lists the Member properties that are made available to this collection by the MSOLAP provider.

TABLE 10.13: Member Properties Collection

Name	Description
EXPRESSION	The source formula from which a calculated member is derived.
MEMBER_KEY	A value that can be used to uniquely identify this member within its parent collection.
IS_DATAMEMBER	A Boolean value that indicates whether the member contains data.
<custom>	Members can also contain custom properties, defined within the Cube Editor in Analysis Manager.

The EXPRESSION property is used within calculated members to provide information on how the calculated member has been derived. For example, within the FoodMart 2000 Sales cube, the Profit measure contains the value `[Measures].[Store Sales]-[Measures].[Store Cost]` for this property.

The MEMBER_KEY property, new in the SQL Server 2000 release of Analysis Services, can be used to uniquely identify a particular member within a collection. This can be particularly useful where multiple members have the same name, such as within the Time dimension. Although each year within a Time dimension might have quarters named Q1, Q2, Q3, and Q4, these members will have distinguishing member keys that can be used to access each one individually. This property is generated automatically.

A Schema Example

Figure 10.10 shows the output of a procedure within the ADOChapter10 sample project. This procedure, called from the Get Schema button on the sample form, uses the schema objects to traverse the hierarchy of a cube.

FIGURE 10.10:

Information retrieved via the schema objects

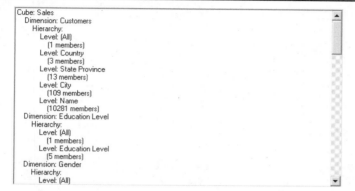

```
Cube: Sales
   Dimension: Customers
      Hierarchy:
         Level: (All)
            (1 members)
         Level: Country
            (3 members)
         Level: State Province
            (13 members)
         Level: City
            (109 members)
         Level: Name
            (10281 members)
   Dimension: Education Level
      Hierarchy:
         Level: (All)
            (1 members)
         Level: Education Level
            (5 members)
   Dimension: Gender
      Hierarchy:
         Level: (All)
```

The code that generates this listing uses nested loops to navigate through the ADO MD hierarchy. You can view it in Listing 10.3.

Listing 10.3:   **Retrieving the Schema of a Cube**

```vb
Private Sub cmdGetSchema_Click()
    Dim cnn As New ADODB.Connection
    Dim cat As New ADOMD.Catalog
    Dim cub As ADOMD.CubeDef
    Dim dmn As ADOMD.Dimension
    Dim hrc As ADOMD.Hierarchy
    Dim lvl As ADOMD.Level

    On Error GoTo HandleErr

    cnn.Open "Provider=MSOLAP;Data Source=localhost;" & _
      "Initial Catalog=FoodMart 2000"
    Set cat.ActiveConnection = cnn
    Set cub = cat.CubeDefs("Sales")

    lboSchema.Clear

    lboSchema.AddItem "Cube: Sales"
    For Each dmn In cub.Dimensions
        lboSchema.AddItem "    Dimension: " & dmn.Name
        For Each hrc In dmn.Hierarchies
            lboSchema.AddItem "        Hierarchy: " & hrc.Name
```

```
        For Each lvl In hrc.Levels
            lboSchema.AddItem "                    Level: " & lvl.Name
            lboSchema.AddItem "                    (" & _
            lvl.Members.Count & " members)"
        Next lvl
    Next hrc
Next dmn

' Clean up
cnn.Close
Set cnn = Nothing
Set cat = Nothing
Set cub = Nothing
Set dmn = Nothing
Set hrc = Nothing
Set lvl = Nothing

ExitHere:
    Exit Sub

HandleErr:
    MsgBox "Error " & Err.Number & ": " & Err.Description, _
      vbOKOnly, "cmdGetSchema"
    Resume ExitHere
    Resume

End Sub
```

Note that the code merely counts the members within each level rather than try to enumerate them. If you refer to Figure 10.10, you'll see that some levels in this particular cube have more than 10,000 members. Generally, you'll find the Member object more useful for retrieving information about a particular member than for browsing through members.

NOTE   The cube schema objects within ADO MD offer strictly read-only access to information about a cube. There's no equivalent within ADO MD to the Append methods of the ADOX collections. You can create new cubes through code, but you'll need to execute complex MDX statements to do so. I won't cover that technique in this book.

Data Objects

In addition to allowing you to retrieve schema information about a cube, ADO MD provides features to support querying of a cube using the MDX language. Results from querying a cube are returned in a structure called a Cellset, which you can think of as a multidimensional analog to the familiar ADO Recordset. I'll discuss the syntax of MDX later in this chapter, but first, let's go through the objects pertaining to multidimensional Cellset manipulation.

The Cellset Object

In the same way as the ADO object model contains a Recordset object that can be used to store the results of a (relational) SQL query, ADO MD contains an equivalent Cellset object, which can be used to store the results of a multidimensional MDX query. Table 10.14 shows the interface of the Cellset object.

TABLE 10.14: Cellset Object Details

Name	Type	Explanation
ActiveConnection	P	A valid OLE DB connection string or ADO Connection object, against which MDX queries should be executed.
Axes	C	A collection containing an Axis object for each of the axes within the result set.
Close	M	Closes the currently open connection.
FilterAxis	P	An Axis object containing information about the slicer dimensions used to return this Cellset.
Item	*P*	*An individual cell, specified by the index or array.*
Open	M	Opens the connection and returns a Cellset based on the results of an MDX query against the active connection.
Properties	C	A collection containing an object for each property relating to the Cellset that has been exposed by the data provider (read-only).
Source	P	Sets the MDX query used to generate the resultant Cellset.
State	P	Indicates whether the Cellset is open or closed.

Cellset objects are created based on an MDX query to an active connection. To fill a Cellset with data, you must complete the following steps:

1. Create a new Cellset object.

2. Set the ActiveConnection property to a valid OLE DB connection string or existing ADO Connection object.

3. Set the Source property to a valid MDX query string.

4. Call the Open method on the Cellset object to perform the query and populate the object.

You saw an example of these steps earlier in this chapter:

```
With cst
    .ActiveConnection = "Provider=MSOLAP;" & _
    "Data Source=localhost;" & _
    "Initial Catalog=FoodMart 2000"
    .Source = "SELECT {Product.Children} ON COLUMNS, " & _
    "{[Store Type].Children} ON ROWS " & _
```

```
        "FROM [Sales] " & _
        "WHERE ([Store].[All Stores].[USA])"
      .Open
    End With
```

Once you have finished using a Cellset object, you should close it in order to release the resources it was holding. This is as simple as calling the Close method:

```
cst.Close
```

Once a Cellset is open, you have two choices: You can either read individual cells in a random-access fashion, selecting the desired cell by an index representing its location, or use the inherent structure of the Cellset to break the cells down by axis, position, and ultimately, member. To select a cell by index, you can use the Cellset's Item property. To select a cell by structure, you start with the Cellset's Axes collection of Axis objects, which is covered in the next section.

The Item property is comparatively simple to use. You simply specify the cell you want, either as an ordinal number index starting from 0 and working along columns and then rows, or as an array index. Figure 10.11 shows a sample Cellset.

FIGURE 10.11:

A two-dimensional Cellset

	1999	2000	2001
Groceries	4261	3802	423
Books	3490	317	4556
Sundries	123	13678	11240

The shaded cell in this figure could be specified in any of the following ways:

```
Set cll = cst(5)
Set cll = cst.Item(2, 1)
Set cll = cst("2001", "Books")
```

TIP   The Item collection, like other ADO MD collections, is numbered starting at zero.

A Cellset object has a Properties collection that is designed to hold provider-supplied properties. However, the versions of the MSOLAP provider included with SQL Server 2000 don't actually place any properties in this collection; it is always empty.

The Cell Object

The Cell object represents a single unit of the data contained within the Cellset (and is therefore analogous to the Field object within ADO). Ultimately, any code that works with a Cellset will operate on Cell objects to display the values of the Cellset, usually by iterating through the Cellset and retrieving Cells individually.

A Cell can be retrieved from the parent Cellset using the Cellset.Item property, as described above. Table 10.15 shows the properties and collections that can be accessed on the Cell object.

TABLE 10.15: Cell Object Details

Name	Type	Explanation
FormattedValue	P	Returns a string containing the value in the appropriate format for that value (e.g., "2,187") as defined by the FORMAT_STRING property associated with a cell.
Ordinal	P	A number representing the index of the cell within its parent Cellset (starting with 0).
Positions	C	A collection containing the individual positions that together represent the location of the cell on an axis.
Properties	C	A collection of extended properties relating to the cell; this is populated by the appropriate OLE DB provider.
Value	P	The value of a cell in raw, unformatted form (e.g., 2187).

It shouldn't surprise you to discover that the Cell object contains two kinds of information: the location of the cell (as provided by the Ordinal and Positions properties) and the data contained within the cell (as provided by the FormattedValue and Value properties).

Cell objects have a Properties collection that can hold provider-supplied properties. Table 10.16 lists some of these properties.

TABLE 10.16: Cell Properties Collection

Name	Description
VALUE	The value of the cell
FORMATTED_VALUE	The value of the cell formatted for display
CELL_ORDINAL	The ordinal number of the cell in the parent Cellset

The Axis Object

An Axis object corresponds to an individual axis from an MDX query. The axes are specified within an MDX statement as ON <axis>, as shown in the following example:

```
SELECT
{[Product].Children} ON COLUMNS,
{[Store Type].Children} ON ROWS,
{[Customers].Children} ON PAGES
FROM Sales
```

This example has three axes: columns, rows, and pages; if you executed the statement, the resultant Cellset would contain an Axes collection of three Axis objects: Cellset.Axis(0), Cellset.Axis(1), and Cellset.Axis(2), denoting columns, rows, and pages, respectively.

Table 10.17 shows the interface details of the Axis object.

TABLE 10.17: Axis Object Details

Name	Type	Explanation
DimensionCount	P	Returns the number of dimensions contained within the axis.
Name	P	Returns the name of the axis, if stored.
Positions	C	A collection containing a Position object for each slice or point within the axis.
Properties	C	A collection containing extended properties for the object as exposed by the provider.

Like the Properties collection of a Cellset object, the Properties collection of an Axis object is always empty if you're using the current Microsoft OLE DB drivers.

The Position Object

You've seen already that an axis contains one or more dimensions and that the corresponding Axis object contains a collection of positions. An individual position is simply a point along the axis. Each position may contain one or more members, depending on the level of the position.

Table 10.18 shows the interface details of the Position object.

TABLE 10.18: Position Object Details

Name	Type	Explanation
Members	C	A collection containing a Member object for each member contained within the position
Ordinal	P	A number representing the index of the position within the axis (read-only)

Unlike most of the other ADO MD objects, the Position object has no Properties collection. Because each position has at least one corresponding Member object, the properties are contained within the member itself.

The Member Object (Again)

In addition to being a child of the Level object, the Member object is also a child of the Position object. The Members of a Position provide a description of the values that were chosen to filter the Cellset at that position.

Table 10.19 shows which of the properties of the Member object are valid, depending on whether it is a child of the Level object or the Position object.

TABLE 10.19: Availability of Member Properties through Level and Position Objects

Name	Level	Position
Caption	Available	Available
ChildCount	Available	Available
Children	Available	Available, but never contains information
Description	Available	Available
DrilledDown	Not available	Available
LevelDepth	Available	Available
LevelName	Available	Available
Name	Available	Available
Parent	Available	Not available
ParentSameAsPrev	Not available	Available
Properties	Available	Available
Type	Available	Not available
UniqueName	Available	Available

Retrieving Multidimensional Data

The major use of ADO MD for most developers is for retrieving results from multidimensional data sources. At this point, I've reviewed all the objects that you'll need for this purpose. However, there's still more to learn before you can use ADO MD for data retrieval in your own applications. You need to understand the fundamentals of the MDX language. Just as SQL is the standard for retrieving results from relational databases, MDX is the standard for retrieving results from multidimensional databases.

In this section, I'll introduce you to the basics of the MDX language, so that you'll be able to understand simple MDX queries. At the end of the chapter, I'll put this language together with the ADO MD objects to actually retrieve some data.

NOTE
There is much more to MDX than I can cover in a single chapter. You'll find a complete reference in the MDX section of the SQL Server Books Online.

MDX is very similar to SQL in syntax, although simpler in many ways. Whereas most implementations of SQL include a large number of different operations (such as SELECT, UPDATE, INSERT, and DELETE), MDX itself fundamentally supports just a few operations. In particular, MDX is not designed to update data. However, as you'll see in this section, the MDX SELECT statement is itself quite complex.

The SELECT statement is the core of the MDX language. An MDX SELECT statement allows you to choose just about any view of an Analysis Services cube that you want to see. You can specify dimensions and measures, slice the data, or apply a variety of functions to the source data to produce the SELECT output. In this section, I'll discuss the basics of the SELECT statement and show you how it works on some sample cube data.

Anatomy of an MDX Statement

By far the most common task you will do using MDX is querying an OLAP database that has already been created. The tool for doing this is the SELECT statement. At the simplest level, every MDX query follows a similar structure:

```
SELECT <axis> [, <axis>,...]
FROM <cube>
WHERE <slicer>
```

The three basic SELECT clauses describe the data that will be retrieved by the query and how it will be aggregated. They include the following:

- One or more axis clauses specifying what information should be returned and how it should be displayed

- A FROM clause, specifying which cube contains the required data

- A WHERE clause, specifying the subset of data that is relevant (how the data should be *sliced*)

In MDX, a query can return any number of dimensions (up to the total number of dimensions in the source cube), and rows and columns have no semantic meaning of their own (unlike SQL queries, where rows represent records and columns represent fields). When you execute an MDX query, the resulting Cellset represents a subset of the queried multidimensional database with the specified number of dimensions.

NOTE   In theory at least, MDX is a database-neutral language that can support any OLE DB for OLAP provider. For example, the OLE DB for OLAP documentation (part of the MDAC SDK available from www.microsoft.com/data) describes the use of MDX in a provider-neutral language. In reality, however, this presently boils down to a single choice, the Microsoft OLE DB Provider for OLAP Services, although this may change in the future.

Simple MDX Queries

To demonstrate the concepts behind MDX, I'll use the Sales cube in the FoodMart 2000 sample database that is installed as part of Analysis Services. This cube contains five measures and 12 dimensions, as shown in Table 10.20.

TABLE 10.20: Structure of the Sales Sample Cube

Name	Type	Comments
Customers	Dimension	Purchaser of the product
Education Level	Dimension	Customer's education level
Gender	Dimension	Customer's gender
Marital Status	Dimension	Customer's marital status
Product	Dimension	Product that was sold
Promotion Media	Dimension	Location of advertising for the product
Promotions	Dimension	Type of advertising for the product
Sales Count	Measure	Quantity sold
Store	Dimension	Store where the sale was made
Store Cost	Measure	Cost of the item wholesale
Store Sales	Measure	Total purchase price
Store Sales Net	Measure	Profit on the sale
Store Size in SQFT	Dimension	Size of the store
Store Type	Dimension	Type of the store
Time	Dimension	Date of sale
Unit Sales	Measure	Price per unit sold
Yearly Income	Dimension	Customer's annual income

Let's start with a relatively simple MDX query:

```
SELECT
[Time].[1997].Children ON COLUMNS,
[Product].[Food].Children ON ROWS
FROM [Sales]
WHERE [Measures].[Unit Sales]
```

NOTE   If you're following the examples on your computer, you'll need an OLAP query tool that supports MDX. Analysis Services ships with the MDX Sample Application, which you can use to evaluate the queries in this section. You can launch this application from Programs ➤ Microsoft SQL Server ➤ Analysis Services ➤ MDX Sample Application.

This query produces the result shown in Figure 10.12.

FIGURE 10.12:

A basic MDX query

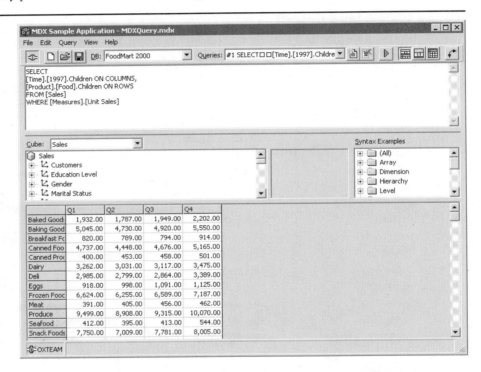

The preceding query has two axes: columns and rows. In the columns axis, it displays an entry for each quarter in the year 1997; in the rows axis, it displays an entry for each type of food product. In each cell of the result set, the query displays the total unit sales for that product in that quarter.

TIP   MDX allows keywords (such as COLUMNS or WHERE) to appear in any case. In this chapter, I'm using the SQL convention of showing keywords entirely in uppercase characters.

It's relatively easy to correlate this back to the original MDX query. In the query, I used the clause [Time].[1997].Children to describe the columns axis. The [Time] portion represents the Time dimension, with `[1997].Children` as a set function returning the child members (that is, quarters) in 1997.

You can use a similar syntax to view any individual member of a dimension. For example, to specify the month of March 1997 alone, you could use the clause `[Time].[1997].[Q1].[3]`. If you're interested in viewing selected members together, you can group them with curly braces (`{` and `}`) to specify a set, as in the following example:

```
SELECT
{[Time].[1997].[Q1].[3],
[Time].[1997].[Q2].[6],
[Time].[1997].[Q3].[9],
[Time].[1997].[Q4].[12]} ON COLUMNS,
{[Store].[USA].[CA],
[Store].[USA].[OR],
[Store].[USA].[WA]} ON ROWS
FROM [Sales]
WHERE [Measures].[Unit Sales]
```

This query produces the results shown in Figure 10.13: the sales for the last month in each quarter in 1997 for selected states.

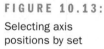

FIGURE 10.13:

Selecting axis positions by set

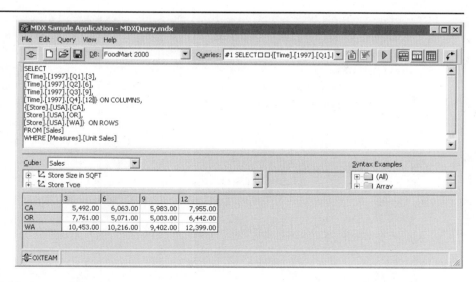

The FROM clause of an MDX SELECT statement is quite simple: It specifies the cube(s) that contain the data you are searching for. If the name of the cube contains a space, you must enclose it in square brackets.

Transact-SQL allows the use of quotation marks as well as square brackets to delimit identifiers in certain circumstances. MDX allows only square brackets as a delimiter. Square brackets are sometimes required (as in the case of an object name with spaces) but never forbidden. In this chapter, I have usually followed the convention of using square brackets around every identifier, whether required or not.

The final clause in the SELECT statement is the WHERE clause. This clause is used to "slice" the data into a subset. In the preceding examples, [Measures].[Unit Sales] is used to limit the result set to contain only one measure (Unit Sales). As with the axis specification, you can use more than one clause to limit the returned set still further, as in the following example:

```
SELECT
[Time].[1997].Children ON COLUMNS,
[Product].[Product Family].Members ON ROWS
FROM [Sales]
WHERE ([Measures].[Unit Sales],
       [Store Type].[All Store Type].[Mid-Size Grocery],
       [Gender].[All Gender].[M])
```

This example filters the Cellset to include only sales made in midsize grocery stores to male shoppers. The slicer dimensions (that is, any dimensions listed in the WHERE clause) can be any or all of the dimensions or measures within the cube, except for those that are used within the axis specification. So, in the preceding example, it wouldn't be acceptable to use the Product dimension in the WHERE clause, since the dimension has already been used in specifying the ROWS axis.

Where a dimension is not explicitly specified within the SELECT statement as a whole, the default member is implicit within the WHERE clause. For a dimension x, the default member is typically equivalent to [x].[All x].

This SELECT statement also introduces a new set function: Members. This function returns a complete set of each of the underlying members for that level, dimension, or hierarchy. For example,

```
[Product].[Product Family].Members
```

returns

```
{[Product].[Drink], [Product].[Food]. [Product].[Non-Consumable]}
```

(in other words, all the members of the Product Family level in the Product dimension).

Using the Members and Children Keywords

There's often confusion at first as to when the Children keyword should be used and when the Members keyword should be used to represent the underlying set of members. A simple rule to remember is that levels have members, and members have children (which are themselves members).

Don't forget that a level is a generic description of a particular point in the dimension hierarchy (for example, year, country, or store). Conversely, a member is one value from that level (for example, 1999, Germany, or Store 35, respectively). So `[Time].[2000].Children` is valid, as is `[Time].[Year].Members`; but `[Time].[Year].Children` and `[Time].[2000].Members` are semantically incorrect. If you are getting the error message "Formula error: invalid bind request: in a <level> base object," chances are you've got the two keywords switched.

You can also use both Members and Children keywords at the Dimension level, with different results from each. Here, Members returns *all* descendant members, whereas Children returns just the direct child members of a dimension. Thus, in the FoodMart 2000 database, `[Products].Children` returns the top-level members (Drink, Food, and Non-Consumable), whereas `[Products].Members` returns all 1500+ descendant members (including the [All Product] member that represents the grand total of all products). So be careful which you choose!

Designing an MDX Query

Here's a step-by-step guide to building an MDX query:

1. *Consider what information you are trying to show.* Will your result set contain measures that already exist within the database? Or will the cells contain the results of a calculation or formula based on other values?

2. *Think about the dimensions by which you want to break down the result set.* How many different ways will the data be broken down? How many levels deep do you want to include in the result set? If you will be writing the client yourself, consider whether you should retrieve more levels than you actually need at once or whether you will issue further queries for more information. Do you need to display all the members at a particular level or only selected members?

3. *Consider how the information should be handled within the Cellset.* Which dimensions will you place on each axis? If you are returning three or more dimensions, do you want to return an axis for each dimension, or will you present several dimensions on one axis? (Note that many OLAP clients can display only two axes at the same time.)

Although it's entirely possible to put together a one-off query without "designing" it, if your query will be hard-coded or parameterized into a client application, some extra thought at the authoring stage can pay dividends in the long run.

Unique Names in MDX

As a language, MDX tries to be relatively forgiving about layout. It allows you to insert white space (spaces and tabs) or carriage returns throughout the query and allows you to leave out unnecessary detail in specifying cube members. For instance, the following query is valid:

```
SELECT
[Beer and Wine].Children ON COLUMNS,
{[Bellflower]} ON ROWS
FROM [Sales]
```

Because there is only one member within the cube for each of the names referenced above within the cube, this query has no ambiguity in its meaning. Another equivalent (albeit long-winded) way of writing the same query would be as follows:

```
SELECT
[Product].[All Products].[Drink].[Alcoholic Beverages].
➥ [Beer and Wine].Children ON COLUMNS,
{[Customers].[All Customers].[USA].[CA].[Bellflower]} ON ROWS
FROM [Sales]
```

This time, all the parent levels for each member are fully described. A member name containing all its ancestor members is known as a *fully qualified* name. In Analysis Services, fully qualified names can be used to avoid ambiguity wherever a member reference is required. Like square brackets, fully qualified names are always allowed—so the simple rule is to always qualify the name if you have any doubt.

Be aware that in some cases, a member will need to be at least partially qualified. For example, if the Time dimension for a particular cube contains Year and Month levels, the reference [January] is likely to be ambiguous because there will be more than one member with the name (unless the cube contains data for a single year only). In such a case, the member will need to be more fully described, as in [2000].[January]. Members that exist in multiple hierarchies will also require such treatment. For example, if both the CustomerLocation and SupplierLocation dimensions contain cities, a reference to [New York] will need to be qualified as [CustomerLocation].[New York], for example.

Remember, members have two Name properties that can be retrieved via ADO MD: Name and UniqueName. The Name property always contains the name of the member itself (for example, PCs). The UniqueName property contains a unique reference to the member; in Analysis Services, this is the qualified name itself.

Axes and Dimensions

Up to this point, all the examples I've chosen have involved information taken from two dimensions displayed in a grid structure. This is a common scenario, but often it's necessary in real-world applications to query against three or more dimensions at once.

MDX will happily return an *n*-dimensional Cellset in response to such a query, and it includes several keywords to support this. I've used the terms COLUMNS and ROWS to support two dimensions thus far, but the keywords PAGES, SECTIONS, and CHAPTERS can be used additionally to represent the third, fourth, and fifth axes, respectively. MDX can return up to 127 dimensions; indeed, each of these can be on a separate axis if necessary. Although there are keywords for only the first five axes, you can also specify an arbitrary number of axes by using AXIS(*x*), where *x* represents an index number for the axis, starting from 0. Table 10.21 summarizes the relationships between the keywords and axis numbers.

TABLE 10.21: Keywords for Representing Axes

Dimension	Keyword	Synonym
1	COLUMNS	AXIS(0)
2	ROWS	AXIS(1)
3	PAGES	AXIS(2)
4	SECTIONS	AXIS(3)
5	CHAPTERS	AXIS(4)
6	(not applicable)	AXIS(5)
...	...	...
127	(not applicable)	AXIS(126)

WARNING   Many OLAP clients that support MDX are limited to displaying a maximum of two axes at any one time. For example, the MDX Sample Application can display only two axes.

It's entirely possible to create a one- or even zero-dimensional result set. Consider the following:

```
SELECT
[Product].[All Products].[Drink].[Alcoholic Beverages].
➥ [Beer and Wine].[Beer].Children ON AXIS(0)
FROM [Sales]
```

The resulting Cellset is shown in Figure 10.14.

FIGURE 10.14:

A one-dimensional
MDX query

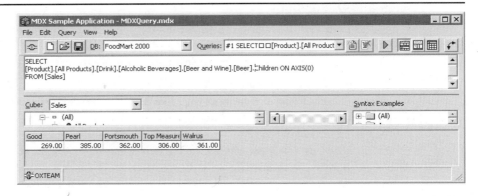

Or consider the simplest possible query:

```
SELECT FROM [Sales]
```

This query will return the total value across all dimensions of the Sales cube for the default member—in this case, 266,773.00.

You must be sure to never leave gaps in the axis definitions. The axes within a particular query must be a continuous set starting at AXIS(0) or COLUMNS, although they can appear in any order within the query. Thus, the following query is invalid and will return an error:

```
SELECT [1997].Children ON ROWS,
[Products].Children ON PAGES
FROM [Sales]
```

In this case, the command will fail because it skips an axis. This query uses ROWS (the second axis) and PAGES (the third axis) without using COLUMNS (the first axis) and will therefore be rejected by the MDX query processor.

Collapsing Multiple Dimensions onto an Axis

In most cases, a better way of handling a Cellset containing three or more dimensions is to collapse them into a smaller number of axes. You've seen how to specify the positions on an axis in terms of individual members in a set, as in the following example:

```
{[USA], [Canada], [Mexico]}
```

An axis specified in those terms would contain three positions: USA, Canada, and Mexico. However, you can combine two or more members from different dimensions to form what is called a *tuple*, as in this example:

```
{([USA], [1997]), ([USA], [1998]),
 ([Canada], [1997]), ([Canada], [1998]),
 ([Mexico], [1997]), ([Mexico], [1998])}
```

Such an axis would contain six positions, one for each tuple: USA/1997, USA/1998, Canada/1997, Canada/1998, Mexico/1997, and Mexico/1998. Each position would contain the relevant sales made in a particular region in a particular year, so USA/1998, for example, would include all sales made within the USA in 1998. Thus, the following MDX query produces the result shown in Figure 10.15:

```
SELECT
    {([USA], [1997]), ([USA], [1998]),
     ([Canada], [1997]), ([Canada], [1998]),
     ([Mexico], [1997]), ([Mexico], [1998])} ON COLUMNS,
    [All Products].Children ON ROWS
FROM [Sales]
WHERE [Measures].[Unit Sales]
```

FIGURE 10.15:

Defining columns with tuples

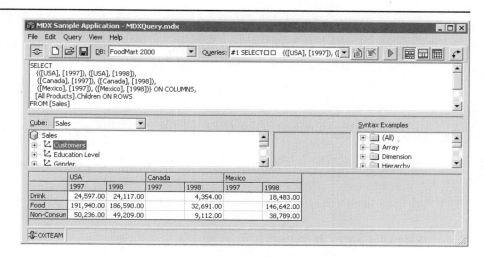

A simpler way of writing the same query is to use the CROSSJOIN function, which combines two sets to produce a set of tuples containing every possible permutation containing one member from each set. Thus, the preceding example could alternatively be stated this way:

```
SELECT
CROSSJOIN ({[USA], [Canada], [Mexico]}, {[1997], [1998]}) ON COLUMNS,
[All Products].Children ON ROWS
FROM [Sales]
WHERE [Measures].[Unit Sales]
```

TIP   The CROSSJOIN function will combine only two sets at any one time; to combine three or more sets, simply nest several CROSSJOIN statements.

Notes on Query Syntax

Earlier in the chapter, I mentioned some of the syntactical issues surrounding MDX SELECT statements. Now I'd like to formally explain the rules for a few things:

- Case and white space
- Comments
- Delimiters

Case of Expressions and Comments

I've already mentioned that MDX is a case-insensitive language. In practice, common convention is to capitalize keywords (such as SELECT) for the sake of clarity, and to enter other elements of MDX syntax in their original case. White space is also ignored; thus, for ease of readability, you can use tabs, space characters, or carriage returns to format MDX queries.

You can, of course, include comments that describe a query within MDX. You can use one or more of the following styles for your comments:

Double hyphens (i.e., --) Any characters following a double hyphen, up to the end of a line, are ignored.

C++-style comments (i.e., //) Any characters following a double slash, up to the end of a line, are ignored.

C-style comments (i.e., /* ... */) Any characters contained within the opening comment marker (/*) and the closing comment marker (*/) are treated as comments. C-style comments can span multiple lines.

Member Name Delimiters

Although you will often see MDX examples with brackets around every member name, they are *required* only in the following cases, to avoid ambiguity:

- The member contains a space, as in `All Products`.
- The member is an MDX reserved word or keyword, such as `Order`.
- The member contains nonalphanumeric characters, such as the `(All)` default member.
- The member's name begins with a number.

Usage is optional in all other cases. You may wish to simply enclose all member names in square brackets to avoid any risk of a conflict, particularly if you generate MDX programmatically. If you use square brackets, each individual item should be delimited to avoid ambiguity. In other words, you should use `[Product].[Small Ticket].[Ornaments]` rather than `[Product.Small Ticket.Ornaments]`.

MDX Functions

You've seen how you can use MDX to query an Analysis Services cube and return a subset of that cube, by specifying members to be displayed across several axes with measures returned in the body of the Cellset. However, MDX goes somewhat further than this; in particular, it includes well over 100 intrinsic functions that operate on various elements of a query component.

The functions available fall into nine categories:

- Set functions, such as the CROSSJOIN() function described previously, that operate on one or more sets and return a set

- Member functions that return an individual member based on input parameters

- Dimension, hierarchy, and level functions that return information about a member's ancestors

- Tuple functions that return a tuple from a set, based on user-defined criteria

- Numeric functions that calculate a value based on a series of measures

- Logical functions that return a Boolean value based on the output of an expression

- Array functions that manipulate a tuple or set and return an array

- String functions that manipulate a tuple or set and return a string

For details about MDX functions, refer to the MDX Function Reference in Analysis Services Books Online.

Opening a Cellset

Now that you've seen all of the necessary technology, let's put the pieces together to retrieve data from an Analysis Services server to the user interface of an application. Figure 10.16 shows an example Visual Basic form from this chapter's sample project.

FIGURE 10.16:

Displaying an MDX query in Visual Basic

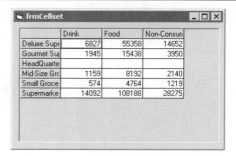

Listing 10.4 shows the code that generated this display.

Listing 10.4:   **Displaying Cube Data on a Grid Control**

```
Private Sub Form_Load()

    Dim cst As New ADOMD.Cellset
    Dim intI As Integer
    Dim intJ As Integer
    Dim pos As ADOMD.Position

    On Error GoTo HandleErr

    ' Get some data
    With cst
        .ActiveConnection = "Provider=MSOLAP;" & _
         "Data Source=localhost;" & _
         "Initial Catalog=FoodMart 2000"
        .Source = "SELECT {Product.Children} ON COLUMNS, " & _
         "{[Store Type].Children} ON ROWS " & _
         "FROM [Sales] " & _
         "WHERE ([Store].[All Stores].[USA])"
        .Open
    End With

    ' Make the FlexGrid match the results on the fly
    With hfgCellset
        .Clear
        .Cols = cst.Axes(0).Positions.Count + 1
        .Rows = cst.Axes(1).Positions.Count + 1
        .FixedCols = 1
        .FixedRows = 1
    End With

    ' Create the column and row headers from the Positions
    intI = 1
    For Each pos In cst.Axes(0).Positions
        hfgCellset.TextMatrix(0, intI) = pos.Members(0).Caption
        intI = intI + 1
    Next

    'Add row headers.
    intI = 1
    For Each pos In cst.Axes(1).Positions
        hfgCellset.TextMatrix(intI, 0) = pos.Members(0).Caption
        intI = intI + 1
    Next

    ' And now copy the data to the FlexGrid
```

```
    For intI = 0 To cst.Axes(0).Positions.Count - 1
        For intJ = 0 To cst.Axes(1).Positions.Count - 1
            ' Nulls are not valid in the .TextMatrix property.
            ' Append an empty string to convert them to strings.
            hfgCellset.TextMatrix(intJ + 1, intI + 1) = _
                cst(intI, intJ).Value & ""
        Next intJ
    Next intI

    ' Clean up
    cst.Close
    Set cst = Nothing
    Set pos = Nothing

ExitHere:
    Exit Sub

HandleErr:
    MsgBox "Error " & Err.Number & ": " & Err.Description, _
      vbOKOnly, "Form_Load"
    Resume ExitHere
    Resume

End Sub
```

The procedure to display this data starts by constructing an MDX query and using the Cellset object to execute it against the local Analysis Services server. Note that this code uses a connection string to set the ActiveConnection property of the Cellset, rather than create an explicit Connection object. ADO MD will still create the Connection object implicitly, but because the code uses this object only once, there's no drawback to this method.

Once the Cellset is returned, the code modifies the FlexGrid to have enough room to display the results. By modifying the FlexGrid at runtime, this code can be general-purpose. To display the results of a different MDX query, you need only to embed the query in the code; the display code can remain the same (assuming that the query has only two axes).

Finally, the code loops through the Cellset and transfers its contents to the FlexGrid. This tedious method of display is necessary because the FlexGrid can't be bound directly to a Cellset object.

Creating a Recordset from a Cellset

It's also possible to use ADO to create a Recordset from an implicit Cellset. Figure 10.17 shows the results of creating a Recordset with this technique.

A bound Recordset
from OLAP data

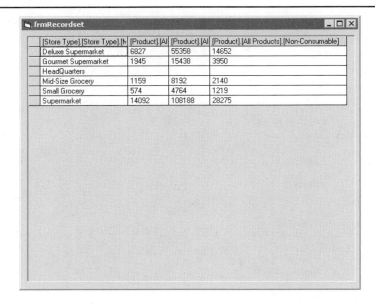

[Store Type].[Store Type].[M	[Product].[Al	[Product].[Al	[Product].[All Products].[Non-Consumable]
Deluxe Supermarket	6827	55358	14652
Gourmet Supermarket	1945	15438	3950
HeadQuarters			
Mid-Size Grocery	1159	8192	2140
Small Grocery	574	4764	1219
Supermarket	14092	108188	28275

The code for this technique, in fact, doesn't use any ADO MD objects at all. Rather, it uses the standard ADO Connection and Recordset objects, together with an ADO MD connection string and an MDX query, as shown in Listing 10.5.

Listing 10.5:   Creating a Recordset from an Implicit Cellset

```
Private Sub Form_Load()

    Dim cnn As New adodb.Connection
    Dim rst As New adodb.Recordset

    On Error GoTo HandleErr

    hfgRecordset.Clear

    ' Get some data
    cnn.Open "Provider=MSOLAP;" & _
      "Data Source=localhost;" & _
      "Initial Catalog=FoodMart 2000"

    rst.Source = "SELECT {Product.Children} ON COLUMNS, " & _
      "{[Store Type].Children} ON ROWS " & _
      "FROM [Sales] " & _
```

```
        "WHERE ([Store].[All Stores].[USA])"
    Set rst.ActiveConnection = cnn
    rst.Open

    ' Bind the data to the FlexGrid
    With hfgRecordset
        Set .DataSource = rst
        .Refresh
    End With

    ' Clean up
    cnn.Close
    Set cnn = Nothing
    rst.Close
    Set rst = Nothing

ExitHere:
    Exit Sub

HandleErr:
    MsgBox "Error " & Err.Number & ": " & Err.Description, _
        vbOKOnly, "Form_Load"
    Resume ExitHere
    Resume

End Sub
```

The provider follows three rules in creating the Recordset:

- There is one row in the Recordset for each combination of members on the row axis of the implied Cellset.

- There is one field in the Recordset for each combination of members on the column axis of the implied Cellset.

- The values returned at the intersection of these records and fields are derived from the unformatted Value property of the cells in the implied Cellset.

The major advantage of returning a Recordset instead of a Cellset is that the Recordset can be used in any context where a regular ADO Recordset is valid. For example, it can be bound to a grid control (as in this example) or even passed back over HTTP via RDS. On the other hand, the formatting of the Recordset is uninspiring, and the concatenated field names can be difficult to work with. If you're developing an interface that allows people to work interactively with multidimensional data, you're almost certainly better off using Cellsets than Recordsets.

Summary

In this chapter, you learned the basics of working with the ADO MD library:

- The basic architecture and terminology of OLAP applications
- The ADO MD object model
- The MDX query language

ADO MD is a specialized part of ADO that's not needed in many applications. Fortunately, the modular ADO architecture allows you to load these objects only when they are needed. If you're summarizing large amounts of data for analysis, you should definitely investigate using ADO MD and an OLAP database such as Analysis Server.

At this point, you've seen the major portions of ADO as it existed at the start of 2001. If you've been paying attention, though, you know that there is a major revolution going on in the world of application development with Microsoft software. The new .NET Framework vastly changes many parts of the development landscape, and ADO is no exception. In Part III of this book, I'll look at the .NET Framework, and in Part IV, I'll dig into the details of ADO.NET.

PART III

Understanding .NET

CHAPTER II

Introduction to .NET

- .NET architecture

- Building a .NET application

- Understanding namespaces

In the preceding eight chapters, you explored the ADO object model and the tasks that it can perform. As recently as the start of 2001, that was the latest and greatest data access that Microsoft had to offer. But that was before .NET, including ADO.NET, burst onto the scene. Even though, as I write this, .NET has yet to ship in final form, it's already clear that .NET represents a major shift in the way that many software applications will be designed and written.

.NET is a huge subject—and a new one to many developers. The sheer amount of documentation that ships with the .NET Framework and Visual Studio .NET can be overwhelming and even frightening. This chapter and the next two will provide an overview of .NET. I'll teach you the basics of the .NET architecture, discuss the .NET languages, and show you how you can still use your existing ADO code from .NET. Then, in Part IV of the book, I'll drill into ADO.NET and see what this new set of classes means for data access.

NOTE   The .NET content in this book is based on Microsoft's beta 2 release. Although this version is stable and usable, it's not the final software. Be sure to check out the book's web page for any last-minute changes that affect my .NET coverage. (Go to Sybex's website, www.sybex.com; in the Search box, type the book's ISBN code, **2994**, or the book's title.)

.NET Architecture

Microsoft describes the .NET Framework variously as "a new computing platform designed to simplify application development in the highly distributed environment of the Internet" and as "an XML Web services platform that will enable developers to create programs that transcend device boundaries and fully harness the connectivity of the Internet." While such descriptions give you some sense of *what* .NET can do, you, as a working developer, are probably more interested in *how* it can do those things. In this section, I'll describe some of the features and innovations that are the underpinnings of the .NET Framework:

- The Common Language Runtime (CLR)
- Managed execution
- The Common Type System (CTS)
- Cross-language interoperability
- The .NET Framework class library
- Namespaces
- Assemblies

- Application domains
- Security
- Deploying and configuring .NET applications
- Web services
- Windows Forms
- ASP.NET

The Common Language Runtime

The Common Language Runtime (CLR) is the core of the .NET Framework. All code written in the .NET languages is executed via the CLR. In that respect, the CLR is similar to previous runtimes such as the Visual Basic runtime. Visual Basic code is executed via the Visual Basic runtime, which translates the VB language into low-level Windows API calls.

The CLR is a much more active component of applications than the VB runtime is. In fact, the CLR takes such an active role in the execution of code that code written for the CLR is referred to as *managed code*. That's because, in addition to executing code, the CLR provides services. For example, the CLR takes care of all memory management and garbage collection (reusing memory occupied by objects that are no longer in use) for .NET applications.

The CLR is responsible for enforcing various rules that are designed to make .NET applications robust. These include constraints on datatypes, memory usage, and application security. Because all of this management is taking place in the CLR, it's impossible for even poorly written .NET code to contain many common types of errors. For example, memory leaks (where an object is instantiated and never destroyed) are impossible in managed code. And this protection comes at no cost to the developer. You don't have to write a single line of code to be assured that your application won't contain memory leaks.

Managed Execution

The entire process of turning your source code into a running application in the .NET Framework is referred to as *managed execution*. This process consists of four steps from start to finish:

1. You create your program's source code using a specialized development environment such as Visual Studio .NET or a general-purpose tool such as a text editor.

2. You use a .NET compiler to turn the source code into a form known as Microsoft Intermediate Language (MSIL). MSIL files typically have the file extension .dll or .exe; they look like executable files to the operating system, although they cannot run without the

CLR. The MSIL format is independent of any particular operating system or hardware architecture.

3. When you run a .NET executable, the .NET Framework uses a just-in-time (JIT) compiler to translate the MSIL instructions into actual hardware-specific instructions that can be executed by your computer's CPU.

4. The CLR passes the compiled code to the CPU, monitoring its execution to perform management services such as memory management, security checking, and versioning support.

Figure 11.1 shows the managed execution process schematically.

FIGURE 11.1:

The managed execution process

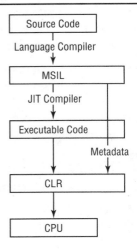

As Figure 11.1 shows, the MSIL version of your application contains information other than the code to perform the application's functions. This *metadata* is a separate section of the MSIL file that describes the contents of the file. This metadata is used by the CLR to ensure proper operation of the code. For example, the metadata contains descriptions of the datatypes exposed by your application; the CLR can use these descriptions to make sure it properly interoperates with other applications.

The .NET Framework includes a tool that you can use to examine the contents of an MSIL file. This tool is the IL disassembler, or ILDASM. To run ILDASM, follow these steps:

1. Choose Start ➢ Programs ➢ Microsoft Visual Studio .NET 7.0 ➢ Visual Studio .NET Tools ➢ Visual Studio .NET Command Prompt.

2. At the command prompt, type **ILDASM**.

3. Choose File ➢ Open to load an MSIL file into ILDASM.

Figure 11.2 shows a simple "Hello, World" program written in Visual Basic .NET and opened in ILDASM. The treeview shows the information contained in the metadata, while the separate window shows the actual MSIL code for the selected component.

FIGURE 11.2:

Examining MSIL with ILDASM

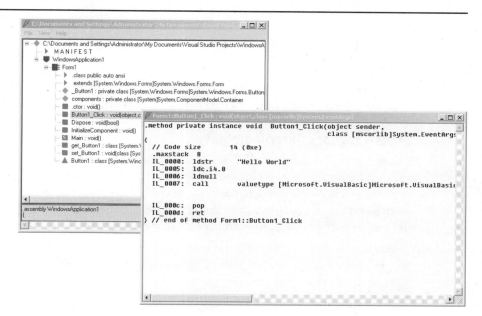

The Common Type System

The CLR defines the Common Type System (CTS). At its most basic level, you can think of the CTS as defining all the datatypes that managed code is allowed to use. It also defines rules for creating, persisting, using, and binding to types.

Because the CTS includes rules for creating new types, you're not limited to a small set of datatypes. In particular, you can define your own values (for example, Visual Basic .NET enumerations) or your own classes such that they will be acceptable to the CTS. Indeed, as long as you're using a .NET language, the operation of defining CTS-acceptable types is transparent to the developer. The compiler will take care of following the CTS rules.

The CTS manages many categories of types, including these:

- Built-in value types such as byte or Int32 (a 32-bit signed integer)
- User-defined value types (for example, you could write code to define a complex number type)
- Enumerations

- Pointers
- Classes from the .NET Framework class library
- User-defined classes
- Arrays
- Delegates (pointers to functions)
- Interfaces

All types managed by the CTS are guaranteed to be *type safe*. That means that the CLR and CTS ensure that an instance of a type cannot overwrite memory that doesn't belong to it.

Cross-Language Interoperability

Because the CLR manages all .NET code, regardless of the language in which it's written, the .NET Framework is an ideal environment for cross-language interoperability. That is, code written in one .NET language can be easily used from another .NET language. This interoperability is pervasive. For example, you can define a class in VB .NET and then call the methods of that class, or even derive a new class from the original class, in C# code.

The key to interoperability is the metadata contained in MSIL files. Because this metadata is standardized across all .NET languages, a component written in one language can use the metadata to figure out the proper way to call a component written in another language.

However, not every .NET language can use all the features of the CLR. For example, the CTS defines a 64-bit unsigned integer datatype, but not all languages allow you to define variables using that type. To ease this problem, .NET defines the Common Language Specification, or CLS. The CLS is a set of rules that dictate a minimum core set of .NET constructs that every .NET language must support. If you write components that conform to the CLS, you can be sure that they will be usable by components written in other .NET languages.

The .NET Framework Class Library

The other major component of the .NET Framework, besides the CLR, is the .NET Framework class library. A *class library* is a set of predefined classes that can be used to access common functionality. By supplying a class library, the .NET Framework keeps developers from having to "reinvent the wheel" in many cases.

If you've used Visual Basic 6, you're already familiar with the notion of a class library, although you may not recognize it by that name. Built-in Visual Basic objects such as the Err and Debug objects, are part of the class library that ships with Visual Basic.

The .NET Framework class library is exceptionally rich, containing several hundred classes. These classes encapsulate functionality such as the following:

- Defining data with the CLR datatypes

- Defining data structures, including lists, queues, and hash tables

- Installing software

- Debugging applications

- Globalizing software

- Reading and writing data

- Interoperating with unmanaged code

- Managing threads

- Handling security

WARNING   If you're not comfortable with concepts such as classes, objects, properties, and methods, you'll need to remedy this before you start working with .NET.

Namespaces

Classes within the .NET Framework class library are arranged in *namespaces*, groups of objects that perform similar functions. Namespaces also contain other .NET entities, such as structures, enumerations, delegates, and interfaces. Namespaces, in turn, are arranged into a hierarchy. For example, one class you'll see used in ADO.NET code is named System.Data .OleDb.OleDbConnection. An object instantiated from this class represents a single connection to an OLE DB database. This is the OleDbConnection class within the System.Data.OleDb namespace (a collection of classes dealing with access to OLE DB data), which is, in turn, contained within the System.Data namespace (a collection of classes dealing with data access), which is, in turn, contained within the System namespace (which is the root namespace for almost all the .NET Framework class library namespaces).

The .NET Framework class library contains nearly 100 namespaces. A complete listing would be exhausting and (because such a listing already appears in the .NET Framework SDK documentation) pointless. Table 11.1 lists some of the namespaces that you'll see as you dig into ADO.NET.

TABLE 11.1: Selected .NET Framework Namespaces

Namespace	Content
System.Collections	Abstract data structures, including lists, hash tables, queues, and dictionaries
System.Data	The root namespace for the ADO.NET classes
System.Data.Common	Classes shared by all .NET data providers
System.Data.OleDb	The OLE DB .NET data provider
System.Data.SqlClient	The SQL Server .NET data provider
System.Data.SqlTypes	Implementations of the SQL Server native datatypes
System.Diagnostics	Debugging and tracing aids
System.DirectoryServices	An interface to the Windows Active Directory
System.Drawing.Printing	Printer functionality
System.Globalization	Classes useful in globalizing an application
System.IO	Classes for reading and writing streams and files
System.Messaging	Inter-application messaging support
System.Net	Network protocol support
System.Resources	Resource file support
System.Runtime.Remoting	Support for distributed applications
System.Runtime.Serialization	Support for saving objects to files or streams
System.Security	Security and permissions functionality
System.Web	Support for communication with web browsers
System.Windows.Forms	Stand-alone user interface components
System.XML	Classes for using XML

Assemblies

.NET groups code into units called *assemblies*. An assembly can consist of a single file or of components distributed across multiple files. In all cases, there is one file that contains the *assembly manifest*, a part of the metadata that lists the contents of the assembly.

When you're writing .NET code, you can designate which files will go into an assembly, and which other assemblies a particular assembly is designed to work with. The CLR uses assemblies as a fundamental unit of management in many respects:

- Permissions are requested and granted on an assembly as a whole.

- A type retains its identity within an assembly. That is, if you declare a type named CustomType within an assembly, that type will be identical in all files contained in the assembly. But different assemblies may contain two different types named CustomType.

- The assembly manifest specifies which types may be used by code outside the assembly.

- Version tracking is done on the assembly level. An assembly can specify the version of another assembly that it requires, but it cannot specify a version for an individual file within an assembly.

- Assemblies are deployed as a unit. When an application requests code contained in an assembly, it must install the entire assembly.

.NET also allows "side-by-side" assemblies. That is, you can have two versions of the same assembly installed on the same computer, and different applications can use them simultaneously.

Application Domains

Application domains provide a second level of code grouping in .NET. An application domain is composed of a group of assemblies loaded together. The CLR enforces isolation between application domains, such that code running in one application domain cannot directly manipulate objects in another application domain.

NOTE	The CLR provides services for allowing cross-domain calls. You can manipulate objects across application domain boundaries by copying them between application domains or by constructing a proxy to forward the calls.

Application domains are not the same as Windows processes. On the Windows level, all of the code within a single application (such as Internet Explorer) runs in a single operating system process. But on the .NET level, multiple application domains can be contained within a single process. This allows, for example, several .NET-developed controls to be used on the same ASP.NET web page without any risk that one will corrupt the other.

Security

.NET is the first of Microsoft's development environments to be designed with serious attention to security. It's a fact of life that security holes have become more critical as more applications are connected to the Internet, where a wide variety of people with bad intentions can attempt to exploit any holes.

The .NET Framework implements both *code access security* and *role-based security*. Code access security is designed to protect the operating system from malicious code by granting permissions to resources based on the source of code and the operations that the code is attempting to perform. You can mark various classes and their members within your application to deny unknown code from using those resources.

Role-based security allows you to grant or deny access to resources based on credentials supplied by users. In role-based security, a user's identity determines the roles to which the user belongs, and permissions are granted to roles. The identity can be determined either by the user's Windows login credentials or by a custom scheme used only by your application.

Deploying and Configuring .NET Applications

The .NET Framework is designed to make deploying applications simple and less likely than current models to cause conflicts with existing applications. Because assemblies contain metadata that describes their contents, there is no need to make Registry entries or transfer files to the system directory in order to use an assembly. In fact, the simplest possible deployment is often appropriate for a .NET application: Just use XCOPY or FTP to move the application's files to a directory on the target machine, and then run the application. The CLR in conjunction with the metadata will take care of the rest.

The .NET Framework also supports version 2 of the Windows Installer. By using this installer to package and deploy your application, you can offer a wider variety of options to the user, including the option to install only portions of the application.

The .NET Framework also supports a mechanism for changing the behavior of applications after they are deployed. This mechanism is the *configuration file*, which is a file of settings stored as XML that the CLR can parse. Such files can include information on local security settings, on the location of particular assemblies, and on performance-related settings. You can also use configuration files to hold parameters for your own applications.

Web Services

As .NET catches on, you're going to hear a lot (if you haven't heard enough already!) about *web services*. You may also read a lot of complex, confusing explanations of the architecture of these web services. But at their most basic level, web services are simple: They are a means for interacting with objects over the Internet.

The key to web services is that they are built with common, pervasive Internet protocols: All communication between web services clients and servers is over HTTP and XML by default (although developers may use other protocols if they wish). For this to work, there has to be a way to translate objects (as well as their methods and properties) into XML. That way is called SOAP, the Simple Object Access Protocol. SOAP is a way to encapsulate object calls as XML sent via HTTP.

There are two major advantages to using SOAP to communicate with web services. First, because HTTP is so pervasive, it can travel to almost any point on the Internet, regardless of intervening hardware or firewalls. Second, because SOAP is XML-based, it can be interpreted by a wide variety of software on many operating systems.

There are two other important acronyms you'll run into when learning about web services in .NET. UDDI stands for Universal Discovery, Description, and Integration; it's a method for finding new web services by referring to a central directory. WSDL stands for Web Services Description Language, a standard by which a web service can tell clients what messages it accepts and which results it will return.

Using the .NET tools, you can take any data and define it as a web service. For example, you could develop a Customer object that retrieves address information from a database via ADO.NET, and wrap it as a web service. Once you've done that, client programs will be able to create new Customer objects and retrieve addresses from anywhere on the Internet.

Windows Forms

.NET also includes a new visual programming model called Windows Forms. Windows Forms is based on the MFC and Visual Basic forms models, and it provides a powerful way to design the user interface for .NET applications. Windows Forms was designed to fit well with the rest of the .NET universe: It includes easy connections to ADO.NET data as well as support for CLR features such as versioning, licensing, and security.

I'll show you some simple Windows Forms code later in this chapter.

ASP.NET

.NET was designed from the ground up to run code on web servers as well as on stand-alone and networked computers. ASP.NET is Microsoft's server-based framework for running .NET code on web servers. ASP.NET still uses the CLR to execute and manage .NET code, but it's tightly integrated into the web development process.

Conceptually, the ASP.NET processor is very similar to the existing ASP processor that you'll find in Internet Information Server (IIS). The user sends, via a web browser, a request to open a page—in this case, one with the extension .aspx. The ASP.NET process on the server executes the .NET code that is contained within the requested page and sends only the results of the execution back to the client.

Because ASP.NET is layered on top of the CLR, the entire spectrum of .NET code is available for ASPX web pages. The distinction between scripting languages (such as VBScript) and "real" languages (such as Visual Basic) found in previous server-side development systems is gone in .NET.

ASP.NET also includes a new visual programming model called Web Forms. These forms are very similar in appearance to Windows Forms and share many of the same controls. Web Forms provide an easy way to handle such tasks as data input, validation, and display.

You'll learn more about ASP.NET in Chapter 19, "Managing Data on the Web with ASP.NET."

Building a .NET Application

Windows Forms are text files, just like any other source files in .NET. You can, if you like, write a Windows Form in a text editor, compile it into your .NET application, and have it work perfectly. However, most developers are unlikely to do so. That's because Visual Studio .NET includes a Windows Forms designer that provides a graphical design surface. This designer translates the graphical design into the textual source code for you.

In this section, I'll show you the Windows Forms designer as part of the process of designing a simple .NET application. You'll see that the built-in tools in .NET make using ADO.NET to display and edit data a very simple task. But don't be fooled by the power of the design tools— there's still a lot to understand in ADO.NET. Although in this example, I'll let the tools write the code, in the chapters to come, I'll show you how to write your own data access code using ADO.NET.

This and the other examples in this book use Visual Basic .NET as their language. I've chosen this language because it's most likely to be familiar to the majority of the readers, who will probably recognize the Visual Basic underpinnings of this language. It's important to remember, though, that none of the functionality I demonstrate is specific to Visual Basic .NET. All of the .NET Framework is available to any .NET language.

Creating a New Application

To create a new application that uses Visual Basic .NET and Windows Forms, follow these steps:

1. Select Start ➢ Programs ➢ Microsoft Visual Studio .NET 7.0 ➢ Microsoft Visual Studio .NET 7.0.

2. If this is your first time to launch Visual Studio .NET, the Start Page will open to the My Profile section, shown in Figure 11.3. If you're an experienced Visual Basic developer, or just want to make your screen look the same as it does in my screen shots, you should use the settings shown in Figure 11.3.

3. Click Get Started on the left side of the Start Page.

4. Click the New Project button. This will open the New Project dialog box shown in Figure 11.4.

5. Select Visual Basic Projects as the project type, and Windows Application as the template for the project.

6. Name the new project ADOChapter11; then click OK to create the project.

TIP   I've provided the source code for this project on the companion CD.

FIGURE 11.3:
Visual Studio .NET
Start Page

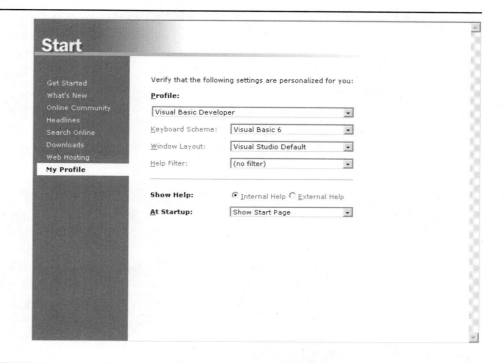

FIGURE 11.4:
New Project dialog box

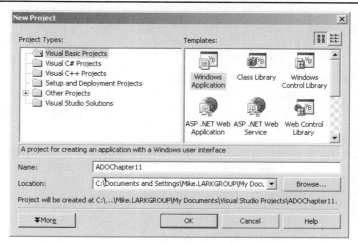

The Visual Basic .NET Design Environment

When you first open a Visual Basic .NET project, you may be overwhelmed by the sheer number of windows and buttons available. Here's what you'll find in the default set of Visual Basic .NET windows:

- In the center of the work area is the *designer*. This is the portion of Visual Basic .NET where you can design forms and write code, as well as design other specialized objects.

- In the upper-right corner of the work area, the *Solution Explorer* and *Class View* share a window. Tabs at the bottom of the window let you move back and forth between these two tools. The Solution Explorer provides a file-based view of the components within your Visual Basic .NET project. You can double-click a file here to open it in the designer. The Solution Explorer also shows you the .NET namespaces and other components that you have referenced from the current project. The Class View provides a logical view of the classes within your project. It presents a treeview that lets you drill down to individual classes, methods, and properties.

- In the lower-right corner of the work area, the *Properties window* and the *Dynamic Help* share a window. Tabs at the bottom of the window let you move back and forth between these two tools. The Properties window shows you the properties of the object currently selected in the Solution Explorer or the designer. Buttons on this window's toolbar let you choose whether to view the properties alphabetically or by category. The Dynamic Help window provides you with hyperlinks to the Visual Studio .NET help files that match what you're doing in the design interface. For example, if you select the Month-Calendar in the Toolbox, the Dynamic Help window will show you topic titles related to the MonthCalendar. If you click one of these titles, the corresponding help topic will open in the main designer window.

- At the bottom of the work area, you'll see the *Output Window*. Visual Basic .NET uses this window to send you informational messages. For example, when you run a Visual Basic .NET project, this window will tell you exactly which .NET assemblies are loaded, to provide functionality for the project.

- The *Toolbox* is to the left of the design surface. It contains controls and other components that you can add to your project. Some of these are Windows Forms controls, while others (for example, those on the Data tab) are nongraphical controls. The tabs on the Toolbox (Data, Components, Windows Forms, Clipboard Ring, and General, by default) allow you to keep components sorted into various categories. You can right-click the Toolbox and select Add Tab to add your own custom categories to the list.

- At the far left of the design surface, you'll see a tab for the Server Explorer. If you hover over this tab, the Server Explorer window will slide out and cover the Toolbox. You can control this sliding behavior by clicking the tiny pushpin icon in the Server Explorer's title bar. The Server Explorer lets you explore databases and other system services that are available to your application.

Of course, the entire Visual Basic .NET interface is customizable. You can drag windows around, leave them free-floating or dock them, and hide or display them. The View menu offers options to display the default windows as well as some other useful windows like the Object Browser and the Command Window.

Connecting to Data

In this example, I'll develop a project that allows you to edit data from a table in the SQL Server Northwind sample database.

NOTE Before proceeding, you need to be able to connect to and log in to a SQL Server that has the Northwind sample database installed. If you don't already have SQL Server installed on your network, you can install the SQL Server Desktop Edition (MSDE) from the Visual Studio .NET CD-ROMs.

To connect your application to the Customers table in the SQL Server Northwind database, follow these steps:

1. Hover the mouse cursor over the Server Explorer tab. This will cause the Server Explorer window to slide out from the left-hand edge of the screen. Click the pushpin icon to anchor the Server Explorer window while you're working with it.

2. Expand the Servers node in the treeview. This will show you the servers that Visual Studio .NET knows about on your network. To start, it will show only the computer where you are actually running Visual Studio .NET. If this is the same computer where you have SQL Server installed, you can continue with step 4. Otherwise, you'll need to add a server.

3. Right-click the Servers node and select Add Server. In the Add Server dialog box, enter the computer name or the IP address of the computer where SQL Server is installed. Click OK to add the server.

4. Expand the node for the server where SQL Server is installed, and then expand the SQL Servers node. Continue expanding to drill into the SQL Server, then the Northwind database, and then the tables in Northwind. Figure 11.5 shows the fully expanded tree in Server Explorer.

FIGURE 11.5:

Locating a database
table in Server
Explorer

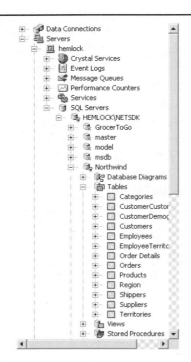

5. Drag the Customers table from the Server Explorer to the designer, and drop it on the
   design surface of the default Form1. Visual Basic .NET will create two objects for you
   when you do this: SqlConnection1 and SqlDataAdapter1. These will appear in a window
   at the bottom of the designer.

6. Click the pushpin icon in Server Explorer again and move your cursor elsewhere to allow
   the Server Explorer window to slide back off-screen.

7. Click SqlDataAdapter1 in the designer. The Properties window will show you the properties of the DataAdapter object, as well as some hyperlinks for working with the object.
   Click the Generate Dataset link. This will open the Generate Dataset dialog box, shown
   in Figure 11.6. Accept the default choices in this dialog box and then click OK. This will
   add a third item, DataSet11, to the designer.

The Connection, DataAdapter, and DataSet objects are ADO.NET objects that handle the
task of moving data from a database to a local cache. You'll learn more about these objects in
Chapter 14, "Using the ADO.NET Objects to Retrieve Data."

Generating a DataSet

Creating the User Interface

Now you can create a user interface for the data and bind the data in the DataSet to the user interface. To finish the project, follow these steps:

1. In the designer, use the sizing handle at the lower-right corner of Form1 to resize it to fill most of the available space.

2. Click the DataGrid control in the Toolbox. Click and drag the mouse on Form1 to create an instance of the DataGrid control that fills most of the available area.

3. In the Properties window, locate the DataSource property for the DataGrid control. When you click this property, it becomes a drop-down list. Use the list to set the property to DataSet11.Customers (the Customers table that has been retrieved into the DataSet).

4. Now you need to write just a little code to glue everything together. Select View ➤ Code to open the code for Form1.vb in the designer. You'll see that there is already some code in the window. In fact, there's quite a bit of code. If you click the + sign next to the box that says "Windows Form Designer generated code," you'll see all the code that Visual Basic .NET has written for you so far.

5. In the Method Name drop-down list at the top of the designer, select New. This will expand the generated code and show you the New procedure that's executed every time an instance of this form is created. You'll find a comment telling you where to add your

own initialization code. Add three lines of code after the comment that Visual Basic .NET supplies, as follows:

```
'Add any initialization after the InitializeComponent() call
SqlConnection1.Open()
SqlDataAdapter1.Fill(DataSet11)
SqlConnection1.Close()
```

This code will open a connection to the SQL Server and retrieve the Customers data whenever you open the form.

6. Select (Base Class Events) in the Class Name drop-down list at the top of the designer, and then select Closing in the Method Name drop-down list. This will create a blank Closing event procedure (which is executed whenever you close the form). Add one line of code to the empty procedure:

```
Private Sub Form1_Closing(ByVal sender As Object, _
  ByVal e As System.ComponentModel.CancelEventArgs) _
  Handles MyBase.Closing
     SqlDataAdapter1.Update(DataSet11)
End Sub
```

This code will save any changes to the bound DataSet whenever you close the form.

Running the Project

Now you're ready to run the project. Select Release from the Solution Configurations combo box on the toolbar. This defaults to Debug; for this test, though, you don't need to capture debugging information, and the project will run faster in Release mode. Then click the Start button on the toolbar or press F5 to start the project. You should see a form similar to the one shown in Figure 11.7, displaying the data from the Customers table in the Northwind database.

You'll find that you can edit the data on this form by typing in the cells, and you can add records via the blank row at the end of the grid. You can also delete records by highlighting them and pressing the Delete key. If you make some changes, close the form, and run the project again, you'll see that your changes have been saved back to the database.

If you think about previous data access solutions, this example should convince you that ADO.NET is a powerful alternative that's well integrated with the Visual Studio .NET user interface. It takes very little effort to write an application to edit data. There's also an interesting feature hidden in the few lines of code that you added: The code closes the connection to the SQL Server database as soon as the DataSet has been retrieved. This demonstrates that ADO.NET is designed from the start for disconnected data access—a useful feature for distributed databases.

FIGURE 11.7:

Customers data on a
Visual Basic .NET form

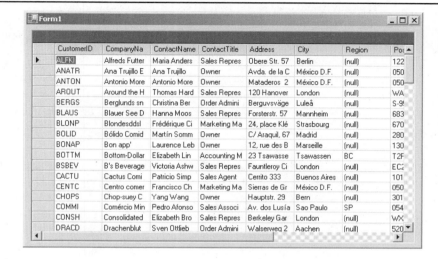

NOTE   You may wish to inspect some of the Windows Forms designer-generated code to get a
sense of the ADO.NET syntax at this point. I'll cover the details in Part IV of this book.

Understanding Namespaces

As mentioned earlier in the chapter, a namespace is a group of objects that perform similar
functions. But as you start investigating .NET namespaces in search of the functionality that
you need for your applications, you'll find a confusing variety of objects. In this section, I'll
explore a bit of the System.Data namespace to introduce you to the types of built-in objects
you can expect to find in .NET namespaces.

The System.Data Namespace

The System.Data namespace contains the fundamental classes for representing data in
ADO.NET. Namespaces are designed to hold a group of related classes, and they may also
contain other namespaces that provide additional functionality. System.Data is the root of a
hierarchy of namespaces:

System.Data: classes for representing data

System.Data.Common: classes shared by all data providers

System.Data.OleDb: the OLE DB data provider

System.Data.SqlClient: the SQL Server data provider

System.Data.SqlTypes: SQL Server datatypes

Typically, you'll use classes from several namespaces together in your applications. For example, to retrieve data from a SQL Server database to a DataSet in memory, you'll need to use classes from the System.Data, System.Data.Common, and System.Data.SqlClient namespaces.

Some namespaces also have links to other namespaces in different parts of the .NET Framework class library. For example, if you're using XML to transmit the structure of a DataSet to another computer over an Internet connection, you'll need to work with the System.Xml.Schema namespace as well as the System.Data namespaces.

Classes

Of course, one thing that you'll find in a namespace is a set of *classes*. The System.Data namespace contains a total of 44 classes. You'll use some of these more often than others. For example, any data access with ADO.NET will probably use the DataSet class, while you won't need to use the ReadOnlyException class unless your code might try to change the value of a read-only column.

Each class in .NET represents a particular entity. An instance of the DataSet class (part of the System.Data namespace), for example, represents an in-memory cache of data from some data source. Classes have members (constructors, methods, properties, and events). Table 11.2 lists the members of the DataSet class.

TABLE 11.2: Members of the System.Data.DataSet Class

	Public	Protected
Constructor	DataSet Constructor	DataSet Constructor
Properties	CaseSensitive	Events
	Container	
	DataSetName	
	DefaultViewManager	
	DesignMode	
	EnforceConstraints	
	ExtendedProperties	
	HasErrors	
	Locale	
	Namespace	
	Prefix	
	Relations	
	Site	
	Tables	

continued on next page

TABLE 11.2 CONTINUED: Members of the System.Data.DataSet Class

	Public	Protected
Methods	AcceptChanges	Dispose
	BeginInit	Finalize
	Clear	GetSchemaSerializable
	Clone	GetSerializationData
	Dispose	HasSchemaChanged
	EndInit	MemberwiseClone
	Equals	OnPropertyChanging
	GetChanges	OnRemoveRelation
	GetHashCode	OnRemoveTable
	GetService	RaisePropertyChanging
	GetType	ReadXmlSerializable
	GetXml	ShouldSerializeRelations
	GetXmlSchema	ShouldSerializeTables
	HasChanges	
	InferXmlSchema	
	Merge	
	ReadXml	
	ReadXmlSchema	
	Reset	
	ToString	
	WriteXml	
	WriteXmlSchema	
Events	Disposed	
	MergeFailed	

As you can see in Table 11.2, the members of a class are divided into public members and protected members. Public members can be called by code that's external to the class; protected members can be called only by code within the class, or within a class that inherits from the class. That is, in .NET, you can create your own class that inherits all the members of the DataSet class; within your own class, you are free to use the protected members. For the most part, your ADO.NET code will be concerned with only the public members of the ADO.NET classes.

Classes have four types of members:

Constructors   These are the special methods that are called when you create a new instance of a class. A class can have multiple constructor methods. For example, in Visual Basic .NET, you can create a DataSet using a constructor with or without a string parameter, as shown in these two examples:

```
Dim dsNew As DataSet
dsNew = New DataSet

Dim dsNew As DataSet
dsNew = New DataSet("DataSetName")
```

In both cases, the New keyword represents the constructor. In the second case, the code uses a form of the constructor that takes a name for the new DataSet object as a parameter.

Properties   Properties are the members that describe the class. They can return simple values (for instance, the System.Data.DataSet.Name property returns a string containing the name of the DataSet), or they can return other classes (for example, the DataSet.Relations property returns a System.Data.DataRelationCollection object).

Methods   Methods are the members that represent actions that a class can perform. Members can return output (for example, the Copy method returns a new DataSet object that is a copy of the current DataSet), but they are not required to do so (the Clear method, which clears the contents of a DataSet, has no return value).

Events   Events are things that can happen within a class that your code can monitor. For example, the DataSet.MergeFailed event is raised whenever you call the Merge method on a pair of DataSets, the EnforceConstraints property is set to True, and two rows have the same primary key.

Interfaces

Many namespaces also define *interfaces*. An interface resembles a class, in that it is a piece of functionality that can have properties, methods, and events. The big difference is that application code never creates instances of interfaces directly. Instead, your application code can create an instance of a class that implements an interface. Interfaces are normally pieces of functionality that are common across several classes. The interface resembles a contract that guarantees that the functionality will work the same way in all the classes that implement the interface.

An example may make this clearer. The System.Data namespace defines an interface named IDbTransaction. This interface represents a database transaction. The IDbTransaction interface defines three members: an IsolationLevel property, a Commit method, and a Rollback method.

The SqlTransaction class (part of the System.Data.SqlClient namespace) represents a transaction against a SQL Server database. This class implements the IDbTransaction interface. As a result, the SqlTransaction class includes an IsolationLevel property and Commit and Rollback methods. It also includes other methods, such as Save, that are not part of this interface.

The OleDbTransaction class (part of the System.Data.OleDb namespace) represents a transaction against an OLE DB database. This class also implements the IDbTransaction interface. As a result, the OleDbTransaction class includes an IsolationLevel property and Commit and Rollback methods. It also includes other methods, such as Begin, that are not part of this interface.

Because both SqlTransaction and OleDbTransaction implement that IDbTransaction interface, you can write code that expects an instance of this interface that will work equally well when passed an instance of either class.

Delegates

Namespaces can also include *delegates*. Like interfaces, delegates represent a sort of code contract. In this case, they define a method that you can write in your code that will be called from within a class (as opposed to interfaces, which define methods within classes that you can call from within your code).

In the .NET Framework class library, the primary use of delegates is defining the parameters that event-handling functions must implement. For example, the System.Data namespace defines a delegate named DataRowChangeEventHandler. This delegate has this programming signature:

```
Public Delegate Sub DataRowChangeEventHandler( _
  ByVal sender As Object, _
  ByVal e As DataRowChangeEventArgs)
```

Any function that has these parameters can be used to respond to the DataRowChange event of the DataTable object (which is what this delegate represents). In Visual Basic .NET, you use the AddHandler keyword to add a delegate. The following block of code will create a DataTable object and set up a delegate to handle its DataRowChange event:

```
Private dtMain As DataTable


Private Sub Setup
    dtMain = New DataTable("Customers")
    AddHandler dtMain.RowChanged, AddressOf dtMain_Changed
End Sub


Protected Sub dtMain_Changed _
  (sender As Object, e As System.Data.DataRowChangeEventArgs)
    ' code to handle event goes here
End Sub
```

Enumerations

Finally, a namespace may contain *enumerations*. An enumeration is a set of constants that are defined for a particular purpose. For example, the System.Data namespace includes an enumeration named DataRowState. As you might guess from the name, this enumeration includes the possible values for the RowState property of the DataRow class:

- Added
- Deleted
- Detached
- Modified
- Unchanged

If you retrieve the DataRow.RowState property for a particular row in your code, you're guaranteed to get back one of these values.

Summary

In this chapter, you saw some of the basic underpinnings of the .NET Framework. Some parts of .NET, such as objects with interfaces, Windows Forms, and XML, may look very familiar. Other areas, including the Common Language Runtime and the .NET deployment model, are new to Windows programming. Overall, the .NET Framework includes a great deal of innovation, and you'll need to work with it for some time before you feel comfortable with all of the new concepts.

In the next chapter, I'll dig a bit further into .NET by looking at some of the programming languages that are available within the .NET Framework. You'll see how .NET makes cross-language interoperability simple to implement.

CHAPTER 12

Understanding .NET Languages

- Visual Basic .NET

- The C# language

- Other languages

- Language interoperability via the CLR

Although the .NET Framework can be called by code from many languages, you'll still need to learn new programming constructs to make effective use of .NET. Even Microsoft's own core languages such as Visual Basic and Visual C++ are being overhauled to work well in the .NET world. In this chapter, I'll take a look at the latest version of Visual Basic, now called Visual Basic .NET, and at the new C# programming language. I'll also briefly consider other .NET languages and show you how code from different languages can interoperate, thanks to the .NET Common Language Runtime.

Visual Basic .NET

For most of the examples in this book, I'm using Visual Basic .NET, the latest version of Microsoft's 10-year-old Visual Basic (VB) language. I've chosen Visual Basic .NET because it's a mature, flexible, and accessible language (and also because I've been working with Visual Basic for years). Although much of Visual Basic .NET will be familiar to experienced VB developers, Microsoft has substantially extended and enhanced the language in this release. In this section, I'll introduce you to some of the new features of Visual Basic .NET and work through a couple of examples to demonstrate how this new version of the language integrates with the rest of the .NET Framework.

NOTE   In this section, I'm assuming familiarity with Visual Basic. For an introduction to Visual Basic .NET from the ground up, refer to the Visual Basic and Visual C# section in the Visual Studio .NET documentation.

What's New in Visual Basic .NET?

Although most existing Visual Basic code will port without major changes to Visual Basic .NET, there are also many changes to the language. Understanding the new capabilities of Visual Basic .NET will help you write efficient .NET programs. Here's a list of some of the most significant language changes:

- Inheritance
- Shared members
- Overloading and overriding
- Explicit constructors and destructors
- Declaring and implementing interfaces
- Structured exception handling
- Delegates
- Namespaces

In addition to these changes, there are many other enhancements and improvements to the Visual Basic language and to the various graphical designers in the product. For example, you can now write multithreaded code with Visual Basic .NET. For a complete list of all the changes, refer to the Visual Studio .NET documentation.

Inheritance

Inheritance is a simple but powerful idea (and one that has been missing from Visual Basic for years, much to the dismay of object-oriented purists). It's based on the notion that classes of things come in natural hierarchies, based on "is a" relationships. For example, in the natural world, you might observe that:

- A horse is an animal.

- A sheep is an animal.

If you know the general rules about how animals behave, you know something about how horses and sheep behave. On the other hand, there are specific things about horses and sheep (for example, their diets) that distinguish them from other animals.

In the business world, you also run into inheritance hierarchies. For example, in a sales application, you might notice that:

- A preferred customer is a customer.

- A suspended customer is a customer.

Here again, knowing how customers behave in your system tells you most of what you need to know about preferred customers and suspended customers, but not everything.

Visual Basic .NET includes new keywords for implementing inheritance. Listing 12.1 shows some code for three simple classes, named Animal, Horse, and Sheep.

NOTE   You'll find all the code from this chapter in the ADOChapter12 sample project on the companion CD. The code from all of the listings is combined into integrated classes. In each of the listings, I've excerpted the appropriate lines of code to demonstrate specific techniques.

Listing 12.1:   **Using Inheritance in Classes**

```
Public Class Animal

    Private mstrName As String

    Public Property Name() As String
        Get
            Name = mstrName
```

```
            End Get
            Set(ByVal Value As String)
                mstrName = Value
            End Set
        End Property

        Public Function Move() As String
            Move = mstrName & " walked across the farm."
        End Function

        Overridable Function Eat() As String
            Eat = mstrName & " ate."
        End Function

    End Class

    Public Class Horse
        Inherits Animal

        Sub New()
            MyBase.Name = "The horse"
        End Sub

        Overrides Function Eat() As String
            Eat = MyBase.Name & " ate some oats."
        End Function

    End Class

    Public Class Sheep
        Inherits Animal

        Sub New()
            MyBase.Name = "The sheep"
        End Sub

        Overrides Function Eat() As String
            Eat = MyBase.Name & " ate some grass."
        End Function

    End Class
```

You should notice a few things as you inspect this code:

- You don't have to do anything special to define a class (such as Animal in this example) as a *base class* (one that other classes can inherit from) in Visual Basic .NET. Any class is, by default, inheritable. You can use the NotInheritable modifier when defining a class to prevent it from being a base class. On the other hand, you can use the MustInherit modifier to specify that a class can be used only as a base class, with no instance ever being declared directly.

- The Inherits keyword specifies the base class for a class. A class can have only a single base class. If you like, you can build hierarchies, where class A is inherited by class B, which in turn is inherited by class C, and so on.

- The Overridable modifier declares a base class member to be one that a derived class can override—that is, the derived class can implement its own version of that member.

- The MyBase keyword, when used within a derived class, refers to the underlying base class.

Figure 12.1 shows the result of calling these classes from the btnInheritance button in this chapter's sample project:

```
Private Sub btnInheritance_Click(ByVal sender As System.Object, _
    ByVal e As System.EventArgs) Handles btnInheritance.Click

    Dim h As New Horse()
    Dim s As New Sheep()

    lboResults.Items.Add(h.Move)
    lboResults.Items.Add(s.Move)
    lboResults.Items.Add(h.Eat)
    lboResults.Items.Add(s.Eat)

End Sub
```

Note the difference between the Move method, which isn't overridden in the derived classes, and the Eat method, which is overridden.

FIGURE 12.1:

Using derived classes

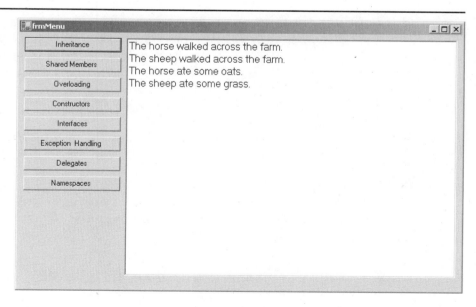

TIP There is no need to set object variables to Nothing in .NET when you've finished using them. The Common Language Runtime (CLR) will take care of cleaning things up for you, whether you do this or not.

Shared Members

Sometimes it's convenient to have a single instance of a property shared among all instances of a class. If the shared property belongs to a base class, it will be shared among all instances of any class derived from that base class. For example, in my imaginary world of animals, I might specify a location for my farm. If I were to change that location, I would want to change it once and have the change apply to all the animals on the farm.

Visual Basic .NET uses the Shared keyword to indicate a shared member. The sample project uses this code to demonstrate this keyword:

```
Public Class Animal
    Public Shared Location As String
End Class

Public Class Horse
    Inherits Animal
End Class

Public Class Sheep
    Inherits Animal
End Class

    Private Sub btnSharedMembers_Click(ByVal sender As System.Object, _
    ByVal e As System.EventArgs) Handles btnSharedMembers.Click

        Dim h As New Horse()
        Dim s As New Sheep()

        h.Location = "Oregon"
        lboResults.Items.Add(h.Name & " lives in " & h.Location)
        lboResults.Items.Add(s.Name & " lives in " & s.Location)

    End Sub
```

Figure 12.2 shows the result of calling the code from the btnSharedMembers button in the sample project. You can see that setting the Location property for the Horse object also sets the property for the Sheep object.

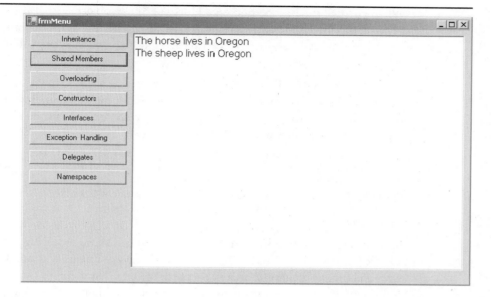

Using a shared property

Overloading and Overriding

Overloading and *overriding* are two ways to provide different behavior for the same method applied to two different objects. Basically, overriding applies within a class, while overloading applies to methods external to a class.

You've already seen overloading in the discussion of inheritance. If a base class method is overridable, the derived classes can use the Overrides keyword to provide their own implementation of the class. For example, the Eat methods of the Horse and Sheep objects override the Eat method of the Animal base class:

```
Public Class Animal
    Overridable Function Eat() As String
        Eat = mstrName & " ate."
    End Function
End Class
Public Class Horse
    Inherits Animal
    Overrides Function Eat() As String
        Eat = MyBase.Name & " ate some oats."
    End Function
End Class
Public Class Sheep
    Inherits Animal
    Overrides Function Eat() As String
        Eat = MyBase.Name & " ate some grass."
    End Function
End Class
```

When you call the Eat method on a Horse or Sheep object, Visual Basic .NET will execute the Eat method from the corresponding class. If you declare another class, say Pig, that also inherits from Animal but doesn't override the Eat method, the class will use the Eat method declared in the base class.

Overloading, on the other hand, allows you to define a single function name that can be called with different sets of parameters. This is useful, for example, in cases where you need two types of objects to be treated differently. For instance, the sample project contains these definitions of a Feed function:

```
Private Overloads Function Feed(ByVal h As Horse) As String
    Feed = "You give the horse some oats."
End Function
Private Overloads Function Feed(ByVal s As Sheep) As String
    Feed = "You turn the sheep loose to graze."
End Function
```

Both of these definitions are in the code behind frmMenu, not in any class. When you call the Feed function, Visual Basic .NET compares the arguments you supply with the various overloaded function definitions, and executes the one that matches (or returns an error if there is no match). In the sample project, btnOverloading uses this code to demonstrate both overriding and overloading:

```
Private Sub btnOverloading_Click(ByVal sender As System.Object, _
ByVal e As System.EventArgs) Handles btnOverloading.Click

    Dim h As New Horse()
    Dim s As New Sheep()

    lboResults.Items.Add(Feed(h))
    lboResults.Items.Add(h.Eat)
    lboResults.Items.Add(Feed(s))
    lboResults.Items.Add(s.Eat)

End Sub
```

Figure 12.3 shows the results of executing this code.

Overloading is much more flexible than this simple example demonstrates:

- You can have as many different versions of the same procedure as you like, as long as each one has a distinct argument list.

- You can have a different order of arguments between different overloaded versions of a procedure.

- Overloaded versions of a procedure can have different return datatypes (although they must also have different argument lists).

FIGURE 12.3:

Overriding and overloading methods

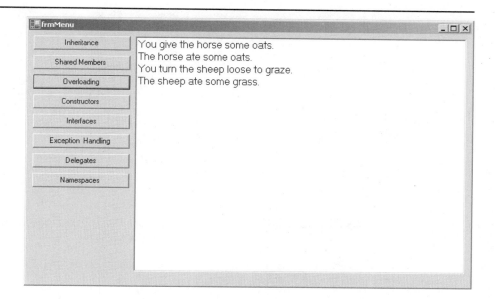

Explicit Constructors and Destructors

A *constructor* is a procedure that is called when an object is first created, and a *destructor* is a procedure that is called when an object is destroyed. Visual Basic 6 allowed you to write explicit constructors and destructors in a class module by using the Initialize and Terminate procedures. Visual Basic .NET goes a step further by providing constructors and destructors for all objects, including system objects such as WinForms and other instances of .NET Framework classes.

One major difference between Visual Basic 6 and Visual Basic .NET lies in when the destructor for a class is called. In Visual Basic 6, it's called when the last reference to an object is dropped. This led to a problem in which circular references prevented objects from terminating properly. Visual Basic .NET (and the other .NET languages) uses a scheme called *garbage collection*. With garbage collection, the CLR keeps track of objects, and when there are no more references to an object from your application, it will clean the references up, even if they're involved in a circular reference. The disadvantage of garbage collection is that you never know precisely when the destructor for an object will be called.

Visual Basic .NET uses a Sub New procedure as a constructor, and a Sub Finalize procedure as a destructor. For example, here's an extremely simple class that exists only to demonstrate this code:

```
Public Class EmptyClass

    Sub New()
        MyBase.New()
```

```
        MsgBox("The constructor has been called")
    End Sub

    Protected Overrides Sub Finalize()
        MsgBox("The destructor has been called")
        MyBase.Finalize()
    End Sub
End Class
```

NOTE   In a derived class, you should call the New and Finalize methods of the base class, as shown in this example. Because all classes are derived from System.Object if they're not otherwise declared, you should always do this.

This class is used from the Constructors button on the sample form:

```
Private Sub btnConstructor_Click(ByVal sender As System.Object, _
  ByVal e As System.EventArgs) Handles btnConstructor.Click
    Dim EC As New EmptyClass()
    MsgBox("Click OK to end the procedure and destroy the EmptyClass")
End Sub
```

If you run this code, you'll find that the constructor for EmptyClass is called as soon as you click the button, but the destructor is not called until you close the form. That's because EmptyClass uses so few resources that the CLR garbage collection mechanism doesn't waste time cleaning it up until the project is closing down.

NOTE   If you have resources in a class that you'd like to free when you're done with the class, you should write a Sub Dispose procedure in that class and call it explicitly, rather than wait for the Finalize to be called.

Declaring and Implementing Interfaces

An *interface* defines a set of methods, properties, and events that can be used by multiple classes. Visual Basic 6 includes the Implements keyword so that Visual Basic classes can use interfaces defined by other components. Visual Basic .NET adds the Interface keyword, which allows you to define interfaces directly within Visual Basic .NET.

The sample project includes an interface definition in Main.vb:

```
Module Main

    Interface Care
        Function Groom() As String
        Function Deworm() As String
    End Interface

End Module
```

Like a base class definition, an interface represents a contract on the part of your code to adhere to a certain structure. But interfaces have advantages in some situations over using base classes and inheritance. First, interfaces tend to be less complex than base classes, and thus more easily maintained. Second, a single class can implement multiple interfaces, which allows you to simulate inheritance from multiple base classes simultaneously.

Both the Horse and the Sheep class implement the Care interface:

```
Public Class Horse
    Inherits Animal
    Implements Care

    Function Groom() As String Implements Care.groom
        Groom = "You brush the horse."
    End Function

    Function Deworm() As String Implements Care.Deworm
        Deworm = "You give the horse a dose of dewormer."
    End Function

End Class
Public Class Sheep
    Inherits Animal
    Implements Care

    Function Groom() As String Implements Care.groom
        Groom = "You shear the sheep."
    End Function

    Function Deworm() As String Implements Care.Deworm
        Deworm = "You give the sheep a dose of dewormer."
    End Function

End Class
```

When you implement an interface, the return type of all properties and methods must exactly match the definition in the interface itself. Also, interfaces must be implemented completely. For example, if you left the Deworm function out of the Sheep class after declaring that the class would implement the Care interface, you would get an error while trying to run the code.

The menu form in the sample project contains code to call the implemented interface members:

```
Private Sub btnInterfaces_Click(ByVal sender As System.Object, _
  ByVal e As System.EventArgs) Handles btnInterfaces.Click

    Dim h As New Horse()
```

```
Dim s As New Sheep()

lboResults.Items.Add(h.Groom)
lboResults.Items.Add(s.Groom)
lboResults.Items.Add(h.Deworm)
lboResults.Items.Add(s.Deworm)

End Sub
```

Figure 12.4 shows the result of running this code.

FIGURE 12.4:

Calling implemented interfaces

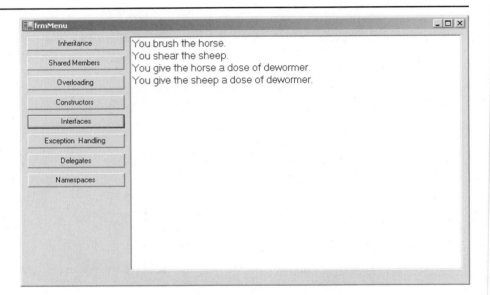

Structured Exception Handling

Visual Basic .NET adds a number of improvements to error handling, compared with previous versions. Chief among these is *structured exception handling*, implemented in a Try…Catch…Finally block. The Try keyword tells Visual Basic .NET that this is the beginning of a structured exception handling block. The Catch keyword indicates a point where code execution should be transferred if an error occurs. The Finally keyword marks a block of code that will always be executed, whether or not an error occurs.

The sample project includes a very simple structured exception handling example:

```
Private Sub btnExceptionHandling_Click(ByVal sender As System.Object, _
    ByVal e As System.EventArgs) Handles btnExceptionHandling.Click

    Dim b As Byte
```

```
 ' Set up a structured exception handling block
 Try
     b = 255
     b = 3 * b
 Catch ex As Exception
     lboResults.Items.Add(ex.Message)
     lboResults.Items.Add(ex.StackTrace)
 Finally
     lboResults.Items.Add("Executing the Finally block")
 End Try

End Sub
```

Any error within the Try...End Try markers will cause execution to resume at the Catch line. The Finally block is executed regardless. Figure 12.5 shows the result of running this code.

FIGURE 12.5:

Structured exception handling

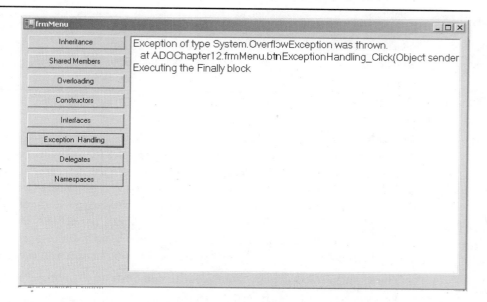

A great deal of flexibility is built into the Catch keyword beyond what is shown here. The Catch block can open with a *filter* to catch only specific exceptions, and it can be repeated. For example, this is the skeleton of a valid structured exception handling block:

```
Try
    …
Catch e As System.IO.EndOfStreamException
    …
Catch When ErrNum = conErrMyError
    …
```

```
Catch e As Exception
   ...
Finally
   ...
End Try
```

As you can see, a filter can be either a particular type of exception (all exceptions are sub-classes of the Exception class) or a Boolean expression. When an error occurs, the CLR inspects all Catch blocks until it finds the first one that matches the current exception.

The Exception class has a number of useful properties. Table 12.1 summarizes them.

TABLE 12.1: Properties of the Exception Class

Property	Explanation
HelpLink	Link to a help file explaining the exception
Message	Text of the error message
Source	Application or object that caused the error
StackTrace	Trace of the call stack that led to this exception
TargetSite	Method that threw the exception

Delegates

Delegates provide Visual Basic .NET with a way to refer to procedures at runtime (delegates are sometimes called *type-safe function pointers*). You can use delegates in any situation where you want to decide at runtime which procedure to call in response to a particular event. Although delegates are a general-purpose concept, they are most useful in Visual Basic .NET as a way to handle events dynamically at runtime. Visual Basic .NET includes the AddHandler and RemoveHandler statements. The former connects an event to a procedure by creating a new delegate; the latter removes an existing connection between an event and a procedure.

The sample project contains some code to demonstrate changing event handlers at runtime:

```
Private Sub btnDelegates_Click(ByVal sender As System.Object, _
  ByVal e As System.EventArgs) Handles btnDelegates.Click
    lboResults.Items.Add("In btnDelegates_Click")
    AddHandler btnDelegates.Click, AddressOf EH1
    RemoveHandler btnDelegates.Click, AddressOf btnDelegates_Click
End Sub

Private Sub EH1(ByVal sender As System.Object, _
  ByVal e As System.EventArgs)
    lboResults.Items.Add("In EH1")
```

```
        AddHandler btnDelegates.Click, AddressOf EH2
        RemoveHandler btnDelegates.Click, AddressOf EH1
    End Sub

    Private Sub EH2(ByVal sender As System.Object, _
      ByVal e As System.EventArgs)
        lboResults.Items.Add("In EH2")
        AddHandler btnDelegates.Click, AddressOf EH1
        RemoveHandler btnDelegates.Click, AddressOf EH2
    End Sub
```

Each of these three procedures has the right argument list to be an event handler for a button Click event. The first is the default event handler that the Windows Forms package creates for btnDelegates' Click event. This procedure uses the AddHandler statement to add the EH1 procedure to the list of handlers for the event, and then uses RemoveHandler to remove itself from the list. Note that both AddHandler and RemoveHandler take two parameters:

- The name of an event

- A pointer to a procedure to handle that event, obtained with the AddressOf operator

The other two procedures also use AddHandler and RemoveHandler to alternate handling the event.

Figure 12.6 shows the result of repeatedly clicking the Delegates button.

FIGURE 12.6:

Using AddHandler and RemoveHandler

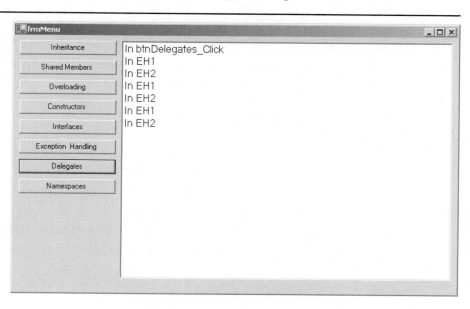

Namespaces

Chapter 11, "Introduction to .NET," introduced you to the concept of *namespaces*: groups of objects that perform similar functions. Namespaces are also useful for avoiding name collisions. That is, two classes may have the same class name without causing an error, as long as they are located in different namespaces.

In addition to being able to use the namespaces of the .NET Framework class library, in Visual Basic .NET, you may also declare your own namespaces. Here's a small bit of sample code from the Namespaces.vb file in this chapter's sample project:

```
Namespace Farm
    Public Class Fork
        Public Length As String = "7 feet"
    End Class
End Namespace

Namespace Kitchen
    Public Class Fork
        Public Length As String = "6 inches"
    End Class
End Namespace
```

Just like a Class declaration statement, a Namespace declaration statement must be matched to a corresponding End Namespace statement. This particular bit of code declares two namespaces, Farm and Kitchen, each of which contains a Fork class. The fully qualified names of the classes are Farm.Fork and Kitchen.Fork, and you can use those names elsewhere in your code:

```
Private Sub btnNamespaces_Click(ByVal sender As System.Object, _
    ByVal e As System.EventArgs) Handles btnNamespaces.Click

    Dim Fork1 As New Farm.Fork()
    Dim Fork2 As New Kitchen.Fork()

    lboResults.Items.Add(Fork1.Length)
    lboResults.Items.Add(Fork2.Length)

End Sub
```

Even though the classes have the same unqualified name, they can both be used in the same program without conflict because they are in different namespaces.

You can nest Namespace statements to create a hierarchy of namespaces, as in this example:

```
Namespace Vehicle
    Namespace Passenger
        Class Sedan
```

```
        End Class
        Class StationWagon

        End Class
    End Namespace
End Namespace
```

This declares two classes, Vehicle.Passenger.Sedan and Vehicle.Passenger.StationWagon.

Creating a Class Library with Visual Basic .NET

As an example of creating a component with Visual Basic .NET, I'll build a very small class library. In fact, the class library is so small that it contains only a single class, named TipList. This class represents a list of tips such as you might see when you launch a new software application. The TipList class will have an AddTip method, to allow you to add new tips to the list, and a RandomTip method, to return a random tip from the list.

The TipServer project on the companion CD contains this class. If you'd like to build this project from scratch, follow these steps:

1. Open Visual Studio .NET and choose New Project from the Start Page.

2. Select Visual Basic Projects from the treeview on the left-hand side of the screen.

3. Select Class Library as the project template.

4. Set the name of the application to TipServer and click OK to create the project.

5. Highlight the class called Class1.vb in the Solution Explorer window and rename it TipList.vb.

6. Select the code for Class1 in TipList.vb (this will be an empty class definition) and replace it with the code shown in Listing 12.2.

7. Choose File ➢ Save All to save your work, and then choose Build ➢ Build to compile the project.

Listing 12.2:   **The TipList Class**

```
Imports System.Collections
Imports System.Io
Imports System.Xml.Serialization

Public Class TipList

    ' List of tips maintained by this server
    Private mTipList As New System.Collections.ArrayList()

    Public Sub New()
```

```vb
    Dim Serializer As XmlSerializer
    Dim Reader As TextReader

    Try
        ' Read the data from the XML file back into the list
        Serializer = New XmlSerializer(GetType(_
        System.Collections.ArrayList))
        Reader = New StreamReader("TipList.XML")
        mTipList = CType(Serializer.Deserialize(Reader), _
        System.Collections.ArrayList)
        Reader.Close()
        ' Initialize the random number generator
        Randomize()
    Catch e As System.Io.FileNotFoundException
        ' This is expected the first time we call
        ' the class, because there will be no saved
        ' file. So just fall through.
    End Try

End Sub

Public Sub AddTip(ByVal strTip As String)
    ' Accept a new tip from the client, adding it to the internal list
    mTipList.Add(strTip)
End Sub

Public ReadOnly Property RandomTip() As String
    ' Return a random tip from the list
    Get
        Dim intI As Integer
        If mTipList.Count > 0 Then
            intI = Int(Rnd(1) * mTipList.Count)
            RandomTip = mTipList.Item(intI)
        Else
            RandomTip = ""
        End If
    End Get
End Property

Protected Overrides Sub Finalize()
    ' Write the current list out to an XML file
    Dim Serializer As XmlSerializer
    Dim Writer As TextWriter

    Serializer = New XmlSerializer(GetType(System.Collections.ArrayList))
    Writer = New StreamWriter("TipList.XML")
    Serializer.Serialize(Writer, mTipList)
    Writer.Close()

    ' Remember to call the Finalize for the base class
    MyBase.Finalize()
End Sub
End Class
```

Although there's not a lot of code in the TipList class, it demonstrates some of the useful functionality that's built into the .NET Framework class library. For instance, rather than build my own data structure to house the list of tips, I've taken advantage of the System.Collections namespace. This namespace includes a number of data structure classes, including ArrayList, the class that I used to hold the tips. This class implements a list by storing it into an array and allowing random access to the stored items via an Item method.

The code in the TipList class also takes advantage of one of the key facets of the .NET Framework class library: Nearly every class in the framework can be saved to an XML file and later rebuilt from that XML file. This process is known as *serialization to XML*, and it's handled by classes from the System.Io and System.Xml.Serialization namespaces.

To understand how serialization to XML works, first look at the Finalize method in the class. This is the class destructor, called whenever an instance of the class is being cleaned up by .NET. At that point, when the object is being removed from memory, I invoke code to save its contents to an XML file on disk:

```
Dim Serializer As XmlSerializer
Dim Writer As TextWriter

Serializer = New XmlSerializer(GetType(System.Collections.ArrayList))
Writer = New StreamWriter("TipList.XML")
Serializer.Serialize(Writer, mTipList)
Writer.Close()
```

The StreamWriter class provides an abstract interface to a disk file (or other location for a character stream). The XMLSerializer provides an interface between a class and an XML file. By using these two classes together, the Finalize code essentially tells the ArrayList to write itself out as an XML file.

Conversely, the New method reads in the XML file, if it exists, and reconstitutes the ArrayList. The following code uses an XMLSerializer object together with a StreamReader class:

```
Try
    ' Read the data from the XML file back into the list
    Serializer = New XmlSerializer(GetType( _
     System.Collections.ArrayList))
    Reader = New StreamReader("TipList.XML")
    mTipList = CType(Serializer.Deserialize(Reader), _
     System.Collections.ArrayList)
    Reader.Close()
    ' Initialize the random number generator
    Randomize()
Catch e As System.Io.FileNotFoundException
    ' This is expected the first time we call
```

```
         ' the class, because there will be no saved
         ' file. So just fall through.
    End Try
```

Note the use of a structured exception handling block here to automatically ignore the error that happens when you try to read a nonexistent file.

Creating a User Interface with Visual Basic .NET

The second Visual Basic .NET program, TipClient, presents a user interface to the TipList class implemented in the TipServer project. The TipClient project on the companion CD contains this user interface. If you'd like to build this project from scratch, follow these steps:

1. Open Visual Studio .NET and choose New Project from the Start Page.

2. Select Visual Basic Project from the treeview on the left side of the screen.

3. Select Windows Application as the project template.

4. Set the name of the application to TipClient and click OK to create the project.

5. Highlight the form called Form1.vb in the Solution Explorer window and rename it frmTips.vb.

6. Create the form shown in Figure 12.7 by adding the appropriate controls and setting the properties of those controls, as outlined in Table 12.2.

FIGURE 12.7:

The Tips form in design view

TABLE 12.2: Controls for the Tips Form

Control	Property	Value
Form	Text	Tips
TextBox	Name	txtTip
	Text	(blank)
	MultiLine	True
Button	Name	btnAddTip
	Text	Add Tip
Button	Name	btnGetTip
	Text	Get Tip

7. Select Project ➢ Add Reference to display the Add Reference dialog box. Click the Browse button and browse to the compiled `TipServer.dll`. By default, this will be in `Visual Studio Projects\TipServer\bin`. Click Open. Click OK to add a reference to the TipServer project to this TipClient project.

8. Select View ➢ Code to open the code module for the form.

9. Add the following line of code above the code generated by Windows Forms Designer:

```
Private TL As New TipServer.TipList()
```

10. Add this code to the code generated by Windows Forms Designer:

```
Private Sub btnAddTip_Click(ByVal sender As System.Object, _
  ByVal e As System.EventArgs) Handles btnAddTip.Click
    TL.AddTip(InputBox("Enter your tip:", "New Tip"))
End Sub

Private Sub btnGetTip_Click(ByVal sender As System.Object, _
  ByVal e As System.EventArgs) Handles btnGetTip.Click
    txtTip.Text = TL.RandomTip
End Sub
```

11. Select Debug ➢ Start to start the project.

Figure 12.8 shows the TipClient project in action, displaying one tip while the user is entering another tip. If you run the project several times, you'll find that the list of tips persists between sessions. The file `TipList.xml` will be created in the same directory as the Tip-Client project, and will resemble this example:

```
<?xml version="1.0" encoding="utf-8"?>
<ArrayList xmlns:xsi="http://www.w3.org/2001/XMLSchema-instance"
➥ xmlns:xsd="http://www.w3.org/2001/XMLSchema">
  <Object xsi:type="xsd:string">Don't run with scissors.</Object>
  <Object xsi:type="xsd:string">A bird in the hand is worth two in the
bush.</Object>
  <Object xsi:type="xsd:string">Neither a borrower nor a lender be.</Object>
  <Object xsi:type="xsd:string" />
  <Object xsi:type="xsd:string">If pigs had wings, they'd be pigeons.</Object>
</ArrayList>
```

NOTE   The project directory—where the XML file will be created—is the /bin subdirectory of the main `TipClient` directory. Visual Basic .NET, unlike Visual Basic 6, stores source code and executable code in separate directories by default.

FIGURE 12.8:

Running the TipClient project

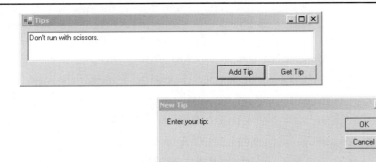

C#

Another major language in the .NET development framework is C# (pronounced "see-sharp"). C# was designed at Microsoft specifically as a component of .NET, and it combines some of the best features of other languages such as C++ and Java. Just like Visual Basic .NET, C# is a first-class .NET language, having access to all the features of the CLR. In fact, because so much of the .NET functionality is inherent in the CLR, a list of the features of C# would be very similar to a list of features of Visual Basic .NET. Both support the creation of rich hierarchies of classes with inheritance, explicit constructors and destructors, structured exception handling, and so on. And Visual Studio .NET supports both with the same integrated development environment (IDE). Whether you're building a Windows Form with Visual Basic .NET or with C#, you use the same visual designer for the task.

To a great extent, you can choose between Visual Basic .NET and C# based on your own preferences in language syntax and style. If you like BASIC-derived languages, stick with Visual Basic .NET. But if you prefer, or are more familiar with, C-derived languages, C# is the natural way for you to work with .NET.

TIP Another choice for C-oriented programmers is the Managed Extensions for C++. This is a component of Visual Studio .NET that lets you take full advantage of the CLR within existing C++ code.

To demonstrate the close similarities between Visual Basic .NET and C#, I'll re-implement the TipServer code into C#. This project, TipServer2, is on the companion CD. To recreate it from scratch, follow these steps:

1. Open Visual Studio .NET and choose New Project from the Start Page.

2. Select Visual C# Projects from the treeview on the left-hand side of the screen.

3. Select Class Library as the project template.

4. Set the name of the application to TipServer2 and click OK to create the project.

5. Highlight the class called Class1.cs in the Solution Explorer window and rename it TipList.cs.

6. Select the code for Class1 in TipList.cs (this will be an empty class definition) and replace it with the code shown in Listing 12.3.

7. Choose File ➤ Save All to save your work, and then choose Build ➤ Build to compile the project.

Listing 12.3: **The TipList Class in C#**

```csharp
using System;
using System.Collections;
using System.IO;
using System.Xml.Serialization;

namespace TipServer2
{

    public class TipList
    {
        System.Collections.ArrayList mTipList;
        System.Random R;

        public TipList()
        {
            XmlSerializer Serializer;
            TextReader Reader;

            mTipList = new System.Collections.ArrayList();
            // Initialize the random number generator
            R = new Random();

            try {
                // Read the data from the XML file back into the list
                Serializer = new XmlSerializer(mTipList.GetType());
                Reader = new StreamReader("TipList.XML");
                mTipList = _
                  (System.Collections.ArrayList)Serializer.Deserialize(Reader);
                Reader.Close();
            }
            catch(System.IO.FileNotFoundException) {
                // This is expected the first time we call
                // the class, because there will be no saved
                // file. So just fall through.
            }
        }
```

```
public void AddTip(System.String strTip)
{
    // Accept a new tip from the client, adding it to the _
     internal list
    mTipList.Add(strTip);
}

public System.String RandomTip
{
    // Return a random tip from the list
    get
    {
        int intI;
        if (mTipList.Count>0)
        {
            intI = (int)(R.NextDouble() * mTipList.Count);
            return (string)mTipList[intI];
        }
        else
            return "";
    }
}

~TipList()
{
    // Write the current list out to an XML file
    XmlSerializer Serializer;
    TextWriter Writer;

    Serializer = new XmlSerializer(mTipList.GetType());
    Writer = new StreamWriter("TipList.XML");
    Serializer.Serialize(Writer, mTipList);
    Writer.Close();
}

    }
}
```

Even if you're not a C-language programmer, you should be able to compare Listing 12.2 with Listing 12.3 and see the similarities between Visual Basic .NET and C#. The differences are in the details of the syntax, not in the concepts that the languages implement.

Other Languages

.NET programming is not limited to Visual Basic .NET, C#, and Visual C++. Indeed, it's not limited to Microsoft languages at all. Microsoft has published the specifications for the CLR so that other language vendors can implement .NET-compliant languages. These languages use the same datatypes, compile to the same MSIL code, and otherwise interoperate perfectly with the .NET languages from Microsoft.

I can't cover all of the available languages here, in part because .NET is still in beta as I write this and it's hard to know exactly what will be released. But in this section, I can give you a peek at some of the options that are already announced or available. These include the following languages:

- Perl
- Python
- XSLT
- APL
- COBOL
- Pascal
- Smalltalk

Perl, Python, and XSLT

ActiveState (`http://aspn.activestate.com/ASPN/`) has produced integrated versions of three languages for Visual Studio .NET. These include compilers for Perl and Python and an editing environment for XSLT files.

Although Perl was originally developed as a scripting or "glue" language for Unix, it has been widely implemented on a variety of operating systems. Many implementations of Perl are open-source and freely available. Perl is especially popular for server-side web programming among developers working with non-Microsoft web servers (and a few working with ASP pages on IIS as well). Perl is simple to get started with, but it's also an extremely powerful language—although it has a reputation for encouraging hard-to-read source code. ActiveState offers Visual Perl as a way to integrate Perl directly into the Visual Studio .NET programming environment.

Python is another popular scripting language. Like Perl, most Python implementations are freeware. Python was designed from the ground up as an object-oriented scripting language; all variables in Python are actually objects (just as they are in .NET). This object orientation, along with some other advanced features, makes Python a good match for the .NET CLR. ActiveState offers Visual Python as a way to integrate Python directly into the Visual Studio .NET programming environment.

XSLT (Extensible Stylesheet Language Transformations) is one of a growing number of XML standards. By using XSLT, you can transform a raw XML document into almost any presentation format you can imagine. ActiveState's Visual XSLT product adds an XSLT editor to Visual Studio .NET and lets you debug the process of applying an XSL transform to an XML file.

Figure 12.9 shows a Python program open in Visual Studio .NET after I installed Visual Python on my test computer. As you can see, the Python editor is completely integrated with the rest of the Visual Studio .NET development environment.

FIGURE 12.9:

Using Visual Python

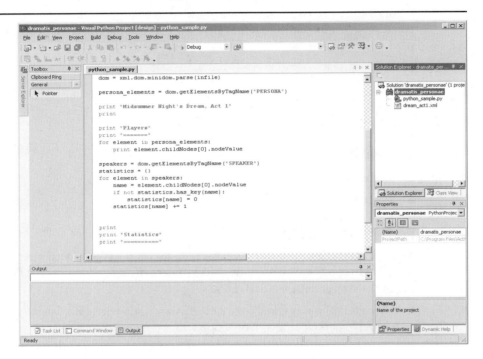

APL

APL is a general-purpose programming language that's perhaps best known for its use of a number of symbols that aren't in the ASCII character set, including Greek letters, to represent operators and other programming concepts. APL is an very terse language, with sorting, searching, and looping built right into many of the basic features of the language. This makes it possible for a short APL program to be extremely powerful. Dyadic (www.dyadic.com/) is building a version of its Dyalog APL for the .NET environment.

COBOL

COBOL (Common Business-Oriented Language) is one of the most pervasive programming languages in the mainframe world. Originally conceived as an alternative to FORTRAN that was more suitable for day-to-day business operations, COBOL has been extended to just about every operating system and computing platform ever invented, and there is a vast supply of professional developers having COBOL knowledge. Fujitsu (`www.adtools.com/info/whitepaper/net.html`) is porting its version of the COBOL language to the .NET platform.

As Fujitsu points out, porting COBOL to .NET enables the existing gargantuan inventory of business applications written in COBOL to be extended to new platforms without being completely rewritten. For example, COBOL programmers will be able to write web services or ASP+ pages, as the following fragment demonstrates:

```
<%@ page language="COBOL" %>
<script runat="server">
OBJECT.
DATA DIVISION.
WORKING-STORAGE SECTION.
77 FONT-SIZE PIC S9(9) COMP-5.
END OBJECT.

</script>
<% PERFORM VARYING FONT-SIZE FROM 1 BY 1 UNTIL FONT-SIZE > 7 %>
<font size="<%=FONT-SIZE%>"> Hello, COBOL world! </font> <br>
<% END-PERFORM. %>
```

Pascal

Pascal is a venerable language that has perhaps had its greatest impact in computer science courses, where it has been quite popular. Component Pascal is an object-oriented extension of Pascal that is used in teaching and research. The Queensland University of Technology has integrated its Gardens Point Component Pascal with the .NET Framework. The university's website (`www2.fit.qut.edu.au/CompSci/PLAS//ComponentPascal/`) offers a freeware compiler that can turn Component Pascal source code into MSIL.

Note that this is a different approach to .NET integration. Rather than use the Visual Studio .NET development environment, the Component Pascal authors modified their existing command-line tools to target MSIL directly. This is a perfectly acceptable strategy for achieving .NET compatibility. There's no requirement to use Microsoft's IDE to achieve interoperability with other .NET code. You just have to be able to produce MSIL that the CLR considers acceptable.

Smalltalk

Smalltalk was one of the first object-oriented languages invented and an early competitor to C++. Indeed, Alan Kay, the original developer of Smalltalk, invented the term *object-oriented*. In fact, everything in Smalltalk is an object, and the language pioneered concepts such as metadata to enable objects to describe themselves. Smalltalk has an extremely active user community, and it has been implemented on many operating systems. QKS (`www.qks.com/`) is implementing a compiler for its Smallscript language (an extended version of Smalltalk) for the .NET platform.

Language Interoperability via the CLR

For several years, COM, the Component Object Model, has offered component-level interoperability between components written in different languages. Of course, this level of interoperability still exists in .NET. For example, the TipClient application (written in Visual Basic .NET) uses a class from the TipServer application (also written in Visual Basic .NET). By changing the reference, TipClient could equally well use a class from the TipServer2 application (written in C#).

The .NET Framework, via the CLR, offers a deeper level of cross-language interoperability that is new to the Windows development universe. This interoperability comes as a natural consequence of three facets of the .NET Framework:

- All code is compiled to the language-neutral MSIL.

- MSIL code contains metadata that describes the types and members within that code.

- The Common Type System (CTS) ensures that types from all .NET-compliant languages are compatible.

This leveling effect from MSIL and the CTS means that:

- A class can inherit from a base class written in another language.

- An object written in one language can pass an object written in another language to a method of an object written in yet another language.

- Tools such as debuggers or code verifiers can work with classes written in any .NET language.

- An exception raised by an object written in one language can be caught by a structured exception handling block written in another language.

As an example of this level of interoperability, I'll demonstrate a third version of the TipServer code. This version will use inheritance to add a property to the TipList class that keeps track of the number of tips delivered. But I'll develop this version in Visual Basic .NET, even though the new class is going to inherit from the TipServer2.TipList base class written in C#.

The TipServer3 project is on the companion CD, but if you'd like to build this project from scratch, follow these steps:

1. Open Visual Studio .NET and choose New Project from the Start Page.

2. Select Visual Basic Projects from the treeview on the left-hand side of the screen.

3. Select Class Library as the project template.

4. Set the name of the application to TipServer3 and click OK to create the project.

5. Highlight the class called `Class1.vb` in the Solution Explorer window and rename it `TipList.vb`.

6. Select Project ➢ Add Reference to display the Add Reference dialog box. Click the Browse button and browse to the compiled `TipServer2.dll`. By default, this will be in `Visual Studio Projects\TipServer2\bin\release`. Click Open. Click OK to add a reference to the TipServer2 project to this TipServer3 project.

7. Select the code for Class1 in `TipList.vb` (this will be an empty class definition) and replace it with the code shown in Listing 12.4.

8. Choose File ➢ Save All to save your work, and then choose Build ➢ Build to compile the project.

Listing 12.4:   **Code for *TipList.vb* in TipServer3**

```vb
Public Class TipList
    Inherits TipServer2.TipList

    Private mintCount As Integer

    Public Shadows Sub AddTip(ByVal strTip As String)
        MyBase.AddTip(strTip)
    End Sub

    Public Shadows ReadOnly Property RandomTip() As String
        Get
            RandomTip = MyBase.RandomTip
            mintCount = mintCount + 1
        End Get
    End Property

    Public ReadOnly Property TipCount() As Integer
        Get
            TipCount = mintCount
        End Get
    End Property

End Class
```

There are a couple of points to note when inspecting the code in Listing 12.4. First, a class in one project can inherit from a class in another project, even when the two projects use different programming languages, so long as you set a reference from the inheriting project to the inherited project. Second, note the use of the Shadows keyword in defining versions of AddTip and RandomTip. The Shadows keyword allows you to use a member name from a base class within an inherited class, even if the base class wasn't defined as overridable. In this case, both of these members use the MyBase keyword to call the member of the same name in the base class.

If you create a client project, you'll discover that TipServer3.TipList works just like the other two implementations of TipList, but that it also offers another property named TipCount. You'll also find that you need to set references to both TipServer2 (the library that contains the base class) and TipServer3 (the library that contains the derived class) in order to use the derived class.

Summary

In this chapter, you learned about some of the languages that can be used to develop applications within the .NET Framework. I discussed Visual Basic .NET and its improvements over Visual Basic 6 and showed how you can use Visual Basic .NET to build class libraries and user interfaces. I also introduced the C# programming language and reviewed some of the other .NET languages that are or will be available. Finally, I showed how the CLR leads to rich code interoperability, even across language boundaries.

Now it's time to move forward with data access in the .NET Framework. Before I start looking at ADO.NET in detail, I'll use the next chapter to cover a hybrid situation: calling the COM-based ADO library from within .NET code.

CHAPTER 13

Using ADO from .NET

- .NET–COM interoperability

- A sample hybrid application

- Upgrading an existing application

- Filling a DataSet from an ADO Recordset

Before digging into the details of ADO.NET, I'd like to cover a transitional solution that you might use as you migrate your development from older languages to .NET. The .NET languages have the ability to use COM components from within .NET code. This means that it's possible to use your existing ADO skills and code as you create .NET solutions. In this chapter, I'll introduce you to the "plumbing" that makes it possible to use the existing COM ADO libraries from your .NET code, and show you how this code looks in practice. I'll also cover a technique for importing an ADO Recordset to the new .NET DataSet object.

.NET–COM Interoperability

Changing development environments is always a tricky process. Not only do you need to learn the new environment (far from a trivial task when that environment is as rich and complex as .NET), you also need to plan to migrate your code from your old environment. If you've been working with a COM-based development language such as Visual Basic 6 for several years, you have built up a large store of both knowledge and components written in that language. If you had to throw out those stores entirely, moving to .NET would be a severe blow to your productivity.

Fortunately, switching from COM to .NET involves no such radical loss of productivity. There are two key concepts that make it much easier to move from COM development to .NET development without any loss of code base or productivity:

- .NET components can call COM components.
- COM components can call .NET components.

That is, there is two-way interoperability between COM and .NET. As you learn the intricacies of .NET, you can continue to use COM components, as both client components and server components. There are several situations where this interoperability is useful:

- You won't know everything about .NET instantly. Since it takes time to learn the .NET programming concepts and implementation, you'll probably need to continue critical development in COM. This applies to all the pieces of .NET. For example, you'll see in the coming chapters that ADO.NET is distinctly different from the ADO libraries that you used in COM applications. While you're just learning .NET, you may find it convenient to continue using ADO for data access.

- Although Visual Basic 6 code can be ported to .NET, the conversion isn't perfect. You may have components that can't be moved to .NET because of implementation or language quirks.

- You can't write all the code for a large application immediately in a new system such as .NET. It makes much more sense to write components individually and test them one at a time, while still interoperating with your existing code.

- You may be using third-party COM components for which you don't have source code.

In this section, I'll discuss some of the details of calling COM servers from .NET clients. Although the Visual Studio .NET development environment will handle most of the messy details for you, it can be helpful to have a mental map of what's going on when you make such cross-product calls.

> **NOTE**   In this book, I won't discuss the details of calling .NET code from COM clients.

Unmanaged Code and Runtime-Callable Wrappers

You'll recall from Chapter 11, "Introduction to .NET," that code that operates within the .NET Common Language Runtime (CLR) is called *managed code*. This code has access to all the services that the CLR brings to the table, such as cross-language integration, security and versioning support, and garbage collection. Code that does not operate within the CLR is called *unmanaged code*. COM components are, by definition, unmanaged code. Because COM was designed before the CLR existed, and COM code doesn't operate within the framework provided by the CLR, it can't use any of the CLR services.

The problem with mixing managed and unmanaged code in a single application is that the unmanaged code isn't recognized in the CLR environment. Managed code components not only depend on the CLR, they expect other components with which they interact to depend on the CLR as well.

The way out of this dilemma is to use a *proxy*. In general terms, a proxy is a piece of software that accepts commands from a component, modifies them, and forwards them to another component. The particular type of proxy used in calling unmanaged code from managed code is known as a Runtime-Callable Wrapper, or RCW. Figure 13.1 shows conceptually how RCWs straddle the boundary between managed and unmanaged code. This figure illustrates how a .NET application named DbUi.exe could use an RCW to call objects from the COM ADO library.

FIGURE 13.1:

Calling COM code from .NET code

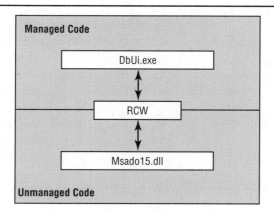

Converting Metadata with Tlbimp

COM components have public interfaces described by their type libraries. Type library information may be contained in a stand-alone file (typically with the extension .tlb or .olb) or embedded within a DLL or EXE program. A type library is a repository of metadata, similar to (but not directly compatible with) the metadata that's contained in an MSIL file created by a .NET programming language. The job of an RCW is to convert COM metadata to .NET metadata, so that .NET components can call code from the COM components.

One tool for performing this conversion is called *tlbimp* (type library importer), and it's provided as part of the .NET Framework SDK (Software Developer Kit). Tlbimp reads the metadata from a COM type library and creates a matching CLR assembly for calling the COM component.

Tlbmp is a command-line tool with a number of options for such things as signing the output assembly with a cryptographic key or resolving external references in the type library. Table 13.1 shows the options for tlbimp. The most important option is /out, which lets you specify a name for the resulting .NET assembly. For example, to convert a Visual Basic ActiveX DLL named Customers.dll to a matching .NET assembly with the name NETCustomers.dll, you could use this command line:

```
tlbimp Customers.dll /out:NETCustomers.dll
```

TABLE 13.1: Command-Line Options for Tlbimp

Option	Usage
/? Or /help	Displays usage information.
/asmversion:Version	Specifies a version for the output assembly.
/delaysign	Sets up the output assembly for delayed signing.
/keycontainer:Filename	Key container containing a strong name key pair.
/keyfile:Filename	File containing a strong name key pair.
/namespace:Namespace	Specifies a namespace for the output assembly.
/nologo	Don't display the tlbimp logo.
/out:Filename	Specifies an output filename.
/primary	Produces a primary interop assembly.
/publickey:Filename	File containing a public key from a strong name key pair.
/reference:Filename	Filename of an assembly to use to resolve external references.
/silent	Don't display any output except errors.
/strictref	Refers only to /reference-specified assemblies to resolve references.
/sysarray	Converts COM SAFEARRAY types to the System.Array class.
/unsafe	Omits .NET Framework security checks from the output assembly.
/verbose	Displays verbose debugging information.

Using COM Components Directly

As a Visual Basic .NET developer, you also have the option of using COM components directly. At least, that's what it looks like, although programmatically, you're still using an RCW to get to objects in unmanaged code. If you're working within a Visual Basic .NET project, you can follow these steps to add a reference to a COM component:

1. Choose Project ➢ Add Reference.

2. Select the COM tab in the Add Reference dialog box.

3. Select the type library you wish to use from the list and click Select, or use the Browse button to locate a component that's not listed. The selected components will be added to the lower listview in the dialog box.

4. Click OK to add the selected type libraries to your VB .NET project. If an RCW already exists for the type library, Visual Basic .NET will use that RCW. Otherwise, it will create a new RCW just for this project.

When you do this, you'll find that Visual Basic .NET actually creates a DLL in your project's /Bin folder, with a name derived from the original COM component name. For example, if you reference BackEnd.dll version 2.0 in this manner, Visual Basic .NET will create the RCW in the file Interop.BackEnd_2_0.dll.

The major drawback to this shortcut method of using a COM component directly is that there's no opportunity to sign the resulting code. As a result, if there isn't already an RCW for the component, you cannot place the code in the Global Assembly Cache (GAC); this, in turn, makes it impossible to share the component among multiple .NET applications.

The Primary Interop Assembly

Although anyone can use tlbimp to create an RCW for a COM component, that's not always the best way to proceed. On a recommended (rather than enforced) level, .NET introduces the concept of a *Primary Interop Assembly*. A Primary Interop Assembly (PIA) is an RCW that has been signed (with a strong name key pair) by the original publisher of the COM component.

If you create your own RCW for a COM component, you may find that your code doesn't work on someone else's computer. .NET won't recognize RCWs as identical unless they have identical signatures. The best way to ensure this recognition is to obtain a PIA from the original publisher of the COM component whenever possible.

When you have a PIA for a COM component, and you set a reference to that component from Visual Basic .NET, the assembly is automatically added to the Global Assembly Cache. The GAC contains components that can be used by any .NET application on the system.

TIP   Microsoft provides PIAs for the core ADODB library when you install the .NET Framework on a computer.

Choosing between Tlbimp and Direct Reference

Although either method of using a COM component allows .NET code to call your COM component, there are some reasons to choose one over the other:

- For a COM component that will be used in only a single VB .NET project, and which you wrote yourself, use direct reference rather than do any extra work. This method is suitable only for a truly private component that doesn't need to be shared.

- If a COM component is shared among multiple projects, use tlbimp so that you can sign the resulting assembly and place it in the GAC. Shared code *must* be signed. This method also allows you to create the RCW with a specific name in a specific location.

- If you need to control advanced details of the created assembly, such as its namespace or version number, you must use tlbimp. The direct reference method gives you no control over these details.

- If you didn't write the COM component, *none of these methods is acceptable*. That's because you aren't allowed to sign code written by another developer. What you need to do in that case is obtain a Primary Interop Assembly from the original developer of the component. If a PIA was installed on your computer as part of .NET setup (as is the case for ADO components), you can use the direct reference method to use this primary assembly.

A Sample Hybrid Application

The ADOChapter13 sample project on the companion CD demonstrates the hybrid approach of using the COM ADO library from within a .NET application. This project demonstrates several features:

- Opening an ADO data connection
- Retrieving an ADO Recordset and displaying it on a .NET user interface
- Deleting and editing data by executing SQL strings

Figure 13.2 shows the user interface of this sample application. It starts by displaying a set of Customer ID values in a listbox. When the user clicks a Customer ID, the application retrieves some of the details of that customer to a set of text boxes. The user can click Delete to remove the customer from the database, or make changes and then click Save Changes to persist the changes to the database.

FIGURE 13.2:

A sample hybrid application

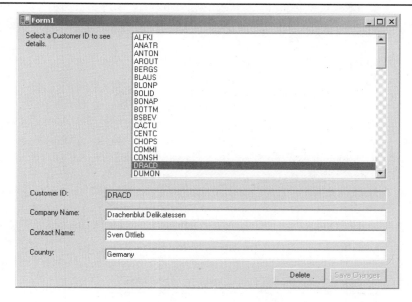

It's worthwhile to put some extra effort into the design of a hybrid application so that future upgrades to ADO.NET will be easier. As you examine the code in the sample application, you'll see that all of the data access code is in a class module, separated from the user interface code. By carefully maintaining this separation, the application makes it easier to swap out ADO and swap in ADO.NET in the future.

NOTE   This procedure assumes that you've done a full default install of the Enterprise Edition of Visual Studio .NET. If you've done so, the `nwind.mdb` file will be in the indicated spot. If not, you can substitute any copy of the Northwind sample database from Visual Basic or Access to test the code.

The Customers Class

All of the ADO code in this particular application is encapsulated in a single class named Customers. In this section, you'll walk through the code for the Customers class. You'll see some concepts that are familiar from your previous work with ADO, as well as some new code that's not possible without using the .NET Framework.

The file containing the class, `Customers.vb`, starts with an Imports statement:

```
Imports System.Collections
```

Note that the Imports statement actually precedes the start of the code for the class. In fact, you can place an Imports statement in any file in your application, and it will have global scope. The effect of this statement is to make all the classes contained within the System.Collections namespace available anywhere within the application.

Next, the code begins the class and declares some class-level variables:

```
Public Class Customers

    Private mcnn As New ADODB.Connection()
    Private mrst As New ADODB.Recordset()
    Private mlstCustomers As New System.Collections.SortedList()
```

Two of these variables (the Connection and the Recordset) are ADODB datatypes. The third is an instance of the SortedList class from the System.Collections namespace that I imported. The SortedList class consists of a set of pairs of keys and values, and it's kept in order by the keys. You can retrieve a value by knowing its key or by knowing its index within the SortedList. Both the keys and the values can be arbitrary objects. In the sample project, the keys are strings, and the values are instances of a simple Customer class.

Table 13.2 lists the members of the SortedList class.

TABLE 13.2: Members of the SortedList Class

Member	Type	Description
Add	Method	Adds a new entry to the SortedList.
Capacity	Property	The number of entries (key-value pairs) that the SortedList can contain. If the SortedList fills up, it will automatically double its capacity.
Clear	Method	Removes all entries from the SortedList.
Clone	Method	Creates a shallow copy of the SortedList.
Contains	Method	Returns True if a particular key is contained in the SortedList.
ContainsKey	Method	Returns True if a particular key is contained in the SortedList.
ContainsValue	Method	Returns True if a particular value is contained in the SortedList.
CopyTo	Method	Copies the contents of the SortedList to an Array object.
Count	Property	The number of entries contained in the SortedList.
GetByIndex	Method	Returns the value at a specific index.
GetEnumerator	Method	Returns an IDictionaryEnumerator interface that can be used to enumerate the elements in the SortedList.
GetKey	Method	Gets the key at a specified index.
GetKeyList	Method	Returns an IList interface containing the keys in the SortedList.
GetValueList	Method	Returns an IList interface containing the values in the SortedList.
IndexOfKey	Method	Returns the index of a specified key.
IndexOfValue	Method	Returns the index of a specified value.

continued on next page

TABLE 13.2 CONTINUED: Members of the SortedList Class

Member	Type	Description
IsFixedSize	Property	Set this property to True to prevent the addition or removal of any entries. It defaults to False.
IsReadOnly	Property	Returns True if the SortedList is read-only.
IsSynchronized	Property	Returns True if the SortedList has been declared in a fashion that is thread-safe.
Item	Property	Returns the value associated with a particular key.
Keys	Property	Returns an ICollection interface containing all the keys from the SortedList.
Remove	Method	Removes an element from the SortedList by specifying its key.
RemoveAt	Method	Removes an element from the SortedList by specifying its index.
SetByIndex	Method	Replaces the value at a particular index.
Synchronized	Method	Returns a thread-safe wrapper for the SortedList.
SyncRoot	Property	Returns an ICollection interface that can be used for thread-safe operations.
TrimToSize	Method	Sets the capacity to the number of entries actually in the SortedList. Useful for recovering memory when you've finished adding entries to the list.
Values	Property	Returns an ICollection interface containing all the values from the SortedList.

You'll notice that all the variables are declared using the As New syntax. Many developers (including me) recommended against using the As New syntax in Visual Basic 6 because of two drawbacks. First, because the object was actually instantiated the first time it was used, you could never be quite sure, when looking at the code for a complex application, precisely when the variable actually referred to an object. Second, this "instantiate when used" policy meant that Visual Basic had to check the status of the object variable every time it was used, and instantiate it if necessary, adding overhead to your application.

Fortunately, these drawbacks are gone with Visual Basic .NET. Now, a statement such as the following one is executed as soon as it's encountered (in a class module, it's executed just before the constructor runs):

```
Private mcnn As New ADODB.Connection()
```

This makes the object lifetime predictable and removes the overhead of checking the object status.

The next piece of code in the class module is the constructor:

```
Public Sub New()
    ' Connect to the database and retrieve all of the
```

```
' Customer IDs when this class is instantiated
mcnn.Open("Provider=Microsoft.Jet.OLEDB.4.0;" & _
  "Data Source=c:\Program Files\Microsoft Visual Studio.NET\" & _
  "Common7\Tools\Bin\nwind.mdb;")
mrst.Open("SELECT CustomerID FROM Customers", _
  mcnn, ADODB.CursorTypeEnum.adOpenDynamic, _
  ADODB.LockTypeEnum.adLockOptimistic)
End Sub
```

This procedure is called whenever an application creates a new instance of the Customers class. It opens an ADO Connection to an Access database and then opens an ADO Recordset on that Connection. You can see that this code is practically identical to ADO code that you would have written in Visual Basic 6. The only difference is that references to the ADO constants (such as adOpenDynamic) are fully qualified with the name of the ADODB namespace (created by the RCW for ADO) and the name of the enumeration that contains the constant.

The constructor establishes the Connection to the database and retrieves the initial data, but it doesn't do anything else with the data. The code defers moving the data to a .NET data structure until a client application tries to retrieve it. This happens in the CustomerList property procedure:

```
Public ReadOnly Property CustomerList() As System.Collections.SortedList
    Get
        ' Check to see whether we've stocked the SortedList. We
        ' assume that there's at least one customer in the database
        If mlstCustomers.Count = 0 Then
            mrst.MoveFirst()
            Do Until mrst.EOF
                ' Only add Customer IDs initially. There's no point in
                ' wasting time to retrieve details unless someone
                ' wants to see them
                mlstCustomers.Add(mrst.Fields("CustomerID").Value, Nothing)
                mrst.MoveNext()
            Loop
        End If
        CustomerList = mlstCustomers
    End Get
End Property
```

The first time this property is called, there won't be any entries in the mlstCustomers data structure. In that case, the code uses a familiar ADO loop to step through all the records in the Recordset and transfer them to the SortedList. But it doesn't bother to retrieve any customer details yet, because it's quite possible that individual customer details will never be required by the rest of the application.

The ReadOnly keyword explicitly marks the CustomerList property as read-only. If you omit this keyword, Visual Basic .NET will require you to write both Set and Get procedures for the property. There's also a corresponding WriteOnly keyword for write-only properties.

When the application needs the details of a customer, it calls the GetCustomer method, supplying a Customer ID:

```
Public Function GetCustomer(ByVal CustomerID As String) As Customer
    Dim TempCustomer As Customer
    Dim rstCustomer As New ADODB.Recordset()

    ' First make sure this is a valid CustomerID
    If mlstCustomers.ContainsKey(CustomerID) Then
        TempCustomer = mlstCustomers.Item(CustomerID)
        ' Now see if we have a Customer object for this customer
        If TempCustomer Is Nothing Then
            ' If not, create an object and retrieve the details
            ' from the database
            TempCustomer = New Customer()
            rstCustomer.Open("SELECT CustomerID, CompanyName," & _
              "ContactName, Country FROM Customers WHERE CustomerID = """ & _
              CustomerID & """", mcnn, _
              ADODB.CursorTypeEnum.adOpenForwardOnly, _
              ADODB.LockTypeEnum.adLockReadOnly)
            With TempCustomer
                .CustomerID = CustomerID
                .CompanyName = rstCustomer.Fields("CompanyName").Value
                .ContactName = rstCustomer.Fields("ContactName").Value
                .Country = rstCustomer.Fields("Country").Value
            End With
            mlstCustomers.Item(CustomerID) = TempCustomer
        End If
        ' By now we've got the details into the SortedList
        GetCustomer = mlstCustomers.Item(CustomerID)
    Else ' This is not a valid CustomerID
        GetCustomer = Nothing
    End If
End Function
```

The GetCustomer method starts by using the ContainsKey method of the SortedList class as a fast way of determining whether it was passed a valid Customer ID. Assuming it was, it next tries to retrieve a Customer object (detailed later in this chapter) from the CustomerList. If it gets back Nothing, you know that this particular Customer hasn't been instantiated yet. If that's the case, it's time to go back to the database via ADO, retrieving the fields that you're interested in. The code here uses a SELECT statement to get the data; you could get a bit more speed by creating a stored procedure in the database and calling that instead. Once the customer details are available, the new Customer object is both saved to the SortedList and returned to the calling code.

The DeleteCustomer method handles any deletions from the database:

```
Public Sub DeleteCustomer(ByVal CustomerID As String)
    ' Need to remove Orders before Customers due to RI
    mcnn.Execute("DELETE FROM Orders WHERE CustomerID=""" & _
    CustomerID & """")
    mcnn.Execute("DELETE FROM Customers WHERE CustomerID=""" & _
    CustomerID & """")
    ' Keep the SortedList in sync with the database
    mlstCustomers.Remove(CustomerID)
End Sub
```

Once again, this procedure uses a combination of .NET and ADO to do its work. The ADO code deletes the customer and related orders from the database, while the Remove method of the SortedList class is used to delete the object (and its key) from the mlstCustomers object.

Similar code handles updates:

```
Public Sub UpdateCustomer(ByVal UpdatedCustomer As Customer)
    With UpdatedCustomer
        ' Update the database...
        mcnn.Execute("UPDATE Customers SET " & _
         "CompanyName = """ & .CompanyName & """, " & _
         "ContactName = """ & .ContactName & """, " & _
         "Country = """ & .Country & """ WHERE " & _
         "CustomerID = """ & .CustomerID & """")
        ' ...and update the SortedList
        mlstCustomers.Item(.CustomerID) = UpdatedCustomer
    End With
End Sub
```

The UpdateCustomer method accepts a Customer object from the application. This object is saved directly to the SortedList, and its properties are used to update the database via another ADO Execute statement.

The Customer Class

Individual customers in this application are represented by a simple Customer class:

```
Public Class Customer

    Public CustomerID As String
    Public CompanyName As String
    Public ContactName As String
```

```
    Public Country As String

End Class
```

The Customer class is really nothing more than a handy container that keeps together in one spot all the fields that the code uses from the database. It doesn't have to contain any code, because all the work with the database is done with methods of the parent class, Customers.

The User Interface Code

Finally, I'll review the user interface code that lets the user interact with the Customers class. Notice as you go through this code that there are no ADO objects or methods directly visible to the user interface; all of the ADO is hidden behind the interface of the Customers class. This isolation means that upgrading this application to use ADO.NET would require no changes to the user interface code.

The code behind the user interface form starts by declaring a local variable to hold an instance of the Customers class:

```
Private mCustomers As New Customers()
```

This object will be instantiated (and, in turn, will execute the constructor of the Customers class) as soon as the form is read into memory. So, by the time the form is visible on-screen, the Customer IDs that it uses will already be completely loaded. The form's Load event then takes these Customer IDs and displays them in the listbox on-screen:

```
Private Sub Form1_Load(ByVal sender As System.Object, _
  ByVal e As System.EventArgs) Handles MyBase.Load
    ' Stock the listbox with all the Customer IDs
    Dim IDList As IList = mCustomers.CustomerList.GetKeyList
    Dim intI As Integer

    For intI = 0 To mCustomers.CustomerList.Count - 1
        lboCustomers.Items.Add(IDList(intI))
    Next
End Sub
```

When the user clicks an item in the listbox, the SelectedIndexChanged event is fired:

```
Private Sub lboCustomers_SelectedIndexChanged( _
  ByVal sender As System.Object, ByVal e As System.EventArgs) _
  Handles lboCustomers.SelectedIndexChanged
    Dim Cust As New Customer()
    ' When a customer is selected in the listbox, retrieve
    ' and display their details
    Cust = mCustomers.GetCustomer(lboCustomers.SelectedItem)
    With Cust
        txtCustomerID.Text = .CustomerID
```

```
            txtCompanyName.Text = .CompanyName
            txtContactName.Text = .ContactName
            txtCountry.Text = .Country
        End With
        btnDelete.Enabled = True
        btnSaveChanges.Enabled = False
    End Sub
```

In response to this event, the form's code calls the GetCustomer method of the Customers class to obtain the details for the selected customer and display them on the user interface.

The Delete button is an interface to the DeleteCustomer method of the Customers class:

```
Private Sub btnDelete_Click(ByVal sender As System.Object, _
  ByVal e As System.EventArgs) Handles btnDelete.Click
    ' Confirm deletion, because this is drastic
    If MsgBox("Clicking Yes will delete this customer and " & _
      "all of their orders", MsgBoxStyle.YesNo + MsgBoxStyle.Critical, _
      "Delete Confirmation") = MsgBoxResult.Yes Then
        ' Delete from the database
        mCustomers.DeleteCustomer(txtCustomerID.Text)
        ' And clean up the UI
        lboCustomers.Items.Remove(lboCustomers.SelectedItem)
        txtCustomerID.Text = ""
        txtCompanyName.Text = ""
        txtContactName.Text = ""
        txtCountry.Text = ""
        btnDelete.Enabled = False
        btnSaveChanges.Enabled = False
    End If
End Sub
```

Because the effect of the DeleteCustomer method is so drastic, I've chosen to ask the user explicitly to confirm this action. Note also that there's code to keep the list in the listbox up to date after a deletion.

Similarly, the Save Changes button is a wrapper around the UpdateCustomer method of the Customers class:

```
Private Sub btnSaveChanges_Click(ByVal sender As System.Object, _
  ByVal e As System.EventArgs) Handles btnSaveChanges.Click
    ' Create a customer object from the UI...
    Dim Cust As New Customer()
    With Cust
        .CustomerID = txtCustomerID.Text
        .CompanyName = txtCompanyName.Text
        .ContactName = txtContactName.Text
        .Country = txtCountry.Text
    End With
```

```
' ...and hand it back to the Customers class to do the updates
   mCustomers.UpdateCustomer(Cust)
End Sub
```

The remaining user interface code handles enabling the Save Changes button only when the user makes a change to the currently displayed customer:

```
' Enable the "Save Changes" button when any field is edited
Private Sub txtCompanyName_TextChanged(ByVal sender As Object, _
 ByVal e As System.EventArgs) Handles txtCompanyName.TextChanged
    btnSaveChanges.Enabled = True
End Sub
Private Sub txtContactName_TextChanged(ByVal sender As Object, _
 ByVal e As System.EventArgs) Handles txtContactName.TextChanged
    btnSaveChanges.Enabled = True
End Sub
Private Sub txtCountry_TextChanged(ByVal sender As Object, _
 ByVal e As System.EventArgs) Handles txtCountry.TextChanged
    btnSaveChanges.Enabled = True
End Sub
```

Upgrading an Existing Application

Another option for working with ADO inside a .NET application is to upgrade an existing Visual Basic 6 application that uses ADO for data access. Visual Basic .NET offers easy upgrading for Visual Basic 6 projects. To demonstrate this capability, I'll upgrade the sample application from Chapter 3 to a .NET application.

Using the Upgrade Wizard

To upgrade the ADOChapter3 sample application, follow these steps:

1. Copy the source code for the ADOChapter3 sample project to a folder on a computer where Visual Basic .NET is installed.

2. Select Start ➢ Programs ➢ Microsoft Visual Studio .NET 7.0 ➢ Microsoft Visual Studio .NET 7.0 to launch the Visual Studio .NET IDE.

3. Choose Open Project on the Start Page. Navigate to the ADOChapter3.vbp file and then click Open.

4. Visual Basic .NET will recognize this as a Visual Basic 6 project and launch the Visual Basic Upgrade Wizard. This wizard starts with an introductory page explaining its function. Click Next.

5. The second panel of the wizard allows you to select the type of Visual Basic .NET project that the wizard should create. You have no choices on this panel, because the Visual Basic 6 project is an EXE project. Click Next.

6. The third panel of the wizard allows you to specify a location for the new .NET project. Either accept the default or choose your own location, and then click Next. If the target folder doesn't already exist, you will be prompted to create it.

7. The next panel of the wizard warns you that the upgrade process may be time-consuming. Click Next. During the upgrade process, the Upgrade Wizard will display a progress bar and the estimated time to complete the upgrade, as shown in Figure 13.3.

FIGURE 13.3:

The Upgrade Wizard performing an upgrade

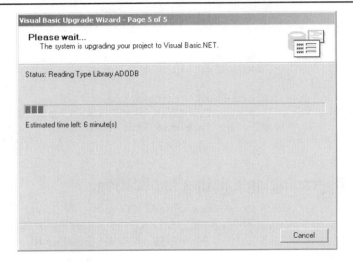

8. When the Upgrade Wizard completes its work, it will load the new project into the Visual Basic .NET interface. One of the components it creates is a web page named _UpgradeReport.htm. You can double-click this component to open it in the IDE. Figure 13.4 shows the upgrade report for the ADOChapter3 sample project.

As you can see, the Upgrade Wizard had no problem in upgrading this particular project to Visual Basic .NET. If you run the project, you'll discover that all of the functionality from the Visual Basic 6 project is still present (you may have to ensure that the connection strings point to valid databases in your new environment).

The major advantage to using the Upgrade Wizard is that it can provide you with a fast way to move ADO or other Visual Basic code to the .NET environment. The major disadvantage is that the automated upgrade offers you no chance to rewrite the application as part of the migration process. For example, there's no way to make the wizard wrap ADO data access in class modules as in the earlier example in this chapter.

Upgrade Report for ADOChapter3.vbp

Time of Upgrade: 11/20/2001 12:34 PM

List of Project Files

New Filename	Original Filename	File Type	Status	Errors	Warnings	Total Issues
⊞ (Global Issues)				0	0	0
⊞ basMain.vb	basMain.bas	Module	Upgraded	0	0	0
⊞ frmCodeSamples.vb	frmCodeSamples.frm	Form	Upgraded	0	0	0
⊞ frmRecordsetProperties.vb	frmRecordsetProperties.frm	Form	Upgraded	0	0	0
3 File(s)		Forms: 2 Modules: 1	Upgraded: 3 Not upgraded: 0	0	0	0

Click here for help with troubleshooting upgraded projects

Upgrade Settings

GenerateInterfacesForClasses: 0
LogFile: ADOChapter3.log
MigrateProjectTo: WinExe
OutputDir: C:\Documents and Settings\Mike\My Documents\Visual Studio Projects\Chapter3.NET
OutputName: ADOChapter3.vbproj
ProjectName: ADOChapter3
ProjectPath: \\Skyrocket\My Documents\Sybex\ADO DH\Samples\Chapter 3\ADOChapter3.vbp

Preparing for a Clean Upgrade

Although the Upgrade Wizard generally does a good job of moving Visual Basic 6 code to
Visual Basic .NET, it's not perfect; some of the Visual Basic 6 coding practices just don't
translate well to .NET. But there are some things you can do in your Visual Basic 6 source
code to make the job easier. Many of these are good programming practices in any case.
Here is a list of things to check before you run the Upgrade Wizard:

- Use early binding wherever possible.

- Use strongly typed datatypes rather than variants for your data.

- Use explicit conversions (such as CStr() or CInt()) when converting from one datatype to
  another, rather than depend on the implicit conversions built into Visual Basic 6.

- Use the Date datatype (instead of the Double datatype) to store dates.

- Use explicit IsNull() tests rather than rely on null propagation.

- Use zero as the lower bound of all arrays.

- Don't call ReDim on an array without declaring it using Dim first.

- Use symbolic constants instead of magic numbers.

- Remove DefBool, DefInt, and the other Def<type> statements.
- Remove On X GoTo and On X GoSub statements.
- Remove GoSub/Return statements.
- Remove Option Base statements.
- Remove VarPtr, VarPtrArray, VarPtrStringArray, ObjPtr, and StrPtr statements.
- Remove LSet statements.

If you don't follow these recommendations, the Upgrade Wizard will still attempt to upgrade your code, but it will insert comments in the result where it was unable to perform the upgrade.

> **TIP**   For more details on the upgrading process, download the Microsoft white paper "Preparing Your Visual Basic 6.0 Applications for the Upgrade to Visual Basic .NET" from `http://msdn.microsoft.com/library/default.asp?url=/library/en-us/dnvb600/html/vb6tovbdotnet.asp?frame=true`.

Filling a DataSet from an ADO Recordset

ADO.NET also has one built-in link to the older COM-based ADO library: You can fill an ADO.NET DataSet object from an ADO Recordset object. In this section, I'll show you how this technique works, and how you can use it to integrate Recordsets delivered by ActiveX server components into an ADO.NET application.

The DataSet and DataAdapter Objects

I'll give you a thorough introduction to the ADO.NET object model in Chapter 14, "Using the ADO.NET Objects to Retrieve Data." For this particular technique, though, I need to introduce two of those objects here: the DataSet and DataAdapter objects.

The key object for representing data in the .NET Framework, and the closest equivalent to an ADO Recordset, is the DataSet. Unlike an ADO Recordset, a DataSet can contain data from multiple tables as well as the relationships between those tables. These are represented by subsidiary DataTable and DataRelation objects within the DataSet object.

The DataSet object is the central point for all .NET code involving data access. It can be loaded with data by communicating with a .NET data provider by various means. It also implements methods to save its contents to XML, or to reconstruct an XML stream into the data that it represents, among many other capabilities.

The DataAdapter provides one of the ways to load data into a DataSet. The DataAdaper acts as a conduit between a data source and a DataSet. You call the DataAdapter's Fill method with various arguments to load data into the DataSet object. In particular, one of the over-loaded versions of the Fill method accepts an ADO Recordset as the source of the data to be loaded into the DataSet:

```
DataAdapter.Fill(DataSet, RecordSet, TableName)
```

As you can see, there are three arguments:

- *DataSet* is an ADO.NET DataSet object.

- *RecordSet* is an ADO Recordset object.

- *TableName* is the name of a table contained in the Recordset that will be loaded into the DataSet.

> **TIP**   Although you'll find many references to a DataAdapter class in the .NET help files, actually there is no such class. Rather, there are several classes that implement the necessary interfaces to work as a DataAdapter. In this chapter, I'll work with an instance of the OleDbDataAdapter class that works with OLE DB data sources. There's also a Sql-DataAdapter class that works with SQL Server data sources, and there will probably be other DataAdapter classes implemented by third parties.

A Sample ActiveX Server

The sample Visual Basic 6 ActiveX server that I'm going to use from a .NET project is called SQLSchema, and it includes a single class named SchemaInfo. This class has two public properties:

- ServerName is the name of a computer running SQL Server.

- DatabaseName is the name of a database on that SQL Server.

The class also provides three methods:

- Tables returns a Recordset with information about tables in the specified database.

- Columns returns a Recordset with information about columns in the specified database.

- Views returns a Recordset with information about views in the specified database.

The information returned by the SchemaInfo class is retrieved by executing select queries that use the schema information views that are built into SQL Server 2000. Listing 13.1 shows the code for the SchemaInfo class.

> **WARNING**   This code lacks some error checking that should be present in actual production code. For example, it doesn't attempt to verify that the server is running SQL Server 2000. The class passes any errors that it encounters back to the client.

Listing 13.1:   The SchemaInfo Class

```
Option Explicit

Const conErrBase = vbObjectError + 2000

Public ServerName As String
Public DatabaseName As String

Public Function Tables() As ADODB.Recordset
    Dim cnn As ADODB.Connection
    Dim rst As ADODB.Recordset

    On Error GoTo HandleErr

    If ServerName = "" Then
        Err.Raise conErrBase + 1, "SQLSchema.SchemaInfo", _
          "ServerName not set"
    ElseIf DatabaseName = "" Then
        Err.Raise conErrBase + 2, "SQLSchema.SchemaInfo", _
          "DatabaseName not set"
    Else
        Set cnn = New ADODB.Connection
        cnn.Open "Provider=SQLOLEDB;Server=" & ServerName & _
          ";Initial Catalog=" & DatabaseName & ";Integrated Security=SSPI"
        Set rst = New ADODB.Recordset
        rst.Open "SELECT * FROM " & DatabaseName & _
          ".INFORMATION_SCHEMA.TABLES", cnn, adOpenStatic, _
          adLockReadOnly
        Set Tables = rst
    End If

ExitHere:
    Exit Function

HandleErr:
    Err.Raise Err.Number, Err.Source, Err.Description

End Function

Public Function Columns() As ADODB.Recordset
    Dim cnn As ADODB.Connection
    Dim rst As ADODB.Recordset

    On Error GoTo HandleErr

    If ServerName = "" Then
        Err.Raise conErrBase + 1, "SQLSchema.SchemaInfo", _
          "ServerName not set"
    ElseIf DatabaseName = "" Then
        Err.Raise conErrBase + 2, "SQLSchema.SchemaInfo", _
```

```
                "DatabaseName not set"
        Else
            Set cnn = New ADODB.Connection
            cnn.Open "Provider=SQLOLEDB;Server=" & ServerName & _
                ";Initial Catalog=" & DatabaseName & ";Integrated Security=SSPI"
            Set rst = New ADODB.Recordset
            rst.Open "SELECT * FROM " & DatabaseName & _
                ".INFORMATION_SCHEMA.COLUMNS", cnn, adOpenStatic, _
                adLockReadOnly
            Set Columns = rst
        End If

ExitHere:
        Exit Function

HandleErr:
        Err.Raise Err.Number, Err.Source, Err.Description

End Function

Public Function Views() As ADODB.Recordset
        Dim cnn As ADODB.Connection
        Dim rst As ADODB.Recordset

        On Error GoTo HandleErr

        If ServerName = "" Then
            Err.Raise conErrBase + 1, "SQLSchema.SchemaInfo", _
                "ServerName not set"
        ElseIf DatabaseName = "" Then
            Err.Raise conErrBase + 2, "SQLSchema.SchemaInfo", _
                "DatabaseName not set"
        Else
            Set cnn = New ADODB.Connection
            cnn.Open "Provider=SQLOLEDB;Server=" & ServerName & _
                ";Initial Catalog=" & DatabaseName & ";Integrated Security=SSPI"
            Set rst = New ADODB.Recordset
            rst.Open "SELECT * FROM " & DatabaseName & _
                ".INFORMATION_SCHEMA.VIEWS", cnn, adOpenStatic, _
                adLockReadOnly
            Set Views = rst
        End If

ExitHere:
        Exit Function

HandleErr:
        Err.Raise Err.Number, Err.Source, Err.Description

End Function
```

Integrating a Recordset into ADO.NET

Figure 13.5 shows a .NET client application that uses the SQLSchema server to retrieve information. In this case, it's displaying information about the views in the Northwind database on a server named OXTEAM. The name of the client project is NetSchemaClient.

> **TIP**   If you'd like to compare the .NET code with the corresponding COM code, you can find a VB 6 implementation of the client in the SchemaClient project.

FIGURE 13.5:

Displaying an ADO
Recordset on a .NET
user interface

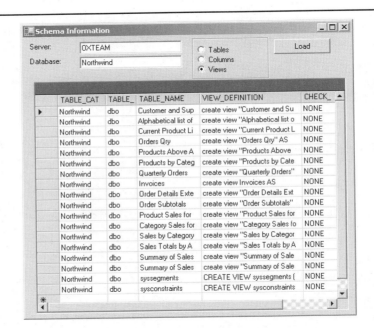

The application shown here, named NetSchemaClient, has references to both the SQLSchema server and ADO 2.6. These references allow it to work with the SchemaInfo and Recordset objects.

> **TIP**   When you're using a Recordset from an ActiveX server in .NET, you must set a reference to the same version of ADO that the ActiveX server uses to create the Recordset.

The code in Listing 13.2 integrates the ADO Recordset with the .NET DataSet.

Listing 13.2:   **Filling a DataSet from a Recordset**

```
Imports System.Data
Imports System.Data.OleDb
...
    Private Sub btnLoad_Click( _
    ByVal sender As System.Object, _
    ByVal e As System.EventArgs) Handles btnLoad.Click

        Dim rst As ADODB.Recordset
        Dim objSchema As New SQLSchema.SchemaInfo()
        Dim da As New OleDb.OleDbDataAdapter()
        Dim ds As New DataSet()

        Try

            objSchema.DatabaseName = txtDatabase.Text
            objSchema.ServerName = txtServer.Text
            If rbTables.Checked Then
                rst = objSchema.Tables
                da.Fill(ds, rst, "TABLES")
                dgMain.DataSource = ds.Tables("TABLES")
            ElseIf rbColumns.Checked Then
                rst = objSchema.Columns
                da.Fill(ds, rst, "COLUMNS")
                dgMain.DataSource = ds.Tables("COLUMNS")
            Else
                rst = objSchema.Views
                da.Fill(ds, rst, "VIEWS")
                dgMain.DataSource = ds.Tables("VIEWS")
            End If
        Catch ex As Exception
            MsgBox("Error " & ex.Message)
        End Try

    End Sub
```

The two Imports statements bring in the namespaces that contain the objects that this code uses. The System.Data namespace contains the DataSet object, while the System.Data .OleDb namespace contains the OleDbDataAdapter object.

When the user clicks the Load button, the procedure shown here first sets the ServerName and DatabaseName properties of a SchemaInfo object. It then calls the appropriate method (Tables, Columns, or Views) to retrieve the desired information. These methods return a Recordset object, which is stored in a local variable named rst. Then the code calls the Fill method of the DataAdapter object to move the table from the Recordset to the DataSet. This table is then bound to the DataGrid on the user interface by setting the DataSource property of the DataGrid to the appropriate DataTable within the DataSet.

You can use this technique any time you have an ADO Recordset to work with. This method is best suited to read-only data that is displayed but not changed by your application. That's because the DataAdapter doesn't set up any two-way communication between the DataSet and the Recordset. If you make changes to the DataSet, you'll have to write application code to capture those changes and apply them back to the data in the Recordset.

Summary

In this chapter, you learned about ways to use ADO from within the .NET Framework:

- Employing Runtime-Callable Wrappers to use the ADO classes directly
- Migrating Visual Basic 6 code to Visual Basic .NET
- Using the DataAdapter and DataSet objects to extract information from an ADO Recordset

All of these are transitional techniques, best used while you are in the process of migrating from ADO to ADO.NET. In the next chapter, you'll start looking at pure ADO.NET techniques, which are faster and more flexible than the hybrid code that I demonstrated in this chapter.

Part IV

Understanding ADO.NET

CHAPTER 14

Using the ADO.NET Objects to Retrieve Data

- The ADO.NET object model

- .NET data providers

- Using DataSets

- Finding and sorting data in DataSets

- Running stored procedures

Now that you understand the basics of .NET and have seen how to use your legacy ADO code in the .NET environment, it's time to tackle the new world of data access provided by ADO.NET. In this chapter, I'll introduce you to the ADO.NET objects and the available data providers. Then you'll see how to use the DataSet object to work with data, and the Command object to interface directly with a database.

The ADO.NET Object Model

The ADO.NET object model is broken up into two distinct sets of objects: data provider objects and DataSet objects. There are two sets of objects because the .NET Framework separates the task of using data from the task of storing data. The DataSet objects provide a memory-resident, disconnected set of objects that you can load with data. The provider objects handle the task of working directly with data sources. One of the provider objects, the DataAdapter object, serves as a conduit between the two sets of objects. By using a DataAdapter, you can load data into a DataSet and later save changes back to the original data source.

Figure 14.1 provides an overview of the ADO.NET object model.

In this section, I'll describe the various ADO.NET objects so that you can get the overall picture before digging into the actual mechanics of using these objects.

FIGURE 14.1:

ADO.NET objects

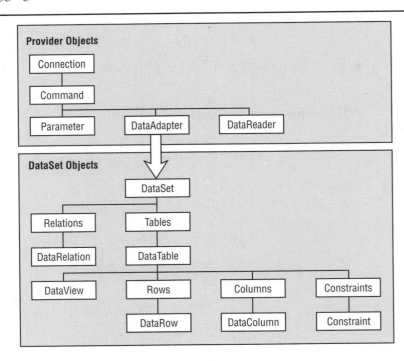

The Data Provider Objects

Depending on how you look at it, there are either four or twelve main data provider objects. How can this be? The answer is that there are four important types of data provider objects, but each of these is implemented within several .NET namespaces. These four objects are as follows:

- Connection
- Command
- DataReader
- DataAdapter

The .NET data provider namespaces are as follows:

- System.Data.OleDb
- System.Data.SqlClient
- System.Data.Odbc

Thus, there are twelve objects to learn about, as shown in Table 14.1. But the only major difference between the objects is the data sources with which they work. For example, the OleDbConnection, SqlConnection, and OdbcConnection all implement the same methods and properties. The difference is that they are used with OLE DB data sources, SQL Server data sources, and ODBC data sources, respectively.

TABLE 14.1: Core Data Provider Objects

Object	Implementations
Connection	OleDbConnection, SqlConnection, OdbcConnection
Command	OleDbCommand, SqlCommand, OdbcCommand
DataReader	OleDbDataReader, SqlDataReader, OdbcDataReader
DataAdapter	OleDbDataAdapter, SqlDataAdapter, OdbcDataAdapter

In the discussion that follows, I'll refer mostly to the generic object names. In actual code, you'll see the particular class names. I'll continue the discussion of the .NET data providers after you've seen the objects in the ADO.NET object model.

There are sometimes minor differences between the implementations of these objects. For example, both the OdbcConnection and the OleDbConnection implement a ReleaseObject-Pool method, which is not shared by the SqlConnection object.

NOTE   Data providers also implement some helper objects, such as the Parameter object, which can be used to supply parameters to a Command object. Like the objects discussed above, these helper objects come in multiple versions.

Connection

The Connection object in ADO.NET, just like its namesake in ADO, represents a single persistent connection to a data source. ADO.NET automatically handles connection pooling, which contributes to better application performance. When you close a Connection, it is returned to a connection pool. Connections in a pool are not immediately destroyed by ADO.NET. Instead, they're available for reuse if another part of your application requests a connection that matches in details a previously closed connection.

Table 14.2 lists the important members of the Connection object.

TABLE 14.2: Connection Members

Name	Type	Description
BeginTransaction	Method	Start a new transaction on this Connection.
ChangeDatabase	Method	Switch current databases.
Close	Method	Close the Connection and return it to the connection pool.
ConnectionString	Property	Connection string that determines the data source to be used for this Connection.
ConnectionTimeout	Property	Number of seconds to wait before timing out when connecting.
CreateCommand	Method	Returns a new Command object.
Database	Property	Name of the current database open on this Connection.
DataSource	Property	Name of the current server for this Connection.
Driver	Property	ODBC driver in use by this Connection. Applies to Odbc-Connection only.
GetOleDbSchemaTable	Method	Returns schema information from the data source. Applies to OleDbConnection only.
InfoMessage	Event	Fired when the server sends an informational message.
Open	Method	Opens the Connection.
PacketSize	Property	Size of network packets (in bytes) used by this Connection. Applies to SqlConnection only.
Provider	Property	OLE DB provider in use by this Connection. Applies to OleDb-Connection only.
ReleaseObjectPool	Method	Releases Connections held in the connection pool. Applies to OdbcConnection and OleDbConnection.
ServerVersion	Property	String containing the version number of the server.
State	Property	State of the Connection.
StateChange	Event	Fired when the state of the Connection changes.
WorkstationID	Property	String that identifies the connection client. Applies to Sql-Connection only.

Here's some code to open a connection to a SQL Server data source, from the frmObjects form in the ADOChapter14 sample project. You'll see that it's very similar to ADO code that performs the same task.

```
Private Sub btnConnection_Click(ByVal sender As System.Object, _
    ByVal e As System.EventArgs) Handles btnConnection.Click

    Dim cnn As New SqlClient.SqlConnection()

    Try
        lboResults.Items.Clear()
        cnn.ConnectionString = "Data Source=SKYROCKET;" & _
          "Initial Catalog=Northwind;Integrated Security=SSPI"
        cnn.Open()
        With lboResults.Items
            .Add("Connection succeeded:")
            .Add("Database = " & cnn.Database)
            .Add("DataSource = " & cnn.DataSource)
            .Add("ServerVersion = " & cnn.ServerVersion)
        End With
        cnn.Close()
    Catch ex As Exception
        MsgBox("Error: " & ex.Source & ": " & ex.Message, _
          MsgBoxStyle.OKOnly, "btnConnection")
    End Try

End Sub
```

WARNING   The examples in this chapter use a SQL Server named SKYROCKET as their data source. You'll need to change this to the name of your server in the source code.

Command

The ADO.NET Command object is also very close in meaning to its ADO counterpart. The Command object represents a string (such as a SQL statement or a stored procedure name) that can be executed through a Connection. Table 14.3 lists the important members of the Command object.

TABLE 14.3: Command Members

Name	Type	Description
Cancel	Method	Cancels execution of the Command.
CommandText	Property	Statement to be executed at the data source.
CommandTimeout	Property	Number of seconds to wait for a Command to execute.

continued on next page

TABLE 14.3 CONTINUED: Command Members

Name	Type	Description
CommandType	Property	An enumeration indicating the type of Command. Possible values are StoredProcedure, TableDirect, and Text. You can omit this property, in which case the data provider will determine the appropriate Command type.
Connection	Property	Connection through which this Command will be executed.
CreateParameter	Method	Creates a new Parameter object for the Command.
ExecuteNonQuery	Method	Executes a Command that does not return results.
ExecuteReader	Method	Executes a Command and puts the results in a DataReader object.
ExecuteScalar	Method	Executes a Command and returns the value of the first column of the first row of results. Any other results are discarded.
ExecuteXmlReader	Method	Executes a Command and puts the results in an XmlReader object. Applies to SqlCommand only.
Parameters	Property	Collection of Parameter objects (if any) for this Command.
Prepare	Method	Prepares the Command for faster execution.
ResetCommandTimeout	Method	Resets the CommandTimeout property to its default value.

As an example of the use of the Command object, here's some code from the frmObjects form in this chapter's sample project; it uses the ExecuteScalar method to return the results of a SELECT COUNT statement:

```
Private Sub btnCommand_Click(ByVal sender As System.Object, _
  ByVal e As System.EventArgs) Handles btnCommand.Click

    Dim cnn As New SqlClient.SqlConnection()
    Dim cmd As New SqlClient.SqlCommand()

    Try
        lboResults.Items.Clear()
        cnn.ConnectionString = "Data Source=SKYROCKET;" & _
          "Initial Catalog=Northwind;Integrated Security=SSPI"
        cnn.Open()
        cmd = cnn.CreateCommand
        cmd.CommandText = "SELECT COUNT(*) FROM Customers"
        lboResults.Items.Add("Customer count:")
        lboResults.Items.Add(cmd.ExecuteScalar)
        cnn.Close()
    Catch ex As Exception
        MsgBox("Error: " & ex.Source & ": " & ex.Message, _
          MsgBoxStyle.OKOnly, "btnCommand")
    End Try

End Sub
```

Like the ADO Command object, the ADO.NET Command object includes a collection of Parameter objects. I'll discuss the use of Parameters later in the chapter, in the "Running Stored Procedures" section.

DataReader

The DataReader object has no direct analog in the old ADO way of doing things. The closest ADO concept is that of a forward-only, read-only Recordset. The DataReader gives you a "firehose" set of results based on a Command. You can create a DataReader only from a Command (not by declaring it using the New keyword), and you can only move forward in the data. The DataReader represents the fastest, but least flexible, way to retrieve data in ADO.NET.

Table 14.4 lists the important members of the DataReader object.

TABLE 14.4: DataReader Members

Name	Type	Description
Close	Method	Closes the DataReader.
Depth	Property	Depth of nesting for the current row of the DataReader.
FieldCount	Property	Number of columns in the current row of the DataReader.
GetBoolean	Method	Gets a Boolean value from the specified column.
GetByte	Method	Gets a byte value from the specified column.
GetBytes	Method	Gets a stream of bytes from the specified column.
GetChar	Method	Gets a character from the specified column.
GetChars	Method	Gets a stream of characters from the specified column.
GetDataTypeName	Method	Gets the name of the source datatype for a column.
GetDateTime	Method	Gets a date/time value from the specified column.
GetDecimal	Method	Gets a decimal value from the specified column.
GetDouble	Method	Gets a double value from the specified column.
GetFieldType	Method	Gets the ADO.NET field type for a column.
GetFloat	Method	Gets a floating-point value from the specified column.
GetGuid	Method	Gets a GUID from the specified column.
GetInt16	Method	Gets a 16-bit integer from the specified column.
GetInt32	Method	Gets a 32-bit integer from the specified column.
GetInt64	Method	Gets a 64-bit integer from the specified column.
GetName	Method	Gets the name of the specified column.
GetOrdinal	Method	Gets the column ordinal, given the column name.
GetSchemaTable	Method	Returns schema information for the DataReader object.
GetString	Method	Gets a string value from the specified column.
GetTimeSpan	Method	Gets a time value from the specified column.

continued on next page

TABLE 14.4 CONTINUED: DataReader Members

Name	Type	Description
GetValue	Method	Gets a value from the specified column in its native format.
GetValues	Method	Gets an entire row of data into an array of objects.
IsClosed	Property	A Boolean value that indicates whether the DataReader is closed.
IsDbNull	Method	Indicates whether the specified column contains a Null.
Item	Property	Gets a value from the specified column in its native format.
NextResult	Method	Retrieves the next result set from the Command object.
Read	Method	Loads the next row of data into the DataReader object.
RecordsAffected	Property	Number of rows changed by the DataReader's SQL statement.

NOTE The SqlDataReader also has methods such as GetSqlBinary and GetSqlBoolean that retrieve data into native objects from the System.Data.SqlClient namespace. Refer to the .NET Framework help for details on these methods.

Here's an example of using the DataReader class, once again with the SQL Server versions of the ADO.NET objects; it's from the frmObjects form in this chapter's sample project:

```
Private Sub btnDataReader_Click(ByVal sender As System.Object, _
ByVal e As System.EventArgs) Handles btnDataReader.Click

    Dim cnn As New SqlClient.SqlConnection()
    Dim cmd As New SqlClient.SqlCommand()
    Dim dr As SqlClient.SqlDataReader

    Try
        lboResults.Items.Clear()
        cnn.ConnectionString = "Data Source=SKYROCKET;" & _
         "Initial Catalog=Northwind;Integrated Security=SSPI"
        cnn.Open()
        cmd = cnn.CreateCommand
        cmd.CommandText = "SELECT CustomerID, CompanyName FROM Customers"
        dr = cmd.ExecuteReader
        While dr.Read
            lboResults.Items.Add(dr.GetString(0) & " " & dr.GetString(1))
        End While
        dr.Close()
        cnn.Close()
    Catch ex As Exception
```

```
        MsgBox("Error: " & ex.Source & ": " & ex.Message, _
          MsgBoxStyle.OKOnly, "btnDataReader")
      End Try

    End Sub
```

Figure 14.2 shows the results of running this procedure in the sample database.

FIGURE 14.2:

Retrieving data with a
DataReader object

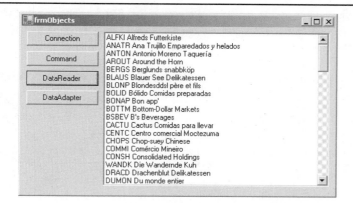

DataAdapter

The DataAdapter object has no direct equivalent in old-style ADO. This object provides the essential link between the data provider objects and the DataSet (which I'll discuss in the next section). The DataAdapter is a two-way pipeline between the data as it's stored and the data in a more abstract form that's designed for manipulation. Methods of the DataAdapter can be used to move the data back and forth between the two representations.

Table 14.5 lists the important members of the DataAdapter object.

TABLE 14.5: DataAdapter Members

Name	Type	Description
AcceptChangesDuringFill	Property	If True, all rows in the DataSet are marked as committed when they're added with the Fill method. Not available for OdbcDataAdapter.
ContinueUpdateOnError	Property	If True, updates continue even after updating a single row fails. Not available for OdbcDataAdapter.
DeleteCommand	Property	SQL statement used to delete records from the data source.
Fill	Method	Transfers data from the data source to the DataSet.

continued on next page

TABLE 14.5 CONTINUED: DataAdapter Members

Name	Type	Description
FillError	Event	Fires when an error occurs during the Fill method.
FillSchema	Method	Adjusts the schema of the DataSet to match the schema of the data source.
GetFillParameters	Method	Gets any parameters supplied to the SelectCommand.
InsertCommand	Property	SQL statement used to insert records into the data source.
RowUpdated	Event	Fires during the Update method just after a row is updated.
RowUpdating	Event	Fires during the Update method just before a row is updated.
SelectCommand	Property	SQL statement used to select records from the data source.
TableMappings	Property	Specifies the mapping between tables in the data source and DataTables in the DataSet.
Update	Method	Transfers data from the DataSet to the data source.
UpdateCommand	Property	SQL statement used to update records in the data source.

The following code for the DataAdapter, from the frmObjects form in this chapter's sample project, makes use of several objects that you won't meet until later in the chapter. Note that filling the DataSet from the DataAdapter requires that the SelectCommand property of the DataAdapter be set, but not the other Command properties (DeleteCommand, InsertCommand, and UpdateCommand). Those properties are needed only to move information back from the DataSet to the data source.

```
Private Sub btnDataAdapter_Click(ByVal sender As System.Object, _
  ByVal e As System.EventArgs) Handles btnDataAdapter.Click
    Dim cnn As New SqlClient.SqlConnection()
    Dim cmd As New SqlClient.SqlCommand()
    Dim da As New SqlClient.SqlDataAdapter()
    Dim ds As New DataSet()
    Dim drw As DataRow

    Try
        lboResults.Items.Clear()
        cnn.ConnectionString = "Data Source=SKYROCKET;" & _
         "Initial Catalog=Northwind;Integrated Security=SSPI"
        cnn.Open()
        cmd = cnn.CreateCommand
        cmd.CommandText = "SELECT CustomerID, CompanyName FROM Customers"
        da.SelectCommand = cmd
        da.Fill(ds, "Customers")
        For Each drw In ds.Tables("Customers").Rows
```

```
                lboResults.Items.Add(drw.Item(0) & " " & drw.Item(1))
            Next
            cnn.Close()
        Catch ex As Exception
            MsgBox("Error: " & ex.Source & ": " & ex.Message, _
             MsgBoxStyle.OKOnly, "btnDataAdapter")
        End Try

    End Sub
```

Minor Data Provider Objects

There are a number of other objects supplied by the data provider namespaces that are used less often than the four I've already covered. Table 14.6 summarizes these objects.

TABLE 14.6: Other Data Provider Objects

Object	Description
CommandBuilder	Automatically generates the DeleteCommand, InsertCommand, and Update-Command properties for a DataAdapter object.
Error	Provides information on an error returned by the data source.
ErrorCollection	A collection of Error objects.
Parameter	A single Parameter to a Command object.
ParameterCollection	A collection of Parameter objects.
Transaction	A database transaction in progress.

The DataSet Objects

Unlike the ADO.NET data provider objects, there is only one set of DataSet objects, implemented in the System.Data namespace. These objects provide an abstract, disconnected way to manipulate almost any sort of data. You can use a DataSet to represent a table or set of tables from a relational data source, an XML document, or any other data that you can access via an OLE DB provider. You can also create completely synthetic DataSets and load them with data directly from your application. In this section, I'll introduce the DataSet and the major objects that it contains:

- DataSet
- DataTable
- DataRelation
- DataRow

- DataColumn
- Constraint
- DataView

DataSet

The DataSet object itself is a memory-resident representation of data. It's designed to be self-contained and easy to move around between the various components of a .NET application. Table 14.7 lists some of the important members of the DataSet object.

TABLE 14.7: DataSet Members

Name	Type	Description
AcceptChanges	Method	Commits all changes made to the DataSet since it was loaded or since the previous call to AcceptChanges.
Clear	Method	Removes all data in the DataSet.
DataSetName	Property	Name of the DataSet.
EnforceConstraints	Property	If True, constraints are enforced during updates.
GetChanges	Method	Gets a DataSet containing only the changed rows from the DataSet.
GetXml	Method	Returns an XML representation of the DataSet.
GetXmlSchema	Method	Returns an XSD schema of the DataSet.
HasChanges	Method	Returns True if the DataSet has changes that have not yet been committed.
Merge	Method	Merges two DataSets.
ReadXml	Method	Loads the DataSet from an XML file.
ReadXmlSchema	Method	Loads the DataSet schema from an XSD file.
RejectChanges	Method	Discards all changes made to the DataSet since it was loaded or since the previous call to AcceptChanges.
Relations	Property	The collection of DataRelation objects within the DataSet.
Tables	Property	The collection of DataTable objects within the DataSet.
WriteXml	Method	Writes the DataSet out as XML.
WriteXmlSchema	Method	Writes the DataSet schema out as an XML schema (XSD) file.

DataTable

As you might guess from the name, the DataTable object represents a single table within a DataSet. A DataSet can contain multiple DataTables. Table 14.8 lists some of the important members of the DataTable object.

TABLE 14.8: DataTable Members

Name	Type	Description
AcceptChanges	Method	Commits all changes to this DataTable since it was loaded or since the last call to AcceptChanges.
CaseSensitive	Property	Read-write property that returns True if string comparisons within this DataTable are case-sensitive.
ChildRelations	Property	The collection of DataRelation objects that refer to children of this DataTable.
Clear	Method	Clears all data from the DataTable.
ColumnChanged	Event	Fires when the data in any row of a specified column has been changed.
ColumnChanging	Event	Fires when the data in any row of a specified column is about to change.
Columns	Property	The collection of DataColumn objects in this DataTable.
Constraints	Property	The collection of Constraint objects for this table.
GetChanges	Method	Gets a DataTable containing only the changed rows from this DataTable.
ImportRow	Method	Imports a DataRow into this DataTable.
LoadDataRow	Method	Finds and updates a row in this DataTable.
NewRow	Method	Creates a new, blank row in the DataTable.
ParentRelations	Property	The collection of DataRelation objects that refer to parents of this DataTable.
PrimaryKey	Property	Array of columns that provide the primary key for this DataTable.
RejectChanges	Method	Discards all changes to this DataTable since it was loaded or since the last call to AcceptChanges.
RowChanged	Event	Fires when any data in a DataRow is changed.
RowChanging	Event	Fires when any data in a DataRow is about to change.
RowDeleted	Event	Fires when a row is deleted.
RowDeleting	Event	Fires when a row is about to be deleted.
Rows	Property	The collection of DataRow objects in this DataTable.
Select	Method	Selects an array of DataRow objects that meet specified criteria.
TableName	Property	The name of this DataTable.

WARNING Unlike other object models with which you may be familiar, the ADO.NET object model doesn't necessarily use the same name for a property and the object that it returns. For example, the Rows property of a DataTable returns a DataRowCollection object, which contains a collection of DataRows. In practice, this seldom causes confusion because you're less likely to operate directly on the collection objects.

DataRelation

The DataRelation object represents a relation between two DataTables. The DataSet has a Relations collection that contains all of the DataRelation objects defined within the DataSet. In addition, Each DataTable has ChildRelations and ParentRelations collections containing the DataRelation objects that refer to that DataTable. Each DataRelation is made up of DataColumn objects that specify the relationship between the DataTables involved. You can optionally use a Constraint object (discussed later in this section) to add cascading deletes or updates to a DataRelation. Table 14.9 lists some of the important members of the DataRelation object.

TABLE 14.9: DataRelation Members

Name	Type	Description
ChildColumns	Property	Collection of DataColumn objects that define the child side of the DataRelation.
ChildKeyConstraint	Property	Returns the foreign key constraint for the DataRelation.
ChildTable	Property	Returns the child DataTable for the DataRelation.
ParentColumns	Property	Collection of DataColumn objects that define the parent side of the DataRelation.
ParentKeyConstraint	Property	Returns the primary key constraint for the DataRelation.
ParentTable	Property	Returns the parent DataTable for the DataRelation.
RelationName	Property	Name of the DataRelation.

DataRow

The DataRow object provides row-by-row access to the data contained in a DataTable. When you're selecting, inserting, updating, or deleting data, you'll usually work with DataRow objects. I'll discuss data selection later in this chapter and data manipulation in the next chapter. Table 14.10 lists some of the important members of the DataRow object.

TABLE 14.10: DataRow Members

Name	Type	Description
AcceptChanges	Property	Commits changes made to this row since the last time AcceptChanges was called.
BeginEdit	Method	Starts editing the DataRow.
CancelEdit	Method	Discards an edit in progress.
Delete	Method	Deletes the DataRow from its parent DataTable.

continued on next page

TABLE 14.10 CONTINUED: DataRow Members

Name	Type	Description
EndEdit	Method	Ends an editing session on the DataRow.
GetChildRows	Method	Gets the child rows related to this DataRow.
GetParentRow	Method	Gets the parent row related to this DataRow.
Item	Property	Returns the data from a particular column of the DataRow.
ItemArray	Property	Returns the data from the entire DataRow as an array.
IsNull	Method	Returns True if a specified column is Null.
RejectChanges	Method	Discards changes made to this row since the last time AcceptChanges was called.
RowState	Property	Returns information on the current state of the DataRow (for example, whether the row has been modified).

DataColumn

The DataColumn object represents a single column in a DataTable. By manipulating the DataColumns in a DataTable, you can investigate and even change the DataTable's schema. Table 14.11 lists some of the important members of the DataColumn object.

TABLE 14.11: DataColumn Members

Name	Type	Description
AllowDbNull	Property	True if the DataColumn can contain Nulls.
AutoIncrement	Property	True if the DataColumn automatically assigns new values to new rows.
AutoIncrementSeed	Property	Starting value for an AutoIncrement DataColumn.
AutoIncrementStep	Property	Increment value for an AutoIncrement DataColumn.
Caption	Property	Caption for the DataColumn.
ColumnName	Property	Name of the DataColumn.
DataType	Property	Datatype for the DataColumn.
DefaultValue	Property	Default value for this DataColumn in new rows of the DataTable.
MaxLength	Property	Maximum length of a text DataColumn.
Ordinal	Property	Position of the DataColumn in the Columns collection of the parent DataTable.
ReadOnly	Property	True if the value in the DataColumn cannot be changed after it has been set.
Unique	Property	True if values in the DataColumn must be unique.

Constraint

The Constraint object comes in two varieties: The ForeignKeyConstraint object represents a foreign key, while the UniqueConstraint object represents a unique constraint. DataTable objects have a Constraints collection that contains both types of Constraint objects. Table 14.12 lists some of the important members of the Constraint objects.

TABLE 14.12: Constraint Members

Name	Type	Description
AcceptRejectRule	Property	Constant that specifies cascading commit behavior. Applies to ForeignKeyConstraint only.
Columns	Property	Array of DataColumns that are affected by this Constraint.
DeleteRule	Property	Constant that specifies cascading delete behavior. Applies to ForeignKeyConstraint only.
ConstraintName	Property	Name of the Constraint.
RelatedColumns	Property	Collection of DataColumns that are the parent of this Constraint. Applies to ForeignKeyConstraint only.
RelatedTable	Property	DataTable that is the parent table of this Constraint. Applies to ForeignKeyConstraint only.
IsPrimaryKey	Property	True if this Constraint represents a primary key. Applies to UniqueConstraint only.
UpdateRule	Property	Constant that specifies cascading update behavior. Applies to ForeignKeyConstraint only.

DataView

The DataView object represents a view of the data contained in a DataTable. This view can contain all of the data from the DataTable, or it can be filtered to return only specific rows. You can filter either with SQL expressions or by looking for rows in a particular state. For example, a DataView could show only selected columns from a DataTable, or it could show only rows that have been modified since the last call to the AcceptChanges method. Table 14.13 lists some of the important members of the DataView object.

TABLE 14.13: DataView Members

Name	Type	Description
AddNew	Method	Adds a new row to the DataView.
AllowDelete	Property	True if deletions can be performed via this DataView.

continued on next page

TABLE 14.13 CONTINUED: DataView Members

Name	Type	Description
AllowEdit	Property	True if updates can be performed via this DataView.
AllowNew	Property	True if new rows can be added via this DataView.
Count	Property	Number of records contained in this DataView.
Delete	Method	Deletes a row from the DataView.
Find	Method	Searches for a specified row in the DataView.
FindRows	Method	Returns an array of rows matching a filter expression.
Item	Property	Returns the data from a particular row of the DataView in a DataRowView object.
ListChanged	Event	Fired when the data in this DataView changes.
RowFilter	Property	Filter expression to limit the data returned in the DataView.
RowStateFilter	Property	Filter to limit the data returned in the DataView by the state of the rows.
Sort	Property	Sorts columns and order for the DataView.

.NET Data Providers

Just as ODBC data access uses ODBC drivers, and ADO data access uses OLE DB providers, ADO.NET data access uses .NET data providers. In all three cases, the purpose is the same: to provide a layer of software that can hide the differences between various data sources by presenting a uniform interface to the more abstract objects (in ADO.NET, these more abstract objects are the DataSet and its child objects).

As of this writing, the .NET Framework includes two data providers: the SQL Server .NET Data Provider and the OLE DB .NET Data Provider. In addition, there is an ODBC .NET Data Provider available as a separate download; it's not clear whether this provider will remain as a download or will ship as part of the final product.

NOTE   During the beta period, the ODBC .NET Data Provider was available from msdn .microsoft.com/downloads/sample.asp?url=/MSDN-FILES/027/001/668/ msdncompositedoc.xml&frame=true. This may change in the final release.

The SQL Server .NET Data Provider

The SQL Server .NET Data Provider can be used with SQL Server data sources that use SQL Server 7 or later. This data provider uses the native SQL Server protocols to talk directly to the database server, without any intervening OLE DB or ODBC layers. This allows it to deliver the fastest possible performance with SQL Server data, at the expense of not working with any other data source.

The SQL Server .NET Data Provider is implemented in the System.Data.SqlClient namespace. As with ADO, you control the data that will be returned by setting the ConnectionString property of the SqlConnection object. The ConnectionString property syntax is similar (but not identical) to that of the SQLOLEDB provider used by traditional ADO. The ConnectionString property must contain a semicolon-delimited set of property-value pairs:

```
Property1=Value1;Property2=Value2...
```

Table 14.14 lists the properties that are recognized in the SqlConnection.ConnectionString property. Note that some of these properties have alternative names, separated by *or* in the table.

TABLE 14.14: Arguments for the SqlConnection.ConnectionString Property

Property	Description
Application Name	Name of the connecting application. Defaults to ".NET Sql-Client Data Provider."
AttachDbFilename or Initial File Name	Name of a database file to attach.
Connect Timeout or Connection Timeout	Number of seconds to wait for the Connection to contact the server. Defaults to 15 seconds.
Connection Lifetime	Maximum age (in seconds) for a Connection returned to the connection pool before it is automatically destroyed.
Connection Reset	True if Connections are reset when they are returned to the connection pool.
Current Language	The SQL Server language used by this Connection.
Data Source or Server or Address or Addr or Network Address	The server to connect to. This can be a machine name, the special name (local), or a network address.
Enlist	Specifies whether to enlist the Connection in the calling thread's transaction context. Defaults to True.
Initial Catalog or Database	Database to connect to.
Integrated Security or Trusted_Connection	Set to True or SSPI to use Windows integrated security. Otherwise, uses SQL Server security, which is the default.
Max Pool Size	Maximum number of Connections to pool. Defaults to 100.
Min Pool Size	Minimum number of Connections to pool. Defaults to 0.
Network Library or Net	Name of the SQL Server network DLL used by this Connection.
Packet Size	Packet Size to use when communicating with the server. Defaults to 8,192.
Password or Pwd	SQL Server password.

continued on next page

TABLE 14.14: Arguments for the SqlConnection.ConnectionString Property

Property	Description
Persist Security Info	Set to True to save passwords in the connection string. Defaults to False.
Pooling	Set to True (the default) to enable Connection pooling.
User ID	SQL Server username.
Workstation ID	Name of the computer that's connecting to SQL Server. Defaults to the local computer name.

The OLE DB .NET Data Provider

The OLE DB .NET Data Provider is used for connecting to data sources from .NET via existing OLE DB providers. Microsoft has implemented a special OLE DB service component to handle connection pooling and transactions on such providers. This sounds like it should be a universal solution, but, unfortunately, the only supported OLE DB data providers are these:

- Microsoft OLE DB Provider for SQL Server
- Microsoft OLE DB Provider for Oracle
- OLE DB Provider for Microsoft Jet (4.0 version only)

Some OLE DB providers are known definitely not to work with this .NET data provider. These include the OLE DB Provider for ODBC, the Microsoft OLE DB Provider for Exchange, and the Microsoft OLE DB Provider for Internet Publishing. You may have success with other OLE DB providers, but you should thoroughly test your solution before depending on an unsupported provider.

Although the OLE DB .NET Data Provider works with the Microsoft OLE DB Provider for SQL Server, you should reserve this solution for SQL Server 6.5 and earlier versions. For SQL Server 7 or later, you'll get better performance by using the SQL Server .NET Data Provider instead.

The OLE DB .NET Data Provider is implemented in the System.Data.OleDb namespace. The ConnectionString syntax for this provider is the same as for the underlying OLE DB providers.

> **TIP** Connection strings for the SQL Server, Oracle, and Jet OLE DB providers are discussed in Chapter 3, "Using the ADO Objects to Retrieve Data."

The ODBC .NET Data Provider

The ODBC .NET Data Provider supplies data access through ODBC drivers, similar to the way in which the OLE DB .NET Data Provider supplies data access through OLE DB providers. There is a short list of ODBC drivers that are supported with this data provider:

- Microsoft SQL ODBC Driver
- Microsoft ODBC Driver for Oracle
- Microsoft Jet ODBC Driver

Other ODBC drivers may work with this data provider, but once again, you'll need to thoroughly test such solutions before depending on them in a production setting.

The OdbcConnection.ConnectionString property is passed through unchanged to the ODBC Manager and ODBC driver that are being used. Thus, the syntax for the connection string precisely matches that of the underlying drivers.

Using DataSets

In this section, you'll learn the basic syntax for working with DataSets. This chapter concentrates on populating a DataSet and retrieving the data that it contains. Chapter 15, "Editing Data with ADO.NET," discusses the use of the DataSet to change data and to persist the changes back to the original data source.

Populating a DataSet from a Database

If you want to display data from a database without writing changes back to the database, you can do so by using the data provider objects to move data from the database to a DataSet, and then using the DataGrid control on a Windows Form to display the data. To do so, follow these steps:

1. Open a Connection to the database containing the data.
2. Create a Command that retrieves the data that you wish to display.
3. Create a DataAdapter and set its SelectCommand property to point to the Command object.
4. Create a DataSet by calling the Fill method of the DataAdapter.
5. Set the DataSource property of a DataGrid control to refer to the DataSet.
6. Set the DataMember property of a DataGrid control to refer to the table that you wish to display.

Here's some code from frmDataSet in this chapter's sample project that carries out these steps:

```
Private Sub btnPopulateDatabase_Click(ByVal sender As System.Object, _
  ByVal e As System.EventArgs) Handles btnPopulateDatabase.Click
    Dim cnn As New SqlClient.SqlConnection()
    Dim cmd As New SqlClient.SqlCommand()
    Dim da As New SqlClient.SqlDataAdapter()
    Dim ds As New DataSet()

    Try
        cnn.ConnectionString = "Data Source=SKYROCKET;" & _
         "Initial Catalog=Northwind;Integrated Security=SSPI"
        cnn.Open()
        cmd = cnn.CreateCommand
        cmd.CommandText = "SELECT * FROM Customers"
        da.SelectCommand = cmd
        da.Fill(ds, "Customers")
        cnn.Close()

        dgMain.DataSource = ds
        dgMain.DataMember = "Customers"

    Catch ex As Exception
        MsgBox("Error: " & ex.Source & ": " & ex.Message, _
          MsgBoxStyle.OKOnly, "btnPopulateDatabase")
    End Try

End Sub
```

Figure 14.3 shows the result of running this code.

Note that this code actually closes the connection to the database before displaying the data. Once the DataSet has been filled, it doesn't need the connection to the data source any longer; the data is entirely contained in memory. Of course, you need to reconnect to the data source to save any changes in the data. You'll see that technique in the next chapter.

The name supplied to the Fill method of the DataAdapter object is not the name of the table in the original data source, but rather the name of the DataTable to be created within the DataSet. The Fill method creates this DataTable and then fills it with whatever data is returned by the SelectCommand. The DataMember property of the DataGrid also holds a DataTable name, not an original table name. Thus, you could replace the fill and display portions of the preceding code snippet with this code, and it would work as well:

```
da.Fill(ds, "Peanuts")
cnn.Close()

dgMain.DataSource = ds
dgMain.DataMember = "Peanuts"
```

FIGURE 14.3:

Data on a DataGrid control

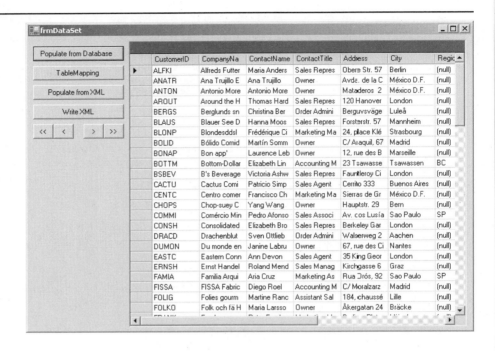

TIP   Of course, for code readability and maintainability, you'll probably want to use the same names for DataTable objects as for the tables that they are filled from!

Although the preceding code does produce the desired result, it's not the best way to solve the problem in a distributed environment such as .NET. In practice, you should strive to minimize the amount of time that you hold an open Connection. You can do this by letting the DataAdapter implicitly open the Connection when it needs it. Here's the actual code that's used in the sample project:

```
Private Sub btnPopulateDatabase_Click(ByVal sender As System.Object, _
  ByVal e As System.EventArgs) Handles btnPopulateDatabase.Click
    Dim cnn As SqlClient.SqlConnection = _
    New SqlClient.SqlConnection("Data Source=SKYROCKET;" & _
    "Initial Catalog=Northwind;Integrated Security=SSPI")
    Dim cmd As New SqlClient.SqlCommand()
    Dim da As New SqlClient.SqlDataAdapter()
    Dim ds As New DataSet()

    Try
        cmd = cnn.CreateCommand
        cmd.CommandText = "SELECT * FROM Customers"
```

```
        da.SelectCommand = cmd
        da.Fill(ds, "Customers")

        dgMain.DataSource = ds
        dgMain.DataMember = "Customers"

    Catch ex As Exception
        MsgBox("Error: " & ex.Source & ": " & ex.Message, _
        MsgBoxStyle.OKOnly, "btnPopulateDatabase")
    End Try

End Sub
```

This version of the code places the connection string directly into the constructor for the Connection object. In this case, the DataAdapter will open the Connection when its own Fill method is invoked, and close it immediately after it has retrieved the necessary data.

NOTE   If you perform multiple operations requiring an open Connection in a single procedure, it will be more efficient to call the Open and Close methods of the Connection object explicitly than to allow other objects to manage the Connection implicitly.

You've already seen that you can specify the name of the DataTable object in the call to the DataAdapter's Fill method. More generally, you can specify both the DataTable name and the names of the DataColumn objects within the DataTable by using the System.Data .Common.DataTableMapping object. This object lets you set up a series of associations between source table and column names and the destination DataTable and DataColumn names. Here's an example:

```
Private Sub btnTableMapping_Click(ByVal sender As System.Object, _
  ByVal e As System.EventArgs) Handles btnTableMapping.Click
    Dim cnn As SqlClient.SqlConnection = _
     New SqlClient.SqlConnection("Data Source=SKYROCKET;" & _
     "Initial Catalog=Northwind;Integrated Security=SSPI")
    Dim cmd As New SqlClient.SqlCommand()
    Dim da As New SqlClient.SqlDataAdapter()
    Dim ds As New DataSet()

    Try
        cmd = cnn.CreateCommand
        cmd.CommandText = "SELECT * FROM Customers"
        da.SelectCommand = cmd

        Dim dtm As System.Data.Common.DataTableMapping = _
         da.TableMappings.Add("Table", "CurrentCustomers")
        With dtm.ColumnMappings
            .Add("CustomerID", "Identifier")
```

```
            .Add("CompanyName", "Company")
            .Add("ContactName", "Contact")
        End With

        da.Fill(ds)

        dgMain.DataSource = ds
        dgMain.DataMember = "CurrentCustomers"

    Catch ex As Exception
        MsgBox("Error: " & ex.Source & ": " & ex.Message, _
          MsgBoxStyle.OKOnly, "btnPopulateDatabase")
    End Try

    End Sub
```

The new DataTableMapping object is created by calling the Add method of the DataAdapter's TableMappings collection. This method takes the name of the table as seen by the DataAdapter (which defaults to "Table" in the case of a result set that returns a single table) and the name of the DataTable to deliver. In turn, the DataTableMapping object has a collection of DataColumnMapping objects that associate source columns with destination DataColumns. Figure 14.4 shows the result of running this code.

FIGURE 14.4:

Table displayed with column names specified by mapping

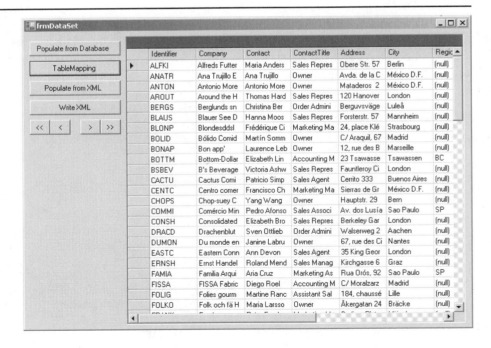

As you can see in Figure 14.4, the DataAdapter object uses the source column name as the destination DataColumn name for any column that doesn't appear in the ColumnMappings collection.

Using XML with the DataSet Object

The .NET Framework supplies close connections between the DataSet object and XML. DataSets can be loaded from XML or persisted to XML files. One way to think about the connection is that XML can be used to provide a transmission format for the DataSet. By converting a DataSet to XML, you end up with a representation of the DataSet in a format that can be easily moved around without your worrying about the problems of transmitting binary data past firewalls.

Populating a DataSet from an XML file is simple. For example, this code from the frm-DataSet form in this chapter's sample project will do just that:

```
Private Sub btnPopulateXML_Click(ByVal sender As System.Object, _
  ByVal e As System.EventArgs) Handles btnPopulateXML.Click

    Try
        Dim ds As DataSet = New DataSet()
        Dim sr As StreamReader = New StreamReader("Customers.xml")
        ds.ReadXml(sr)

        dgMain.DataSource = ds
        dgMain.DataMember = "Customers"

    Catch ex As Exception
        MsgBox("Error: " & ex.Source & ": " & ex.Message, _
          MsgBoxStyle.OKOnly, "btnPopulateXML")
    End Try

End Sub
```

As you can see, the DataSet object's ReadXml method can be used to directly read an XML file into the DataSet. The StreamReader object (part of the System.IO namespace) simply provides a way to read a disk file. In this particular case, the XML file was created by exporting the Customers table from the Access 2002 version of the Northwind sample database. Here's a portion of that file:

```
<?xml version="1.0" encoding="UTF-8"?>
<dataroot xmlns:od="urn:schemas-microsoft-com:officedata">
<Customers>
<CustomerID>ALFKI</CustomerID>
<CompanyName>Alfreds Futterkiste</CompanyName>
<ContactName>Maria Anders</ContactName>
<ContactTitle>Sales Representative</ContactTitle>
```

```
<Address>Obere Str. 57</Address>
<City>Berlin</City>
<PostalCode>12209</PostalCode>
<Country>Germany</Country>
<Phone>030-0074321</Phone>
<Fax>030-0076545</Fax>
</Customers>
<Customers>
<CustomerID>ANATR</CustomerID>
<CompanyName>Ana Trujillo Emparedados y helados</CompanyName>
<ContactName>Ana Trujillo</ContactName>
<ContactTitle>Owner</ContactTitle>
...
```

This file contains all the data from the original Customers table, but none of the schema information. So, how does .NET know what to do with it? It infers a schema by looking at the data and making the best choices that it can about data types. The ReadXml method actually takes two parameters:

```
DataSet.ReadXml(Stream, XmlReadMode)
```

The XmlReadMode parameter can be any one of the constants listed in Table 14.15.

TABLE 14.15: XmlReadMode Constants

Constant	Meaning
Auto	If the XML file is recognized as a DiffGram, read it as a DiffGram. If it's not a Diff-gram but there is schema information in the XML file or in an associated XSD file, use that schema to build the DataSet. Otherwise, infer the schema from the data. This is the default.
DiffGram	Treats the XML file as a DiffGram. A DiffGram is a special format that specifies changes to a DataSet by supplying original rows and change information.
Fragment	Reads XML files containing inline XDR schema information.
IgnoreSchema	Ignores any schema information contained in the XML file and attempts to fit the data into the current schema of the DataSet.
InferSchema	Infers the schema of the XML file by examining the data.
ReadSchema	Uses XSD information to define the schema of the DataSet.

WARNING   Although Access 2002 can save XSD information when exporting an XML file, the XSD file from Access uses an XML namespace that .NET doesn't recognize.

The DataSet object also provides several ways to convert its contents to XML. First, there's the GetXml method, which returns an XML representation of the DataSet as a string:

```
Dim strXML As String = ds.GetXml()
```

The GetXml method is useful when you want to make a DataSet available as XML through an object property or when you want to display the XML on the user interface.

There's also the WriteXml method, which can persist the XML representation of the DataSet directly to a file:

```
ds.WriteXml("SavedCustomers.xml")
```

The WriteXml method takes an optional second parameter to specify schema behavior. This parameter can be one of three constants from the XmlWriteMode enumeration, as shown in Table 14.16.

TABLE 14.16: XmlWriteMode Constants

Constant	Meaning
IgnoreSchema	Writes the XML file without any schema information. This is the default.
WriteSchema	Writes XSD information directly to the XML file.
Diffgram	Writes the DataSet out in DiffGram format.

The Write XML button on frmDataSet in the sample application calls code to write a DataSet out as XML:

```
Private Sub btnWriteXml_Click(ByVal sender As System.Object, _
  ByVal e As System.EventArgs) Handles btnWriteXml.Click
    Dim cnn As SqlClient.SqlConnection = _
     New SqlClient.SqlConnection("Data Source=SKYROCKET;" & _
     "Initial Catalog=Northwind;Integrated Security=SSPI")
    Dim cmd As New SqlClient.SqlCommand()
    Dim da As New SqlClient.SqlDataAdapter()
    Dim ds As New DataSet()

    Try
        cmd = cnn.CreateCommand
        cmd.CommandText = "SELECT * FROM Customers"
        da.SelectCommand = cmd
        da.Fill(ds, "Customers")
        ds.WriteXml("SQLCustomers.xml", XmlWriteMode.WriteSchema)

    Catch ex As Exception
        MsgBox("Error: " & ex.Source & ": " & ex.Message, _
         MsgBoxStyle.OKOnly, "btnWriteXml")
    End Try

End Sub
```

Listing 14.1 shows the beginning of the resulting file.

Listing 14.1: **A DataSet Saved as XML with Schema Information**

```xml
<?xml version="1.0" standalone="yes"?>
<NewDataSet>
  <xs:schema id="NewDataSet" xmlns=""
➥ xmlns:xs="http://www.w3.org/2001/XMLSchema"
➥ xmlns:msdata="urn:schemas-microsoft-com:xml-msdata">
    <xs:element name="NewDataSet" msdata:IsDataSet="true">
      <xs:complexType>
        <xs:choice maxOccurs="unbounded">
          <xs:element name="Customers">
            <xs:complexType>
              <xs:sequence>
                <xs:element name="CustomerID"
➥ type="xs:string" minOccurs="0" />
                <xs:element name="CompanyName"
➥ type="xs:string" minOccurs="0" />
                <xs:element name="ContactName"
➥ type="xs:string" minOccurs="0" />
                <xs:element name="ContactTitle"
➥ type="xs:string" minOccurs="0" />
                <xs:element name="Address" type="xs:string" minOccurs="0" />
                <xs:element name="City" type="xs:string" minOccurs="0" />
                <xs:element name="Region" type="xs:string" minOccurs="0" />
                <xs:element name="PostalCode"
➥ type="xs:string" minOccurs="0" />
                <xs:element name="Country" type="xs:string" minOccurs="0" />
                <xs:element name="Phone" type="xs:string" minOccurs="0" />
                <xs:element name="Fax" type="xs:string" minOccurs="0" />
              </xs:sequence>
            </xs:complexType>
          </xs:element>
        </xs:choice>
      </xs:complexType>
    </xs:element>
  </xs:schema>
  <Customers>
    <CustomerID>ALFKI</CustomerID>
    <CompanyName>Alfreds Futterkiste</CompanyName>
    <ContactName>Maria Anders</ContactName>
    <ContactTitle>Sales Representative</ContactTitle>
    <Address>Obere Str. 57</Address>
    <City>Berlin</City>
    <PostalCode>12209</PostalCode>
    <Country>Germany</Country>
    <Phone>030-0074321</Phone>
    <Fax>030-0076545</Fax>
  </Customers>
  <Customers>
    <CustomerID>ANATR</CustomerID>
    <CompanyName>Ana Trujillo Emparedados y helados</CompanyName>
```

```
        <ContactName>Ana Trujillo</ContactName>
        <ContactTitle>Owner</ContactTitle>
        <Address>Avda. de la Constitución 2222</Address>
        <City>México D.F.</City>
        <PostalCode>05021</PostalCode>
        <Country>Mexico</Country>
        <Phone>(5) 555-4729</Phone>
        <Fax>(5) 555-3745</Fax>
    </Customers>
```

The information at the top of the file, in the xs: namespace, is the XSD schema information created by the WriteXml method. This information includes the field names and datatypes for the columns within the DataSet.

TIP   For more information on XSD and other XML topics, refer to *XML Schemas* by Chelsea Valentine, Lucinda Dykes, and Ed Tittel (Sybex, 2002).

Moving Around in DataSets and Retrieving Data

In some ways, the DataSet requires completely different thinking than the ADO Recordset. Moving around in the data is a case in point. A Recordset, of course, consists of a set of rows plus a current-row pointer (a cursor). A DataSet doesn't have a concept of a current row. In this respect, it's much closer to a traditional SQL View, which is a set of records of no particular order that is processed as a group.

So forget about the EOF and BOF properties and the various Move methods when you migrate from Recordsets to DataSets. You can still move around in the data, but the code is a bit different. At first, you might feel a bit lost without your trusty MoveNext method, but after a while, it will seem simple. Instead of having their own particular methods, DataSets work like any other collection.

In particular, the DataSet contains a Tables collection made of DataTable objects. The DataTable, in turn, contains a Rows collection of DataRow objects, and a Columns collection of DataColumn objects. A DataRow has an Item collection (its default) that is indexed by column number and returns data. You can move through all these collections with a zero-based index or by name, or by using a For Each loop. So, to dump all the data in a DataSet, you could use code like this:

```
Dim dt As DataTable
Dim dr As DataRow
Dim dc As DataColumn
For Each dt In ds.Tables
    For Each dr In dt.Rows
        For each dc In dt.Columns
```

```
            Console.WriteLine(dr(dc))
        Next dc
    Next dr
Next dt
```

If you want to do some sort of row-based navigation, you'll need to maintain your own current-record pointer. The navigation buttons on the DataSet form in this chapter's sample application take this approach. The form's New event is used to instantiate a DataSet:

```
Dim mds As DataSet = New DataSet()
Dim mlngCurRow As Long

Public Sub New()

    MyBase.New()

    'This call is required by the Windows Form Designer.
    InitializeComponent()

    'Add any initialization after the InitializeComponent() call
    Dim cnn As SqlClient.SqlConnection = _
     New SqlClient.SqlConnection("Data Source=SKYROCKET;" & _
     "Initial Catalog=Northwind;Integrated Security=SSPI")
    Dim cmd As New SqlClient.SqlCommand()
    Dim da As New SqlClient.SqlDataAdapter()

    Try
        cmd = cnn.CreateCommand
        cmd.CommandText = "SELECT * FROM Customers"
        da.SelectCommand = cmd
        da.Fill(mds, "Customers")
        mlngCurRow = 0

    Catch ex As Exception
        MsgBox("Error: " & ex.Source & ": " & ex.Message, _
          MsgBoxStyle.OKOnly, "New")
    End Try

End Sub
```

The individual navigation buttons then manipulate the current row number and call a common subroutine to display the first couple of columns from that row:

```
Private Sub DisplayCurrentRow()
    MsgBox(mds.Tables("Customers").Rows(mlngCurRow).Item(0) & ": " & _
      mds.Tables("Customers").Rows(mlngCurRow).Item(1))
End Sub
```

```
Private Sub btnFirst_Click(ByVal sender As System.Object, _
 ByVal e As System.EventArgs) Handles btnFirst.Click
    mlngCurRow = 0
    DisplayCurrentRow()
End Sub

Private Sub btnPrevious_Click(ByVal sender As System.Object, _
 ByVal e As System.EventArgs) Handles btnPrevious.Click
    mlngCurRow = Math.Max(mlngCurRow - 1, 0)
    DisplayCurrentRow()
End Sub

Private Sub btnNext_Click(ByVal sender As System.Object, _
 ByVal e As System.EventArgs) Handles btnNext.Click
    mlngCurRow = Math.Min(mlngCurRow + 1, _
     mds.Tables("Customers").Rows.Count - 1)
    DisplayCurrentRow()
End Sub

Private Sub btnLast_Click(ByVal sender As System.Object, _
 ByVal e As System.EventArgs) Handles btnLast.Click
    mlngCurRow = mds.Tables("Customers").Rows.Count - 1
    DisplayCurrentRow()
End Sub
```

Note the use of the Math.Min and Math.Max methods to make sure that the current-row pointer always stays between zero and one less than the number of rows in the DataTable. This is necessary because DataTables have no EOF or BOF property to trap.

Using Strongly Typed Datasets

The DisplayCurrentRow method in the preceding code uses the Item method of the Rows collection to return data. There are several equivalent ways to return information with this method. Assuming dt is a DataTable variable, all of these statements are equivalent:

```
dt.Rows(0).Item(0)
dt.Rows(0)(0)
dt.Rows(0).Item("CustomerID")
dt.Rows(0)("CustomerID")
dt.Rows(0)!CustomerID
```

All of these syntaxes have one thing in common: They're all late-bound. That is, .NET doesn't know until runtime that "CustomerID" is a valid column name in the DataTable. One of the innovations of the .NET Framework is the concept of a strongly typed DataSet, in which the columns actually become properties of the row. With such a DataSet, an early-bound version of the data-retrieval code becomes available:

```
dt.Rows(0).CustomerID
```

In addition to being faster than the late-bound syntax, this syntax also has the benefit that the column names show up in the IntelliSense list that Visual Studio .NET displays when you type the dot after Rows(0).

There are several ways to create a strongly typed DataSet. One is to craft an XSD schema file representing the DataSet and then use the command-line xsd.exe tool to generate source code that you can then compile into your application. In practice, though, you're more likely to use the visual tools built into Visual Studio .NET to hide the command-line tool. Here's how to add a strongly typed DataSet to an existing project through the Visual Basic .NET interface:

1. Select Project ➤ Add New Item from the Visual Basic .NET menu. Select the DataSet object, give it a name (I'll use Customers.xsd for this example), and click Open. Visual Basic .NET will add the new schema file to the Solution Explorer and open the blank object in the designer. At the bottom of the designer, you'll see tabs for DataSet and XML; these let you toggle between a data-oriented view of the schema and the XML view.

2. In the Server Explorer window, right-click the Data Connections node and select Add Connection. The Data Link Properties dialog box will open. Fill in appropriate connection information and then click OK.

3. Expand the Data Connections tree to find the table, stored procedure, or view that you'd like to use in the DataSet. Drag the object (the Customers table in my example) from the Server Explorer to the design surface. You can drag selected columns if you don't need all the columns in a source table. You can also drag multiple source objects to create a DataSet that contains multiple DataTables.

4. Save the XSD file or the entire project. This step is important, because Visual Basic .NET doesn't generate the class file corresponding to the XSD file until the XSD file is saved.

Figure 14.5 shows the visual representation of the Customers table as an XSD file on the DataSet tab of the XSD designer. The "E" icons indicate that each row of the table has been rendered as an XML element.

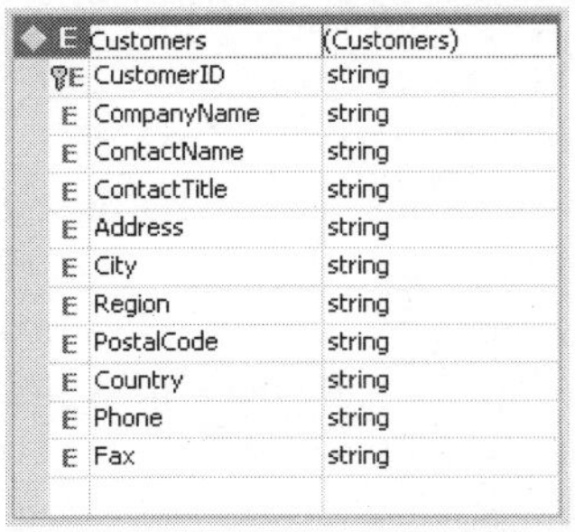

FIGURE 14.5:

XSD schema in the designer

E Customers	(Customers)
E CustomerID	string
E CompanyName	string
E ContactName	string
E ContactTitle	string
E Address	string
E City	string
E Region	string
E PostalCode	string
E Country	string
E Phone	string
E Fax	string

At this point, your project contains a new class named Customers. This class consists of a DataSet that implements strong typing based on the Customers table. With this class, you can write code such as this:

```
Private Sub btnOpen_Click(ByVal sender As System.Object, _
 ByVal e As System.EventArgs) Handles btnOpen.Click

    Dim cnn As SqlClient.SqlConnection = _
     New SqlClient.SqlConnection("Data Source=SKYROCKET;" & _
     "Initial Catalog=Northwind;Integrated Security=SSPI")
    Dim cmd As New SqlClient.SqlCommand()
    Dim da As New SqlClient.SqlDataAdapter()
    Dim cust As New Customers()
    Dim custRow As Customers.CustomersRow

    Try
        cmd = cnn.CreateCommand
        cmd.CommandText = "SELECT * FROM Customers"
        da.SelectCommand = cmd
        da.Fill(cust, "Customers")

        For Each custRow In cust.Customers
            lboData.Items.Add(custRow.CustomerID & _
             " " & custRow.CompanyName)
        Next custRow

    Catch ex As Exception
        MsgBox("Error: " & ex.Source & ": " & ex.Message, _
         MsgBoxStyle.OKOnly, "btnOpen")
    End Try

End Sub
```

As you can see, using the Customers class to define a DataSet lets you treat the Customers DataTable as a property of the DataSet. The class also defines a Customers.CustomersRow class to represent a single DataRow in the DataTable, and it creates properties of this class to represent each column in the DataRow.

To see the code that Visual Basic .NET generated for the class, select the project in Solution Explorer and click the Show All Files button. This will let you expand the Customers.xsd file in the tree and display the Customers.vb file beneath it. You may also see a Customers.xsx file that holds layout information for the XSD design surface. You can load the Customers.vb file into the design window to view the auto-generated code that makes the strong typing possible.

WARNING Any changes that you make to the auto-generated code will be lost the next time that you save the XSD file that was used to create it.

DataSets with Multiple Tables

So far, each of the DataSets that you've seen in this chapter contains only one DataTable. But DataSets are much more flexible than that; they may contain as many DataTables as you need to represent your data. In this section, I'll show you four different ways to load multiple tables from a data source into a DataSet:

- Using a join
- Using the Shape provider
- Using multiple result sets
- Using multiple DataAdapters

Using a Join

The easiest way to bring data from multiple tables together into a single DataSet is to join the tables in the Command that initializes the DataAdapter:

```
Private Sub btnJoin_Click(ByVal sender As System.Object, _
ByVal e As System.EventArgs) Handles btnJoin.Click
    Dim cnn As SqlClient.SqlConnection = _
    New SqlClient.SqlConnection("Data Source=SKYROCKET;" & _
    "Initial Catalog=Northwind;Integrated Security=SSPI")
    Dim cmd As New SqlClient.SqlCommand()
    Dim da As New SqlClient.SqlDataAdapter()
    Dim ds As New DataSet()

    Try
        cmd = cnn.CreateCommand
        cmd.CommandText = "SELECT * FROM Customers " & _
         "INNER JOIN Orders " & _
         "ON Customers.CustomerID = Orders.CustomerID"
        da.SelectCommand = cmd
        da.Fill(ds, "Customers")

        dgMain.DataSource = ds
        dgMain.DataMember = "Customers"

    Catch ex As Exception
        MsgBox("Error: " & ex.Source & ": " & ex.Message, _
         MsgBoxStyle.OKOnly, "btnJoin")
    End Try

End Sub
```

As I mentioned, even though the DataTable in the DataSet is assigned the name *Customers*, the content of this table is determined by the SQL statement that's used to fill it. Figure 14.6 shows the result of running this code: a single virtual table that includes columns from both Customers and Orders, with the customer information repeated multiple times.

FIGURE 14.6:

DataTable based on a join

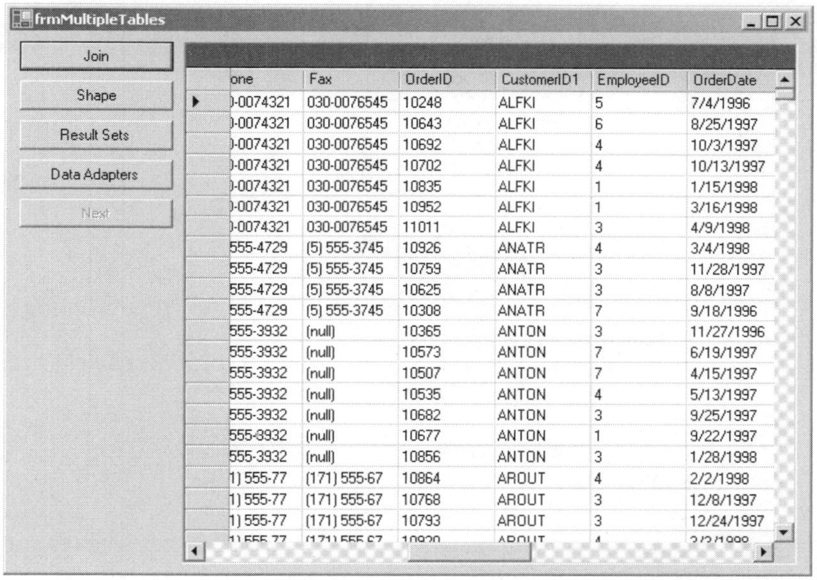

one	Fax	OrderID	CustomerID1	EmployeeID	OrderDate
)-0074321	030-0076545	10248	ALFKI	5	7/4/1996
)-0074321	030-0076545	10643	ALFKI	6	8/25/1997
)-0074321	030-0076545	10692	ALFKI	4	10/3/1997
)-0074321	030-0076545	10702	ALFKI	4	10/13/1997
)-0074321	030-0076545	10835	ALFKI	1	1/15/1998
)-0074321	030-0076545	10952	ALFKI	1	3/16/1998
)-0074321	030-0076545	11011	ALFKI	3	4/9/1998
555-4729	(5) 555-3745	10926	ANATR	4	3/4/1998
555-4729	(5) 555-3745	10759	ANATR	3	11/28/1997
555-4729	(5) 555-3745	10625	ANATR	3	8/8/1997
555-4729	(5) 555-3745	10308	ANATR	7	9/18/1996
555-3932	(null)	10365	ANTON	3	11/27/1996
555-3932	(null)	10573	ANTON	7	6/19/1997
555-3932	(null)	10507	ANTON	7	4/15/1997
555-3932	(null)	10535	ANTON	4	5/13/1997
555-3932	(null)	10682	ANTON	3	9/25/1997
555-3932	(null)	10677	ANTON	1	9/22/1997
555-3932	(null)	10856	ANTON	3	1/28/1998
1) 555-77	(171) 555-67	10864	AROUT	4	2/2/1998
1) 555-77	(171) 555-67	10768	AROUT	3	12/8/1997
1) 555-77	(171) 555-67	10793	AROUT	3	12/24/1997

Using the Shape Provider

Another way to bring multiple tables into a DataSet is to use the Shape provider along with a SQL statement that creates a hierarchical view of a data source. This method actually produces multiple DataTables within the DataSet (one for each result set within the hierarchy).

TIP

For more information on the Shape provider and hierarchical result sets, see Chapter 7, "Data Shaping."

Here's an example of this technique from the sample project for this chapter:

```
Private Sub btnShape_Click(ByVal sender As System.Object, _
 ByVal e As System.EventArgs) Handles btnShape.Click
    Dim cnn As OleDbConnection = _
     New OleDbConnection("Provider=MSDataShape;" & _
     "Data Provider=SQLOLEDB;Data Source=SKYROCKET;" & _
```

```
                "Initial Catalog=Northwind;Integrated Security=SSPI")
            Dim cmd As New OleDbCommand()
            Dim da As New OleDbDataAdapter()
            Dim ds As New DataSet()

            Try
                cmd = cnn.CreateCommand
                cmd.CommandText = "SHAPE {SELECT CustomerID, " & _
                  "CompanyName FROM Customers} " & _
                  "APPEND ({SELECT * FROM Orders} " & _
                  "RELATE CustomerID to CustomerID)"

                da.SelectCommand = cmd
                da.Fill(ds, "Customers")

                dgMain.DataSource = ds
                dgMain.DataMember = "Customers"

            Catch ex As Exception
                MsgBox("Error: " & ex.Source & ": " & ex.Message, _
                  MsgBoxStyle.OKOnly, "btnShape")
            End Try

        End Sub
```

NOTE   This example uses the OLE DB data provider classes instead of the SQL Server data provider classes. That's because the SQL Server data provider classes don't allow you to use any OLE DB provider other than the SQL Server provider, and the SHAPE syntax requires the use of the MSDataShape provider.

Figure 14.7 shows two views of the resulting DataSet on a DataGrid control. The initial view, shown in the background on the figure, displays the parent result set. You can click the plus sign next to the parent to see the name of the child result set, and click the hyperlinked name to view the child result set, as shown in the foreground.

Although the DataGrid uses this rather complex user interface to show the entire contents of the DataSet, there are two distinct DataTables within the DataSet: Customers and CustomersChapter1. When the DataAdapter's Fill method hits a chapter column, it automatically creates a new DataTable to hold the child rows. All child rows from the same position in the result set hierarchy are stored in a single DataTable. The Fill method adds a column to the parent and child result sets that serves to link the parent and child DataTables together.

FIGURE 14.7:

Hierarchical result sets on a DataGrid

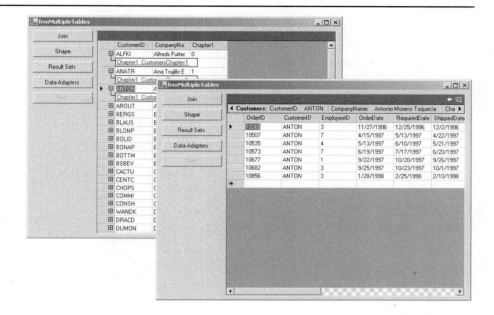

Using Multiple Result Sets

A third option for populating a DataSet with multiple DataTables is to use a stored procedure or SQL statement that returns multiple result sets as the Command for the DataAdapter. Listing 14.2 shows an example.

Listing 14.2:   Using a SQL Statement to Display Data from Multiple Tables

```
Private Sub btnResultSets_Click(ByVal sender As System.Object, _
ByVal e As System.EventArgs) Handles btnResultSets.Click
    Dim cnn As SqlClient.SqlConnection = _
     New SqlClient.SqlConnection("Data Source=SKYROCKET;" & _
     "Initial Catalog=Northwind;Integrated Security=SSPI")
    Dim cmd As New SqlClient.SqlCommand()
    Dim da As New SqlClient.SqlDataAdapter()
    Dim ds As New DataSet()

    Try
        cmd = cnn.CreateCommand
        cmd.CommandText = "SELECT * FROM Customers " & _
         "WHERE Country = 'Germany' " & _
         "SELECT * FROM Customers " & _
         "WHERE Country = 'Venezuela'"
        da.SelectCommand = cmd
        da.Fill(ds, "Customers")
```

```
        dgMain.DataSource = ds
        dgMain.DataMember = "Customers"

        btnNext.Enabled = True

    Catch ex As Exception
        MsgBox("Error: " & ex.Source & ": " & ex.Message, _
         MsgBoxStyle.OKOnly, "btnResultSets")
    End Try

End Sub

Private Sub btnNext_Click(ByVal sender As System.Object, _
  ByVal e As System.EventArgs) Handles btnNext.Click
    Try
        dgMain.DataMember = "Customers1"
        btnNext.Enabled = False
    Catch ex As Exception
        MsgBox("Error: " & ex.Source & ": " & ex.Message, _
         MsgBoxStyle.OKOnly, "btnNext")
    End Try
End Sub
```

In this case, no connection between the two result sets is specified, so the DataGrid control doesn't know how to display both of them at the same time. The code assigns the contents of the Customers DataTable to the DataGrid and then enables the Next button on the form's user interface. When you click the Next button, the code assigns the other DataTable, Customers1, to the DataGrid. The Fill method of the DataAdapter automatically serializes DataTable naming in this way if it encounters multiple result sets.

Using Multiple DataAdapters

Finally, you can use more than one DataAdapter object to fill a single DataSet. This allows you complete control of the DataTables that the DataSet contains. You can also use DataRelation objects to specify how these DataTables are related.

TIP   The DataAdapters don't all need to use the same data source for their data. The DataSet, remember, is a completely virtual view of the data. As such, it has no problem combining results from multiple heterogeneous data sources.

Listing 14.3 shows the code for a sample procedure that uses three different DataAdapter objects, all of which draw from the same data source to create a DataSet containing Customers, Orders, and Order Details.

Listing 14.3:   **Using Multiple DataAdapters to Display Data from Multiple Tables**

```
Private Sub btnDataAdapters_Click(ByVal sender As System.Object, _
  ByVal e As System.EventArgs) Handles btnDataAdapters.Click
    Dim cnn As SqlClient.SqlConnection = _
     New SqlClient.SqlConnection("Data Source=SKYROCKET;" & _
     "Initial Catalog=Northwind;Integrated Security=SSPI")
    Dim cmdCustomers As New SqlClient.SqlCommand()
    Dim daCustomers As New SqlClient.SqlDataAdapter()
    Dim cmdOrders As New SqlClient.SqlCommand()
    Dim daOrders As New SqlClient.SqlDataAdapter()
    Dim cmdOrderDetails As New SqlClient.SqlCommand()
    Dim daOrderDetails As New SqlClient.SqlDataAdapter()
    Dim ds As New DataSet()

    Try
        cmdCustomers = cnn.CreateCommand
        cmdCustomers.CommandText = "SELECT * FROM Customers"
        daCustomers.SelectCommand = cmdCustomers
        daCustomers.Fill(ds, "Customers")

        cmdOrders = cnn.CreateCommand
        cmdOrders.CommandText = "SELECT * FROM Orders"
        daOrders.SelectCommand = cmdOrders
        daOrders.Fill(ds, "Orders")

        cmdOrderDetails = cnn.CreateCommand
        cmdOrderDetails.CommandText = "SELECT * FROM [Order Details]"
        daOrderDetails.SelectCommand = cmdOrderDetails
        daOrderDetails.Fill(ds, "Order Details")

        Dim relCustOrder As DataRelation = _
         ds.Relations.Add("CustOrder", _
         ds.Tables("Customers").Columns("CustomerID"), _
         ds.Tables("Orders").Columns("CustomerID"))

        Dim relOrderOrderDetail As DataRelation = _
         ds.Relations.Add("OrderOrderDetail", _
         ds.Tables("Orders").Columns("OrderID"), _
         ds.Tables("Order Details").Columns("OrderID"))

        dgMain.DataSource = ds
        dgMain.DataMember = "Customers"

    Catch ex As Exception
        MsgBox("Error: " & ex.Source & ": " & ex.Message, _
        MsgBoxStyle.OKOnly, "btnJoin")
    End Try

End Sub
```

Creating the DataRelation objects sets up primary key–foreign key relationships between the DataTable objects. The Add method of the Relations collection of the DataSet takes three arguments:

- A name for the DataRelation object to be created
- The column from the primary key side of the relationship
- The column from the foreign key side of the relationship

The DataGrid control contains built-in logic to help navigate between related DataTables in a DataSet. Figure 14.8 shows three successive stages of drilling into the information from this example. Note the rows of information above the grid area that provide context for the currently displayed information.

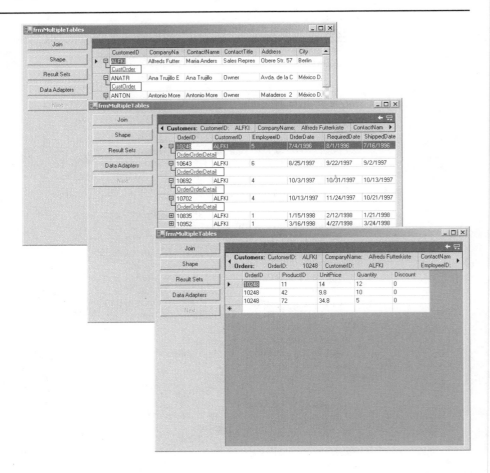

Finding and Sorting Data in DataSets

The DataSet objects offer a variety of ways to find and sort data. Some of these are similar to methods you already know from ADO Recordsets, but others are new to the ADO.NET world. In this section, I'll explain the basics:

- Using the DataRowCollection.Find method to find rows
- Using the DataTable.Select method to filter and sort rows
- Using a DataView to filter and sort rows

The DataSet object has no equivalent of the Recordset.Supports method. Because all DataSets are completely present in memory, they all have the same capabilities. The old distinction between client-side and server-side cursors no longer applies.

Using the DataRowCollection.Find Method to Find Rows

If you go looking for familiar methods in ADO.NET, you'll find the Find method of the DataRowCollection object. The DataRowCollection is the strongly typed collection that's returned by the Rows property of the DataTable object; it contains all of the DataRow objects within the DataTable.

The Find method does indeed enable you to find a particular DataRow within a Data-Table. However, there's a catch: It searches only for a matching value in the primary key of the table. See Listing 14.4, for example, which shows code from this chapter's sample project.

Listing 14.4:   **Using the Find Method to Locate Data**

```
Private Sub btnFind_Click(ByVal sender As System.Object, _
  ByVal e As System.EventArgs) Handles btnFind.Click
    Dim cnn As SqlClient.SqlConnection = _
     New SqlClient.SqlConnection("Data Source=SKYROCKET;" & _
      "Initial Catalog=Northwind;Integrated Security=SSPI")
    Dim cmd As New SqlClient.SqlCommand()
    Dim da As New SqlClient.SqlDataAdapter()
    Dim ds As New DataSet()
    Dim dr As DataRow
    Dim dc As DataColumn
    Dim pk(1) As DataColumn

    Try
        lboResults.Items.Clear()

        cmd = cnn.CreateCommand
        cmd.CommandText = "SELECT * FROM Customers"
        da.SelectCommand = cmd
        da.Fill(ds, "Customers")
        pk(0) = ds.Tables("Customers").Columns("CustomerID")
        ds.Tables("Customers").PrimaryKey = pk
```

```
        dr = ds.Tables("Customers").Rows.Find("BONAP")
        If Not dr Is Nothing Then
            For Each dc In ds.Tables("Customers").Columns
                lboResults.Items.Add(dr(dc))
            Next
        Else
            lboResults.Items.Add("Not Found")
        End If

    Catch ex As Exception
        MsgBox("Error: " & ex.Source & ": " & ex.Message, _
         MsgBoxStyle.OKOnly, "btnFind")
    End Try

End Sub
```

You might be surprised to see the two lines of code in this snippet that set the primary key for this table by assigning an array of columns (that happens to have only a single member) to the PrimaryKey property of the DataTable. That's necessary because the DataAdapter.Fill method doesn't move any schema information other than column names to the DataTable. An alternative would be to use an XSD schema to define a strongly typed DataSet that includes primary key information.

You can also use the Find method to find DataRows that have a multiple-part primary key. In that case, you supply an array of objects as the argument to the Find method. Each object is the value to be found in one column of the primary key.

Using the DataTable.Select Method to Filter and Sort Rows

The Find method is quick and useful, but inflexible: It can find only a single row, and it searches only the primary key field of the DataTable. For a more flexible way to filter and sort DataTables, take a look at the DataTable.Select method. This method allows you to extract an array of DataRow objects from a DataTable. When building the array, you can specify a filter expression to select DataRows, a sort expression to sort the DataRows in the array, and a state constant to select only DataRows in a particular state.

If you call the Select method with no arguments, it selects all the DataRows in the DataTable. This is a quick way to get an array that holds the content of a DataTable:

```
Dim adrAll() As DataRow = dt.Select()
```

To select a subset of the DataRows in the DataTable, you can supply a filter expression. Filter expressions are essentially SQL WHERE clauses constructed according to these rules:

- Column names containing special characters should be enclosed in square brackets.

- String constants should be enclosed in single quotes.

- Date constants should be enclosed in pound signs.

- Numeric expressions can be specified in decimal or scientific notation.

- Expressions can be created using AND, OR, NOT, parentheses, IN, LIKE, comparison operators, and arithmetic operators.

- The + operator is used to concatenate strings.

- Either * or % can be used as a wildcard to match any number of characters. Wildcards may be used only at the start or end of strings.

- Columns in a child table can be referenced with the expression Child.Column. If the table has more than one child table, use the expression Child(RelationName).Column to choose a particular child table.

- The Sum, Avg, Min, Max, Count, StDev, and Var aggregates can be used with child tables.

- Supported functions include CONVERT, LEN, ISNULL, IIF, and SUBSTRING.

TIP　　For more details on the syntax of filter expressions, see the .NET Framework help for the DataColumn.Expression property.

If you don't specify a sort order in the Select method, the rows are returned in primary key order, or in the order of addition if the table doesn't have a primary key. You can also specify a sort expression consisting of one or more column names and the keywords ASC or DESC to specify ascending or descending sorts. For example, this is a valid sort expression:

```
Country ASC, CompanyName DESC
```

That expression will sort first by country in ascending order, and then by company name within each country in descending order.

Finally, you can also select DataRows according to their current state by supplying one of the DataViewRowState constants. Table 14.17 shows these constants.

TABLE 14.17: DataViewRowState Constants

Constant	Meaning
Added	A new row that has not yet been committed.
CurrentRows	All current rows, including unchanged, modified, and new rows.
Deleted	A row that has been deleted.
ModifiedCurrent	A row that has been modified.
ModifiedOriginal	The original data from a row that has been modified.
None	Does not match any rows in the DataTable.
OriginalRows	Original rows, including rows that have since been modified or deleted.
Unchanged	Rows that have not been changed.

Listing 14.5 contains a snippet from this chapter's sample project that demonstrates the use of the Select method with a filter and a sort. This code extracts all the DataRows for customers in Venezuela to an array and sorts them by the ContactName field. Figure 14.9 shows the results of running this code.

Listing 14.5:   **Using the Select Method to Locate Data**

```
Private Sub btnSelect_Click(ByVal sender As System.Object, _
ByVal e As System.EventArgs) Handles btnSelect.Click
    Dim cnn As SqlClient.SqlConnection = _
    New SqlClient.SqlConnection("Data Source=SKYROCKET;" & _
    "Initial Catalog=Northwind;Integrated Security=SSPI")
    Dim cmd As New SqlClient.SqlCommand()
    Dim da As New SqlClient.SqlDataAdapter()
    Dim ds As New DataSet()
    Dim dr As DataRow
    Dim dc As DataColumn
    Dim pk(1) As DataColumn

    Try
        lboResults.Items.Clear()

        cmd = cnn.CreateCommand
        cmd.CommandText = "SELECT * FROM Customers"
        da.SelectCommand = cmd
        da.Fill(ds, "Customers")
        pk(0) = ds.Tables("Customers").Columns("CustomerID")
        ds.Tables("Customers").PrimaryKey = pk

        Dim adr() As DataRow = ds.Tables("Customers").Select( _
        "Country = 'Venezuela'", "ContactName ASC")

        For Each dr In adr
            lboResults.Items.Add(dr(0) & " " & dr(1) & " " & dr(2))
        Next

    Catch ex As Exception
        MsgBox("Error: " & ex.Source & ": " & ex.Message, _
        MsgBoxStyle.OKOnly, "btnSelect")
    End Try

End Sub
```

FIGURE 14.9:

Array of rows produced by the DataTable.Select method.

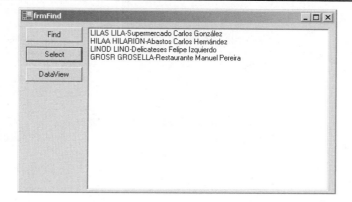

Using a DataView to Filter and Sort Rows

Another alternative for presenting a filtered or sorted subset of the data in a DataTable is to use one or more DataView objects. The DataView is derived from a DataTable and has the same rows-and-columns structure, but it allows you to specify sorting and filtering options. One great advantage of using the DataView object in a user interface application is that it can be bound to controls.

Table 14.18 lists some of the important members of the DataView object.

TABLE 14.18: DataView Members

Name	Type	Description
AddNew	Method	Adds a new row to the DataView.
AllowDelete	Property	True if deletions through this DataView are allowed.
AllowEdit	Property	True if edits through this DataView are allowed.
AllowNew	Property	True if new rows can be added through this DataView.
Count	Property	Number of records in the DataView.
Delete	Method	Deletes a row from the DataView.
Find	Method	Finds a row in the DataView by matching the primary key.
FindRows	Method	Finds a row in the DataView with columns matching a specified set of values.
Item	Property	Returns a single DataRow from the DataView.
ListChanged	Event	Fires when the list of rows managed by the DataView changes.
RowFilter	Property	Sets a filter expression using a WHERE clause to limit the rows in the DataView.
RowStateFilter	Property	Sets a filter expression using a DataViewRowState constant to limit the rows in the DataView.
Sort	Property	Sets the sort order for the DataView.

Figure 14.10 shows a form with two DataGrid controls bound to different DataViews based on the same underlying DataTable object. Here's the code that was used to instantiate this form:

```
Private Sub frmDataView_Load(ByVal sender As System.Object, _
  ByVal e As System.EventArgs) Handles MyBase.Load
    Dim cnn As SqlClient.SqlConnection = _
     New SqlClient.SqlConnection("Data Source=SKYROCKET;" & _
     "Initial Catalog=Northwind;Integrated Security=SSPI")
    Dim cmd As New SqlClient.SqlCommand()
    Dim da As New SqlClient.SqlDataAdapter()
    Dim ds As New DataSet()

    Try
        cmd = cnn.CreateCommand
        cmd.CommandText = "SELECT * FROM Customers"
        da.SelectCommand = cmd
        da.Fill(ds, "Customers")

        Dim dv1 As DataView = New DataView(ds.Tables("Customers"))
        dv1.RowFilter = "Country = 'Germany'"
        dv1.Sort = "CompanyName DESC"
        dg1.DataSource = dv1

        Dim dv2 As DataView = New DataView(ds.Tables("Customers"))
        dv2.RowFilter = "Country = 'Brazil'"
        dv2.Sort = "CompanyName ASC"
        dg2.DataSource = dv2

    Catch ex As Exception
        MsgBox("Error: " & ex.Source & ": " & ex.Message, _
         MsgBoxStyle.OKOnly, "btnPopulateDatabase")
    End Try

End Sub
```

Running Stored Procedures

Like classic ADO, ADO.NET also allows you to retrieve data by using a stored procedure. As you'll recall from Chapter 3, a stored procedure is a SQL statement or collection of SQL statements saved as a persistent object on the database server. By supplying values for the input parameters of the stored procedure, you can determine which records it will retrieve. By moving this piece of logic from the client to the server, you can both increase performance and make sure that particular business rules are enforced. Some databases precompile statements saved as stored procedures so that they will execute more quickly. In addition, you may find it easier to maintain the logic of your application by using stored procedures, which provide a central point for modification.

FIGURE 14.10:

Multiple DataViews based on a single table

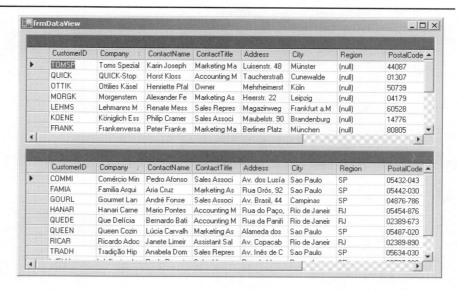

In this section, I'll demonstrate the use of an ADO.NET Command object to return a DataSet based on a stored procedure.

Using the Command Object

I'll start the discussion with another look at the "Ten Most Expensive Products" stored procedure from the Northwind database. As you saw in Chapter 3, this stored procedure is defined with this SQL statement:

```
CREATE PROCEDURE "Ten Most Expensive Products" AS
SET ROWCOUNT 10
SELECT Products.ProductName AS TenMostExpensiveProducts,
 Products.UnitPrice
FROM Products
ORDER BY Products.UnitPrice DESC
```

This stored procedure returns a result set consisting of the 10 most expensive products stored in the Products table.

To open a DataSet based on the results of a stored procedure such as this one, you can use a Command object in conjunction with a DataAdapter object:

```
Private Sub btnWithoutParameters_Click(ByVal sender As System.Object, _
  ByVal e As System.EventArgs) Handles btnWithoutParameters.Click
    Dim cnn As SqlClient.SqlConnection = _
    New SqlClient.SqlConnection("Data Source=SKYROCKET;" & _
    "Initial Catalog=Northwind;Integrated Security=SSPI")
```

```
Dim cmd As New SqlClient.SqlCommand()
Dim da As New SqlClient.SqlDataAdapter()
Dim ds As New DataSet()

Try
    cmd = cnn.CreateCommand
    cmd.CommandText = "[Ten Most Expensive Products]"
    cmd.CommandType = CommandType.StoredProcedure
    da.SelectCommand = cmd
    da.Fill(ds, "Products")

    dgMain.DataSource = ds
    dgMain.DataMember = "Products"

Catch ex As Exception
    MsgBox("Error: " & ex.Source & ": " & ex.Message, _
      MsgBoxStyle.OKOnly, "btnWithoutParameters")
End Try

End Sub
```

The connection to the database is made via the Command object. Because this object was created with the CreateCommand method of the Connection object, it uses that Connection to retrieve data. The CommandText property holds the name of the stored procedure to be executed by the command. Calling the DataAdapter's Fill method tells the database to execute the stored procedure and returns the results to the specified DataSet.

TIP Explicitly setting the Command object's CommandType property to CommandType.Stored-Procedure is not a requirement. The code will run without this setting, but it will run faster if you use this property to tell ADO.NET what type of object it's dealing with.

In this particular case, using a stored procedure with the Command object offers no advantage over filling the DataSet directly from the text of the SQL statement. In general, though, you'll find that stored procedures are useful and necessary. That's because you can use parameters to customize a stored procedure to return only the desired rows, as shown in the next section.

Using Parameters

Stored procedures can take input parameters and return output parameters. For example, in the Northwind SQL Server database, there's a stored procedure named SalesByCategory. Here's the SQL that creates that stored procedure:

```
CREATE PROCEDURE SalesByCategory
    @CategoryName nvarchar(15),
    @OrdYear nvarchar(4) = '1998'
```

```
AS
IF @OrdYear != '1996'
 AND @OrdYear != '1997'
 AND @OrdYear != '1998'
BEGIN
    SELECT @OrdYear = '1998'
END
SELECT ProductName,
    TotalPurchase=ROUND(SUM(CONVERT(decimal(14,2),
    OD.Quantity * (1-OD.Discount) * OD.UnitPrice)), 0)
FROM [Order Details] OD, Orders O, Products P, Categories C
WHERE OD.OrderID = O.OrderID
    AND OD.ProductID = P.ProductID
    AND P.CategoryID = C.CategoryID
    AND C.CategoryName = @CategoryName
    AND SUBSTRING(CONVERT(
    nvarchar(22), O.OrderDate, 111), 1, 4) = @OrdYear
GROUP BY ProductName
ORDER BY ProductName
```

Here, @CategoryName and @OrdYear are a pair of input parameters to the stored procedure, both defined as being of the nvarchar datatype. The stored procedure uses these parameters to filter a Recordset of order information. The Recordset becomes the return value of the stored procedure.

Retrieving a DataSet from a stored procedure with input parameters is a four-step process:

1. Create a Command object and connect it to a data source.

2. Supply values for the input parameters.

3. Use the Command object as the SelectCommand for a DataAdapter.

4. Use the DataAdapter's Fill method to retrieve the data to a DataSet object.

As an example, consider the code in Listing 14.6, which is from this chapter's sample project.

Listing 14.6:   Retrieving a DataSet from a Stored Procedure

```
Private Sub btnWithParameters1_Click(ByVal sender As System.Object, _
  ByVal e As System.EventArgs) Handles btnWithParameters1.Click
    Dim cnn As SqlClient.SqlConnection = _
      New SqlClient.SqlConnection("Data Source=SKYROCKET;" & _
      "Initial Catalog=Northwind;Integrated Security=SSPI")
    Dim cmd As New SqlClient.SqlCommand()
    Dim da As New SqlClient.SqlDataAdapter()
    Dim ds As New DataSet()
    Dim cb As SqlClient.SqlCommandBuilder
    Dim prm As SqlClient.SqlParameter
```

```
Try
        cmd = cnn.CreateCommand
        cmd.CommandText = "SalesByCategory"
        cmd.CommandType = CommandType.StoredProcedure

        cnn.Open()
        cb.DeriveParameters(cmd)
        cnn.Close()
        For Each prm In cmd.Parameters
            If (prm.Direction = ParameterDirection.Input) Or _
             (prm.Direction = ParameterDirection.InputOutput) Then
                prm.Value = InputBox(prm.ParameterName, _
                 "Enter parameter value")
            End If
        Next

        da.SelectCommand = cmd
        da.Fill(ds, "Products")

        dgMain.DataSource = ds
        dgMain.DataMember = "Products"

    Catch ex As Exception
        MsgBox("Error: " & ex.Source & ": " & ex.Message, _
          MsgBoxStyle.OKOnly, "btnWithParameters1")
    End Try

End Sub
```

TIP   To test the code in Listing 14.6, try Beverages for the category name and 1996 for the order year.

WARNING   This procedure requires a build of .NET later than beta 2 to execute.

This code starts by defining a Connection to the Northwind database on a SQL Server named SKYROCKET, using Windows NT security. (As always, if your environment is different, you may have to modify the connection string.) Then it creates a Command object and loads it with the SalesByCategory stored procedure.

The code then opens the Connection and calls the DeriveParameters method of a Sql-CommandBuilder object. This call tells ADO to query the data source and find out what parameters are required by this stored procedure. Once the Parameters collection is populated, the code walks through it one parameter at a time and prompts the user for values for all input parameters.

Finally, the DataAdapter is used to fill the DataSet, just as in the previous example, and the results are displayed on the form.

Although this method works, it's not the most efficient way to execute a stored procedure. The bottleneck is the DeriveParameters call. This method requires you to open a Connection to the server and transmits information both ways to do its job. If you already know the details of the stored procedure, you can avoid using this method by creating your own parameters. This method is also demonstrated in the sample project for this chapter; you'll find the subroutine in Listing 14.7.

Listing 14.7:   Creating Parameters for a Stored Procedure

```
Private Sub btnWithParameters2_Click(ByVal sender As System.Object, _
  ByVal e As System.EventArgs) Handles btnWithParameters2.Click
    Dim cnn As SqlClient.SqlConnection = _
     New SqlClient.SqlConnection("Data Source=SKYROCKET;" & _
     "Initial Catalog=Northwind;Integrated Security=SSPI")
    Dim cmd As New SqlClient.SqlCommand()
    Dim da As New SqlClient.SqlDataAdapter()
    Dim ds As New DataSet()
    Dim prm As SqlClient.SqlParameter
    Dim strCategoryName As String
    Dim strOrderYear As String

    Try
        cmd = cnn.CreateCommand
        cmd.CommandText = "SalesByCategory"
        cmd.CommandType = CommandType.StoredProcedure

        strCategoryName = InputBox("Enter category name:")
        strOrderYear = InputBox("Enter order year:")

        prm = cmd.Parameters.Add("@CategoryName", _
         SqlDbType.NVarChar, 15)
        prm.Value = strCategoryName
        prm = cmd.Parameters.Add("@OrdYear", SqlDbType.NVarChar, 4)
        prm.Value = strOrderYear

        da.SelectCommand = cmd
        da.Fill(ds, "Products")

        dgMain.DataSource = ds
        dgMain.DataMember = "Products"

    Catch ex As Exception
        MsgBox("Error: " & ex.Source & ": " & ex.Message, _
         MsgBoxStyle.OKOnly, "btnWithParameters2")
    End Try

End Sub
```

The difference between this procedure and the previous one is in the method used to populate the Parameters collection of the Command object. This procedure uses the Add method of the Command object's Parameters collection:

```
Cmd.Parameters.Add(Name, Type, Size)
```

The Add method takes three arguments:

- The *Name* argument must match exactly the name that the underlying data source is expecting for the parameter.

- The *Type* argument specifies a datatype for the parameter. These datatypes are expressed by constants supplied by the data provider—in this case, the SQL Server .NET Data Provider. If you have trouble determining the required type, you can first use the CommandBuilder .DeriveParameters method to get the parameter from the server and then examine the Type property of the returned parameter. Once you know what this type is, you can create your own matching parameter in the future.

- The *Size* argument specifies the size of the parameter. You don't need to specify a size for fixed-length datatypes such as integer or datetime.

All these arguments are optional when you're calling the Add method. You can create parameters and then set the properties afterward if you prefer not to do the entire operation in one line of code.

In general, if you're writing code that will always call the same stored procedure, it's worth your while to explicitly code the parameters using the Add method of the Parameters collection. You should save the CommandBuilder.DeriveParameters method for situations in which you don't know in advance what the Parameters collection should contain.

Summary

In this chapter, you've seen the basics of using ADO.NET to retrieve data from a data source. You learned about the two broad groups of ADO.NET objects: data provider objects and DataSet objects. You saw that multiple versions of the data provider objects exist to facilitate connections to different data sources, but that a single group of DataSet objects provides a uniform representation in code of diverse data.

You also learned a variety of methods for retrieving data in ADO.NET applications. These include the use of the DataAdapter object to fill a DataSet, the construction of strongly typed DataSets through the user interface, and the use of multiple tables or stored procedures to provide the data for a DataSet. You also saw several methods for sorting and filtering the data in a DataTable.

As you can tell by now, ADO.NET offers a great deal of flexibility (and complexity!) in its operations. And that's without even having edited any of the data that the samples have retrieved. Editing data is the subject of the next chapter.

CHAPTER 15

Editing Data with ADO.NET

- Updating, adding, and deleting data

- Using auto-generated commands

- Adding primary keys to a DataSet

- Working with ADO.NET events

- Managing concurrency and transactions

When you're working with a data source, retrieving the data for display is normally only one of the requirements. Often, making changes to data is even more important. As you'd expect, ADO.NET provides support for the full suite of editing operations, including updating existing data, adding new data, and deleting existing data. In this chapter, I'll explore the syntax for these fundamental data operations in ADO.NET. I'll also introduce you to the events supported by the DataSet and DataTable objects, and discuss concurrency and transactions in ADO.NET.

Updating Data

At the highest level, you can think of updating data with ADO.NET as a three-part task. That's because updates have to take into account the fact that the DataSet is designed to be kept in a disconnected state.

1. Use the Fill method of the DataAdapter object to retrieve the data into a DataSet.

2. Edit the data in the DataSet.

3. Use the Update method of the DataAdapter to reconcile changes with the original data source.

In this section, I'll go into each of those topics in more depth.

Filling the DataSet

You've already seen many examples of filling a DataSet from a DataAdapter in Chapter 14, "Using the ADO.NET Objects to Retrieve Data." But there's a problem with those examples. The code in Chapter 14 sets the SelectCommand property of the DataAdapter but sets none of its other Command-related properties. As a result, although those examples are useful for filling DataSets, they lack the ability to persist any changes back to the original data source.

The key to enabling two-way communication between the DataSet and the original data source is to supply Command objects for all four of the Command-related properties of the DataAdapter. To recap, these Commands and their functions are as follows:

SelectCommand   Called by the DataAdapter.Fill method to load the initial data into the DataSet.

UpdateCommand   Called by the DataAdapter.Update method to save changes to existing rows of the DataSet.

InsertCommand   Called by the DataAdapter.Update method to save new rows of the DataSet.

DeleteCommand   Called by the DataAdapter.Update method to delete existing rows from the DataSet.

Listing 15.1 shows an example of setting up a DataAdapter with all four Commands. This code is from the frmUpdate form in the ADOChapter15 sample project.

Listing 15.1:   Setting Up a DataAdapter to Persist Changes

```
Dim mda As New SqlClient.SqlDataAdapter()
Dim mds As New DataSet()

Private Sub frmUpdate_Load(ByVal sender As System.Object, _
 ByVal e As System.EventArgs) Handles MyBase.Load
    Dim cnn As SqlClient.SqlConnection = _
     New SqlClient.SqlConnection("Data Source=SKYROCKET;" & _
     "Initial Catalog=Northwind;Integrated Security=SSPI")
    Dim cmdSelect As New SqlClient.SqlCommand()
    Dim cmdUpdate As New SqlClient.SqlCommand()
    Dim cmdInsert As New SqlClient.SqlCommand()
    Dim cmdDelete As New SqlClient.SqlCommand()
    Dim prm As SqlClient.SqlParameter

    Try
        ' Create the Select command to grab the initial data
        cmdSelect = cnn.CreateCommand
        cmdSelect.CommandText = "SELECT CustomerID, CompanyName, " & _
         "ContactName FROM Customers"
        mda.SelectCommand = cmdSelect

        ' The Update command handles updates to existing rows
        cmdUpdate = cnn.CreateCommand
        cmdUpdate.CommandText = "UPDATE Customers " & _
         "SET CompanyName = @CompanyName, " & _
         "ContactName = @ContactName " & _
         "WHERE CustomerID = @CustomerID"
        ' Now create the parameters that will be
        ' passed to this command
        prm = cmdUpdate.Parameters.Add("@CompanyName", _
         SqlDbType.NVarChar, 40, "CompanyName")
        prm = cmdUpdate.Parameters.Add("@ContactName", _
         SqlDbType.NVarChar, 30, "ContactName")
        prm = cmdUpdate.Parameters.Add("@CustomerID", _
         SqlDbType.NChar, 5, "CustomerID")
        prm.SourceVersion = DataRowVersion.Original
        mda.UpdateCommand = cmdUpdate

        ' The Delete command handles deletions of existing rows
        cmdDelete = cnn.CreateCommand
        cmdDelete.CommandText = "DELETE FROM Customers " & _
         "WHERE CustomerID = @CustomerID"
        ' Now create the parameter that will be
        ' passed to this command
        prm = cmdDelete.Parameters.Add("@CustomerID", _
         SqlDbType.NChar, 5, "CustomerID")
```

```
    prm.SourceVersion = DataRowVersion.Original
    mda.DeleteCommand = cmdDelete

    ' And the Insert command adds new rows
    cmdInsert = cnn.CreateCommand
    cmdInsert.CommandText = "INSERT INTO Customers " & _
      "(CustomerID, CompanyName, ContactName) " & _
      "VALUES(@CustomerID, @CompanyName, @ContactName)"
    ' Now create the parameters that will be
    ' passed to this command
    prm = cmdInsert.Parameters.Add("@CompanyName", _
      SqlDbType.NVarChar, 40, "CompanyName")
    prm = cmdInsert.Parameters.Add("@ContactName", _
      SqlDbType.NVarChar, 30, "ContactName")
    prm = cmdInsert.Parameters.Add("@CustomerID", _
      SqlDbType.NChar, 5, "CustomerID")
    mda.InsertCommand = cmdInsert

    ' Fill the DataSet and display it on the UI
    mda.Fill(mds, "Customers")
    dgMain.DataSource = mds
    dgMain.DataMember = "Customers"

  Catch ex As Exception
    MsgBox("Error: " & ex.Source & ": " & ex.Message, _
      MsgBoxStyle.OKOnly, "btnPopulateDatabase")
  End Try

End Sub

Private Sub btnSaveUpdates_Click(ByVal sender As System.Object, _
  ByVal e As System.EventArgs) Handles btnSaveUpdates.Click

  Try
    mda.Update(mds, "Customers")
  Catch ex As Exception
    MsgBox("Error: " & ex.Source & ": " & ex.Message, _
      MsgBoxStyle.OKOnly, "frmUpdate_Load")
  End Try

End Sub
```

Of particular interest for the task of editing data is the block that creates the Command object that is assigned to the DataAdapter.UpdateCommand property. This Command is based on a SQL statement with three parameters:

```
UPDATE Customers
  SET CompanyName = @CompanyName,
  ContactName = @ContactName
  WHERE CustomerID = @CustomerID
```

After the code creates the Command with this CommandText, it calls the Parameters.Add method of the Command once for each of the three parameters. In this case, the format of the Add method used takes four arguments:

- The name of the parameter to create
- The datatype of the parameter
- The size of the parameter
- The source column to which this parameter will be bound

Supplying the source column is essential to transferring updates seamlessly from the DataSet back to the original data source.

Editing Data

Editing data in a DataSet is easy. You don't need to worry about entering some special editing mode, as was the case with some of the older data access libraries. Instead, you can simply assign a new value to the appropriate item in the DataRow of interest. For example, here's some code that finds a particular row and then prompts the user for a new value of the ContactName column in that row:

```
Private Sub btnPromptedEdit_Click(ByVal sender As System.Object, _
  ByVal e As System.EventArgs) Handles btnPromptedEdit.Click

    Dim strCustomerID As String
    Dim strContactName As String
    Dim dr As DataRow

    Try
        strCustomerID = InputBox("Customer ID to edit:")
        Dim adrEdit() = mds.Tables("Customers").Select( _
         "CustomerID = '" & strCustomerID & "'")
        If UBound(adrEdit, 1) > -1 Then
            dr = adrEdit(0)
            strContactName = InputBox("New contact name:", , _
             dr("ContactName"))
            dr("ContactName") = strContactName
        Else
            MsgBox(strCustomerID & " not found!")
        End If

    Catch ex As Exception
        MsgBox("Error: " & ex.Source & ": " & ex.Message, _
         MsgBoxStyle.OKOnly, "btnPromptedEdit")
    End Try
End Sub
```

Note the check of the upper bound of the array after the call to the Select method, to make sure that a matching row was found. Generally, you'd need to write code to loop through the entire array. In this case, though, because the filtering is on the primary key of the underlying table, you know that there can be, at most, one matching row.

The edit is performed by this line:

```
dr("ContactName") = strContactName
```

This line of code simply assigns a new value to the ContactName column in the selected DataRow.

Although this sort of editing is convenient when you're performing some operation entirely in code, in many cases it will be easier to allow the Windows Forms user interface to handle the editing chore. Figure 15.1 shows the frmUpdate form open, with a row being edited via the user interface. The DataGrid is displaying the Customers member from the DataSet. As you can see, the DataGrid allows editing in place.

In fact, the DataGrid allows all three of the fundamental editing operations:

- To update the data in a row, click in the column to be updated and type a new value.

- To add a new row, scroll to the end of the list and type the values for the row into the last row of the grid.

- To delete an existing row, click on the record selector to the left of the row and then press the Delete key on the keyboard.

TIP   To selectively disable any of these features, build a DataView based on the DataTable that you wish to edit, and set the AllowEdit, AllowNew, or AllowDelete property of the DataView to False. Then bind the DataView rather than the DataTable to the DataGrid.

Reconciling Changes

Changes in the DataSet affect only the in-memory copy of the data. To actually write the changes back to the original data source, you need to call the Update method of the DataAdapter object. The frmUpdate form in this chapter's sample project includes a button to perform this task:

```
Private Sub btnSaveUpdates_Click(ByVal sender As System.Object, _
  ByVal e As System.EventArgs) Handles btnSaveUpdates.Click

    Try
        mda.Update(mds, "Customers")
    Catch ex As Exception
        MsgBox("Error: " & ex.Source & ": " & ex.Message, _
          MsgBoxStyle.OKOnly, "btnSaveUpdates")
    End Try

End Sub
```

FIGURE 15.1:

Editing a row via the DataGrid control

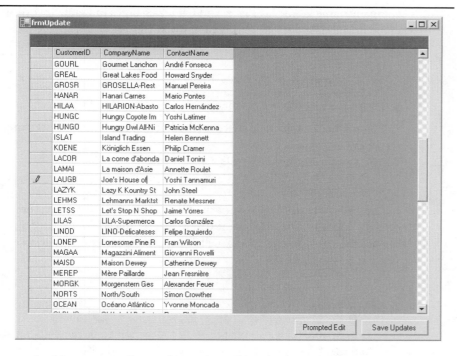

The Update method is syntactically similar to the Fill method. It takes as its parameters the DataSet to be reconciled with the data source and the name of the DataTable whose changes should be saved back to the data source.

You don't need to worry about how many changes were made to the data in the DataSet, or which columns were changed. The DataAdapter automatically locates the changed rows and executes the UpdateCommand for each of them, filling in the parameters of the Command from the data in the DataSet.

If you need finer control over the updates, you can pass a subset of the rows in the DataSet to the DataAdapter to be updated. There's no requirement to make the entire DataTable available. For example, you could save new rows to the data source, without committing any edits or deletions, by calling the Update method this way:

```
Mda.Update(mds.Tables("Customers").Select( _
   Nothing, Nothing, DataViewRowState.Added))
```

In most cases, editing conflicts between different users will be resolved with a simple optimistic-locking rule of "last edit wins." For example, suppose both Cindy and Chuck are editing the Customers table. Cindy changes the record whose key is ALFKI so that the company name is Alfreds Place, and Chuck changes the same record so that the contact name is Maria Anderson. In this case, when Cindy's change is reconciled with the database, the Update method will run this SQL statement:

```
UPDATE Customers
SET CompanyName = 'Alfreds Place',
ContactName = 'Maria Anders'
WHERE CustomerID = 'ALFKI'
```

When Chuck calls the Update method, it will run this SQL statement:

```
UPDATE Customers
SET CompanyName = 'Alfreds Futterkiste',
ContactName = 'Maria Anderson'
WHERE CustomerID = 'ALFKI'
```

The net effect will be to overwrite Cindy's change. Of course, some changes can't be reconciled that way. For example, if Cindy deletes the ALFKI record and then Chuck tries to update the same record, Chuck will receive a concurrency violation error. I'll discuss concurrency issues in more detail later in the chapter.

Adding Data

The DataAdapter can also recognize new rows added to the DataSet and save them back to the database. It does this by invoking the Command referred to by the InsertCommand property. In the example you saw earlier, this Command uses an INSERT INTO SQL statement:

```
INSERT INTO Customers
  (CustomerID, CompanyName, ContactName)
  VALUES(@CustomerID, @CompanyName, @ContactName)
```

The parameters for this statement are defined just as they are for the UpdateCommand.

In this particular case, that statement is sufficient because all the data to be inserted comes from the user. Tables that use autonumber or identity keys require a bit more effort to keep the DataSet and the underlying data source synchronized in the case of added rows. The problem, of course, is that the autonumber column is generated at the data source at the time the new row is added. To make this column available to the user interface, the DataAdapter must actually return data as part of its InsertCommand.

The solution is to use a stored procedure with an output parameter on the server to perform the insert and then return the autonumber. Listing 15.2 shows an example, from frm-Products in this chapter's sample project.

Listing 15.2: Using a Stored Procedure to Update an Identity Column

```
Dim mda As New SqlClient.SqlDataAdapter()
Dim mds As New DataSet()

Private Sub frmProducts_Load(ByVal sender As System.Object, _
ByVal e As System.EventArgs) Handles MyBase.Load
    Dim cnn As SqlClient.SqlConnection = _
     New SqlClient.SqlConnection("Data Source=SKYROCKET;" & _
     "Initial Catalog=Northwind;Integrated Security=SSPI")
    Dim cmdCreate As New SqlClient.SqlCommand()
    Dim cmdSelect As New SqlClient.SqlCommand()
    Dim cmdUpdate As New SqlClient.SqlCommand()
    Dim cmdInsert As New SqlClient.SqlCommand()
    Dim cmdDelete As New SqlClient.SqlCommand()
    Dim prm As SqlClient.SqlParameter
    Dim strCreate As String

    Try
        ' Make sure the stored proc we need
        ' for inserts exists in the database
        strCreate = "CREATE PROC spInsertProduct " & _
         "@ProductName nvarchar(40), " & _
         "@ProductID int OUT " & _
         "AS " & _
         " INSERT INTO Products(ProductName)" & _
         "   VALUES(@ProductName) " & _
         "SET @ProductID = @@Identity"
        cmdCreate = cnn.CreateCommand
        cmdCreate.CommandText = strCreate
        cnn.Open()
        cmdCreate.ExecuteNonQuery()
        cnn.Close()
    Catch
        ' We don't care if it fails because
        ' the stored proc already exists
    End Try

    Try
        ' Create the Select command to grab the initial data
        cmdSelect = cnn.CreateCommand
        cmdSelect.CommandText = "SELECT ProductID, ProductName " & _
         "FROM Products"
        mda.SelectCommand = cmdSelect

        ' The Update command handles updates to existing rows
        cmdUpdate = cnn.CreateCommand
        cmdUpdate.CommandText = "UPDATE Products " & _
         "SET ProductName = @ProductName " & _
         "WHERE ProductID = @CustomerID"
        ' Now create the parameters that will be
        ' passed to this command
```

```
        prm = cmdUpdate.Parameters.Add("@ProductName", _
         SqlDbType.NVarChar, 40, "ProductName")
        prm = cmdUpdate.Parameters.Add("@ProductID", _
         SqlDbType.Int)
        prm.SourceColumn = "ProductID"
        prm.SourceVersion = DataRowVersion.Original
        mda.UpdateCommand = cmdUpdate

        ' The Delete command handles deletions of existing rows
        cmdDelete = cnn.CreateCommand
        cmdDelete.CommandText = "DELETE FROM Products " & _
         "WHERE ProductID = @ProductID"
        ' Now create the parameter that will be
        ' passed to this command
        prm = cmdDelete.Parameters.Add("@ProductID", _
         SqlDbType.Int)
        prm.SourceColumn = "ProductID"
        prm.SourceVersion = DataRowVersion.Original
        mda.DeleteCommand = cmdDelete

        ' And the Insert command adds new rows
        cmdInsert = cnn.CreateCommand
        cmdInsert.CommandText = "spInsertProduct"
        cmdInsert.CommandType = CommandType.StoredProcedure
        ' Now create the parameters that will be
        ' passed to this command
        prm = cmdInsert.Parameters.Add("@ProductName", _
         SqlDbType.NVarChar, 40, "ProductName")
        prm = cmdInsert.Parameters.Add("@ProductID", _
         SqlDbType.Int)
        prm.SourceColumn = "ProductID"
        prm.Direction = ParameterDirection.Output
        mda.InsertCommand = cmdInsert

        ' Fill the DataSet and display it on the UI
        mda.Fill(mds, "Products")
        dgMain.DataSource = mds
        dgMain.DataMember = "Products"

    Catch ex As Exception
        MsgBox("Error: " & ex.Source & ": " & ex.Message, _
         MsgBoxStyle.OKOnly, "frmProducts_Load")
    End Try

End Sub

Private Sub btnMain_Click(ByVal sender As System.Object, _
 ByVal e As System.EventArgs) Handles btnMain.Click

    Try

        mda.Update(mds, "Products")
```

```
Catch ex As Exception
    MsgBox("Error: " & ex.Source & ": " & ex.Message, _
    MsgBoxStyle.OKOnly, "btnMain")
End Try

End Sub
```

Most of this is very similar to the code you already saw for the frmUpdate form. The difference is in the InsertCommand. The frmProducts_Load procedure starts by creating a stored procedure on the target SQL Server:

```
CREATE PROC spInsertProduct
@ProductName nvarchar(40),
@ProductID int OUT
AS
INSERT INTO Products(ProductName)
VALUES(@ProductName)
SET @ProductID = @@Identity
```

This stored procedure inserts a new row into the table and then uses the *@@Identity* system variable to retrieve the most recent identity value used by the connection (this, of course, will be the new ProductID value in this case). There are some minor differences in setting up the InsertCommand for the DataAdapter:

```
' And the Insert command adds new rows
cmdInsert = cnn.CreateCommand
cmdInsert.CommandText = "spInsertProduct"
cmdInsert.CommandType = CommandType.StoredProcedure
' Now create the parameters that will be
' passed to this command
prm = cmdInsert.Parameters.Add("@ProductName", _
 SqlDbType.NVarChar, 40, "ProductName")
prm = cmdInsert.Parameters.Add("@ProductID", _
 SqlDbType.Int)
prm.SourceColumn = "ProductID"
prm.Direction = ParameterDirection.Output
mda.InsertCommand = cmdInsert
```

Note that the CommandType is explicitly set to CommandType.StoredProcedure; without this, you'll get a syntax error when trying to execute the update. Also, the Direction property of the Parameter object representing the @ProductID parameter must be set to Parameter-Direction.Output to tell the DataAdapter that this is information that should be sent back to the DataSet.

To try this code out, follow these steps:

1. Run the sample project.

2. Open the Products form.

3. Scroll to the end of the DataGrid and enter a new name in the ProductName column.

4. Click the Update button.

You'll see the newly assigned ProductID automatically appear on the DataGrid when the DataAdapter finishes the update process.

Deleting Data

As you've no doubt guessed by now, deleting data is a matter of supplying an appropriate DeleteCommand to the DataAdapter. Here's the version from the code you saw in Listing 15.1:

```
' The Delete command handles deletions of existing rows
cmdDelete = cnn.CreateCommand
cmdDelete.CommandText = "DELETE FROM Customers " & _
 "WHERE CustomerID = @CustomerID"
' Now create the parameter that will be
' passed to this command
prm = cmdDelete.Parameters.Add("@CustomerID", _
 SqlDbType.NChar, 5, "CustomerID")
prm.SourceVersion = DataRowVersion.Original
mda.DeleteCommand = cmdDelete
```

The DeleteCommand can be simpler than the InsertCommand or UpdateCommand in most cases. All it needs to do is locate the appropriate row in the original source table by using a WHERE clause that includes all the columns of the primary key, and then delete that row.

Using Auto-Generated Commands

In some cases, you can avoid the tedium of writing your own SQL strings to manage updates, insertions, and deletions. The .NET data providers include an object called the Command-Builder (depending on the provider, this will be the OleDbCommandBuilder, SqlCommand-Builder, or OdbcCommandBuilder object). You saw this object briefly in Chapter 14, where I used its DeriveParameters method to automatically retrieve the parameters for a stored procedure. But there's a lot more to the CommandBuilder object than that: It also knows how to build the Command objects required by the DataAdapter object in simple cases.

In particular, there are three constraints in using the CommandBuilder object to automatically configure a DataAdapter:

- The SelectCommand property of the DataAdapter must be set first.

- The SelectCommand can draw columns from only a single database table.

- The columns loaded by the SelectCommand must include at least one primary key or unique constraint.

The frmUpdate2 form in this chapter's sample project demonstrates the syntax. Listing 15.3 presents the code.

Listing 15.3:   **Generating Commands with the SqlCommandBuilder Object**

```
Private Sub frmUpdate2_Load(ByVal sender As System.Object, _
 ByVal e As System.EventArgs) Handles MyBase.Load
    Dim cnn As SqlClient.SqlConnection = _
     New SqlClient.SqlConnection("Data Source=SKYROCKET;" & _
     "Initial Catalog=Northwind;Integrated Security=SSPI")
    Dim cmdSelect As New SqlClient.SqlCommand()

    Try
        ' Create the Select command to grab the initial data
        cmdSelect = cnn.CreateCommand
        cmdSelect.CommandText = "SELECT CustomerID, CompanyName, " & _
         "ContactName FROM Customers"
        mda.SelectCommand = cmdSelect

        ' Automatically generate the Update, Insert,
        ' and Delete commands
        Dim cb As SqlClient.SqlCommandBuilder = _
         New SqlClient.SqlCommandBuilder(mda)

        ' Fill the DataSet and display it on the UI
        mda.Fill(mds, "Customers")
        dgMain.DataSource = mds
        dgMain.DataMember = "Customers"

    Catch ex As Exception
        MsgBox("Error: " & ex.Source & ": " & ex.Message, _
         MsgBoxStyle.OKOnly, "frmUpdate_Load")
    End Try

End Sub

Private Sub btnSaveUpdates_Click(ByVal sender As System.Object, _
 ByVal e As System.EventArgs) Handles btnSaveUpdates.Click

    Try
        mda.Update(mds, "Customers")
    Catch ex As Exception
        MsgBox("Error: " & ex.Source & ": " & ex.Message, _
         MsgBoxStyle.OKOnly, "btnSaveUpdates")
    End Try

End Sub
```

If you compare this with the code for frmUpdate, you'll see that the CommandBuilder object can considerably simplify the task of setting up a DataAdapter for two-way communication between a DataSet and a data source. But remember, if your data source is complex, you'll probably have to write the Commands that modify the data by hand, because the CommandBuilder won't work for SelectCommands based on multiple tables. Also, because the CommandBuilder has to retrieve schema information from the data source to do its job, you'll have one more round-trip to the database server in your code, which may slow things down a bit (especially if you're working over a slow link).

The CommandBuilder object won't overwrite properties that are set manually. So it's possible to craft a custom Command for, say, the UpdateCommand property and still let the CommandBuilder do the work of building the InsertCommand and the DeleteCommand.

When it's building the UpdateCommand and DeleteCommand, the CommandBuilder object creates WHERE clauses that check the values of all the columns in the DataTable. This ensures that updates will be made only if no other user has changed the row since it was loaded.

Adding Primary Keys to a DataSet

One of the problems with the Fill method of the DataAdapter is that it transfers only data to the DataSet; it doesn't transfer any of the constraints from the data source to the DataSet. This means that you can, for example, add rows with a duplicate primary key to a DataTable in that DataSet. Although these rows cannot be saved back to the data source (the problem will cause an error to be raised when you call the DataAdapter.Update method), it's much better practice to prevent the user from entering these rows in the first place. That's the purpose of adding constraints to a DataSet.

The most important constraints to add to the DataSet are primary keys. There are three ways to take care of adding primary keys when filling a DataSet:

- Call the DataAdapter.FillSchema method.
- Set the DataAdapter.MissingSchemaAction property.
- Create the primary key in code.

The DataAdapter.FillSchema method copies primary key constraint information from a specified data source table to the DataSet. You can see an example in frmConstraints in this chapter's sample project. That form's code is shown in Listing 15.4.

Listing 15.4:   **Copying Constraint Information to a DataSet**

```
Private Sub btnFillSchema_Click(ByVal sender As System.Object, _
ByVal e As System.EventArgs) Handles btnFillSchema.Click
    Dim cnn As SqlClient.SqlConnection = _
     New SqlClient.SqlConnection("Data Source=SKYROCKET;" & _
      "Initial Catalog=Northwind;Integrated Security=SSPI")
    Dim cmdSelect As New SqlClient.SqlCommand()

    Try
        ' Create the Select command to grab the initial data
        cmdSelect = cnn.CreateCommand
        cmdSelect.CommandText = "SELECT CustomerID, CompanyName, " & _
         "ContactName FROM Customers"
        mda.SelectCommand = cmdSelect

        ' Automatically generate the Update, Insert,
        ' and Delete commands
        Dim cb As SqlClient.SqlCommandBuilder = _
         New SqlClient.SqlCommandBuilder(mda)

        ' Fill the DataSet and display it on the UI
        mds.Clear()
        mda.FillSchema(mds, SchemaType.Source, "Customers")
        mda.Fill(mds, "Customers")
        dgMain.DataSource = mds
        dgMain.DataMember = "Customers"

    Catch ex As Exception
        MsgBox("Error: " & ex.Source & ": " & ex.Message, _
         MsgBoxStyle.OKOnly, "btnFillSchema")
    End Try

End Sub
```

When you call the FillSchema method in this case, it will add the primary key constraint to the Customers DataTable within the specified DataSet. This has the effect of bringing primary key validation to the user interface, before any call to the DataAdapter.Fill method. If you try to enter a row whose primary key duplicates that of an existing row, you'll get the warning message shown in Figure 15.2.

If you answer Yes to this prompt, you'll be returned to the row on the DataGrid to continue editing. If you answer No, the row with the duplicate primary key will be erased from the DataGrid and discarded.

NOTE   Remember, any edits you make through the DataGrid are reflected in the DataSet, but not saved to the original data source. To save the changes permanently, you'll need to click the Save Updates button.

FIGURE 15.2:

Trapping a duplicate
primary key with a
DataTable constraint

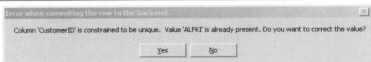

You can also copy schema information to the DataTable at the time the Fill method is
called by setting the MissingSchemaAction property of the DataAdapter to AddWithKey. Listing 15.5 shows this technique in action.

Listing 15.5:   Adding Schema Information to a DataTable Automatically

```
Private Sub btnMissingSchemaAction_Click(ByVal sender As System.Object, _
ByVal e As System.EventArgs) Handles btnMissingSchemaAction.Click
    Dim cnn As SqlClient.SqlConnection = _
    New SqlClient.SqlConnection("Data Source=SKYROCKET;" & _
    "Initial Catalog=Northwind;Integrated Security=SSPI")
    Dim cmdSelect As New SqlClient.SqlCommand()

    Try
        ' Create the Select command to grab the initial data
        cmdSelect = cnn.CreateCommand
        cmdSelect.CommandText = "SELECT CustomerID, CompanyName, " & _
        "ContactName FROM Customers"
        mda.SelectCommand = cmdSelect

        ' Automatically generate the Update, Insert,
        ' and Delete commands
        Dim cb As SqlClient.SqlCommandBuilder = _
        New SqlClient.SqlCommandBuilder(mda)

        ' Fill the DataSet and display it on the UI
        mds.Clear()
        mda.MissingSchemaAction = MissingSchemaAction.AddWithKey
```

```
        mda.Fill(mds, "Customers")
        dgMain.DataSource = mds
        dgMain.DataMember = "Customers"

    Catch ex As Exception
        MsgBox("Error: " & ex.Source & ": " & ex.Message, _
        MsgBoxStyle.OKOnly, "btnFillSchema")
    End Try

End Sub
```

This code is nearly identical to that of Listing 15.4, and it has the same effect on the user interface. The MissingSchemaAction property does allow some additional flexibility. This property is checked whenever you're adding a new column to the DataSet, and the DataSet doesn't contain a matching DataColumn. The property can take any of these values:

- MissingSchemaAction.Add to just add the column

- MissingSchemaAction.AddWithKey to add the column and any primary key constraint that includes the column

- MissingSchemaAction.Error to throw a runtime error

- MissingSchemaAction.Ignore to ignore the column

Using the FillWithSchema method or the MissingSchemaAction property has the same drawback as using the CommandBuilder object: It requires additional trips to the data source to retrieve the schema information, with the consequent performance penalty. If you know the structure of the data in advance, you may wish to create the primary key constraint directly in code instead. To do this, you actually need to build the entire DataTable in code. Listing 15.6 provides an example.

Listing 15.6:   **Creating a DataTable from Scratch**

```
Private Sub btnCreatePK_Click(ByVal sender As System.Object, _
  ByVal e As System.EventArgs) Handles btnCreatePK.Click
    Dim cnn As SqlClient.SqlConnection = _
    New SqlClient.SqlConnection("Data Source=SKYROCKET;" & _
    "Initial Catalog=Northwind;Integrated Security=SSPI")
    Dim cmdSelect As New SqlClient.SqlCommand()

    Try
        ' Create the Select command to grab the initial data
        cmdSelect = cnn.CreateCommand
        cmdSelect.CommandText = "SELECT CustomerID, CompanyName, " & _
        "ContactName FROM Customers"
        mda.SelectCommand = cmdSelect
```

```
        ' Automatically generate the Update, Insert,
        ' and Delete commands
        Dim cb As SqlClient.SqlCommandBuilder = _
        New SqlClient.SqlCommandBuilder(mda)

        ' Create the DataTable with a PK
        Dim dtCustomers As DataTable = _
        mds.Tables.Add("Customers")
        Dim dcPK As DataColumn = dtCustomers.Columns.Add( _
        "CustomerID", Type.GetType("System.String"))
        dtCustomers.Columns.Add("CompanyName", _
        Type.GetType("System.String"))
        dtCustomers.Columns.Add("ContactName", _
        Type.GetType("System.String"))
        dtCustomers.PrimaryKey = New DataColumn() {dcPK}

        ' Fill the DataSet and display it on the UI
        mds.Clear()
        mda.Fill(mds, "Customers")
        dgMain.DataSource = mds
        dgMain.DataMember = "Customers"

    Catch ex As Exception
        MsgBox("Error: " & ex.Source & ": " & ex.Message, _
        MsgBoxStyle.OKOnly, "btnFillSchema")
    End Try

End Sub
```

As you can see, building a DataTable is a relatively straightforward process:

1. Create the DataTable by calling the Add method of the DataSet.Tables collection.

2. Create the individual DataColumn objects in the DataTable by calling the Add method of the DataTable.Columns method. Note that this method takes system datatypes rather than data source datatypes.

3. Set the PrimaryKey property of the DataTable to point to one of the just-created columns. The code shows how to do this by creating a new DataColumn object from an existing DataColumn.

Although this method is the most tedious of the three demonstrated in this section, it's also the fastest (because it doesn't have to query the data source for schema information). At run-time, this code has the same effect as the FillSchema or MissingSchemaAction method; you'll get the same warning prompt if you try to enter a duplicate primary key.

TIP   In Chapter 27, "Using ADO.NET from Visual Basic .NET," you'll see some of the design-time tools that Visual Basic .NET provides to make this process less tedious.

Working with ADO.NET Events

Working with data always presents challenges. The user may enter data that makes no sense in the context of the application, you might need to do special processing for certain values, or you might be faced with the necessity to keep a record of changes for audit trail purposes. Fortunately, ADO.NET provides a reasonably rich set of events to allow you to intervene in the data editing process with your own code. In this section, I'll discuss the two main objects in the ADO.NET model that support data-related events:

- DataTable events
- DataAdapter events

Figure 15.3 shows the frmEvents form in this chapter's sample project. This form dumps information on events to the listbox as they happen. You can use it to see how user interaction with a DataSet triggers the various events. Listing 15.7 shows the code from frmEvents.

FIGURE 15.3:

Events during an editing session

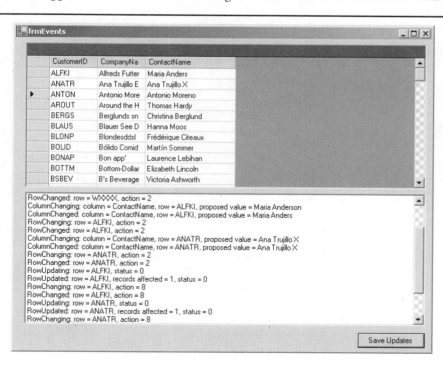

Listing 15.7:   frmEvents Source Code

```vb
Dim mda As New SqlClient.SqlDataAdapter()
Dim mds As New DataSet()

Private Sub frmEvents_Load(ByVal sender As System.Object, _
 ByVal e As System.EventArgs) Handles MyBase.Load
    Dim cnn As SqlClient.SqlConnection = _
     New SqlClient.SqlConnection("Data Source=SKYROCKET;" & _
     "Initial Catalog=Northwind;Integrated Security=SSPI")
    Dim cmdSelect As New SqlClient.SqlCommand()
    Dim cmdUpdate As New SqlClient.SqlCommand()
    Dim cmdInsert As New SqlClient.SqlCommand()
    Dim cmdDelete As New SqlClient.SqlCommand()
    Dim prm As SqlClient.SqlParameter

    Try
        ' Create the Select command to grab the initial data
        cmdSelect = cnn.CreateCommand
        cmdSelect.CommandText = "SELECT CustomerID, CompanyName, " & _
         "ContactName FROM Customers"
        mda.SelectCommand = cmdSelect

        ' The Update command handles updates to existing rows
        cmdUpdate = cnn.CreateCommand
        cmdUpdate.CommandText = "UPDATE Customers " & _
         "SET CompanyName = @CompanyName, " & _
         "ContactName = @ContactName " & _
         "WHERE CustomerID = @CustomerID"
        ' Now create the parameters that will be
        ' passed to this command
        prm = cmdUpdate.Parameters.Add("@CompanyName", _
         SqlDbType.NVarChar, 40, "CompanyName")
        prm = cmdUpdate.Parameters.Add("@ContactName", _
         SqlDbType.NVarChar, 30, "ContactName")
        prm = cmdUpdate.Parameters.Add("@CustomerID", _
         SqlDbType.NChar, 5, "CustomerID")
        prm.SourceVersion = DataRowVersion.Original
        mda.UpdateCommand = cmdUpdate

        ' The Delete command handles deletions of existing rows
        cmdDelete = cnn.CreateCommand
        cmdDelete.CommandText = "DELETE FROM Customers " & _
         "WHERE CustomerID = @CustomerID"
        ' Now create the parameter that will be
        ' passed to this command
        prm = cmdDelete.Parameters.Add("@CustomerID", _
         SqlDbType.NChar, 5, "CustomerID")
        prm.SourceVersion = DataRowVersion.Original
        mda.DeleteCommand = cmdDelete
```

```
            ' And the Insert command adds new rows
            cmdInsert = cnn.CreateCommand
            cmdInsert.CommandText = "INSERT INTO Customers " & _
             "(CustomerID, CompanyName, ContactName) " & _
             "VALUES(@CustomerID, @CompanyName, @ContactName)"
            ' Now create the parameters that will be
            ' passed to this command
            prm = cmdInsert.Parameters.Add("@CompanyName", _
             SqlDbType.NVarChar, 40, "CompanyName")
            prm = cmdInsert.Parameters.Add("@ContactName", _
             SqlDbType.NVarChar, 30, "ContactName")
            prm = cmdInsert.Parameters.Add("@CustomerID", _
             SqlDbType.NChar, 5, "CustomerID")
            mda.InsertCommand = cmdInsert

            ' Fill the DataSet and display it on the UI
            mda.Fill(mds, "Customers")
            dgMain.DataSource = mds
            dgMain.DataMember = "Customers"

            ' Set up event handlers
            AddHandler mds.Tables("Customers").ColumnChanging, _
             New DataColumnChangeEventHandler(AddressOf Column_Changing)
            AddHandler mds.Tables("Customers").ColumnChanged, _
             New DataColumnChangeEventHandler(AddressOf Column_Changed)
            AddHandler mds.Tables("Customers").RowChanging, _
             New DataRowChangeEventHandler(AddressOf Row_Changing)
            AddHandler mds.Tables("Customers").RowChanged, _
             New DataRowChangeEventHandler(AddressOf Row_Changed)
            AddHandler mds.Tables("Customers").RowDeleting, _
             New DataRowChangeEventHandler(AddressOf Row_Deleting)
            AddHandler mds.Tables("Customers").RowDeleted, _
             New DataRowChangeEventHandler(AddressOf Row_Deleted)
            AddHandler mda.RowUpdated, _
             New SqlClient.SqlRowUpdatedEventHandler(AddressOf Row_Updated)
            AddHandler mda.RowUpdating, _
             New SqlClient.SqlRowUpdatingEventHandler(AddressOf Row_Updating)

        Catch ex As Exception
            MsgBox("Error: " & ex.Source & ": " & ex.Message, _
            MsgBoxStyle.OKOnly, "frmUpdate_Load")
        End Try

    End Sub

    Private Sub btnSaveUpdates_Click(ByVal sender As System.Object, _
     ByVal e As System.EventArgs) Handles btnSaveUpdates.Click

        Try
            mda.Update(mds, "Customers")
        Catch ex As Exception
```

```vbnet
        MsgBox("Error: " & ex.Source & ": " & ex.Message, _
          MsgBoxStyle.OKOnly, "btnSaveUpdates")
      End Try

End Sub

Private Sub Column_Changing(ByVal sender As Object, _
 ByVal e As DataColumnChangeEventArgs)
    lboEvents.Items.Add("ColumnChanging: column = " & _
     e.Column.ColumnName & ", row = " & e.Row("CustomerID") & _
     ", proposed value = " & e.ProposedValue)
    If MsgBox("Cancel column change?", MsgBoxStyle.YesNo) = _
     MsgBoxResult.Yes Then
        e.ProposedValue = e.Row(e.Column.ColumnName)
    End If
End Sub

Private Sub Column_Changed(ByVal sender As Object, _
 ByVal e As DataColumnChangeEventArgs)
    lboEvents.Items.Add("ColumnChanged: column = " & _
     e.Column.ColumnName & ", row = " & e.Row("CustomerID") & _
     ", proposed value = " & e.ProposedValue)
End Sub

Private Sub Row_Changing(ByVal sender As Object, _
 ByVal e As DataRowChangeEventArgs)
    lboEvents.Items.Add("RowChanging: row = " & _
     e.Row("CustomerID") & _
     ", action = " & e.Action)
End Sub

Private Sub Row_Changed(ByVal sender As Object, _
 ByVal e As DataRowChangeEventArgs)
    lboEvents.Items.Add("RowChanged: row = " & _
     e.Row("CustomerID") & _
     ", action = " & e.Action)
End Sub

Private Sub Row_Deleting(ByVal sender As Object, _
 ByVal e As DataRowChangeEventArgs)
    lboEvents.Items.Add("RowDeleting: row = " & _
     e.Row("CustomerID") & _
     ", action = " & e.Action)
End Sub

Private Sub Row_Deleted(ByVal sender As Object, _
 ByVal e As DataRowChangeEventArgs)
    lboEvents.Items.Add("RowDeleted: " & _
     "action = " & e.Action)
End Sub
```

```
Private Sub Row_Updated(ByVal sender As Object, _
  ByVal e As SqlClient.SqlRowUpdatedEventArgs)
    lboEvents.Items.Add("RowUpdated: row = " & _
      e.Row("CustomerID") & _
      ", records affected = " & e.RecordsAffected & _
      ", status = " & e.Status)
End Sub

Private Sub Row_Updating(ByVal sender As Object, _
  ByVal e As SqlClient.SqlRowUpdatingEventArgs)
    lboEvents.Items.Add("RowUpdating: row = " & _
      e.Row("CustomerID") & _
      ", status = " & e.Status)
End Sub
```

DataTable Events

When you're editing data in a DataTable, you can monitor events on either a row-by-row or column-by-column basis. The six events supported by the DataTable come in three pairs, whose before-and-after structure will be familiar to you if you've looked at ADO Recordset events:

- ColumnChanging and ColumnChanged
- RowChanging and RowChanged
- RowDeleting and RowDeleted

The ColumnChanging and ColumnChanged Events

The ColumnChanging and ColumnChanged events fire whenever the data in a column of a DataSet is changed. The ColumnChanging event fires just before the change is committed to the DataSet; the ColumnChanged event fires just after the change is made.

ADO.NET passes to each of these events an argument whose type is DataColumnChangeEventArgs. This argument has three properties containing information about the event:

Column   The DataColumn object whose contents are being changed

ProposedValue   The new value being assigned to the data

Row   The DataRow object whose contents are being changed

Although the ColumnChanging event doesn't have an explicit Cancel argument, you can achieve the effect of cancelling the change by reassigning the original data to the ProposedValue property within the event procedure. The code for frmEvents prompts the user with a message box asking whether to discard the change:

```
If MsgBox("Cancel column change?", MsgBoxStyle.YesNo) = _
  MsgBoxResult.Yes Then
      e.ProposedValue = e.Row(e.Column.ColumnName)
  End If
```

The ColumnChanging and ColumnChanged events fire as soon as you leave the affected column. If you're editing multiple columns in the same row of data, these events will fire once per column. They fire when you're adding a new row of data to a DataSet, as well as when you're editing an existing row.

The RowChanging and RowChanged Events

The RowChanging and RowChanged events fire whenever the data in a row of a DataSet is changed. The RowChanging event fires just before the change is committed to the DataSet; the RowChanged event fires just after the change is made. These events fire once per row, regardless of how many columns are edited in the row. The RowChanging and RowChanged events fire after all of the ColumnChanging and ColumnChanged events for the row.

ADO.NET passes to each of these events an argument whose type is DataRowChange-EventArgs. This argument has two properties containing information about the event:

Action Specifies the action that fired the event. Table 15.1 lists the values for this property.

Row The DataRow whose contents are being changed.

TABLE 15.1: Action Values

Value	Meaning
Add	The row has been added to the table.
Change	The row has been edited.
Commit	The changes in the row have been committed.
Delete	The row has been deleted from the table.
Nothing	The row has not changed.
Rollback	A change has been rolled back.

The RowDeleting and RowDeleted Events

The RowDeleting and RowDeleted events fire whenever a row is deleted from the DataSet. The RowDeleting event fires just before the row is deleted; the RowDeleted event fires just after the deletion is final. These events fire once per row. Deletions do not trigger any column-level events.

ADO.NET passes to each of these events an argument whose type is DataRowChange-EventArgs. This argument has two properties containing information about the event:

Action   Specifies the action that fired the event. Table 15.1 lists the values for this property.

Row   The DataRow whose contents are being changed.

The Row property isn't valid in the RowDeleted event, because by then the row has already been deleted.

You might think that you could cancel a deletion by setting the Action property to DataRowAction.Nothing, but the Action property is read-only in these events. You can't cancel a deletion within these events. Remember, though, that you have full control over whether the deletion is committed back to the underlying data source through your calls to the DataAdapter.Update method, as you saw earlier in the chapter. Alternatively, you could carry out the deletion in the context of a transaction and commit or roll back the transaction as you see fit. I'll discuss transactions later in the chapter.

DataAdapter Events

The DataAdapter, too, has a pair of data-related events: RowUpdated and RowUpdating. These events fire when data is being written back to the data source in the course of the DataAdapter.Update method.

The RowUpdating and RowUpdated Events

When you call the DataAdapter.Update method, the following sequence of actions and events occurs:

1. The values in the DataRow are moved to the parameters of the appropriate Command (InsertCommand, UpdateCommand, or DeleteCommand).

2. The RowUpdating event fires.

3. The appropriate Command is executed.

4. Any output parameters are copied back to the DataRow.

5. The RowUpdated event fires.

6. The DataRow.AcceptChanges method is called.

These actions happen once for each row that's being altered by the Update method.

ADO.NET passes an argument of type SqlRowUpdatingEventArgs to the RowUpdating event. This argument has these properties:

Command   The Command about to be executed.

Errors   Any errors generated by the Command.

Row   The DataRow being updated.

StatementType   The type of SQL statement being executed (Select, Insert, Update, or Delete).

Status   The UpdateStatus of the change. See Table 15.2 for the possible values of this argument.

TableMapping   The TableMapping object being changed by this update.

TABLE 15.2: UpdateStatus Values

Value	Meaning
Continue	Continue processing rows.
ErrorsOccurred	Errors occurred during this update.
SkipAllRemainingRows	Stop updating entirely.
SkipCurrentRow	Skip this row and continue updating.

ADO.NET passes an argument of type SqlRowUpdatedEventArgs to the RowUpdated event. This argument has these properties:

Command   The Command that was executed.

Errors   Any errors generated by the Command.

RecordsAffected   The number of rows in the data source affected by the Command.

Row   The DataRow being updated.

StatementType   The type of SQL statement being executed (Select, Insert, Update, or Delete).

Status   The UpdateStatus of the change. See Table 15.2 for the possible values of this argument.

TableMapping   The TableMapping object being changed by this update.

Order of Updating Events

If you're monitoring all the events for the DataTable and DataAdapter, you'll discover that the events of both objects fire when you call the DataAdapter.Update method. Here's the order of update events:

1. The RowUpdating event fires for the appropriate row.

2. The RowUpdated event fires for the appropriate row.

3. The RowChanging event fires for the appropriate row with an Action value of `DataRowAction.Commit`. This is the result of the call to AcceptChanges in the update sequence.

4. The RowChanged event fires for the appropriate row with an Action value of `DataRowAction.Commit`.

Managing Concurrency and Transactions

Just about any data access library offers facilities for dealing with multiuser issues, and ADO.NET is no exception. Broadly speaking, these facilities break down into two areas:

- *Concurrency* deals with the problems that come about when multiple users work with the same data at the same time.

- *Transactions* deal with the problems that arise when multiple tables need to be updated in a single operation.

In this section, I'll demonstrate the concurrency and transaction support in ADO.NET.

Concurrency

You're probably familiar with the distinction between optimistic locking and pessimistic locking from libraries such as ADO:

With *optimistic locking*, users are prevented from updating a record while another user is updating that record.

With *pessimistic locking*, users are prevented from editing a record while another user is editing that record.

In ADO.NET, the choices change somewhat. That's because disconnected DataSets (the core data-editing tool in ADO.NET) are fundamentally inconsistent with pessimistic locking. In almost all applications, it doesn't make sense to lock records for the entire time that someone has them loaded into a DataSet, which is what you'd need to do to implement pessimistic locking.

Instead, ADO.NET lets you choose between two strategies when you're creating the Command objects that will be used with a DataAdapter to update data:

- With optimistic concurrency control, you can update a row only if no one else has updated that row since you loaded it into your DataSet.

- With "last one wins" concurrency control, you can always update a row, whether another user has changed it or not.

The frmConcurrency form in this chapter's sample project lets you experiment with these two strategies. It does this by switching the Commands for the DataAdapter between two versions. To illustrate, Listing 15.8 shows the bit of code that sets the UpdateCommand property.

Listing 15.8:   **Switching Versions of the UpdateCommand**

```
If rbOptimistic.Checked Then
    ' Optimistic concurrency

    ' The Update command handles updates to existing rows
    cmdUpdate = cnn.CreateCommand
    cmdUpdate.CommandText = "UPDATE Customers " & _
      "SET CompanyName = @CompanyName, " & _
      "ContactName = @ContactName " & _
      "WHERE CustomerID = @CustomerID AND " & _
      "CompanyName = @CompanyNameOrig AND " & _
      "ContactName = @ContactNameOrig"
    ' Now create the parameters that will be
    ' passed to this command
    prm = cmdUpdate.Parameters.Add("@CompanyName", _
      SqlDbType.NVarChar, 40, "CompanyName")
    prm = cmdUpdate.Parameters.Add("@ContactName", _
      SqlDbType.NVarChar, 30, "ContactName")
    prm = cmdUpdate.Parameters.Add("@CustomerID", _
      SqlDbType.NChar, 5, "CustomerID")
    prm.SourceVersion = DataRowVersion.Original
    prm = cmdUpdate.Parameters.Add("@CompanyNameOrig", _
      SqlDbType.NVarChar, 40, "CompanyName")
    prm.SourceVersion = DataRowVersion.Original
    prm = cmdUpdate.Parameters.Add("@ContactNameOrig", _
      SqlDbType.NVarChar, 30, "ContactName")
    prm.SourceVersion = DataRowVersion.Original
    mda.UpdateCommand = cmdUpdate
  ' other code omitted
Else
    ' "Last one wins" concurrency

    ' The Update command handles updates to existing rows
    cmdUpdate = cnn.CreateCommand
    cmdUpdate.CommandText = "UPDATE Customers " & _
      "SET CompanyName = @CompanyName, " & _
      "ContactName = @ContactName " & _
      "WHERE CustomerID = @CustomerID"
    ' Now create the parameters that will be
    ' passed to this command
    prm = cmdUpdate.Parameters.Add("@CompanyName", _
      SqlDbType.NVarChar, 40, "CompanyName")
    prm = cmdUpdate.Parameters.Add("@ContactName", _
      SqlDbType.NVarChar, 30, "ContactName")
```

```
    prm = cmdUpdate.Parameters.Add("@CustomerID", _
      SqlDbType.NChar, 5, "CustomerID")
    prm.SourceVersion = DataRowVersion.Original
    mda.UpdateCommand = cmdUpdate
  ' other code omitted
  End If
```

To implement optimistic concurrency, the code uses a SQL WHERE clause that checks to see that every column in the data source exactly matches the original value of that column in the DataSet. This ensures that the record will be found (and therefore updated) only if no other user has changed the record. To implement last-one-wins concurrency, the code locates the record by primary key only and then updates it regardless of what values are in the other columns. Figure 15.4 shows this form in action.

FIGURE 15.4:

Experimenting with concurrency

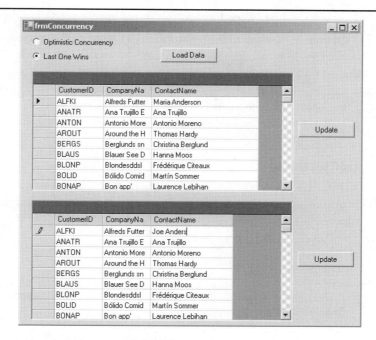

To see the effects of these two choices, follow these steps:

1. Run the sample project and open the Concurrency form.

2. Select the Optimistic Concurrency radio button and click the Load Data button.

3. Make a change to the first row of the first DataGrid.

4. Make a different change to the first row of the second DataGrid.

5. Click the Update button for the first DataGrid.

6. Click the Update button for the second DataGrid.

7. Click the Load Data button. You'll see that only the first update was made to the data. That's because when you clicked the second Update button, the WHERE clause didn't match any records; thus, the update was silently discarded.

8. Select the Last One Wins radio button and click the Load Data button.

9. Make a change to the first row of the first DataGrid.

10. Make a different change to the first row of the second DataGrid.

11. Click the Update button for the first DataGrid.

12. Click the Update button for the second DataGrid.

13. Click the Load Data button. You'll see that the second update overwrote the first update.

Of course, you're not limited to a silent failure in the case of an optimistic update that can't find a row. You can, for example, return the record count from the SQL statement and check that to find out whether an update was rejected.

TIP In Chapter 27, you'll see the built-in tools that Visual Basic .NET provides for managing concurrency via the user interface.

Transactions

ADO.NET also provides built-in support for transactions (provided that the underlying data provider supports transactions). This support is implemented through three methods of two objects:

```
Connection.BeginTransaction
Transaction.Commit
Transaction.Rollback
```

NOTE If you need a refresher on the ACID properties that characterize transactions, refer to Chapter 4, "Editing Data with ADO."

When you call the BeginTransaction method of the Connection object, the Connection's underlying data provider will return a Transaction object if the data provider supports transactions. It then starts grouping all subsequent data changes associated with this object into a transaction. This includes updates, additions, and deletions. None of these changes will be immediately written to the database.

When you call the Commit method of the Transaction object, all data changes associated with that Transaction object are committed to the database.

When you call the Rollback method of the Transaction object, all data changes associated with that Transaction object are discarded.

By associating transactions with a particular object, ADO.NET allows you to execute both transacted and non-transacted operations on the same Connection at the same time. This is an improvement over ADO, in which all operations on the Connection are part of a single transaction.

The btnTransactions_Click procedure in the frmMenu form in this chapter's sample project demonstrates the use of the transaction methods. Listing 15.9 shows the code behind this form.

Listing 15.9:   **Using Transactions with ADO.NET**

```
Private Sub btnTransactions_Click(ByVal sender As System.Object, _
  ByVal e As System.EventArgs) Handles btnTransactions.Click
    Dim cnn As SqlClient.SqlConnection = _
     New SqlClient.SqlConnection("Data Source=SKYROCKET;" & _
     "Initial Catalog=Northwind;Integrated Security=SSPI")
    ' Start a transaction
    cnn.Open()
    Dim trn As SqlTransaction = cnn.BeginTransaction()
    Try
        ' Create a command and associate it with the transaction
        Dim cmd As SqlCommand = New SqlCommand()
        cmd.Transaction = trn
        ' Now execute a couple of SQL statements on the transaction
        cmd.CommandText = "INSERT INTO Customers " & _
         "CustomerID, CompanyName " & _
         "VALUES ('ZZZZZ', 'Z Industries')"
        cmd.ExecuteNonQuery()
        cmd.CommandText = "INSERT INTO Customers " & _
         "CustomerID, CompanyName " & _
         "VALUES ('ZZZZZ', 'Zebra Riders Inc.')"
        cmd.ExecuteNonQuery()
        ' And try to commit the transaction
        trn.Commit()
        MsgBox("Transaction succeeded")
    Catch ex As Exception
        ' In case of any problem, roll back the whole transaction
        trn.Rollback()
        MsgBox("Transaction failed")
    Finally
        cnn.Close()
    End Try
End Sub
```

In this particular case, you'll see the "Transaction failed" message. That's because the second Command tries to insert a record in the table that would duplicate the key of the record that the first Command loaded. This causes an error, which forces the code into the Catch block, where it executes the Rollback method.

Summary

In this chapter, you saw how to use ADO.NET to perform the basic data-editing operations of updating an existing record, adding a new record, and deleting an existing record. The key to all these operations lies in the proper configuration of the DataAdapter object. You also learned how to use the CommandBuilder object to eliminate some code, how to use primary key constraints, and how to monitor ADO.NET data events. Finally, you saw how to use particular Command objects to give you some control over concurrency and how to work with transactions in ADO.NET.

In the next chapter, I'll dig further into the notion of disconnected data, which lies at the heart of ADO.NET, and show how you can easily move data between components of a distributed application.

CHAPTER 16

Working with Disconnected DataSets

- Converting DataSets to XML

- Reconstituting an XML DataSet

- DataSets via web services

N ow that you've seen the basic DataSet operations, it's time to dig a bit further into how ADO.NET fits with the rest of the .NET Framework. In this chapter, I'll look at how XML provides facilities for disconnected DataSets. As you already know, *all* DataSets are disconnected. The purpose of this chapter is to show you how to convert those DataSets into an XML format that's easier to move around among components in multitiered applications.

Converting DataSets to XML

ADO.NET DataSets are designed to be easily converted to XML representations. In fact, the conversion is very flexible: You can decide whether to include an XSD schema, and even control the way that each column is represented in the resulting XML file. There are four methods of the DataSet that work together to produce XML:

- *GetXml* returns an XML representation of the DataSet as a string.
- *GetXmlSchema* returns an XSD representation of the DataSet's schema as a string.
- *WriteXml* writes an XML representation of the DataSet (with or without schema information) to a file, stream, TextWriter, or XmlWriter object.
- *WriteXmlSchema* writes an XSD representation of the DataSet's schema to a file, stream, TextWriter, or XmlWriter object.

I'll explain each of these methods in more depth in this section.

Using GetXml

The simplest way to retrieve an XML representation of a DataSet is to use the GetXml method of the DataSet object. Listing 16.1 is an example of code from frmGetXML in the ADOChapter16 sample project; it first loads two tables into a DataSet and then uses the GetXml method to return the XML representation of that DataSet.

Listing 16.1:   **Using the GetXml Method**

```
Dim mds As New DataSet()

Public Sub New()
    MyBase.New()

    'This call is required by the Windows Form Designer
    InitializeComponent()

    'Add any initialization after the InitializeComponent() call
    Dim cnn As SqlConnection = _
     New SqlClient.SqlConnection("Data Source=SKYROCKET;" & _
     "Initial Catalog=Northwind;Integrated Security=SSPI")
```

```
        Dim cmdCustomers As New SqlCommand()
        Dim daCustomers As New SqlDataAdapter()
        Dim cmdOrders As New SqlCommand()
        Dim daOrders As New SqlDataAdapter()

        Try
            mds.DataSetName = "CustomerOrders"

            cmdCustomers = cnn.CreateCommand
            cmdCustomers.CommandText = "SELECT * FROM Customers"
            daCustomers.SelectCommand = cmdCustomers
            daCustomers.Fill(mds, "Customers")

            cmdOrders = cnn.CreateCommand
            cmdOrders.CommandText = "SELECT * FROM Orders"
            daOrders.SelectCommand = cmdOrders
            daOrders.Fill(mds, "Orders")

            Dim relCustOrder As DataRelation = _
             mds.Relations.Add("CustOrder", _
             mds.Tables("Customers").Columns("CustomerID"), _
             mds.Tables("Orders").Columns("CustomerID"))

        Catch ex As Exception
            MsgBox("Error: " & ex.Source & ": " & ex.Message, _
            MsgBoxStyle.OKOnly, "New")
        End Try

    End Sub

    Private Sub btnGetXml_Click(ByVal sender As System.Object, _
     ByVal e As System.EventArgs) Handles btnGetXml.Click

        Try
            txtXML.Text = mds.GetXml
        Catch ex As Exception
            MsgBox("Error: " & ex.Source & ": " & ex.Message, _
            MsgBoxStyle.OKOnly, "btnGetXml_Click")
        End Try

    End Sub
```

If you run this code and inspect the resulting XML, you'll find that it looks something like Listing 16.2.

Listing 16.2:   **A DataSet Converted to XML**

```
<CustomerOrders>
  <Customers>
    <CustomerID>ALFKI</CustomerID>
```

```
        <CompanyName>Alfreds Futterkiste</CompanyName>
        <ContactName>Maria Anders</ContactName>
        <ContactTitle>Sales Representative</ContactTitle>
        <Address>Obere Str. 57</Address>
        <City>Berlin</City>
        <PostalCode>12209</PostalCode>
        <Country>Germany</Country>
        <Phone>030-0074321</Phone>
        <Fax>030-0076545</Fax>
      </Customers>
      <Customers>
        <CustomerID>ANATR</CustomerID>
        <CompanyName>Ana Trujillo Emparedados y helados</CompanyName>
        <ContactName>Ana Trujillo</ContactName>
        <ContactTitle>Owner</ContactTitle>
        <Address>Avda. de la Constitución 2222</Address>
        <City>México D.F.</City>
        <PostalCode>05021</PostalCode>
        <Country>Mexico</Country>
        <Phone>(5) 555-4729</Phone>
        <Fax>(5) 555-3745</Fax>
      </Customers>
Additional Customers omitted...
      <Orders>
        <OrderID>10248</OrderID>
        <CustomerID>ALFKI</CustomerID>
        <EmployeeID>5</EmployeeID>
        <OrderDate>1996-07-04T00:00:00.0000000-07:00</OrderDate>
        <RequiredDate>1996-08-01T00:00:00.0000000-07:00</RequiredDate>
        <ShippedDate>1996-07-16T00:00:00.0000000-07:00</ShippedDate>
        <ShipVia>3</ShipVia>
        <Freight>32.38</Freight>
        <ShipName>Vins et alcools Chevalier</ShipName>
        <ShipAddress>59 rue de l'Abbaye</ShipAddress>
        <ShipCity>Reims</ShipCity>
        <ShipPostalCode>51100</ShipPostalCode>
        <ShipCountry>France</ShipCountry>
      </Orders>
      <Orders>
        <OrderID>10249</OrderID>
        <CustomerID>TOMSP</CustomerID>
        <EmployeeID>6</EmployeeID>
        <OrderDate>1996-07-05T00:00:00.0000000-07:00</OrderDate>
        <RequiredDate>1996-08-16T00:00:00.0000000-07:00</RequiredDate>
        <ShippedDate>1996-07-10T00:00:00.0000000-07:00</ShippedDate>
        <ShipVia>1</ShipVia>
        <Freight>11.62</Freight>
        <ShipName>Toms Spezialitäten</ShipName>
        <ShipAddress>Luisenstr. 48</ShipAddress>
        <ShipCity>Münster</ShipCity>
        <ShipPostalCode>44087</ShipPostalCode>
```

```
    <ShipCountry>Germany</ShipCountry>
  </Orders>
Additional Orders omitted...
</CustomerOrders>
```

The outermost element, CustomerOrders, has the name of the DataSet (as assigned in the code with the `DataSet.DataSetName` property). Then come all the rows from the first Data-Table in the DataSet. Then come all the rows from the second table in the DataSet, and so on.

As you can see, the default XML created by a DataSet doesn't intermingle the rows from different DataTables, even if the DataTables are related. Every field in each row is saved as a separate XML element; this is sometimes called *element-centric* XML. The alternative to element-centric XML is *attribute-centric* XML, in which every field is saved as an attribute of a single XML element that represents an entire row. Later in the chapter, I'll show you how to produce attribute-centric XML, or to change some of the other defaults used by .NET in producing XML from a DataSet.

Using GetXmlSchema

The GetXmlSchema method of the DataSet object is just as simple as the GetXml method:

```
Private Sub btnGetXmlSchema_Click(ByVal sender As System.Object, _
  ByVal e As System.EventArgs) Handles btnGetXmlSchema.Click

    Try
        txtXML.Text = mds.GetXmlSchema
    Catch ex As Exception
        MsgBox("Error: " & ex.Source & ": " & ex.Message, _
          MsgBoxStyle.OKOnly, "btnGetXmlSchema_Click")
    End Try

End Sub
```

The output from calling this method, shown in Listing 16.3, is a properly formed XSD document describing the contents of the CustomerOrders DataSet:

Listing 16.3:   **An XML Schema File**

```
<?xml version="1.0" encoding="utf-16"?>
<xs:schema id="CustomerOrders" xmlns=""
➥    xmlns:xs="http://www.w3.org/2001/XMLSchema"
➥    xmlns:msdata="urn:schemas-microsoft-com:xml-msdata">
  <xs:element name="CustomerOrders" msdata:IsDataSet="true">
    <xs:complexType>
      <xs:choice maxOccurs="unbounded">
        <xs:element name="Customers">
```

```
<xs:complexType>
  <xs:sequence>
    <xs:element name="CustomerID" type="xs:string"
    minOccurs="0" />
    <xs:element name="CompanyName" type="xs:string"
    minOccurs="0" />
    <xs:element name="ContactName" type="xs:string"
    minOccurs="0" />
    <xs:element name="ContactTitle" type="xs:string"
    minOccurs="0" />
    <xs:element name="Address" type="xs:string" minOccurs="0" />
    <xs:element name="City" type="xs:string" minOccurs="0" />
    <xs:element name="Region" type="xs:string" minOccurs="0" />
    <xs:element name="PostalCode" type="xs:string"
    minOccurs="0" />
    <xs:element name="Country" type="xs:string" minOccurs="0" />
    <xs:element name="Phone" type="xs:string" minOccurs="0" />
    <xs:element name="Fax" type="xs:string" minOccurs="0" />
  </xs:sequence>
</xs:complexType>
</xs:element>
<xs:element name="Orders">
  <xs:complexType>
    <xs:sequence>
      <xs:element name="OrderID" type="xs:int" minOccurs="0" />
      <xs:element name="CustomerID" type="xs:string"
      minOccurs="0" />
      <xs:element name="EmployeeID" type="xs:int" minOccurs="0" />
      <xs:element name="OrderDate" type="xs:dateTime"
      minOccurs="0" />
      <xs:element name="RequiredDate" type="xs:dateTime"
      minOccurs="0" />
      <xs:element name="ShippedDate" type="xs:dateTime"
      minOccurs="0" />
      <xs:element name="ShipVia" type="xs:int" minOccurs="0" />
      <xs:element name="Freight" type="xs:decimal"
      minOccurs="0" />
      <xs:element name="ShipName" type="xs:string"
      minOccurs="0" />
      <xs:element name="ShipAddress" type="xs:string"
      minOccurs="0" />
      <xs:element name="ShipCity" type="xs:string"
      minOccurs="0" />
      <xs:element name="ShipRegion" type="xs:string"
      minOccurs="0" />
      <xs:element name="ShipPostalCode" type="xs:string"
      minOccurs="0" />
      <xs:element name="ShipCountry" type="xs:string"
      minOccurs="0" />
    </xs:sequence>
  </xs:complexType>
```

```
          </xs:element>
        </xs:choice>
      </xs:complexType>
      <xs:unique name="Constraint1">
        <xs:selector xpath=".//Customers" />
        <xs:field xpath="CustomerID" />
      </xs:unique>
      <xs:keyref name="CustOrder" refer="Constraint1">
        <xs:selector xpath=".//Orders" />
        <xs:field xpath="CustomerID" />
      </xs:keyref>
    </xs:element>
  </xs:schema>
```

Although I introduced XSD documents in Chapter 14, "Using the ADO.NET Objects to Retrieve Data," I haven't taken a close look at the XSD syntax yet. This document will serve well to demonstrate the key pieces of XSD that ADO.NET uses.

TIP Formally, XSD documents are described by the XML Schema specification endorsed by the W3C. You can find much more information about XSD online at www.w3.org/XML/Schema.

As with any other XML file, an XSD file starts with a section of declarations:

```
<?xml version="1.0" encoding="utf-16"?>
<xs:schema id="CustomerOrders" xmlns=""
➥   xmlns:xs="http://www.w3.org/2001/XMLSchema"
➥   xmlns:msdata="urn:schemas-microsoft-com:xml-msdata">
```

The first of these, of course, identifies the document as being XML. The second points to the official XML Schema specification. The third points to a proprietary Microsoft name-space that extends the XML Schema.

The next thing the file does is specify that it's a description of the CustomerOrders object, which is a DataSet:

```
<xs:element name="CustomerOrders" msdata:IsDataSet="true">
  <xs:complexType>
```

The <xs:complexType> tag indicates that CustomerOrders is a datatype that consists of other datatypes. Child tags of this tag indicate the internal structure of the CustomerOrders datatype. Consider this part of the XSD document:

```
<xs:element name="CustomerOrders" msdata:IsDataSet="true">
  <xs:complexType>
    <xs:choice maxOccurs="unbounded">
      <xs:element name="Customers">
        <xs:complexType>
...
```

```
          </xs:complexType>
        </xs:element>
        <xs:element name="Orders">
          <xs:complexType>
...
          </xs:complexType>
        </xs:element>
      </xs:choice>
    </xs:complexType>
```

The `<xs:choice>` tag indicates that the CustomerOrders type can contain any of the child datatypes of the `<xs:choice>` tag. The `maxOccurs="unbounded"` attribute of this tag indicates that you can make an unlimited number of choices. The children of this tag are two other XSD elements, named Customers and Orders. Each of these is itself a complex datatype. The net effect of this section is to specify that the CustomerOrders type (which, remember, represents the entire DataSet) can contain an unlimited number of children, each of which can be either an instance of the Customers datatype or an instance of the Orders datatype.

Now focus on the description of the Customers datatype:

```
<xs:element name="Customers">
  <xs:complexType>
    <xs:sequence>
      <xs:element name="CustomerID" type="xs:string"
    minOccurs="0" />
      <xs:element name="CompanyName" type="xs:string"
    minOccurs="0" />
      <xs:element name="ContactName" type="xs:string"
    minOccurs="0" />
      <xs:element name="ContactTitle" type="xs:string"
    minOccurs="0" />
      <xs:element name="Address" type="xs:string" minOccurs="0" />
      <xs:element name="City" type="xs:string" minOccurs="0" />
      <xs:element name="Region" type="xs:string" minOccurs="0" />
      <xs:element name="PostalCode" type="xs:string"
    minOccurs="0" />
      <xs:element name="Country" type="xs:string" minOccurs="0" />
      <xs:element name="Phone" type="xs:string" minOccurs="0" />
      <xs:element name="Fax" type="xs:string" minOccurs="0" />
    </xs:sequence>
  </xs:complexType>
```

The `<xs:sequence>` tag specifies that the elements within the Customers datatype must appear in the specified order. This means that the XML preserves the column ordering of the DataTable. Each of the child elements (for example, `<xs:element name="City" type="xs:string" minOccurs="0" />`) specifies one column in the DataTable with a column name, a datatype, and information about repetition. Here, each column is specified to occur at least zero times; there's an implied maximum of one time if the XSD doesn't specify a maxOccurs argument. The non-complex datatypes (such as string, int, and datetime) are part of the XSD specification.

The section following the description of the Customers DataTable is a description of the Orders DataTable. Finally, the XSD description captures the information that describes the DataRelation that connects the two tables:

```
<xs:unique name="Constraint1">
  <xs:selector xpath=".//Customers" />
  <xs:field xpath="CustomerID" />
</xs:unique>
<xs:keyref name="CustOrder" refer="Constraint1">
  <xs:selector xpath=".//Orders" />
  <xs:field xpath="CustomerID" />
</xs:keyref>
```

This section uses the XPath language (another of the array of XML standards) to specify that CustomerIDs in the Customers DataTable are unique and that CustomerIDs in the Orders DataTable refer to those unique IDs.

NOTE   For more details on XPath, see Chapter 18, "Synchronizing DataSets with XML."

Using WriteXml

WriteXml provides another way to turn a DataSet into XML. It features some enhancements over GetXml:

- Because it can send information directly to a stream or file, it's faster for many applications than GetXml.

- It offers a choice of XML formats, including XML with embedded XSD information and the DiffGram format.

The general syntax of the WriteXml method is as follows:

```
DataSet.WriteXml(Destination, WriteMode)
```

The *Destination* parameter can be any of the following:

- A Stream object
- The name of a file to write to
- A TextWriter object
- An XmlWriter object

The *WriteMode* parameter can be any one of the XmlWriteMode constants shown in Table 16.1.

TABLE 16.1: XmlWriteMode Constants

Constant	Meaning
WriteSchema	Embed XSD schema information directly in the XML file. This is the default.
IgnoreSchema	Do not include any schema information. With IgnoreSchema, the WriteXml method produces the same XML as the GetXml method.
DiffGram	Write the entire DataSet as a DiffGram.

The frmWriteXml form in this chapter's sample project lets you experiment with different combinations of destination objects and write modes. In each case, the code writes the resulting XML to a disk file, but the syntax for doing so varies. The code behind this form starts by creating a DataSet and then uses the user's choice on the form to pick the proper XmlWriteMode constant:

```
' Get the write mode
Dim xm As New XmlWriteMode()
If rbWriteSchema.Checked Then
    xm = XmlWriteMode.WriteSchema
ElseIf rbIgnoreSchema.Checked Then
    xm = XmlWriteMode.IgnoreSchema
Else
    xm = XmlWriteMode.DiffGram
End If
```

Another set of conditional statements then determines the destination to use with the WriteXml method. For starters, here's some code that uses WriteXml to write to a Stream:

```
If rbStream.Checked Then
    ' Write to stream
    Dim sfd As New SaveFileDialog()
    sfd.Filter = "XML files (*.xml)|*.xml|All Files(*.*)|*.*"
    sfd.ShowDialog()
    Dim strFileName As String = sfd.FileName
    If Len(strFileName) > 0 Then
        Dim fs As New System.IO.FileStream _
            (strFilename, System.IO.FileMode.Create)
        ds.WriteXml(fs, xm)
    End If
```

TIP   The SaveFileDialog class displays the operating system's Save File dialog box when you invoke the SaveFileDialog.ShowDialog method. The filename the user selected (if any) is returned in the SaveFileDialog.FileName property.

Here, the particular Stream is a FileStream object, which inherits from the basic Stream class, and which writes directly to a file. Other implementations of the Stream class that can be used here are the BufferedStream class (which uses a memory buffer to accumulate the data being written, to minimize the performance impact of the disk writes) and the Memory-Stream class (which stores its data in memory rather than on disk, thus providing a fast implementation for temporary files).

The advantage of using the Stream class to handle this task is that you can pass different implementations of Stream to your code, allowing you, for example, to switch easily between file and memory storage. If you're going to write the XML only to a disk file, it's simpler to pass the filename to the WriteXml method directly:

```
ElseIf rbFileName.Checked Then
    ' Write to file by name
    Dim sfd As New SaveFileDialog()
    sfd.Filter = "XML files (*.xml)|*.xml|All Files(*.*)|*.*"
    sfd.ShowDialog()
    Dim strFileName As String = sfd.FileName
    If Len(strFileName) > 0 Then
        ds.WriteXml(strFileName, xm)
    End If
```

The code that uses a TextWriter object is very similar to the two versions you've already seen:

```
ElseIf rbTextWriter.Checked Then
    ' Write to TextWriter
    Dim sfd As New SaveFileDialog()
    sfd.Filter = "XML files (*.xml)|*.xml|All Files(*.*)|*.*"
    sfd.ShowDialog()
    Dim strFileName As String = sfd.FileName
    If Len(strFileName) > 0 Then
        Dim tw As TextWriter = New StreamWriter(strFileName)
        ds.WriteXml(tw, xm)
    End If
```

This particular piece of code uses a StreamWriter object as an implementation of the Text-Writer class. The StreamWriter acts as a pipeline between the WriteXml method and the actual destination of the data—in this case, a text file. Other implementations of TextWriter include these:

- System.Web.HttpWriter, which sends its output through an HttpResponse object to a web page

- System.IO.StreamWriter, which writes to file streams

- System.IO.StringWriter, which writes its output to a string

You'll probably want to use the TextWriter class for writing XML only when you need to build in the flexibility to handle these (and other) destinations.

Finally, the code that uses an XmlWriter object looks like this:

```
Else
    ' Write to XmlWriter
    Dim sfd As New SaveFileDialog()
    sfd.Filter = "XML files (*.xml)|*.xml|All Files(*.*)|*.*"
    sfd.ShowDialog()
    Dim strFileName As String = sfd.FileName
    If Len(strFileName) > 0 Then
        Dim fs As New FileStream _
            (strFileName, FileMode.Create)
        Dim xw As New System.Xml.XmlTextWriter _
            (fs, System.Text.Encoding.Unicode)
        xw.WriteStartDocument()
        ds.WriteXml(xw, xm)
        xw.Close()
    End If
```

This code uses the XmlTextWriter implementation of XmlWriter to send the output to a file via a FileStream object. The best thing about using the XmlWriter (or its subclasses) is that it actually has proper XML syntax built in, making it possible to modify the generated XML without fear of syntactical errors. For example, the call to the WriteStartDocument method of the XmlTextWriter object adds a proper XML header to the start of the file.

The exact format of the XML created by WriteXml depends on the XmlWriteMode constant that you select, and whether there are any changes in the DataSet that haven't already been persisted. If you use the IgnoreSchema constant, you'll get the same XML from WriteXml that you would from GetXml. If you use WriteSchema, you'll get a file that first has the schema information and then the data information. This is almost (but not quite) a combination of the formats provided by GetXml and GetXmlSchema. Listing 16.4 shows a sample of the XML produced by calling the WriteXml method.

Listing 16.4:   **XML Created by WriteXml with WriteSchema**

```
<?xml version="1.0" standalone="yes"?>
<CustomerOrders>
  <xs:schema id="CustomerOrders" xmlns=""
➥ xmlns:xs="http://www.w3.org/2001/XMLSchema"
➥ xmlns:msdata="urn:schemas-microsoft-com:xml-msdata">
Other XSD information omitted...
  </xs:schema>
  <Customers>
    <CustomerID>ALFKI</CustomerID>
```

```
         <CompanyName>Alfreds Futterkiste</CompanyName>
         <ContactName>Joe Graham</ContactName>
         <ContactTitle>Sales Representative</ContactTitle>
         <Address>Obere Str. 57</Address>
         <City>Berlin</City>
         <PostalCode>12209</PostalCode>
         <Country>Germany</Country>
         <Phone>030-0074321</Phone>
         <Fax>030-0076545</Fax>
      </Customers>
Additional Customers omitted...
      <Orders>
         <OrderID>10248</OrderID>
         <CustomerID>ALFKI</CustomerID>
         <EmployeeID>5</EmployeeID>
         <OrderDate>1996-07-04T00:00:00.0000000-07:00</OrderDate>
         <RequiredDate>1996-08-01T00:00:00.0000000-07:00</RequiredDate>
         <ShippedDate>1996-07-16T00:00:00.0000000-07:00</ShippedDate>
         <ShipVia>3</ShipVia>
         <Freight>32.38</Freight>
         <ShipName>Vins et alcools Chevalier</ShipName>
         <ShipAddress>59 rue de l'Abbaye</ShipAddress>
         <ShipCity>Reims</ShipCity>
         <ShipPostalCode>51100</ShipPostalCode>
         <ShipCountry>France</ShipCountry>
      </Orders>
Additional Orders omitted...
   </CustomerOrders>
```

This isn't quite a combination of the separate XML and XSD files, because an XML file can have only a single root element. So the XSD information is inserted into the file as the first child of the <CustomerOrders> root element, and it's then followed by the Customer and Order information.

The third possible value for the WriteMode parameter, DiffGram, is used to transmit enough information to identify both the original and current contents of the DataSet and to allow the receiving component to match up original and current versions of changed rows. Listing 16.5 shows the pertinent points of a DiffGram that includes a single changed row.

Listing 16.5:   A DiffGram Showing Changes to a DataSet

```
<?xml version="1.0" standalone="yes"?>
<diffgr:diffgram xmlns:msdata="urn:schemas-microsoft-com:xml-msdata"
➥   xmlns:diffgr="urn:schemas-microsoft-com:xml-diffgram-v1">
   <CustomerOrders>
      <Customers diffgr:id="Customers1" msdata:rowOrder="0"
➥   diffgr:hasChanges="modified">
         <CustomerID>ALFKI</CustomerID>
```

```
      <CompanyName>Alfreds Futterkiste</CompanyName>
      <ContactName>Joe Graham</ContactName>
      <ContactTitle>Sales Representative</ContactTitle>
      <Address>Obere Str. 57</Address>
      <City>Berlin</City>
      <PostalCode>12209</PostalCode>
      <Country>Germany</Country>
      <Phone>030-0074321</Phone>
      <Fax>030-0076545</Fax>
    </Customers>
    <Customers diffgr:id="Customers2" msdata:rowOrder="1">
      <CustomerID>ANATR</CustomerID>
      <CompanyName>Ana Trujillo Emparedados y helados</CompanyName>
      <ContactName>Ana Trujillo</ContactName>
      <ContactTitle>Owner</ContactTitle>
      <Address>Avda. de la Constitucion 2222</Address>
      <City>Mexico D.F.</City>
      <PostalCode>05021</PostalCode>
      <Country>Mexico</Country>
      <Phone>(5) 555-4729</Phone>
      <Fax>(5) 555-3745</Fax>
    </Customers>
Additional Customers and Orders omitted...
  </CustomerOrders>
  <diffgr:before>
    <Customers diffgr:id="Customers1" msdata:rowOrder="0">
      <CustomerID>ALFKI</CustomerID>
      <CompanyName>Alfreds Futterkiste</CompanyName>
      <ContactName>Maria Anders</ContactName>
      <ContactTitle>Sales Representative</ContactTitle>
      <Address>Obere Str. 57</Address>
      <City>Berlin</City>
      <PostalCode>12209</PostalCode>
      <Country>Germany</Country>
      <Phone>030-0074321</Phone>
      <Fax>030-0076545</Fax>
    </Customers>
  </diffgr:before>
</diffgr:diffgram>
```

As you can see, the DiffGram adds a new root tag, <diffgr>, which indicates (along with the XML namespace declarations) that this is a DiffGram. Then comes the current data from every row in the DataSet. Rows with uncommitted changes are identified by the diffgr: hasChanges="modified" attribute. Then, at the end of the file, the WriteXml method writes the original data from the changed rows. The diffgr:id attributes allow the receiving code to match up the changed rows with their original version.

Using WriteXmlSchema

The fourth method for writing XML from a DataSet is the WriteXmlSchema method. This method takes a single parameter, which indicates the destination for the schema. This parameter can be one of the following:

- A Stream object
- The name of a file to write to
- A TextWriter object
- An XmlWriter object

The XSD information from the WriteXmlSchema method matches exactly the information from the GetXmlSchema method. Thus, you can choose between the two based on where you need the information. To display the XSD schema in a control or to store it in a string, you should use GetXmlSchema. But to place the same schema in a file, on a web page, or in memory, you should use WriteXmlSchema.

Writing Only Changes to XML

If you examine the DiffGrams produced by using WriteXml on the original DataSet, you'll find that they contain much more information than is necessary for some purposes. In particular, they contain the entire contents of all the unchanged rows of the DataSet, as well as the original and current versions of the changed rows. If you're using DiffGrams to send changes from one distributed component to another, sending the unchanged rows clearly wastes many bytes.

Fortunately, you can avoid this waste by using the DataSet.GetChanges method to create a cloned DataSet that contains only changed rows, and by using WriteXml on that version of the DataSet. Figure 16.1 shows the frmChanges form in this chapter's sample project, which uses this technique to populate a text box on the form with a DiffGram containing changes made since the form was loaded.

Here's the code that fills the text box with the DiffGram:

```
Private Sub btnGetDiffGram_Click(ByVal sender As System.Object, _
  ByVal e As System.EventArgs) Handles btnGetDiffGram.Click

    Try
        Dim dsChanges As DataSet = mds.GetChanges
        Dim sb As New StringBuilder()
        Dim sw As New StringWriter(sb)
        dsChanges.WriteXml(sw, XmlWriteMode.DiffGram)
        txtDiffGram.Text = sb.ToString
    Catch ex As Exception
```

```
        MsgBox("Error: " & ex.Source & ": " & ex.Message, _
          MsgBoxStyle.OKOnly, "btnGetDiffGram_Click")
      End Try

    End Sub
```

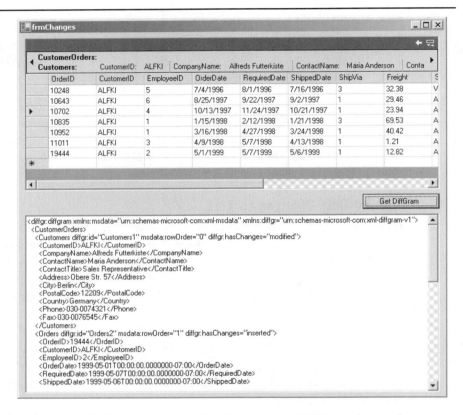

Most of the complexity of this code lies in piping the generated XML to the text box, rather than in generating the XML itself. The code takes these steps:

1. Call the GetChanges method on the original DataSet to return a new DataSet containing only rows that have been changed in some way.

2. Create a StringBuilder object. The StringBuilder can accept a stream of text and convert it into a string.

3. Create a StringWriter object that writes to the StringBuilder. Because the StringWriter is a subclass of the TextWriter, it can serve as a destination for the WriteXml method.

4. Call the DataSet.WriteXml method on the new DataSet, using the StringWriter as the destination. The results are automatically piped to the StringBuilder object.

5. Call the ToString method of the StringBuilder object to retrieve the XML as a string that can be displayed in the text box.

Listing 16.6 is a sample of the generated XML.

Listing 16.6: **An XML DiffGram**

```
<diffgr:diffgram xmlns:msdata="urn:schemas-microsoft-com:xml-msdata"
    xmlns:diffgr="urn:schemas-microsoft-com:xml-diffgram-v1">
  <CustomerOrders>
    <Customers diffgr:id="Customers1" msdata:rowOrder="0">
      <CustomerID>ALFKI</CustomerID>
      <CompanyName>Alfreds Futterkiste</CompanyName>
      <ContactName>Maria Anders</ContactName>
      <ContactTitle>Sales Representative</ContactTitle>
      <Address>Obere Str. 57</Address>
      <City>Berlin</City>
      <PostalCode>12209</PostalCode>
      <Country>Germany</Country>
      <Phone>030-0074321</Phone>
      <Fax>030-0076545</Fax>
    </Customers>
    <Customers diffgr:id="Customers2" msdata:rowOrder="1">
      <CustomerID>BONAP</CustomerID>
      <CompanyName>Bon app'</CompanyName>
      <ContactName>Laurence Lebihan</ContactName>
      <ContactTitle>Owner</ContactTitle>
      <Address>12, rue des Bouchers</Address>
      <City>Marseille</City>
      <PostalCode>13008</PostalCode>
      <Country>France</Country>
      <Phone>91.24.45.40</Phone>
      <Fax>91.24.45.41</Fax>
    </Customers>
    <Orders diffgr:id="Orders1" msdata:rowOrder="0"
      diffgr:hasChanges="modified">
      <OrderID>10254</OrderID>
      <CustomerID>ALFKI</CustomerID>
      <EmployeeID>5</EmployeeID>
      <OrderDate>1996-07-11T00:00:00.0000000-07:00</OrderDate>
      <RequiredDate>1996-07-01T00:00:00.0000000-07:00</RequiredDate>
      <ShippedDate>1996-07-23T00:00:00.0000000-07:00</ShippedDate>
      <ShipVia>2</ShipVia>
      <Freight>22.98</Freight>
      <ShipName>Chop-suey Chinese</ShipName>
      <ShipAddress>Hauptstr. 31</ShipAddress>
      <ShipCity>Bern</ShipCity>
```

```
            <ShipPostalCode>3012</ShipPostalCode>
            <ShipCountry>Switzerland</ShipCountry>
          </Orders>
          <Orders diffgr:id="Orders3" msdata:rowOrder="2"
➡          diffgr:hasChanges="inserted">
            <OrderID>19444</OrderID>
            <CustomerID>BONAP</CustomerID>
            <EmployeeID>2</EmployeeID>
            <OrderDate>1999-07-08T00:00:00.0000000-07:00</OrderDate>
            <RequiredDate>1999-07-16T00:00:00.0000000-07:00</RequiredDate>
            <ShippedDate>1999-07-09T00:00:00.0000000-07:00</ShippedDate>
            <ShipVia>2</ShipVia>
            <Freight>1.15</Freight>
            <ShipName>Bon app'</ShipName>
          </Orders>
        </CustomerOrders>
        <diffgr:before>
          <Orders diffgr:id="Orders1" msdata:rowOrder="0">
            <OrderID>10254</OrderID>
            <CustomerID>CHOPS</CustomerID>
            <EmployeeID>5</EmployeeID>
            <OrderDate>1996-07-11T00:00:00.0000000-07:00</OrderDate>
            <RequiredDate>1996-08-08T00:00:00.0000000-07:00</RequiredDate>
            <ShippedDate>1996-07-23T00:00:00.0000000-07:00</ShippedDate>
            <ShipVia>2</ShipVia>
            <Freight>22.98</Freight>
            <ShipName>Chop-suey Chinese</ShipName>
            <ShipAddress>Hauptstr. 31</ShipAddress>
            <ShipCity>Bern</ShipCity>
            <ShipPostalCode>3012</ShipPostalCode>
            <ShipCountry>Switzerland</ShipCountry>
          </Orders>
          <Orders diffgr:id="Orders2" msdata:rowOrder="1">
            <OrderID>10595</OrderID>
            <CustomerID>ERNSH</CustomerID>
            <EmployeeID>2</EmployeeID>
            <OrderDate>1997-07-10T00:00:00.0000000-07:00</OrderDate>
            <RequiredDate>1997-08-07T00:00:00.0000000-07:00</RequiredDate>
            <ShippedDate>1997-07-14T00:00:00.0000000-07:00</ShippedDate>
            <ShipVia>1</ShipVia>
            <Freight>96.78</Freight>
            <ShipName>Ernst Handel</ShipName>
            <ShipAddress>Kirchgasse 6</ShipAddress>
            <ShipCity>Graz</ShipCity>
            <ShipPostalCode>8010</ShipPostalCode>
            <ShipCountry>Austria</ShipCountry>
          </Orders>
        </diffgr:before>
      </diffgr:diffgram>
```

This DiffGram was generated by editing one order, adding one order, and deleting one order. If you examine the DiffGram, you'll find these sections in it:

1. The current row for customer ALFKI. This row is included because it is the customer for the edited order, even though the customer row wasn't modified.

2. The current row for customer BONAP. This row is included because it is the customer for the inserted order, even though the customer row wasn't modified.

3. The current row for order 10254. This row has the attribute `diffgr:hasChanges=` `"modified"`, indicating that it is the current version of an edited row.

4. The current row for order 19444. This row has the attribute `diffgr:hasChanges="inserted"`, indicating that it is a new order.

5. The original row for order 10254.

6. The original row for order 10595. You can tell that this is a deleted order, because no row for this order appears in the current row section of the DiffGram.

You should be able to see that this DiffGram includes all the information necessary to reconstruct the changes to the DataSet. By including the original rows, it also makes it possible for the receiving component to check that no other component modified these rows after they were loaded; thus, the DiffGram can be used to enforce optimistic concurrency.

TIP   Later in the chapter, you'll see that the ReadXml method can merge a DiffGram with a copy of the original DataSet to reconstruct the changed DataSet.

Handling DataRelations

The XML files that you've seen so far in this chapter have grouped the information they contain by DataTable: All the customers are listed first, followed by all the orders. It's sometimes more useful to have child rows (such as orders) included as child elements of their parents (such as customers). ADO.NET makes it extremely easy to generate XML that has this parent-and-child structure, as frmWriteXmlNested in this chapter's sample project demonstrates. In fact, only a single line of code distinguishes this form from the nonnested version that you saw earlier in the chapter:

```
relCustomerOrder.Nested = True
```

Setting the Nested property of a DataRelation object to True tells the DataSet to generate XML with the child rows nested inside the parent rows. Listing 16.7 is an example of the resulting XML, generated with an embedded schema.

Listing 16.7:   **XML File with Nested Child Rows**

```
<CustomerOrders>
  <xs:schema id="CustomerOrders" xmlns=""
➥ xmlns:xs="http://www.w3.org/2001/XMLSchema"
➥ xmlns:msdata="urn:schemas-microsoft-com:xml-msdata">
    <xs:element name="CustomerOrders" msdata:IsDataSet="true">
      <xs:complexType>
        <xs:choice maxOccurs="unbounded">
          <xs:element name="Customers">
            <xs:complexType>
              <xs:sequence>
                <xs:element name="CustomerID" type="xs:string"
➥ minOccurs="0" />
                <xs:element name="CompanyName" type="xs:string"
➥ minOccurs="0" />
                <xs:element name="ContactName" type="xs:string"
➥ minOccurs="0" />
                <xs:element name="ContactTitle" type="xs:string"
➥ minOccurs="0" />
                <xs:element name="Address" type="xs:string"
➥ minOccurs="0" />
                <xs:element name="City" type="xs:string" minOccurs="0" />
                <xs:element name="Region" type="xs:string"
➥ minOccurs="0" />
                <xs:element name="PostalCode" type="xs:string"
➥ minOccurs="0" />
                <xs:element name="Country" type="xs:string"
➥ minOccurs="0" />
                <xs:element name="Phone" type="xs:string" minOccurs="0" />
                <xs:element name="Fax" type="xs:string" minOccurs="0" />
                <xs:element name="Orders" minOccurs="0"
➥ maxOccurs="unbounded">
                  <xs:complexType>
                    <xs:sequence>
                      <xs:element name="OrderID" type="xs:int"
➥ minOccurs="0" />
                      <xs:element name="CustomerID" type="xs:string"
➥ minOccurs="0" />
                      <xs:element name="EmployeeID" type="xs:int"
➥ minOccurs="0" />
                      <xs:element name="OrderDate" type="xs:dateTime"
➥ minOccurs="0" />
                      <xs:element name="RequiredDate"
➥ type="xs:dateTime" minOccurs="0" />
                      <xs:element name="ShippedDate" type="xs:dateTime"
➥ minOccurs="0" />
                      <xs:element name="ShipVia" type="xs:int"
➥ minOccurs="0" />
                      <xs:element name="Freight" type="xs:decimal"
➥ minOccurs="0" />
```

```
                          <xs:element name="ShipName" type="xs:string"
➡ minOccurs="0" />
                          <xs:element name="ShipAddress" type="xs:string"
➡ minOccurs="0" />
                          <xs:element name="ShipCity" type="xs:string"
➡ minOccurs="0" />
                          <xs:element name="ShipRegion" type="xs:string"
➡ minOccurs="0" />
                          <xs:element name="ShipPostalCode"
➡ type="xs:string" minOccurs="0" />
                          <xs:element name="ShipCountry" type="xs:string"
➡ minOccurs="0" />
                      </xs:sequence>
                    </xs:complexType>
                  </xs:element>
                </xs:sequence>
              </xs:complexType>
            </xs:element>
          </xs:choice>
        </xs:complexType>
        <xs:unique name="Constraint1">
          <xs:selector xpath=".//Customers" />
          <xs:field xpath="CustomerID" />
        </xs:unique>
        <xs:keyref name="CustOrder" refer="Constraint1" msdata:IsNested="true">
          <xs:selector xpath=".//Orders" />
          <xs:field xpath="CustomerID" />
        </xs:keyref>
      </xs:element>
</xs:schema>
<Customers>
  <CustomerID>ALFKI</CustomerID>
  <CompanyName>Alfreds Futterkiste</CompanyName>
  <ContactName>Joe Graham</ContactName>
  <ContactTitle>Sales Representative</ContactTitle>
  <Address>Obere Str. 57</Address>
  <City>Berlin</City>
  <PostalCode>12209</PostalCode>
  <Country>Germany</Country>
  <Phone>030-0074321</Phone>
  <Fax>030-0076545</Fax>
  <Orders>
    <OrderID>10248</OrderID>
    <CustomerID>ALFKI</CustomerID>
    <EmployeeID>5</EmployeeID>
    <OrderDate>1996-07-04T00:00:00.0000000-07:00</OrderDate>
    <RequiredDate>1996-08-01T00:00:00.0000000-07:00</RequiredDate>
    <ShippedDate>1996-07-16T00:00:00.0000000-07:00</ShippedDate>
    <ShipVia>3</ShipVia>
    <Freight>32.38</Freight>
    <ShipName>Vins et alcools Chevalier</ShipName>
```

```
            <ShipAddress>59 rue de l'Abbaye</ShipAddress>
            <ShipCity>Reims</ShipCity>
            <ShipPostalCode>51100</ShipPostalCode>
            <ShipCountry>France</ShipCountry>
         </Orders>
    Additional Orders for first Customer omitted...
      </Customers>
      <Customers>
         <CustomerID>ANATR</CustomerID>
         <CompanyName>Ana Trujillo Emparedados y helados</CompanyName>
         <ContactName>Ana Trujillo</ContactName>
         <ContactTitle>Owner</ContactTitle>
         <Address>Avda. de la Constitucion 2222</Address>
         <City>Mexico D.F.</City>
         <PostalCode>05021</PostalCode>
         <Country>Mexico</Country>
         <Phone>(5) 555-4729</Phone>
         <Fax>(5) 555-3745</Fax>
         <Orders>
            <OrderID>10308</OrderID>
            <CustomerID>ANATR</CustomerID>
            <EmployeeID>7</EmployeeID>
            <OrderDate>1996-09-18T00:00:00.0000000-07:00</OrderDate>
            <RequiredDate>1996-10-16T00:00:00.0000000-07:00</RequiredDate>
            <ShippedDate>1996-09-24T00:00:00.0000000-07:00</ShippedDate>
            <ShipVia>3</ShipVia>
            <Freight>1.61</Freight>
            <ShipName>Ana Trujillo Emparedados y helados</ShipName>
            <ShipAddress>Avda. de la Constitucion 2222</ShipAddress>
            <ShipCity>Mexico D.F.</ShipCity>
            <ShipPostalCode>05021</ShipPostalCode>
            <ShipCountry>Mexico</ShipCountry>
         </Orders>
    Additional Orders for second Customer omitted...
    Additional Customers with their Orders omitted...
      </CustomerOrders>
```

As you can see, the nested format includes changes to both the XSD schema information and the XML data information. That makes sense, because the schema has to change to describe the nested information, by showing the Orders complex type as an element of the Customers complex type.

Fine-Tuning Column Mappings

All the XML files you've seen in this chapter so far have been element-centric. ADO.NET is also perfectly capable of creating attribute-centric XML files.

In fact, you can control the XML output on a column-by-column basis by setting the ColumnMapping property of the DataColumn objects within a DataSet. Table 16.2 lists the possible values for this property.

TABLE 16.2: ColumnMapping Values

Value	Meaning
MappingType.Element	Output as an XML element.
MappingType.Attribute	Output as an XML attribute.
MappingType.Hidden	Do not include in the XML.
MappingType.SimpleText	Output as the text for the parent element in the XML. This value cannot be used if there are any columns in the table set to MappingType.Element, or if there is a nested relation that includes the table.

TIP   All of the XML output methods (GetXml, GetXmlSchema, WriteXml, and WriteXmlSchema) support these settings.

Figure 16.2 shows the frmColumnMappings form from this chapter's sample project. This form allows you to experiment with different column mappings for the Customers table, as well as choose whether or not the Orders table should be included via a nested relation.

Listing 16.8 shows a portion of the XML file created by the settings shown in Figure 16.2.

FIGURE 16.2:

Choosing column mappings

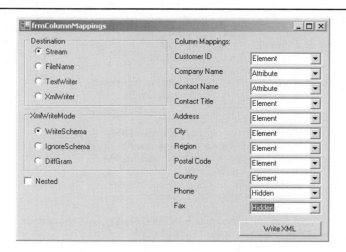

Listing 16.8: **XML File with Custom Column Mappings**

```
<CustomerOrders>
  <xs:schema id="CustomerOrders" xmlns=""
➡ xmlns:xs="http://www.w3.org/2001/XMLSchema"
➡ xmlns:msdata="urn:schemas-microsoft-com:xml-msdata">
    <xs:element name="CustomerOrders" msdata:IsDataSet="true">
      <xs:complexType>
        <xs:choice maxOccurs="unbounded">
          <xs:element name="Customers">
            <xs:complexType>
              <xs:sequence>
                <xs:element name="CustomerID" type="xs:string"
➡ minOccurs="0" msdata:Ordinal="0" />
                <xs:element name="ContactTitle" type="xs:string"
➡ minOccurs="0" msdata:Ordinal="3" />
                <xs:element name="Address" type="xs:string"
➡ minOccurs="0" msdata:Ordinal="4" />
                <xs:element name="City" type="xs:string" minOccurs="0"
➡ msdata:Ordinal="5" />
                <xs:element name="Region" type="xs:string"
➡ minOccurs="0" msdata:Ordinal="6" />
                <xs:element name="PostalCode" type="xs:string"
➡ minOccurs="0" msdata:Ordinal="7" />
                <xs:element name="Country" type="xs:string"
➡ minOccurs="0" msdata:Ordinal="8" />
              </xs:sequence>
              <xs:attribute name="CompanyName" type="xs:string" />
              <xs:attribute name="ContactName" type="xs:string" />
              <xs:attribute name="Phone" type="xs:string"
➡ use="prohibited" />
              <xs:attribute name="Fax" type="xs:string"
➡ use="prohibited" />
            </xs:complexType>
          </xs:element>
Additional schema information omitted...
  </xs:schema>
  <Customers CompanyName="Alfreds Futterkiste"
➡ ContactName="Joe Graham">
    <CustomerID>ALFKI</CustomerID>
    <ContactTitle>Sales Representative</ContactTitle>
    <Address>Obere Str. 57</Address>
    <City>Berlin</City>
    <PostalCode>12209</PostalCode>
    <Country>Germany</Country>
  </Customers>
  <Customers CompanyName="Ana Trujillo Emparedados y helados"
➡ ContactName="Ana Trujillo">
    <CustomerID>ANATR</CustomerID>
    <ContactTitle>Owner</ContactTitle>
    <Address>Avda. de la Constitucion 2222</Address>
```

```
      <City>Mexico D.F.</City>
      <PostalCode>05021</PostalCode>
      <Country>Mexico</Country>
   </Customers>
Additional Customers and Orders omitted...
</CustomerOrders>
```

The hidden columns still appear in the schema portion of the XML file, so that the DataSet structure can be reconstructed, but the data from those columns will be lost if this XML file is used to reconstruct the DataSet.

The code behind this form is mainly a tedious exercise in converting user interface choices to object properties. Here's a sample that shows how the ColumnMapping property for the CustomerID column gets set; the code for the other columns is similar:

```
Dim dt As DataTable = ds.Tables("Customers")
Select Case cboCustomerID.Text
    Case "Element"
        dt.Columns(0).ColumnMapping = MappingType.Element
    Case "Attribute"
        dt.Columns(0).ColumnMapping = MappingType.Attribute
    Case "Hidden"
        dt.Columns(0).ColumnMapping = MappingType.Hidden
End Select
```

Reconstituting an XML DataSet

Of course, saving DataSets to XML is only half the story. It's equally important to be able to recreate a DataSet from the saved XML. Fortunately, the .NET Framework offers flexible functionality in this area as well. You can create a DataSet from an XML file, merge an XML file into an existing DataSet, or just use the XML or XSD file as a source of schema information for a DataSet. I'll cover all of these techniques in this section.

The main tool for converting XML files back into DataSets is the DataSet.ReadXml method. Just like the WriteXml method, ReadXml is overloaded so that it can import XML from a variety of sources. The source of the XML can be any of the following:

- A Stream object
- A file identified by a string containing a filename
- A TextReader object
- An XmlReader object

In other words, ReadXml can read from any source that WriteXml can use as a destination.

ReadXml also accepts an optional second parameter that controls its operations. This second parameter can be any of the XmlReadMode values listed in Table 16.3.

TABLE 16.3: XmlReadMode Values

Constant	Meaning
Auto	If the XML file is recognized as a DiffGram, read it as a DiffGram. If the XML file is not recognized as a Diffgram but there is schema information in the XML file or in an associated XSD file, use that schema to build the DataSet. Otherwise, infer the schema from the data. This is the default.
DiffGram	Treats the XML file as a DiffGram.
Fragment	Reads XML information from an XmlReader that may already be positioned in the middle of an XML file.
IgnoreSchema	Ignores any schema information contained in the XML file and attempts to fit the data into the current schema of the DataSet.
InferSchema	Infers the schema of the XML file by examining the data.
ReadSchema	Uses XSD information to define the schema of the DataSet.

Figure 16.3 shows the frmReadXml form from this chapter's sample project. This form allows you to select an XML file and an XmlReadMode, and then see the results of reading that XML file with that XmlReadMode on the DataGrid.

FIGURE 16.3:

Reading an XML file to a DataGrid

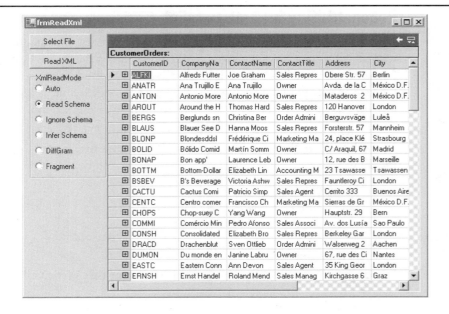

Here's the code that frmReadXml uses to do its job. The DataSet object doesn't require any special initialization; ADO.NET will construct a DataSet schema that matches that found in the XML file.

```
Private Sub btnReadXml_Click(ByVal sender As System.Object, _
  ByVal e As System.EventArgs) Handles btnReadXml.Click
    Dim rm As New XmlReadMode()
    Dim ds As New DataSet()

    If Len(mstrFileName) = 0 Then
        Exit Sub
    End If

    Try
        If rbAuto.Checked Then
            rm = XmlReadMode.Auto
        ElseIf rbDiffGram.Checked Then
            rm = XmlReadMode.DiffGram
        ElseIf rbFragment.Checked Then
            rm = XmlReadMode.Fragment
        ElseIf rbIgnoreSchema.Checked Then
            rm = XmlReadMode.IgnoreSchema
        ElseIf rbInferSchema.Checked Then
            rm = XmlReadMode.InferSchema
        Else
            rm = XmlReadMode.ReadSchema
        End If

        ds.ReadXml(mstrFileName, rm)
        dgMain.DataSource = ds
    Catch ex As Exception
        MsgBox("Error: " & ex.Source & ": " & ex.Message, _
        MsgBoxStyle.OKOnly, "btnReadXml")
    End Try

End Sub
```

By experimenting with the forms in this chapter's sample project, you can see how the various choices in writing XML translate to the end result when that same XML is read back into a DataSet. In general, ReadXml can read anything that WriteXml can write. In the rest of this section, I'll address a few special cases:

- Merging XML data

- Merging a DiffGram

- Reading a schema

- Inferring a schema

Merging XML Data

There are times when, rather than load XML into an empty DataSet, you'd like to merge it into an existing DataSet. The ReadXml method supports this operation by default. Rows in the XML are added to the end of the DataSet, provided the DataSet already contains a DataTable with the same schema as the XML file. If the DataSet doesn't contain a corresponding DataTable, the information in the XML file will be added as a new DataTable.

The frmMerge form in this chapter's sample project demonstrates the use of WriteXml and ReadXml to merge two DataSets. The form opens with an empty DataGrid and a second DataGrid containing customer information. You can add rows to the empty DataGrid and click the Merge button to add these rows to the DataSet containing customer information. Here's the code that performs the merge:

```
Private Sub btnMerge_Click(ByVal sender As System.Object, _
  ByVal e As System.EventArgs) Handles btnMerge.Click

    Try
        Dim ms As New System.IO.MemoryStream()
        mdsNew.WriteXml(ms, XmlWriteMode.IgnoreSchema)
        ms.Seek(0, SeekOrigin.Begin)
        mdsMain.ReadXml(ms, XmlReadMode.IgnoreSchema)
        mdsNew.Clear()
        mdsMain.AcceptChanges()
    Catch ex As Exception
        MsgBox("Error: " & ex.Source & ": " & ex.Message, _
          MsgBoxStyle.OKOnly, "btnFillSchema")
    End Try

End Sub
```

This code writes the entire contents of the mdsNew DataSet to a MemoryStream object and then reads those contents into the mdsMain DataSet. By using a MemoryStream and by not writing any schema information (because the two DataSets already have the same structure), this code can transfer the information very quickly. The call to the Seek method of the Memory-Stream "rewinds" the stream so that the ReadXml method will start reading at its beginning.

TIP	If the two DataSets exist in the same component, you can also use the DataSet.Merge method to combine their information. The technique shown in this section is more useful when the two DataSets exist in different components.

Merging a DiffGram

If you try to use the frmMerge form to make changes to an existing row, you'll get a result such as that shown in Figure 16.4. Rather than overwrite the existing row, the ReadXml record will attempt to add a new row to the DataSet, possibly causing a primary key violation.

Primary key violation caused by merging DataSets

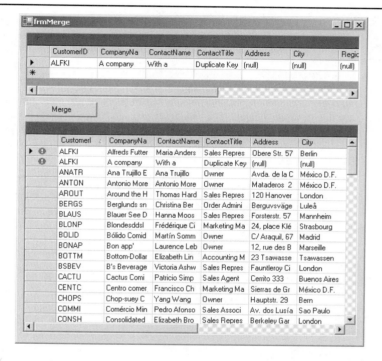

To merge changes to an existing version of a DataSet, you should use DiffGrams. The frm-MergeDiffGram form takes this approach. It starts by opening two copies of the same DataSet, each containing all the customers. You can make any changes you like to the DataSet displayed at the top of the form, and then click the Merge button. At that point, the form will use a DiffGram to merge those changes into the copy of the DataSet displayed at the bottom of the form. Here's the code that handles the merge, once again by using a MemoryStream object as a pipeline between the two DataSets:

```
Private Sub btnMerge_Click(ByVal sender As System.Object, _
  ByVal e As System.EventArgs) Handles btnMerge.Click

    Try
        Dim ms As New System.IO.MemoryStream()
        mdsNew.WriteXml(ms, XmlWriteMode.DiffGram)
        ms.Seek(0, SeekOrigin.Begin)
        mdsMain.ReadXml(ms, XmlReadMode.DiffGram)
        mdsMain.AcceptChanges()
```

```
Catch ex As Exception
    MsgBox("Error: " & ex.Source & ": " & ex.Message, _
    MsgBoxStyle.OKOnly, "btnFillSchema")
End Try

End Sub
```

TIP You can omit the XmlReadMode.DiffGram constant from the ReadXml call if you like, because ReadXml will automatically determine that the XML is formatted as a DiffGram and perform the correct operations. But the code will execute faster if you explicitly specify the DiffGram format.

Reading a Schema

The ReadXml method reads the schema information from the XML file, in addition to the data. But what if you want to read only the schema—for example, to create a new DataSet with the same schema as an existing one? In that case, you can use the ReadXmlSchema method of the DataSet.

The frmMerge form uses the ReadXmlSchema method as part of copying the schema from dsMain to dsNew:

```
Dim ms As New System.IO.MemoryStream()
mdsMain.WriteXmlSchema(ms)
ms.Seek(0, SeekOrigin.Begin)
mdsNew.ReadXmlSchema(ms)
```

As with the earlier code that moves data from one DataSet to another, this code uses a MemoryStream object for speed. Like ReadXml, ReadXmlSchema can read information from a stream, a file, a TextReader object, or an XmlReader object. It can read a schema either from a pure schema XSD document or from an XML document with or without embedded schema information. If there is no embedded schema information, ReadXmlSchema infers the schema according to the rules in the next section.

Inferring a Schema

As mentioned above, if the ReadXml or ReadXmlSchema method doesn't find schema information within the source that it's reading, it will try to infer an appropriate DataSet schema to hold the XML data. Here are the rules that these methods use to infer a schema:

1. Elements that have attributes are assumed to be tables.

2. Elements that have child elements are assumed to be tables.

3. Repeating elements are mapped to a single table. That is, if you have multiple <Customer> elements in the XML file, ADO.NET will create a single Customer DataTable to hold them all.

4. Attributes are assumed to be columns.

5. Nonrepeating elements that have no attributes or child elements are assumed to be columns.

6. If the root element has attributes or child elements that are assumed to be columns, it is assumed to be a table. Otherwise, it is assumed to be a DataSet.

7. If two tables are nested in the XML, ADO.NET adds a column named TableName_ID to each table and then uses that column to create a nested DataRelation between the tables.

8. If an element is assumed to be a table and has no child elements, ADO.NET creates a single column named TableName_Text for the table and initializes it with the text of the element. If the element has child elements, any text in the element is ignored.

With no schema information, there's no way to tell what the original datatype of a column was when the XML file was created. Some products (for example, Excel and Access) attempt to determine a plausible column type in analogous situations. ADO.NET doesn't do this. All columns in an inferred schema will be text columns with the System.String datatype.

Note that the inference process isn't perfect (if it were, we wouldn't need XSD schemas at all!). Consider this very simple XML document:

```
<Customers>
    <Customer>ALFKI</Customer>
</Customers>
```

In this case, the `<Customer>` element is assumed to be a column (rule 5), and then the `<Customers>` element is assumed to be a table (rule 6). The result is a DataSet with the arbitrary name of NewDataSet, containing a single table named Customers. The table has a single column named Customer. There will be one row in the table, with the value ALFKI in the Customer column.

On the other hand, a slightly different XML file produces a result that seems more likely to be correct:

```
<Customers>
    <Customer>ALFKI</Customer>
    <Customer>BONAP</Customer>
</Customers>
```

In this case, the `<Customer>` element is assumed to be a table (rule 3), and the text is assumed to be a single column in the table (rule 8). Then the `<Customers>` element is assumed to be a DataSet (rule 6). The result is a DataSet named Customers, containing a single table named Customer. The Customer table will have a single column named Customer_Text. There will be two rows in the table, with the values ALFKI and BONAP in the Customer_Text column.

Generally, the inference process will produce reasonable results, but to be absolutely certain of the correct results, you should supply an XSD schema.

DataSets via Web Services

In actual distributed applications, you may find that you don't worry too much about the details of saving DataSets to XML and then recreating them in another component. That's because the .NET environment provides higher-level abstractions that hide some of the details of what's going on. The most important of these abstractions is the *web service*.

A web service is a programmable application that's accessible over common web protocols. Web services communicate with clients via SOAP, the Simple Object Access Protocol. Because SOAP transforms objects into XML files that can be sent as standard HTTP messages, it allows applications to use distributed objects without application-specific programming. In this section, I'll show you what it takes to build and use a simple data-based web service.

To create a simple web service that returns a DataSet, follow these steps:

1. Launch Visual Studio .NET and choose New Project from the Start Page.

2. Select the ASP.NET Web Service project in the Visual Basic Projects folder. Specify `http://localhost/Customers` as the location of the web service and then click OK. This will open the design surface for the code module of Service1.asmx, which is the main programmatic interface for the new web service.

3. Expand the tree in the Server Explorer to find a SQL Server database table. I used an existing SQL Server connection, but you can also create a new connection. Drag the table and drop it on the Service1.asmx design surface. This will create SqlConnection1 and SqlDataAdapter1 objects. For this example, I chose to use the Customers table from a copy of the SQL Server version of the Northwind database.

4. Select the SqlDataAdapter1 object. At the bottom of the Properties window, click the Generate DataSet... hyperlink.

5. In the Generate DataSet dialog box, choose to create a new DataSet named DataSet1, select the Customers table, and choose the check box to add the DataSet to the designer. Click OK. This will add a third object, a DataSet named DataSet11, to the design surface.

6. Right-click on the design surface and select View Code. This will open the code-behind-page window for Service1.asmx.

7. Enter this code to create a new WebMethod as a part of the Service1 class:

```
<WebMethod()> Public Function GetCustomers() As DataSet
    SqlDataAdapter1.Fill(DataSet11)
    GetCustomers = DataSet11
End Function
```

(Except for the `<WebMethod>` tag, this is exactly the code that you could use to create a method named GetCustomers in a regular Windows application.)

At this point, you're ready to test the web service. To do so, follow these steps:

1. Save the project and select Debug ➤ Start to run it. This will open a page with general information on the web service, including a hyperlink to the GetCustomers method.

2. Click the GetCustomers link. This will open a page of information about the GetCustomers method, as shown in Figure 16.5. Included are details of the SOAP messages that can be used to invoke the GetCustomers method.

3. Click the Invoke button. This will open a second browser window with the results of the GetCustomers call. You'll see the XML version of the Customers table, together with the XSD schema information. The web services infrastructure automatically takes care of generating this for you.

4. Close the browser windows to stop the debugging session.

FIGURE 16.5:

GetCustomers information

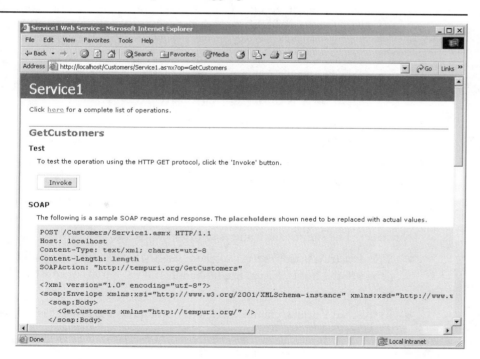

If all you wanted was the raw XML, you could stop here. A web service can deliver the XML representation of an object to any browser that can send HTTP messages and receive the returned HTML. But you can go further and present a seamless user interface by building a web client for the web service. Here's how:

1. Launch Visual Studio .NET and choose New Project from the Start Page.

2. Select the ASP.NET Web Application project in the Visual Basic Projects folder. Specify http://localhost/CustomersClient as the location of the web application and then click OK. This will open the design surface for an ASP.NET page named WebForm1.aspx.

3. Select Project ➢ Add Web Reference. In the Add Web Reference dialog box, click the Web References on Local Web Server hyperlink. In the Available References list, click the hyperlink for http://localhost/Customers.vsdisco. Click the Add Reference button.

4. Add a DataGrid control to the WebForm1.aspx design surface and give it an ID property of dgMain.

5. Double-click on the design surface of WebForm1.aspx to open the code-behind window for this web form. Add this code to the web form:

```
Private Sub Page_Load(ByVal sender As System.Object, _
  ByVal e As System.EventArgs) Handles MyBase.Load
    'Put user code to initialize the page here
    Dim cust As New CustomersClient.localhost.Service1()
    dgMain.DataSource = cust.GetCustomers
    dgMain.DataMember = "Customers"
    dgMain.DataBind()
End Sub
```

6. Choose Debug ➢ Start to launch the WebForm1.aspx page in your web browser. It should appear as shown in Figure 16.6.

What's significant here is not that the web form displays a table of customer information in a grid; you already know that .NET makes this sort of web interface to a database easy to construct. The significant features of this example are as follows:

- The data travels from server to client via XML, without your having to do anything to generate the XML. Visual Studio handles all the details of constructing the XML and the SOAP message that contains it.

- In the .NET arena, client-server web development is just as easy as client-server network development.

Customer information retrieved from a web service

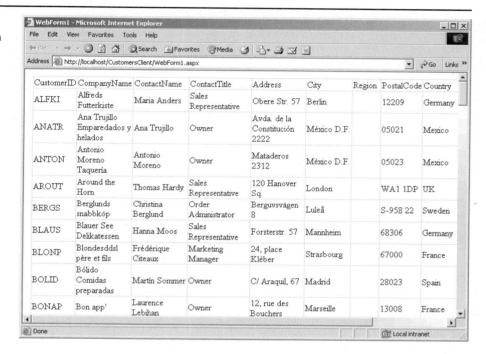

Summary

In this chapter, you learned how to use XML to store a DataSet and how to recreate a DataSet from stored XML. Along the way, I discussed schema generation, customizing the XML, and the rules that ADO.NET uses to infer a schema from an XML file when a formal XSD definition isn't present. Finally, you saw how to use a web service to make a DataSet available remotely over standard web protocols.

In the next chapter, I'll look at some further applications of DataSets, this time on Windows Forms.

CHAPTER 17

Using Windows Forms with ADO.NET

- Data binding with Windows Forms

- Manipulating data through Windows Forms

- A more complex sample

Windows Forms provide the user interface for Windows applications built with the .NET development languages. Over the course of the past several chapters, you've seen many examples of Windows Forms. But the code in those chapters has concentrated on the data, not on its connection with the user interface. In this chapter, I'll look at some of the finer points of using Windows Forms with ADO.NET data.

Data Binding with Windows Forms

Data binding refers to the action of making a persistent connection between some element of the Windows Forms user interface and a source of data such as a DataSet. Data binding can be broken down into two main classes:

- *Simple data binding* means connecting a single value from a data source to a single property of a control.

- *Complex data binding* means connecting a collection of values from a data source to a control.

Most of the examples you've seen so far in this book have used complex data binding to display an entire DataSet on a DataGrid control. In this section, I'll demonstrate the flexibility that both simple and complex data binding offer beyond that model of user interface for data.

Simple Data Binding

Simple data binding can be performed from either the Visual Studio .NET design interface or entirely in code. First, I'll discuss the user interface actions that you can use to bind data; then I'll show you how to achieve the same effect entirely in code.

Data Binding in the IDE

In this example, I'll bind the Text property of a control to a field from a query contained in the Access database `ADOChapter17.mdb`, which is included on this book's companion CD. To create this example of simple data binding, follow these steps:

1. Launch Visual Studio .NET and create a new Visual Basic .NET Windows application.

2. Open the Server Explorer window. Right-click the Data Connections node and select Add Connection.

3. In the Data Link Properties dialog box, select the Provider tab and then choose the Microsoft Jet 4.0 OLE DB provider.

4. In the Data Link Properties dialog box, select the Connection tab and use the browse button to locate the `ADOChapter17.mdb` database in the `/bin` directory of the sample project. Click Open. Click OK to create the new Data Connection.

5. Expand the new Data Connection in Server Explorer and then expand the Views node. Drag qryOrderTotals from the Views node and drop it on your form. You'll get a Data Adapter configuration error, because this query is a totals query and thus isn't an appropriate target for updating. That's not a problem; click OK to continue, and Visual Basic .NET will automatically create an OleDbConnection object and an OleDbDataAdapter object for this query.

6. Select the OleDbDataAdapter object. In the Properties window, click the Generate DataSet hyperlink.

7. In the Generate DataSet dialog box, click the New radio button and name the new DataSet **dsTotals**. Select the Add This DataSet to the Designer check box. Click OK.

8. Add a TextBox control to the form. Name the text box **txtCompanyName**.

9. Expand the DataBindings section at the top of the Properties window. Select the drop-down arrow for the Text property. Expand the tree that drops down and then click the CompanyName field.

10. Double-click the form to open the code editor with the form's Load event procedure selected. Enter this code to fill the DataSet when you open the form:

    ```
    OleDbDataAdapter1.Fill(DsTotals1)
    ```

11. Run the project. You should see the name of the first customer from the database on your form.

Data Binding from Code

It's also possible to bind fields to properties in code without using the user interface. Here's how to add a second binding to the same form by using code:

1. Add a second TextBox control to the form. Name the text box **txtTotalBusiness**.

2. Add this code to the form's Load event procedure:

    ```
    txtTotalBusiness.DataBindings.Add( _
      "Text", DsTotals1.Tables("qryOrderTotals"), "TotalBusiness")
    ```

3. Run the project. You should see the TotalOrders value from the first row of the DataSet on your form, along with the customer name.

   This sort of runtime data binding uses the DataBindings property of the control to associate properties of the control with properties of an object. The DataBindings property returns a ControlBindingsCollection object, which, in turn, returns individual Binding objects.

The object that supplies the properties that are bound to a control need not be a data object. The .NET Framework generalizes the notion of bindings to include many binding sources. For example, you can bind an array to a property. In this chapter, I'll discuss bindings only as they relate to objects from the System.Data namespace.

The ControlBindingsCollection object supports a standard set of collection methods and properties. In particular, you can use the methods and properties shown in Table 17.1 to manage this collection in code.

TABLE 17.1: ControlBindingsCollection Interfaces

Name	Type	Description
Add	Method	Adds a Binding object to the collection.
Clear	Method	Removes all Binding objects from the collection.
Control	Property	Returns the control that owns this collection.
Count	Property	Total number of active Bindings.
Item	Property	Returns a specific Binding object.
Remove	Method	Removes a particular Binding object from the collection.

The most common form of the Add method of the ControlBindingsCollection takes three parameters:

propertyName   The name of the property of the control to which this binding is attached

dataSource   The object that provides the data for the binding

dataMember   The property of the object that should be bound to the control

Unlike data binding in earlier versions of Visual Basic, .NET data binding allows you to choose which property of a control should be bound. I'll discuss this more in the next section.

The ControlBindingsCollection.Add method returns a Binding object. You can use properties of the Binding object to retrieve all the information originally passed to the Add method, or a pointer back to the control to which the Binding object is attached. The Binding object also supports a Parse event, which is fired whenever the value of the control changes. In some circumstances, you may wish to trap this event to react to the data with custom code, rather than write it back to the original data source.

Data Binding to Other Properties

As I mentioned in the preceding section, you can bind to properties other than the Text property. In fact, you can do so from either the user interface or code. To see this capability in action, follow these steps:

1. Add a Panel control to the form. Name this control **pnlTotalOrders**.

2. Expand the DataBindings section at the top of the Properties window. You'll see that the default property for data binding on a Panel control is the Tag property. Click in the (Advanced) section of the DataBindings section and then click the build button. This will open the Advanced Data Binding dialog box shown in Figure 17.1.

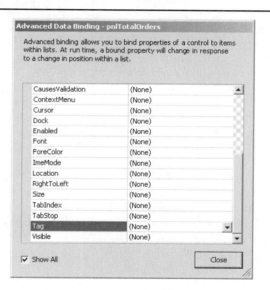

3. Select the right column of the dialog box for any property, and you'll find that you can browse to almost any member of the DsTotals1 DataSet for binding.

4. To bind to a member that doesn't appear in the Advanced Data Binding dialog box, close the dialog box and enter this line of code in the form's Load procedure:

```
pnlTotalOrders.DataBindings.Add( _
    "Width", DsTotals1.Tables("qryOrderTotals"), "TotalOrders")
```

5. Run the project. The result will be a Panel whose Width property is set at runtime to a value drawn from the TotalOrders field in the data source.

TIP The user interface method doesn't let you bind to all the properties of the control, even if you select the Show All check box on the dialog box. In particular, the Advanced Data Binding dialog box doesn't let you bind to properties such as X or Width that are grouped into more complex properties within the Properties window. Fortunately, you can bind any of these properties in code, as this example shows.

You can even bind multiple properties of the same control to fields at the same time. To see this in action, first look at the actual data returned by qryOrderTotals, shown in Figure 17.2.

FIGURE 17.2: Source data for simple data binding

qryOrderTotals : Select Query

Customer ID	Company Name	TotalOrders	TotalBusiness	Color
ALFKI	Alfreds Futterkiste	12	4270	Yellow
ANATR	Ana Trujillo Emparedados y helados	10	1401	Red
ANTON	Antonio Moreno Taquería	17	7018	Yellow
AROUT	Around the Horn	30	13384	Yellow
BERGS	Berglunds snabbköp	52	24912	Green
BLAUS	Blauer See Delikatessen	14	3239	Yellow
BLONP	Blondel père et fils	26	18529	Yellow
BOLID	Bólido Comidas preparadas	6	4230	Red
BONAP	Bon app'	44	21945	Green
BOTTM	Bottom-Dollar Markets	35	20793	Yellow
BSBEV	B's Beverages	22	6088	Yellow
CACTU	Cactus Comidas para llevar	11	1813	Yellow
CENTC	Centro comercial Moctezuma	2	100	Red

Record: 1 of 89

In addition to the columns that I've already added to the form, this query returns a column named Color that specifies a color associated with the record. This column is calculated by the query at runtime using this expression:

```
Color:
IIf(Count([Orders.OrderID])>10,
IIf(Count([Orders.OrderID])>35,"Green","Yellow"),"Red")
```

In Microsoft Access syntax, this expression instructs the query to return the value *Red* if the count of orders is 10 or less, *Yellow* if the count is between 11 and 35, and *Green* for a count greater than 35.

If you inspect the Properties window for the Panel control, you might think that you could simply bind this column to the BackColor property. After all, Red, Yellow, and Green are valid values for that property in the IDE. Unfortunately for this idea, the BackColor property takes values from the System.Drawing.Color class, and there's a difference between Green and System.Drawing.Color.Green. Worse yet, .NET provides no automatic conversion between strings and system color values.

Fortunately, you can get around this problem in code. The frmSimple form in the ADOChapter17 sample project demonstrates a technique for doing so. Listing 17.1 shows the code from the form's Load event.

Listing 17.1:   **Binding an Enumerated Property**

```
Private Sub frmSimple_Load(ByVal sender As System.Object, _
  ByVal e As System.EventArgs) Handles MyBase.Load
    Dim dr As DataRow

    Try
        OleDbDataAdapter1.Fill(DsTotals1)
        DsTotals1.Tables("qryOrderTotals"). _
         Columns.Add("TranslatedColor", GetType(Color))
        For Each dr In DsTotals1.Tables("qryOrderTotals").Rows
            Select Case dr("Color")
                Case "Red"
                    dr("TranslatedColor") = Color.Red
                Case "Yellow"
                    dr("TranslatedColor") = Color.Yellow
                Case "Green"
                    dr("TranslatedColor") = Color.Green
            End Select
        Next
        txtCompanyName.DataBindings.Add( _
         "Text", DsTotals1.Tables("qryOrderTotals"), "CompanyName")
        txtTotalBusiness.DataBindings.Add( _
         "Text", DsTotals1.Tables("qryOrderTotals"), "TotalBusiness")
        pnlTotalOrders.DataBindings.Add( _
         "Width", DsTotals1.Tables("qryOrderTotals"), "TotalOrders")
        pnlTotalOrders.DataBindings.Add( _
         "BackColor", DsTotals1.Tables("qryOrderTotals"), "TranslatedColor")

    Catch ex As Exception
        MsgBox("Error: " & ex.Source & ": " & ex.Message, _
         MsgBoxStyle.OKOnly, "frmSimple_Load")
    End Try

End Sub
```

The approach that this code takes to the problem is to add an extra column to the DataSet after it has been filled by the DataAdapter. DataSet columns added in this manner are not limited to datatypes that can be stored in a database; the columns can use any available datatype. The GetType function returns the datatype of the specified class. After the code adds the column, it runs through all the rows in the DataSet with a For Each loop, and uses a Select Case statement to insert appropriate values in the new column. This new column can then be bound to the BackColor property of the Panel control.

Navigating in the Data

So far, all the samples in this chapter have had one failing: They retrieve the first record from the DataTable and sit there. In the real world, you need a way to navigate between the rows that are bound to the user interface. Fortunately, .NET provides a robust way to do this. Figure 17.3 shows the finished frmSimple, with its navigation buttons.

FIGURE 17.3:

Navigating through simple-bound data

You may recall that a DataTable doesn't map well to a traditional database cursor. In particular, the DataTable doesn't have any concept of a current row; it's just a collection of rows. But to navigate between rows, the concept of a cursor is necessary. Bound forms solve this problem by introducing a new object, the CurrencyManager object. This object adds a current row to a data source (whether that data source is a DataTable or some other bindable data source).

Table 17.2 lists some of the important members of the CurrencyManager. I'll be using some of the editing methods later in the chapter.

TABLE 17.2: CurrencyManager Interface

Name	Type	Description
AddNew	Method	Add a new row to the underlying data source.
Bindings	Property	The collection of Binding objects managed by this CurrencyManager.
CancelCurrentEdit	Method	Cancel any editing operation in progress.
EndCurrentEdit	Method	Commit any editing operation in progress.
Count	Property	Number of rows in the data source being managed.
Current	Property	Current row for this CurrencyManager.
Position	Property	Number of the current row within the data source. The Position property is zero-based, with valid values running from zero to Count minus one.
Refresh	Method	Repopulate all controls managed by this CurrencyManager.
RemoveAt	Method	Remove a row from the underlying data source.

You can retrieve a CurrencyManager object using the BindingContext property of a form or a control. The navigation code for frmSimple, shown in Listing 17.2, makes extensive use of the CurrencyManager object for this form.

Listing 17.2:   **Navigation Code for frmSimple**

```
Private Sub btnNext_Click(ByVal sender As System.Object, _
 ByVal e As System.EventArgs) Handles btnNext.Click

    Try
        Me.BindingContext( _
        DsTotals1.Tables("qryOrderTotals")).Position += 1
        Me.lblPosition.Text = ((Me.BindingContext( _
        DsTotals1.Tables("qryOrderTotals")).Position + 1).ToString _
        + " of  " + Me.BindingContext( _
        DsTotals1.Tables("qryOrderTotals")).Count.ToString)

    Catch ex As Exception
        MsgBox("Error: " & ex.Source & ": " & ex.Message, _
        MsgBoxStyle.OKOnly, "btnNext_Click")
    End Try

End Sub

Private Sub btnFirst_Click(ByVal sender As System.Object, _
 ByVal e As System.EventArgs) Handles btnFirst.Click

    Try
        Me.BindingContext( _
        DsTotals1.Tables("qryOrderTotals")).Position = 0
        Me.lblPosition.Text = ((Me.BindingContext( _
        DsTotals1.Tables("qryOrderTotals")).Position + 1).ToString _
        + " of  " + Me.BindingContext( _
        DsTotals1.Tables("qryOrderTotals")).Count.ToString)

    Catch ex As Exception
        MsgBox("Error: " & ex.Source & ": " & ex.Message, _
        MsgBoxStyle.OKOnly, "btnFirst_Click")
    End Try

End Sub

Private Sub btnPrevious_Click(ByVal sender As System.Object, _
 ByVal e As System.EventArgs) Handles btnPrevious.Click

    Try
        Me.BindingContext( _
        DsTotals1.Tables("qryOrderTotals")).Position -= 1
        Me.lblPosition.Text = ((Me.BindingContext( _
        DsTotals1.Tables("qryOrderTotals")).Position + 1).ToString _
        + " of  " + Me.BindingContext( _
        DsTotals1.Tables("qryOrderTotals")).Count.ToString)

    Catch ex As Exception
        MsgBox("Error: " & ex.Source & ": " & ex.Message, _
        MsgBoxStyle.OKOnly, "btnNext_Click")
```

```
        End Try

    End Sub

    Private Sub btnLast_Click(ByVal sender As System.Object, _
     ByVal e As System.EventArgs) Handles btnLast.Click

        Try
            Me.BindingContext( _
             DsTotals1.Tables("qryOrderTotals")).Position = _
            Me.BindingContext( _
             DsTotals1.Tables("qryOrderTotals")).Count - 1
            Me.lblPosition.Text = ((Me.BindingContext( _
             DsTotals1.Tables("qryOrderTotals")).Position + 1).ToString _
             + " of " + Me.BindingContext( _
             DsTotals1.Tables("qryOrderTotals")).Count.ToString)

        Catch ex As Exception
            MsgBox("Error: " & ex.Source & ": " & ex.Message, _
             MsgBoxStyle.OKOnly, "btnLast_Click")
        End Try
```

As you can probably guess from looking at Listing 17.2, the BindingContext property of the form actually returns a collection of CurrencyManager objects. That makes sense, because a form can have many different controls bound to many different data sources. Each data source that is used for data binding is represented by a separate CurrencyManager object. All the CurrencyManager objects are accessible through the BindingContext property.

Complex Data Binding

If that was simple data binding, you may be wondering how tough the code might be for complex data binding! Fortunately, complex data binding isn't really any more complicated than simple data binding; it's just a different way to hook up a control to data. With complex data binding, instead of connecting a property to a single value from a data source, you connect a property to a collection of values from a data source. That collection might be one-dimensional (such as all the values in a particular column), two-dimensional (such as all the values in a particular table), or even more complex (such as all the values in an entire DataSet).

Binding Data to a ListBox, CheckedListBox, or ComboBox

The ListBox, CheckedListBox, and ComboBox controls can each be bound to a Data-Column. To do so, you need to set two properties of the control:

- The *DataSource* property specifies a DataTable or DataView that contains the DataColumn to be bound.

- The *DisplayMember* property specifies the DataColumn to be bound.

The frmComplex sample form includes one of each of these controls. They're all bound to SQL Server data in the form's Load event, as shown in the following code.

NOTE The Load procedure for this form connects to data on a server named SKYROCKET. To run the project, you'll need to change this to match the name of your own server.

```
cmdEmployees = cnn.CreateCommand
cmdEmployees.CommandText = _
  "SELECT FirstName + ' ' + LastName AS FullName FROM Employees"
daEmployees.SelectCommand = cmdEmployees
daEmployees.Fill(dsMain, "Employees")

lboEmployees.DataSource = dsMain.Tables("Employees")
lboEmployees.DisplayMember = "FullName"

cmdProducts = cnn.CreateCommand
cmdProducts.CommandText = _
  "SELECT ProductName FROM Products"
daProducts.SelectCommand = cmdProducts
daProducts.Fill(dsMain, "Products")

clbProducts.DataSource = dsMain.Tables("Products")
clbProducts.DisplayMember = "ProductName"

cmdShippers = cnn.CreateCommand
cmdShippers.CommandText = _
  "SELECT ShipperID, CompanyName FROM Shippers"
dashippers.SelectCommand = cmdShippers
dashippers.Fill(dsMain, "Shippers")

cboShippers.DataSource = dsMain.Tables("Shippers")
cboShippers.DisplayMember = "CompanyName"
cboShippers.ValueMember = "ShipperID"
```

NOTE This code stores three DataTables in a single DataSet without creating any relationships between the DataTables. The DataSet is just used as a container to hold all the DataTables.

The code to initialize the cboShippers ComboBox control demonstrates that you can use these controls to perform database lookups by utilizing their ValueMember property as well as their DisplayMember property. (Although it's not shown in this sample, the ListBox and CheckedListBox controls share these properties.) The DisplayMember property provides the data to be displayed in the control, but the ValueMember property provides the data for the SelectedValue property of the control. The sample form includes a small bit of code to display the SelectedValue in a TextBox control whenever the user selects a row in the ComboBox:

```
Private Sub cboShippers_SelectedIndexChanged( _
  ByVal sender As System.Object, ByVal e As System.EventArgs) _
  Handles cboShippers.SelectedIndexChanged

    Try
        txtShipperID.Text = cboShippers.SelectedValue
    Catch
    End Try

End Sub
```

Binding Data to a DataGrid

The next step up in complexity is to bind a DataTable to a DataGrid. The DataGrid, of course, can display data in both rows and columns—the perfect visual metaphor for a table of data. To display a DataTable on a DataGrid, simply supply the DataSet object as the Data-Source property for the DataGrid and supply the name of the DataTable as the DataMember property of the DataGrid:

```
dgShippers.DataSource = dsMain
dgShippers.DataMember = "Shippers"
```

You can also bind an entire DataSet to a DataGrid. The frmComplex form includes code to build a DataSet containing two different DataTables. The code then binds this to a pair of DataGrids in two ways:

```
Dim cmdCustomers As New SqlCommand()
Dim daCustomers As New SqlDataAdapter()
Dim cmdOrders As New SqlCommand()
Dim daOrders As New SqlDataAdapter()

cmdCustomers = cnn.CreateCommand
cmdCustomers.CommandText = _
  "SELECT * FROM Customers"
daCustomers.SelectCommand = cmdCustomers
daCustomers.Fill(dsCustomerOrders, "Customers")

cmdOrders = cnn.CreateCommand
cmdOrders.CommandText = _
  "SELECT * FROM Orders"
daOrders.SelectCommand = cmdOrders
daOrders.Fill(dsCustomerOrders, "Orders")

Dim relCustOrder As DataRelation = _
  dsCustomerOrders.Relations.Add("CustOrder", _
  dsCustomerOrders.Tables("Customers").Columns("CustomerID"), _
  dsCustomerOrders.Tables("Orders").Columns("CustomerID"))
```

```
dgCustomerOrders1.DataSource = dsCustomerOrders
dgCustomerOrders2.DataSource = dsCustomerOrders
dgCustomerOrders2.DataMember = "Customers"
```

Figure 17.4 shows the completed frmComplex with its variety of complex data-bound controls.

FIGURE 17.4:

Complex data binding

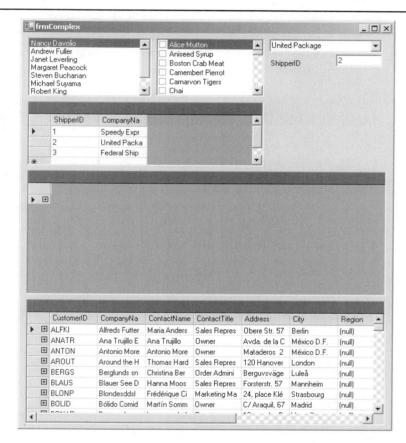

The differences in appearance of the three DataGrid controls result from the differences in the ways that they were bound:

- A DataGrid bound to a single DataTable that isn't related to any other DataTables, or to a DataTable that doesn't have any child DataTables, loads and displays all the rows of the DataTable when it is instantiated.

- A DataGrid bound to an entire DataSet shows only a single record selector with the + expander button when it is instantiated. Clicking the expander button will show hyperlinks to all the DataTables within the DataSet. Clicking one of those hyperlinks will load and display all the rows of the selected DataTable. You can click the Back button in the upper-right corner of the DataGrid to return to the hyperlinks after loading a DataTable.

- A DataGrid bound to a DataTable that does have child DataTables loads and displays all the rows of the parent DataTable and displays a + expander button with each row when it is instantiated. Clicking the expander button will show hyperlinks to all the DataRelations in which this DataTable is the parent. Clicking a hyperlink from the list will load and display the related child rows, and compress the parent row to a header row in the DataGrid. You can click the Back button in the upper-right corner of the DataGrid to return to the parent DataTable after loading a child DataTable.

Manipulating Data through Windows Forms

In addition to displaying data on a Windows Form in bound controls, you can save changes in that data back to the original data source. With complex-bound controls such as the Data-Grid, manipulating the data is just a matter of making changes through the user interface. If the DataSet that provides the data was instantiated with enough information (via the Command properties of the DataAdapter), changes will automatically be passed back to the data source when you call the Update method of the DataAdapter. This technique is covered in Chapter 15, "Editing Data with ADO.NET."

If you're using simple-bound controls, there's a bit more to learn. As I hinted earlier in the chapter, you can use methods of the CurrencyManager class to edit data shown in simple-bound controls. In this section, I'll show how you can use these methods to perform the fundamental data manipulation tasks:

- Editing existing data
- Adding new data
- Deleting existing data

In this chapter's sample project, the frmCustomers form demonstrates all of these tasks, as well as navigation and saving the changes back to the original data source. Listing 17.3 shows the code that runs this form. The form itself is shown in Figure 17.5.

TIP   Although this chapter will teach you to write the code for manipulating data in bound forms, you may find that you never actually have to write that code yourself. You'll learn about the built-in Data Form Wizard in Chapter 27, "Using ADO.NET from Visual Basic .NET." It's important, though, that you understand the code before you start using the wizard, so that you can tune it for your own use.

TIP   In Listing 17.3, you'll see that the data is loaded from a database in AppDomain.Current-Domain.BaseDirectory. That's the closest equivalent that Visual Basic .NET offers for the App.Path property of Visual Basic 6. It gives you the directory from which the current assembly was loaded. This is not guaranteed to be the source code directory—the assembly, for example, could have been placed in the Global Assembly Cache—but in the case of simple applications like this, it's likely to be correct.

FIGURE 17.5:

The frmCustomers form

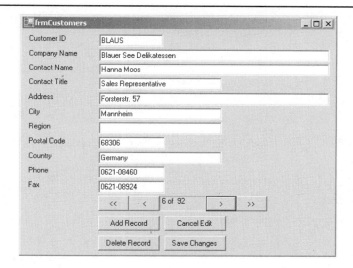

Listing 17.3:   Code for frmCustomers

```
Dim daCustomers As New OleDbDataAdapter()
Dim dsCustomers As New DataSet()

Private Sub frmCustomers_Load(ByVal sender As System.Object, _
 ByVal e As System.EventArgs) Handles MyBase.Load

    Dim cnn As OleDbConnection = New OleDbConnection( _
      "Provider=Microsoft.Jet.OLEDB.4.0;" & _
      "Data Source=" & AppDomain.CurrentDomain.BaseDirectory & _
      "ADOChapter17.mdb")
    Dim cmdCustomers As New OleDbCommand()

    Try
        cmdCustomers = cnn.CreateCommand
        cmdCustomers.CommandText = _
          "SELECT * FROM Customers"
        daCustomers.SelectCommand = cmdCustomers
        ' Automatically generate the Update, Insert,
        ' and Delete commands
```

```vb
            Dim cb As OleDbCommandBuilder = _
            New OleDbCommandBuilder(daCustomers)
            daCustomers.Fill(dsCustomers, "Customers")

            txtCustomerID.DataBindings.Add( _
             "Text", dsCustomers.Tables("Customers"), "CustomerID")
            txtCompanyName.DataBindings.Add( _
             "Text", dsCustomers.Tables("Customers"), "CompanyName")
            txtContactName.DataBindings.Add( _
             "Text", dsCustomers.Tables("Customers"), "ContactName")
            txtContactTitle.DataBindings.Add( _
             "Text", dsCustomers.Tables("Customers"), "ContactTitle")
            txtAddress.DataBindings.Add( _
             "Text", dsCustomers.Tables("Customers"), "Address")
            txtCity.DataBindings.Add( _
             "Text", dsCustomers.Tables("Customers"), "City")
            txtRegion.DataBindings.Add( _
             "Text", dsCustomers.Tables("Customers"), "Region")
            txtPostalCode.DataBindings.Add( _
             "Text", dsCustomers.Tables("Customers"), "PostalCode")
            txtCountry.DataBindings.Add( _
             "Text", dsCustomers.Tables("Customers"), "Country")
            txtPhone.DataBindings.Add( _
             "Text", dsCustomers.Tables("Customers"), "Phone")
            txtFax.DataBindings.Add( _
             "Text", dsCustomers.Tables("Customers"), "Fax")

            UpdatePosition()

    Catch ex As Exception
        MsgBox("Error: " & ex.Source & ": " & ex.Message, _
        MsgBoxStyle.OKOnly, "frmCustomers_Load")
    End Try

End Sub

Private Sub UpdatePosition()
    Me.lblPosition.Text = ((Me.BindingContext( _
    dsCustomers.Tables("Customers")).Position + 1).ToString _
    + " of " + Me.BindingContext( _
    dsCustomers.Tables("Customers")).Count.ToString)
End Sub

Private Sub btnNext_Click(ByVal sender As System.Object, _
 ByVal e As System.EventArgs) Handles btnNext.Click

    Try
        Me.BindingContext( _
         dsCustomers.Tables("Customers")).Position += 1
        UpdatePosition()

    Catch ex As Exception
        MsgBox("Error: " & ex.Source & ": " & ex.Message, _
        MsgBoxStyle.OKOnly, "btnNext_Click")
```

```vb
        End Try

    End Sub

    Private Sub btnFirst_Click(ByVal sender As System.Object, _
      ByVal e As System.EventArgs) Handles btnFirst.Click

        Try
            Me.BindingContext( _
              dsCustomers.Tables("Customers")).Position = 0
            UpdatePosition()

        Catch ex As Exception
            MsgBox("Error: " & ex.Source & ": " & ex.Message, _
              MsgBoxStyle.OKOnly, "btnFirst_Click")
        End Try

    End Sub

    Private Sub btnPrevious_Click(ByVal sender As System.Object, _
      ByVal e As System.EventArgs) Handles btnPrevious.Click

        Try
            Me.BindingContext( _
              dsCustomers.Tables("Customers")).Position -= 1
            UpdatePosition()

        Catch ex As Exception
            MsgBox("Error: " & ex.Source & ": " & ex.Message, _
              MsgBoxStyle.OKOnly, "btnNext_Click")
        End Try

    End Sub

    Private Sub btnLast_Click(ByVal sender As System.Object, _
      ByVal e As System.EventArgs) Handles btnLast.Click

        Try
            Me.BindingContext( _
              dsCustomers.Tables("Customers")).Position = _
              Me.BindingContext( _
              dsCustomers.Tables("Customers")).Count - 1
            UpdatePosition()

        Catch ex As Exception
            MsgBox("Error: " & ex.Source & ": " & ex.Message, _
              MsgBoxStyle.OKOnly, "btnLast_Click")
        End Try

    End Sub

    Private Sub btnSaveChanges_Click(ByVal sender As System.Object, _
      ByVal e As System.EventArgs) Handles btnSaveChanges.Click
```

```
    Try
        Me.BindingContext( _
         dsCustomers.Tables("Customers")).EndCurrentEdit()
        daCustomers.Update(dsCustomers.Tables("Customers"))

    Catch ex As Exception
        MsgBox("Error: " & ex.Source & ": " & ex.Message, _
         MsgBoxStyle.OKOnly, "btnSaveChanges_Click")
    End Try

End Sub

Private Sub btnCancelEdit_Click(ByVal sender As System.Object, _
 ByVal e As System.EventArgs) Handles btnCancelEdit.Click

    Try
        Me.BindingContext( _
         dsCustomers.Tables("Customers")).CancelCurrentEdit()
        UpdatePosition()

    Catch ex As Exception
        MsgBox("Error: " & ex.Source & ": " & ex.Message, _
         MsgBoxStyle.OKOnly, "btnCancelEdit_Click")
    End Try

End Sub

Private Sub btnAddRecord_Click(ByVal sender As System.Object, _
 ByVal e As System.EventArgs) Handles btnAddRecord.Click

    Try
        Me.BindingContext( _
         dsCustomers.Tables("Customers")).EndCurrentEdit()
        Me.BindingContext( _
         dsCustomers.Tables("Customers")).AddNew()
        UpdatePosition()

    Catch ex As Exception
        MsgBox("Error: " & ex.Source & ": " & ex.Message, _
         MsgBoxStyle.OKOnly, "btnAddRecord_Click")
    End Try

End Sub

Private Sub btnDeleteRecord_Click(ByVal sender As System.Object, _
 ByVal e As System.EventArgs) Handles btnDeleteRecord.Click

    Try
        Me.BindingContext( _
         dsCustomers.Tables("Customers")).RemoveAt(Me.BindingContext( _
         dsCustomers.Tables("Customers")).Position)
```

```
        UpdatePosition()

    Catch ex As Exception
        MsgBox("Error: " & ex.Source & ": " & ex.Message, _
          MsgBoxStyle.OKOnly, "btnAddRecord_Click")
    End Try

End Sub
```

Editing a Row of Data

You don't have to do anything special to edit data in bound controls (you may have noticed that there's no BeginEdit method in Listing 17.3). Once the control is bound, changes to the data are automatically reflected in the underlying DataSet. But there are two methods of the CurrencyManager object that you may need to use in the course of editing data:

- The CancelCurrentEdit method throws away any changes that have been made to the current row of data before they can be saved to the DataSet.

- The EndCurrentEdit method takes all the changes to the current row of data and saves them to the DataSet. Changes are also saved whenever you navigate to another row by changing the Position property of the CurrencyManager object.

Remember, though, that any changes you make by editing data in a bound control are made only to the DataSet and not to the underlying data source. You still need to call the Update method of the appropriate DataAdapter (which must have the appropriate Command properties filled in) to finally save the changes. That's the purpose of the code that gets called from the Save Changes button:

```
    Private Sub btnSaveChanges_Click(ByVal sender As System.Object, _
      ByVal e As System.EventArgs) Handles btnSaveChanges.Click

        Try
            Me.BindingContext( _
              dsCustomers.Tables("Customers")).EndCurrentEdit()
            daCustomers.Update(dsCustomers.Tables("Customers"))

        Catch ex As Exception
            MsgBox("Error: " & ex.Source & ": " & ex.Message, _
              MsgBoxStyle.OKOnly, "btnSaveChanges_Click")
        End Try

    End Sub
```

The call to EndCurrentEdit makes sure that any changes to the current record are saved to the DataSet before the DataSet, in turn, is saved to the data source.

Adding a Row of Data

To add a fresh row of data to the DataSet, call the AddNew method of the CurrencyManager object:

```
Private Sub btnAddRecord_Click(ByVal sender As System.Object, _
  ByVal e As System.EventArgs) Handles btnAddRecord.Click

    Try
        Me.BindingContext( _
          dsCustomers.Tables("Customers")).EndCurrentEdit()
        Me.BindingContext( _
          dsCustomers.Tables("Customers")).AddNew()
        UpdatePosition()

    Catch ex As Exception
        MsgBox("Error: " & ex.Source & ": " & ex.Message, _
          MsgBoxStyle.OKOnly, "btnAddRecord_Click")
    End Try

End Sub
```

This procedure calls the EndCurrentEdit method before it calls the AddNew method. This avoids losing any changes that might have been pending on the current record when the user clicks the Add Record button.

If you call the AddNew method, and then call the CancelCurrentEdit method without either moving off the record or calling the EndCurrentEdit method, the new row will not be added to the DataSet.

Deleting a Row of Data

Deleting a row of data via simple-bound controls requires a call to the RemoveAt method of the CurrencyManager object. There isn't any DeleteRow method to operate on the current row. Instead, the RemoveAt method removes a row at a particular index in the data source. Fortunately, you can use the Position property of the CurrencyManager to get the index of the current row:

```
Private Sub btnDeleteRecord_Click(ByVal sender As System.Object, _
  ByVal e As System.EventArgs) Handles btnDeleteRecord.Click

    Try
        Me.BindingContext( _
          dsCustomers.Tables("Customers")).RemoveAt(Me.BindingContext( _
          dsCustomers.Tables("Customers")).Position)
        UpdatePosition()

    Catch ex As Exception
        MsgBox("Error: " & ex.Source & ": " & ex.Message, _
```

```
        MsgBoxStyle.OKOnly, "btnAddRecord_Click")
    End Try

End Sub
```

Note that there isn't any "undo" for a deletion. If you call RemoveAt and then call Cancel-CurrentEdit, the deletion won't be cancelled. Of course, if you don't call the Update method of the DataAdapter, the deletions won't be made in the original data source.

TIP   You can prevent any deletions being made in the original data source by removing the Data-Adapter's DeleteCommand before calling its Update method.

A More Complex Sample

As a final example, I'll look at the order entry form shown in Figure 17.6. This form lets you browse and alter the data in three related tables (Customers, Orders, and Order Details). Listing 17.4 contains the code for this form.

FIGURE 17.6:

The frmOrderEntry form

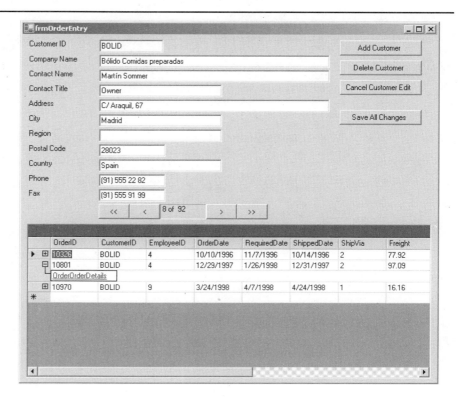

Listing 17.4:   **Code for frmOrderEntry**

```
Dim daCustomers As New OleDbDataAdapter()
Dim daOrders As New OleDbDataAdapter()
Dim daOrderDetails As New OleDbDataAdapter()
Dim dsMain As New DataSet()

Private Sub frmOrderEntry_Load(ByVal sender As System.Object, _
 ByVal e As System.EventArgs) Handles MyBase.Load

    Dim cnn As OleDbConnection = New OleDbConnection( _
     "Provider=Microsoft.Jet.OLEDB.4.0;" & _
     "Data Source=" & AppDomain.CurrentDomain.BaseDirectory & _
     "ADOChapter17.mdb")
    Dim cmdCustomers As New OleDbCommand()
    Dim cmdOrders As New OleDbCommand()
    Dim cmdOrderDetails As New OleDbCommand()

    Try
        cmdCustomers = cnn.CreateCommand
        cmdCustomers.CommandText = _
         "SELECT * FROM Customers"
        daCustomers.SelectCommand = cmdCustomers
        Dim cbCustomers As OleDbCommandBuilder = _
         New OleDbCommandBuilder(daCustomers)
        daCustomers.Fill(dsMain, "Customers")

        cmdOrders = cnn.CreateCommand
        cmdOrders.CommandText = _
         "SELECT * FROM Orders"
        daOrders.SelectCommand = cmdOrders
        Dim cbOrders As OleDbCommandBuilder = _
         New OleDbCommandBuilder(daOrders)
        daOrders.Fill(dsMain, "Orders")

        cmdOrderDetails = cnn.CreateCommand
        cmdOrderDetails.CommandText = _
         "SELECT * FROM [Order Details]"
        daOrderDetails.SelectCommand = cmdOrderDetails
        Dim cbOrderDetails As OleDbCommandBuilder = _
         New OleDbCommandBuilder(daOrderDetails)
        daOrderDetails.Fill(dsMain, "OrderDetails")

        Dim relCustOrder As DataRelation = _
         dsMain.Relations.Add("CustOrder", _
         dsMain.Tables("Customers").Columns("CustomerID"), _
         dsMain.Tables("Orders").Columns("CustomerID"))

        Dim relOrderOrderDetails As DataRelation = _
         dsMain.Relations.Add("OrderOrderDetails", _
         dsMain.Tables("Orders").Columns("OrderID"), _
         dsMain.Tables("OrderDetails").Columns("OrderID"))
```

```
            txtCustomerID.DataBindings.Add( _
             "Text", dsMain, "Customers.CustomerID")
            txtCompanyName.DataBindings.Add( _
             "Text", dsMain, "Customers.CompanyName")
            txtContactName.DataBindings.Add( _
             "Text", dsMain, "Customers.ContactName")
            txtContactTitle.DataBindings.Add( _
             "Text", dsMain, "Customers.ContactTitle")
            txtAddress.DataBindings.Add( _
             "Text", dsMain, "Customers.Address")
            txtCity.DataBindings.Add( _
             "Text", dsMain, "Customers.City")
            txtRegion.DataBindings.Add( _
             "Text", dsMain, "Customers.Region")
            txtPostalCode.DataBindings.Add( _
             "Text", dsMain, "Customers.PostalCode")
            txtCountry.DataBindings.Add( _
             "Text", dsMain, "Customers.Country")
            txtPhone.DataBindings.Add( _
             "Text", dsMain, "Customers.Phone")
            txtFax.DataBindings.Add( _
             "Text", dsMain, "Customers.Fax")

            dgOrders.DataSource = dsMain
            dgOrders.DataMember = "Customers.CustOrder"

            UpdatePosition()

        Catch ex As Exception
            MsgBox("Error: " & ex.Source & ": " & ex.Message, _
            MsgBoxStyle.OKOnly, "frmOrderEntry_Load")
        End Try

    End Sub

    Private Sub UpdatePosition()
        Me.lblPosition.Text = ((Me.BindingContext( _
         dsMain, "Customers").Position + 1).ToString _
        + " of " + Me.BindingContext( _
         dsMain, "Customers").Count.ToString)
    End Sub

    Private Sub btnNext_Click(ByVal sender As System.Object, _
     ByVal e As System.EventArgs) Handles btnNext.Click

        Try
            Me.BindingContext( _
             dsMain, "Customers").Position += 1
            UpdatePosition()

        Catch ex As Exception
            MsgBox("Error: " & ex.Source & ": " & ex.Message, _
            MsgBoxStyle.OKOnly, "btnNext_Click")
```

```vbnet
            End Try

    End Sub

    Private Sub btnFirst_Click(ByVal sender As System.Object, _
      ByVal e As System.EventArgs) Handles btnFirst.Click

        Try
            Me.BindingContext( _
             dsMain, "Customers").Position = 0
            UpdatePosition()

        Catch ex As Exception
            MsgBox("Error: " & ex.Source & ": " & ex.Message, _
             MsgBoxStyle.OKOnly, "btnFirst_Click")
        End Try

    End Sub

    Private Sub btnPrevious_Click(ByVal sender As System.Object, _
      ByVal e As System.EventArgs) Handles btnPrevious.Click

        Try
            Me.BindingContext( _
             dsMain, "Customers").Position -= 1
            UpdatePosition()

        Catch ex As Exception
            MsgBox("Error: " & ex.Source & ": " & ex.Message, _
             MsgBoxStyle.OKOnly, "btnNext_Click")
        End Try

    End Sub

    Private Sub btnLast_Click(ByVal sender As System.Object, _
      ByVal e As System.EventArgs) Handles btnLast.Click

        Try
            Me.BindingContext( _
             dsMain, "Customers").Position = _
             Me.BindingContext( _
             dsMain, "Customers").Count - 1
            UpdatePosition()

        Catch ex As Exception
            MsgBox("Error: " & ex.Source & ": " & ex.Message, _
             MsgBoxStyle.OKOnly, "btnLast_Click")
        End Try

    End Sub
```

```
Private Sub btnSaveChanges_Click(ByVal sender As System.Object, _
 ByVal e As System.EventArgs) Handles btnSaveChanges.Click

    Try
        Me.BindingContext( _
         dsMain, "Customers").EndCurrentEdit()
        daCustomers.Update(dsMain.Tables("Customers"))

    Catch ex As Exception
        MsgBox("Error: " & ex.Source & ": " & ex.Message, _
         MsgBoxStyle.OKOnly, "btnSaveChanges_Click")
    End Try

End Sub

Private Sub btnCancelEdit_Click(ByVal sender As System.Object, _
 ByVal e As System.EventArgs) Handles btnCancelEdit.Click

    Try
        Me.BindingContext( _
         dsMain, "Customers").CancelCurrentEdit()
        UpdatePosition()

    Catch ex As Exception
        MsgBox("Error: " & ex.Source & ": " & ex.Message, _
         MsgBoxStyle.OKOnly, "btnCancelEdit_Click")
    End Try

End Sub

Private Sub btnAddRecord_Click(ByVal sender As System.Object, _
 ByVal e As System.EventArgs) Handles btnAddRecord.Click

    Try
        Me.BindingContext( _
         dsMain, "Customers").EndCurrentEdit()
        Me.BindingContext( _
         dsMain, "Customers").AddNew()
        UpdatePosition()

    Catch ex As Exception
        MsgBox("Error: " & ex.Source & ": " & ex.Message, _
         MsgBoxStyle.OKOnly, "btnAddRecord_Click")
    End Try

End Sub

Private Sub btnDeleteRecord_Click(ByVal sender As System.Object, _
 ByVal e As System.EventArgs) Handles btnDeleteRecord.Click

    Try
```

```
        Me.BindingContext( _
          dsMain, "Customers").RemoveAt(Me.BindingContext( _
          dsMain, "Customers").Position)
        UpdatePosition()

    Catch ex As Exception
        MsgBox("Error: " & ex.Source & ": " & ex.Message, _
        MsgBoxStyle.OKOnly, "btnAddRecord_Click")
    End Try

End Sub
```

Most of this code should be familiar to you from earlier in the chapter, but it's worthwhile to take a close look at the data-binding code. If you try the form, you'll discover that the Customer data and the DataGrid that shows Orders and Order Details all remain synchronized. For this to happen, all of these controls must share the same CurrencyManager, which means that they must all use the same binding object. This results in some syntactical differences from the code that I used earlier in the chapter.

For example, here's the code that sets up the data binding for the txtCustomerID control:

```
txtCustomerID.DataBindings.Add( _
  "Text", dsMain, "Customers.CustomerID")
```

Rather than specify the DataTable as the object to bind (as did the examples earlier in the chapter), this line of code uses the entire DataSet as the object to bind. The item to bind is specified by the format *DataTable.DataColumn*—here, the CustomerID column in the Customers table.

Similarly, the DataGrid is also bound to the dsMain DataSet, specifically to the CustOrder relation within the DataSet:

```
dgOrders.DataSource = dsMain
dgOrders.DataMember = "Customers.CustOrder"
```

Specifying a DataRelation rather than a DataTable as the top level to bind to the DataGrid means that the form will know how to keep this DataTable synchronized with the other controls on the form. Because all the display controls are based on the Customers table at their top level, they can all be manipulated by using a CurrencyManager that specifies that table. For instance, here's the code that moves forward in the DataSet (and thus updates all the controls on the form to display data from the next row of the DataSet):

```
Private Sub btnNext_Click(ByVal sender As System.Object, _
  ByVal e As System.EventArgs) Handles btnNext.Click

    Try
        Me.BindingContext( _
          dsMain, "Customers").Position += 1
        UpdatePosition()
```

```
Catch ex As Exception
    MsgBox("Error: " & ex.Source & ": " & ex.Message, _
    MsgBoxStyle.OKOnly, "btnNext_Click")
End Try

End Sub
```

As you can see, the BindingContext property is overloaded to allow you to specify both the object and the path within the object that supplies the binding in which you are interested.

Summary

In this chapter, you've learned about using both simple- and complex-bound controls on Windows Forms to display ADO.NET data. You saw how to hook these controls to data from the Visual Basic .NET interface (which provides rapid development capabilities) as well as from code (which provides more control over the results). You also learned how to navigate through data with bound controls and how to use bound controls to alter the data.

In the next chapter, I'm going to look at some of the features that .NET provides for synchronizing DataSets and XML beyond the disconnected DataSet features that you already saw in Chapter 16.

CHAPTER 18

Synchronizing DataSets with XML

- Understanding XmlDataDocuments

- Synchronizing a DataSet with an XmlDataDocument

- Using synchronized objects

In Chapter 16, "Working with Disconnected DataSets," you saw how you could use XML as a transmission format for the DataSet. But the connections between the DataSet and XML in .NET go much deeper than that. In this chapter, I'll introduce you to the XmlData-Document class, which provides you with a general tool to represent any XML document. Then you'll see how to synchronize a DataSet with an XmlDataDocument, and I'll explore the powerful processing that this synchronization makes possible.

Understanding XmlDataDocuments

The key .NET Framework class for synchronizing a DataSet with an XML representation of the same data is the XmlDataDocument. Before you can understand this class, though, you should have a grasp of the XmlDocument class, since XmlDataDocument inherits from and extends XmlDocument. The XmlDocument class, in turn, is an implementation of the Document Object Model. So, to start working with DataSets and XML, the first thing to explore is the Document Object Model.

The Document Object Model

The Document Object Model, or DOM, is an Internet standard for representing the information contained in an HTML or XML document as a tree of nodes. Like many other Internet standards, the DOM is an official standard of the W3C. According to the W3C, the DOM specification "defines the Document Object Model, a platform- and language-neutral interface that will allow programs and scripts to dynamically access and update the content, structure, and style of documents. The Document Object Model provides a standard set of objects for representing HTML and XML documents, a standard model of how these objects can be combined, and a standard interface for accessing and manipulating them."

Despite the existence of the DOM specifications, though, there are numerous differences in DOM implementations by different vendors. Microsoft is no exception here. The .NET Framework includes support for the DOM Level 1 Core and DOM Level 2 Core specifications, but it also extends the DOM by adding additional objects, methods, and properties to the specifications. This is typical of Internet vendors. While a grasp of the applicable standard will get you started understanding a technology such as the DOM, you'll need to look at a particular vendor's tools to determine exactly how that technology is implemented by that vendor.

NOTE   For the official DOM specifications, see www.w3.org/DOM. The XML Cover Pages website also has a nice set of DOM-related links at www.oasis-open.org/cover/dom.html.

To explore the DOM, I'll use an XML file containing a few customers, their associated orders, and the schema information necessary to reconstitute this XML file as a DataSet. This file is shown in Listing 18.1.

Listing 18.1:   CustOrders.xml

```
<?xml version="1.0" standalone="yes"?>
<CustomerOrders>
  <xs:schema id="CustomerOrders" xmlns=""
➥ xmlns:xs="http://www.w3.org/2001/XMLSchema"
➥ xmlns:msdata="urn:schemas-microsoft-com:xml-msdata">
    <xs:element name="CustomerOrders" msdata:IsDataSet="true">
      <xs:complexType>
        <xs:choice maxOccurs="unbounded">
          <xs:element name="Customers">
            <xs:complexType>
              <xs:sequence>
                <xs:element name="ContactName" type="xs:string"
➥ minOccurs="0" msdata:Ordinal="2" />
                <xs:element name="ContactTitle" type="xs:string"
➥ minOccurs="0" msdata:Ordinal="3" />
                <xs:element name="Address" type="xs:string"
➥ minOccurs="0" msdata:Ordinal="4" />
                <xs:element name="City" type="xs:string" minOccurs="0"
➥ msdata:Ordinal="5" />
                <xs:element name="Region" type="xs:string"
➥ minOccurs="0" msdata:Ordinal="6" />
                <xs:element name="PostalCode" type="xs:string"
➥ minOccurs="0" msdata:Ordinal="7" />
                <xs:element name="Country" type="xs:string"
➥ minOccurs="0" msdata:Ordinal="8" />
                <xs:element name="Phone" type="xs:string" minOccurs="0"
➥ msdata:Ordinal="9" />
                <xs:element name="Fax" type="xs:string" minOccurs="0"
➥ msdata:Ordinal="10" />
                <xs:element name="Orders" minOccurs="0"
➥ maxOccurs="unbounded">
                  <xs:complexType>
                    <xs:sequence>
                      <xs:element name="OrderID" type="xs:int"
➥ minOccurs="0" />
                      <xs:element name="CustomerID" type="xs:string"
➥ minOccurs="0" />
                      <xs:element name="EmployeeID" type="xs:int"
➥ minOccurs="0" />
                      <xs:element name="OrderDate" type="xs:dateTime"
➥ minOccurs="0" />
                      <xs:element name="RequiredDate" type="xs:dateTime"
➥ minOccurs="0" />
                      <xs:element name="ShippedDate" type="xs:dateTime"
➥ minOccurs="0" />
```

```
                            <xs:element name="ShipVia" type="xs:int"
➡ minOccurs="0" />
                            <xs:element name="Freight" type="xs:decimal"
➡ minOccurs="0" />
                            <xs:element name="ShipName" type="xs:string"
➡ minOccurs="0" />
                            <xs:element name="ShipAddress" type="xs:string"
➡ minOccurs="0" />
                            <xs:element name="ShipCity" type="xs:string"
➡ minOccurs="0" />
                            <xs:element name="ShipRegion" type="xs:string"
➡ minOccurs="0" />
                            <xs:element name="ShipPostalCode"
➡ type="xs:string" minOccurs="0" />
                            <xs:element name="ShipCountry" type="xs:string"
➡ minOccurs="0" />
                          </xs:sequence>
                        </xs:complexType>
                      </xs:element>
                    </xs:sequence>
                    <xs:attribute name="CustomerID" type="xs:string" />
                    <xs:attribute name="CompanyName" type="xs:string" />
                  </xs:complexType>
                </xs:element>
              </xs:choice>
            </xs:complexType>
            <xs:unique name="Constraint1">
              <xs:selector xpath=".//Customers" />
              <xs:field xpath="@CustomerID" />
            </xs:unique>
            <xs:keyref name="CustOrder" refer="Constraint1"
➡ msdata:IsNested="true">
              <xs:selector xpath=".//Orders" />
              <xs:field xpath="CustomerID" />
            </xs:keyref>
          </xs:element>
        </xs:schema>
        <Customers CustomerID="ALFKI" CompanyName="Alfreds Futterkiste">
          <ContactName>Joe Graham</ContactName>
          <ContactTitle>Sales Representative</ContactTitle>
          <Address>Obere Str. 57</Address>
          <City>Berlin</City>
          <PostalCode>12209</PostalCode>
          <Country>Germany</Country>
          <Phone>030-0074321</Phone>
          <Fax>030-0076545</Fax>
          <Orders>
            <OrderID>10248</OrderID>
            <CustomerID>ALFKI</CustomerID>
            <EmployeeID>5</EmployeeID>
            <OrderDate>1996-07-04T00:00:00.0000000-07:00</OrderDate>
```

```
            <RequiredDate>1996-08-01T00:00:00.0000000-07:00</RequiredDate>
            <ShippedDate>1996-07-16T00:00:00.0000000-07:00</ShippedDate>
            <ShipVia>3</ShipVia>
            <Freight>32.38</Freight>
            <ShipName>Vins et alcools Chevalier</ShipName>
            <ShipAddress>59 rue de l'Abbaye</ShipAddress>
            <ShipCity>Reims</ShipCity>
            <ShipPostalCode>51100</ShipPostalCode>
            <ShipCountry>France</ShipCountry>
         </Orders>
         <Orders>
            <OrderID>10643</OrderID>
            <CustomerID>ALFKI</CustomerID>
            <EmployeeID>6</EmployeeID>
            <OrderDate>1997-08-25T00:00:00.0000000-07:00</OrderDate>
            <RequiredDate>1997-09-22T00:00:00.0000000-07:00</RequiredDate>
            <ShippedDate>1997-09-02T00:00:00.0000000-07:00</ShippedDate>
            <ShipVia>1</ShipVia>
            <Freight>29.46</Freight>
            <ShipName>Alfreds Futterkiste</ShipName>
            <ShipAddress>Obere Str. 57</ShipAddress>
            <ShipCity>Berlin</ShipCity>
            <ShipPostalCode>12209</ShipPostalCode>
            <ShipCountry>Germany</ShipCountry>
         </Orders>
Additional Orders omitted here...
      </Customers>
      <Customers CustomerID="ANATR" CompanyName="Ana Trujillo Emparedados y
helados">
         <ContactName>Ana Trujillo</ContactName>
         <ContactTitle>Owner</ContactTitle>
         <Address>Avda. de la Constitución 2222</Address>
         <City>México D.F.</City>
         <PostalCode>05021</PostalCode>
         <Country>Mexico</Country>
         <Phone>(5) 555-4729</Phone>
         <Fax>(5) 555-3745</Fax>
Orders omitted here...
      </Customers>
Additional Customers and Orders omitted here...
   </CustomerOrders>
```

NOTE   This XML file contains embedded schema information in XSD format. You'll find an introduction to XSD schemas in Chapter 16, "Working with Disconnected DataSets."

Structurally, an XML document is a series of nested items, including elements and attributes. Any nested structure can be transformed to an equivalent tree structure by making the outermost nested item the root of the tree, the next-in items the children of the root, and so on. Figure 18.1 shows a schematic representation of a portion of the CustOrders.xml file as a tree.

FIGURE 18.1:

Portion of an XML doc-
ument represented as
a tree

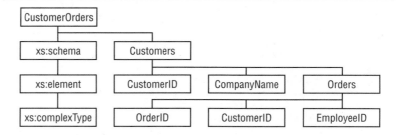

In converting an XML document to a tree, many different items may become nodes. In Figure 18.1, for example, Customers and Orders are nodes based on elements in the original XML, while CustomerID and CompanyName are nodes based on attributes. The DOM assigns a node type to each node to identify its source in the XML. The .NET Framework includes an XmlNodeType enumeration that distinguishes the possible node types in Microsoft's DOM implementation. Table 18.1 lists the members of this enumeration.

TIP The XmlNodeType enumeration, as well as the other XML classes discussed in this chapter, is a member of the System.Xml namespace.

TABLE 18.1: XmlNodeType Enumeration

Member	Represents
Attribute	An XML attribute
CDATA	An XML CDATA section
Comment	An XML comment
Document	The outermost element of the XML document (that is, the root of the tree representation of the XML)
DocumentFragment	The outermost element of a subsection of an XML document
DocumentType	A Document Type Description (DTD) reference
Element	An XML element
EndElement	The closing tag of an XML element
EndEntity	The end of an included entity
Entity	An XML entity declaration
EntityReference	A reference to an entity
None	Indication of an XmlReader that has not been initialized
Notation	An XML notation
ProcessingInstruction	An XML processing instruction
SignificantWhitespace	White space that must be preserved to recreate the original XML document
Text	The text content of an attribute, element, or other node
Whitespace	Space between actual XML markup items
XmlDeclaration	The XML declaration

Technically, attributes are not part of the DOM tree. Rather, they're considered properties of their parent element. Later in the chapter, you'll see how to retrieve a collection containing all the attributes belonging to a particular element.

Individual nodes in the DOM representation of an XML document are represented in the .NET Framework by XmlNode objects. After instantiating an XmlNode object that represents a particular portion of an XML file, you can alter the properties of the XmlNode object and then write the changes back to the XML file. The DOM provides two-way access to the underlying XML and is thus a convenient means for manipulating XML files.

The System.Xml namespace also contains a set of classes that represent particular types of nodes: XmlAttribute, XmlComment, XmlElement, and so on. These classes all inherit from the XmlNode class.

Table 18.2 lists some of the important methods and properties of the XmlNode object.

TABLE 18.2: XmlNode Members

Member	Type	Description
AppendChild	Method	Adds a new child node to the end of this node's list of children.
Attributes	Property	Returns the attributes of the node as an XmlAttributeCollection.
ChildNodes	Property	Returns all child nodes of this node.
CloneNode	Method	Creates a duplicate of this node.
FirstChild	Property	Returns the first child node of this node.
HasChildNodes	Property	True if this node has any children.
InnerText	Property	The value of the node and all its children.
InnerXml	Property	The markup representing only the children of this node.
InsertAfter	Method	Inserts a new node after this node.
InsertBefore	Method	Inserts a new node before this node.
LastChild	Property	Returns the last child node of this node.
Name	Property	The name of the node.
NextSibling	Property	Returns the next child of this node's parent node.
NodeType	Property	The type of this node.
OuterXml	Property	The markup representing this node and its children.
OwnerDocument	Property	The XmlDocument object that contains this node.
ParentNode	Property	Returns the parent of this node.
PrependChild	Method	Adds a new child node to the beginning of this node's list of children.

continued on next page

TABLE 18.2 CONTINUED: XmlNode Members

Member	Type	Description
PreviousSibling	Property	Returns the previous child of this node's parent node.
RemoveAll	Method	Removes all children of this node.
RemoveChild	Method	Removes a specified child of this node.
ReplaceChild	Method	Replaces a child of this node with a new node.
SelectNodes	Method	Selects a group of nodes matching an XPath expression.
SelectSingleNode	Method	Selects the first node matching an XPath expression.
WriteContentTo	Method	Writes all children of this node to an XmlWriter object.
WriteTo	Method	Writes this node to an XmlWriter.

As you can see, the XmlNode object has a comparatively rich interface. Figure 18.2 shows how some of the properties of this object work together to allow you to navigate within the DOM tree.

FIGURE 18.2:

Navigational properties of the XmlNode object

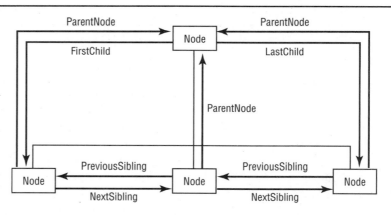

Note that although every node has a property to navigate directly to its parent node, the parent node doesn't have a property for every child node.

The XmlDocument Class

The XmlNode class represents one particular piece of an XML document. To represent the document as a whole, you need another class. Not surprisingly, this is the XmlDocument class. An instance of the XmlDocument class can be instantiated from an XML document, and it then provides access to the individual XmlNode objects that describe the document. The XmlDocument class has a rich interface, with many properties, methods, and events. Some of these are shown in Table 18.3.

TABLE 18.3: XmlDocument Members

Member	Type	Description
CreateAttribute	Method	Creates an attribute node.
CreateElement	Method	Creates an element node.
CreateNode	Method	Creates an XmlNode object.
DocumentElement	Property	Returns the root XmlElement for this document.
DocumentType	Property	Returns the node containing the DTD declaration for this document, if it has one.
GetElementsByTagName	Method	Returns a list of all elements with the specified tag name.
ImportNode	Method	Imports a node from another XML document.
Load	Method	Loads an XML document into the XmlDocument.
LoadXml	Method	Loads the XmlDocument from a string of XML data.
NodeChanged	Event	Fires after the value of a node has been changed.
NodeChanging	Event	Fires when the value of a node is about to be changed.
NodeInserted	Event	Fires when a new node has been inserted.
NodeInserting	Event	Fires when a new node is about to be inserted.
NodeRemoved	Event	Fires when a node has been removed.
NodeRemoving	Event	Fires when a node is about to be removed.
PreserveWhitespace	Property	True if white space in the document should be preserved when loading or saving the XML.
Save	Method	Saves the XmlDocument as a file or stream.
WriteTo	Method	Saves the XmlDocument to an XmlWriter.

By using the XmlDocument and XmlNode classes, you can produce a visual representation of any XML document as a treeview. Figure 18.3 shows the frmDOM form from the ADOChapter18 sample project. This form allows you to browse to any XML document on your hard drive and then view the DOM using a TreeView control.

The code for frmDOM makes use of the XmlDocument class to represent the document and uses the TreeView class (part of the System.Windows.Forms namespace) to represent the DOM visually on the screen. The TreeView contains a collection of TreeNode objects that form a tree and is thus a good match for a visual representation of the XmlDocument.

The code starts by declaring some necessary objects:

```
Dim dlgOpen As New OpenFileDialog()
Dim xnod As XmlNode
Dim tnod As TreeNode
```

Because this form juggles two different kinds of Node objects, a naming convention is essential. I've chosen to give all the XmlNode objects names beginning with "xnod," and all the TreeNode objects names beginning with "tnod."

FIGURE 18.3:

CustOrders.xml
translated into a
DOM tree

FIGURE 18.3:

CustOrders.xml
translated into a
DOM tree

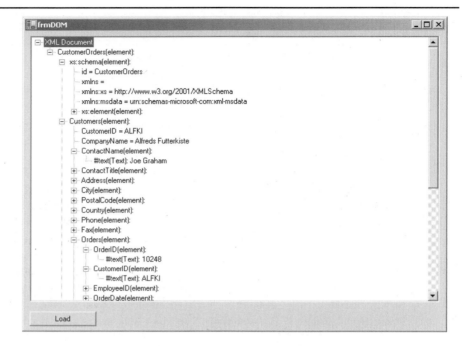

The first step in displaying the DOM is to select a file and to load it into an XmlDocument object:

```
dlgOpen.ShowDialog()
If Len(dlgOpen.FileName) > 0 Then

    Dim xtr As New XmlTextReader(dlgOpen.FileName)
    xtr.WhitespaceHandling = WhitespaceHandling.None
    Dim xdCustOrders As XmlDocument = New XmlDocument()
    xdCustOrders.Load(xtr)
```

The OpenFileDialog object displays the standard Windows File Open dialog when you call its ShowDialog method. If the user actually selects a file, there will be a FileName to read, and the code will proceed. The XmlTextReader class provides a pipeline between a disk file and another object (in this case, an XmlDocument object). Setting the Whitespace-Handling property of the XmlReader to `WhitespaceHandling.None` tells it that I'm not interested in white space for this example. When the XmlDocument object calls its Load method and supplies the XmlReader object, the entire contents of the selected XML file (except for, in this case, any white space) are brought into the XmlDocument.

TIP
The XmlDocument.Load method can load XML from a stream, a URL, a TextReader, or an XmlReader.

The code then creates a TreeNode to represent the root of the XmlDocument:

```
tnod = New TreeNode("XML Document")
tvwDOM.Nodes.Add(tnod)
```

When you call the TreeNode constructor, you can supply a string of text to be displayed in the TreeView for that TreeNode. In this case, the string is static text to give the TreeView a starting point. After constructing a new TreeNode, you can add it to the TreeView by calling the Add method of the TreeView's Nodes collection.

The main function finishes by retrieving the DocumentElement node from the XmlDocument and calling the AddChildren procedure:

```
xnod = xdCustOrders.DocumentElement
AddChildren(xnod, tnod)
```

AddChildren is a procedure that takes an XmlNode object and a TreeNode object, and adds XmlNode to the TreeView as a child of the supplied TreeNode. The AddChildren procedure then calls itself recursively to walk through the entire DOM tree. AddChildren starts by declaring some variables:

```
Dim xnodWorking As XmlNode
Dim tnodWorking As TreeNode
Dim tnodAttribute As TreeNode
```

AddChildren then adds the supplied XmlNode object to the TreeView:

```
tnodWorking = New TreeNode(xnod.Name & "(" & _
  GetNodeType(xnod.NodeType) & "): " & xnod.Value)
tnod.Nodes.Add(tnodWorking)
```

Here, the string displayed in the TreeNode is built up from the name of the XmlNode, the NodeType of the XmlNode, and the value of the XmlNode. The name of the XmlNode varies with the node type; for an element, it is the element name. The GetNodeType helper function translates the XmlNodeType enumeration values into corresponding strings. Listing 18.2 shows this function.

The new TreeNode is added to the Nodes collection of the TreeNode that was passed into AddChildren, not to the Nodes collection of the TreeView. That's what makes the new TreeNode a child of the supplied TreeNode.

If the current XmlNode represents an XML element, the AddChildren procedure has to run some special code to extract the attributes (if any) of the element:

```
If xnod.NodeType = XmlNodeType.Element Then
    Dim mapAttributes As XmlNamedNodeMap = xnod.Attributes
    Dim xnodAttribute As XmlNode
```

```
    For Each xnodAttribute In mapAttributes
        tnodAttribute = New TreeNode(xnodAttribute.Name & " = " & _
         xnodAttribute.Value)
        tnodWorking.Nodes.Add(tnodAttribute)
    Next
End If
```

Remember, attributes are not represented as children of the elements in the DOM. The XmlNamedNodeMap class can hold a collection of arbitrary XmlNode objects. In this case, it's filled from the Attributes property of the XmlNode that represents an element. The code uses a simple For Each loop to add all the attributes to the TreeView.

Finally, the AddChildren procedure checks to see whether the current XmlNode has any children; if so, it calls itself recursively:

```
If xnod.HasChildNodes Then
    xnodWorking = xnod.FirstChild
    While Not IsNothing(xnodWorking)
        AddChildren(xnodWorking, tnodWorking)
        xnodWorking = xnodWorking.NextSibling
    End While
End If
```

Listing 18.2:   GetNodeType Function

```
Private Function GetNodeType(ByVal typ As XmlNodeType) As String

    Try
        Select Case typ
            Case XmlNodeType.Attribute
                GetNodeType = "Attribute"
            Case XmlNodeType.CDATA
                GetNodeType = "CDATA"
            Case XmlNodeType.Comment
                GetNodeType = "Comment"
            Case XmlNodeType.Document
                GetNodeType = "Document"
            Case XmlNodeType.DocumentFragment
                GetNodeType = "Document Fragment"
            Case XmlNodeType.DocumentType
                GetNodeType = "Document Type"
            Case XmlNodeType.Element
                GetNodeType = "element"
            Case XmlNodeType.EndElement
                GetNodeType = "End Element"
            Case XmlNodeType.EndEntity
                GetNodeType = "End Entity"
            Case XmlNodeType.Entity
                GetNodeType = "Entity"
            Case XmlNodeType.EntityReference
                GetNodeType = "Entity Reference"
```

```
            Case XmlNodeType.None
                GetNodeType = "None"
            Case XmlNodeType.Notation
                GetNodeType = "Notation"
            Case XmlNodeType.ProcessingInstruction
                GetNodeType = "Processing Instruction"
            Case XmlNodeType.SignificantWhitespace
                GetNodeType = "Significant Whitespace"
            Case XmlNodeType.Text
                GetNodeType = "Text"
            Case XmlNodeType.Whitespace
                GetNodeType = "Whitespace"
            Case XmlNodeType.XmlDeclaration
                GetNodeType = "XML Declaration"
        End Select

    Catch ex As Exception
        MsgBox("Error: " & ex.Source & ": " & ex.Message, _
        MsgBoxStyle.OKOnly, "GetNodeType")
    End Try

End Function
```

The XmlDataDocument Class

The XmlDocument class is useful for working with XML via the DOM, but it's not a data-enabled class. To bring the DataSet class into the picture, you need to use an XmlDataDocument class, which inherits from the XmlDocument class. Table 18.4 shows the additional members that the XmlDataDocument class adds to the XmlDocument class.

TABLE 18.4: XmlDataDocument Members

Member	Type	Description
DataSet	Property	Retrieves a DataSet representing the data in the XmlDataDocument.
GetElementFromRow	Method	Retrieves an XmlElement representing a specified DataRow.
GetRowFromElement	Method	Retrieves a DataRow representing a specified XmlElement.
Load	Method	Loads the XmlDataDocument and synchronizes it with a DataSet.

Figure 18.4 shows the frmXmlDataDocument form in this chapter's sample project. This form loads an XML document selected by the user into an XmlDataDocument and DataSet together; then it simultaneously displays the XmlDataDocument in a TreeView control and the DataSet in a DataGrid control.

FIGURE 18.4:

Two views of an XML
document

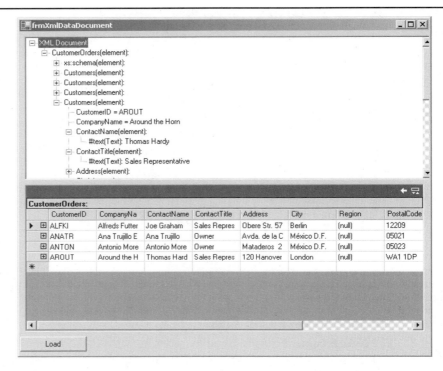

Nearly all the code behind the frmXmlDataDocument form is identical to the code that
you've already seen for the frmDOM form. The only changes are in the btnLoad_Click procedure that does the initial data loading. Listing 18.3 shows the code for this procedure.

Listing 18.3:   **Loading an XmlDataDocument and a DataSet Together**

```
Private Sub btnLoad_Click(ByVal sender As System.Object, _
  ByVal e As System.EventArgs) Handles btnLoad.Click
    Dim dlgOpen As New OpenFileDialog()
    Dim xnod As XmlNode
    Dim tnod As TreeNode

    Try
        dlgOpen.ShowDialog()
        If Len(dlgOpen.FileName) > 0 Then

            Dim xtr As New XmlTextReader(dlgOpen.FileName)
            Dim xddCustOrders As XmlDataDocument = New XmlDataDocument()
            Dim dsCustOrders As DataSet = xddCustOrders.DataSet
            dsCustOrders.ReadXmlSchema(xtr)
            xtr = New XmlTextReader(dlgOpen.FileName)
```

```
        xtr.WhitespaceHandling = WhitespaceHandling.None
        xddCustOrders.Load(xtr)

        tnod = New TreeNode("XML Document")
        tvwDOM.Nodes.Add(tnod)

        xnod = xddCustOrders.DocumentElement
        AddChildren(xnod, tnod)

        dgMain.DataSource = dsCustOrders

    End If

Catch ex As Exception
    MsgBox("Error: " & ex.Source & ": " & ex.Message, _
      MsgBoxStyle.OKOnly, "btnLoad_Click")
End Try

End Sub
```

If you compare Listing 18.3 with the code you saw earlier, you'll find several changes:

- The object to hold the DOM is declared as XmlDataDocument rather than XmlDocument.

- The DataSet is retrieved directly from the DataSet property of the XmlDataDocument object.

- The code initializes the schema of the DataSet by calling its ReadXmlSchema method, using the same XmlTextReader that will be used by the XmlDataDocument object. This ensures that both the DataSet and the XmlDataDocument will have the same schema.

- The code recreates the XmlTextReader after using it to initialize the DataSet. That's because the XmlTextReader provides forward-only access to the underlying XML.

- The DataGrid is filled by setting its DataSource property to the new DataSet.

WARNING   There's no code in this sample to synchronize the TreeView and DataGrid controls. In a production application, you might trap the events for both controls and use them to ensure that corresponding items will always be selected in both controls.

Synchronizing a DataSet with an XmlDataDocument

The code behind frmXmlDataDocument creates the XmlDataDocument first and then creates a DataSet from that XmlDataDocument. That's only one of several methods for synchronizing a DataSet with an XmlDataDocument. You can start the synchronization process with any of these objects:

- A full DataSet
- A schema-only DataSet
- An XmlDataDocument

I'll discuss these three options in this section.

Starting with a Full DataSet

One way to end up with a DataSet synchronized to an XmlDataDocument is to start with a DataSet. Here's some sample code for doing this. You'll find it, along with the other code in this section, behind frmSynchronize in this chapter's sample project.

```
dsCustOrders.ReadXml(dlgOpen.FileName, _
  XmlReadMode.ReadSchema)
Dim xddCustOrders As XmlDataDocument = _
  New XmlDataDocument(dsCustOrders)
```

Here, dsCustOrders is a DataSet that is initialized by using its ReadXml method to read in an XML file. After creating the DataSet (in this fashion or in any other), you can simply create a new XmlDataDocument by calling an overloaded constructor that takes the DataSet as an argument. This is very convenient if you already have the DataSet in your code.

Starting with a Schema-Only DataSet

The second way to synchronize the two objects is to follow a three-step recipe:

1. Create a new DataSet with the proper schema, but no data.
2. Create the XmlDataDocument from the DataSet.
3. Load the XML document into the XmlDataDocument.

   Here's some code that carries out these steps:

```
dsCustOrders.ReadXmlSchema(dlgOpen.FileName)
Dim xddCustOrders As XmlDataDocument = _
  New XmlDataDocument(dsCustOrders)
Dim xtr As XmlTextReader = _
  New XmlTextReader(dlgOpen.FileName)
xtr.WhitespaceHandling = WhitespaceHandling.None
xddCustOrders.Load(xtr)
```

The advantage to using this technique is that you don't have to represent the entire XML document in the DataSet schema; the schema only needs to include the XML elements that you wish to work with. For example, you could create a DataSet that included only the customer fields, and still use this technique to synchronize that DataSet with the entire XML document of customers and orders. This technique allows you to create a DataSet that is a view into a larger XML document. The XmlDataDocument still contains the entire XML document, and it can still be used to write changes back to the entire document.

Starting with an XmlDataDocument

The third method to synchronize a DataSet and an XmlDataDocument is to start with the XmlDataDocument and to retrieve the DataSet from its DataSet property:

```
Dim xtr As New XmlTextReader(dlgOpen.FileName)
Dim xddCustOrders As XmlDataDocument = New XmlDataDocument()
Dim dsCustOrders As DataSet = xddCustOrders.DataSet
dsCustOrders.ReadXmlSchema(xtr)
xtr = New XmlTextReader(dlgOpen.FileName)
xtr.WhitespaceHandling = WhitespaceHandling.None
xddCustOrders.Load(xtr)
```

Even when you're creating the DataSet from the XmlDataDocument, you must still explicitly create the schema of the DataSet before it will contain data. That's because, in this technique, you can also use a DataSet that represents only a portion of the XmlDataDocument.

Using Synchronized Objects

By now, you may be wondering what's the point of all this maneuvering. Sure, it's interesting that you can create two different objects to represent the same underlying XML file, but why would you want to? There are two general reasons that this technique may be useful in your code.

First, the XmlDataDocument object can be used to read and write XML with complete fidelity. If you load an XML document into a DataSet object with the DataSet's ReadXml method, and later write the DataSet back to an XML document with the WriteXml method, you may find that the document has changed in unexpected ways. In particular, white space from the original file may be missing from the re-created file, and the order of elements may be changed. In contrast, if you read and write the XML file by using the methods of the XmlDataDocument object, the re-created document will preserve the formatting of the original document.

Second, there are some things that are easier to do with an XmlDataDocument than with a DataSet. By loading a DataSet and then synchronizing it with an XmlDataDocument, you can get the best of both worlds. For conventional database operations, you can use the objects and interfaces of the DataSet. For other operations, you can use the XmlDataDocument and its associated objects. In this section, I'll explore two useful things that you can do with this technique:

- Selecting data with an XPath query
- Transforming data with XSLT

Using XPath Queries with a DataSet

XPath is yet another W3C standard. More formally known as the XML Path Language, it's described by the W3C as "a language for addressing parts of an XML document." The .NET implementation of XPath supports the Version 1.0 Recommendation standard for XPath.

TIP   For more information on XPath, visit `www.w3.org/TR/xpath`.

Just as SQL allows you to select a set of information from a table or group of tables, XPath allows you to select a set of nodes from a DOM. In this section, I'll introduce you to the basic syntax of XPath and then explain how you can use an XPath query to retrieve a set of DataRow objects from a DataSet.

Understanding XPath

XPath is not itself an XML standard; rather, it's a language for talking *about* XML. By writing an appropriate XPath expression, you can select particular elements or attributes within an XML document. XPath starts with a notion of *current context*. The current context defines the set of nodes that will be inspected by an XPath query. In general, there are four choices for specifying the current context for an XPath query:

- `./` uses the current node as the current context.
- `/` uses the root of the XML document as the current context.
- `.//` uses the entire XML hierarchy, starting with the current node, as the current context.
- `//` uses the entire XML document as the current context.

The full XPath syntax is rather complex, but the basics are easy to describe. I'll start with the syntaxes for identifying elements and identifying attributes.

To identify a set of elements using XPath, you use the path down the tree structure to those elements, separating tags by forward slashes. For example, this XPath expression selects all the Orders elements in the `CustOrders.xml` file:

```
/CustomerOrders/Customers/Orders
```

You can also select all the Orders elements without worrying about the full path to them by using this expression:

```
//Orders
```

You can use * as a wildcard at any level of the tree. For example, this expression selects all the Orders that are grandchildren of the CustomerOrders node:

```
/CustomerOrders/*/Orders
```

XPath expressions select a set of elements, not a single element. Thus, in the context of the XmlDataDocument, an XPath expression can be used to select a set of XmlNode objects to operate on later.

To identify a set of attributes, you trace the path down the tree to the attributes, just as you do with elements. The only difference is that attribute names must be prefixed with an @ character. For example, this XPath expression selects all the CompanyName attributes from Customers in the CustOrders.xml file:

```
//Customers/@CompanyName
```

Because only Customers have a CompanyName attribute in the CustOrders.xml file, this XPath expression is equivalent to the preceding one:

```
//@CompanyName
```

TIP   The expression with the explicit path (//Customers/@CompanyName) will execute much more quickly than the expression that searches all levels of the XML hierarchy (//@CompanyName) because the former has to search only a limited number of nodes to return results.

You can select multiple attributes with the @* operator. To select all attributes of Customers anywhere in the XML, use this expression:

```
//Customers/@*
```

XPath also offers a predicate language to allow you to specify smaller groups of nodes or even individual nodes in the XML tree. You might think of this as a filtering capability similar to a SQL WHERE clause. One thing you can do is specify the exact value of the node that you'd like to work with. For example, to find all EmployeeID nodes with the value *4*, you could use this XPath expression:

```
/CustomerOrders/Customers/Orders/EmployeeID[.="4"]
```

Here, the dot operator stands for the current node.

Alternatively, you could find all Orders taken by the employee with the EmployeeID of 4:

```
/CustomerOrders/Customers/Orders[./EmployeeID="4"]
```

TIP   There is no forward slash between an element and a filtering expression in XPath.

You can also use operators and Boolean expressions within filtering specifications. For example, you might want to find Orders where the Freight amount is 20 or more:

```
/CustomerOrders/Customers/Orders[./Freight>=20]
```

Because the current node is the default context, you can simplify this expression a little:

```
/CustomerOrders/Customers/Orders[Freight>=20]
```

Of course, you can filter on attributes as well as on elements. For example, to get all Customers whose CustomerID starts with *A*, you could use this XPath expression:

```
/CustomerOrders/Customers[starts-with(@CustomerID,"A")]
```

If you were expecting to see a wildcard test in that expression, you might have been surprised. Instead of wildcards, XPath supports a selection of functions. Some XPath functions are listed in Table 18.5. For a complete guide to these functions, see the XPath specification.

TABLE 18.5: Selected XPath Functions

Function	Description
concat	Concatenates strings.
contains	Determines whether one string contains another.
count	Counts the number of nodes in an expression.
last	Last element in a collection.
normalize-space	Removes white space from a string.
not	Negates the function's argument.
number	Converts the function's argument to a number.
position	Ordinal of a node within its parent.
starts-with	Determines whether one string starts with another.
string-length	Returns the number of characters in a string.
substring	Returns a substring from a string.

Square brackets are also used to indicate indexing. Collections are indexed starting at 1. To return the first Customers node, for example, you would use this expression:

```
/CustomerOrders/Customers[1]
```

This expression returns the first order of the first customer:

```
/CustomerOrders/Customers[1]/Orders[1]
```

And this one returns the first order in the XML file, regardless of the customer:

```
(/CustomerOrders/Customers/Orders)[1]
```

The parentheses are necessary because the square brackets have a higher operator precedence than the path operators.

There's also a last() function that you can use to return the last element in a collection, without needing to know how many elements are in the collection:

```
/CustomerOrders/Customers[last()]
```

Another useful operator is the vertical bar, which is used to form the union of two sets of nodes. This expression returns all the orders for the customers with the CustomerID values of ALFKI or AROUT:

```
/CustomerOrders/Customers[@CustomerID="ALFKI"]/Orders|
➥ /CustomerOrders/Customers[@CustomerID="AROUT"]/Orders
```

> **NOTE** There's more to XPath than I've covered here. Refer to the W3C XPath specification for full details.

To test your knowledge of XPath expressions, you can use the frmXPath form in this chapter's sample project. Figure 18.5 shows this form. The Load button retrieves an XML file and displays its contents in the TreeView and DataGrid controls. The Execute button executes the supplied XPath expression and displays the results in the listbox.

The code that handles loading the XML is identical to the code that you already saw from the frmXmlDataDocument form. The new code is in the Click event procedure for the Execute button. Listing 18.4 shows this code.

FIGURE 18.5:

Testing XPath

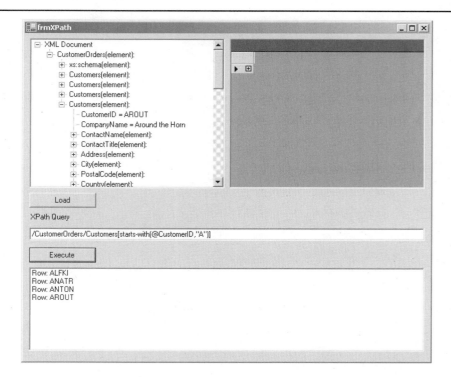

Listing 18.4:   **Using XPath to Retrieve Data**

```
Private Sub btnExecute_Click(ByVal sender As System.Object, _
 ByVal e As System.EventArgs) Handles btnExecute.Click
    Dim dr As DataRow
    Dim xnod As XmlNode

    Try

        Me.Cursor = Cursors.WaitCursor

        lboResults.Items.Clear()

        Dim xnl As XmlNodeList = mxddCustOrders.DocumentElement. _
         SelectNodes(txtXPath.Text)
        If xnl.Count = 0 Then
            MsgBox("No nodes returned")
        Else
            For Each xnod In xnl
                If xnod.NodeType = XmlNodeType.Element Then
                    dr = mxddCustOrders.GetRowFromElement( _
                     CType(xnod, XmlElement))
                    If Not dr Is Nothing Then
                        lboResults.Items.Add("Row: " & dr(0).ToString())
                    Else
                        lboResults.Items.Add("Element " & xnod.Name & _
                         " (" & xnod.Value & ")")
                    End If
                ElseIf xnod.NodeType = XmlNodeType.Attribute Then
                    lboResults.Items.Add("Attribute " & xnod.Name & _
                     " (" & xnod.Value & ")")
                Else
                    lboResults.Items.Add("Other")
                End If
            Next
        End If

    Catch ex As Exception
        MsgBox("Error: " & ex.Source & ": " & ex.Message, _
         MsgBoxStyle.OKOnly, "btnExecute_Click")
    Finally
        Me.Cursor = Cursors.Default
    End Try

End Sub
```

The key line of code in this example is the call to the SelectNodes method of the Xml-DataDocument object:

```
Dim xnl As XmlNodeList = mxddCustOrders.DocumentElement. _
    SelectNodes(txtXPath.Text)
```

The SelectNodes method takes an XPath expression as its argument and returns a collection of nodes that result from executing that XPath expression on the XmlDataDocument. The rest of the code in Listing 18.4 simply loops through the returned XmlNode objects and prints some basic information about each one to the listbox.

Retrieving Rows with XPath

For another example of this technique, take a look at frmXPathRows in this chapter's sample project. This form, shown in Figure 18.6, uses the now-familiar technique of loading an XML document into an XmlDataDocument and a DataSet at the same time. The user can then enter a CustomerID, and the form will create a new DataSet containing only that customer and that customer's orders and will bind the DataSet to a DataGrid.

FIGURE 18.6:

Retrieving information about a single customer

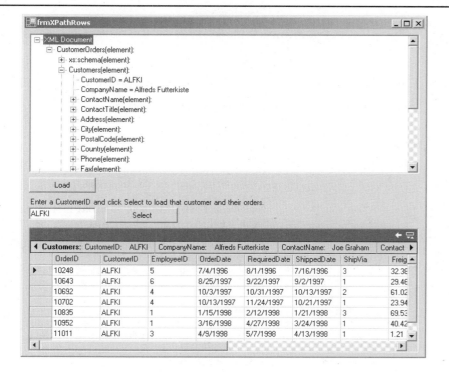

The code that does the new work here is, of course, in the Click event procedure that handles the Select button. Listing 18.5 shows this procedure.

Listing 18.5: **Using XPath to Build a DataSet**

```
Private Sub btnSelect_Click(ByVal sender As System.Object, _
  ByVal e As System.EventArgs) Handles btnSelect.Click
    Dim dr As DataRow
    Dim xnod As XmlNode
    Dim strXPath As String

    Try

        Me.Cursor = Cursors.WaitCursor

        ' First, build an XPath expression that takes the union of the
        ' specified customer and all of its orders
        strXPath = "/CustomerOrders/Customers[@CustomerID=""" & _
          txtCustomerID.Text & """]|/CustomerOrders/Customers" & _
          "[@CustomerID=""" & txtCustomerID.Text & """]/Orders"

        ' Execute the XPath query
        Dim xnl As XmlNodeList = mxddCustOrders.DocumentElement. _
          SelectNodes(strXPath)

        ' Clone the DataSet that holds the original data
        Dim dsResults As DataSet = mdsCustOrders.Clone()

        ' Walk through the returned nodes
        If xnl.Count = 0 Then
            MsgBox("No nodes returned")
        Else
            For Each xnod In xnl
                ' Get the row from the original DataSet
                dr = mxddCustOrders.GetRowFromElement( _
                  CType(xnod, XmlElement))
                ' And import it into the new DataSet
                dsResults.Tables(dr.Table.TableName).ImportRow(dr)
            Next
        End If

        ' Display the results on the grid
        dgResults.DataSource = dsResults.Tables("Customers")

    Catch ex As Exception
        MsgBox("Error: " & ex.Source & ": " & ex.Message, _
          MsgBoxStyle.OKOnly, "btnExecute_Click")
    Finally
        Me.Cursor = Cursors.Default
    End Try

End Sub
```

The code starts by assuming that the user has entered a valid customer ID and builds an XPath expression from that customer ID. Remember, a pair of quotation marks inside a string gets translated into a single quotation mark. With that in mind, you should be able to see that the XPath expression will be something like this:

```
/CustomerOrders/Customers[@CustomerID="ALFKI"]|
➥ /CustomerOrders/Customers[@CustomerID="ALFKI"]/Orders
```

A rough translation of this into English would be, fetch the Customers nodes whose CustomerID is "ALFKI," and also fetch the Orders nodes whose parent Customers node has the CustomerID of "ALFKI." In other words, this expression returns a set of nodes representing the specified customer and all the orders placed by that customer.

After the code executes the query and builds an XmlNodeList with the results, it uses the Clone method of the original DataSet (the one that was built when the XML document was loaded) to produce a new DataSet. The new DataSet will have exactly the same schema (including DataTables, DataColumns, and DataRelations) as the original, but will not contain any data.

The next step is to loop through all the XmlNode objects in the XmlNodeList. From the way that the original XPath expression was designed, you can be certain that all the nodes are elements that map to DataSet rows; there's nothing in the expression to retrieve an attribute or a column. The code calls GetRowFromElement to retrieve the corresponding DataRow from the original DataSet for each XmlNode. Then it calls the ImportRow method of a table in the new DataSet to stick this DataRow object into the appropriate DataTable in that DataSet. ImportRow is a method of the DataTable object. The code knows the DataTable to which each DataRow should be imported because the DataRow's TableName property contains the name of the original source table.

Finally, when all the DataRows have been imported to the cloned DataSet, the code uses this DataSet as the source for the DataGrid, which then displays the selected data.

Using XSLT with a DataSet

My second example of adding functionality to a DataSet by using an XmlDataDocument involves the use of XSLT, the Extensible Stylesheet Language Transformations standard. XSLT provides a flexible way to control the formatting of XML data. In this section, I'll introduce the basics of XSLT and then show you how to use it to dress up your DataSets.

NOTE As you've probably guessed by now, XSLT is another of the W3C standards. You'll find the official specification online at www.w3.org/TR/xslt. The .NET implementation of XSLT conforms to the XSL Transformations Version 1.0 Recommendation.

Understanding XSLT

XML is all about representing information. Think about the examples you've seen so far in this chapter: They describe customers and orders. Each element in the XML file contains raw information about some characteristic of a customer or an order. But that's all that the XML file contains. In particular, there is nothing in an XML file that dictates a presentation format for the information in the file.

Of course, sooner or later, this poses a problem—when you want to see the information. To solve this problem, you can use XSLT. XSLT files (which usually have the extension .xsl and are sometimes called stylesheets) are combined with XML files by an XSLT processor, producing an output file. That output file might be HTML, pure text, a Word document, or just about anything else. Figure 18.7 shows this process schematically.

FIGURE 18.7:

Displaying XML with XSLT

When you open an XML file in Internet Explorer, for example, you're actually using a default XSLT file that's built into Internet Explorer. This XSLT file transforms the XML into the color-coded treeview that IE then displays. Figure 18.8 shows the CustOrders.xml file displayed with Internet Explorer's default stylesheet.

Visual Studio .NET also has a default stylesheet built in for use with XML files. Figure 18.9 shows the same CustOrders.xml file, this time open in Visual Studio .NET. You'll see that the color coding is a bit different in VS .NET than it is in IE, and that the VS .NET version lacks the ability to expand and collapse portions of the file. The differences between the two are strictly a matter of presentation; the XML data is exactly the same in both cases.

An XSLT Example

To demonstrate XSLT in action, I'll start with CustOrders1.xsl, which looks like this:

```
<HTML xmlns:xsl="http://www.w3.org/1999/XSL/Transform" xsl:version="1.0">
<BODY>
    <xsl:for-each select="/CustomerOrders/Customers">
        <p><b>Customer</b>
         <br><xsl:value-of select="@CustomerID"/></br>
         <br><xsl:value-of select="@CompanyName"/></br>
         <br><xsl:value-of select="ContactName"/></br></p>
    </xsl:for-each>
</BODY>
</HTML>
```

FIGURE 18.8:

CustOrders.xml in
Internet Explorer 6

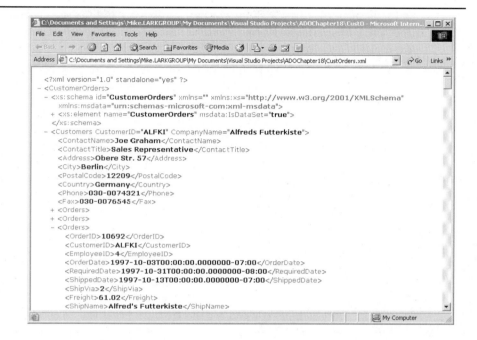

FIGURE 18.9:

CustOrders.xml in
Visual Studio .NET

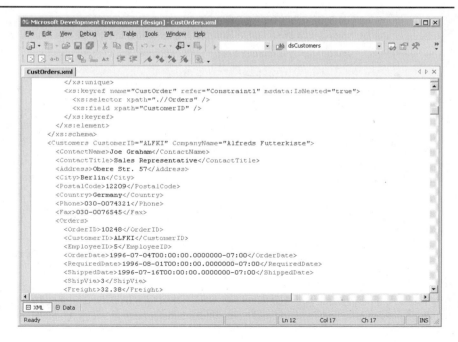

I'll discuss how this XSLT file works in a moment, but first you need to know how to apply the XSLT file to the XML file. There are three main alternatives you can use when you're experimenting with XSLT:

- You can modify the XML file to contain a hard-coded reference to a particular XSLT file. For example, you could insert this XML processing directive into CustOrders.xml directly after the XML declaration:

  ```
  <?xml-stylesheet type="text/xsl" href="CustOrders1.xsl"?>
  ```

  This processing directive will be read by any XSLT processor that is handed this XML file. It specifies a stylesheet of XSLT commands named CustOrders1.xsl, in the same folder as the XML file (you could also use an absolute URL rather than a relative URL). For example, opening the XML file with Internet Explorer will automatically use the specified XSLT file instead of IE's default stylesheet.

- You can use a command-line XSLT engine to combine the XML and XSLT files. Although neither Windows nor .NET contains such a tool, there are several available for free on the Internet. Two popular options are the Unicorn XSLT Processor (www.unicorn-enterprises.com/products_uxt.html) and the Saxon XSLT Processor (http://saxon.sourceforge.net). With these products, you can execute a command line to see the results. For example, you can use the Unicorn processor to combine CustOrders.xml with CustOrders1.xsl to produce CustOrders1.html by executing this command line:

  ```
  uxt CustOrders.xml CustOrders1.xsl CustOrders1.html
  ```

  The equivalent command line for the Saxon processor is:

  ```
  saxon -o CustOrders1.html CustOrders.xml CustOrders1.xsl
  ```

- You can use a full-fledged XML editor that includes XSL capabilities. Two popular visual editors are XML Spy (www.xmlspy.com) and MarrowSoft Xselerator (www.marrowsoft.com). Figure 18.10 shows MarrowSoft Xselerator displaying the results of applying CustOrders1.xsl to CustOrders.xml. Such programs are not free, but they're a worthwhile investment if you're going to be working with XML on a regular basis.

WARNING   You'll find minor variations in the output of different XSLT engines. For example, some XSLT engines handle break tags in HTML files in idiosyncratic ways. In this chapter, I'll be displaying the output that's created by the MSXML engine that ships as part of Internet Explorer 6.

Here's the output generated by applying CustOrders1.xsl to CustOrders1.xml:

```
<HTML>
<BODY>
<p><b>Customer</b><br>ALFKI<br>Alfreds Futterkiste<br>Joe Graham</p>
```

```
<p><b>Customer</b><br>ANATR<br>
➤ Ana Trujillo Emparedados y helados<br>Ana Trujillo</p>
<p><b>Customer</b><br>ANTON<br>
➤ Antonio Moreno Taquería<br>Antonio Moreno</p>
<p><b>Customer</b><br>AROUT<br>Around the Horn<br>Thomas Hardy</p>
</BODY>
</HTML>
```

FIGURE 18.10:

MarrowSoft Xselerator

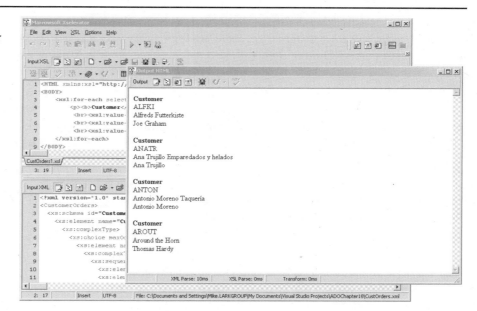

Understanding the Example

The simplest way to understand the output of this process is to start with the XSLT file. Anything in this file that's not tagged with the xsl: namespace prefix is simply copied verbatim to the output file. So, in this case, the output (which is what Internet Explorer displays) starts with this:

```
<HTML xmlns:xsl="http://www.w3.org/1999/XSL/Transform" xsl:version="1.0">
<BODY>
```

NOTE   Note that the namespace information for XSLT is packed into the HTML tag. The XSLT processor can still find it there, and it has no effect on the output file's presentation as HTML.

At least, that's what you would *expect* to happen (and what will happen with many XSLT processors). However, the MSXML parser recognizes HTML output as a special case and deletes the extra information from the HTML tag; thus, this is what you actually get for the start of the output:

```
<HTML>
<BODY>
```

The next thing in the XSLT file is the starting tag of a `for-each` element in the XSL namespace:

```
<xsl:for-each select="/CustomerOrders/Customers">
```

The `/CustomerOrders/Customers` attribute in this element matches every Customers element that is a child of the CustomerOrders element in the XML document. If you refer to the XML document, you'll see that there is one such tag for each customer.

All the code within the `for-each` element (which, of course, ends with the `</xsl:for-each>` tag) is executed once for each instance of the `tblCustomer1` element in the XML file. This code starts by simply outputting some more literal text (which happens to be HTML, although, of course, the XSLT processor has no knowledge of how its output will be used):

```
<p><b>Customer</b>
 <br>
```

Next comes an XSLT `value-of` element:

```
<xsl:value-of select="@CustomerID"/>
```

The `value-of` element is similar to the Eval() function in Access. It returns the value of the element to which it refers. The value of an XML element is just the text within that element, with all tags stripped away. For example, the value of

```
<ContactName>Joe Graham</ContactName>
```

is

```
Joe Graham
```

The `@` character in the `value-of` element above indicates that CustomerID refers to an attribute rather than to an element. The value of an XML attribute is the quoted text that follows the attribute name. For example, the value of

```
CustomerID="ALFKI"
```

is

```
ALFKI
```

For each customer, then, this XSLT file inserts the value of the CustomerID and Company-Name attributes and the ContactName element, with HTML break tags used to place them on separate lines when the HTML is displayed.

TIP Note that the <br> tags in the XSLT file are terminated explicitly with </br> tags. Although HTML doesn't require the closing tag here, XML does, and XSLT files must be well formed by the rules of XML. When it's creating an HTML file, the MSXML parser drops the closing </br> tags.

Finally, the XSLT file ends its output with two more literal HTML tags:

```
</BODY>
</HTML>
```

Putting the pieces together, here's the generated HTML once again:

```
<HTML>
<BODY>
<p><b>Customer</b><br>ALFKI<br>Alfreds Futterkiste<br>Joe Graham</p>
<p><b>Customer</b><br>ANATR<br>
➥ Ana Trujillo Emparedados y helados<br>Ana Trujillo</p>
<p><b>Customer</b><br>ANTON<br>
➥ Antonio Moreno Taquería<br>Antonio Moreno</p>
<p><b>Customer</b><br>AROUT<br>Around the Horn<br>Thomas Hardy</p>
</BODY>
</HTML>
```

TIP If you're using Internet Explorer to view this example (by inserting an xml-stylesheet directive in the XML file), the only way to see the generated HTML is to work it out for yourself. If you choose View ➢ Source in IE, you'll see the XML file, not the generated HTML.

You'll notice that most of the information in CustOrders.xml is discarded by this stylesheet. XSLT picks and chooses the information to output. XSLT is much more complex than this simple example can demonstrate. However, if you grasp this example, you understand how XSLT works, which is the important thing in this chapter.

Transforms and the XmlDataDocument

Suppose that you have a DataSet that contains the customer and order information that's stored in CustOrders.xml, and you want to create HTML from it that shows the customer information (similar to the output in Figure 18.10). You could do this by using the DataSet's WriteXml method to write the data out as an XML file, and then apply an XSL transform to the results. But this is another case where the XmlDataDocument provides an easier way to get the same results.

The key to this functionality is the XslTransform class. This class is dedicated to the transformation of XML documents using XSLT stylesheets. To use the XslTransform class, you load an XSLT document and then use it to transform an XML document. Table 18.6 shows two of the important members of the XslTransform class.

TABLE 18.6: XslTransform Members

Member	Type	Description
Load	Method	Loads an XSLT stylesheet into the XslTransform object.
Transform	Method	Transforms the input XML using the loaded stylesheet, and outputs the results.

Figure 18.11 shows frmTransform from this chapter's sample project. When you click the Transform button, this form prompts you to select an XML document and an XSLT document from your hard drive. It then applies the XSLT to the XML and shows the results in the text box. Listing 18.6 shows the code that accomplishes this task.

FIGURE 18.11:

Applying an XSL transform

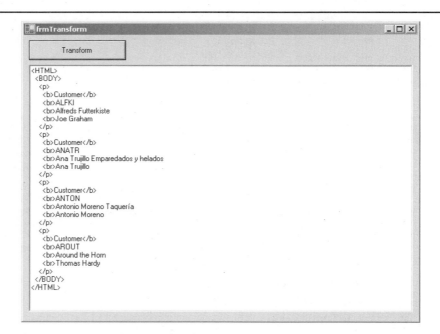

Listing 18.6:   **Applying an XSL Transform to a DataSet**

```
Private Sub btnTransform_Click(ByVal sender As System.Object, _
ByVal e As System.EventArgs) Handles btnTransform.Click
    Dim dlgOpen As New OpenFileDialog()
    Dim dsCustOrders As New DataSet()

    Try
        ' First, load the XML file
```

```
dlgOpen.Title = "Select XML file"
dlgOpen.ShowDialog()
If Len(dlgOpen.FileName) > 0 Then

    ' Create DataSet and XmlDataDocument from the XML
    dsCustOrders.ReadXml(dlgOpen.FileName, _
     XmlReadMode.ReadSchema)
    Dim xddCustOrders As XmlDataDocument = _
     New XmlDataDocument(dsCustOrders)

    ' Now, load an XSLT file
    dlgOpen.Title = "Select XSLT file"
    dlgOpen.FileName = ""
    dlgOpen.ShowDialog()
    If Len(dlgOpen.FileName) > 0 Then

        ' Load the XSLT into an XslTransform
        Dim xslt As XslTransform = New XslTransform()
        xslt.Load(dlgOpen.FileName)

        Dim stm As MemoryStream = New MemoryStream()
        xslt.Transform(xddCustOrders, Nothing, stm)
        stm.Position = 1
        Dim sr As New StreamReader(stm)
        txtResults.Text = sr.ReadToEnd

    End If
End If

Catch ex As Exception
    MsgBox("Error: " & ex.Source & ": " & ex.Message, _
     MsgBoxStyle.OKOnly, "btnTransform_Click")
End Try

End Sub
```

The btnTransform_Click event procedure starts by loading a DataSet and then creating a synchronized XmlDataDocument from the DataSet. Next, it prompts the user to select an XSLT file and then uses the Load method to get that XSLT file into an XslTransform object. The Transform method of the XslTransform object is used to apply the transformation. This method takes three arguments:

- The first argument is the source of the XML to be transformed.

- The second argument is a list of additional arguments to be used in the transformation. This is an advanced capability that can be used to supply information such as the current time or the username to the transformation. In this example, I've passed Nothing in this argument.

- The third argument is the destination of the transformation. This can be a string that is interpreted as a filename, an XmlReader object, an XmlWriter object, a TextWriter object, or a Stream object. In this case, I've used a Stream object implemented as a Memory-Stream. That has the effect of writing the transformed XML to a location in memory, where it's held as a series of bytes.

Setting the MemoryStream's Position property to 1 has the effect of "rewinding" the stream after it has been written. After that, the StreamReader object can extract the text from the stream and supply it to another component—in this case, the Text property of the text box on the form.

Summary

In this chapter, you saw some of the strong similarities between the DataSet class and the XmlDataDocument class. You saw how to load data into these classes and how to synchronize them with one another. You then learned how you can take advantage of this similarity to apply XML concepts, such as XPath queries and XSL transforms, to the contents of a DataSet.

In the next chapter, you'll learn about one more place where you can use ADO.NET: on the Web, by connecting ADO.NET to ASP.NET.

CHAPTER 19

Managing Data on the Web with ASP.NET

- Introducing ASP.NET

- Displaying bound data using ASP.NET

- Using the DataList control

- Using legacy ADO with ASP.NET

One of the facets of the .NET development environment that I haven't yet discussed in this book is ASP.NET. As you can guess from the name, ASP.NET is an upgrade to Microsoft's server-side ASP environment for web page development. Although ASP.NET can use all of the ADO.NET code that you saw in the last several chapters, it also has some unique connections to ADO.NET built into its programming and user interface model. In this chapter, I'll introduce ASP.NET and show how it can work with ADO.NET to enable database-driven web pages on your web server.

> **NOTE**   ASP.NET is a huge topic in its own right—entire books can be (and have been) written about it. In this chapter, I'm going to try to give you a taste of ASP.NET development without trying to teach you all the details of this development environment. Throughout the chapter, you'll see that I work with familiar ADO.NET objects. Most of the code and concepts you've learned in previous chapters can be transferred directly to ASP.NET.

Introducing ASP.NET

ASP (Active Server Pages) was Microsoft's original solution for server-side web server development. In server-side development, code runs on the web server rather than on the client, and only the results of the code are sent back to the client. This is in contrast to client-side development, where the server sends programming code to the client to be executed within the client's web browser. Server-side programming generally offers benefits in speed and security over client-side programming.

Rather than modify ASP for the .NET environment, Microsoft chose to build ASP.NET from scratch, with an entirely new architecture. Indeed, ASP code won't even run in ASP.NET, because the VBScript language used in ASP isn't supported by ASP.NET. However, this doesn't mean that installing ASP.NET on an Internet Information Server (IIS) computer will break existing ASP pages. That's because ASP.NET pages use ASPX as an extension. Only ASPX files are handled by the new ASP.NET processor; existing ASP pages continue to go through the existing ASP processor. Over the long run, you'll probably want to rewrite existing ASP pages to use ASP.NET, but there's no need to do so just to start using ASP.NET on the same server.

ASP.NET offers enhanced performance compared with ASP. That's because ASP.NET is actually built on top of the .NET Common Language Runtime (CLR), so that it offers all the CLR benefits, including just-in-time compilation, type safety, and early binding. By contrast, the older ASP engine was strictly an interpreter and required all the variables within its code to be late-bound variants. Code for ASPX pages can be written in Visual Basic .NET, C#, or JScript (I'll use Visual Basic .NET for my examples).

The first time that a client requests an ASPX file, the ASP.NET processor parses and compiles the file into a .NET Framework class. This class then dynamically processes incoming requests for the ASPX page. The compiled instance is reused across multiple requests, so that the time taken to compile the page isn't significant after the first request for the page.

As you'll see later in the chapter, ASP.NET also offers an excellent development environment. Building ASPX pages and the other parts of an ASP.NET application is integrated directly into the Visual Studio .NET IDE and shares tools with other Visual Studio .NET applications.

Because it's built on the CLR, ASP.NET offers interoperability with the rest of the .NET Framework. You can use .NET classes and call code in any .NET application from within an ASP.NET page. You can also use the .NET Framework's interoperability features to integrate ASP.NET pages with existing COM-based components.

Web Forms

ASP.NET introduces *Web Forms*. Web Forms are text files with the `.aspx` extension. Although they are text files "under the covers," Visual Studio .NET includes a designer that lets you work with Web Forms just as you can with Windows Forms, complete with a Toolbox, the capability to move and size controls via the mouse, properties that can be set, and so on. I'll be using the Web Forms designer extensively later in this chapter.

There are two programming models for Web Forms. The first follows the traditional ASP programming model, in which HTML is intermingled with code. In this model, your code is set off within script blocks within the web page. The second model, *code-behind* Web Forms, associates a class module with each Web Form. In this model, the ASPX file contains the HTML and control declarations for the Web Form, while a separate Visual Basic .NET, JScript, or C# file contains the code that will handle events on the form. The Visual Studio .NET Web Forms designer makes it easy to write code-behind Web Forms, and I find the separation of code from markup to be an aid to understanding. All the examples in this chapter will use code-behind Web Forms.

Disconnected Data Architecture

ASP.NET is designed to support a disconnected data architecture. That is, data is moved to the client when requested; there is no persistent connection to the server. This design decision is a natural outgrowth of ASP.NET using HTTP (Hypertext Transfer Protocol) to communicate between client and server. HTTP is a stateless protocol: The client sends a request, the server returns a page, and that's it. The server doesn't maintain any memory of the client, and if the client requests more data, the server simply renders the page anew.

The ASP.NET controls use the ADO.NET DataSet object as their data source. As you know from the last several chapters, the DataSet is a passive container for data. Once you've filled the DataSet (from a DataAdapter or by some other method), it can be disconnected from the original data source with no loss of integrity. If the data in the original data source needs to be changed, you can reconnect the DataSet and send updates back to the data source.

When it's transmitting a DataSet from one component to another (for example, from server to client), ASP.NET automatically converts the DataSet to its XML representation at the sending end, and then back into a DataSet at the receiving end. By using XML as the data transmission protocol for data, ASP.NET can successfully operate through most firewalls.

Deployment in ASP.NET

If you have a web server set up on your development computer, it's easy to test ASP.NET applications during the development cycle. When you create a new ASP.NET application, Visual Studio .NET will automatically create a virtual root on your local web server that references this application.

ASP.NET was designed for ease of deployment to production servers after the development cycle is finished. You can use FTP or XCOPY to copy all the files in the application to the production server, and set up a virtual root pointing to the files—and everything will work. ASP.NET also allows you to designate an assembly cache directory on your production server. When you copy an assembly into this directory, ASP.NET automatically registers it. There's no need to log on to the server or manually register the assembly.

When users interact with an application, ASP.NET makes shadow copies of the files in the application and runs from the shadow copies. At any time, you can upgrade an application by copying new files into the application's directory. ASP.NET monitors the files in an application for changes, and loads newer versions as they are detected. The end result is that you should never have to shut down a web server to upgrade an ASP.NET application.

Displaying Bound Data Using ASP.NET

One typical use of ASP.NET pages is displaying data from some data source in a bound control. ASP.NET ships with DataList and DataGrid controls that can be bound directly to a data source. To create the data source, you use the same Connection and Command objects that you've seen in the last several chapters. I'll start this exploration of ASP.NET by creating a simple application to display bound data and then enhancing it.

Displaying Data in a DataGrid

In this section, I'll walk through the steps necessary to build an ASP.NET application that displays SQL Server data in a DataGrid control. The final application is available on this book's companion CD as the ADOChapter19 sample project, but you may want to follow along with my instructions so that you can see the intermediate stages of constructing this application. To recreate this project, follow these steps:

1. Launch Visual Studio .NET.

2. On the Start Page, select New Project. Navigate to the Visual Basic Projects node in the Project Types control. Select ASP.NET Web Application as the template. Name the project **ADOChapter 19** and then click OK. Table 19.1 shows the components that Visual Studio .NET will create in the new web project.

TABLE 19.1: Components of a New Web Application

Component	Type	Description
System	Reference	.NET Framework class library root namespace
System.Data	Reference	Classes for working with data
System.Drawing	Reference	Classes for basic graphics functionality
System.Web	Reference	Classes for browser/server communication
System.Web.Services	Reference	Classes for building and using web services
System.XML	Reference	Classes for working with XML
<ProjectName>.vsdisco	Dynamic discovery document	Information for discovering web services and schemas
AssemblyInfo.vb	Assembly information file	Assembly name, version, and other configuration information
Global.asax	Global application class	Handlers for application-level events
Styles.css	Cascading style sheet	Styles for displaying visual components
Web.config	Configuration document	XML document with configuration information for this web
WebForm1.aspx	Web Form	The visual interface for the web application

3. Select WebForm1.aspx in the Solution Explorer window and change its name to **Customers.aspx**.

4. Click the Data tab in the Toolbox to display the data components available to the Web Forms designer.

5. Drag a SqlConnection object from the Toolbox to the Customers.aspx form. You can drop the object anywhere; Visual Basic .NET will display the control in a special window at the bottom of the form designer. This area is reserved for components, such as the Sql-Connection object, that don't have a visual representation.

6. In the Properties window, click the ConnectionString property to display the drop-down arrow for this property. Click the drop-down arrow. Select <New Connection> from the list of connections. This will open the Data Link Properties dialog box. Set the data link properties to retrieve a copy of the Northwind database from a SQL Server on your net-work. Click OK to save the connection string.

TIP   If you did a full install of Visual Studio .NET, including the samples, you'll have a named instance of SQL Server named NetSDK available on the computer where you are running Visual Studio .NET.

WARNING   The SQLConnection objects in the ADOChapter19 sample project point to my development server, named THISTLE. You'll need to change this to your server name in the Connection-String properties before you can run this sample on your own computer.

7. Drag a SqlCommand object from the Toolbox to the Customers.aspx form.

8. In the Properties window, click the Connection property to display the drop-down arrow for this property. Click the drop-down arrow. Expand the Existing node in the treeview that displays in the drop-down list and then select the SqlConnection1 connection.

9. Click the CommandText property to display the build button. Click the build button to open the Query Builder. Select the Customers table in the Add Table dialog box and click Add; then click Close. Select the CustomerID, CompanyName, and Country fields by checking them as shown in Figure 19.1. Click OK to save the command text.

10. Click the Web Forms tab in the Toolbox to display the visual controls that you can place on a Web Form.

11. Click the DataGrid control, then click and drag on the Web Form design surface to cre-ate an instance of the control. Click the AutoFormat link at the bottom of the Properties box and then select the Professional 2 format. Click OK. Figure 19.2 shows the data form in the designer. Note that at this point, I haven't done anything to connect the DataGrid to the SqlConnection and SqlCommand controls.

FIGURE 19.1:

Creating a command text in the Query Builder

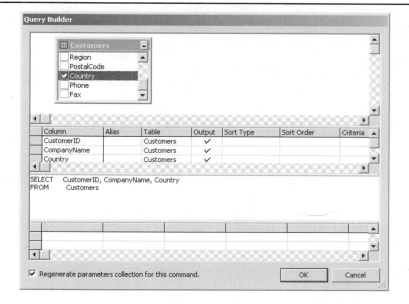

FIGURE 19.2:

Creating a Web Form

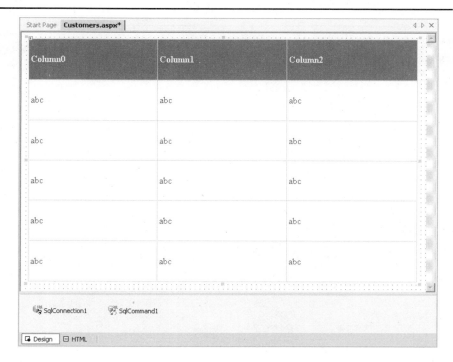

12. Double-click outside the DataGrid in the form designer to open the code editor for the Web Form. Modify the Page_Load procedure to include this code:

```
Private Sub Page_Load(ByVal sender As System.Object, _
  ByVal e As System.EventArgs) Handles MyBase.Load
    SqlConnection1.Open()
    Dim dr As System.Data.SqlClient.SqlDataReader
    dr = SqlCommand1.ExecuteReader()
    DataGrid1.DataSource = dr
    DataGrid1.DataBind()
    dr.Close()
    SqlConnection1.Close()
End Sub
```

When a browser requests this page, the code will open a connection to the SQL Server database and use the SqlCommand object to load the Customers table into the DataReader object. The DataReader is ideal in this case because it offers fast forward-only access to the data, which is all the DataGrid needs in order to show the data. Once the data has been bound to the DataGrid, all the connections to the database can be closed.

13. Select File ➤ Save All to save the project.

14. Right-click on Customers.aspx in the Solution Explorer and select Build and Browse. Figure 19.3 shows the resulting web page.

FIGURE 19.3:

Browsing customers on a web page

CustomerID	CompanyName	Country
ALFKI	Alfreds Futterkiste	Germany
ANATR	Ana Trujillo Emparedados y helados	Mexico
ANTON	Antonio Moreno Taquería	Mexico
AROUT	Around the Horn	UK
BERGS	Berglunds snabbköp	Sweden
BLAUS	Blauer See Delikatessen	Germany
BLONP	Blondesddsl père et fils	France
BOLID	Bólido Comidas preparadas	Spain
BONAP	Bon app'	France
BOTTM	Bottom-Dollar Markets	Canada
BSBEV	B's Beverages	UK
CACTU	Cactus Comidas para llevar	Argentina
CENTC	Centro comercial Moctezuma	Mexico
CHOPS	Chop-suey Chinese	Switzerland
COMMI	Comércio Mineiro	Brazil
CONSH	Consolidated Holdings	UK
DRACD	Drachenblut Delikatessen	Germany
DUMON	Du monde entier	France
EASTC	Eastern Connection	UK
ERNSH	Ernst Handel	Austria

If you right-click in the browser displaying the page and select View Source, you'll find one of the nicest features of ASP.NET. Although the designer uses all sorts of fancy components, all of the magic is going on at the server. As far as the client is concerned, the generated page is straight HTML. There's no trace of ActiveX controls, Java applets, or other heavy, client-side components. Here's a portion of the generated page:

```
<tr style="color:White;background-color:#006699;font-weight:bold;">
    <td>
        CustomerID
    </td><td>
        CompanyName
    </td><td>
        Country
    </td>
</tr><tr style="color:#000066;">
    <td>
        ALFKI
    </td><td>
        Alfreds Futterkiste
    </td><td>
        Germany
    </td>
</tr><tr style="color:#000066;">
    <td>
        ANATR
    </td><td>
        Ana Trujillo Emparedados y helados
    </td><td>
        Mexico
    </td>
</tr><tr style="color:#000066;">
    <td>
        ANTON
    </td><td>
        Antonio Moreno Taquería
    </td><td>
        Mexico
    </td>
```

TIP   The HTML that ASP.NET sends to the browser follows the HTML 3.2 or 4.0 standards, depending on the browser that requests the page. Any browser currently in wide use can display this HTML.

Parameterizing the Displayed Data

As it stands, the Customers.aspx page displays every row in the Customers table. Normally, this isn't the best way to handle data displayed in a web browser. Displaying entire tables forces the user to scroll excessively and increases the amount of data that must be pushed over a possibly slow connection. In this section, I'll modify this chapter's sample project to display only the customers from a selected country. To perform these modifications yourself, follow these steps:

1. Close the HTML and source views of Customers.aspx, then double-click the Customers .aspx file in the Solution Explorer to reopen the page in design view.

2. Using the Web Forms tab of the Toolbox, add a DropDownList control to the page. Name the DropDownList **ddlCountries**.

3. Set the AutoPostBack property of the ddlCountries DropDownList to True. This tells the page to send the new value of the list to the server, where it can trigger events, whenever the selection in the list is changed.

4. Drag a DataSet object from the Data tab of the Toolbox to the page. This is just a shortcut for declaring a DataSet object in code. When you do this, the Add Dataset dialog box will appear. Choose Untyped Dataset and then click OK.

5. Select the DataGrid control and set its EnableViewState property to False. This will prevent the page from returning information about the (read-only) DataGrid to the server whenever a new value is posted from the DropDownList.

6. Select the SqlCommand1 object and click its CommandText property in the Properties window. Click the build button to load the Query Builder. In the Criteria column for the Country field, enter **=@Country**. Click OK to save the change. This change allows you to supply a runtime parameter to filter the records returned by the query.

7. In the code editor for the page, modify the Page_Load procedure as follows:

```
Private Sub Page_Load(ByVal sender As System.Object, _
ByVal e As System.EventArgs) Handles MyBase.Load
    If Not IsPostBack Then
        Dim da As System.Data.SqlClient.SqlDataAdapter
        SqlConnection1.Open()

        da = New System.Data.SqlClient.SqlDataAdapter( _
          "SELECT DISTINCT Country FROM Customers", SqlConnection1)
        DataSet1 = New DataSet()
        da.Fill(DataSet1, "Customers")

        ddlCountries.DataSource = DataSet1.Tables("Customers")
        ddlCountries.DataValueField = "Country"
        ddlCountries.DataBind()
        SqlConnection1.Close()
    End If
End Sub
```

Now, when the user loads this page, the DropDownList control will be initialized to show a list of all the countries from the Customers table in the database. Because the DataGrid isn't bound at all at this point, it won't even be displayed. The check for the IsPostBack property prevents this code from running when the user makes a selection in the Drop-DownList control.

8. Add code to run when the user makes a selection in the ddlCountries control:

```
Private Sub ddlCountries_SelectedIndexChanged( _
 ByVal sender As Object, ByVal e As System.EventArgs) _
 Handles ddlCountries.SelectedIndexChanged
     Dim dr As System.Data.SqlClient.SqlDataReader
     SqlConnection1.Open()
     SqlCommand1.Parameters("@Country").Value = _
      ddlCountries.SelectedItem.Value
     dr = SqlCommand1.ExecuteReader()
     DataGrid1.DataSource = dr
     DataGrid1.DataBind()
     dr.Close()
     SqlConnection1.Close()
 End Sub
```

When the user makes a selection in the DropDownList, the SelectedIndexChanged procedure runs on the server (because the AutoPostBack property of the control is set to True). At that point, the code sets the @Country parameter in the query to the value from the ddlCountries control and then uses the SqlCommand and SqlDataReader objects to load the DataGrid.

9. Select File ➢ Save All to save the project.

10. Right-click on Customers.aspx in the Solution Explorer and select Build and Browse. Select a country from the DropDownList control. Figure 19.4 shows the resulting web page.

Note the three-step process used to bind the DropDownList control. Unlike the DataGrid control, the DropDownList cannot be bound to an entire DataSet. Rather, you need to follow these steps:

1. Set the DataSource property of the control to the name of a table within a DataSet.

2. Set the DataValueField property of the control to the name of a field within the specified table.

3. Call the control's DataBind method.

CustomerID	CompanyName	Country
BLONP	Blondesddsl père et fils	France
BONAP	Bon app'	France
DUMON	Du monde entier	France
FOLIG	Folies gourmandes	France
FRANR	France restauration	France
LACOR	La corne d'abondance	France
LAMAI	La maison d'Asie	France
PARIS	Paris spécialités	France
SPECD	Spécialités du monde	France
VICTE	Victuailles en stock	France
VINET	Vins et alcools Chevalier	France

Viewing Detail Information

A common scenario in database access involves master and detail information stored in tables
with a one-to-many relationship. For example, one customer has many orders. In this section, I'll extend my sample to retrieve order information for a selected customer. To add this
capability, follow these steps:

1. Close the browser displaying the page and navigate to the Customers.aspx page in the
    forms designer. Click the DataGrid control to select it. Click the Property Builder link at
    the bottom of the Properties window. This will open the DataGrid Property Builder.

2. In the Property Builder, click Hyperlink Column in the Available Columns list. Click
    the > button to make a hyperlink column in the Selected Columns list. Set the Header
    Text property of the new column to **Click for details**. Set the Text property to **Orders**.
    Set the URL Field property to **CustomerID**. Set the URL Format String property to
    Orders.aspx?CustomerID={0}. Figure 19.5 shows the filled-in Property Builder. Click
    OK to save the changes.

FIGURE 19.5:

Adding a hyperlink column to the DataGrid

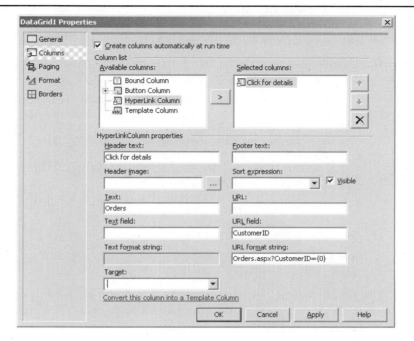

3. Now you need to create the Orders.aspx page. Select Project ➤ Add Web Form. Name the new Web Form **Orders.aspx** and then click Open.

4. Drag a SqlConnection object from the Data tab of the Toolbox to the Orders.aspx form.

5. In the Properties window, click the ConnectionString property to display the drop-down arrow for this property. Click the drop-down arrow. Select the connection string that you created for the Customers.aspx page from the list.

6. Drag a SqlCommand object from the Toolbox to the Customers.aspx form.

7. In the Properties window, click the Connection property to display the drop-down arrow for this property. Click the drop-down arrow. Expand the Existing node in the treeview that displays in the drop-down list and select the SqlConnection1 connection.

8. Click the CommandText property to display the build button. Click the build button to open the Query Builder. Select the Orders table in the Add Table dialog box and click Add; then click Close. Select the OrderID, CustomerID, and OrderDate fields by checking them. Uncheck the Output column for the CustomerID field. Enter **=@CustomerID** in the Criteria column for the CustomerID field. Click OK to save the command text.

9. Click the DataGrid control in the Web Forms tab of the Toolbox, then click and drag on the Web Form design surface to create an instance of the control. Click the AutoFormat link at the bottom of the Properties box and then select the Professional 2 format. Click OK.

10. Double-click outside the DataGrid in the form designer to open the code editor for the Web Form. Modify the Page_Load procedure to include this code:

```
Private Sub Page_Load(ByVal sender As System.Object, _
 ByVal e As System.EventArgs) Handles MyBase.Load
    SqlConnection1.Open()
    SqlCommand1.Parameters("@CustomerID").Value =
Request.QueryString("CustomerID")
    Dim dr As System.Data.SqlClient.SqlDataReader
    dr = SqlCommand1.ExecuteReader
    DataGrid1.DataSource = dr
    DataGrid1.DataBind()
    dr.Close()
    SqlConnection1.Close()
End Sub
```

11. Select File ➤ Save All to save the project.

12. Right-click on Customers.aspx in the Solution Explorer and select Build and Browse. Select a country from the DropDownList control. Then click the Orders link for any customer. Figure 19.6 shows the resulting web page.

FIGURE 19.6:

Browsing orders for a particular customer

OrderID	OrderDate
10408	1/8/1997 12:00:00 AM
10480	3/20/1997 12:00:00 AM
10634	8/15/1997 12:00:00 AM
10763	12/3/1997 12:00:00 AM
10789	12/22/1997 12:00:00 AM

13. Use the Back button in the browser to return to the Customers page, and select the Orders link for another customer. You should find that the Orders page loads much more quickly the second time, because it has already been compiled into memory.

This example demonstrates two important techniques. First, the FormatString property of the hyperlink column in the DataGrid shows how you can easily construct a hyperlink that differs for every row of a table. At runtime, the {0} in the FormatString is replaced with the value of the CustomerID field for the current row. As you saw in this example, you can also supply other literal characters in the format string. You can even have multiple replaceable parameters in the format string; {1} is the second replacement token, {2} is the third replacement token, and so on.

Second, this example shows how you can use a parameter passed as part of the address of a page to parameterize the records for the page. The code for the Page_Load event in this section is almost identical to the code in the preceding section that is used to select a set of customers when the user chooses a country. The major difference is that the code for Page_Load uses the Request.QueryString method to retrieve the value of the parameter from the command line.

Editing and Deleting Data

The DataGrid control includes built-in support for editing and deleting data. Although you still have to hook code up by hand to use this support, the designers of the control provided a workable overall framework for such data changes. To add edit and deletion capabilities to the Orders.aspx page, follow these steps:

1. Close the browser displaying the page and navigate to the Orders.aspx page in the form designer. Click the DataGrid control to select it. Click the Property Builder link at the bottom of the Properties window. This will open the DataGrid Property Builder.

2. Select the Columns section of the Property Builder. Expand the Button Column node in the Available Columns list. Select the Edit, Update, Cancel, and Delete column types and click the > button to place them in the Selected Columns list.

3. Still in the Property Builder, select Bound Column in the Available Columns list and add two bound columns to the Selected Columns list. For the first of these, set the Header Text to **Order ID**, set the Data Field to **OrderID**, and check the Read Only box. For the second bound column, set the Header Text to **Order Date** and the Data Field to **OrderDate**.

4. At the top of the Property Builder, uncheck the Create Columns Automatically at Run Time check box. Click OK to save your changes.

5. Set the DataKeyField property of the DataGrid control to **OrderID**.

6. Replace the code behind Orders.aspx with the code shown in Listing 19.1.

7. Select File ➢ Save All to save the project.

8. Right-click on Customers.aspx in the Solution Explorer and select Build and Browse. Select a country from the DropDownList control. Then click on the Orders link for any customer. Click the Edit link for any row, and you can edit the order date, as shown in Figure 19.7. Click Cancel to cancel the update, or Update to save the changes. Click the Delete link for any row to delete that order.

FIGURE 19.7:

Editing order data

		Order ID	Order Date
Edit	Delete	10363	11/26/1996 12:00:00 AM
Edit	Delete	10391	12/23/1996 12:00:00 AM
Update Cancel	Delete	10797	12/25/1997 12:00:00 AM
Edit	Delete	10825	1/9/1998 12:00:00 AM
Edit	Delete	11036	4/20/1998 12:00:00 AM
Edit	Delete	11067	5/4/1998 12:00:00 AM

Listing 19.1:   Code for Edits and Deletions on Orders.aspx

```
Private Sub Page_Load(ByVal sender As System.Object, _
 ByVal e As System.EventArgs) Handles MyBase.Load
    If Not IsPostBack Then
        BindData()
    End If
End Sub

Private Sub BindData()
    ' Initialize or reinitialize the grid
```

```
        SqlConnection1.Open()
        SqlCommand1.Parameters("@CustomerID").Value = _
         Request.QueryString("CustomerID")
        Dim dr As System.Data.SqlClient.SqlDataReader
        dr = SqlCommand1.ExecuteReader
        DataGrid1.DataSource = dr
        DataGrid1.DataBind()
        dr.Close()
        SqlConnection1.Close()
End Sub

Private Sub DataGrid1_DeleteCommand( _
 ByVal source As Object, _
 ByVal e As System.Web.UI.WebControls.DataGridCommandEventArgs) _
 Handles DataGrid1.DeleteCommand

        Dim com As System.Data.SqlClient.SqlCommand
        Dim strDeleteDetail As String = _
         "DELETE FROM [Order Details] WHERE OrderID = @OrderID"
        Dim strDelete As String = _
         "DELETE FROM Orders WHERE OrderID = @OrderID"

        ' Need to delete details before orders due to RI
        com = New System.Data.SqlClient.SqlCommand( _
         strDeleteDetail, SqlConnection1)
        com.Parameters.Add(New System.Data.SqlClient.SqlParameter( _
         "@OrderID", SqlDbType.Int))
        com.Parameters("@OrderID").Value = _
         DataGrid1.DataKeys(e.Item.ItemIndex)
        com.Connection.Open()
        com.ExecuteNonQuery()
        com.Connection.Close()

        com = New System.Data.SqlClient.SqlCommand( _
         strDelete, SqlConnection1)
        com.Parameters.Add(New System.Data.SqlClient.SqlParameter( _
         "@OrderID", SqlDbType.Int))
        com.Parameters("@OrderID").Value = _
         DataGrid1.DataKeys(e.Item.ItemIndex)
        com.Connection.Open()
        com.ExecuteNonQuery()
        com.Connection.Close()

        BindData()
End Sub

Private Sub DataGrid1_CancelCommand( _
 ByVal source As Object, _
 ByVal e As System.Web.UI.WebControls.DataGridCommandEventArgs) _
 Handles DataGrid1.CancelCommand
        ' To cancel an edit in progress, tell the grid that
```

```
        ' there is no edited item
        DataGrid1.EditItemIndex = -1
        BindData()
    End Sub

    Private Sub DataGrid1_EditCommand( _
     ByVal source As Object, _
     ByVal e As System.Web.UI.WebControls.DataGridCommandEventArgs) _
     Handles DataGrid1.EditCommand
        ' To edit a row, tell the grid which row to edit
        DataGrid1.EditItemIndex = CInt(e.Item.ItemIndex)
        BindData()
    End Sub

    Private Sub DataGrid1_UpdateCommand(ByVal source As Object, _
     ByVal e As System.Web.UI.WebControls.DataGridCommandEventArgs) _
     Handles DataGrid1.UpdateCommand

        Dim ds As DataSet
        Dim cmd As System.Data.SqlClient.SqlCommand

        Dim strUpdate As String = _
         "UPDATE Orders SET OrderDate = @OrderDate WHERE OrderID = @OrderID"

        cmd = New System.Data.SqlClient.SqlCommand( _
         strUpdate, SqlConnection1)

        cmd.Parameters.Add(New System.Data.SqlClient.SqlParameter( _
         "@OrderDate", SqlDbType.DateTime))
        cmd.Parameters.Add(New System.Data.SqlClient.SqlParameter( _
         "@OrderID", SqlDbType.Int))

        ' Order ID to edit is the current value of the DataKeys collection
        cmd.Parameters("@OrderID").Value = _
         DataGrid1.DataKeys(CInt(e.Item.ItemIndex))
        ' Retrieve the new order date from the text box
        Dim txtDate As TextBox
        txtDate = e.Item.Cells(3).Controls(0)
        cmd.Parameters("@OrderDate").Value = txtDate.Text
        cmd.Connection.Open()
        cmd.ExecuteNonQuery()

        ' Tell the grid we're done editing
        DataGrid1.EditItemIndex = -1

        cmd.Connection.Close()
        BindData()
    End Sub
```

The DataGrid control uses the EditItemIndex property to indicate which row (if any) is currently being edited. This property is read/write. If you set the property to a row number, the DataGrid replaces the static display labels for that row with text boxes, to allow you to edit the data. If you read the property, you can determine which row is currently being edited. The special value –1 indicates that no row is currently being edited.

The code for editing or deleting records works by constructing parameterized queries in SQL and then executing them using information from the form for the parameters. There are a few things you should note about this code:

- The DataKeys property of the DataGrid control retrieves the primary key for the row that the user is currently working with. This works only because the code sets the DataKeyField property of the control to the appropriate field name.

- The code for the Delete command has to delete order details and then orders, because there is a relationship defined between the two tables without cascading deletes.

- When retrieving a value from the row being edited, you first have to cast the appropriate member of the Controls collection of the DataGrid to a TextBox control before you can retrieve the Value property of the control.

- The cmd.ExecuteNonQuery() method is the appropriate way to pass action query SQL statements to the database.

- You need to call the BindData procedure after every data change to update the display of records on the DataGrid.

Adding New Records

The last requirement I'll tackle for the sample application is that of adding new data to the database from a Web Form. There's no particular capability built into the DataGrid for this task, so I'll add separate controls to the Orders.aspx Web Form to handle this task. To make these modifications, follow these steps:

1. Close the browser displaying the page and navigate to the Orders.aspx page in the form designer.

2. Using the Web Forms tab on the Toolbox, add two labels, a text box, and a button to the form, as shown in Figure 19.8. Set the (ID) property of the TextBox control to **txtOrder-Date** and the (ID) property of the button to **btnAdd**.

3. Add this line of code at the end of the Page_Load procedure to show today's date in the txtOrderDate control when the user loads the Orders page:

```
txtOrderDate.Text = Date.Today
```

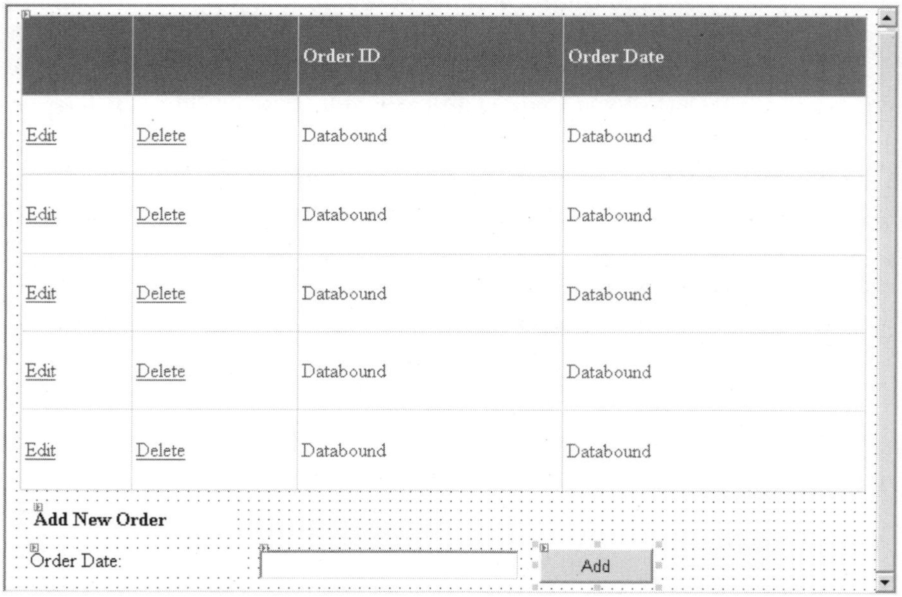

FIGURE 19.8:

Adding controls to the orders form

4. Add code behind the Orders.aspx form to handle the button click event from the Add button:

```
Private Sub btnAdd_Click(ByVal sender As Object, _
  ByVal e As System.EventArgs) Handles btnAdd.Click
    Dim ds As DataSet
    Dim cmd As System.Data.SqlClient.SqlCommand

    Dim strInsert As String = "INSERT INTO Orders " & _
      "(CustomerID, OrderDate)VALUES (@CustomerID, @OrderDate)"

    cmd = New System.Data.SqlClient.SqlCommand(strInsert, SqlConnection1)

    cmd.Parameters.Add(New System.Data.SqlClient.SqlParameter( _
      "@CustomerID", SqlDbType.NVarChar, 5))
    cmd.Parameters("@CustomerID").Value = _
      Request.QueryString("CustomerID")

    cmd.Parameters.Add(New System.Data.SqlClient.SqlParameter( _
      "@OrderDate", SqlDbType.DateTime))
    cmd.Parameters("@OrderDate").Value = txtOrderDate.Text
```

```
        cmd.Connection.Open()
        cmd.ExecuteNonQuery()

        cmd.Connection.Close()

        BindData()
    End Sub
```

In the same manner as the code for edits and deletes from the preceding section, this code uses a parameterized query to pass information from the form back to the database, and then calls the BindData procedure to reload the grid, showing the new data.

5. Select File ➤ Save All to save the project.

6. Right-click on Customers.aspx in the Solution Explorer and select Build and Browse. Select a country from the DropDownList control. Then click the Orders link for any customer. Fill in data for an order and then click the Add button to add the new order.

Using the DataList Control

The DataGrid control is convenient for displaying records from a database on a web page, but it's not very flexible. Although you can control visual aspects of the grid, such as foreground and background colors, fonts, and row and column size, the grid will remain a grid. For more flexibility in data display, you'll want to use the DataList control instead of the DataGrid control.

Displaying Data with a DataList

In this section, I'll show you how to add a DataList control to the sample project and to use it to browse data from the Employees table. To make these modifications, follow these steps:

1. Close the browser displaying the page.

2. Now you need to create the Employees.aspx page. Select Project ➤ Add Web Form. Name the new Web Form **Employees.aspx** and then click Open.

3. This time, instead of hooking up data in code, you'll do it all through the designer. Drag a SqlDataAdapter object from the Data tab of the Toolbox and drop it on the Employees.aspx form. This will launch the Data Adapter Configuration Wizard. Read the introductory panel on the wizard and then click Next.

4. On the Choose Your Data Connection panel, choose the existing data connection to the Northwind database and then click Next.

5. On the Choose a Query Type panel, choose Use SQL Statements and then click Next.

6. On the Generate SQL Statements panel, enter this code as the SQL statement:

   ```
   SELECT Employees.* FROM Employees
   ```
   Click Next.

7. After a short delay, you should see the View Wizard Results panel, as shown in Figure 19.9. As you can see, the wizard does quite a bit of work to hook your DataAdapter up to the database. By default, it prepares all the necessary SQL statements to handle insertions, updates, and deletions, as well as a simple data display. Click Finish to close the wizard.

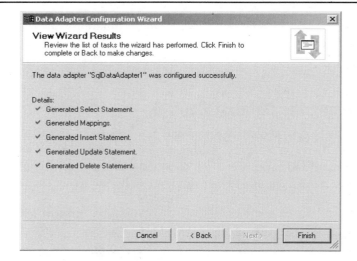

8. The wizard will generate both a SqlDataAdapter and a SqlConnection object on your form. Select the SqlDataAdapter object and then click the Generate Dataset link under the Properties window. This will open the Generate Dataset dialog box. Accept all the defaults in this dialog box and then click OK to generate a DataSet object.

9. Drag an instance of the DataList control from the Web Forms tab of the Toolbox to your form.

10. With the DataList control selected, click the Property Builder link under the Properties window to open the Properties dialog box for the DataList. Select DataSet1 as the data source for the DataList; then select Employees as the DataMember and select EmployeeID as the Data Key field. Set the Columns property under Repeat Layout to 2. Click OK to save the changes.

11. Double-click on the background of the Web Form to open its code module. Modify the Page_Load procedure as follows:

```
Private Sub Page_Load(ByVal sender As System.Object, _
  ByVal e As System.EventArgs) Handles MyBase.Load
    SqlDataAdapter1.Fill(DataSet11, "Employees")
    DataList1.DataBind()
End Sub
```

At load time, this code will fill the DataSet from the DataAdapter, and then bind the results to the DataList. The DataList control is now wired to the data in the Employees table. However, it won't display anything on the form until you provide it with one or more templates. A template is a set of HTML controls that the DataList can use to display the data that it contains. To create your first template for the DataList, continue with the next steps.

12. Right-click the DataList control and then select Edit Template ➤ Item Templates.

13. Drag a Label control from the Web Forms section of the Toolbox and drop it in the ItemTemplate area of the DataList. Set the ForeColor property of this label to Dark Gray and set the (ID) property to **lblEmployeeID**. Type several spaces and drag a second Label control to the ItemTemplate area. Set the (ID) property of the second label to **lblEmployeeName**.

14. Select the lblEmployeeID label, click its DataBindings property in the Properties window, and click the build button. In the DataBindings dialog box, select Text as the bindable property, select Simple binding, and expand the treeview to select the Container.DataItem.EmployeeID property to bind to this control. Click OK.

15. Select the lblEmployeeName label, click its DataBindings property in the Properties window, and click the build button. In the DataBindings dialog box, select Text as the bindable property and select Custom as the type of binding expression. Set the expression as follows:

```
DataBinder.Eval(Container, "DataItem.FirstName") & " " &
➥ DataBinder.Eval(Container, "DataItem.LastName")
```

16. Press Enter to make the ItemTemplate space taller. Figure 19.10 shows the finished design of the template.

17. Select File ➤ Save All to save the project.

18. Right-click on Employees.aspx in the Solution Explorer and select Build and Browse. You'll see a list of the employees in the database, as shown in Figure 19.11.

FIGURE 19.10:

Designing the
ItemTemplate

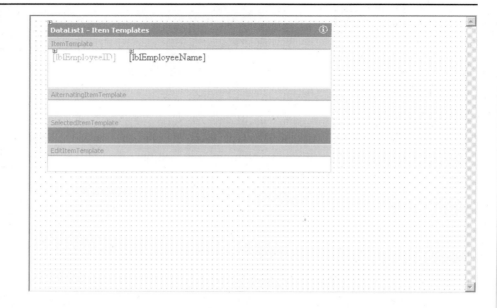

FIGURE 19.11:

Browsing employees
in a DataList control

As you can see, the DataList takes the data to which it's bound and renders it using the controls in the appropriate template. The DataList supports up to seven templates, although only the ItemTemplate is required. Table 19.2 lists the possible templates for a DataList.

TABLE 19.2: DataList Templates

Template	Use
ItemTemplate	Renders each row of data.
AlternatingItemTemplate	If supplied, renders alternate rows of data.
SelectedItemTemplate	Renders the currently selected row of data.
EditItemTemplate	Renders a row of data that is being edited.
HeaderTemplate	Appears once at the top of the DataList.
FooterTemplate	Appears once at the bottom of the DataList.
SeparatorTemplate	Functions as a separator between rows of data.

Using the SelectedItemTemplate

The DataList has a built-in understanding of several commands. One of these is Select. If you execute a Select in a DataList, it will take the row that issued the command and redisplay it using the SelectedItemTemplate. Here's an example:

1. Close the browser displaying the page.

2. Navigate to the Employees.aspx Web Form, right-click in the DataList, and choose Edit Template ➤ Item Templates.

3. Drag a LinkButton control from the Web Forms section of the Toolbox to the existing ItemTemplate. Set the Text property of this new control to Select, and set the Command-Name property to Select.

4. Copy the two label controls and the intervening spaces from the ItemTemplate section of the Item Templates view to the SelectedItemTemplate section.

5. Select File ➤ Save All to save the project.

6. Right-click on Employees.aspx in the Solution Explorer and select Build and Browse. You'll see a list of the employees in the database. Click the Select link for an employee, and that employee will be displayed in the style of the SelectedItemTemplate, as shown in Figure 19.12.

Of course, this is a trivial example intended only to demonstrate the technique. In an actual application, you might use this technique to display a selected item with additional detail fields. You can also create an explicit DataList_SelectedIndexChanged procedure in your code and use it to perform other actions when a row is selected.

The DataList also supports EditCommand, UpdateCommand, CancelCommand, and DeleteCommand procedures. These work exactly as they do in the DataGrid. Because I already demonstrated these commands in the context of the DataGrid control earlier in the chapter, I won't run through another example here. The only difference is that you gain finer control of the appearance of a row that's being edited by using the EditItemTemplate property of the DataList control.

NOTE   There's one more data-bound server control, the Repeater control. The Repeater is essentially a stripped-down version of the DataList control. It doesn't offer the layout flexibility of the DataList, and it has templates for only the header, footer, and item it's currently displaying. For most serious applications, you'll want to use a DataList instead of a Repeater.

Using Legacy ADO with ASP.NET

By now, you may be worried if you've already got a collection of ASP pages that use ADO to access databases and display results. ASP.NET is undeniably a very different development environment, and most of the code you've seen in this chapter bears very little relationship to traditional ADO code behind ASP pages.

There's good news, though: ASP.NET supports your legacy ADO code unchanged, because it implements the Server.CreateObject method that ASP uses to create late-bound objects. This means that you can move your existing ASP pages to an ASP.NET server, rename them to ASPX pages, and have them almost ready to run in the ASP.NET environment.

There are some changes you'll need to make to move ASP pages to ASPX, including these:

- Add `<%@ Page ASPCompat=true %>` to the top of each page.
- Declare all variables explicitly.

- Spell out all default properties.
- Remove all use of the Set and Let keywords.
- Enclose all argument lists in parentheses, even if there is no return value.

Listing 19.2 shows a simple ASP page that uses ADO to retrieve information from the Northwind Products table. Listing 19.3 shows the equivalent ASPX page, with the changes marked in boldface.

Listing 19.2:   **Data Access with ASP and ADO**

```
<!DOCTYPE HTML PUBLIC "-//W3C//DTD HTML 4.0 Transitional//EN">
<html>
  <%@ Language=VBScript %>
  <head>
    <title>Products</title>
  </head>
  <body>
    <h1>
      Product Information
    </h1>
    <%
    strConn = "Provider=SQLOLEDB;Data Source=THISTLE\NetSDK;" & _
     "Initial Catalog=Northwind;Integrated Security=SSPI"
    Set cnn = Server.CreateObject("ADODB.Connection")
    cnn.open strConn
    strQuery = "SELECT ProductName, UnitPrice FROM PRODUCTS"
    Set rstProducts = cnn.Execute(strQuery)
    %>
    <table>
      <tr>
        <td>
          <b>Product Name</b>
        </td>
        <td>
          <b>Unit Price</b>
        </td>
      </tr>
      <% Do While Not rstProducts.EOF %>
      <tr>
        <td>
          <%= rstProducts("ProductName") %>
        </td>
        <td>
          <%= rstProducts("UnitPrice") %>
        </td>
      </tr>
      <%
      rstProducts.MoveNext
    Loop
```

```
      rstProducts.Close
      Set rstProducts=Nothing
      cnn.close
      Set cnn=Nothing
   %>
      </table>
   </body>
</html>
```

Listing 19.3:   **Data Access with ASP.NET and ADO.NET**

```
<!DOCTYPE HTML PUBLIC "-//W3C//DTD HTML 4.0 Transitional//EN">
<html>
   <%@ Page ASPCompat=true Language=VBScript %>
   <head>
     <title>Products</title>
   </head>
   <body>
     <h1>
       Product Information
     </h1>
     <%
     Dim strConn
     Dim cnn
     Dim strQuery
     Dim rstProducts

     strConn = "Provider=SQLOLEDB;Data Source=THISTLE\NetSDK;" & _
       "Initial Catalog=Northwind;Integrated Security=SSPI"
     cnn = Server.CreateObject("ADODB.Connection")
     cnn.open(strConn)
     strQuery = "SELECT ProductName, UnitPrice FROM PRODUCTS"
     rstProducts = cnn.Execute(strQuery)
   %>
     <table>
       <tr>
         <td>
           <b>Product Name</b>
         </td>
         <td>
           <b>Unit Price</b>
         </td>
       </tr>
       <% Do While Not rstProducts.EOF %>
       <tr>
         <td>
           <%= rstProducts("ProductName").Value %>
         </td>
         <td>
           <%= rstProducts("UnitPrice").Value %>
```

```
        </td>
      </tr>
      <%
      rstProducts.MoveNext
    Loop
    rstProducts.Close
    rstProducts=Nothing
    cnn.close
    cnn=Nothing
  %>
    </table>
  </body>
</html>
```

The code from Listing 19.3 is stored in this chapter's sample project as `Products.aspx`. Figure 19.13 shows this page open in the built-in browser.

Product Name	Unit Price
Chai	18
Chang	19
Aniseed Syrup	10
Chef Anton's Cajun Seasoning	22
Chef Anton's Gumbo Mix	21.35
Grandma's Boysenberry Spread	25
Uncle Bob's Organic Dried Pears	30
Northwoods Cranberry Sauce	40
Mishi Kobe Niku	97
Ikura	31
Queso Cabrales	21
Queso Manchego La Pastora	38
Konbu	6
Tofu	23.25
Genen Shouyu	15.5
Pavlova	17.45
Alice Mutton	39
Carnarvon Tigers	62.5
Teatime Chocolate Biscuits	9.2
Sir Rodney's Marmalade	81

Product Information

Objects created with Server.CreateObject are automatically late-bound. You can gain a bit of performance by using early-bound COM objects in your ASP.NET code. To do so, you'll need to create Runtime-Callable Wrappers (RCWs) for the COM objects. For more information on RCWs, see Chapter 13, "Using ADO from .NET."

You should consider both of these solutions (Server.CreateObject and RCWs) to be interim solutions for using existing COM objects in ASP.NET. Over the long run, you'll want to rewrite your COM components to be .NET components, and replace ADO code with ADO.NET code. That's because there can be a severe performance disadvantage to using COM components (including ADO) from an ASP.NET application. First, the COM components will run in a single-threaded apartment, which may not mix well with the multi-threaded apartment that .NET uses by default. Second, converting from COM to .NET and vice versa requires extra time to marshal data between the two models.

Summary

In this chapter, you learned about using ADO.NET with ASP.NET. I covered the basics of ASP.NET, the use of the DataGrid and DataList controls, and the use of legacy ADO code from .NET. Along the way, you learned how to design Web Forms, to use the tools in Visual Studio .NET to create data components quickly, and to write code to handle common database operations such as adding a record, editing a record, and deleting a record.

Now it's time to turn our attention from the client to the server. Although ADO and ADO.NET are intended to be universal solutions, the databases that they can use differ in many respects from one another. In the next part of the book, I'll look at specific issues that you may face when using ADO with particular databases.

Part V

Specific Provider Issues

CHAPTER 20

ADO and SQL Server

- SQL Server versions

- SQL Server connection strings

- Dynamic properties of ADO objects

- Using linked servers to access heterogeneous data

- Using OPENXML

- SQL Server tips and quirks

I n the previous sections of this book, I've emphasized the universal nature of ADO, which allows you to use identical code for working with data from many different sources. Now it's time to drill a bit deeper. Although ADO can treat all data sources alike, it's not required to do so. The ADO developers created various mechanisms to allow data providers to expose unique functionality from the data sources that they manage. In the next several chapters, I'll look at some of this unique functionality. I'll start by examining some of the details of ADO's interactions with Microsoft SQL Server. This chapter also covers some of the unique functionality of SQL Server that is most interesting from an ADO perspective.

NOTE   This chapter includes some examples of Transact-SQL stored procedures and scripts. You can run these by using the command-line `osql` utility (type **osql /?** at a command prompt for the syntax of this utility) or the graphical SQL Query Analyzer program. Refer to the SQL Server documentation for more details on using these programs.

SQL Server Versions

ADO works with SQL Server 6.5, SQL Server 7, and SQL Server 2000. Of course, you will find occasional places where version 6.5 or 7 doesn't offer the full feature set of SQL Server 2000, and in those cases, ADO can't do anything to provide the missing functionality. For example, linked servers (discussed later in this chapter) don't exist on SQL Server 6.5.

ADO also works well across the entire range of SQL Server editions, including the Personal, Desktop, Developer, Standard, and Enterprise editions. ADO and OLE DB communicate directly with the core database engine, and this core engine is the same across the entire SQL Server product line.

There is one important catch to watch out for when using ADO with earlier versions of SQL Server. ADO makes use of *catalog stored procedures*, a set of system stored procedures that can obtain object information from the system tables on SQL Server. These stored procedures have changed as later versions of ADO and SQL Server have been released, and you should make sure that the latest version of ADO is installed on any server that you're trying to access via ADO. You'll find a file named `instcat.sql` in the `i386` directory on the SQL Server 2000 installation CD, or in the `Program Files\Microsoft SQL Server\MSSQL\Install` directory of a SQL Server installation on a server. If you're running SQL 7 or 6.5 servers and you'd like to use the latest version of ADO with these servers, you should copy the updated `instcat.sql` file to those older servers and then run it using the `isql` utility that ships with SQL Server. You can use a command line to run the script with `isql`:

```
isql /Uusername /Ppassword /Sservername /iInstcat.sql
```

Of course, you should supply the actual username, password, and server name information for your SQL Server as part of the command line.

SQL Server Connection Strings

In addition to the standard connection string parameters supplied by ADO itself (see Chapter 3, "Using the ADO Objects to Retrieve Data"), the SQL Server OLE DB provider supports 10 provider-specific connection string parameters. Table 20.1 lists these parameters, all of which are optional.

TABLE 20.1: SQL Server OLE DB Connection String Parameters

Parameter	Description
Application Name	Arbitrary string identifying the client application.
Auto Translate	Set to Yes to tell the OLE DB provider to perform ANSI/OEM character translation on string data, or No to skip such translation. The default is Yes.
Current Language	A SQL Server language name to use for system message selection and formatting.
Integrated Security	Can be set to SSPI (Secured Support Provider Interface) to use Windows integrated security, or omitted to use SQL Server login authentication. You should not include both the Integrated Security and Trusted_Connection parameters in the same connection string.
Network Address	The TCP/IP network address of the server to connect with. If you specify a value for the Network Address parameter, you can omit the Data Source parameter that normally holds the server name.
Network Library	Specifies the network protocol library to use. Possible values are dbnmntw for named pipes, dbmssocn for TCP/IP, dsmsspxn for SPX/IPX, dbmsvinn for Vines, and dbmsrpcn for the multi-protocol library. If you omit this parameter, ADO defaults to using the network library specified as the default in the client library setup.
Packet Size	Network packet size in bytes, from 512 to 32,767. The default is 4,096.
Trusted_Connection	Can be set to Yes to use Windows integrated security, or to No to use SQL Server login authentication. If Trusted_Connection is set to Yes, settings for the User ID and Password parameters are ignored. You should not include both the Integrated Security and Trusted_Connection parameters in the same connection string.
Use Procedure for Prepare	Can be set to Yes to tell SQL Server to create temporary stored procedures to handle prepared commands.
Workstation ID	Arbitrary string identifying the client workstation.

TIP   To connect to a named instance of SQL Server 2000, include the instance name after the server name in the Data Source parameter of the connection string. For example, to connect to a named instance named NetSDK on a server named SAILBOAT, you'd use `"Data Source=SAILBOAT\NetSDK"`.

Dynamic Properties of ADO Objects

OLE DB providers are allowed to add custom properties to the various objects that ADO provides. These properties are called *dynamic properties*, and can be found in the Properties collections of the appropriate objects. The SQL Server OLE DB provider adds a great many dynamic properties to the Connection, Command, and Recordset objects.

Connection Object Dynamic Properties

The SQL Server OLE DB provider adds about 60 dynamic properties to the Connection object. Many of these are of interest only to developers who are writing ADO tools that have to interoperate with multiple data providers and need a way to query for supported functionality. For example, the Identifier Case Sensitivity property will always return the constant *8* (indicating that identifiers are case-insensitive but stored in mixed case).

Table 20.2 shows a few of the important Connection object dynamic properties.

TABLE 20.2: Selected Dynamic Properties of the Connection Object

Property	Meaning
DBMS Version	Returns the version of SQL Server, including the minor version. For example, the initial release of SQL Server 2000 returns 08.00.0194.
OLE DB Version	Returns the version of OLE DB supported by the provider. For the SQL Server provider, this is normally the same as the ADO version.
Read-Only Datasource	Returns True or False to indicate whether or not you can modify data via this connection.
Server Name	Returns the name of the SQL Server to which you are connected. This returns the actual computer name if you've used the (local) shortcut in the connection string. For a non-default instance of SQL Server 2000, the Server Name property includes the instance name as well as the server name.

Because the Properties collection contains all of the dynamic properties, you can retrieve these properties by iterating through the collection. For example, the code in Listing 20.1 (contained in the frmDynamicProperties form in the ADOChapter20 sample project) will retrieve all the properties for a connection to the local SQL Server.

Listing 20.1:   **Retrieving the Dynamic Properties of a Connection Object**

```
Private Sub cmdConnection_Click()
    ' Retrieve dynamic properties for a connection
    Dim cnn As ADODB.Connection
    Dim prp As ADODB.Property
    Dim li As ListItem

    On Error GoTo HandleErr

    lvwProperties.ListItems.Clear

    Set cnn = New ADODB.Connection
    cnn.Open "Provider=SQLOLEDB;Data Source=(local);" & _
      "Initial Catalog=Northwind;Integrated Security=SSPI"

    For Each prp In cnn.Properties
        Set li = _
          lvwProperties.ListItems.Add(, prp.Name, prp.Name)
        li.SubItems(1) = prp.Value
    Next prp

    ' Clean up
    cnn.Close
    Set cnn = Nothing
    Set prp = Nothing
    Set li = Nothing
ExitHere:
    Exit Sub

HandleErr:
    MsgBox "Error " & Err.Number & ": " & Err.Description, _
      vbOKOnly, "cmdConnection"
    Resume ExitHere
    Resume

End Sub
```

Figure 20.1 shows the result of running this code. As you can see, the dynamic properties are not in any particular order in the Properties collection.

It's useful to be able to retrieve dynamic properties this way, because the list of available dynamic properties changes every time the SQL Server OLE DB provider is updated. If you run this code after installing a new version of the provider, you may well discover new and useful properties. The challenge, of course, is figuring out the meaning of these new properties. Your best bet for this is probably to download the latest MDAC SDK from the Microsoft Universal Data Access website (www.microsoft.com/data).

Retrieving dynamic
properties of a Con-
nection object

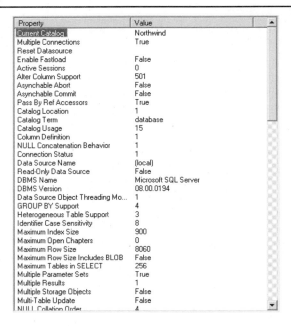

Property	Value
Current Catalog	Northwind
Multiple Connections	True
Reset Datasource	
Enable Fastload	False
Active Sessions	0
Alter Column Support	501
Asynchable Abort	False
Asynchable Commit	False
Pass By Ref Accessors	True
Catalog Location	1
Catalog Term	database
Catalog Usage	15
Column Definition	1
NULL Concatenation Behavior	1
Connection Status	1
Data Source Name	(local)
Read-Only Data Source	False
DBMS Name	Microsoft SQL Server
DBMS Version	08.00.0194
Data Source Object Threading Mo...	1
GROUP BY Support	4
Heterogeneous Table Support	3
Identifier Case Sensitivity	8
Maximum Index Size	900
Maximum Open Chapters	0
Maximum Row Size	8060
Maximum Row Size Includes BLOB	False
Maximum Tables in SELECT	256
Multiple Parameter Sets	True
Multiple Results	1
Multiple Storage Objects	False
Multi-Table Update	False
NULL Collation Order	4

Command Object Dynamic Properties

The SQL Server OLE DB provider adds about 75 dynamic properties to Command objects.
Table 20.3 shows a few of the more useful Command dynamic properties.

TABLE 20.3:   Selected Dynamic Properties of the Command Object

Property	Meaning
Maximum Rows	The maximum number of rows that this Command will fetch from the database. Any attempt to read more than this number of rows will return EOF. You can use this property to limit any chance of being overwhelmed by a larger-than-expected amount of data from a Command.
Others' Changes Visible	True if changes made to a Recordset based on this Command by other sessions are visible in this session.
Others' Inserts Visible	True if new records added to a Recordset based on this Command by other sessions are visible in this session.
Own Changes Visible	True if changes made to a Recordset based on this Command are visible without re-executing the Command.
Own Inserts Visible	True if new records added to a Recordset based on this Command are visible without re-executing the Command.
XML Root	Can be used to set a root tag so that the result of a FOR XML query is a proper XML document.
XSL	An XSL document or URL that will be used to format the results of a FOR XML query.

As with the dynamic properties of the Connection object, most of the dynamic properties of the Command object exist for the benefit of tool and utility writers who may be working with multiple providers. Many of these properties indicate whether particular OLE DB interfaces can be used with the provider. For example, the IRowsetChange property indicates whether the provider supports the IRowsetChange interface. You're unlikely to need any of these properties in ADO development.

The frmDynamicProperties form in this chapter's sample project contains code to display the properties of a simple Command object. Figure 20.2 shows the results of running this code.

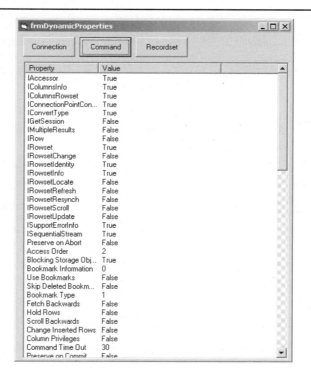

Recordset Object Dynamic Properties

The SQL Server OLE DB provider also adds about 70 dynamic properties to the Recordset object. If you use the ADOChapter20 sample project to inspect these properties, you'll discover that many of them are identical to the dynamic properties of a Command object. That's because many of the Command object properties refer to the details of a Recordset created from that Command.

Table 20.4 shows some of the Recordset dynamic properties.

TABLE 20.4:   Selected Dynamic Properties of the Command Object

Property	Meaning
Immobile Rows	True if newly inserted and updated rows are kept in proper order in the Recordset. False if updated rows remain in their current position and newly inserted rows are added to the end of the Recordset.
Maximum Rows	The maximum number of rows that this Recordset will fetch from the database. Any attempt to read more than this number of rows will return EOF.
Others' Changes Visible	True if changes made to this Recordset by other sessions are visible in this session.
Others' Inserts Visible	True if new records added to this Recordset by other sessions are visible in this session.
Own Changes Visible	True if changes made to this Recordset are visible without re-executing the Command.
Own Inserts Visible	True if new records added to this Recordset are visible without re-executing the Command.

The frmDynamicProperties form in this chapter's sample project contains code to display the properties of a simple Recordset object. Figure 20.3 shows the results of running this code.

FIGURE 20.3:

Retrieving properties
of a Recordset object

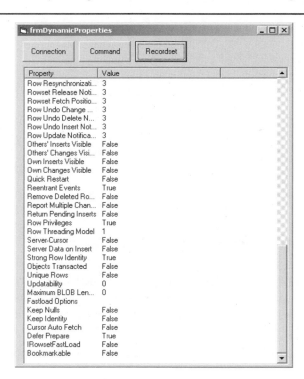

Using Linked Servers to Access Heterogeneous Data

SQL Server, starting with version 7, provides an interesting and useful feature, *linked servers*, that allows you to use the SQL Server OLE DB driver to work with data from a variety of data sources. One way to think of a linked server is as an OLE DB forwarding service. For example, if you link a Microsoft Access database to a SQL Server, you can send queries to the SQL Server that are destined for that Access database. The SQL Server, in turn, uses the Jet OLE DB provider to retrieve the data from the Access database, and then returns it to the ultimate client application. Figure 20.4 shows schematically how linked servers function.

In this section, I'll show you how you can use ADO to create a linked server, and then how you can create an ADO Recordset containing data from the linked server.

FIGURE 20.4:

SQL Server linked server architecture

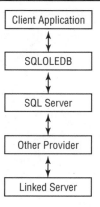

Linked servers provide SQL Server with support for distributed heterogeneous queries. That is, you can write a single Transact-SQL query that draws data from a variety of data sources, including non–SQL Server data sources. This can be a useful alternative to opening multiple Recordset objects by going directly to the data sources and trying to match up the information in code.

Creating a Linked Server

To create a linked server, you need to run the sp_addlinkedserver stored procedure:

```
sp_addlinkedserver [ @server = ] 'server'
  [ , [ @srvproduct = ] 'product_name' ]
  [ , [ @provider = ] 'provider_name' ]
  [ , [ @datasrc = ] 'data_source' ]
  [ , [ @location = ] 'location' ]
  [ , [ @provstr = ] 'provider_string' ]
  [ , [ @catalog = ] 'catalog' ]
```

This stored procedure takes up to seven arguments, although only the first one is required:

- *@server* is the local name of the linked server—that is, it's the name by which you will refer to the linked server within the current database. If you specify no other arguments, SQL Server assumes that this is also the name of a remote SQL Server that you wish to link to the current server.

- *@srvproduct* is the product name for the server being linked. For SQL Server data sources, this must be the string "SQL Server"; for other data sources, this string can be anything.

- *@provider* is the name of an OLE DB provider for the server being linked.

- *@datasrc* is the value to pass to the Data Source parameter of the OLE DB provider.

- *@location* is the value to pass to the Location parameter of the OLE DB provider.

- *@provstr* is the value to pass to the Provider String parameter of the OLE DB provider.

- *@catalog* is the value to pass to the Initial Catalog parameter of the OLE DB provider.

Here are some examples of calls to sp_addlinkedserver. To create a link to a SQL Server named Hornet:

```
sp_addlinkedserver @server = 'Hornet', @srvproduct = 'SQL Server'
```

To create a link to a Microsoft Access database:

```
sp_addlinkedserver @server = 'AccServer', @srvproduct = 'Jet',
  @provider = 'Microsoft.Jet.OLEDB.4.0',
  @datasrc = 'C:\Temp\Northwind.mdb'
```

To create a link to an Oracle database:

```
sp_addlinkedserver @server = 'TestOracle', @srvproduct = 'Oracle',
  @provider = 'MSDAORA', @datasrc = 'Customers'
```

Because creating a linked server is just a matter of running a stored procedure, it's possible to create linked servers directly from ADO code. You can do this by using a Command object to execute the appropriate SQL. I'll show you an example a bit later in this chapter.

TIP   SQL Server doesn't check the information you supply to sp_addlinkedserver when it creates the linked server. In particular, if you get the OLE DB provider name or the server name wrong, the linked server will be created, but queries sent to that linked server will fail. You can find the valid OLE DB provider names on your server by executing the xp_enum_oledb_providers extended stored procedure.

Adding Linked Server Logins

By default, SQL Server simply passes user credentials through to linked servers. That is, if you're logged on to SQL Server as user *Bill* with password *Foo*, SQL Server will supply that username and password when attempting to log on to a linked server. You can change this default behavior by using the `sp_addlinkedsrvlogin` stored procedure to create specific login mappings:

```
sp_addlinkedsrvlogin [ @rmtsrvname = ] 'rmtsrvname'
  [ , [ @useself = ] 'useself' ]
  [ , [ @locallogin = ] 'locallogin' ]
  [ , [ @rmtuser = ] 'rmtuser' ]
  [ , [ @rmtpassword = ] 'rmtpassword' ]
```

The five parameters accepted by this stored procedure are as follows:

- *@rmtsrvname* is the local name of the linked server.

- *@useself* is True if the login credentials used to connect to SQL Server should be passed directly to the linked server, or False if a new set of credentials should be created.

- *@locallogin* is the local user login to be mapped. This can be either the name of a SQL Server account or the name of a Windows account. It can also be Null, to specify that the mapping being created should apply to all users.

- *@rmtuser* is the username to supply to the linked server.

- *@rmtpassword* is the password to supply to the linked server.

For example, to use an unsecured Access database as a linked server, you should specify that all local accounts map to the Admin user with no password:

```
sp_addlinkedsrvlogin @rmtsrvname = 'AccServer',
  @useself = False,
  @locallogin = Null,
  @rmtuser = 'Admin',
  @rmtpassword = Null
```

Later in this section, I'll show you an example of the code to execute this stored procedure via an ADO Command object.

Deleting a Linked Server

To delete a linked server, you use the `sp_dropserver` stored procedure:

```
sp_dropserver [ @server = ] 'server'
  [ , [ @droplogins = ] { 'droplogins' | NULL} ]
```

Here the *@server* parameter is the local name of the linked server, and the *@droplogins* parameter tells SQL Server whether it should also delete any logins that were created for this linked server.

The code in this chapter's sample project uses `sp_dropserver` to remove any existing server with the name AccServer, so that the Visual Basic procedure can be run multiple times without error.

Example: Linking an Access Database

The frmLinkedServers form in this chapter's sample project contains code demonstrating the creation of a linked server and a default login for that linked server. This particular piece of code links a local Access database to the local SQL Server. Of course, you could generalize this to use any Access and SQL Server databases that you can access from your computer. Listing 20.2 shows the sample code.

Listing 20.2:   **Creating a Linked Server**

```
Private Sub cmdCreateLink_Click()

    Dim cnn As ADODB.Connection
    Dim cmd As ADODB.Command
    Dim strSQL As String

    On Error Resume Next

    ' Connect to the local SQL Server
    Set cnn = New ADODB.Connection
    cnn.Open "Provider=SQLOLEDB;Data Source=(local);" & _
      "Initial Catalog=master;Integrated Security=SSPI"

    ' Drop the linked server, in case it was created
    ' already by a previous run through this code
    strSQL = "sp_dropserver @server = 'AccServer', " & _
      "@droplogins = 'droplogins'"
    Set cmd = New ADODB.Command
    cmd.CommandType = adCmdText
    cmd.CommandText = strSQL
    Set cmd.ActiveConnection = cnn
    cmd.Execute

    On Error Goto HandleErr

    ' Build the SQL to link in the Access database
    ' that's in the same folder as the sample project
    strSQL = "sp_addlinkedserver @server = 'AccServer', " & _
      "@srvproduct = 'Jet', " & _
      "@provider = 'Microsoft.Jet.OLEDB.4.0', " & _
      "@datasrc = '" & App.Path & "\Customers.mdb'"

    ' And execute it via a command
    Set cmd = New ADODB.Command
    cmd.CommandType = adCmdText
    cmd.CommandText = strSQL
    Set cmd.ActiveConnection = cnn
    cmd.Execute

    ' Map all logins to the Access Admin account
```

```
      strSQL = "sp_addlinkedsrvlogin @rmtsrvname = 'AccServer', " & _
       "@useself = False, " & _
       "@locallogin = Null, " & _
       "@rmtuser = 'Admin', " & _
       "@rmtpassword = NULL "

      Set cmd = New ADODB.Command
      cmd.CommandType = adCmdText
      cmd.CommandText = strSQL
      Set cmd.ActiveConnection = cnn
      cmd.Execute

      ' Clean up
      cnn.Close
      Set cnn = Nothing
      Set cmd = Nothing
      MsgBox "Created linked server AccServer", vbInformation

ExitHere:
    Exit Sub

HandleErr:
    MsgBox "Error " & Err.Number & ": " & Err.Description, _
     vbOKOnly, "cmdCreateLink"
    Resume ExitHere
    Resume

End Sub
```

All of the work done by this code is accomplished via an ADO Command object connected to the (local) SQL Server. The Command object provides a simple way to execute stored procedures on the server. There are three steps to the process:

1. Drop the linked server (if it exists) along with the associated logins by using sp_dropserver. In production code, you might want to trap the error that occurs if you try instead to create an already-existing linked server. Including this step ensures that you can run the sample code more than once without a runtime error. In this example, I've placed this code in an On Error Resume Next block so that it will still work, even if you attempt to drop a linked server that doesn't exist.

2. Create the linked server by using sp_addlinkedserver.

3. Create a default login (used by any SQL Server user who tries to retrieve data from the server) that is mapped to the Access Admin user by using sp_addlinkedsrvlogin.

After you've executed this code, you can open SQL Server Enterprise Manager and confirm that the linked server was successfully created by navigating to the Linked Servers node beneath the Security node in the treeview. You can also list the tables and views on the linked server, as shown in Figure 20.5.

FIGURE 20.5:

A linked server in SQL
Server Enterprise
Manager

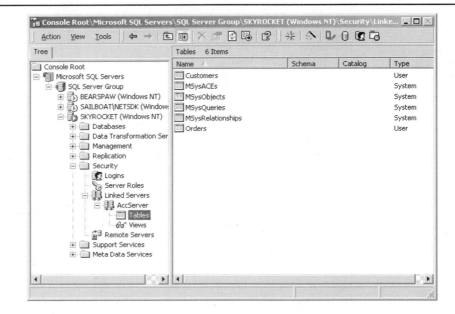

Using a Linked Server

After you've created a linked server, you can execute queries against it using the regular ADO
Connection, Command, and Recordset objects. The key to querying linked servers is to use a
four-part name for the table or view that holds the data:

```
Server.Catalog.Schema.Object
```

The four parts of the name are as follows:

- *Server* is the name that was defined for the linked server in the call to
  sp_addlinkedserver.

- *Catalog* is the catalog or database name on the linked server.

- *Schema* is the schema or owner name on the linked server.

- *Object* is the table or view name on the linked server.

Some linked servers may not require all of this information, depending on the type of
server. For example, Microsoft Jet has no concept of catalogs or schemas, so those parts of
the four-part name are nonexistent for Jet databases. But you still need to supply the server
and object names, and to include the separating dots.

The frmLinkedServers form in this chapter's sample project contains a procedure to retrieve data from the linked server that was created by the cmdCreateLink_Click procedure. Listing 20.3 shows this procedure.

Listing 20.3:   **Retrieving Data from a Linked Server**

```
Private Sub cmdRetrieveData_Click()
    ' Retrieve data from a linked server
    Dim cnn As ADODB.Connection
    Dim rst As ADODB.Recordset

    On Error GoTo HandleErr

    lboResults.Clear

    ' Connect to the local SQL Server
    Set cnn = New ADODB.Connection
    cnn.Open "Provider=SQLOLEDB;Data Source=(local);" & _
     "Initial Catalog=master;Integrated Security=SSPI"

    ' Open a Recordset from the linked server
    Set rst = New ADODB.Recordset
    rst.Open "SELECT CustomerID FROM AccServer...Customers", cnn

    ' And dump it to the user interface
    Do Until rst.EOF
        lboResults.AddItem rst.Fields("CustomerID").Value
        rst.MoveNext
    Loop

    ' Clean up
    rst.Close
    Set rst = Nothing
    cnn.Close
    Set cnn = Nothing (AU - Ok here? - TE)
....
ExitHere:
    Exit Sub

HandleErr:
    MsgBox "Error " & Err.Number & ": " & Err.Description, _
     vbOKOnly, "cmdRetrieveData"
    Resume ExitHere
    Resume

End Sub
```

You can see the four-part server object name in the SELECT statement that this procedure uses to retrieve data.

NOTE   Once the linked server is added, you don't need to know anything about its location to retrieve data from it.

You must always use the fully qualified object name when working with linked servers, even in situations where SQL Server would normally allow you to omit some of the information. For example, if BIGDOG is a linked SQL Server, this query won't work:

```
SELECT * FROM BIGDOG.Northwind..Customers
```

You must supply the owner name even when it is dbo:

```
SELECT * FROM BIGDOG.Northwind.dbo.Customers
```

TIP   Because the four-part name completely specifies the data source, it doesn't matter what SQL Server database you use in the connection string when you're running a query to retrieve data from a linked server.

You can also use the Distributed Query button on the frmLinkedServers form to demonstrate the ability of SQL Server to transparently combine data from SQL Server and linked data sources. Listing 20.4 shows the code that this button runs.

Listing 20.4:   **Retrieving Data from a Distributed Query**

```
Private Sub cmdDistributed_Click()
    ' Retrieve data from a distributed
    ' heterogeneous query
    Dim cnn As ADODB.Connection
    Dim rst As ADODB.Recordset

    On Error GoTo HandleErr

    lboResults.Clear

    ' Connect to the local SQL Server
    Set cnn = New ADODB.Connection
    cnn.Open "Provider=SQLOLEDB;Data Source=(local);" & _
      "Initial Catalog=Northwind;Integrated Security=SSPI"

    ' Open a Recordset from the linked server
    Set rst = New ADODB.Recordset
    rst.Open "SELECT C.CustomerID, " & _
      "COUNT(OrderID) " & _
      "FROM AccServer...Customers AS C INNER JOIN Orders " & _
      "ON C.CustomerID = " & _
      "Orders.CustomerID GROUP BY C.CustomerID " & _
      "ORDER BY COUNT(OrderID)", cnn
```

```
      ' And dump it to the user interface
      Do Until rst.EOF
          lboResults.AddItem rst.Fields(0).Value & _
          " - " & rst.Fields(1).Value
          rst.MoveNext
      Loop

      ' Clean up
      rst.Close
      Set rst = Nothing
      cnn.Close
      Set cnn = NothingExitHere:
      Exit Sub

HandleErr:
      MsgBox "Error " & Err.Number & ": " & Err.Description, _
      vbOKOnly, "cmdDistributed"
      Resume ExitHere
      Resume

End Sub
```

As you can see, it's easier to work with linked servers if you assign an alias to the table name. Here's the SQL statement that this example runs, stripped of the Visual Basic string syntax:

```
SELECT C.CustomerID
COUNT(OrderID)
FROM AccServer...Customers AS C INNER JOIN Orders
ON C.CustomerID =
Orders.CustomerID GROUP BY C.CustomerID
ORDER BY COUNT(OrderID)
```

Figure 20.6 shows the results of running this query in the sample application.

Ad Hoc Linking

SQL Server also supports *ad hoc linking*. With ad hoc linking, you can retrieve information into a distributed heterogeneous query without creating a linked server. This method has advantages and disadvantages compared with creating a linked server. The advantage of an ad hoc link is that you can create and run the entire query in a single statement, rather than first linking the server and then running a second query to retrieve data from the server. But there are some drawbacks to be aware of when using this method:

- You cannot specify login mappings when using ad hoc links.

- Ad hoc links are slower than permanent links.

- You cannot retrieve a list of tables or views from an ad hoc link.

FIGURE 20.6:

Results of a distributed heterogeneous query

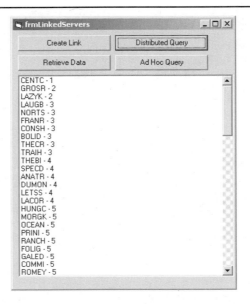

Generally, you should use ad hoc links only in cases where a particular server will be queried only a few times.

There are two T-SQL keywords that you can use to perform ad hoc linked queries: OPEN-ROWSET and OPENDATASOURCE. To choose between them, consider these differences:

- OPENROWSET can be used with any OLE DB provider that returns rowsets. It can be used in place of a table name in any SQL statement.

- OPENDATASOURCE can be used only with OLE DB providers that use the catalog.schema.object notation to specify rowsets. It can be used in any SQL statement where a linked server name can be used.

The syntax of OPENROWSET is as follows:

```
OPENROWSET( 'provider_name',
  { 'datasource' ; 'user_id' ; 'password'
  | 'provider_string' },
  { [ catalog. ] [ schema. ] object
    | 'query' }
        )
```

The parameters to OPENROWSET are as follows:

- *Provider_name* is the name of an OLE DB provider.

- *Datasource* is a connection string for that provider.

- *User_id* is the username to use when logging on to the linked server.

- *Password* is the password to use when logging on to the linked server.

- *Provider_string* is an additional connection string containing provider-specific information.

- *Catalog*, *schema*, *object*, and *query* identify the source of the data within the specified server.

OPENROWSET is most useful with data sources, such as Jet databases, that don't support the catalog.schema.object naming scheme. Although OPENROWSET can be used with data sources that do support this scheme (such as SQL Server or Oracle), the OPENDATA-SOURCE statement has a simpler syntax for these databases:

```
OPENDATASOURCE( provider_name, init_string )
```

In the OPENDATASOURCE statement, *provider_name* is the name of an OLE DB provider, and *init_string* is an OLE DB connection string.

The frmLinkedServers form in this chapter's sample project contains an example of using OPENROWSET to retrieve data from a Jet database. Listing 20.5 shows this procedure.

Listing 20.5:   **Retrieving Data from an Ad Hoc Linked Server**

```
Private Sub cmdAdHoc_Click()
    ' Retrieve data from an
    ' ad hoc linked server
    Dim cnn As ADODB.Connection
    Dim rst As ADODB.Recordset

    On Error GoTo HandleErr

    lboResults.Clear

    ' Connect to the local SQL Server
    Set cnn = New ADODB.Connection
    cnn.Open "Provider=SQLOLEDB;Data Source=(local);" & _
      "Initial Catalog=master;Integrated Security=SSPI"

    ' Open a Recordset from the linked server
    Set rst = New ADODB.Recordset
    rst.Open "SELECT CustomerID FROM " & _
      " OPENROWSET('Microsoft.Jet.OLEDB.4.0', " & _
      "'" & App.Path & "\Customers.mdb';'Admin';'', " & _
      "Customers)", cnn

    ' And dump it to the user interface
    Do Until rst.EOF
        lboResults.AddItem rst.Fields("CustomerID").Value
        rst.MoveNext
    Loop

    ' Clean up
    rst.Close
    Set rst = Nothing
```

```
        cnn.Close
        Set cnn = Nothing
    ExitHere:
        Exit Sub

    HandleErr:
        MsgBox "Error " & Err.Number & ": " & Err.Description, _
          vbOKOnly, "cmdAdHoc"
        Resume ExitHere
        Resume

    End Sub
```

Using OPENXML

With the increasing popularity of XML as a data interchange format, it's likely that at some point, you'll want to create a Recordset from an XML file. In Chapter 18, "Synchronizing DataSets with XML," you learned how to do this using classes from the .NET Framework class library. But what can you do if you're using traditional ADO rather than the newer ADO.NET? One answer is to use SQL Server 2000's OPENXML statement to parse the contents of an XML file. With OPENXML, you can treat a set of nodes within an XML file as a rowset source, just like a table or a view. In this section, I'll explain the syntax of OPENXML and show you some examples.

Understanding XPath

Before you can understand the syntax of OPENXML, you need to understand the basics of XPath. XPath is not itself an XML standard; rather, it's a language for talking *about* XML. By writing an appropriate XPath expression, you can select particular elements or attributes within an XML document. To explore XPath and OPENXML, I'll use the OrdersQuery.xml file shown in Listing 20.6.

Listing 20.6:   *OrdersQuery.xml*

```xml
<?xml version="1.0" ?>
<ROOT>
  <Order>
    <OrderID Status="Shipped" Rating="High">10643</OrderID>
    <CustomerID>ALFKI</CustomerID>
    <EmployeeID>6</EmployeeID>
    <OrderDate>1997-08-25T00:00:00</OrderDate>
    <RequiredDate>1997-09-22T00:00:00</RequiredDate>
    <ShippedDate>1997-09-02T00:00:00</ShippedDate>
    <ShipVia>1</ShipVia>
    <Freight>29.46</Freight>
```

```
    </Order>
    <Order>
      <OrderID Status="Returned" Rating="Low">10692</OrderID>
      <CustomerID>ALFKI</CustomerID>
      <EmployeeID>4</EmployeeID>
      <OrderDate>1997-10-03T00:00:00</OrderDate>
      <RequiredDate>1997-10-31T00:00:00</RequiredDate>
      <ShippedDate>1997-10-13T00:00:00</ShippedDate>
      <ShipVia>2</ShipVia>
      <Freight>61.02</Freight>
    </Order>
    <Order>
      <OrderID Status="Shipped" Rating="High">10702</OrderID>
      <CustomerID>ALFKI</CustomerID>
      <EmployeeID>4</EmployeeID>
      <OrderDate>1997-10-13T00:00:00</OrderDate>
      <RequiredDate>1997-11-24T00:00:00</RequiredDate>
      <ShippedDate>1997-10-21T00:00:00</ShippedDate>
      <ShipVia>1</ShipVia>
      <Freight>23.94</Freight>
    </Order>
    <Order>
      <OrderID Status="Shipped" Rating="Medium">10835</OrderID>
      <CustomerID>ALFKI</CustomerID>
      <EmployeeID>1</EmployeeID>
      <OrderDate>1998-01-15T00:00:00</OrderDate>
      <RequiredDate>1998-02-12T00:00:00</RequiredDate>
      <ShippedDate>1998-01-21T00:00:00</ShippedDate>
      <ShipVia>3</ShipVia>
      <Freight>69.53</Freight>
    </Order>
    <Order>
      <OrderID Status="Shipped" Rating="High">10952</OrderID>
      <CustomerID>ALFKI</CustomerID>
      <EmployeeID>1</EmployeeID>
      <OrderDate>1998-03-16T00:00:00</OrderDate>
      <RequiredDate>1998-04-27T00:00:00</RequiredDate>
      <ShippedDate>1998-03-24T00:00:00</ShippedDate>
      <ShipVia>1</ShipVia>
      <Freight>40.42</Freight>
      <ShipName>Alfreds Futterkiste</ShipName>
    </Order>
    <Order>
      <OrderID Status="Shipped" Rating="Low">11011</OrderID>
      <CustomerID>ALFKI</CustomerID>
      <EmployeeID>3</EmployeeID>
      <OrderDate>1998-04-09T00:00:00</OrderDate>
      <RequiredDate>1998-05-07T00:00:00</RequiredDate>
      <ShippedDate>1998-04-13T00:00:00</ShippedDate>
      <ShipVia>1</ShipVia>
      <Freight>1.21</Freight>
    </Order>
  </ROOT>
```

The `OrdersQuery.xml` file is based on data from the Northwind sample database. As you can see, it contains some information on orders for a particular customer. Some of the information, such as the CustomerID, is stored in elements. Other information, such as the Status of the order, is stored in attributes of the OrderID element.

To understand XPath, it's helpful to think of an XML file as a tree of information. Figure 20.7 shows a portion of the `OrdersQuery.xml` file rendered as a tree using Microsoft's XML Notepad application.

TIP   You can download XML Notepad from `http://msdn.microsoft.com/library/default.asp?url=/library/en-us/dnxml/html/xmlpaddownload.asp`.

FIGURE 20.7:

Tree structure of `OrderQuery.xml`

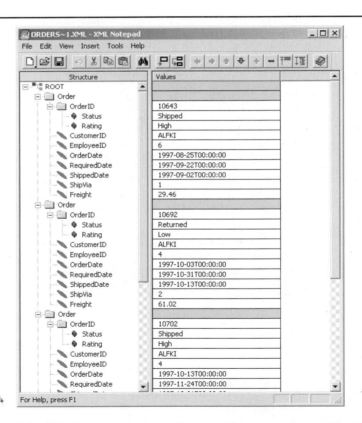

There are two parts of the XPath syntax that are of interest for our purposes: identifying elements and identifying attributes. These are the parts of an XML file that OPENXML can work with.

NOTE   The full XPath specification is much more comprehensive than the pieces that I'm using here. For details, refer to the W3C XPath recommendation at www.w3.org/TR/XPath.html.

To identify a set of elements using XPath, you use the path down the tree structure to those elements, separating tags with forward slashes. For example, this XPath expression selects all of the Order elements in the `OrderQuery.xml` file:

```
/ROOT/Order
```

Similarly, this XPath expression selects all of the OrderDate elements:

```
/ROOT/Order/OrderDate
```

XPath expressions select a set of elements, not a single element. This makes them roughly analogous, in this case, to fields in a table or view.

WARNING   The XPath specification allows the use of a single forward slash to specify the root of the entire XML document. SQL Server 2000 doesn't allow this in the XPath that it uses. You need to specify the root element by name.

To identify a set of attributes, you trace the path down the tree to the attributes, just as you do with elements. The only difference is that attribute names must be prefixed with the @ character. For example, this XPath expression selects all of the Status attributes in the `Open-Query.xml` file:

```
/ROOT/Order/OrderID/@Status
```

XPath also offers a predicate language to allow you to specify smaller groups of nodes or even individual nodes in the XML tree. You might think of this as a filtering capability similar to a SQL WHERE clause. One thing you can do is specify the exact value of the node that you'd like to work with. For example, to find all CustomerID nodes with the value ALFKI, you could use this XPath expression:

```
/ROOT/Order/CustomerID[.="ALFKI"]
```

Here the dot operator stands for the current node.

You can also filter using values of elements or attributes within the current node. For example, to find Order nodes where the ShipVia element has the value *1*, you'd use this expression:

```
/ROOT/Order[ShipVia="1"]
```

Or to find OrderID elements with a Rating attribute having the value *Low*, you'd use this:

```
/ROOT/Order/OrderID[@Rating="Low"]
```

TIP   There is no forward slash between an element and a filtering expression in XPath.

You can also use operators and Boolean expressions within filtering specifications. For example, you might want to find Orders where the Freight amount is between 20.00 and 50.00:

```
/ROOT/Order[Freight>=20 and Freight<=50]
```

TIP   The full XPath specification includes operators for such things as finding ancestors, descendants, and siblings of a particular node in the XML tree. I won't be using any of these operators in the examples.

OPENXML Syntax

OPENXML works in concert with two stored procedures, sp_xml_preparedocument and sp_xml_removedocument. The first of these converts an XML document represented as a string of text into a treeview and stores it in SQL Server's memory. The second removes such a parsed version of an XML document from the SQL Server memory when you're done with it.

WARNING   sp_xml_preparedocument uses the MSXML parser to do its job, and allots one-eighth of SQL Server's total memory setting to this task. It's important to remember to call sp_xml_removedocument to free this memory when you're done with it.

The syntax for sp_xml_preparedocument is as follows:

```
sp_xml_preparedocument hdoc OUTPUT
   [, xmltext]
   [, xpath_namespaces]
```

This stored procedure has three parameters:

- *Hdoc* is an integer variable that will contain a returned document handle. You need this document handle for the calls to OPENXML and sp_xml_removedocument; it identifies the particular XML document to SQL Server.

- *Xmltext* is the text of the XML document to be parsed by the procedure.

- *Xpath_namespaces* allows you to specify a namespace to define additional information about the XML document. You're unlikely to need this optional parameter.

When you're done using a particular XML document in T-SQL, you should call the sp_xml_removedocument stored procedure:

```
sp_xml_removedocument hdoc
```

In this stored procedure, the single parameter is the document handle that was originally retrieved from sp_xml_preparedocument.

Between the calls to sp_xml_preparedocument and sp_xml_removedocument, you can use OPENXML to retrieve data from the document. Here's the syntax of OPENXML:

```
OPENXML(idoc, rowpattern, [flags])
   [WITH (SchemaDeclaration | TableName)]
```

The parameters of OPENXML are as follows:

- *Idoc* is a document handle returned by `sp_xml_preparedocument`.

- *Rowpattern* is an XPath expression that indicates the nodes that should be treated as rows in the resulting rowset.

- *Flags* is a value that specifies how to process the XML into columns. Table 20.5 shows the possible values for this parameter.

- *SchemaDeclaration* specifies the column mapping between the XML and the resulting rowset. I'll discuss this parameter in more detail later in this section.

- *TableName* is the name of an existing table that has the structure of the rowset that should be created.

TABLE 20.5: Values of the Flags Parameter for OPENXML

Value	Meaning
0 (default)	Attribute-centric mapping.
1	Attribute-centric mapping (same effect as a value of 0).
2	Element-centric mapping.
3	Attribute-centric mapping, followed by element-centric mapping for any remaining columns.
8	Add to any of the other values to discard data that won't fit in a column, rather than save it in a metaproperty.

If you omit the optional WITH clause, the results are returned in *edge table* format. An edge table provides a full description of all the nodes that are at the "edge" of the XML parse tree. Table 20.6 lists the columns that are returned in edge table format.

TABLE 20.6: Edge Table Format

Column	Meaning
id	Unique identifier of this node
parentid	Identifier of the parent of this node
nodetype	1 for an element, 2 for an attribute, 3 for text
localname	Name of the node
prefix	Namespace prefix for the node
namespaceuri	Namespace URI for the node
datatype	Datatype of the node
prev	Identifier of the previous sibling of the node
text	Node content in text form

Although the edge table completely describes the XML, it's not very useful as a rowset if you want to work with the data rather than examine its schema. In most cases, you'll want to use the WITH clause to supply a *schema definition*. A schema definition is a string of fields for the output rowset in this format:

```
ColName ColType [ColPattern | MetaProperty]
    [, ColName ColType [ColPattern | MetaProperty]...]
```

A schema definition uses these four parameters:

- *ColName* is the name to use for the output column in the rowset.

- *ColType* is the datatype of the column.

- *ColPattern* is an XPath expression that describes the data to map in relation to the row-pattern parameter of the OPENXML statement.

- *MetaProperty* is a name of an OPENXML metaproperty. Metaproperties allow you to use information such as the namespace of nodes in the output rowset.

NOTE   Refer to SQL Server Books Online for more information about OPENXML metaproperties.

OPENXML Examples

This chapter's sample project includes a form, frmOPENXML, that lets you experiment with the OPENXML statement. To use this form:

1. Type in or load an XML file to be processed.

2. Type in or load an OPENXML query to run on the XML. Use **@hDoc** to indicate the document handle parameter.

3. Click the Execute button to load the resulting rowset into the grid.

The code behind the Execute button, shown in Listing 20.7, handles the task of calling `sp_xml_preparedocument` and `sp_xml_removedocument` for you.

Listing 20.7:   **Executing an OPENXML Query via ADO**

```
Private Sub cmdExecute_Click()
    ' Execute the OPENXML query

    Dim cnn As ADODB.Connection
    Dim cmd As ADODB.Command
    Dim rst As ADODB.Recordset

    On Error GoTo HandleErr

    Set cnn = New ADODB.Connection
```

```
    cnn.CursorLocation = adUseClient
    cnn.Open "Provider=SQLOLEDB;Data Source=(local);" & _
     "Initial Catalog=master;Integrated Security=SSPI"

    ' Create the appropriate stored proc
    ' and query calls
    Set cmd = New ADODB.Command
    Set cmd.ActiveConnection = cnn
    cmd.CommandType = adCmdText
    cmd.CommandText = "DECLARE @hDoc int " & vbCrLf & _
     "EXEC sp_xml_preparedocument @hDoc OUTPUT, " & vbCrLf & _
     "N'" & txtXML.Text & "'" & vbCrLf & _
     txtQuery.Text & vbCrLf & _
     "EXEC sp_xml_removedocument @hDoc"

    Debug.Print cmd.CommandText

    ' Execute them all, putting the results in the grid
    Set rst = cmd.Execute()
    Set hfgResults.Recordset = rst

    ' Clean up
    rst.Close
    Set rst = Nothing
    Set cmd = Nothing
    cnn.Close
    Set cnn = Nothing

ExitHere:
    Exit Sub

HandleErr:
    MsgBox "Error " & Err.Number & ": " & Err.Description, _
     vbOKOnly, "cmdExecute"
    Resume ExitHere
    Resume

End Sub
```

You can use this form, together with the OrdersQuery.xml file and the saved query files (all of which are supplied on the companion CD), to run the examples from this section. The query files are named Query1.sql through Query6.sql.

The simplest OPENXML query retrieves the information from the XML file in edge table format:

```
SELECT * FROM OPENXML(@hDoc, '/ROOT')
```

Figure 20.8 shows the results of running this query.

FIGURE 20.8:
OrdersQuery.xml in
edge table format

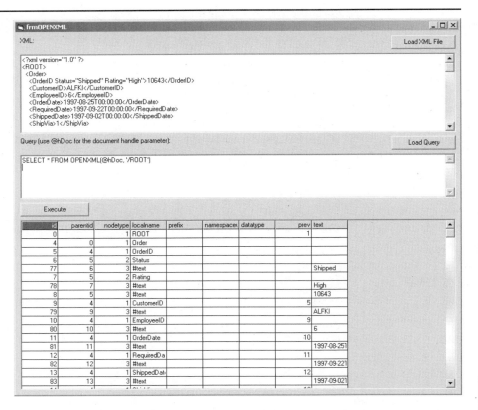

FIGURE 20.8:
OrdersQuery.xml in
edge table format

To retrieve a Recordset with OrderID and CustomerID information, you can use this
query:

```
SELECT * FROM OPENXML(@hDoc, '/ROOT/Order', 2)
    WITH (OrderID varchar(5), CustomerID varchar(5))
```

As you can see, there's no need to supply the ColPattern parameter in the WITH clause if
the column names in the rowset are the same as the tag names in the XML document. Also
note the use of 2 as a value for the flags parameter. If you omit this, you'll still get a Recordset with five rows, but all the values will be empty because OPENXML will be looking for
attributes with the names OrderID and CustomerID rather than elements.

To retrieve information from the attributes of the Orders, you can use a query such as this:

```
SELECT * FROM OPENXML(@hDoc, '/ROOT/Order', 3)
    WITH (OrderID varchar(5),
      Status varchar(10) 'OrderID/@Status',
      Rating varchar(10) 'OrderID/@Rating')
```

Here the flags value of 3 allows mixed evaluation of elements and attributes in building the rowset.

You can retrieve the same results with this query:

```
SELECT * FROM OPENXML(@hDoc, '/ROOT/Order/OrderID', 3)
  WITH (OrderID varchar(5) '.',
    Status varchar(10) './@Status',
    Rating varchar(10) './@Rating')
```

Here the OrderID has been pushed up into the XPath expression that specifies the nodes to retrieve. Note the use of the dot operator in the XPath expressions for columns to indicate the current node.

You can also use XPath filtering expressions within the definition of the rows to be retrieved. For example, this query retrieves information from three of the orders that meet the specified criteria on the value of the Freight element:

```
SELECT * FROM OPENXML(@hDoc,
  '/ROOT/Order[Freight>=20 and Freight<=50]', 3)
  WITH (OrderID varchar(5), CustomerID varchar(5), Freight money)
```

Because OPENXML returns a SQL rowset, you can also filter it using a WHERE clause after processing the rows. The following query will give the same results as the preceding one:

```
SELECT * FROM OPENXML(@hDoc, '/ROOT/Order', 3)
  WITH (OrderID varchar(5), CustomerID varchar(5), Freight money)
  WHERE Freight >= 20 AND Freight <=50
```

As this last statement demonstrates, you can treat OPENXML as the equivalent of a table within a T-SQL statement. You can use an OPENXML statement anywhere in T-SQL that a table name would be valid.

SQL Server Tips and Quirks

ADO is an ambitious undertaking. The idea that all data sources can be accessed using the same code, by changing only a connection string, is not always successful in practice. With SQL Server (as with any other OLE DB data source), you'll find various quirks and bugs that you need to be aware of when using ADO.

If possible, your first line of defense against problems should be to use the latest versions of both SQL Server and ADO. But in many organizations, that's not possible. Because SQL Server tends to be used for mission-critical data, system administrators are generally loathe to upgrade without a very good reason and extensive testing and planning. In situations where you can't upgrade, you'll need to know about the problems and (where they exist) the workarounds.

Tips for All Versions of SQL Server

SQL Server allows only one "firehose" (forward-only, read-only) cursor to be active on a connection at a time. This can lead to additional connections being opened without your knowledge. For example, consider this code snippet:

```
Dim cnn As New ADODB.Connection
Dim rst1 As New ADODB.Recordset
Dim rst2 As New ADODB.Recordset
cnn.Open "Provider=SQLOLEDB;Data Source=(local);" & _
    "Initial Catalog=Northwind;Integrated Security=SSPI"
rst1.Open "Customers", cnn
rst2.Open "Orders", cnn
```

SQL Server will create an additional Connection when you open the second Recordset. This Connection won't participate in connection pooling, which may result in poorer-than-expected performance.

You may receive error 80020009 when retrieving data from SQL Server tables containing text or ntext tables. If you do get this error, check the order of columns in your SELECT statement. The text or ntext columns should be last in the list, after all other columns.

The SQL Server OLE DB provider imposes some limits on your use of ADOX. In particular, it doesn't implement these ADOX features:

- The Catalog.Create method
- The Append and Delete methods of the Procedures and Keys collections
- The ability to modify properties of existing Table objects
- The Procedure.Command property
- The Views, Users, and Groups collections

NOTE   For more information on ADOX, see Chapter 9, "Using ADOX for Data Definition and Security Operations."

You may experience difficulty trying to retrieve the value of output parameters from stored procedures that return Recordsets. A typical symptom is that the output parameter has the Null value even though it has been executed and you have retrieved data from the Recordset. That's because SQL Server doesn't send the output parameters until the entire result of the stored procedure has been sent, which requires retrieving all the records. There are two possible workarounds for this. First, you can continue to use the default server-side cursor, but move to the end of the Recordset before you try to retrieve the value of the output parameters. Second, you can use a client-side Recordset, which SQL Server will fill completely as soon as you execute the stored procedure.

Tips for SQL Server 7

When using SQL Server 7, you may find that custom errors raised in a stored procedure using the RAISERROR statement are not propagated to the ADO Errors collection. The way to solve this problem is to issue the SET NOCOUNT ON statement before running a stored procedure that might return custom errors.

With SQL Server 7 SP2, you'll get a syntax error when trying to use column names that contain spaces in conjunction with server-side cursors. There are three possible ways to fix this bug:

- Remove the spaces from the column names.

- Use client-side cursors rather than server-side cursors.

- Apply SQL Server 7 SP4.

You may receive an error when calling the Update or AddNew method on a Recordset that uses a client-side cursor:

```
Run-time error '-2147217900 (80040e14)':
Line 1: Syntax error near 'table'
```

This error will occur only if your SQL Server has its quoted identifier option set to Off. There are two possible fixes:

- Use server-side cursors instead of client-side cursors.

- Execute the set quoted_identifier on T-SQL statement at the server before attempting to update the Recordset.

Performance Tips

No application is ever fast enough to satisfy all its users. When using ADO to retrieve data from SQL Server, there are many things to consider in a quest for maximum performance. Most of these boil down to particular examples of one general principle:

Send as little data across the network as possible.

Here's a list of things to investigate when trying to improve the performance of an application that uses ADO to work with SQL Server data. Most of these tips apply equally well to any client-server database:

- When opening a Recordset, include only the fields that your application works with. SELECT * is convenient but often wastes time returning data that you'll never use.

- Beware of returning unexpectedly large amounts of data. When in doubt, consider adding the TOP keyword to SELECT queries so that you can specify the maximum number of records returned.

- When possible, use stored procedures to manipulate data rather than the Update, AddNew, or Delete methods of the Recordset object. By doing updates via a stored procedure, you keep the entire operation on the server without needless network traffic.

- If you don't need to edit data, use a read-only Recordset. If you don't need to move backward in the data, use a forward-only Recordset. Forward-only, read-only Recordsets are the fastest type. Beware, though, of opening a second forward-only, read-only Recordset before you've reached the end of one that is already open; this will cause ADO to open a second Connection to the database.

- If you're working with a parameterized query, create the parameters yourself rather than rely on the Parameters.Refresh method to fetch them from the server.

- Transactions will be faster if you execute them on the server in a stored procedure rather than depend on the transaction methods of the ADO Connection object.

- If you'll need to filter or sort the same data in multiple ways, start by retrieving the data into a client-side Recordset. Then you can use the ADO Sort and Filter methods to manipulate the data without any further trips to the server.

- If there's little chance of multiple users editing the same data simultaneously, use batch optimistic locking and the UpdateBatch method to group multiple edits into a single trip to the server.

- For editable Recordsets, consider increasing the CacheSize property of the Recordset from the default value of 1 to a value such as 100. This will make ADO fetch more records from the server in a single trip, which is more efficient than making many small fetches.

- To return a single row of data, use a stored procedure with an output parameter, rather than open a Recordset.

Summary

In this chapter, you've learned about some of the interactions of ADO in general with SQL Server in particular. You saw the connection string and object properties that are specific to the SQL Server OLE DB driver. I also discussed some of the useful SQL Server techniques that SQL Server makes available to the ADO developer. Linked servers provide a way to use ADO to query heterogeneous data sources in a single query, and the OPENXML statement makes XML documents available as data sources to ADO code. Finally, I considered some of the problems you may face when using ADO with SQL Server.

In the next chapter, I'll examine another of the important OLE DB drivers: the OLE DB driver for Oracle data sources.

CHAPTER 21

ADO and Oracle

- Supported versions of Oracle

- Provider-specific connection string parameters

- Setting up the Oracle environment for ADO

- Limitations of ADO with Oracle data

- Oracle tips and quirks

- An Oracle example

With a market share running somewhere around 30% (depending on which survey you believe), Oracle Corporation remains a major player in the database market. In this chapter, I'll dig into some of the details and quirks involved in working with Oracle via ADO. Unfortunately, as you'll see later in the chapter, the relationship between Microsoft drivers and Oracle databases has been anything but smooth. If you're working with Oracle via ADO, you need to be prepared to do extensive testing before rolling a solution out to production.

> **NOTE**
> In this book, I've chosen to work exclusively with the Microsoft OLE DB Provider for Oracle. Oracle also ships its own Oracle Provider for OLE DB, which is installed when you install the Oracle client components on a computer. Another option is the DataDirect family of products (www.datadirect-technologies.com/ado/connectado/apxconnectado.asp). If you run into serious bugs with the Microsoft provider, you may want to evaluate the Oracle or DataDirect provider as an alternative.

Supported Versions of Oracle

The Microsoft OLE DB Provider for Oracle supports versions 7.3 and later of the Oracle database. You must also install the Oracle client and network software on computers that will use this driver to retrieve Oracle data. If you're retrieving data from an Oracle7 database, you'll need version 7.3.3.4.0 or later of the Oracle client software. If you're retrieving data from an Oracle8 database, you'll need version 8.0.4.1.1c or later of the client software.

> **NOTE**
> While writing this book, I used Oracle client software from the 8.1.6 and 8.1.7 releases of Oracle8i. Both versions worked fine in the sample code.

The Microsoft OLE DB Provider for Oracle does have some limitations when used with Oracle8 servers. In particular, the datatypes introduced in Oracle8, as well as the object extensions to Oracle, are not supported. Table 21.1 shows the limits to datatype support when using the Microsoft OLE DB Provider for Oracle to retrieve data from Oracle databases.

TABLE 21.1: Datatype Support in the Microsoft OLE DB Provider for Oracle

Datatype	Oracle 7.3	Oracle8
BFILE	Not included	Not supported
BLOB	Not included	Not supported
CHAR	Supported	Supported
CLOB	Not included	Not supported

continued on next page

TABLE 21.1 CONTINUED: Datatype Support in the Microsoft OLE DB Provider for Oracle

Datatype	Oracle 7.3	Oracle8
DATE	Supported	Supported
FLOAT	Supported	Supported
INTEGER	Supported	Supported
LONG	Supported	Supported
LONG RAW	Supported	Supported
NCHAR	Not included	Not supported
NCLOB	Not included	Not supported
NUMBER	Supported	Supported
NVARCHAR2	Not included	Not supported
RAW	Supported	Supported
VARCHAR2	Supported	Supported
MLSLABEL	Not supported	Not supported

TIP   The Oracle Provider for OLE DB does support the new datatypes introduced in Oracle8.

If you're using Oracle8i, you should install MDAC version 2.5 or later on your client computers. Earlier versions of the Microsoft OLE DB Provider for Oracle and other MDAC components aren't supported by Microsoft for use with Oracle8i. Additionally, if you're trying to use the MDAC 2.5 version of the OLE DB provider to connect to an Oracle8i database, you may receive this error:

```
"SQLSTATE: NA000
Native error code: 0
Driver Message: [Microsoft][ODBC Driver for Oracle][Oracle]
Do you need any suggestions to avoid the error?"
```

This happens because the MDAC 2.5 installation doesn't make the proper Registry entries to use the Oracle8i networking components. Microsoft has a patch file available at http:// download.microsoft.com/download/odbcdriver/mdac250/250/win98me/en-us/OraReg.exe that contains Registry files with the proper entries to fix this problem. Alternatively, you can upgrade to MDAC 2.6.

Provider-Specific Connection String Parameters

Like most OLE DB providers, the Microsoft OLE DB Provider for Oracle supports both standard and provider-specific keywords. The standard keywords are Provider, Data Source,

User ID, and Password. For example, you might connect to a server named Sample with this connection string:

```
Provider=MSDAORA.1;Password=TIGER;User ID=SCOTT;
➥ Data Source=Sample
```

The Data Source keyword accepts an Oracle net service name (for Oracle8i) or System Identifier (SID, for earlier versions) as the name of the data source. These names encompass connection information including server, database, and communications protocol and port in a single name. That's why you don't need to specify a database name as part of an Oracle connection string. You can define system names and SIDs with Oracle utilities such as Net8 Configuration Assistant or Net8 Assistant.

The Microsoft OLE DB Provider for Oracle also accepts five provider-specific property settings. These settings are described in Table 21.2. All of these keywords are optional in an Oracle connection string.

TABLE 21.2: Provider-Specific Property Settings

Property	Meaning
Extended Properties	Additional settings to be passed directly to the server without interpretation by OLE DB.
Locale Identifier	A Windows LCID that specifies the user-interface language. This affects national language settings such as date and time formatting, string comparisons, and alphabetical order for special characters.
Prompt	Set to Yes to prompt the user for any missing information.
Window Handle	Window handle to use as the parent to any prompt for additional information.

Setting Up the Oracle Environment for ADO

If you haven't worked with Oracle, you may experience some trouble setting up ADO to communicate with an Oracle server. Here's how to install the necessary software and to check your connection to an Oracle database:

These instructions were checked using version 8.1.7 of the Oracle client tools. You may find substantial differences in client tools setup if you're using an earlier version.

1. Obtain connection information for your Oracle database from your Oracle administrator. You'll need to know the Oracle version, server name, communications protocol and port, and service name or SID for the database that you'll be using.

2. Install the current release of the Microsoft Data Access Components (MDAC) on the client computer.

3. Insert the Oracle8i CD into the client computer. Choose Install/Deinstall Products from the Autorun screen to launch the Oracle Universal Installer.

4. Click Next on the Welcome screen to proceed.

5. The next screen of the Oracle Universal Installer, shown in Figure 21.1, asks for source and destination file locations. Generally, you can leave these locations set to their defaults. For the destination, you must specify an Oracle Home name. This is a 1- to 16-character alphanumeric string that identifies this Oracle installation on this computer. Click Next to continue.

FIGURE 21.1:

Choosing the source and destination for an Oracle installation

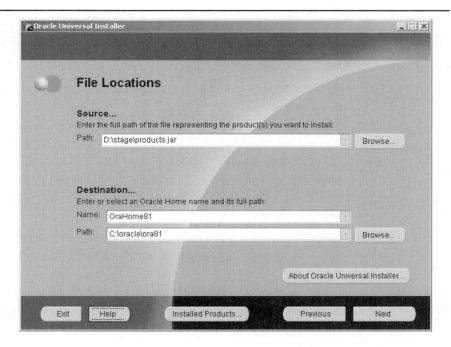

6. Select the Oracle8i Client as the product to install and then click Next.

7. Select the type of installation to perform. If you need to connect only to Oracle databases and don't need to perform any application development, select the Application User installation type. Click Next. The Installer will calculate the size of the installation and present a summary screen.

8. Click Next to perform the installation.

9. When the Oracle client components are installed, the Installer will automatically launch the Net8 Configuration Assistant. Click Next to proceed with the Net8 Configuration Assistant.

10. On the Directory Service Access screen of the Net8 Configuration Assistant, select No and then click Next to skip directory service configuration. You won't need a directory service for the initial test, and you can always add it later.

11. Select Local as your naming method (it should be preselected for you) and then click Next. This will store the connection information for the Oracle server on your local computer. This is a good choice unless the location of the database you're using changes frequently.

12. Select the version of Oracle that your database runs on and then click Next.

13. For an Oracle8i database, enter the service name; for an earlier version, enter the SID. Click Next.

14. Select the network protocol and then click Next (the default for Oracle is TCP).

15. Enter the host (server) name and port and then click Next. Use the standard TCP port 1521 unless instructed otherwise by your Oracle administrator.

16. Select Yes, Perform a Test and then click Next.

TIP   If you're connecting to Oracle's standard sample database, the Net8 Configuration Assistant will automatically fill in the username *Scott* and the password *Tiger,* which are the defaults. Otherwise, you may have to click Change Login and enter a different username and password if the connectivity test fails.

---

17. After the test succeeds, click Next. Enter a net service name to refer to this Oracle database. This is the name that you can use with the OLE DB provider to locate the database in the future. Click Next.

18. Unless you have another server to connect to, click No. If you do have another server, click Yes and repeat the steps above. Click Next three times and then Finish to end the Net8 Configuration Assistant.

19. Click Exit and then Yes to terminate the Oracle Universal Installer.

20. Now you're ready to check that you can connect to the specified server using OLE DB. Right-click any folder in Windows Explorer and select New ➤ Text Document. Name the new document TestOracle.udl.

21. Double-click TestOracle.udl to open the Data Link Properties dialog box.

22. On the Provider tab of the dialog box, choose Microsoft OLE DB Provider for Oracle.

23. On the Connection tab of the Data Link Properties dialog box, enter the net service name that you specified in step 17 as the server name. Enter an appropriate username and password. Click the Test Connection button to verify that you can connect to the Oracle database.

24. Click OK to close the Data Link Properties dialog box.

You can go one step further by testing connectivity from ADO with frmTest in the ADOChapter21 sample project. This form, shown in Figure 21.2, lets you fill in the essential connectivity information. Listing 21.1 provides the code that this form uses to create and open a Connection object.

Listing 21.1: **Connecting to an Oracle Database**

```
Private Sub cmdCheckConnection_Click()

    Dim cnn As ADODB.Connection

    On Error GoTo HandleErr

    Set cnn = New ADODB.Connection
    cnn.ConnectionString = "Provider=MSDAORA;" & _
      "Data Source=" & txtNetServiceName.Text & _
      ";User ID=" & txtUserName.Text & _
      ";Password=" & txtPassword.Text

    cnn.Open

    MsgBox "Test connection to " & _
      txtNetServiceName.Text & " succeeded!"

    ' Clean up
    cnn.Close
    Set cnn = Nothing

ExitHere:
    Exit Sub

HandleErr:
    MsgBox "Error " & Err.Number & ": " & Err.Description, _
      vbOKOnly, "cmdCheckConnection"
    Resume ExitHere
    Resume

End Sub
```

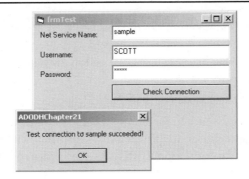

Limitations of ADO with Oracle Data

The Microsoft OLE DB Provider for Oracle doesn't offer native support for two features that are crucial to many applications: scrolling and updating. Fortunately, you can use the Client Cursor Engine to transform a Recordset returned by this provider into a scrollable, updatable Recordset. To use the Client Cursor Engine, you must specify adUseClient as the location of your Recordset. You should use only a server-side Recordset with this provider if a forward-only, read-only Recordset is sufficient for your application.

If you attempt to update a server-side Oracle Recordset, you'll get the error "Object or provider is not capable of performing requested operation." This is a good indication that you neglected to specify the adUseClient flag.

There are also a number of limitations you may run into when dealing with Oracle data:

- If you're using the Oracle7 client software, you can only work with VARCHAR columns containing 2,000 bytes or less, even though Oracle8 allows 4,000-byte VARCHAR columns. You can work around this limitation by upgrading to the Oracle8 client.

- The Oracle server doesn't allow access to all system tables, so you may experience unexpected results when trying to build a Recordset on a system table.

- The Oracle NUMBER datatype stores values with an exponent from -130 to $+125$. The OLE DB DBTYPE_VARNUMERIC datatype has an exponent range of -128 to $+127$. The result is that extremely small values stored in an Oracle NUMBER datatype cannot be retrieved via OLE DB.

- Bookmarks aren't supported by the provider. You can work around this limitation by using the Client Cursor Engine.

- Outer joins may not work properly on Oracle7 servers. The only workaround is to upgrade to Oracle8.

- Oracle converts empty strings to nulls when you execute an update. This leads to the error "The specified row could not be located for updating; some values may have been changed since it was last read" when you execute the Recordset.Update method. That's because the Recordset is looking for an updated row with an empty string that no longer exists. Requery the Recordset in this case to retrieve the most current data.

NOTE Because ADO.NET uses the Microsoft OLE DB Provider for Oracle to connect to Oracle data sources, these limitations are inherited by ADO.NET applications that use Oracle for their data store.

Oracle Tips and Quirks

There are quite a number of issues that you need to watch out for when using the Microsoft OLE DB Provider for Oracle. In this section, I'll review these issues, grouped into three categories: connectivity, SQL, and miscellaneous.

Connectivity Issues

You may experience serious problems when using Oracle from ASP pages on a Microsoft Internet Information Server (IIS) via ADO. In particular, you may encounter any of these symptoms:

- The WWW service may shut down, making the web server unavailable.
- The ASP service may shut down, making all ASP pages on the web server unavailable.
- ASP pages may return the error "ASP 0115: A trappable error has occurred."

The especially insidious thing about this bug is that it won't happen unless there are multiple connections to the server at the same time, so it's more likely to occur in production than in testing. The problems occur because some older versions of the Oracle networking components aren't compatible with a multithreaded environment such as IIS. Fortunately, the fix is simple: Upgrade the Oracle client components on the IIS server to the recommended versions (7.3.3.4.0 or later for Oracle7; 8.0.4.1.1c or later for Oracle8i).

TIP You can quickly check the version of the Oracle client components by running the Oracle SQL*Plus application, which prints out a version string at startup.

The Oracle server, like Microsoft SQL Server, is available in a variety of editions. You shouldn't have any trouble connecting to the Enterprise or Standard edition of Oracle using ADO, but Personal Oracle is another matter. Attempting to log on to Personal Oracle with the Microsoft OLE DB Provider for Oracle will return an error message. That's because Personal Oracle is a file-based database, rather than a stripped-down version of the full Oracle server database. The Microsoft OLE DB Provider for Oracle doesn't support the interfaces that Personal Oracle supplies. The fix is to use the ODBC driver that Personal Oracle installs, via the OLE DB Provider for ODBC data sources.

In general, connectivity to Oracle databases from ASP pages via ADO seems to be one of the more troublesome areas of Oracle–ADO interoperability. This may simply be due to the number of layers of software involved in making this connection. Microsoft has published a Knowledge Base article (Q255084) that offers a step-by-step troubleshooting guide for ASP-to-Oracle connectivity issues. (You can read this article online at http://support.microsoft .com/support/kb/articles/Q255/0/84.ASP.) Here's a summary of the steps that you can take when you're having ASP-to-Oracle problems:

1. Check the obvious: Make sure that you can connect to the target Oracle database from the computer where IIS is running. One way to test this is to run Oracle SQL*Plus. When you start it up, SQL*Plus will ask for a username, password, and host string; the Host String box is where you should enter the service name or SID for your Oracle database. Of course, you should use the same username and password that your ASP pages are using to connect with Oracle. If SQL*Plus connects successfully, it will print a startup message similar to this:

   ```
   SQL*Plus: Release 8.1.7.0.0 - Production on Sat Aug 25 06:49:30 2001
   (c) Copyright 2000 Oracle Corporation.  All rights reserved.

   Connected to:
   Oracle8i Release 8.1.7.0.0 - Production
   JServer Release 8.1.7.0.0 - Production

   SQL>
   ```

2. If you can't connect to the server from SQL*Plus, check the Oracle client setup. You may want to reinstall the client software, following the steps presented in the section "Setting Up the Oracle Environment for ADO" earlier in this chapter.

3. Make sure the IIS computer was rebooted at least once after the Oracle client software was installed.

4. Check the installed version of the Oracle client components.

5. Make sure that the PATH variable doesn't include remote shares or drives that contain versions of the Oracle components. Also check that the PATH variable *does* include the Oracle executables folder; this will be something like c:\oracle\ora81\bin. You can check or modify the PATH variable by launching the System applet from Windows Control Panel, choosing the Advanced tab, and clicking Environment Variables. You'll need to reboot the computer if you make any changes to the PATH variable.

6. Disable SQL*Net authentication by editing the `SQLNET.ora` file from the `Oracle home\network\ADMIN` folder. Add these two lines to the file and then restart IIS:

```
SQLNET.AUTHENTICATION_SERVICES = (none)
SQLNET.AUTHENTICATION = (none)
```

7. If you're still having problems, try using alternative drivers. Although the Microsoft OLE DB Provider for Oracle should work from ASP pages, if you've gotten this far without resolution, you should try the Oracle Provider, and then the ODBC for Oracle driver, to see whether they work in your particular situation.

SQL Issues

Every OLE DB provider needs some way to identify the rows in a Recordset, so that updates to those rows are sent to the proper row when they are transmitted to the server. Oracle SQL implements a *pseudocolumn* (a column in a result set that isn't actually stored in the underlying table) named ROWID. The ROWID column provides a physical address for each row in the result set. That is, by retrieving the ROWID, you can know the precise location of that row on the server.

The Microsoft OLE DB Provider for Oracle uses the ROWID column as a way to identify records uniquely. Whenever you open a Recordset, the provider adds ROWID to the list of retrieved columns and hides the resulting column. When you update a row, the provider uses a WHERE clause similar to this one to make sure the proper row is updated:

```
WHERE ROWID = value
```

This strategy has several consequences that can be undesirable in practice. For starters, because you can have only one ROWID column in a result set, you can't actually display the ROWID in an ADO-based application; the hidden copy of the column takes precedence. Figure 21.3 shows the results of running identical queries in SQL*Plus and a Visual Basic application that uses ADO; the Visual Basic application doesn't display the ROWID values.

> **TIP** The Visual Basic form shown in Figure 21.3 is available in this chapter's sample project. It provides an easy way to test SQL statements in an Oracle database via ADO.

The other consequences of using a ROWID as a unique row identifier are more serious. First, in a multiuser application, this strategy can actually result in updating the wrong row in the database! This can happen as follows:

1. User 1 retrieves a client-side Recordset.

2. User 2 deletes a record from the source table for this Recordset. Suppose for simplicity that the ROWID of this record is 1.

3. User 1 makes a change to the record with ROWID 1 in the user's local Recordset.

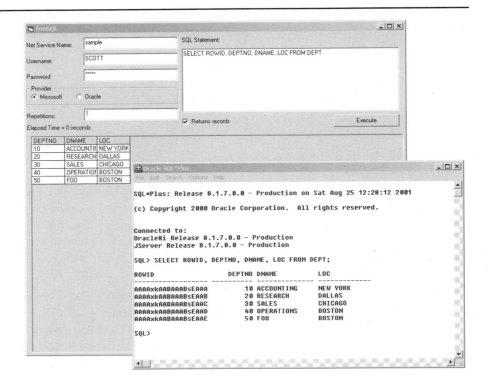

4. User 2 adds a new record to the source table. To conserve space, Oracle may reuse the location that held the old record. Because the ROWID is a physical address, this new record gets assigned the ROWID of 1.

5. User 1 calls the Recordset.Update method. OLE DB sends an update to the server that affects the row with a ROWID of 1—which is *not* the original row!

ROWIDs can also cause problems in multitiered applications. If you perform a data update that adds new records via a middle-tier component, the new ROWIDs will be returned to the middle-tier component, but not to the disconnected Recordset at the client end of the application. This results in an inability to update the new rows without requerying the Recordset. Attempting to update such a new record will return this error message:

```
Run-time error '-2147217864 (80040e38)': Row cannot be located for
updating. Some values may have been changed since it was last read.
```

Fortunately, Microsoft provides a means to turn off the use of ROWIDs for row identification in Recordsets. The alternative is for the OLE DB provider to retrieve the metadata about a table and determine which columns of the table form a primary key or unique index.

To do this, you set a custom property on the Recordset, as demonstrated by the code shown in Listing 21.2 (from frmROWID in this chapter's sample project).

Listing 21.2: **Retrieving Oracle Metadata**

```
Private Sub cmdGetData_Click()

    Dim cnn As ADODB.Connection
    Dim rst As ADODB.Recordset

    On Error GoTo HandleErr

    Set cnn = New ADODB.Connection
    cnn.Open "Provider=MSDAORA;Data Source=sample;" & _
      "User ID=SCOTT;Password=TIGER"

    Set rst = New ADODB.Recordset

    Set rst.ActiveConnection = cnn
    rst.CursorLocation = adUseServer
    rst.Properties("Determine Key Columns For Rowset") = True
    rst.CursorLocation = adUseClient
    rst.Open "SELECT * FROM DEPT", , _
      adOpenStatic, adLockBatchOptimistic

    Set hfgResults.Recordset = rst

    ' Clean up
    rst.Close
    Set rst = Nothing
    cnn.Close
    Set cnn = Nothing

ExitHere:
    Exit Sub

HandleErr:
    MsgBox "Error " & Err.Number & ": " & Err.Description, _
      vbOKOnly, "cmdGetData"
    Resume ExitHere
    Resume

End Sub
```

The sequence of steps used to set this property is important:

1. Instantiate the Connection and Recordset objects and set the Recordset's ActiveConnection property.

2. Set the CursorLocation property of the Recordset to adUseServer.

3. Now you can set the Determine Key Columns For Recordset property to True. This tells OLE DB to use metadata to identify rows. If this property is set to False (the default), OLE DB uses ROWIDs to identify rows.

4. Set the CursorLocation property of the Recordset to adUseClient (this is necessary only if you want a scrolling or updatable Recordset).

5. Open the Recordset without specifying an ActiveConnection in the Open method.

Oracle provides an expression operator, DECODE, that can do inline data lookups:

```
DECODE(expr, search, result [search, result [,…n]], [default])
```

With a DECODE expression, Oracle compares the expr value to each search value in turn, and returns the matching result value when one of the search values matches the expr value. If no match is found among the search values, Oracle returns the default value or, if no default is specified, a Null value.

Using a DECODE expression in an ADO statement executed against an Oracle8 server will raise an error if the expression returns any Nulls. There are three ways to work around this problem:

- Specify adUseServer for the CursorLocation of the Recordset involved.

- Use a non-Null default value in the DECODE expression.

- Upgrade to Oracle8i.

As mentioned earlier in the chapter, the Microsoft OLE DB Provider for Oracle converts empty strings into Nulls when sending them to the Oracle database. This can cause problems, particularly when you've applied the technique above to use keys rather than ROWIDs to locate rows. For example, this sequence of events can occur:

1. You retrieve a Recordset and add a new record with an empty string as part of a multi-part key.

2. You edit the record to change the value in another field.

3. When you call the Recordset.Update method, the OLE DB provider attempts to locate a row with an empty string in the field, rather than a Null, and fails with the error "The specified row could not be located for updating; some values may have been changed since it was last read."

To work around this issue, you should convert empty strings to Nulls before inserting them into an Oracle Recordset. Alternatively, you can call the Recordset.Resync method after making any changes to the Recordset, to ensure that the client-side copy matches the values actually saved on the server.

Oracle SQL allows you to select rows and simultaneously lock them by adding the FOR UPDATE clause to a SELECT statement:

```
SELECT * FROM EMP FOR UPDATE
```

If you execute this statement from ADO on an Oracle8 server, you'll get a "Fetch out of sequence" error. To work around this error, you can either call the Connection.BeginTrans method before issuing the SQL statement or upgrade to Oracle8i.

If you're using ADO 2.5, UNION queries drawn from Oracle data sources may mysteriously lose columns when presented on the client. That is, not every column specified in the SQL statement will actually be returned. The easiest fix in this case is to upgrade to ADO 2.6.

Oracle8i stored procedures that return 50 or more output parameters won't work with the Microsoft OLE DB Provider for Oracle. You'll get an "unspecified error" when you attempt to run such a stored procedure. Most applications should be able to avoid this problem by rewriting the stored procedures to return fewer output parameters. Another alternative is to use ODBC instead of OLE DB to connect to the Oracle database.

Miscellaneous Issues

The Parameters.Refresh method fails for parameterized SELECT queries in all versions of Oracle. As an example, consider the code in Listing 21.3.

Listing 21.3:   **Attempting to Refresh Query Parameters**

```
Private Sub cmdParametersRefresh_Click()

    Dim cnn As ADODB.Connection
    Dim cmd As ADODB.Command

    Set cnn = New ADODB.Connection
    cnn.Open "Provider=MSDAORA;Data Source=sample;" & _
      "User ID=SCOTT;Password=TIGER;"

    Set cmd = New ADODB.Command
    Set cmd.ActiveConnection = cnn
    cmd.CommandText = "SELECT * FROM EMP WHERE EMPNO = ?"
    cmd.CommandType = adCmdText
    cmd.Parameters.Refresh

    Debug.Print cmd.Parameters.Count

    ' Clean up
    cnn.Close
    Set cnn = Nothing
    Set cmd = Nothing

End Sub
```

This code will fail on the boldfaced line, where it attempts to refresh the Parameters collection of the Command object. You'll get the error "The provider cannot derive parameter info, and SetParameterInfo has not been called." To work around this error, you'll need to use the Command.CreateParameter method to create Parameter objects, rather than attempt to retrieve parameter information from the server. If you absolutely must call the Parameters.Refresh method (for example, if you're writing a tool to execute arbitrary stored procedures), you'll need to make a connection to the server using ODBC instead of OLE DB.

The Microsoft OLE DB Provider for Oracle doesn't support setting the Connection.ConnectionTimeout and Command.CommandTimeout properties. For the ConnectionTimeout property, you can work around this limitation by using the adAsyncConnect flag when calling the Connection.Open method, and calling the Connection.Cancel method if the connection isn't made within a specific period. For Commands, no workaround is available.

An Oracle Example

Figure 21.4 shows the frmSQL form from this chapter's sample project. This form is designed to let you execute arbitrary SQL statements against an Oracle database via ADO, and it provides relative execution times for the Microsoft and Oracle providers.

FIGURE 21.4:

Testing a SQL statement in an Oracle database

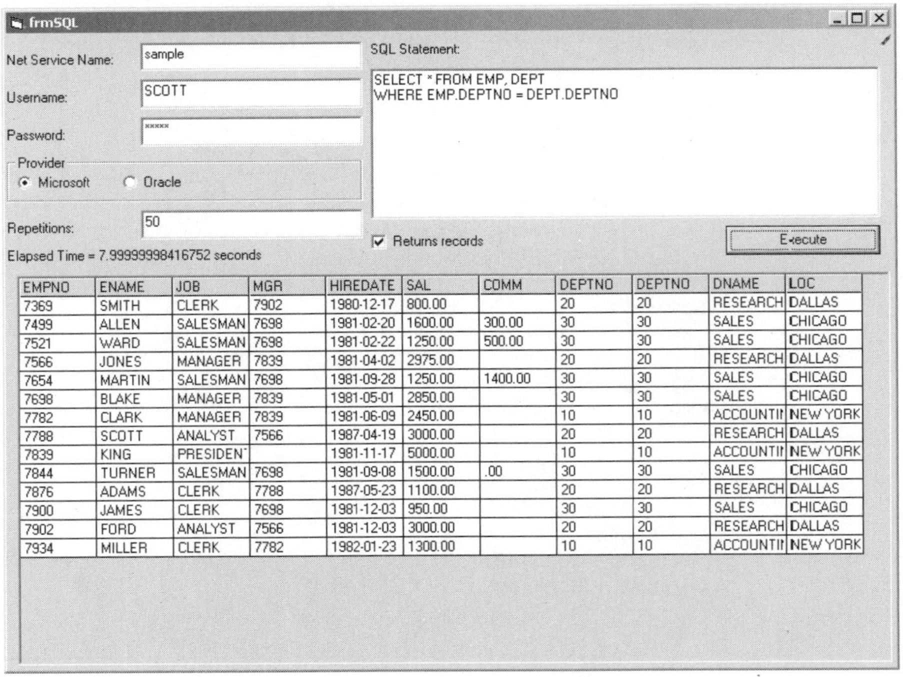
frmSQL
Net Service Name:
sample
Username:
SCOTT
Password:
Provider
Microsoft
Oracle
Repetitions:
50
Elapsed Time = 7.99999998416752 seconds
SQL Statement:
SELECT * FROM EMP, DEPT
WHERE EMP.DEPTNO = DEPT.DEPTNO
Returns records
Execute
EMPNO ENAME JOB MGR HIREDATE SAL COMM DEPTNO DEPTNO DNAME LOC
7369 SMITH CLERK 7902 1980-12-17 800.00 20 20 RESEARCH DALLAS
7499 ALLEN SALESMAN 7698 1981-02-20 1600.00 300.00 30 30 SALES CHICAGO
7521 WARD SALESMAN 7698 1981-02-22 1250.00 500.00 30 30 SALES CHICAGO
7566 JONES MANAGER 7839 1981-04-02 2975.00 20 20 RESEARCH DALLAS
7654 MARTIN SALESMAN 7698 1981-09-28 1250.00 1400.00 30 30 SALES CHICAGO
7698 BLAKE MANAGER 7839 1981-05-01 2850.00 30 30 SALES CHICAGO
7782 CLARK MANAGER 7839 1981-06-09 2450.00 10 10 ACCOUNTII NEW YORK
7788 SCOTT ANALYST 7566 1987-04-19 3000.00 20 20 RESEARCH DALLAS
7839 KING PRESIDEN 1981-11-17 5000.00 10 10 ACCOUNTII NEW YORK
7844 TURNER SALESMAN 7698 1981-09-08 1500.00 .00 30 30 SALES CHICAGO
7876 ADAMS CLERK 7788 1987-05-23 1100.00 20 20 RESEARCH DALLAS
7900 JAMES CLERK 7698 1981-12-03 950.00 30 30 SALES CHICAGO
7902 FORD ANALYST 7566 1981-12-03 3000.00 20 20 RESEARCH DALLAS
7934 MILLER CLERK 7782 1982-01-23 1300.00 10 10 ACCOUNTII NEW YORK

To use this form, follow these steps:

1. Enter the net service name or SID for your Oracle database, your Oracle username, and your Oracle password.

2. Select whether you would like to use the Microsoft or Oracle provider.

3. Enter the number of times you would like to repeat the test. By default, this is 1. If you're trying to time the performance of your system, you should enter a higher number here so that fluctuations in the system load are averaged out.

4. Enter a SQL statement to be executed.

5. If the SQL statement returns records, check the Returns Records check box.

6. Click the Execute button to execute the SQL statement the specified number of times. If the statement returns records, they will be shown on the grid control.

The code that this form uses is straightforward. It's shown in Listing 21.4.

Listing 21.4:   **Executing SQL Statements in an Oracle Database**

```
Private Sub cmdExecute_Click()

    Dim cnn As ADODB.Connection
    Dim cmd As ADODB.Command
    Dim rst As ADODB.Recordset
    Dim strProvider As String
    Dim lngI As Long
    Dim dtnow As Date

    On Error GoTo HandleErr

    If optMicrosoft Then
        strProvider = "MSDAORA"
    Else
        strProvider = "OraOLEDB.Oracle"
    End If

    dtnow = Now
    For lngI = 1 To CLng(txtRepetitions.Text)
        Set cnn = New ADODB.Connection

        cnn.ConnectionString = "Provider=" & strProvider & ";" & _
          "Data Source=" & txtNetServiceName.Text & _
          ";User ID=" & txtUserName.Text & _
          ";Password=" & txtPassword.Text
        cnn.CursorLocation = adUseClient

        cnn.Open
```

```
        Set cmd = New ADODB.Command
        Set cmd.ActiveConnection = cnn
        cmd.CommandType = adCmdText
        cmd.CommandText = txtSQL.Text

        Screen.MousePointer = vbHourglass
        If chkReturnsRecords.Value = vbChecked Then
            Set rst = cmd.Execute()
            Set hfgResults.Recordset = rst
        Else
            cmd.Execute
        End If

        If Not rst Is Nothing Then
            rst.Close
            Set rst = Nothing
        End If
        Set cmd = Nothing
        cnn.Close
        Set cnn = Nothing
    Next lngI
    lblElapsedTime.Caption = "Elapsed Time = " & _
     (Now - dtnow) * 86400 & " seconds"

    ' Clean up
    rst.Close
    Set rst = Nothing
    cnn.Close
    Set cnn = Nothing
    Set cmd = Nothing

ExitHere:
    Screen.MousePointer = vbDefault
    Exit Sub

HandleErr:
    MsgBox "Error " & Err.Number & ": " & Err.Description, _
     vbOKOnly, "cmdExecute"
    Resume ExitHere
    Resume

End Sub
```

You may wish to modify this code to more accurately represent your own environment before testing the performance of the Microsoft and Oracle providers. Here are some modifications you might want to consider:

- If you plan to use persistent connections to a data source, you should move the creation and destruction of the Connection object outside the timing loop.

- If you don't need updatable, scrollable cursors, you should change the CursorLocation property of the Connection to adUseServer.

- If you intend to use keys instead of ROWIDs to identify records, you should incorporate the code from frmROWID into the Recordset creation section of the loop.

For simple examples, I generally find the Microsoft provider to be about 10% faster than the Oracle provider. That's close enough that you should make the decision between the two based on other factors, including which provider better supports your application's requirements and which vendor provides you with better technical support.

Summary

In this chapter, I examined some of the details of setting up the Microsoft OLE DB Provider for Oracle and connecting to Oracle databases. I also looked at some of the problems that you may encounter with this combination of software components. As you've seen, the relationship between Microsoft and Oracle software is not always smooth.

In the next chapter, I'll look at a OLE DB provider that doesn't bring multiple supplier issues into the mix: the OLE DB Provider for Microsoft Jet databases.

CHAPTER 22

ADO and Jet

- Supported versions

- Provider-specific connection string parameters

- Dynamic properties of ADO objects

- Jet tips and quirks

- Using linked tables for distributed queries

- Custom schema rowsets

The third OLE DB provider that I'm going to examine in depth is the Microsoft OLE DB Provider for Microsoft Jet. As you can probably guess, this provider is well supported by Microsoft, and it offers access to almost all the capabilities of the Jet engine. In this chapter, I'll cover the details of this provider and touch on some other Jet-specific topics such as distributed queries and retrieving Jet engine performance statistics.

> **NOTE** You'll probably find two Jet OLE DB providers installed on your computer. In this chapter, you'll be working specifically with the Jet 4.0 version of the provider, which uses the Jet 4.0 data-base engine for data access. The older Jet 3.51 provider is useful mainly in cases where you need to support an older application that was coded around the quirks of this version of the provider.

Supported Versions

Generally, the version number for the Microsoft OLE DB Provider for Microsoft Jet doesn't match the version number for the Microsoft Data Access Components (MDAC). There are three versions of MDAC that you may be concerned with. Both MDAC 2.1 and MDAC 2.5 include the Microsoft.Jet.OLEDB.4.0 provider components. Beginning with MDAC 2.6, though, things have changed. MDAC 2.6 no longer includes the Jet provider. Instead, after installing MDAC 2.6, you should download and install the separate Jet 4.0 Service Pack setup.

> **NOTE** You can usually find the most recent MDAC and Jet releases, as well as several previous versions, at the Microsoft Universal Data Access website, www.microsoft.com/data. As of this writing, the latest version of the Jet 4.0 Service Pack that's available at this web-site is Service Pack 3. A more recent edition, Jet 4.0 Service Pack 5, is available via http://support.microsoft.com/support/kb/articles/q239/1/14.asp.

The Jet 4.0 provider includes complete support for the Jet Engine Installable ISAM (IISAM) technology. This means that you can use this provider to read or manipulate data in a wide variety of file formats, including these:

- Microsoft Access
- Paradox
- dBASE
- Lotus Notes
- Excel
- Microsoft Exchange
- Text
- HTML

Provider-Specific Connection String Parameters

The basic Jet OLE DB provider connection string uses the same parameters that most other providers use:

```
Provider=Microsoft.Jet.OLEDB.4.0;Data Source=Database;
➥ User ID=Username;Password=Password;
```

For the Jet provider, a data source is a Microsoft Jet (.mdb) file. The User ID parameter defaults to the special value *Admin*, and the Password parameter defaults to Null; so for unsecured Jet databases, you can use a simpler version:

```
Provider=Microsoft.Jet.OLEDB.4.0;Data Source=Database;
```

Unlike most other providers, though, the Jet provider supports a rich variety of provider-specific connection string parameters. These parameters, which are listed in Table 22.1, allow fine-tuning of many of the aspects of the Jet engine and its behavior. They can be set in the connection string, or (after you've connected to a database using the Jet provider) set or read from the Connection object's Properties collection.

TABLE 22.1: Jet Connection String Parameters

Parameter	Meaning
Jet OLEDB:Compact Reclaimed Space Amount	An estimate of the number of bytes that can be reclaimed by compacting the database. Read-only, and valid only after connecting to a database. The value is set at connection time and may not be accurate.
Jet OLEDB:Connection Control	Set to 1 to prevent other users from logging on to the database. Set to 2 (the default) to allow other users to continue to log on.
Jet OLEDB:Create System Database	This Boolean property indicates whether the ADOX Catalog.Create method should also create a system database.
Jet OLEDB:Database Locking Mode	Set to 0 for page-level locking, or 1 for row-level locking. Can be set only by the first user to open the database; read-only for all other users.
Jet OLEDB:Database Password	The database password (as distinct from the password of the user opening the database).
Jet OLEDB:Don't Copy Locale on Compact	Set to True to prevent Jet from copying the existing locale information when compacting a database.
Jet OLEDB:Encrypt Database	Set to True to encrypt the database when it's compacted. Set to False to leave the database unencrypted when compacted. If not set, the compacted database will be encrypted only if the original database is encrypted.

continued on next page

TABLE 22.1 CONTINUED: Jet Connection String Parameters

Parameter	Meaning
Jet OLEDB:Engine Type	Set by the Jet Engine to indicate the file format of the database that it has open. See Table 22.2 for the possible values for this property.
Jet OLEDB:Exclusive Async Delay	Maximum number of milliseconds that the engine will delay asynchronous writes when the database is open exclusively.
Jet OLEDB:Flush Transaction Timeout	Number of milliseconds to wait before flushing the write buffer to the disk.
Jet OLEDB:Global Bulk Transactions	Set to 1 to allow bulk queries to succeed partially, or 2 to require all-or-nothing execution.
Jet OLEDB:Global Partial Bulk Ops	Set to 1 to allow inconsistent changes, or 2 to cause bulk transactions to fail if a single error occurs.
Jet OLEDB:Implicit Commit Sync	Set to True to commit implicit transactions synchronously, or False to allow them to write asynchronously.
Jet OLEDB:Lock Delay	Number of milliseconds to wait after a failed locking attempt before trying again.
Jet OLEDB:Lock Retry	Number of times to attempt to set a lock before failing completely.
Jet OLEDB:Max Buffer Size	Number of kilobytes of memory Jet can use before flushing updates to disk.
Jet OLEDB:Max Locks Per File	Number of locks that Jet can place on a file. The default is 9,500.
Jet OLEDB:New Database Password	New database password to be set for this database.
Jet OLEDB:ODBC Command Time Out	Number of milliseconds to wait for an ODBC query to complete.
Jet OLEDB:Page Locks to Table Lock	When this many pages of the same table are locked, Jet will attempt to promote the page lock to a table lock.
Jet OLEDB:Page Timeout	Number of milliseconds before Jet considers a page in the local cache to be stale.
Jet OLEDB:Recycle Long-Valued Pages	Set to True to aggressively recycle pages containing BLOBs.
Jet OLEDB:Registry Path	Windows Registry key containing tuning values for the Jet engine.
Jet OLEDB:Reset ISAM Stats	Set to True to reset the internal performance statistics after they have been retrieved.
Jet OLEDB:Shared Async Delay	Maximum number of milliseconds that the engine will delay asynchronous writes when the database is open in shared mode.
Jet OLEDB:System Database	Path and filename of the workgroup information file to use.

continued on next page

TABLE 22.1 CONTINUED: Jet Connection String Parameters

Parameter	Meaning
Jet OLEDB:Transaction Commit Mode	Set to 0 to write changes in a transaction to the disk asynchronously, or 1 to force synchronous writes as soon as the data is updated.
Jet OLEDB:User Commit Sync	Set to 0 to write user-initiated changes to the disk asynchronously, or 1 to force synchronous writes as soon as the data is updated.

TABLE 22.2: Values for Jet OLEDB:Engine Type

Value	Database Format
0	Unknown
1	Jet 1.0
2	Jet 1.1
3	Jet 2.0
4	Jet 3.x
5	Jet 4.x
10	dBASE III
11	dBASE IV
12	dBASE 5
20	Excel 3.0
21	Excel 4.0
22	Excel 5.0
23	Excel 8.0
24	Excel 9.0
30	Exchange
40	Lotus .WK1
41	Lotus .WK3
42	Lotus .WK4
50	Paradox 3.x
51	Paradox 4.x
52	Paradox 5.x
53	Paradox 7.x
60	Text
70	HTML

In addition, the Connection object supports a property named Extended Properties. The value of this property is passed directly back to the OLE DB provider involved. In the case of the Jet 4.0 provider, this property is used to indicate the format of the file to be opened. Table 22.3 shows the possible values for the Extended Properties property.

TABLE 22.3: Extended Properties Settings

Database Type	Extended Properties
dBASE III	dBASE III
dBASE IV	dBASE IV
dBASE 5	dBASE 5.0
Excel 3	Excel 3.0
Excel 4	Excel 4.0
Excel 5	Excel 5.0
Excel 95	Excel 5.0
Excel 97	Excel 8.0
Excel 2000	Excel 8.0
Lotus .WK1	Lotus WK1
Lotus .WK3	Lotus WK3
Lotus .WK4	Lotus WK4
Paradox 3	Paradox 3.x
Paradox 4	Paradox 4.x
Paradox 5	Paradox 5.x
HTML	HTML Import
Exchange 4.0	Exchange 4.0
Exchange 5.0	Exchange 4.0
Outlook	Exchange 4.0

To open an Excel 2000 or 2002 database, for example, you might use code similar to this:

```
Sub OpenExcel()
    Dim cnn As ADODB.Connection

    Set cnn = New ADODB.Connection

    cnn.ConnectionString = "Provider=Microsoft.Jet.OLEDB.4.0;" & _
      "Data Source=c:\Temp\Test.xls"
    cnn.Properties("Extended Properties") = "Excel 8.0"
    cnn.Open

End Sub
```

Dynamic Properties of ADO Objects

The Microsoft OLE DB Provider for Microsoft Jet also adds dynamic properties to the principal ADO objects (Connection, Command, and Recordset). These properties are added to the objects when they are instantiated on a connection to a database via the Jet engine. In this section, I'll look at some of the most useful of these properties.

Connection Object Dynamic Properties

In addition to the provider-specific connection parameters, the Jet OLE DB provider adds nearly 60 dynamic properties to the Connection object when you call the Connection.Open method. Most of these properties describe the database that you're accessing and the limits that it imposes on your operations. Because the Jet provider can be used to connect to a data from variety of different applications (for example, Lotus, dBase, or Excel) via its Installable ISAM technology, you may find yourself wanting to query some of these properties to find out what you can do with the current data source. A few of these properties are listed in Table 22.4.

TABLE 22.4: Selected Dynamic Properties of the Connection Object

Property	Meaning
Heterogeneous Table Support	1 if you can join tables from multiple databases; 2 if you can join tables from multiple providers.
Maximum Index Size	Number of bytes in the largest possible index.
Maximum Row Size	Number of bytes in the largest possible row.
Multi-Table Update	True if you can update Recordsets derived from more than one table.
NULL Concatenation Behavior	1 if concatenating Null to another value always yields Null; 2 if Nulls are ignored when concatenating values.
Read-Only Data Source	True if you cannot modify the data in this database.

TIP For a complete list of Jet dynamic properties and their meanings, refer to Alyssa Henry's white paper "Migrating from DAO to ADO" at `http://msdn.microsoft.com/library/en-us/dndao/html/daotoadoupdate.asp`.

I've provided the frmConnectionProperties form in the ADOChapter22 sample project to allow you to explore the dynamic properties of ADO Connection objects used with the Microsoft OLE DB Provider for Microsoft Jet. To use this form, follow these steps:

1. Enter an OLE DB connection string.

2. Click Create Connection to instantiate a Connection object using this connection string. At this point, the provider-specific Connection properties are available, and the code will retrieve them to the form.

3. Click Connect to connect to the database. At this point, the dynamic Connection properties are available, and the code will retrieve them to the form.

Figure 22.1 shows this form in action. Listing 22.1 contains the code that's used to implement this form's functionality.

FIGURE 22.1:

Jet OLE DB provider dynamic properties

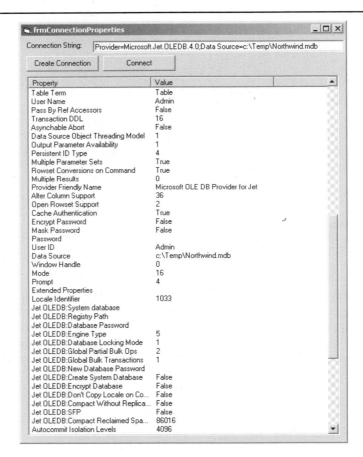

Listing 22.1: **frmConnectionProperties**

```
Option Explicit

Dim mcnn As ADODB.Connection

Private Sub cmdConnect_Click()

    On Error GoTo HandleErr
```

```
    mcnn.Open

    DumpProperties

ExitHere:
    Exit Sub

HandleErr:
    MsgBox "Error " & Err.Number & ": " & Err.Description, _
      vbOKOnly, "cmdConnect"
    Resume ExitHere
    Resume

End Sub

Private Sub cmdCreateConnection_Click()

    On Error GoTo HandleErr

    Set mcnn = New ADODB.Connection
    mcnn.ConnectionString = txtConnectionString.Text

    DumpProperties

ExitHere:
    Exit Sub

HandleErr:
    MsgBox "Error " & Err.Number & ": " & Err.Description, _
      vbOKOnly, "cmdCreateConnection"
    Resume ExitHere
    Resume

End Sub

Private Sub DumpProperties()

    Dim prp As ADODB.Property
    Dim li As ListItem

    On Error GoTo HandleErr

    lvwProperties.ListItems.Clear

    For Each prp In mcnn.Properties
        Set li = lvwProperties.ListItems.Add(, , prp.Name)
        li.SubItems(1) = prp.Value
    Next prp

    ' Clean up
    Set prp = Nothing
    Set li = Nothing
```

```
ExitHere:
    Exit Sub

HandleErr:
    MsgBox "Error " & Err.Number & ": " & Err.Description, _
      vbOKOnly, "DumpProperties"
    Resume ExitHere
    Resume

End Sub
```

Command and Recordset Provider-Specific Properties

The Microsoft OLE DB Provider for Microsoft Jet also adds 13 provider-specific properties to Command and Recordset objects. These properties are mostly the same for both types of objects, so it's convenient to discuss them together. On a Command object, the properties refer for the most part to a Recordset based on that Command; on a Recordset object, the properties refer to the Recordset itself. Table 22.5 lists these provider-specific properties.

TABLE 22.5: Command and Recordset Provider-Specific Properties

Property	Meaning
Jet OLEDB:Bulk Transactions	Set to True to perform bulk SQL operations within a transaction.
Jet OLEDB:Enable Fat Cursors	Set to True to cache multiple rows when populating a Recordset.
Jet OLEDB:Fat Cursor Cache Size	Number of rows to cache if Jet OLEDB:Enable Fat Cursors is True.
Jet OLEDB:Grbit Value	Not used.
Jet OLEDB:Inconsistent	Set to True to allow inconsistent updates.
Jet OLEDB:Locking Granularity	Set to 1 for page-level locking, or 2 for row-level locking.
Jet OLEDB:ODBC Pass-Through Statement	Set to True for a pass-through query (that is, one that should be passed unaltered to a linked table from another data source).
Jet OLEDB:Partial Bulk Ops	Set to 1 to allow inconsistent changes, or 2 to cause bulk transactions to fail if single error occurs.
Jet OLEDB:Pass-Through Query Bulk-Op	Set to True for a pass-through action query.
Jet OLEDB:Pass-Through Query Connect String	Connection string for a pass-through query.
Jet OLEDB:Stored Query	Set to True if the CommandText is the name of a stored query rather than a SQL string.
Jet OLEDB:Use Grbit	Not used.
Jet OLEDB:Validate Rules On Set	If True, validation rules are evaluated when a value is set. If False, validation is deferred until the record is saved.

Command and Recordset Dynamic Properties

The Jet provider also adds about 70 dynamic properties to Command and Recordset objects. As with the Connection object dynamic properties, most of these are read-only properties that describe the objects in more detail. Table 22.6 shows a few of the most useful of these properties.

TABLE 22.6: Selected Dynamic Properties of the Command and Recordset Objects

Property	Meaning
Append-Only Rowset	Set to True to prevent editing or deleting existing records while still allowing new records to be added.
Bookmarks Ordered	Set to True if bookmarks can be directly compared to determine the order of the corresponding rows in the Recordset.
Change Inserted Rows	Set to True if new rows can be edited without resynchronizing the Recordset.
Fetch Backwards	Set to True if you can scroll backward in this Recordset.
Maximum Pending Rows	The number of rows that can have pending updates at one time.
Server Data on Insert	Set to True if new rows are refreshed from the server after being inserted.
Updatability	A bitmask specifying operations that can be performed on the Recordset: 1 for edits, 2 for deletes, 4 for inserts.

Figure 22.2 shows the frmRecordsetProperties form in this chapter's sample project, which lets you explore the provider-specific and dynamic properties of a Recordset. Many of these properties will take on other values if you modify the code behind the form to apply different settings to the CursorLocation, CursorType, or LockType properties of the Recordset object.

Jet Tips and Quirks

Despite the fact that the Jet engine and the Microsoft OLE DB Provider for Microsoft Jet generally work well together, there are some areas where the results are not what you might expect (or just plain wrong). In this section, I'll examine some of these issues, grouped into two major areas: Recordset issues and other issues.

Recordset Issues

The Microsoft OLE DB Provider for Microsoft Jet doesn't support dynamic cursors. If you request a dynamic cursor, the provider will supply a keyset cursor instead. The major difference between a dynamic cursor and a keyset cursor is that the keyset cursor won't show you rows that have been added by other users that should appear in your Recordset. To see new rows with a keyset cursor, you must requery the Recordset.

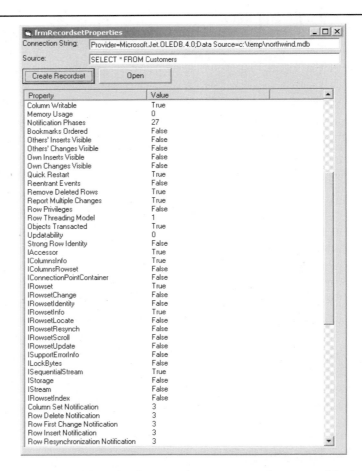

You may find in an application with multiple Recordsets open on the same table that changes to one Recordset don't show up in another. That's a feature of the Jet engine: It can cache changes at the Connection level for up to 5 seconds, to speed performance (by writing when it's not otherwise busy). If you find that you have multiple Recordsets that need to be synchronized, the simplest workaround is to make sure that they all use the same Connection object. You can ensure this by setting the ActiveConnection property of the Recordsets to a persistent Connection, or by setting the ActiveConnection property of one Recordset to another:

```
Set rst1.ActiveConnection = cnn
Set rst2.ActiveConnection = rst1.ActiveConnection
```

WARNING   Be sure to include the Set keyword when you're setting the ActiveConnection property. The code will work without the keyword, but in that case, it will create additional implicit connections, defeating the purpose.

Alternatively, you can adjust the Jet OLEDB:Shared Async Delay property of the Connection objects involved in order to force more frequent writes to the database, but this may impose a performance penalty.

The Jet database engine supports AutoNumber fields—fields that are automatically numbered by the engine when you insert a new record, similar to SQL Server identity fields. But you may not be able to retrieve the value of an AutoNumber field after inserting a record without resynchronizing the Recordset. Whether you can retrieve the value immediately depends on several factors:

- If you're using a server-side cursor (that is, if the CursorLocation property of the Recordset is set to adUseServer), the AutoNumber value is available.

- If you're using a client-side cursor (that is, if the CursorLocation property of the Recordset is set to adUseClient) and the database is in Access 97 format, the AutoNumber value will always return zero.

- If you're using a client-side cursor and the database is in Access 2000 or 2002 format, the AutoNumber value is available.

In the case where the AutoNumber isn't available (client-side cursor and Access 97 file format), you can retrieve the value after you call the Recordset.Resync method.

When you try to set the Index property of a Recordset so that you can use the Seek method, you may receive error 3251, "Current provider does not support the necessary interface for Index functionality." This will happen when you try to set the Index property on a table that is linked to the Access database (as opposed to one that is actually stored in the database). There isn't any workaround for this; the Index property and Seek method are available only on native Jet tables.

Although a Jet Recordset will let you set the MaxRecords property, this property is not supported by the Jet provider. For example, with the following procedure, you'll actually get *all* the records from the query, not just the 10 records you're asking for:

```
Sub TestMaxRecords()
    Dim cnn As ADODB.Connection
    Dim rst As ADODB.Recordset

    Set cnn = New ADODB.Connection
    cnn.Open "Provider = Microsoft.Jet.OLEDB.4.0;" & _
      "Data Source=c:\Temp\Northwind.mdb"
```

```
    Set rst = New ADODB.Recordset
    rst.MaxRecords = 10
    rst.Open "Customers", cnn, adOpenKeyset
    rst.MoveLast

    Debug.Print rst.RecordCount

    'Clean up
    rst.Close
    Set rst = Nothing
    cnn.Close
    Set cnn = Nothing

End Sub
```

To work around this problem, you can use the TOP predicate in a SQL statement rather than use the MaxRecords property:

```
Sub TestTop()
    Dim cnn As ADODB.Connection
    Dim rst As ADODB.Recordset

    Set cnn = New ADODB.Connection
    cnn.Open "Provider = Microsoft.Jet.OLEDB.4.0;" & _
      "Data Source=c:\Temp\Northwind.mdb"

    Set rst = New ADODB.Recordset
    rst.Open "SELECT TOP 10 * FROM Customers", _
      cnn, adOpenKeyset
    rst.MoveLast

    Debug.Print rst.RecordCount

    'Clean up
    rst.Close
    Set rst = Nothing
    cnn.Close
    Set cnn = Nothing

End Sub
```

You may have trouble setting a Recordset filter expression that contains both AND and OR as logical operators. If you do have such a filter expression, you must make sure (by using parentheses) that the OR operations are performed after the AND operations. An example may make this clear. Consider first this bit of code:

```
Sub FilterTest()
    Dim cnn As ADODB.Connection
```

```
        Dim rst As ADODB.Recordset

        Set cnn = New ADODB.Connection
        cnn.Open "Provider=Microsoft.Jet.OLEDB.4.0;" & _
         "Data Source=c:\Temp\Northwind.mdb"

        Set rst = New ADODB.Recordset

        rst.Open "SELECT * FROM Customers", cnn, _
         adOpenKeyset, adLockOptimistic

        ' This filter causes a runtime error
        rst.Filter = "((CustomerID LIKE 'A%') OR " & _
         "(CustomerID LIKE 'D%')) AND (Country <> 'Brazil')"

        rst.MoveFirst
        Do While Not rst.EOF
            Debug.Print rst.Fields(0).Value
            rst.MoveNext
        Loop

        'Clean up
        rst.Close
        Set rst = Nothing
        cnn.Close
        Set cnn = Nothing
    End Sub
```

If you try to run this procedure, you'll get error 3001, "Arguments are of the wrong type, are out of acceptable range, or are in conflict with one another" when you attempt to set the Filter property. You can fix this problem by rewriting the filter expression with a different order of operations:

```
    Sub FilterTest2()
        Dim cnn As ADODB.Connection
        Dim rst As ADODB.Recordset

        Set cnn = New ADODB.Connection
        cnn.Open "Provider=Microsoft.Jet.OLEDB.4.0;" & _
         "Data Source=c:\Temp\Northwind.mdb"

        Set rst = New ADODB.Recordset

        rst.Open "SELECT * FROM Customers", cnn, _
         adOpenKeyset, adLockOptimistic

        ' This filter works, even though it's
```

```
' logically equivalent to the first one
rst.Filter = "(CustomerID LIKE 'A%' AND Country <> 'Brazil') " & _
  "OR (CustomerID LIKE 'D%' AND Country <> 'Brazil')"

rst.MoveFirst
Do While Not rst.EOF
    Debug.Print rst.Fields(0).Value
    rst.MoveNext
Loop

'Clean up
rst.Close
Set rst = Nothing
cnn.Close
Set cnn = Nothing
End Sub
```

You may encounter mysterious failures in ADO when calling queries that work perfectly well from the Access interface. For example, this SQL expression is legal in Access (assuming that the database contains a table named Diagnostics):

```
SELECT * FROM Diagnostics
```

However, trying to run the same query from ADO results in error -2147467259, "Method 'Open' of object '_Recordset' failed":

```
Sub ReservedWordTest()
    Dim cnn As ADODB.Connection
    Dim rst As ADODB.Recordset

    Set cnn = New ADODB.Connection
    cnn.Open "Provider=Microsoft.Jet.OLEDB.4.0;" & _
      "Data Source=c:\Temp\Northwind.mdb"

    Set rst = New ADODB.Recordset

    rst.Open "SELECT * FROM Diagnostics", cnn, _
      adOpenKeyset, adLockOptimistic

    'Clean up
    rst.Close
    Set rst = Nothing
    cnn.Close
    Set cnn = Nothing
End Sub
```

The problem is that the Microsoft OLE DB Provider for Microsoft Jet uses a new flag for the Jet engine to turn on extended ANSI syntax for queries. This flag makes the Jet query processor more compliant with the ANSI-92 SQL standard, including compliance with the complete list of ANSI reserved words. *Diagnostics* is a reserved word in ANSI SQL but not in Jet SQL, which accounts for the different results.

To work around this issue, use square brackets around the reserved word:

```
Sub ReservedWordTest()
    Dim cnn As ADODB.Connection
    Dim rst As ADODB.Recordset

    Set cnn = New ADODB.Connection
    cnn.Open "Provider=Microsoft.Jet.OLEDB.4.0;" & _
     "Data Source=c:\Temp\Northwind.mdb"

    Set rst = New ADODB.Recordset

    rst.Open "SELECT * FROM [Diagnostics]", cnn, _
     adOpenKeyset, adLockOptimistic

    'Clean up
    rst.Close
    Set rst = Nothing
    cnn.Close
    Set cnn = Nothing
End Sub
```

TIP   You can find the complete list of reserved words that the Jet provider respects in Knowledge Base article Q238243 at http://support.microsoft.com/support/kb/articles/q238/2/43.asp.

Other Issues

The Jet Provider is one of the few providers (or perhaps the only one) that supports the adCmdTableDirect Recordset option for low-level access to data in a single table. But you need to be aware that this is a Recordset option only, not a Command type. If you try to use this option with a Command object, as in the following code, you'll get a runtime error:

```
Sub CommandError()
    ' This code won't work
    Dim cnn As ADODB.Connection
    Dim cmd As ADODB.Command

    Set cnn = New ADODB.Connection
    cnn.Open "Provider=Microsoft.Jet.OLEDB.4.0;" & _
     "Data Source=c:\Temp\Northwind.mdb"
```

```
        Set cmd = New ADODB.Command
        Set cmd.ActiveConnection = cnn
        cmd.CommandType = adCmdTableDirect
        cmd.CommandText = "Customers"

        'Clean up
        cnn.Close
        Set cnn = Nothing
        Set cmd = Nothing
    End Sub
```

If you try to run this code, you'll get error 3001, "The application is using arguments that are of the wrong type, are out of acceptable range, or are in conflict with one another" on the line that sets the CommandType property. The problem is that the CommandType of a Command object cannot be adCmdTableDirect, even though this value will show up in the IntelliSense choices for the property. Only Recordsets can use this CommandType. To fix the problem, rewrite the code to use a Recordset object without a Command object:

```
    Sub DirectRecordset()
        Dim cnn As ADODB.Connection
        Dim rst As ADODB.Recordset

        Set cnn = New ADODB.Connection
        cnn.Open "Provider = Microsoft.Jet.OLEDB.4.0; " & _
          "Data Source=c:\Temp\Northwind.mdb"

        Set rst = New ADODB.Recordset
        rst.Open "Customers", cnn, adOpenKeyset, adLockOptimistic, adCmdTableDirect

        Debug.Print rst.RecordCount

        'Clean up
        rst.Close
        Set rst = Nothing
        cnn.Close
        Set cnn = Nothing
    End Sub
```

If you create a view using ADOX, you may find that it's not visible if you open the same database in Microsoft Access. This isn't really a problem with ADO, but rather a limitation in the support of the Jet file format by Access. For example, you can use ADOX to create a new view as follows:

```
    Sub MakeView()
        Dim cnn As ADODB.Connection
```

```
Dim cat As ADOX.Catalog
Dim cmd As ADODB.Command
Dim vw As ADOX.View

Set cnn = New ADODB.Connection
cnn.Open "Provider = Microsoft.Jet.OLEDB.4.0;" & _
  "Data Source=c:\Temp\Northwind.mdb"

Set cat = New ADOX.Catalog
Set cat.ActiveConnection = cnn
Set cmd = New ADODB.Command
cmd.CommandType = adCmdText
cmd.CommandText = "SELECT * FROM Orders"

cat.Views.Append "vwOrders", cmd

'Clean up
cnn.Close
Set cnn = Nothing
Set cat = Nothing
Set cmd = Nothing
Set vw = Nothing
End Sub
```

If you run this procedure, it will create a view named vwOrders in the specified database. The result of opening the same database in Access will then depend on the version of Access that you're using:

- With Access 2000, vwOrders will not be visible in the Queries container.

- With Access 2002, vwOrders will be visible in the Queries container, and will display the proper records if you open it. It will not, however, be portrayed properly in query design view. You can open vwOrders in SQL view to see its source code.

If you use ADOX to create a new Column object and set its Default property, you may find that adding rows to the table containing this column ignores the setting of the Default property. You can work around this problem by using the following SQL statement to set the Default property:

```
ALTER TABLE tablename
ALTER COLUMN columnname
SET DEFAULT newvalue
```

Alternatively, you can upgrade to the latest Jet 4.0 Service Pack; this bug is fixed in Jet 4.0 Service Pack 5.

Using Linked Tables for Distributed Queries

Like SQL Server, the Jet engine is capable of executing distributed heterogeneous queries that draw on data from multiple data sources. In the case of Jet, the key to this technique is the linked table—a table that appears to be in the Jet database even though it's actually stored physically in another database, possibly managed by a completely different database engine. ADO allows you to both create and query linked tables.

Creating Linked Tables with ADOX

You can create linked tables that draw their data from a variety of data sources, including these:

- Microsoft Access
- Paradox
- dBASE
- Lotus Notes
- Excel
- Microsoft Exchange
- Text
- HTML
- ODBC data sources

NOTE   There's no mechanism for linking a table via OLE DB. You need to use either the built-in Jet IISAM drivers or an ODBC driver to communicate with the database that is the source of the linked table.

Creating a linked table via ADOX is very similar to creating a native table:

1. Set a Catalog object to refer to the database where you want the linked table to be available.

2. Create a new Table object and set its properties.

3. Append the Table object to the Tables collection of the Catalog object.

The differences between native and linked tables are in which properties you need to set and to what values. Figure 22.3 shows the frmLink form in the ADOChapter22 sample database, which enables you to experiment with the code for linking tables. Listing 22.2 provides the code that performs the actual linking.

FIGURE 22.3:

Linking a table
between Access
databases

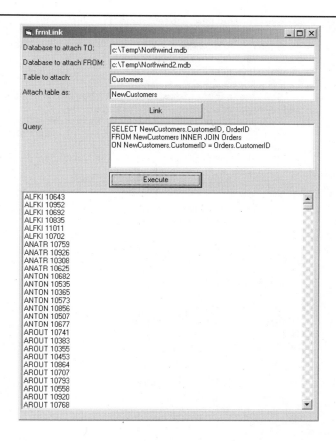

Listing 22.2:   **Creating a Linked Table**

```
Private Sub cmdLink_Click()

    Dim cnn As ADODB.Connection
    Dim cat As ADOX.Catalog
    Dim tbl As ADOX.Table

    On Error GoTo HandleErr

    Set cnn = New ADODB.Connection
    cnn.Open "Provider=Microsoft.Jet.OLEDB.4.0;" & _
      "Data Source=" & txtAttachTo.Text

    Set cat = New ADOX.Catalog
    Set cat.ActiveConnection = cnn
```

```
' Create the new table, name it, and tell
' ADO where it will be saved
Set tbl = New ADOX.Table
tbl.Name = txtAttachName.Text
Set tbl.ParentCatalog = cat

' Set the properties to create the link
tbl.Properties("Jet OLEDB:Create Link") = True
tbl.Properties("Jet OLEDB:Link Datasource") = txtAttachFrom.Text
' You may need a Link Provider String for other properties
' such as username and password
' tbl.Properties("Jet OLEDB:Link Provider String") = _
  ";Uid=Admin;Pwd=Password"
tbl.Properties("Jet OLEDB:Remote Table Name") = txtTableToAttach.Text

' Save the information to the target database
cat.Tables.Append tbl

' Cleanup
Set tbl = Nothing
Set cat = Nothing
cnn.Close
Set cnn = Nothing

MsgBox "Attachment Successful"
ExitHere:
    Exit Sub

HandleErr:
    MsgBox "Error " & Err.Number & ": " & Err.Description, _
     vbOKOnly, "cmdLink"
    Resume ExitHere
    Resume

End Sub
```

The key to creating the linked table with data from another database lies in the settings for the Table object's Properties collection. There are three required properties and one optional property that you can set here:

- Jet OLEDB:Create Link must be set to True to create the linked table.

- Jet OLEDB:Link Datasource must be set to the filename of the database that contains the table to be linked. This property should contain only the filename.

- Jet OLEDB:Remote Table Name must be set to the name of the table in the source database.

- Jet OLEDB:Link Provider String can optionally contain additional parameters to be passed to the source database. For an unsecured Jet database, you can omit this property.

You must set the ParentCatalog property of the Table object before you attempt to set any of these provider-specific properties. Otherwise, ADOX has no way of knowing which property names are valid for the Table object.

If you're linking a table from an ODBC data source, the property usage is somewhat different:

- Jet OLEDB:Create Link must be set to True to create the linked table.
- Jet OLEDB:Link Datasource should be omitted.
- Jet OLEDB:Remote Table Name must be set to the name of the table in the source database.
- Jet OLEDB:Link Provider String must contain the ODBC connection string for the data source, including all required Connection properties.

The linked table need not have the same name in both the source database and the linking database.

Querying Linked Tables with ADO

After you've created a linked table in a Jet database, you can use it in queries as you would any other table in the database. In the case of the frmLink sample form, some simple code, shown in Listing 22.3, executes a SQL query and dumps the results to the user interface.

Listing 22.3:   **Using a Linked Table in a Query**

```
Private Sub cmdExecute_Click()

    Dim cnn As ADODB.Connection
    Dim rst As ADODB.Recordset
    Dim fld As Field
    Dim strTemp As String

    On Error GoTo HandleErr

    lboResults.Clear

    Set cnn = New ADODB.Connection
    cnn.Open "Provider=Microsoft.Jet.OLEDB.4.0;" & _
      "Data Source=" & txtAttachTo.Text

    Set rst = New ADODB.Recordset
    rst.Open txtQuery.Text, cnn

    Do Until rst.EOF
```

```
            strTemp = ""
            For Each fld In rst.Fields
                strTemp = strTemp & fld.Value & " "
            Next fld
            lboResults.AddItem strTemp
            rst.MoveNext
        Loop

        ' Clean up
        rst.Close
        Set rst = Nothing
        Set fld = Nothing
        cnn.Close
        Set cnn = Nothing
    ExitHere:
        Exit Sub

    HandleErr:
        MsgBox "Error " & Err.Number & ": " & Err.Description, _
            vbOKOnly, "cmdExecute"
        Resume ExitHere
        Resume

    End Sub
```

Note that you don't have to do anything special to use the linked table in SQL or in ADO. The only potentially tricky point is that you must refer to the table by the name you used for the Table object in the database that contains the link, not by the table's name in the original source database. These two names may or may not be the same.

Choosing a Distributed Query Strategy

You may be faced with a choice between SQL Server linked servers and Jet linked tables in your application if you need to resolve heterogeneous distributed queries. Here are some things to consider when making this choice:

- To use SQL Server linked servers, you must have OLE DB providers for every data source in the query. If you have only ODBC drivers for some data sources, you can use the OLE DB Provider for ODBC to access those data sources from a SQL Server linked server. In that case, though, you may see a performance boost by using Jet linked tables instead.

- If a large amount of the data to be processed is already in a SQL Server database, you should incline toward using SQL Server linked servers. If a large amount of the data to be processed is already in a Jet database, you should incline toward using Jet linked tables.

- If you need to process ad hoc distributed queries, you should use the SQL Server OPEN-ROWSET or OPENDATASOURCE statements, which don't require creating a permanent link.

- For client-server databases, SQL Server linked servers generally provide better performance.

- For file-based databases that are accessible through the Jet IISAMS, Jet linked tables generally provide better performance.

- SQL Server can handle large amounts of data more gracefully than Jet.

- Jet is less expensive to license than SQL Server.

Custom Schema Rowsets

One interesting bit of functionality that the Microsoft OLE DB Provider for Microsoft Jet enables is the retrieval of the current user roster from a Jet database. Jet is inherently a multiuser database, but there's no easy way to retrieve a list of the currently logged-in users through the Access user interface. The Jet provider makes this task simple by providing a custom schema rowset with user information.

The frmUserRoster form in this chapter's sample project demonstrates the process of retrieving this custom schema rowset. The code in Listing 22.4 does the retrieval.

Listing 22.4:   Retrieving a List of Users from the Jet Engine

```
Const JET_SCHEMA_USERROSTER = _
 "{947bb102-5d43-11d1-bdbf-00c04fb92675}"
Private Sub cmdGetUsers_Click()
    Dim cnn As ADODB.Connection
    Dim rst As ADODB.Recordset

    On Error GoTo HandleErr

    lboUsers.Clear

    Set cnn = New ADODB.Connection
    cnn.ConnectionString = txtConnectionString.Text
    cnn.Open

    ' Open the user roster schema rowset
    Set rst = cnn.OpenSchema(adSchemaProviderSpecific, , _
     JET_SCHEMA_USERROSTER)

    ' And dump to the UI
    Do Until rst.EOF
```

```
            lboUsers.AddItem NullTrim(rst.Fields("LOGIN_NAME").Value) & _
               " on " & NullTrim(rst.Fields("COMPUTER_NAME").Value)
            rst.MoveNext
        Loop

        'Clean up
        rst.Close
        Set rst = Nothing
        cnn.Close
        Set cnn = Nothing
    ExitHere:
        Exit Sub

    HandleErr:
        MsgBox "Error " & Err.Number & ": " & Err.Description, _
           vbOKOnly, "cmdGetUsers"
        Resume ExitHere
        Resume

    End Sub
    Private Function NullTrim(strIn As String) As String
        Dim intNull As Integer
        intNull = InStr(1, strIn, Chr(0))
        NullTrim = Left(strIn, intNull - 1)
    End Function
```

As with all custom schema rowsets, this one is identified by a GUID. The particular GUID for this rowset is stored in a constant (JET_SCHEMA_USERROSTER) to make the code more readable. To get the user roster, all you need to do is to call the OpenSchema method of the Connection object, supplying the appropriate constant (assuming, of course, that the Connection object is open on a Jet database).

This rowset contains four columns:

- COMPUTER_NAME is the name of the computer where the user is working (as set via the Control Panel Network icon).

- LOGIN_NAME is the user's Access username (not the Windows username).

- CONNECTED is True if there is a lock for this user in the LDB file, and False otherwise.

- SUSPECTED_STATE is True if this user did something to leave the database in a suspect state, and Null otherwise.

TIP

The COMPUTER_NAME and LOGIN_NAME fields are returned with null characters at the end of the strings. The NullTrim function in the code snippet in Listing 22.4 takes care of stripping off the extra characters starting with the null.

The Jet provider also supports a second custom schema rowset, JET_SCHEMA_ISAM-STATS. This rowset provides performance information for the Jet engine. Figure 22.4 shows the results of retrieving this schema rowset (which contains a single row with the indicated fields) to the user interface. The code, provided in Listing 22.5, is very similar to the code for returning the user roster.

FIGURE 22.4:

Retrieving ISAM statistics

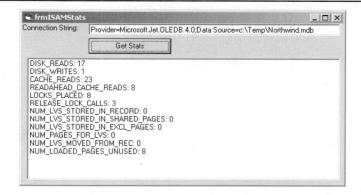

Listing 22.5: **Retrieving Jet Engine Performance Data**

```
Const JET_SCHEMA_ISAMSTATS = _
 "{8703b612-5d43-11d1-bdbf-00c04fb92675}"
Private Sub cmdGetStats_Click()
    Dim cnn As ADODB.Connection
    Dim rst As ADODB.Recordset
    Dim fld As ADODB.Field

    On Error GoTo HandleErr

    lboStats.Clear

    Set cnn = New ADODB.Connection
    cnn.ConnectionString = txtConnectionString.Text
    cnn.Open

    ' Open the user roster schema rowset
    Set rst = cnn.OpenSchema(adSchemaProviderSpecific, , _
     JET_SCHEMA_ISAMSTATS)

    ' And dump to the UI
    For Each fld In rst.Fields
        lboStats.AddItem fld.Name & ": " & fld.Value
    Next fld
```

```
       'Clean up
       rst.Close
       Set rst = Nothing
       Set fld = Nothing
       cnn.Close
       Set cnn = Nothing
   ExitHere:
       Exit Sub

   HandleErr:
       MsgBox "Error " & Err.Number & ": " & Err.Description, _
        vbOKOnly, "cmdGetUsers"
       Resume ExitHere
       Resume

   End Sub
```

Table 22.7 shows the fields that are returned in the ISAM statistics schema rowset.

TABLE 22.7: ISAM Statistics Schema Rowset

Field	Meaning
DISK_READS	Number of reads from disk (as with all the ISAM statistics, this count starts when the connection is made to the database)
DISK_WRITES	Number of writes to disk
CACHE_READS	Number of reads from cache
READAHEAD_CACHE_READS	Number of reads from the read-ahead cache
LOCKS_PLACED	Number of locks placed
RELEASE_LOCK_CALLS	Number of locks released
NUM_LVS_STORED_IN_RECORD	Undocumented
NUM_LVS_STORED_IN_SHARED_PAGES	Undocumented
NUM_LVS_STORED_IN_EXCL_PAGES	Undocumented
NUM_PAGES_FOR_LVS	Undocumented
NUM_LVS_MOVED_FROM_REC	Undocumented
NUM_LOADED_PAGES_UNUSED	Undocumented

NOTE   Microsoft has not documented six of the fields in the ISAM statistics rowset. As far as I can tell in testing, these six fields always return zero. It's possible that these are left over from some internal test or a feature that was never fully implemented.

Although the ISAM statistics are primarily intended for use by the developers at Microsoft when they're fine-tuning data access components, you may occasionally find them useful in optimizing your own applications. For example, if the LOCKS_PLACED statistic consistently runs much higher than the RELEASE_LOCK_CALLS statistic, you might inspect your code for Recordsets that are being held open in a locked state longer than they should be.

Summary

Despite the issues I've mentioned in this chapter, the Microsoft OLE DB Provider for Microsoft Jet is one of the best-supported OLE DB providers. Besides enabling all the common OLE DB and ADO operations, this provider also works well with the SHAPE statement (as you'll see in more detail in Chapter 25, "Using ADO from Microsoft Access"). The Jet provider also offers full support for the DDL and security features of the ADOX library (see Chapter 9, "Using ADOX for Data Definition and Security Operations," for more details on ADOX).

There are many, many other OLE DB providers available today. Although I can't cover them all in this book, the next chapter is devoted to some of the other data sources that are available via OLE DB: Microsoft Exchange, Active Directory, and MySQL.

CHAPTER 23

ADO and Other Providers

- Active Directory

- ADO and Active Directory

- MySQL

There are dozens of OLE DB providers available, with more being developed all the time. I don't want to turn this into a book about OLE DB providers, so I'm not going to try to review them all. But to give you a sense of the universality of OLE DB and ADO, I do want to look at a few more providers. These providers let you do things that would have been impossible with Microsoft's data access libraries a few years ago. In this chapter, I'll cover the use of ADO to retrieve data from the Windows Active Directory as well as the open-source MySQL database.

Active Directory

If you've kept up with Microsoft Windows at all during the last few years, you've heard of Active Directory (AD). Active Directory is Microsoft's implementation of a *directory service*, a single database on the network that stores information about a wide variety of objects. One of the strengths of Active Directory is that it's integrated with other software through standard interfaces and protocols, including ADO. In this section, I'll review the basics of Active Directory (which can be a rather daunting topic if you don't have experience with directory services) and then demonstrate how ADO fits into the Active Directory architecture.

Understanding Active Directory

Active Directory is based on a unified database that's sometimes called simply the *directory*. The directory can store information about any object whatsoever. By default, it stores information on computers, users, groups, printers, servers, and other network components. Each object is characterized by its place in a hierarchy and by a set of attributes (properties) that describe the object. The classes of objects in the directory and the attributes (which can be either mandatory or optional) of each class of objects are defined by the *AD schema*. AD includes tools for extending the schema to include new classes and new attributes, so it's not limited to storing only the information that Microsoft places in the directory. You can add your own classes, attributes, and objects to the directory and benefit from the storage, security, and other features of AD in your own applications.

Information stored in Active Directory is automatically replicated to all domain controllers in the domain. As long as you can connect to any domain controller, you can query AD for the most recent information about the network's resources. Of course, replication isn't instantaneous; you may experience some latency while changed information is propagated around the network, particularly if your network has some domain controllers separated from others by a slow link such as a frame relay line.

In Windows NT, the domain was the largest level of aggregation for computers. Active Directory introduces two new concepts that parallel the hierarchical structure of the directory itself: *domain trees* and *forests*. Depending on its size and the number of managed computers, an organization can choose to aggregate domains hierarchically into a domain tree and to combine multiple domain trees into a forest. Figure 23.1 shows the relationship between domains, domain trees, and forests.

FIGURE 23.1:

Grouping domains into domain trees and forests

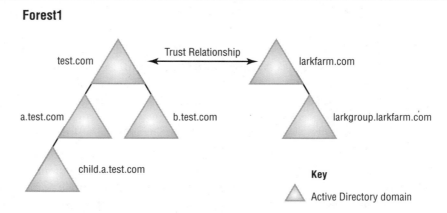

In Figure 23.1, triangles indicate Active Directory domains. As you can see, each domain has a name that fits into the Domain Name System (DNS). Child domains are named hierarchically from their parents, and the names indicate unambiguously how the hierarchy is arranged. For example, you know by looking at the name that the `child.a.test.com` domain is a child of the `a.test.com` domain, which, in turn, is a child of the `test.com` domain. A completely connected hierarchy of domains forms a domain tree. Domain trees, in turn, can be grouped into forests; a forest contains one or more domain trees. Figure 23.1 shows one forest that contains two domain trees and a total of six domains.

Although multiple domain trees in a single forest don't share a DNS namespace, they do share a single directory, and AD information is replicated among all domain controllers in all domain trees. AD automatically sets up two-way transitive trust relationships between the *forest root domain*—the first domain created in each forest—and the root domain of any other domain tree in the same forest. It also automatically sets up two-way transitive trust relationships between parent and child domains. The net effect is that every domain trusts every other domain in the same forest, and users can be authenticated by any domain in the forest.

NOTE   A *trust relationship* means that one computer trusts the actions of another. A *two-way* trust relationship means that the two computers trust one another. A *transitive* trust relationship can be "passed along": For example, if domains A and B share a two-way transitive trust relationship, and domains B and C share a two-way transitive trust relationship, then domains A and C automatically share a two-way transitive trust relationship.

Active Directory assigns names to users and computers based on their location in the domain hierarchy. A user named Fred whose account is located in the larkgroup.larkfarm.com domain has a *user principal name* of Fred@larkgroup.larkfarm.com. Similarly, a computer named ROBOTRON in the domain test.larkfarm.com has a *computer principal name* of ROBOTRON.test.larkfarm.com. You can't have two users with the same name or two computers with the same name within the same domain. Given that restriction, principal names provide unambiguous names that can be used for users and computers across an entire forest.

In addition to domains, AD also organizes computers into *sites*. Sites are meant to reflect the physical structure of an organization rather than the logical structure. A site consists of a group of computers all interconnected by high-speed communication links. One domain may contain several sites; conversely, one site may contain several domains. AD uses sites to make processes such as locating a service or replicating information more efficient, by maximizing communications within sites and minimizing communications between sites.

Another object that you will find within AD is the *organizational unit* (OU). An organizational unit is a container that can hold users, groups, computers, and other organizational units. All of the contents in an OU must come from a single domain. The OU provides a means to model the hierarchy of an organization within a single domain.

The Directory Service

The directory service is the core of Active Directory. Every object stored within the directory service is assigned a unique Lightweight Directory Access Protocol (LDAP) name. LDAP is a standard protocol that has been implemented by many directory vendors. Actually, as you'll see later in this section, LDAP assigns several names to each object. These names are each appropriate in different circumstances.

To understand how LDAP names are constructed, it's helpful to start with the concept of a *naming attribute*. Remember, each object within AD is an instance of a particular class, and each class has attributes that distinguish it from other classes according to the AD schema. One particular attribute of each class is distinguished within the schema as the naming attribute for that class. You'll run across three naming attributes frequently in constructing LDAP names:

- For users and computers, the naming attribute is Common-Name, abbreviated in LDAP as cn.

- For organizational units, the naming attribute is Organizational-Unit-Name, abbreviated in LDAP as ou.

- For domains, the naming attribute is Domain-Components, abbreviated in LDAP as dc.

NOTE   The LDAP standard defines other naming attributes, such as *o* for organization and *c* for country, that are not implemented by AD.

Once you know the location of an object within AD, you can determine its *distinguished name* (DN). The DN is composed of a set of `naming attribute=value` pairs that walk up the hierarchy of containers from the object being named to the root domain of the directory namespace.

An example will help make the concept of the DN clearer. Figure 23.2 shows five AD objects:

- A domain named `larkfarm.com`
- A domain named `larkgroup.larkfarm.com` that is a child of the `larkfarm.com` domain
- An organizational unit named `Support` within the `larkgroup.larkfarm.com` domain
- An organizational unit named `Escalation` within the `Support` OU
- A user named `Fred` within the `Escalation` OU

TIP   On AD diagrams, domains are conventionally represented as triangles, OUs as ellipses, and other objects as rectangles or icons.

FIGURE 23.2:

Nested objects in AD

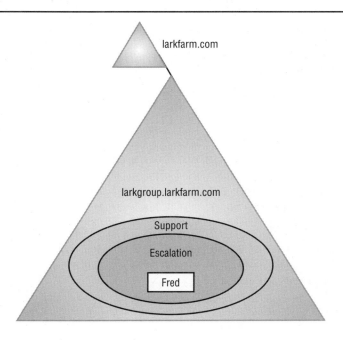

Starting from the top, each of these objects has a distinguished name:

The DN of the `larkfarm.com` domain is `dc=larkfarm,dc=com`.

The DN of the `larkgroup.larkfarm.com` domain is `dc=larkgroup,dc=larkfarm,dc=com`.

The DN of the `Support` OU is `ou=Support,dc=larkgroup,dc=larkfarm,dc=com`.

The DN of the `Escalation` OU is `ou=Escalation,ou=Support,dc=larkgroup,dc=larkfarm,dc=com`.

Finally, the DN of the `Fred` user is `cn=Fred,ou=Escalation,ou=Support,dc=larkgroup,dc=larkfarm,dc=com`.

NOTE Notice that the `com` domain is treated as a separate object for constructing LDAP names, even though it's not under the control of the organization running `larkfarm.com`.

Each Active Directory object also has a *relative distinguished name* (RDN). The RDN is the part of the DN that is an attribute of the object itself—what we generally think of as the object's name. In Figure 23.2, the RDN of the user is Fred, and the RDN of the OU that immediately contains that user is Escalation.

RDNs are unique within their parent container but can be repeated elsewhere in the directory. For example, there could be two users with the RDN Fred, but they might have the full DNs:

```
cn=Fred,ou=Escalation,ou=Support,dc=larkgroup,dc=larkfarm,dc=com
cn=Fred,ou=Advertising,ou=Marketing,dc=larkgroup,dc=larkfarm,dc=com
```

LDAP also specifies a second format for naming objects in a directory: the LDAP Uniform Resource Locator (URL) format. To construct an LDAP URL, you concatenate three items:

- The `LDAP://` protocol specifier
- The name of the server holding the directory information
- The DN of the object

For example, if the root server in the `larkgroup.larkfarm.com` domain were named POTATO, the LDAP URL for the user Fred in Figure 23.2 would be:

```
LDAP://POTATO.larkgroup.larkfarm.com/cn=Fred,
➡ ou=Escalation,ou=Support,dc=larkgroup,dc=larkfarm,dc=com
```

Finally, AD has its own format for *AD canonical names*. A canonical name lists the containers for an object from the top of the hierarchy down, uses the DNS name for the domains in the hierarchy, and omits the names of the naming attributes. The AD canonical name for the user Fred in Figure 23.2 is:

```
larkgroup.larkfarm.com/Support/Escalation/Fred
```

The directory service stores information in a file named ntds.dit. This is the file that is replicated between all of the domain controllers in a forest. It contains three types of information:

- Domain data on the actual objects in the directory

- Configuration data that describes the topology of the directory (for example, which domains, domain trees, and forests are contained in the directory)

- Schema data that describes all of the object classes and attributes that can be stored in the directory

The initial domain controller in a forest also creates a special database called the *global catalog*. The global catalog contains a full replica of all objects from its host domain, and a partial replica of all objects from other domains in the forest. This partial replica stores only key attributes for all objects in the forest, rather than all attributes. The global catalog allows fast searching for objects across an entire forest without having to send queries to every domain within the forest. In addition, it provides universal logon services for the forest by recording user and group information for the entire forest. In a large AD installation, the administrator can configure additional global catalogs to distribute search and logon activity.

ADO and Active Directory

Now that you have some understanding of the basic concepts of Active Directory, it's time to see how you can use ADO to extract information from the directory. When you install Windows 2000 or XP on a computer, or install the Active Directory client on a computer running an earlier Windows operating system, you'll also get a copy of the Microsoft OLE DB Provider for Microsoft Active Directory Service. This provider gives you read-only access to some of the information in Active Directory (as well as in other LDAP-compliant directories such as the Novell Directory Service).

In this section, I'll examine some of the details of working with Active Directory via ADO, as well as via the fuller Active Directory Services Interface (ADSI) COM library. As I proceed, you'll see that these two methods of Active Directory can complement each other. ADO is good at finding information in the directory quickly; ADSI provides broader information about the objects that ADO finds. I'll look at several AD tasks using a sample application:

- Connecting to AD with ADO

- Navigating the AD hierarchy

- Retrieving detailed information on AD objects

- Searching for AD objects

NOTE   To use the code samples in this chapter, your computer must be a member of a domain that uses Active Directory, you must have AD client software installed, and you must know the distinguished name of the domain containing the AD directory service. If you're unsure about any of this information, consult your system administrator.

Connecting to Active Directory Using ADO

The Microsoft OLE DB Provider for Microsoft Active Directory Service supports only three connection string parameters:

- The Provider parameter must be set to ADSDSOObject.

- The User ID parameter can be set to a Windows username. If you omit this parameter, the provider will use the current logon.

- The Password parameter can be set to a Windows password. If you omit this parameter, the provider will use the current logon.

There are no provider-specific connection string parameters for this provider. Thus, opening a connection to Active Directory is much simpler than using other OLE DB providers. Here's a snippet of code from the ADOChapter23 sample project that demonstrates connecting to Active Directory from ADO:

```
Dim cnn As ADODB.Connection
...
Set cnn = New ADODB.Connection
cnn.Provider = "ADSDSOObject"
cnn.Open
```

Navigating the Active Directory Hierarchy

After you've opened a connection to AD, there are several types of information that you can retrieve. For the first part of the example, I'll open Recordsets using the LDAP non-SQL syntax for the CommandText parameter. This syntax uses up to four parameters to indicate the information that should be retrieved from Active Directory:

    <Root>;(Filter);Attributes[;Scope]

These four parameters are as follows:

- *Root* is the DN of the AD node where you wish to start the search.

- *Filter* is a search filter that indicates the information to search for, in the format attribute=value. To search for all objects, use the filter objectClass=*.

- *Attributes* are the attributes to retrieve into the Recordset. If you know enough about the schema you're searching, you can specify a comma-separated list of attributes here. Otherwise, you can use the Name and AdsPath attributes, which are generally implemented on every AD object. The AdsPath attribute returns the DN for the object. You can't use a wildcard in the Attributes parameter.

- *Scope* is an optional parameter that indicates how deeply to perform the search. This can be set to Base to search only the Root object, OneLevel to search direct children of the Root object, or Subtree to search the entire subtree starting at the Root object.

Figure 23.3 shows the frmADExplorer form from this chapter's sample project. This form uses the CommandText syntax repeatedly to populate the treeview of AD objects.

The code for this example begins with frmMenu, which is used to initialize the treeview on frmADExplorer by supplying a root node:

```
Private Sub cmdADExplorer_Click()
    Load frmADExplorer
    frmADExplorer.Root = txtRoot.Text
    frmADExplorer.InitTree
    frmADExplorer.Show
End Sub
```

FIGURE 23.3:

Active Directory
object hierarchy and
attributes

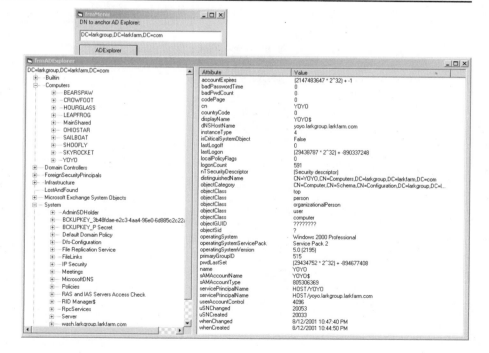

WARNING Although there is a default value on frmMenu for the root DN, this root value won't work on your system. You'll need to substitute the DN of your own AD root or of a node further down in your own directory.

The InitTree method of frmADExplorer does the work of stocking the top level of the treeview. Listing 23.1 shows the code.

Listing 23.1: **Adding Top-Level Nodes to the AD Tree**

```
Public Sub InitTree()

    Dim nodRoot As Node
    Dim nod As Node
    Dim rst As ADODB.Recordset

    On Error GoTo HandleErr

    ' Initialize the module-level connection to AD
    Set mcnn = New ADODB.Connection
    mcnn.Provider = "ADSDSOObject"
    mcnn.Open

    ' Open a Recordset on the top-level objects
    ' NOTE: You'll need to provide the path to your own
    ' root directory here!
    Set rst = New ADODB.Recordset
    rst.Open "<LDAP://" & Root & ">;(objectClass=*);" & _
    "Name,AdsPath;OneLevel", mcnn

    ' Create the root node for the tree
    Set nodRoot = tvwAD.Nodes.Add(, , Root, Root)

    ' Now add children for each top-level object
    Do Until rst.EOF
        Set nod = tvwAD.Nodes.Add(nodRoot, tvwChild, rst.Fields(1).Value, _
            rst.Fields(0).Value)
        ' Add a dummy node to each of these so it will display the + sign
        Set nod = tvwAD.Nodes.Add(nod, tvwChild, "DUMMY" & nod.Key)
        rst.MoveNext
    Loop

    ' And expand the root node
    nodRoot.Expanded = True

    ' Clean up
    rst.Close
    Set rst = Nothing
    Set nod = Nothing
    Set nodRoot = Nothing
```

```
ExitHere:
    Exit Sub

HandleErr:
    MsgBox "Error " & Err.Number & ": " & Err.Description, _
        vbOKOnly, "InitTree"
    Resume ExitHere
    Resume

End Sub
```

This code is a combination of data access code that uses ADO to retrieve information from Active Directory and user interface code that manages the placement of that information on the treeview. If you look at it in small pieces, it should be fairly easy to see how the code functions. After opening a connection to Active Directory, the code opens a Recordset:

```
Set rst = New ADODB.Recordset
rst.Open "<LDAP://" & Root & ">;(objectClass=*);" & _
    "Name,AdsPath;OneLevel", mcnn
```

The Root variable is filled in by the frmMenu form before it calls this procedure. So the actual CommandText executed by the provider will be something like this:

```
<LDAP://DC=larkgroup,DC=larkfarm,DC=com>;
➡ (objectClass=*);Name,AdsPath;OneLevel
```

Given the CommandText syntax that you saw earlier, the four parameters of this query are as follows:

- `<LDAP://DC=larkgroup,DC=larkfarm,DC=com>` is the DN of the root node where the Recordset should be anchored. In this case, it happens to be a domain in the domain tree of my own test forest.

- `(objectClass=*)` is the filter to use. In this case, it's essentially no filter, telling ADO to retrieve all AD objects.

- `Name,AdsPath` are the attributes to retrieve for each object found. These provide the columns for the Recordset.

- `OneLevel` is the scope modifier, which specifies that the Recordset should contain only direct children of the root node.

When you use this CommandText to create a Recordset, the net result is a Recordset that contains the Name and AdsPath of each direct child of the root node. The next step is to walk through this Recordset and use it to build the part of the tree that's visible when you open the form:

```
' Create the root node for the tree
Set nodRoot = tvwAD.Nodes.Add(, , Root, Root)
```

```
' Now add children for each top-level object
Do Until rst.EOF
    Set nod = tvwAD.Nodes.Add(nodRoot, tvwChild, rst.Fields(1).Value, _
      rst.Fields(0).Value)
    ' Add a dummy node to each of these so it will display the + sign
    Set nod = tvwAD.Nodes.Add(nod, tvwChild, "DUMMY" & nod.Key)
    rst.MoveNext
Loop
```

You may not have looked at the object model of the treeview before now. It's a fairly rich model, but this example uses only a small piece of it. The structure of the tree is captured by the treeview's Nodes collection. Each item shown in the tree is a node in this collection. To create a new node, you call the Add method of the collection:

```
Nodes.Add([Relative], [Relationship], [Key], [Text], [Image], [SelectedImage])
```

The parameters to the Add method are as follows:

- *Relative* is a node already in the tree. If not supplied, it defaults to the root of the tree.

- *Relationship* is a constant that indicates the position of the new node with respect to the relative node. If not supplied, it defaults to creating a new node on the same level of the tree.

- *Key* is a unique key that can be used to retrieve the node from the Nodes collection.

- *Text* is the text to display on-screen for this node.

- *Image* is an index of an image drawn from the collection of images in an ImageList control. This index provides an icon to be displayed next to the node when it is not selected.

- *SelectedIndex* is an index into a collection of images in an ImageList control. This index provides an icon to be displayed next to the node when it is selected.

The code in this procedure calls the Add method repeatedly. First, it adds a root node to the treeview, representing the root of the Recordset. Second, it loops through the Recordset, adding a new node as a child of this root node for each row in the Recordset. The AD object's name is used for the text of the node, while its DN is used as the key. Finally, it adds a dummy node as a child of each of the new object nodes. Adding a dummy child node is a treeview trick that causes the treeview to display the plus sign next to the parent node. This is much faster than recursively retrieving all the nodes that make up the entire tree before they're needed.

After adding nodes representing each row in the Recordset (which, in turn, represent the AD objects), the code sets the Expanded property of the root node to True. This causes the treeview to make the children of this node visible. Finally, the code closes the Recordset, because all of its information is now stored on the tree.

When the user clicks the plus sign or double-clicks a node to expand the node, the treeview's Expand event is fired. In this event, the code again makes use of ADO to retrieve information from AD if necessary. Listing 23.2 provides the code.

Listing 23.2:   **Retrieving Child Objects When a Node is Expanded**

```
Private Sub tvwAD_Expand(ByVal Node As MSComctlLib.Node)
    ' When a node is expanded, check to see whether its first
    ' child is a dummy node. If so, delete it and add the real
    ' children (if any)

    Dim nodChild As Node
    Dim rst As ADODB.Recordset

    On Error GoTo HandleErr

    Set nodChild = Node.Child
    If Left(nodChild.Key, 5) = "DUMMY" Then
        tvwAD.Nodes.Remove nodChild.Index

        ' Open a Recordset to get the actual children
        Set rst = New ADODB.Recordset
        rst.Open "<" & Node.Key & ">;(objectClass=*);" & _
         "Name,AdsPath;OneLevel", mcnn

        ' Add these new nodes
        Do Until rst.EOF
            Set nodChild = tvwAD.Nodes.Add(Node, tvwChild, _
             rst.Fields(1).Value, rst.Fields(0).Value)
            ' Add a dummy node to each of these so it
            ' will display the + sign
            Set nodChild = tvwAD.Nodes.Add(nodChild, _
             tvwChild, "DUMMY" & nodChild.Key)
            rst.MoveNext
        Loop

        ' Clean up
        rst.Close
        Set rst = Nothing
        Set nodChild = Nothing

    End If

ExitHere:
    Exit Sub

HandleErr:
    MsgBox "Error " & Err.Number & ": " & Err.Description, _
     vbOKOnly, "tvwAD_Expand"
    Resume ExitHere
    Resume

End Sub
```

The key to this code is the check for whether the first child of the currently selected node is a dummy node:

```
Set nodChild = Node.Child
If Left(nodChild.Key, 5) = "DUMMY" Then
    tvwAD.Nodes.Remove nodChild.Index
```

If the node is a dummy node, the event then opens a new Recordset anchored at the selected node and adds its children to the treeview, just as the original InitTree procedure does. By stocking the treeview in this "just-in-time" fashion, the code provides the ability to retrieve information from anywhere in the directory without any large delays.

Retrieving Object Information from Active Directory

When the user clicks a node in the treeview, the NodeClick event is fired. In this event, I want to retrieve a complete list of properties for the active node and display them in the listview. Because it doesn't offer a way to retrieve a list of all properties for an Active Directory object, ADO isn't an appropriate tool for this task. Instead, the code relies on the Active DS Type Library (the library that implements the Active Directory Services Interface for COM clients) to retrieve the information. This type library provides an implementation of AD that can be called as a set of COM objects.

WARNING   You'll find that the objects in the Active DS Type Library are not entirely friendly to Visual Basic developers. In particular, they don't support all of the functionality necessary for the Locals Window or IntelliSense to provide complete information. Be prepared to spend a lot of time with the documentation when you're trying to use this library.

The code in the NodeClick event uses three objects from this type library (actually, they're interfaces, but to the VB programmer, interfaces and objects look the same):

• IADsPropertyList represents all the attributes of an AD object.

• IADsPropertyEntry represents a single attribute of an AD object.

• IADsPropertyValue represents the value or values of an attribute of an AD object. AD attributes can be multivalued.

The code in the NodeClick event starts by retrieving a list of all the attributes of the AD object represented by the selected node in the treeview:

```
Private Sub tvwAD_NodeClick(ByVal Node As MSComctlLib.Node)

    ' When a node is selected, retrieve its properties

    Dim plstProperties As IADsPropertyList
    Dim pent As IADsPropertyEntry
    Dim intI As Integer
```

```
Dim val As IADsPropertyValue
Dim v As Variant
Dim li As ListItem
Dim lngHigh As Long
Dim lngLow As Long
Dim lngInteger As Long

On Error GoTo HandleErr

lvwProperties.ListItems.Clear

' Get the Property List interface to the selected node
' The Node's key has the LDAP path in it
Set plstProperties = GetObject(Node.Key)
plstProperties.GetInfo
```

Note the use of the Visual Basic GetObject function here. When you pass an LDAP distinguished name (which, you'll remember, is what the code for this project stores in the Key property of the Node object) to GetObject, it returns one of the AD interfaces to the object that the DN represents. Oddly enough, this capability isn't mentioned in the Visual Basic help files.

Once the code has a reference to the IADsPropertyList interface, the next step is to call the GetInfo method of this interface. GetInfo moves information from AD to a client-side cache. This is necessary to populate the attributes for the use of the rest of the code.

TIP   There's another method, GetInfoEx, which you can call if you only need the values of specific attributes. This is faster than calling GetInfo if you need only a few attributes.

Next, the code has to loop through the list of attributes and move them to the user interface. Here's the looping code:

```
' Step through the entries in the list
For intI = 0 To plstProperties.PropertyCount - 1
    Set pent = plstProperties(intI)
    ' Need to use a variant to use the For Each syntax...
    For Each v In pent.Values
        ' ...but then grab the IADsPropertyValue interface
        Set val = v
        ' Code to handle values omitted here
    Next v
Next intI
```

The IADsPropertyList interface has a default Item method that you can use to retrieve individual IADsPropertyEntry objects from the list. It does not, however, support the _NewEnum interface, so you can't use a For Each loop to retrieve the individual attributes. Instead, you must use a For Next loop, as shown here.

Once you've got an IADsPropertyEntry object, you can look at its Name and Value properties. Name is simple: It returns the name of the object. The code uses this to add a new item to the listview. A listview contains a collection of ListItems, each of which represents one row or icon in the listview. The ListItem object, in turn, has a collection of SubItems, which represent the columns of the list after the first column.

```
Set li = lvwProperties.ListItems.Add(, , pent.Name)
```

The real fun starts when you want to retrieve the value of the attribute. The IADsProperty-Entry interface has a Values property, which returns an array of IADsPropertyValue objects in a variant array. As you can see in the looping code above, you can deal with this array by walking through it with a For Each loop, using a variant variable, but then you need to immediately assign the variant to an IADsPropertyValue object to do any useful work. The loop is necessary because attributes can be multivalued. For example, the objectClass property of a User object will often have four values simultaneously: top, person, organizationalPerson, and user. The code deals with this issue by adding each value as a separate ListItem in the listview.

If you look at the IADsPropertyValue object in the Object Browser, you'll discover that it has many properties. It turns out that the key property here is ADsType. This property returns a constant that indicates which of the other properties of the object is actually set. For example, if ADsType returns ADSTYPE_PRINTABLE_STRING, the PrintableString property of the object contains the value, and the other properties are undefined (and you'll get an error trying to retrieve them). The code handles this by using a Select statement that chooses the right property to display, based on the value of the ADsType property:

```
' Retrieving the data depends on checking the
' type of the value
Select Case val.ADsType
    Case ADSTYPE_INVALID
        li.SubItems(1) = "(Invalid data)"
    Case ADSTYPE_DN_STRING
        li.SubItems(1) = val.DNString
    Case ADSTYPE_CASE_EXACT_STRING
        li.SubItems(1) = val.CaseExactString
    Case ADSTYPE_CASE_IGNORE_STRING
        li.SubItems(1) = val.CaseIgnoreString
    Case ADSTYPE_PRINTABLE_STRING
        li.SubItems(1) = val.PrintableString
    Case ADSTYPE_NUMERIC_STRING
        li.SubItems(1) = val.NumericString
    Case ADSTYPE_BOOLEAN
        If val.Boolean Then
            li.SubItems(1) = "True"
        Else
            li.SubItems(1) = "False"
        End If
```

```
        Case ADSTYPE_INTEGER
            li.SubItems(1) = CStr(val.Integer)
        Case ADSTYPE_OCTET_STRING
            li.SubItems(1) = val.OctetString
        Case ADSTYPE_UTC_TIME
            li.SubItems(1) = val.UTCTime
        Case ADSTYPE_LARGE_INTEGER
            lngHigh = val.LargeInteger.HighPart
            lngLow = val.LargeInteger.LowPart
            If lngHigh = 0 Then
                li.SubItems(1) = CStr(lngLow)
            Else
                li.SubItems(1) = "(" & CStr(lngHigh) & _
                  " * 2^32) + " & CStr(lngLow)
            End If
        Case ADSTYPE_PROV_SPECIFIC
            li.SubItems(1) = "(Provider-specific string)"
        Case ADSTYPE_NT_SECURITY_DESCRIPTOR
            li.SubItems(1) = "(Security descriptor)"
        Case Else
            li.SubItems(1) = "Uninterpreted ADsType " & _
              CStr(val.ADsType)
    End Select
```

Searching for Objects in Active Directory

There's one more piece of functionality included in this example. If you right-click an attribute in the listview on frmADExplorer, you'll get a shortcut menu with the single item Find Similar. Clicking this item will retrieve a list of all objects in the directory that share that value of that particular attribute. For example, Figure 23.4 shows all of the AD objects in my test domain where the objectClass attribute has the value *container*.

For searching, this code uses a second format of the CommandText property of a Record-set from the Microsoft OLE DB Provider for Microsoft Active Directory Service. This format may actually look more familiar, because it's expressed as a SQL SELECT statement:

```
SELECT attributes FROM 'LDAP://DN' [WHERE attribute_expression]
```

In this format:

- attributes is a comma-delimited list of AD attributes to use as fields in the resulting Recordset.

- DN is the distinguished name of the AD node where the search should start. When you use this format, the search always proceeds over the entire AD subtree anchored by this node.

- attribute_expression is an expression built up of attribute=value pairs. You can use the AND and OR Boolean operators to build complex expressions here.

For example, this is the CommandText that generated Figure 23.4:

```
SELECT Name, AdsPath
  FROM 'LDAP://DC=larkgroup,DC=larkfarm,DC=com'
  WHERE objectClass='container'
```

The code to execute this expression starts in the procedure on frmADExplorer that responds to the shortcut menu click:

```
Private Sub mnuShortcutFindSimilar_Click()
    ' Find AD objects with the same attribute-value
    ' combination as the selected object

    Load frmFindSimilar
    frmFindSimilar.WhereClause = _
     lvwProperties.SelectedItem.Text & "='" & _
     lvwProperties.SelectedItem.SubItems(1) & "'"
    frmFindSimilar.Find
    frmFindSimilar.Show

End Sub
```

This code loads the frmFindSimilar form (where the results will be displayed) and sets its WhereClause property to an attribute expression built from the attribute and value displayed in the currently selected ListItem. It then calls the Find method of frmFindSimilar to do the actual work:

```
Public Sub Find()

    Dim cnn As ADODB.Connection
    Dim rst As ADODB.Recordset
    Dim li As ListItem

    On Error GoTo HandleErr

    ' Connect to AD
    Set cnn = New ADODB.Connection
    cnn.Provider = "ADSDSOObject"
    cnn.Open

    ' Open a Recordset on the top-level objects
    ' to find the requested data
    Set rst = New ADODB.Recordset
    rst.Open "SELECT Name, AdsPath FROM 'LDAP://" & _
     frmADExplorer.Root & "' WHERE " & WhereClause, cnn

    lvwResults.ListItems.Clear
    Do Until rst.EOF
        Set li = lvwResults.ListItems.Add(, , rst.Fields("Name").Value)
        li.SubItems(1) = rst.Fields("AdsPath").Value
        rst.MoveNext
    Loop

    lblResults.Caption = "Results for query " & WhereClause

    ' Clean up
    rst.Close
    Set rst = Nothing
    cnn.Close
    Set cnn = Nothing
    Set li = Nothing

ExitHere:
    Exit Sub

HandleErr:
    MsgBox "Error " & Err.Number & ": " & Err.Description, _
     vbOKOnly, "Find"
    Resume ExitHere
    Resume

End Sub
```

This code connects to Active Directory, builds a SQL expression for the CommandText of the Recordset, and then opens the Recordset. Because the SELECT starts at the root node displayed on frmADExplorer, the SELECT will always find all matching nodes in the directory. The code then loops through the Recordset and moves the data from the Recordset to the user interface.

If you try this code, you'll discover that it is quite fast, even on a large Active Directory installation. Finding AD objects that match a particular set of attribute values is probably the best use of ADO in Active Directory–related code. Once you've used ADO to locate the object that you want to work with, you can hand it off to other interfaces such as ADSI.

WARNING   The sample code for searching isn't perfect. In particular, it doesn't handle building proper search strings for attributes that have long integer, Boolean, or other values that are formatted differently for display than for storage.

MySQL

One of the advantages of ADO and OLE DB is that you're not limited to accessing Microsoft databases, or even commercial products. The OLE DB specification is public, meaning that anyone with the time and skills can implement an OLE DB provider. The developers of the free, open-source MySQL database have done precisely that.

MySQL implements a relational database management system under the GNU General Public License (GPL). What that means is that you can download MySQL, including the source code, for free—and use it for free. This can result in substantial cost savings over a commercial database such as SQL Server or Oracle.

MySQL offers a number of impressive features, including these:

- Cross-platform support across many versions of Linux, Unix, Windows, and other operating systems
- Support for databases containing up to at least 60,000 tables and five billion rows of data
- File size limits in the terabyte range (depending on the operating system)
- C, C++, Eiffel, Java, Perl, PHP, Python, and Tcl APIs
- Built-in ODBC support and available OLE DB support

Compared with other databases, though, you'll find some things missing from MySQL:

- The SQL supported is only a subset of ANSI SQL-92. Of course, like any other major database, this is balanced by the existence of MySQL-specific extensions to ANSI SQL.

- No support for transactions (although there are extensions available that implement new table types that support transactions).
- No support for row-level locking.
- No support for views.
- No support for stored procedures or triggers.
- No support for declarative referential integrity (DRI).

NOTE   These lists were correct when this chapter was written. Like most open-source projects, though, MySQL is in a constant state of rapid evolution. For the most current information, check the www.mysql.com website.

Like all databases, MySQL is suitable for some applications and unsuitable for others. There are real-world examples of heavily trafficked websites that store all of their data in MySQL. If you're undertaking a new database project and licensing costs are an issue, it's worthwhile to evaluate MySQL as a possible alternative.

In this section, I'll concentrate on getting MySQL up and running on a Windows system and then show how you can use OLE DB and ADO to perform MySQL operations.

Installing MySQL

To install the MySQL database on a Windows system, follow these steps:

1. Connect to the MySQL downloads page at www.mysql.com/downloads/ and click the Mirrors link. This will allow you to choose a download server close to your own location. Click the download server that you'd like to use.

2. Click the Downloads link on the new server.

3. Click the link for the latest stable version of the database. As of this writing, that is version 3.23.

4. Download the Windows binary version of the MySQL distribution.

5. Go back to the Downloads page and follow the link for Other Win32 Downloads.

6. Download the latest version of MyOLEDB.exe. You may also want to download MyOLEDB.chm, the help file for MyOLEDB.

7. Unzip the files for MySQL itself (downloaded in step 4) and run setup.exe to install MySQL. Do this on the computer that you want to use as a MySQL database server. Unless you have a pressing reason to do otherwise, you should accept the default install

location of c:\mysql. If you install MySQL elsewhere, you'll need to do some additional configuration; check the manual for information on the basedir directive.

8. Run the MyOLEDB.exe installation on the computer that you want to use as a MySQL database client.

NOTE   The companion CD contains version 3.23 of MySQL for Windows. You'll need to download MyOLEDB.

Now that you've installed MySQL, you must initialize it and should also test it. The MySQL documentation includes instructions for doing this from the command line; however, the Windows distribution includes a graphical tool that makes the job easier. Follow these steps to make sure MySQL is installed properly:

1. Run the program c:\mysql\bin\winmysqladmin.exe. This will launch the Quick Setup dialog box shown in Figure 23.5.

FIGURE 23.5:

Quick Setup
dialog box from
winmysqladmin.exe

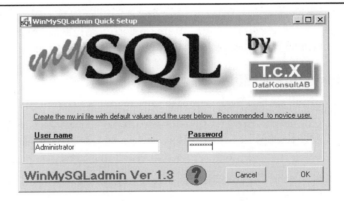

2. Fill in a username and password and then click OK. The username and password that you supply here will be used for administrative privileges by MySQL. One caution: This username and password will be stored in a disk file named my.ini in plain text.

3. WinMySQLadmin will launch and initialize the MySQL server and will place a small stoplight icon in the Windows taskbar. Right-click this icon and choose Show Me to open the WinMySQLadmin interface.

4. Click the Databases tab. You should now see a display similar to that in Figure 23.6, indicating that MySQL has successfully created the mysql and test databases.

5. Right-click anywhere in the application and choose Hide Me to revert the WinMySQL-admin interface to a taskbar icon. (Closing the dialog box will shut down the MySQL server.)

FIGURE 23.6:

Verifying the existence of the mysql and test databases

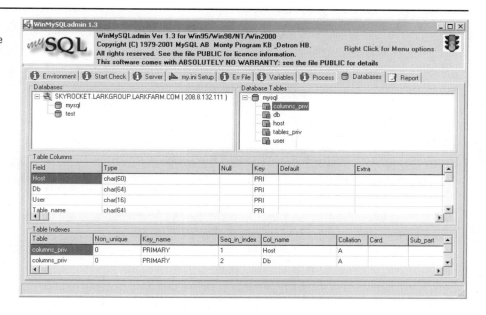

The MySQL documentation contains additional notes on starting MySQL as a service and managing it under various versions of Windows.

One of the nice things about an open-source project like MySQL is that it tends to accumulate contributions from developers. If you browse the Contributed section on the MySQL website's downloads page, you'll find a bunch of interesting stuff. In writing this chapter, I used the mssql2mysql code (`www.kofler.cc/mysql/mssql2mysql.html`) to migrate a copy of the Northwind sample database from SQL Server to MySQL, and it worked fine. Another interesting tool is MySQL Navigator, shown in Figure 23.7. You can download this from `http://sql.kldp.org/mysql/`, although you may find (as I did) that one of the mirror sites offers a faster download.

Connecting to MySQL with OLE DB

The name of the MyOLEDB provider is MySqlProv. This provider can handle connection strings in two different formats:

```
Provider=MySqlProv;Data Source=database;
➡ User ID=username;Password=password;

Provider=MySqlProv;Data Source='server=HostName;DB=database';
➡ User ID=username;Password=password;
```

FIGURE 23.7:

MySQL Navigator

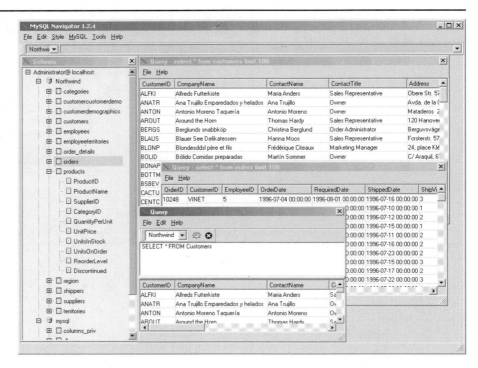

The parameters to the MyOLEDB connection string are as follows:

- *HostName* is the name of the computer where the MySQL server is running. If the server is running on the same computer as the ADO code, you can omit this parameter or use the special name `localhost`.

- *Database* is the name of the MySQL database to use.

- *Username* is the name of the user to log in as.

- *Password* is the password to use to log in.

The frmMySQLConnect form in this chapter's sample project demonstrates connecting to a MySQL server and retrieving the results of a query. This form lets you enter the necessary connection parameters. Figure 23.8 shows this form in action.

By now, the code that does the work behind this form should be perfectly familiar to you. Provided in Listing 23.3, this code builds a connection string from the user interface parameters, then opens the Connection, opens the Recordset, and uses a Hierarchical FlexGrid control to display the results.

Retrieving data from a
MySQL database

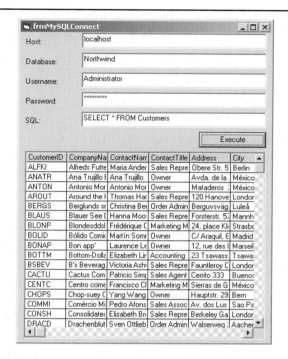

Listing 23.3:   Using ADO to Display MySQL Data

```
Private Sub cmdExecute_Click()

    Dim cnn As ADODB.Connection
    Dim rst As ADODB.Recordset

    On Error GoTo HandleErr

    Set cnn = New ADODB.Connection
    cnn.Open "Provider=MySqlProv;Data Source='server=" & txtHost.Text & _
      ";DB=" & txtDatabase.Text & "';User ID=" & txtUsername.Text & _
      ";Password=" & txtPassword.Text

    Set rst = New ADODB.Recordset
    rst.CursorLocation = adUseServer
    rst.Open txtSQL.Text, cnn
    Set hfgResults.Recordset = rst

    ' Clean up
    rst.Close
    Set rst = Nothing
```

```
        cnn.Close
        Set cnn = Nothing

    ExitHere:
        Exit Sub

    HandleErr:
        MsgBox "Error " & Err.Number & ": " & Err.Description, _
          vbOKOnly, "cmdExecute"
        Resume ExitHere
        Resume

    End Sub
```

Limitations of the MySQL OLE DB Provider

The major limitation of the MySQL OLE DB provider comes from its open-source nature. It appears that the original authors of the provider, SWSoft (www.sw.com.sg/), have ceased development of the provider. That means that bug fixes are currently unlikely. However, because this provider was released under the GPL, it's possible that some other group of developers will pick up where SWSoft left off.

As it currently exists, the MySQL OLE DB provider has uneven support for the various ADO cursor types. This doesn't appear to be documented in the small help file that comes with the provider. However, it's easy enough to determine the rules by running the code in Listing 23.4 (excerpted from the sample project).

Listing 23.4:   **Investigating Cursors with MySQL**

```
    Private Sub cmdMySQLCursors_Click()
        Dim strConn As String
        Dim strSQL As String
        Dim rst As ADODB.Recordset
        Dim intFile As Integer
        Dim intLocation As Integer
        Dim intServer As Integer
        Dim strServerName As String
        Dim intCursorType As Integer
        Dim intLockType As Integer

        On Error Resume Next
        Kill App.Path & "\cursors.txt"
        On Error GoTo HandleErr
        intFile = FreeFile
        Open App.Path & "\cursors.txt" For Output As #intFile
```

```
    Set rst = New ADODB.Recordset

    strConn = "Provider=MySqlProv;Data Source=Northwind;"
    strSQL = "SELECT * FROM Customers"
    strServerName = "MySQL"
    For intLocation = 2 To 3
        Print #intFile, GetLocation(intLocation) & " " & strServerName
        For intCursorType = 0 To 3
            For intLockType = 1 To 4
            rst.CursorLocation = intLocation
                rst.Open strSQL, strConn, intCursorType, intLockType
                Print #intFile, GetCursorType(intCursorType) & " " & _
                GetLockType(intLockType) & vbTab;
                If (intCursorType = rst.CursorType) And _
                 (intLockType = rst.LockType) And _
                 (intLocation = rst.CursorLocation) Then
                    Print #intFile, "Same as requested"
                Else
                    Print #intFile, GetLocation(rst.CursorLocation) & " " & _
                     GetCursorType(rst.CursorType) & " " & _
                     GetLockType(rst.LockType)
                End If
                rst.Close
                Set rst = New ADODB.Recordset
            Next intLockType
        Next intCursorType
        Print #intFile,
    Next intLocation

    Close #intFile

    ' Clean up
    rst.Close
    Set rst = Nothing

ExitHere:
    Exit Sub

HandleErr:
    MsgBox "Error " & Err.Number & ": " & _
     Err.Description, , "cmdMySQLCursors_Click"
    Resume ExitHere
    Resume

End Sub
```

Running this procedure and inspecting the results leads to these conclusions about the provider's cursor support:

- No matter what type of cursor you request on the server, you'll get a dynamic optimistic cursor. That is, once you set the CursorLocation property to adUseServer, the result is a dynamic optimistic cursor. That's true even if you requested a forward-only, read-only, "firehose" cursor.

- If you set the CursorLocation property to adUseClient, you'll get a static cursor no matter what cursor type you request (forward-only, keyset, static, or dynamic). The provider properly supplies read-only, optimistic, and batch optimistic cursors. Pessimistic client-side cursor requests, though, are serviced with batch optimistic cursors, which seems a strange choice.

Table 23.1 provides some additional details about the cursors from the MySQL OLE DB provider. The entries in this table were determined by opening a Recordset and using the Supports method.

TABLE 23.1: Feature Support in MySQL ADO Recordsets

Feature	Server-Side Dynamic Optimistic Cursor	Client-Side Static Optimistic Cursor
Add New	Yes	Yes
Approximate Position	Yes	Yes
Bookmarks	Yes	Yes
Delete	Yes	Yes
Find	Yes	Yes
Hold Records	Yes	Yes
Index	No	No
Move Previous	Yes	Yes
Notify	Yes	Yes
Resync	No	Yes
Seek	Yes	No
Update	Yes	Yes
Batch Update	No	No

NOTE There's an inconsistency in the provider's reporting here: It claims to support Seek on a server-side Recordset, even though it doesn't support setting an index, which is a prerequisite to using Seek. In fact, Seek is not supported.

If you try to call the Connection.BeginTrans, Connection.CommitTrans, or Connection.Rollback Trans method, you'll get an error. That's hardly surprising, given that MySQL itself doesn't support transactions in its base configuration.

Summary

This chapter has, I hope, given you a glimpse of the flexibility of ADO by demonstrating its use with two widely disparate data sources: Microsoft's Active Directory and the open-source MySQL database. On the one hand, ADO is useful for finding resources in an enterprise by searching an LDAP-compliant directory service. On the other hand, ADO can equally well be used with a free database assembled entirely by volunteer developers.

By now, you've been exposed to a good cross section of OLE DB providers: Microsoft Access, Oracle, Microsoft SQL Server, Microsoft Active Directory, and MySQL. Now it's time to turn from the provider to the consumer. In the next section of the book, I'll discuss some of the features that ADO enables in particular client applications, starting with what is perhaps the most widely used ADO client of all, Microsoft Visual Basic.

PART VI

Specific Client Issues

CHAPTER 24

Using ADO from Visual Basic

- Using bound controls to present ADO data

- Using the Data Environment and Data Report

- Data consumers

- Creating an OLE DB provider

I have, of course, used Visual Basic for nearly all the examples that you've seen so far in this book. But from the Visual Basic point of view, those samples have only scratched the surface of Visual Basic's capabilities. Visual Basic 6 is tightly integrated with ADO, and you can do some amazing things with the VB rapid application development (RAD) environment. In this chapter, I'll dig in and show you some of the advanced capabilities of VB 6 when using ADO. I'll start with a review of using simple bound controls to present data on a user interface, and then discuss the Data Environment and Data Report as well as the details of creating your own data consumers and even your own OLE DB providers.

> **WARNING**   Many of the techniques in this chapter don't translate directly to Visual Basic .NET. If you're thinking about implementing a VB/ADO environment, you need to consider when and whether you're going to take that upgrade path before you invest heavily in advanced VB 6 techniques. I'll discuss Visual Basic .NET techniques in Chapter 27, "Using ADO.NET from Visual Basic .NET."

Using Bound Controls to Present ADO Data

Visual Basic popularized the use of *bound controls*, which are user interface widgets that are connected to a data control at design time. All database access is encapsulated within the data control, which acts as a persistent connection to a database for a single form. Historically, bound controls have been frowned on by serious Visual Basic developers. This dates back to Visual Basic 3, where using bound controls with DAO involved serious performance and functionality tradeoffs.

The release of Visual Basic 6, containing a new ADO Data Control, made bound controls a much more appealing development path. This second-generation data control is flexible and fast enough to make serious applications using bound controls a distinct possibility. In this section, I'll look at the ADO Data Control and show you how it can be used to quickly produce some sophisticated data-aware applications.

Using the ADO Data Control

The ADO Data Control provides a way to connect other controls on Visual Basic forms to data via any OLE DB provider. At design time, you set the properties of the control to indicate the desired data source. At runtime, the control makes a connection to the selected provider and retrieves data for other controls on the form. Unless you've hidden it, the ADO Data Control displays buttons for first, last, next, and previous records on the form at runtime, so it can also be used to navigate through the Recordset it has retrieved.

Connecting to Data

As with any other control, the first step when using the ADO Data Control is to place it on a Visual Basic form and set the properties of the control. Don't confuse the ADO Data Control with the standard Data Control that appears by default in the Visual Basic toolbox. You'll have to add this control to the toolbox yourself. The easiest way to do this is to press Ctrl+T and choose Microsoft ADO Data Control 6.0 (OLEDB) from the list of available controls in the Components dialog box. After you've added an ADO Data Control to a form, you can click the builder button for the control's Custom property to open the property pages for the control, shown in Figure 24.1.

FIGURE 24.1:

Property pages for the
ADO Data Control

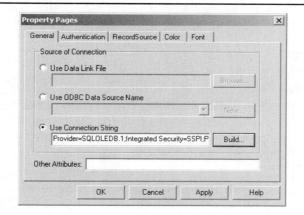

As you can see, there are five tabs in the property pages:

General   Lets you specify the data source to use. This can be a Data Link file, an ODBC data source, or an OLE DB connection string. Data Link files are convenient for applications that connect to a single OLE DB data provider. ODBC connections are useful if you need to connect to an older data source for which an OLE DB provider does not yet exist; if you specify an ODBC file, the data control will use the OLE DB Provider for ODBC to access the data. OLE DB connection strings are most useful if you need to set or alter the properties of the connection in code. This tab also provides a text box where you can enter additional OLE DB attributes to be passed back to the provider.

Authentication   Allows you to specify the username and password that should be used to connect to the OLE DB provider. You can leave this blank if the provider doesn't require this information (for example, if you're using the SQL Server OLE DB provider with integrated security) or if you'd rather supply this information at runtime.

RecordSource   Lets you specify the actual Recordset that this data control will deliver to controls that are bound to the data control. You can choose to supply a table or stored procedure or a SQL statement that returns records. By default, other controls can use the data control to retrieve any Recordset from the data source.

Color   Lets you specify the foreground and background colors that are used to paint the inside of the control at runtime.

Font   Lets you set the font used for the text displayed inside the ADO Data Control.

As soon as you've filled in the General tab of the property pages, you can start binding controls to the data. I'll cover data binding a bit later in the chapter. But first, let's look at some of the other properties of the ADO Data Control.

Creating a Data Link File

One of the problems with the older ODBC standard for connecting to data is that connection information was stored in the Windows Registry, where it was difficult to view and change. (This was fixed in later releases by the introduction of File DSNs.) Data Link files provide a way around this problem for ADO by saving the information necessary to connect to an OLE DB provider into a simple text file.

To create a new Data Link, open Windows Explorer and navigate to the folder where you want to save the file. Right-click in the window and choose New ➤ Text Document. This will create the file and allow you to assign it a name. Choose a name with the extension .udl and confirm the name change. After you've named the file, right-click it and choose Properties—or simply double-click it—to open the Data Link Properties dialog box. This dialog box will let you choose an OLE DB provider and supply other information to connect to the appropriate data source. Once you click OK, you will have created a Data Link file that you can use anywhere in Visual Basic that an OLE DB connection string is expected.

ADO Data Control Properties

Like any other control, the ADO Data Control has a number of standard properties. These properties, such as ToolTipText, Top, Left, and Font, are shared with many other controls, and won't be covered in this book. More important, though, are the data properties that dictate the interaction of the control with its data source. A firm grasp of these properties will help you design applications that use bound controls to retrieve data via ADO.

The BOFAction and EOFAction properties control what happens when the user navigates beyond the beginning or end of the Recordset supplied by the data control. You can set the

BOFAction property to adDoMoveFirst (the default) or adStayBOF. Similarly, you can set the EOFAction property to adDoMoveLast (the default), adStayEOF, or adDoAddNew. If you stick with the defaults, the user can never move outside the retrieved records; they can navigate from one end to the other of the Recordset, but that's it. Setting BOFAction to adStayBOF or EOFAction to adStayEOF allows the user to move "off the end" of the Recordset, with the side effect of validating any changes to the first or last record, but it doesn't allow the user to do anything with the blank record that is displayed. Setting EOF-Action to adDoAddNew automatically adds a new record when the user moves past the end of the Recordset, and then positions the Recordset to that record for editing.

The CacheSize property sets the size of the control's internal cache of records. By default, this is 50; you can set it to any positive long integer. When you first display a form containing an ADO Data Control, it retrieves enough records to fill its internal cache. After this, it doesn't communicate with the server again until the user moves outside the cached records, at which point it will flush the cache and retrieve enough records to fill it again. If there aren't enough records left in the data source to fill the cache, all remaining records are fetched; no error is raised in this case. Data in the cache is kept with the form, so it doesn't reflect any changes other users might make to the data. If you want to make sure the cache contains the latest data, you can call the Resync method of the underlying Recordset. For example, if you have an ADO Data Control named adodcCustomers, you could execute this code:

```
adodcCustomers.Recordset.Resync
```

NOTE   The CacheSize property has no particular effect if you're using client-side cursors, since the client-side cursor engine does its own caching.

The CommandTimeout property sets the maximum number of seconds that the control will wait for data to be returned before giving up and generating an error. By default, this is 30 seconds. You may need to increase the timeout on slow networks, or if you're using the Internet to retrieve data via the Remote Data Service. You can also set this property to zero to force an indefinite wait.

The CommandType property indicates to ADO what the source of the Recordset will be. This is one of the properties that you set on the RecordSource tab of the control's property pages. You can set this to adCmdText to supply a SQL statement as the connection's source, to adCmdTable to supply a table name (in this case, ADO generates its own internal query to return the contents of the table), to adCmdStoredProc to supply a stored procedure name, or to adCmdUnknown if you don't know where the records are coming from. This last choice is useful primarily if you're going to set both the CommandType and CommandText properties at runtime.

The ConnectionString property holds the information that you supply on the General tab of the control's property pages. If you're using a Data Link file, this string will be of this form:

```
FILE NAME=C:\Test\NorthwindSQL.udl
```

If you're using an ODBC data source, this property will have this form:

```
DSN=NorthwindSQL
```

If you're using an OLE DB connection string, this property will contain the full text of the connection string.

The ConnectionTimeout property sets the maximum number of seconds that the control will wait to connect to the data source before giving up and returning an error. By default, this is 15 seconds. You may need to increase the timeout on slow networks, or if you're using the Internet to retrieve data via the Remote Data Service. You can also set this property to zero to force an indefinite wait.

The CursorLocation property controls whether the cursor engine (the part of the data access architecture that returns data) is located on the client or on the server. The possible settings are adUseClient (the default) and adUseServer. Generally, adUseClient is more flexible, but if you need to conserve client-side resources, you may want to switch this to adUseServer. Also, using client-side cursors limits you to using static cursors (see the CursorType property), which may not be what you want.

The CursorType property controls the type of cursor that is used. The default is adOpen-Static, which returns a static set of records that doesn't show changes of any sort by other database users. You can also set this to adOpenKeyset, which will show you changes and deletions, but not additions, by other users, or adOpenDynamic, which shows you all changes that are made by other users.

> **TIP** Don't be confused into thinking that an adOpenStatic cursor represents read-only data. You are quite free to make changes in your copy of the data, and these changes will be saved back to the server (assuming that the data isn't read-only for some other reason).

The LockType property controls the record locking used when you're editing records that are displayed via the ADO Data Control. The default is adLockOptimistic, which (not surprisingly) provides optimistic locking, holding locks only when the record is actually being updated. You can also set this to adLockReadOnly to make your copy of the data read-only; generally, this will consume less resources, and, of course, it prevents users from accidentally altering the data. The adLockPessimistic setting enforces pessimistic locking, which will lock the record as soon as you start updating it. The fourth setting, adLockBatchOptimistic, is used for client-side disconnected Recordsets that may need to be edited when they're not connected to the server. This is the only type of lock that can be used by disconnected Recordsets.

TIP Properties such as CursorLocation, CursorType, and LockType are used by the ADO Data Control to set the corresponding properties of the Recordsets that it retrieves. You can find more information about these properties on Recordsets in Chapter 3, "Using the ADO Objects to Retrieve Data."

The MaxRecords property specifies the maximum number of records that the provider should return from the data source. If you set this to zero, all records are returned without limit. Depending on the OLE DB provider you're using, the MaxRecords property might work by retrieving all records but returning only a certain number of them to the data control. In this case, you won't save any server processing by setting MaxRecords to a small value. You'd be better off limiting the number of records with SET COUNT on the server, a TOP query, or some other server-side means.

The Mode property sets the access permissions on the data. By default, this is set to adMode-Unknown, which indicates that no particular permissions are being requested. Table 24.1 shows the possible settings for the Mode property. You may be able to improve performance by setting the Mode to adModeRead. Setting the Mode property at runtime has no effect if data has already been retrieved by the control.

TABLE 24.1: Settings for the Mode Property

Constant	Description
adModeUnknown	No permissions requested.
adModeRead	Read-only permissions.
adModeWrite	Write-only permissions.
adModeReadWrite	Read/write permissions.
adModeShareDenyRead	Prevents others from opening a connection with read permissions.
adModeShareDenyWrite	Prevents others from opening a connection with write permissions.
adModeShareExclusive	Prevents others from opening a connection at all.
adModeShareDenyNone	Prevents others from opening a connection with any permissions.

The UserName and Password properties supply security settings for the connection to the data source and display the information from the Authentication tab in the control's property pages. You can leave these blank if the provider doesn't require this information or if you want to supply this information at runtime. Remember, if you do provide a password, it will appear in plain text in the control's Password property, and so will be available to anyone who has access to the source code.

The RecordSource property tells the ADO Data Control precisely where to get the data it should display. What you put in this property depends on the setting of the CommandType property. If the CommandType is adCmdText, the RecordSource should be a SQL statement. If the CommandType is adCmdTable, the RecordSource should be a table name (or, with providers that treat views the same as tables, a view name). If the CommandType is adCmdStoredProc, the RecordSource should be a stored procedure name.

For most purposes, you'll probably find that the default settings of these data properties are sufficient. If you need to change or optimize the characteristics of the database connection that's being made, take a look first at the CursorLocation, CursorType, LockType, and Mode properties. If you want to alter the actual data being retrieved, you should be working with the ConnectionString, CommandType, and RecordSource properties instead.

Binding Simple Controls

The ADO Data Control has the ability to bind to any control that has a DataSource property and to display data in that control. This includes not just the controls shipped with Visual Basic, but ActiveX controls from third parties and data-aware UserControls. You can bind any of these controls shipped with the Enterprise Edition of Visual Basic 6 to the ADO Data Control:

- CheckBox
- ComboBox
- DataCombo
- DataGrid
- DataList
- DateTimePicker
- Image
- ImageCombo
- Label
- ListBox
- Microsoft Chart
- Microsoft Hierarchical FlexGrid
- MonthView
- PictureBox
- Rich TextBox
- TextBox

To bind a control to the ADO Data Control, you generally set two properties on the target control. First, set the control's DataSource property to the name of the ADO Data Control. Second, set the control's DataField property to the name of a field in the Recordset supplied by the ADO Data Control. If you set the properties in this order, Visual Basic will helpfully populate the DataField property with a combo box that lets you choose from all available fields.

A Simple Data-Aware Form

For an example of simple data binding, take a look at frmSimpleBound in the ADOChapter24 sample project. Figure 24.2 shows this form.

FIGURE 24.2:

A simple data-bound form

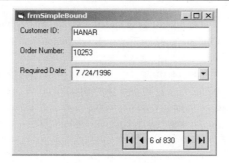

This form contains an ADO Data Control and three bound controls: two text boxes and a date picker. (The date picker, one of the Microsoft Windows Common Controls, provides a calendar-based way to select the value for a date field.) As you navigate through the records by clicking the buttons on the ADO Data Control, you'll find that the data shown in these controls changes as new records are retrieved from the data source. You can also change these values, and the new values will be saved to the data source when you move to another record. The ADO Data Control handles all the necessary calls to the methods of the underlying Recordset to manage these updates.

WARNING   The samples for this section are designed to use the Northwind sample database on a Microsoft SQL Server located on the same computer where the samples are installed. To use the Access version of Northwind, or to use another database server, you'll need to edit the ConnectionString property of the ADO Data Control.

The caption of the ADO Data Control in this sample shows Recordset position information (for example, "6 of 830"). This is not the default behavior; by default, the control's caption is static. To get this dynamic caption, the sample uses the MoveComplete event of the ADO Data Control:

```
Private Sub adodcOrders_MoveComplete( _
  ByVal adReason As ADODB.EventReasonEnum, _
  ByVal pError As ADODB.Error, _
  adStatus As ADODB.EventStatusEnum, _
  ByVal pRecordset As ADODB.Recordset)

    adodcOrders.Caption = _
      adodcOrders.Recordset.AbsolutePosition & " of " & _
      adodcOrders.Recordset.RecordCount

End Sub
```

This event is triggered every time the control is positioned to a new row in the Recordset. Here the code takes advantage of the Recordset property of the ADO Data Control, which returns the underlying ADO Recordset that the control is using to retrieve the data. Once you've retrieved this property, you have complete access to all the ADO Recordset properties and methods. With OLE DB providers that support this functionality (including both the Jet and SQL Server providers), the AbsolutePosition property provides a pretty good indication of where the user is in the Recordset.

WARNING   If you're using the original release of Visual Basic 6, this code sample won't work. If you get an error while trying to run this code, change the last parameter declaration in the event to As ADODB.Recordset20. When Visual Basic creates the event procedure, this parameter will be declared As ADODB.Recordset. You need to make this change manually every time you use an event procedure from the ADO Data Control if that event procedure includes a Recordset object as a parameter. That's because Microsoft changed the Recordset interface between ADO 2.0 (which is the version that the ADO Data Control was compiled with) and ADO 2.5. You can fix this problem permanently by installing the latest Visual Basic service pack, which includes a new version of the ADO Data Control that removes the incompatibility. As of this writing, the most recent service pack for Visual Basic is SP5, which you can download from http://msdn.microsoft.com/vstudio/sp/vs6sp5/default.asp.

The DataList and DataCombo Controls

The DataList and DataCombo controls are designed to help you easily present relational data on a form. Each of these controls can connect to two data sources: one that supplies items for the list of available choices and one that stores the chosen item. These controls are used on frmDatalist in the ADOChapter24 sample project, shown in Figure 24.3.

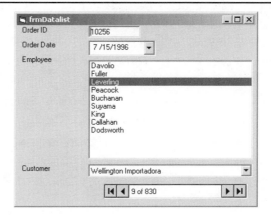

NOTE   If you browse the Components list (from the Project ➤ Components menu) on a computer that has a variety of recent Microsoft software installed, you'll probably find several libraries of data-bound list controls. The library that comes with Visual Basic and is used in this section is called Microsoft DataList Controls 6 (OLEDB).

Because they shuttle data from one table to another, the DataList and DataCombo controls require two ADO Data Controls each. One control supplies the data for the list, and the other tells the list where to save the bound value. There are five essential properties you need to set for these controls:

DataSource   Specifies the name of the ADO Data Control that contains the bound values. This is typically the one side of a one-to-many relationship.

BoundColumn   Specifies the name of the field in the data source to which values are saved.

RowSource   Specifies the name of the ADO Data Control that supplies the list of possible values. This is typically the many side of a one-to-many relationship.

DataField   Specifies the name of the field that actually contains the data to be saved. This is the field that's the same in both tables.

ListField   Specifies the name of the field that should be displayed in the list portion of the DataList or DataCombo. By using different fields for ListField and DataField, you can save a numeric ID while still displaying user-friendly information. Of course, if the RowSource is a view rather than a table, you can also use a calculated field for the ListField.

Figure 24.4 shows these properties for the DataCombo on the sample form. You can think of the DataCombo as a control that takes values from the DataField of the RowSource and stores them in the BoundColumn of the DataSource.

FIGURE 24.4:

Properties for the Customer DataCombo

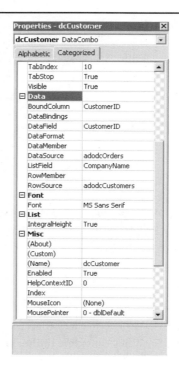

> **NOTE**   Although Figure 24.4 displays only a single ADO Data Control, there are actually three such controls on the form, which you can verify by opening it in Design View. The ADO Data Controls that connect to the Employee and Customer tables have their Visible property set to False, since they are used only by the DataList and DataCombo controls, not directly by the user.

The DataGrid Control

Visual Basic 6 also includes the DataGrid control—more formally, the Microsoft DataGrid Control 6 (OLEDB). This control is useful when you want to display the contents of an entire Recordset in a pseudo-spreadsheet form. No matter how much you explain that databases and spreadsheets are different animals, some users persist in wanting that old familiar grid display. This control, shown in Figure 24.5, fills that need nicely.

FIGURE 24.5:

The DataGrid control in action

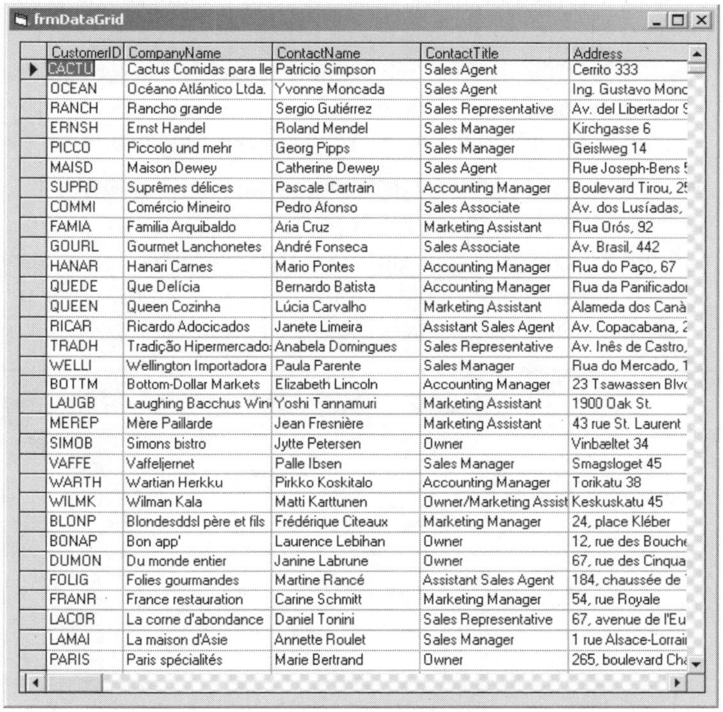

CustomerID	CompanyName	ContactName	ContactTitle	Address
CACTU	Cactus Comidas para lle	Patricio Simpson	Sales Agent	Cerrito 333
OCEAN	Océano Atlántico Ltda.	Yvonne Moncada	Sales Agent	Ing. Gustavo Monc
RANCH	Rancho grande	Sergio Gutiérrez	Sales Representative	Av. del Libertador S
ERNSH	Ernst Handel	Roland Mendel	Sales Manager	Kirchgasse 6
PICCO	Piccolo und mehr	Georg Pipps	Sales Manager	Geislweg 14
MAISD	Maison Dewey	Catherine Dewey	Sales Agent	Rue Joseph-Bens 5
SUPRD	Suprêmes délices	Pascale Cartrain	Accounting Manager	Boulevard Tirou, 25
COMMI	Comércio Mineiro	Pedro Afonso	Sales Associate	Av. dos Lusíadas,
FAMIA	Familia Arquibaldo	Aria Cruz	Marketing Assistant	Rua Orós, 92
GOURL	Gourmet Lanchonetes	André Fonseca	Sales Associate	Av. Brasil, 442
HANAR	Hanari Carnes	Mario Pontes	Accounting Manager	Rua do Paço, 67
QUEDE	Que Delícia	Bernardo Batista	Accounting Manager	Rua da Panificador
QUEEN	Queen Cozinha	Lúcia Carvalho	Marketing Assistant	Alameda dos Canà
RICAR	Ricardo Adocicados	Janete Limeira	Assistant Sales Agent	Av. Copacabana, 2
TRADH	Tradição Hipermercado:	Anabela Domingues	Sales Representative	Av. Inês de Castro,
WELLI	Wellington Importadora	Paula Parente	Sales Manager	Rua do Mercado, 1
BOTTM	Bottom-Dollar Markets	Elizabeth Lincoln	Accounting Manager	23 Tsawassen Blvd
LAUGB	Laughing Bacchus Win	Yoshi Tannamuri	Marketing Assistant	1900 Oak St.
MEREP	Mère Paillarde	Jean Fresnière	Marketing Assistant	43 rue St. Laurent
SIMOB	Simons bistro	Jytte Petersen	Owner	Vinbæltet 34
VAFFE	Vaffeljernet	Palle Ibsen	Sales Manager	Smagsloget 45
WARTH	Wartian Herkku	Pirkko Koskitalo	Accounting Manager	Torikatu 38
WILMK	Wilman Kala	Matti Karttunen	Owner/Marketing Assist	Keskuskatu 45
BLONP	Blondesddsl père et fils	Frédérique Citeaux	Marketing Manager	24, place Kléber
BONAP	Bon app'	Laurence Lebihan	Owner	12, rue des Bouche
DUMON	Du monde entier	Janine Labrune	Owner	67, rue des Cinqua
FOLIG	Folies gourmandes	Martine Rancé	Assistant Sales Agent	184, chaussée de
FRANR	France restauration	Carine Schmitt	Marketing Manager	54, rue Royale
LACOR	La corne d'abondance	Daniel Tonini	Sales Representative	67, avenue de l'Eu
LAMAI	La maison d'Asie	Annette Roulet	Sales Manager	1 rue Alsace-Lorrai
PARIS	Paris spécialités	Marie Bertrand	Owner	265, boulevard Cha

The basic DataGrid is ridiculously simple to set up. All you need to do is place both a DataGrid and an ADO Data Control on the same form, set the data control's properties, and then set the DataGrid's DataSource property to the name of the data control. That's it! The form will display all the data from the table in rows and columns, and allow you to edit values directly in the cells. Note that in the ADOChapter24 sample project, the ADO Data Control has its Visible property set to False, because you can navigate in the Recordset by selecting cells in the grid or using the grid's scroll bars.

The DataGrid is a complex control with many other capabilities. Here are a few of them:

- At runtime, the user can resize either rows or columns by dragging the separator lines with the mouse. If the rows are tall enough, text in a cell will automatically word-wrap, but only while the cell is being edited.
- The user can move from cell to cell with the arrow keys if the AllowArrows property of the control is set to True.
- You can control the user's ability to change data with three Boolean properties: AllowAddNew, AllowDelete, and AllowUpdate. If you set all three of these properties

to False, the grid becomes a read-only view of the data, and is thus safe to turn almost anyone else loose on.

- The DataGrid supports 35 different events that let you react to user editing and navigation actions. You can determine in its object model exactly which data is being changed, and verify or modify it before the data is returned to the data source.

- You can set the font, border, and word wrap properties for each column independently.

- The user can split the DataGrid into multiple views (called splits) at runtime by clicking and dragging the split tab, the small vertical bar to the left of the DataGrid's horizontal scroll bar. Figure 24.6 demonstrates how a split DataGrid lets you see widely separated columns in a single Recordset. You can also control and create splits programatically.

FIGURE 24.6:

A split DataGrid control

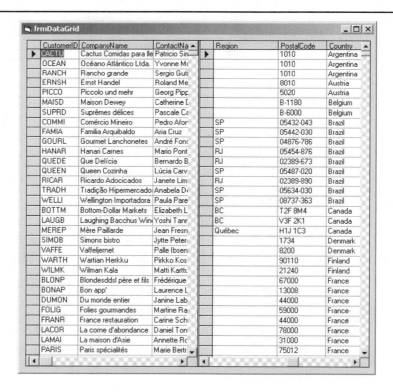

NOTE   If you'd like to learn how to create splits in the DataGrid programatically, refer to the Visual Basic help files. However, before you go too far down that road, you should take a look at the Hierarchical FlexGrid. You may find that this newer control is capable of all the display flexibility you need without the bother of programming splits.

The Data Form Wizard

Building simple data forms can get tedious. Fortunately, Visual Basic 6 includes a tool to make it easier: the Data Form Wizard. To make this wizard available to your copy of Visual Basic, choose Add-Ins ➤ Add-In Manager and select the VB 6 Data Form Wizard as an add-in to be loaded. You may also want to choose to load it on startup to make it available every time you launch Visual Basic.

Once the wizard is loaded, you can launch it by choosing Add-Ins ➤ Data Form Wizard. This will bring up a standard wizard interface. The first panel asks what profile you want to use. A profile is a list of saved settings from a previous use of the wizard. If this is the first time you've used the wizard, you won't have a saved profile, so just click Next.

The next step is to choose a database format. Even though there are a bunch of choices available to you on any VB 6 machine for OLE DB providers, the only choices here are Access and Remote(ODBC). Choosing the former results in a connection string that uses the Jet 3.51 OLE DB provider. Choosing the latter results in a connection through the OLE DB provider for ODBC data sources. Neither of these is really what you want in most cases. Usually, your best choice here is to pick the Remote(ODBC) format and reconfigure the ADO Data Controls that the wizard creates in order to use the appropriate OLE DB provider after the form has been created.

Assuming you choose to create an ODBC connection, the next step is to provide connection information. You can either supply an existing ODBC DSN or supply the necessary information (User ID, Password, Database, Driver, and Server) to allow a DSN-less ODBC connection. This tab verifies the database connection settings you enter before continuing. Note that you cannot create a new DSN from this wizard panel, so if you don't know all your connection information by heart and haven't created a DSN in the past, you'll need to abort here, create the DSN, and restart the wizard.

The next step is to name the form and pick a layout. You can choose from five form layouts:

Single Record　Creates a form with individual controls for each column in the record source. This form will display a single row of data at a time.

Grid (Datasheet)　Uses the DataGrid to display the records on the form.

Master/Detail　Joins several tables to present "drill-down" information on a single form.

MS HFlexGrid　Uses the Hierarchical FlexGrid control to display the data. (This control is covered later in this chapter.)

MS Chart　Uses the Microsoft Chart control to display graphical summaries of the data. This layout isn't especially useful for most database applications, and isn't covered here.

You can also choose the binding type to use on this page. Depending on the layout you choose, you'll have a choice of using the ADO Data Control, straight ADO Code, or a Class module. All the examples in this chapter use the ADO Data Control.

The next panel of the wizard lets you select a record source for your data form and then fields from that record source. You can also choose a single field (column) to sort the records by. The wizard will build a SQL statement based on your choices.

The next panel lets you choose which buttons the wizard should create on the form. You have seven choices here:

Add   Adds new records to the database.

Update   Immediately saves any data changes in the current record back to the database.

Edit   Allows editing the current record. You won't see this option unless you base your form on ADO Code. The ADO Data Control automatically allows editing with no further user interaction.

Delete   Deletes the current record.

Refresh   Requeries the database to get any changes made to the current record while it has been displayed. This button makes sense only if the data source is multiuser.

Close   Closes the form.

Show Data Control   Makes the ADO Data Control visible. (This choice applies only to forms that use the Grid (Datasheet) layout.)

The final screen of the wizard lets you choose a profile name to save the settings you just used. This is useful if either you're going to need to create the same form many times in different applications or you're going to try the form and then possibly make some slight adjustments. The form is then created and added to the current project.

Single Record Forms

Figure 24.7 shows a single record form created by the Data Form Wizard. It's based on the Customers table in the Northwind database and is included in the ADOChapter24 sample project as frmWizardSingleRecord, exactly as it was created by the wizard.

In addition to building the form and its controls, the Data Form Wizard creates some code, most of it tied to events of the ADO Data Control. This code is helpfully commented to allow you to customize it for your own application. The wizard writes procedures for the following events:

- The Error event has a hook for trapping data errors in general.
- The MoveComplete event updates the record counter at the bottom of the form.

A single record form

- The WillChangeRecord event lets you validate data before it's saved to the database. The code that the wizard creates shows you how you can use the adReason argument of this event to validate only in response to certain actions, while ignoring others:

```
Private Sub datPrimaryRS_WillChangeRecord( _
ByVal adReason As ADODB.EventReasonEnum, _
ByVal cRecords As Long, _
adStatus As ADODB.EventStatusEnum, _
ByVal pRecordset As ADODB.Recordset)
  'This is where you put validation code
  'This event gets called when the following actions occur
  Dim bCancel As Boolean

  Select Case adReason
  Case adRsnAddNew
  Case adRsnClose
  Case adRsnDelete
  Case adRsnFirstChange
  Case adRsnMove
  Case adRsnRequery
  Case adRsnResynch
  Case adRsnUndoAddNew
  Case adRsnUndoDelete
  Case adRsnUndoUpdate
  Case adRsnUpdate
  End Select

  If bCancel Then adStatus = adStatusCancel
End Sub
```

The wizard also writes code for all the buttons it creates:

- The Add button calls the Recordset's AddNew method.
- The Delete button calls the Recordset's Delete method and then makes sure that a valid record is displayed.
- The Refresh button calls the data control's Refresh method.
- The Update button calls the Recordset's UpdateBatch method.
- The Close button calls the Form's Unload method.

Grid Forms

Figure 24.8 shows a grid form created by the Data Form Wizard. As you can see, it's very similar to the single record form, except that it uses a DataGrid control rather than a series of text boxes to display the data. This form is saved in the ADOChapter24 sample project as frmWizardGrid.

The grid form also includes a bit more code than the single record form:

- The Form_Resize event is used to automatically adjust the size of the grid itself to fill the bulk of the form. This is an easy way to let the user adjust the view for different video settings or working conditions.
- The code for the Add button uses a hack: It sends the focus to the last row in the grid and then uses SendKeys to send a Down arrow, thus forcing the focus onto the new record row. This is necessary because the grid doesn't have a method for adding a new record programmatically.

Master/Detail Forms

Master/Detail forms, such as the one shown in Figure 24.9, are ideal for displaying both halves of a one-to-many relationship. For example, the master section might display customers one at a time, while the detail section displays the orders for the selected customer. Or the master section might display orders, while the detail section displays the order detail for the selected order. There's a sample Master/Detail form saved in the ADOChapter24 sample project as frmWizardMasterDetail.

FIGURE 24.9:

Master/Detail form created by the Data Form Wizard

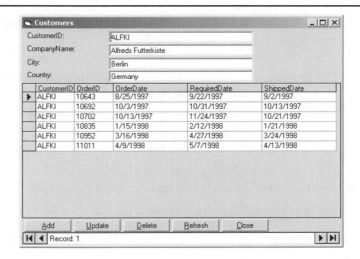

Building a Master/Detail form requires making a couple more choices in the wizard. You'll see the Select Record Source panel of the wizard twice, since you have to tell the wizard which records to use for the master part of the form and which records to use for the detail part of the form. When you've selected both record sources, the wizard will prompt you to select the joining fields so that it can keep the information synchronized.

WARNING   Be sure to select the joining fields as fields to display on the form. Otherwise, you'll get a runtime error when you try to open the form.

The wizard creates a form that uses the OLE DB MSDataShape Provider to retrieve data from the data source. Not surprisingly, the MSDataShape Provider returns *data shapes*, which are most easily thought of as hierarchical Recordsets. The simplest data shape has a parent Recordset that includes a field in each row that is actually a pointer to a child Recordset. When you retrieve the parent row, the child Recordset is automatically constructed and made available. See Chapter 7, "Data Shaping," for much more detail on shaped Recordsets.

Programming the ADO Data Control

Now that you've seen several ways of using the ADO Data Control on a form, it's time to look at what you can do with it programmatically. You had a taste of this when you looked at the wizard-generated code, and the important properties of the control were covered earlier in the chapter. Now let's take a more systematic look at the methods and events supported by the ADO Data Control.

The Refresh Method

There's only one data-related method of the ADO Data Control: the Refresh method. (The control also has some of the standard VB methods, such as Drag, Move, and ZOrder, shared by many controls; those simple visual methods aren't covered in this book.)

The Refresh method of the ADO Data Control essentially tells the control to throw away all the data it has loaded and get all its data anew from the underlying OLE DB provider. There are two main reasons why you might want to use this method:

- The data in the database might actually have changed. This is the case in multiuser applications, and is the reason that the Data Form Wizard puts a Refresh button on the form.

- The properties of the control might have changed. This happens, for example, when you switch a control from one database to another by changing its ConnectionString property.

You need to call the Refresh method for these two cases, but you shouldn't call it more than necessary, since each trip to the server for more data obviously consumes time and system resources.

Events

Although the ADO Data Control shares several events with other controls, the interesting events for ADO programming are the data-related ones. These include the following:

- EndOfRecordset
- Error
- WillMove
- MoveComplete
- WillChangeField
- FieldChangeComplete
- WillChangeRecord
- RecordChangeComplete
- WillChangeRecordset
- RecordsetChangeComplete

Except for the first two, these events fall neatly into "before" and "after" pairs. Let's look at each of them in more detail. The Events form in the ADOChapter24 sample project has message boxes attached to each event to allow you to see in detail when they occur.

You can review the code from this section in the frmEvents form in the ADOChapter24 sample project. That form also contains additional code to prevent the WillMove and MoveComplete events from being fired before the form is fully loaded. If you try to do anything in these events before the form is fully loaded, you'll get data binding errors.

The EndOfRecordset event is called whenever the user navigates past the end of the Recordset in either direction (that is, by going to the previous record from the first record or by going to the next record from the last record). This event occurs before the Recordset is actually repositioned. The event procedure for this event has three arguments, as shown in this example:

```
Private Sub adodcNwind_EndOfRecordset( _
  fMoreData As Boolean, _
  adStatus As ADODB.EventStatusEnum, _
  ByVal pRecordset As ADODB.Recordset)
    Dim intReply As Integer
    intReply = MsgBox("EndOfRecordset event. " & _
     "Do you want to see this event in the future?", _
     vbYesNo)
    If intReply = vbNo Then
        adStatus = adStatusUnwantedEvent
    End If
End Sub
```

The fMoreData argument is used by ADO. If you actually add more records to the Recordset while in this event, you need to set this argument to True.

The adStatus argument is both passed in by ADO and used on its return. This argument will be adStatusOK if the move was successful, or adStatusCantDeny if the move was successful and cannot be cancelled. In addition, you can set this argument to adStatusUnwantedEvent to prevent this event from firing in the future. In cancellable events such as WillMove, you can set this argument to adCancel to tell ADO not to permit the action that caused the event to fire in the first place.

The pRecordset argument contains the actual Recordset that's being manipulated. You can use this argument or the ADO Data Control's Recordset property interchangeably, if you want to work with the underlying data.

The Error event is triggered whenever an OLE DB or ADO error occurs that's not directly caused by your own Visual Basic code. For example, if you change a record and then move to another record using the ADO Data Control (which would automatically save your changes), but the underlying database record is locked by another user, it will raise the Error event. This event comes with a bunch of arguments, nearly all of which just pass information on from the underlying error:

```
Private Sub adodcNwind_Error(ByVal ErrorNumber As Long, _
  Description As String, ByVal Scode As Long, _
  ByVal Source As String, ByVal HelpFile As String, _
  ByVal HelpContext As Long, fCancelDisplay As Boolean)
    Dim intReply As Integer
    intReply = MsgBox("An ADO Error has occured. " & _
     "The error number is " & ErrorNumber & ". The " & _
     "error description is """ & Description & """. " & _
     "The " & _
     "error code on the server is " & Scode & ". The " & _
     "source of the error is """ & Source & """. " & _
     "Do you wish " & _
     "to display the default message?", vbYesNo)
    If intReply = vbNo Then
        fCancelDisplay = True
    End If
End Sub
```

Note that if you don't set the fCancelDisplay argument to True during your procedure, the ADO Data Control will proceed to display its own message after this event procedure is executed.

The WillMove and MoveComplete events are triggered by moving through the Recordset. You'll see the WillMove event before any move, whether the move is to the first record, the last record, or any other record. You can cancel the WillMove event, but even if you do, you'll still get the MoveComplete event. The MoveComplete event is fired whenever you either move successfully to another record or cancel a move in the WillMove event. Here's some code from the frmEvents sample form:

```
Private Sub adodcNwind_MoveComplete( _
  ByVal adReason As ADODB.EventReasonEnum, _
  ByVal pError As ADODB.Error, _
  adStatus As ADODB.EventStatusEnum, _
  ByVal pRecordset As ADODB.Recordset)
    MsgBox "mc"
    If Not mfLoaded Then
        Exit Sub
    End If
    adodcNwind.Caption = _
     adodcNwind.Recordset.AbsolutePosition & " of " & _
     adodcNwind.Recordset.RecordCount
End Sub
```

```
Private Sub adodcNwind_WillMove( _
  ByVal adReason As ADODB.EventReasonEnum, _
  adStatus As ADODB.EventStatusEnum, _
  ByVal pRecordset As ADODB.Recordset)
    Dim intReply As Integer
    intReply = MsgBox("cancel wm", vbYesNo)
    If intReply = vbNo Then
        adStatus = adStatusCancel
    End If
End Sub
```

The WillChangeField and FieldChangeComplete events bracket any change you make to the data in any field that's being retrieved via this data control. Here are the definitions for those two events, taken from the frmEvents form in the ADOChapter24 sample project:

```
Private Sub adodcNwind_WillChangeField( _
  ByVal cFields As Long, _
  Fields As Variant, _
  adStatus As ADODB.EventStatusEnum, _
  ByVal pRecordset As ADODB.Recordset)
    Dim intReply As Integer
    intReply = MsgBox("Cancel WillChangeField?", vbYesNo)
    If intReply = vbYes Then
        adStatus = adStatusCancel
    End If
End Sub

Private Sub adodcNwind_FieldChangeComplete( _
  ByVal cFields As Long, _
  Fields As Variant, _
  ByVal pError As ADODB.Error, _
  adStatus As ADODB.EventStatusEnum, _
  ByVal pRecordset As ADODB.Recordset)
    MsgBox "FieldChangeComplete"
End Sub
```

In these events, the cFields argument tells you how many fields have changes pending, and the Fields argument is an array of ADO Field objects representing those fields. These events can be triggered by anything that sets the Value property of a field, whether that's typing directly into a bound control or altering a field's Value through code.

The WillChangeRecord and RecordChangeComplete events fire any time you're making a change to a record. (This includes making a change to a field; thus, you'll typically see the WillChangeField and WillChangeRecord events occur together.) Here are the procedures for the WillChangeRecord and RecordChangeComplete events:

```
Private Sub adodcNwind_WillChangeRecord( _
  ByVal adReason As ADODB.EventReasonEnum, _
```

```
  ByVal cRecords As Long, _
  adStatus As ADODB.EventStatusEnum, _
  ByVal pRecordset As ADODB.Recordset)
    Dim intReply As Integer
    intReply = MsgBox( _
     "Cancel WillChangeRecord?", vbYesNo)
    If intReply = vbYes Then
        adStatus = adStatusCancel
    End If
End Sub

  Private Sub adodcNwind_RecordChangeComplete( _
  ByVal adReason As ADODB.EventReasonEnum, _
  ByVal cRecords As Long, _
  ByVal pError As ADODB.Error, _
  adStatus As ADODB.EventStatusEnum, _
  ByVal pRecordset As ADODB.Recordset)
    MsgBox "RecordChangeComplete"
End Sub
```

In these events, the EventReasonEnum argument tells you why the event was fired. It can be one of these values:

- adRsnAddNew if a record was added

- adRsnDelete if a record was deleted

- adRsnUpdate if a call to the Update method generated this event

- adRsnUndoUpdate if an Update was undone

- adRsnUndoAddNew if an Add New operation was undone

- adRsnUndoDelete if a Delete operation was undone

- adRsnFirstChange if a field in the record was changed for the first time

In these events, the cRecords argument is set to the number of records with pending changes. The passed Recordset is filtered to hold only the records with pending changes. Because VB itself is using the Filter property, it causes an error to try to change the value of that property during one of these events.

The WillChangeRecordset and RecordsetChangeComplete events surround changes to the overall Recordset contents:

```
  Private Sub adodcNwind_WillChangeRecordset( _
  ByVal adReason As ADODB.EventReasonEnum, _
  adStatus As ADODB.EventStatusEnum, _
  ByVal pRecordset As ADODB.Recordset)
    Dim intReply As Integer
```

```
        intReply = MsgBox( _
          "Cancel WillChangeRecordset?", vbYesNo)
        If intReply = vbYes Then
            adStatus = adStatusCancel
        End If
    End Sub

    Private Sub adodcNwind_RecordsetChangeComplete( _
      ByVal adReason As ADODB.EventReasonEnum, _
      ByVal pError As ADODB.Error, _
      adStatus As ADODB.EventStatusEnum, _
      ByVal pRecordset As ADODB.Recordset)
        MsgBox "RecordsetChangeComplete"
    End Sub
```

In these events, the adReason argument again tells you why the event was fired, but it takes on a different set of values:

- adRsnRequery if the Requery method was called

- adRsnResynch if the Resynch method was called

- adRsnClose if the Recordset was closed

- adRsnOpen if the Recordset is newly opened

Using the Hierarchical FlexGrid Control

The final data-bound control that I'll cover in this section is the Hierarchical FlexGrid control. This control, new to Visual Basic 6, is designed to show hierarchical data from multiple tables in a single read-only control.

Figure 24.10 shows the frmFlexgrid control in the ADOChapter24 sample project. This form uses the Hierarchical FlexGrid control to display information from a single view based on the Northwind Customers, Orders, Order Details, and Products tables. Although the form doesn't allow data editing, it is moderately interactive: It allows the user to drag columns to rearrange them. If the user drags a column, the hierarchy and sorting are automatically recalculated by the form.

Although this form appears to display a hierarchical Recordset, it's actually displaying a single Recordset based on a view. The illusion of hierarchy comes about because the Hierarchical FlexGrid in this case is set to merge adjacent cells in the same column (for instance, the cells in the CompanyName column) that contain the same value.

This form involves two controls, an ADO Data Control and a Hierarchical FlexGrid control. The ADO Data Control has its Visible property set to False, because the entire Recordset is visible at one time in the grid.

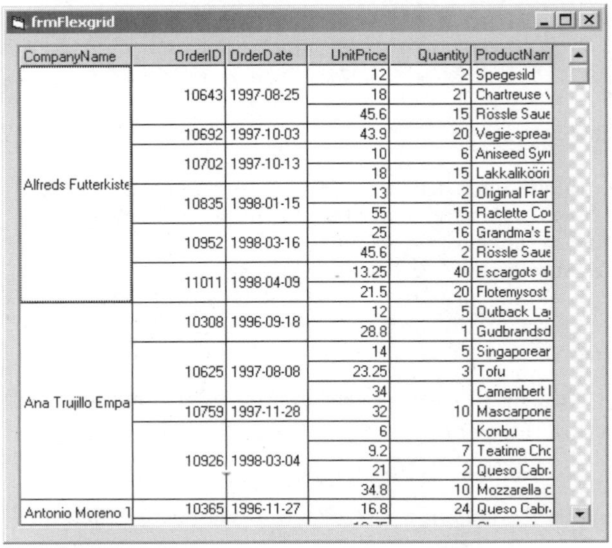

FIGURE 24.10:

Example of a Hierarchical FlexGrid form

The ADO Data Control has its connection set to point to a local copy of the SQL Server Northwind sample database. The CommandType property of this control is set to adCmd-Text, and the CommandText property is set as follows:

```
SELECT Customers.CompanyName, Orders.OrderID,
    Orders.OrderDate, [Order Details].UnitPrice,
    [Order Details].Quantity, Products.ProductName
FROM (((Customers INNER JOIN
    Orders ON
    Customers.CustomerID = Orders.CustomerID) INNER JOIN
    [Order Details] ON
    Orders.OrderID = [Order Details].OrderID) INNER JOIN
    Products ON [Order Details].ProductID = Products.ProductID)
```

Most of the properties of the Hierarchical FlexGrid are at their default settings in this example. These properties are not at their default settings:

- *AllowUserResizing* is set to flexResizeBoth. This allows the user to resize both rows and columns by clicking and dragging with the mouse.

- *DataSource* is set to adodcNorthwind, the name of the ADO Data Control, to bind the grid automatically to the data source.

- *FixedCols* is set to 0, to suppress the blank selection column that normally displays at the left edge of the grid.

- *MergeCells* is set to flexMergeFree, to allow the control to merge adjacent cells that have the same value. This is the setting that makes the grid display the "outline" look.

In addition to setting the MergeCells property, if you want cells to be merged, you need to tell the control what it is allowed to merge. In the ADOChapter24 sample project, there's code in the Form Load event to do this:

```
Private Sub Form_Load()
    Dim intI As Integer
    For intI = 0 To MSHFlexGrid1.Cols - 1
        MSHFlexGrid1.MergeCol(intI) = True
    Next intI
    SortGrid
End Sub
```

The MergeCol property is an array with one entry for each column in the grid. If you set MergeCol for a particular column to True, the control will merge rows in that column that contain identical values. There is a similar MergeRow property that can be used to tell the control to merge identical columns within a particular row.

This form is designed to sort the data on the Hierarchical FlexGrid control. It does so by taking advantage of the built-in sorting capabilities of the control:

```
Public Sub SortGrid()
    With MSHFlexGrid1
        .Col = 0
        .ColSel = .Cols - 1
        .Sort = 1
    End With
End Sub
```

Setting the Col property tells the grid which column to begin the sort with; setting the ColSel property tells the grid which column to end the sort with (columns in the grid have a zero-based numbering). Setting the Sort property to 1 triggers a left-to-right ascending sort—in this case, on the CompanyName column.

There's also code behind this form to enable the column dragging:

```
Private Sub MSHFlexGrid1_MouseDown(Button As Integer, _
  Shift As Integer, x As Single, y As Single)
    With MSHFlexGrid1
        .Tag = ""
        If .MouseRow <> 0 Then
            Exit Sub
        End If
        .Tag = Str(.MouseCol)
        .MousePointer = vbSizeWE
    End With
End Sub

Private Sub MSHFlexGrid1_MouseUp(Button As Integer, _
  Shift As Integer, x As Single, y As Single)
    With MSHFlexGrid1
```

```
            .MousePointer = vbDefault
            If .Tag = "" Then
                Exit Sub
            End If
            .Redraw = False
            .ColPosition(Val(.Tag)) = .MouseCol
            SortGrid
            .Redraw = True
        End With
    End Sub
```

When the user clicks the primary mouse button, the MouseDown code first checks to see whether the user is on the header row of the grid. If so, the Tag property of the grid is set to the column that's being dragged and the mouse pointer is set to a two-headed arrow. In the corresponding MouseUp event, if the Tag property has a value, you know it's time to rearrange and re-sort the data. Setting the ColPosition property of the dragged column to the new mouse position moves that column, and calling the SortGrid procedure re-sorts the data.

Using the Data Environment and Data Report

Early versions of Visual Basic used only forms and modules to create programs. One of the major advances of Visual Basic since then has been the introduction of additional designers. A Visual Basic designer provides a way to manipulate an object and its code within Visual Basic projects—for example, forms are handled by the Forms Designer. Among the new designers in Visual Basic 6 are the Data Environment Designer and the Data Report Designer.

The Data Environment Designer creates and manipulates Data Environment objects, which represent ADO connections and commands. A single Data Environment can contain multiple connections and multiple commands within those connections. You can also attach code to events of objects contained within the Data Environment, just as you can to events of forms within the Forms Designer.

To create a new Data Environment, choose Project ➤ Add Data Environment from the Visual Basic menus, or choose Data Environment from the New Object dropdown button on the Visual Basic standard toolbar. This will create, by default, Data Environment1, containing a connection object named Connection1.

Creating Connections

When you create a new Data Environment, it isn't connected to any particular data source, since Visual Basic doesn't know what you want to do with it. But there is a blank Connection object within the Data Environment just waiting to be connected.

Like any other object within a designer, Connection objects within the Data Environment Designer have properties that show in the Visual Basic properties window. You can dictate which data source a Connection object will use by setting these familiar properties:

- Attributes
- CommandTimeout
- ConnectionSource (this property holds an OLE DB connection string)
- ConnectionTimeout
- CursorLocation (by default, Data Environment connections use client-side cursors)

However, there's an easier way to hook up a connection than composing the OLE DB connection string by hand. Right-click the Connection object within the designer and select Properties, or click the Connection object within the designer and click the Properties button on the designer's toolbar. Either action will open the familiar Data Link Properties dialog box, which allows you to choose an OLE DB provider and set other connection properties.

Of course, you don't have to accept the default name for the Connection object (and probably shouldn't, since more descriptive names are easier to grasp in code). You can assign a name to the object by changing the Name property directly in the object's property sheet, by slowly double-clicking the object and typing a new name, or by right-clicking the object and choosing Rename to specify your own name for the connection.

Connection objects in the Data Environment have two sets of security properties, one for design time and one for runtime. If you use the Categorized tab of the Visual Basic properties window, it's easy to see these two sets of properties. There are four Design Authentication properties:

DesignPassword   Holds the password to use at design time.

DesignPromptBehavior   Specifies when to prompt the user for logon information, and can be set to adPromptAlways, adPromptComplete, adPromptCompleteRequired, or adPromptNever. These correspond to values of the Prompt property on the underlying ADO Connection object.

DesignSaveAuthentication   Tells the designer whether to save the values of Design-Password and DesignUserName in the files that hold the Data Environment Connection object's definition. By default, this property is set to False.

DesignUserName   Holds the username to use at design time.

There are also four Runtime Authentication properties that exactly parallel the Design Authentication properties:

RunPassword   Holds the password to use at runtime.

RunPromptBehavior   Can be set to adPromptAlways, adPromptComplete, adPromptCompleteRequired, or adPromptNever.

RunSaveAuthentication   Tells the designer whether to save the values of RunPassword and RunUserName in the files that hold the Data Environment Connection object's definition. By default, this property is set to False.

RunUserName   Holds the username to use at runtime.

> **WARNING**   If you set DesignSaveAuthentication or RunSaveAuthentication to True, the usernames and passwords you've entered will be available in plain text to anyone who has access to your Visual Basic source code files.

> **TIP**   If you're using SQL Server with Windows integrated authentication in the connection string for the data environment, all of these other security properties are irrelevant.

You're not limited to a single connection within a Data Environment. You can create additional connections by right-clicking the root node in the Data Environment and choosing Add Connection, or by clicking the Add Connection button on the Data Environment Designer toolbar. Either action will create another Connection object with a serialized name within the designer. In addition to appearing in the Data Environment, all Data Environment connections appear in the Data View window (which you can display with View ➢ Data View Window).

It's possible for the information in a connection to change while you're working with it. For example, someone might add new stored procedures to the database, or delete existing tables, or eliminate the user you've specified for retrieving design information. To bring a connection up to date, right-click it and choose Refresh, or select it and click the Refresh button on the Data Environment toolbar. This will refresh all the locally stored metadata about the connection and rebuild the Data Environment's internal lists of objects by querying the data source for current information.

Using Command Objects in the Data Environment

The fact that you can persist a connection to an OLE DB provider via ADO as an object, together with the code attached to it, is moderately interesting. But connections alone won't get you data. For that, you need Command objects. Command objects in the Data Environment are wrappers around ADO Command objects. In this section, you'll learn how to create Command objects and see what you can do with them in the Data Environment.

Creating Command Objects

To create a Command object within a Data Environment, select the Connection or Command object that will be the parent of the new Command object and then click the Add

Command button on the Data Environment toolbar, or right-click the parent object and choose Add Command (if the parent is a connection) or Add Child Command (if the parent is a command). Any of these procedures will create a new, blank Command object. Once again, you should immediately rename the Command object to something more intuitive than the default Command1.

There are three basic properties that determine what data a Command object will retrieve:

ConnectionName   The name of the Connection object that should be used to hook up this Command object. This will be automatically filled in with the name of the parent Connection when you create the Command object.

CommandType   Corresponds to the ADO CommandType property. You can set this to adCmdText (for SQL statements), adCmdTable (for tables), or adCmdStoredProc (for stored procedures).

CommandText   Corresponds to the ADO CommandText property. It will contain the SQL statement, table name, or stored procedure name that this command object should use to retrieve data. If you're entering CommandText directly in the Visual Basic properties window, you have to enter names exactly. However, if you create a Command object, right-click it, and choose Properties, you'll find that you can select the name of a table, view, synonym, or stored procedure from a combo box in the object's property pages.

When you assign these three properties, the Command object node in the Data Environment Designer will automatically retrieve information on the schema of the Recordset that it represents and create child Field objects in the designer. At this time, the Command also retrieves parameter information if it's based on a stored procedure. Figure 24.11 shows what a Data Environment looks like after creating a simple table-based Command object. Note that the status bar in the Data Environment describes the highlighted node of the treeview.

FIGURE 24.11:

A Data Environment
with a single command

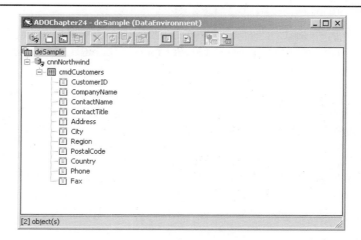

Command objects also have a set of advanced properties (available through their property sheet or property dialog box) that are derived from the properties of the underlying ADO Command object:

CacheSize   Sets the number of records that should be cached locally. (It defaults to 100.)

CallSyntax   Specifies the exact string that ADO should send to the data source to execute the command. For example, if you base a command on a stored procedure named Cust-OrderHist in a SQL Server database, this property will contain {? = CALL dbo.Cust-OrderHist(?)}, which is the ODBC syntax for calling a stored procedure. Unless your data source uses wildly nonstandard syntax for stored procedures, you won't need to alter this property's value.

CommandTimeout   Sets the number of seconds to wait for data to be returned when the Command is executed. (It defaults to 30.)

CursorLocation   Can be set to adUseClient (for client-side cursors, the default) or adUseServer (for server-side cursors).

CursorType   Can be set to adOpenStatic (the default), adOpenDynamic, adOpenKeyset, or adOpenForwardOnly.

GrandTotalName   Applies only to grand total aggregate Commands. These are discussed later in the chapter.

LockType   Can be set to adLockReadOnly (the default), adLockPessimistic, adLock-Optimistic, or adLockBatchOptimistic. Note that by default you won't be able to edit records retrieved by this Command.

MaxRecords   Sets the maximum number of records that should be retrieved from the data provider. By default this is zero, which means that there is no limit on the number of records.

Prepared   Can be set to True to save a compiled version of the Command for faster execution. If the provider doesn't support compiled commands, you'll receive an error when you try to set this property to True.

Because many developers use stored procedures for all data access in client-server environments, there's also a shortcut for creating Command objects based on stored procedures. Select a Connection object and click the Insert Stored Procedures button on the Data Environment toolbar, or right-click the Connection object and choose Insert Stored Procedures. The Data Environment will display the Insert Stored Procedures dialog box. Select as many stored procedures as you like by moving them from the Available listbox to the Add listbox and then click Insert. The Data Environment will automatically create a Command object for each of the stored procedures you've chosen. You can repeat this operation later if you want to add additional Command objects based on other stored procedures. Depending on the source of the Command objects, the Data Environment will display different icons. For example, the icon for a SQL statement is different from that for a stored procedure.

If you display the Data View window, there's another way to create a Command object. Simply expand the Data View until you can see the object you'd like to use as the source for the Data Environment Command object (for example, a table or stored procedure). Then drag that object from the Data View window and drop it in the Data Environment window. If there's already a Data Environment Connection pointing to the same data source, the Data Environment will create a Command for this Connection and automatically hook it up to the object you dragged and dropped. If there's no matching Connection object, the Data Environment will create both the Connection and the Command.

Working with Command Objects

Now that you've created a Command object, you can perform a variety of operations with the object directly within the Data Environment. These include examining the properties of the Command, setting properties for the Field objects contained in this Command, refreshing the Command from the underlying data source, debugging it (if the Command is based on a stored procedure), and designing it (if the Command is based on a SQL string).

To see the properties of a Command object, right-click the object and choose Properties, or select the object and click the Properties button on the Data Environment toolbar. Either action will open the property sheet for the object. This property sheet has six tabs:

General   Lets you choose the data that you want the Command connected to. When you choose an object type from the Database Object list, the Object Name list will automatically be refreshed to indicate which objects of that type are available via the selected Connection. If you choose SQL Statement, the SQL Builder button will launch the Visual Data Tools Query Builder to help you create a SQL statement on the fly.

Parameters   Lets you examine the properties of any parameters your Command contains. Naturally, this makes sense only for Commands based on stored procedures. I'll cover the use of parameterized stored procedures later in this chapter.

Relation, Grouping, and Aggregates   Are used to relate parent and child Commands. You'll see this in the next section, "Command Object Hierarchies."

Advanced   Provides one-stop access to the advanced properties of the Command object (see Figure 24.12). One nice thing about using this method, instead of the Visual Basic properties window, to set these properties is that it won't let you change things that don't make sense. For example, to choose a type of cursor other than static, you must use a server-side cursor.

FIGURE 24.12:

Advanced tab of a
Command object's
property sheet

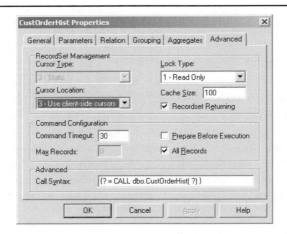

To set properties for a Field object underneath a Command object, right-click the Field object and select Properties, or select the object and click the Properties button on the Data Environment toolbar. This will open the property sheet for the Field object. The property sheet will show you the datatype and size of the field. It also lets you set two properties used when basing form controls on this field: the type of control to use and the caption that should be placed beside the field. You'll learn more about creating forms based on Command objects later in the chapter.

To refresh a Command object, right-click the object and select Refresh, or select the object and click the Refresh button on the Data Environment toolbar. The Data Environment will warn you that any user-defined information stored with the fields of this Command object (such as the preferred display control) will be lost, and will let you abort the process at this point (it does this whether there is any such information or not). If you choose to continue, all the metadata about the object is fetched anew from the data source. This includes information about the Command itself (for example, the current definition of a stored procedure, which might have changed since the command was created) as well as all the Field and Parameter information stored beneath it.

To debug a Command object based on a stored procedure, right-click the object and select Debug. This will load the stored procedure into the T-SQL Debugger. (The Debug menu option will be unavailable if the Command object is not based on a stored procedure.)

To design a Command object based on a SQL statement, right-click the object and choose Design (again, this menu item will be unavailable if the Command object isn't based on a SQL statement), or select it and click the Design button on the Data Environment toolbar. This will load the text of the SQL statement into the Visual Database Tools Query Designer.

Command Object Hierarchies

Were it limited to single Commands, the Data Environment wouldn't offer much advantage over the Data Form Wizard. However, there's much more to the Data Environment than just a wrapper for ADO Command objects. For starters, there's an easy way to design hierarchical Recordsets using the Data Environment. The Data Environment implements the notion of a Command hierarchy—a set of Command objects with particular relations that correspond to an ADO Shape Command.

Later in this chapter, you'll see how to bind the information from Command hierarchies to controls on a form. You can either use a single Hierarchical FlexGrid control to hold the entire hierarchy or bind individual Recordsets and fields to individual controls on a form. But first, you need to understand the types of Recordsets that you can create.

Command hierarchies can represent three basic kinds of information:

- Relation hierarchies
- Grouping hierarchies
- Aggregates

Relation Hierarchies

A *relation hierarchy* contains information from a set of tables that are related in a traditional one-to-many relationship. For example, Figure 24.13 shows the frmRelationHierarchy form in the ADOChapter24 sample project. This form uses the Hierarchical FlexGrid control to display information from the Customers, Orders, and Order Details tables. Note that the grid allows you to use the + and – signs to expand and contract detail information from the three tables. It draws on three Command objects in a Data Environment, each based on a SQL statement.

To create a relation hierarchy, first create a Connection object, and then create a Command object based on a SQL statement, as in this example:

```
SELECT CustomerID, CompanyName FROM Customers
```

The next step is to create a child Command object beneath the first Command object. You can do this by right-clicking the parent Command object and selecting Add Child Command, or by selecting the parent Command object and clicking the Add Child Command button on the Data Environment toolbar. The Data Environment will insert a new Command object in the treeview display beneath the parent Command object. Display the properties for the child command and assign it a SQL statement, as in this example:

```
SELECT OrderID, CustomerID FROM Orders
```

Then select the Relation tab on the property sheet for the child Command object. You need to choose a pair of fields (in this case, the CustomerID field in each statement) and click the Add button to tell the Data Environment how the two tables are related. Figure 24.14 shows the Relation tab (after clicking Add) for this particular case.

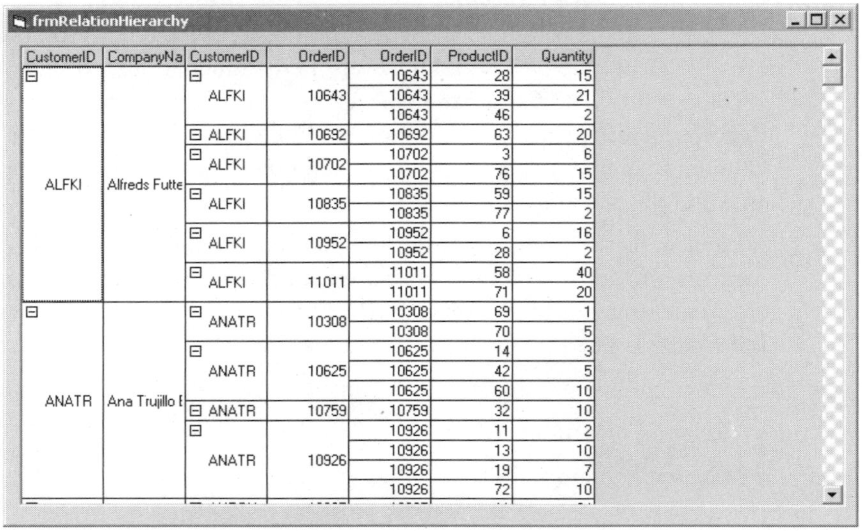

FIGURE 24.13:

Relation hierarchy on a form

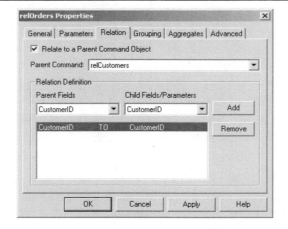

FIGURE 24.14:

Relating two Command objects

You can repeat the same process to create a child Command of the Orders Command object that draws information from the OrderDetails table based on a SQL statement. For example:

```
SELECT OrderID, ProductID, Quantity FROM [Order Details]
```

Once again, you must navigate to the Relation tab and add a relation to specify how this Command is related to its parent.

That's all you have to do to create a relation hierarchy. To produce a quick browse form like the one shown in Figure 24.13, just right-drag the top-level Command object from the hierarchy to an empty form and choose Hierarchical Flex Grid from the context menu that appears when you drop the object.

Grouping Hierarchies

The second type of hierarchy available in the Data Environment is a *grouping hierarchy*. A grouping hierarchy lets you take a single Command object and split it up so that some of the fields are used to group other fields. Figure 24.15 shows the result of displaying a grouping hierarchy on frmGroupingHierarchy in the ADOChapter24 sample project. Here you can see a list of product categories which you can expand or collapse to show their constituent products.

FIGURE 24.15:

Grouping a Command object

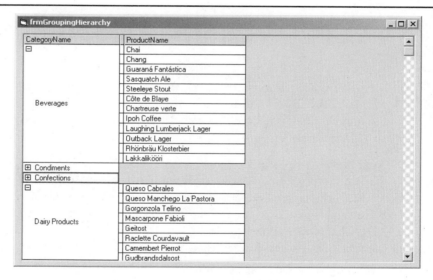

To create this particular form, start with a Command object based on this SQL statement:

```
SELECT Categories.CategoryName, Products.ProductName
FROM Products
INNER JOIN Categories
ON Products.CategoryID = Categories.CategoryID
```

You can convert this Command into a grouping hierarchy by opening its property sheet and setting appropriate properties on the Grouping tab. To do this, first check the Group Command Object check box to tell the Data Environment that this Command will be grouped. Then enter a name for the grouping Command that will be created from this Command—for example, Category. Select the fields that you want to use for grouping and move them from the Fields In Command listbox to the Fields Used For Grouping listbox. Figure 24.16 shows the completed tab on the property sheet.

FIGURE 24.16:

Defining a grouping
Command object

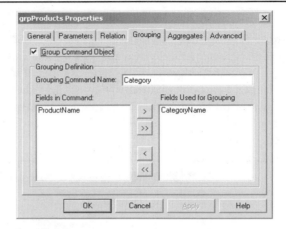

In the Data Environment window, the grouping hierarchy is displayed as a single Command object. However, instead of fields, this object has two child folders—one containing the summary fields that the Command is grouped by and one containing the detail fields that are shown for each record.

Aggregates

The third type of hierarchy, an *aggregate*, lets you add a calculated total to a grouped Command. (Although you can create aggregates on ungrouped Commands, they won't be displayed and thus aren't very useful.) Figure 24.17 shows the frmAggregate form in the ADOChapter24 sample project. Here the TotalOrders column is an aggregate that displays the total of the orders for the listed company.

This form started with a Command object based on this SQL statement:

```
SELECT Customers.CompanyName,
[Order Details].UnitPrice * [OrderDetails].Quantity
AS Total
FROM Customers INNER JOIN Orders
ON Customers.CustomerID = Orders.CustomerID
INNER JOIN [Order Details]
ON Orders.OrderID = [Order Details].OrderID
```

I then used the Grouping tab in the property sheet for the Command to set up a grouping Command named Company that groups on the CompanyName field. The last step was to fill in the necessary information on the Aggregates tab, shown in Figure 24.18:

Name   The name (and default column caption) to use for the calculated field.

Function   Dictates how the field should be calculated. You can choose between Any (which selects a random value from the available choices), Average, Count, Maximum, Minimum, Standard Deviation, and Sum.

Aggregate On   Tells which level of grouping to calculate the total across. In this particular instance, the aggregate is on a group-by-group basis.

Field   Lets you pick the field that should be aggregated.

FIGURE 24.17:

Form with an aggregate

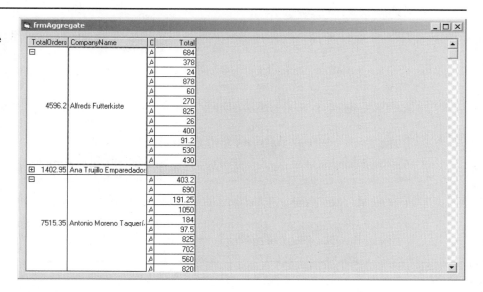

FIGURE 24.18:

Defining an aggregate
Command

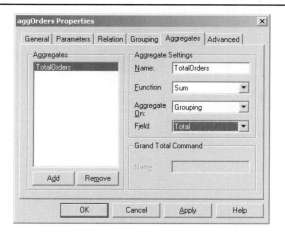

When you create a Command hierarchy (of any of the three types discussed in this section), the Data Environment adds an additional menu item to the shortcut menu for the top-level Command object: Hierarchy Info. This menu item brings up a simple dialog box that will display either the SHAPE statement that the Data Environment has automatically generated or the hierarchy of ADO objects involved in the Command.

With practice, you will be able to tell one type of hierarchical command from another just by looking at them in the Data Environment. Figure 24.19 shows the three Command hierarchies discussed in this section:

- The relation hierarchy is displayed as a series of SQL Command objects, with child Commands being subordinate to their parent Commands.

- The grouping hierarchy is displayed as a single Command object with folders dividing the grouping fields from the detail fields.

- The aggregate field is shown with a special +/– field symbol.

Data Environment Options and Operations

Although most of the operation of the Data Environment is completely automatic, there are a few options that you can set by hand. These fall into two categories:

- *General options* control the overall behavior of the Data Environment.

- *Field Mapping options* are useful when you want to create forms by using drag-and-drop from the Data Environment.

FIGURE 24.19:

Command hierarchies
in the Data Environment

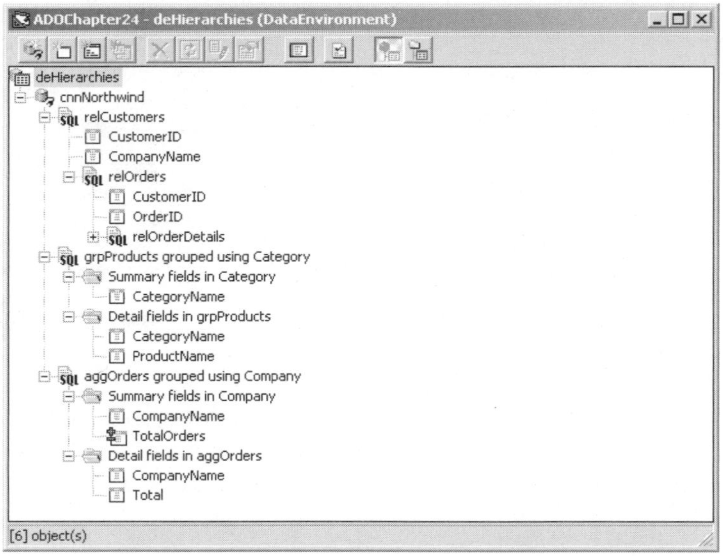

General Options

You can set the general options for the Data Environment by right-clicking the root node in the Data Environment Designer and choosing Options, or by clicking the Options button on the Data Environment toolbar. This will open a dialog box with six check boxes. These options (and the control type options discussed next) are global settings that apply to all Data Environments within your project. Changes take effect as soon as you close the dialog box.

Show Properties Immediately after Object Creation   By default, this option is off. Turning it on is helpful if you're creating many Command and Connection objects from scratch, since it saves having to separately open the property sheet for each object.

Prompt before Deleting Object   By default, this option is on. Turn it off if you'd rather not get a warning when deleting objects from your Data Environment.

Show Status Bar   By default, this option is on, and it causes the status bar to appear at the bottom of the Data Environment.

Show System Objects   By default, this option is off. If you turn it on, any system objects that are part of Commands in this Data Environment will be displayed.

Disable Warnings   By default, this option is off. If you turn it on, it suppresses warning messages when you're doing something that the Data Environment thinks is wrong—for example, saving a Command object that has no CommandText.

Prompt before Executing Command   By default, this option is on. To retrieve metadata from SQL commands or stored procedures, the Data Environment may need to execute the command on the server. Leaving this box checked will ensure that the Data Environment warns you before it does so—probably the better choice, since executing some commands could have drastic side effects such as modifying or deleting data.

Associating Control Types with Data

As you'll see in the next section, one of the most powerful features of the Data Environment is the ability to create data-based forms and reports with simple drag-and-drop operations. The Data Environment Designer ships with a set of default associations between datatypes and fields, but you can change these associations on several levels.

If you like, you can set a control type to be used specifically with a particular Field object within a particular Command object. To do this, open the property sheet for the Field object and select the control you'd like to use from the combo box in the Field Mapping section. This combo box shows all the ActiveX controls registered on your computer, as well as the intrinsic Visual Basic controls; it's likely to contain several controls that are inappropriate, so choose with care. The Data Environment will happily try to create whatever control you choose, defaulting back to creating a text box if, for whatever reason, the control you've chosen can't be created on a Visual Basic form.

If the Field Mapping for a particular control remains set to <Use Default>, the Data Environment next looks to see whether you've specified a control type for the exact datatype of the underlying field in the data source. You can examine these mappings by choosing the Field Mapping tab of the Data Environment Options dialog box. To see some specific datatypes in the list presented by this dialog box, you need to check the Show All Data Types check box. Once again, you can choose control types from a combo box listing all controls registered on your computer.

Finally, if there is no Field Mapping for a particular field and no mapping for the particular datatype used in that field, the Data Environment uses the control type specified for the appropriate datatype category. The Data Environment groups datatypes into categories and specifies a default control for each category. For example, the adChar and adWChar datatypes are grouped in the Text category and displayed by default with a TextBox control.

There are also two special entries on the Data Environment Options list of datatypes:

Caption   Used to determine the type of control to create for the captions of other controls. This property is used only if the Drag and Drop Field Captions check box is checked.

Multiple   Used to determine the type of control to use if you drag and drop an entire Command object. That is, this control is used for each field from the Command object when you drop the Command object rather than drop individual fields.

Table 24.2 shows the default field mappings that the Data Environment is installed with.

TABLE 24.2: Default Field Mappings in the Data Environment

Category	Datatype	Control
Binary		TextBox
	adBinary	<Use default>
	adLongVarBinary	<Use default>
	adVarBinary	<Use default>
Boolean		CheckBox
	adBoolean	<Use default>
Caption		Label
	Caption	<Use default>
Currency		TextBox
	adCurrency	<Use default>
Date		TextBox
	adDate	<Use default>
	adDBDate	<Use default>

continued on next page

TABLE 24.2 CONTINUED: Default Field Mappings in the Data Environment

Category	Datatype	Control
Empty		TextBox
	adEmpty	<Use default>
	adNull	<Use default>
Integer		TextBox
	adBigInt	<Use default>
	adInteger	<Use default>
	adSmallInt	<Use default>
	adTinyInt	<Use default>
	adUnsignedBigInt	<Use default>
	adUnsignedInt	<Use default>
	adUnsignedSmallInt	<Use default>
	adUnsignedTinyInt	<Use default>
Long		TextBox
	adDecimal	<Use default>
	adDouble	<Use default>
	adNumeric	<Use default>
	adSingle	<Use default>
	adVarNumeric	<Use default>
Memo		TextBox
	adLongVarChar	<Use default>
	adLongVarWChar	<Use default>
	adVarChar	<Use default>
	adWVarChar	<Use default>
Multiple		TextBox
	Multiple	<Use default>
Other		TextBox
	adBSTR	<Use default>
	adError	<Use default>
	adGUID	<Use default>
	adIDispatch	<Use default>
	adIUnknown	<Use default>
	adUserDefined	<Use default>
Text		TextBox
	adChar	<Use default>
	adWChar	<Use default>
Time		TextBox
	adDBTime	<Use default>
	adDBTimeStamp	<Use default>
Variant		TextBox
	adVariant	<Use default>

Miscellaneous Data Environment Options

You can also adjust some of the options that control the look of the treeview of objects within the Data Environment. The Data Environment offers two arrangements of its treeview and lets you suppress the display of Field objects.

By default, the Data Environment displays a treeview with Command objects as children of their parent Connection objects. If you prefer, you can choose an alternate display with Connections and Commands in separate folders within the treeview. To display items grouped by folder, right-click the root node and select Arrange By Object, or click the Arrange By Objects button on the Data Environment toolbar. To display items in the default hierarchy, right-click the root node and select Arrange By Connection, or click the Arrange By Connections button on the Data Environment toolbar.

You can also choose to suppress the display of Field objects in the treeview. This is most useful when you want a sense of the overall structure of the Data Environment and don't need to work with the properties of individual fields. To display or hide fields, right-click the root node in the treeview and select Show Fields. This is a toggle menu item, and there is no toolbar equivalent.

Binding Forms to the Data Environment

Once you've created Connection and Command objects to retrieve the data you're interested in, the next step is to display that data to the user somehow. Visual Basic 6 supports binding data from one class to another, and you can bind objects from the Data Environment to user interface objects such as forms and Data Reports. You've already seen some examples of forms bound to Data Environments in the discussion of command hierarchies; in this section, I'll explore bound forms in more depth. I'll cover Data Reports later in the chapter.

Creating Bound Forms

Binding a control on a form to a Data Environment is nearly the same process as binding a control to a data control—except that there's no data control involved. Figure 24.20 shows the frmDEBound form from the ADOChapter24 sample project. This form uses data binding to retrieve data from the Northwind database via a Data Environment.

Four properties control the binding of controls to fields from a Data Environment:

DataSource   Holds the name of the Data Environment itself.

DataMember   Holds the name of the Command object within the Data Environment that contains the field to which the control will be bound.

DataField   Holds the name of the field to which the control will be bound.

DataFormat   Lets you add data formatting to get a nicer display of information. You can set this optional property to General (the default), Number, Currency, Date, Time, Percentage, Scientific, Boolean, Checkbox, Picture, or Custom.

FIGURE 24.20:

FIGURE 24.20:

Form bound to a Data
Environment

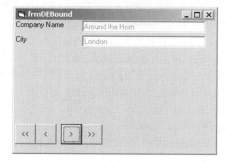

Of course, because no data control is involved, there's no way for the user to navigate between records. To work around this problem, the sample form includes four command buttons to handle navigation:

```
Private deCurrent As Object

Private Sub cmdFirst_Click()
    deCurrent.rscmdCustomers.MoveFirst
End Sub

Private Sub cmdLast_Click()
    deCurrent.rscmdCustomers.MoveLast
End Sub

Private Sub cmdNext_Click()
    With deCurrent.rscmdCustomers
        .MoveNext
        If .EOF Then
            .MoveLast
        End If
    End With
End Sub

Private Sub cmdPrevious_Click()
    With deCurrent.rscmdCustomers
        .MovePrevious
        If .BOF Then
            .MoveFirst
        End If
    End With
End Sub

Private Sub Form_Load()
    Set deCurrent = deNorthwind
End Sub
```

Here, deCurrent is an object reference to the Data Environment. The form sets this reference to the appropriate Data Environment object when you load the form.

If you inspect the ADOChapter24 sample project, you'll find that there is nothing named rscmdCustomers in the deNorthwind Data Environment. Where, then, does this object come from? The answer is that the Data Environment automatically creates an ADO Recordset object corresponding to each Command object within the Data Environment. To avoid ambiguity between the Command and Recordset objects, it automatically prepends *rs* to the Recordset object's name. In this case, the Command is named cmdCustomers, so the corresponding Recordset is rscmdCustomers.

Using Drag-and-Drop

Obviously, building bound forms by setting individual control properties would be just as tedious with the Data Environment as with the ADO Data Control. That's why the Data Environment Designer and the Forms Designer work together to enable drag-and-drop form design. If you arrange a form and a Data Environment in the Visual Basic workspace so that you can see them both, you can perform these drag-and-drop operations:

- If you drag a Command and drop it on a form, you'll get a data entry control for each field in the Command, and a label for each control (assuming you have the Data Environment Field Mapping options set to create labels).

- If you drag a single field and drop it on a form, you'll get a data entry control for just that field, as well as a label.

- If you right-drag a Command and drop it on a form, you'll get the choice of binding the Command to a regular Data Grid control, a Hierarchical FlexGrid control, or a group of bound controls. (That's how the sample forms in the "Command Object Hierarchies" section earlier in the chapter were built.)

- If you drag a Command that's at the top of a relation hierarchy and drop it on a form, you'll get individual data controls for the parent Command and a Hierarchical FlexGrid control for the child Command.

- If you drag a Command that's at the bottom of a relation hierarchy and drop it on a form, you'll get individual data controls for that Command only.

In all these cases, the drag-and-drop operation only creates and binds the controls. You'll still need to add code if you want to allow the user to navigate through the records. You can use the code from the simple bound form in the preceding section to get you started.

Using Parameterized Stored Procedures

If you drag a Command based on a parameterized stored procedure (such as the CustOrderHist procedure in the Northwind sample database) to a form and open the form, you'll find that the form doesn't display any data. This is because the Data Environment opens the Recordset before you have any chance to supply a value for the parameter—so, of course, there are no records in it. In order for you to retrieve data this way, you'll need to first close the empty Recordset, then supply a value for the parameter, then rebind the new Recordset to the controls. Here's some code that does this; it's from frmParameter in the ADOChapter24sample project:

```
Private Sub cmdExecute_Click()
    With deNorthwind
        If .rsdbo_CustOrderHist.State = _
         adStateOpen Then
            .rsdbo_CustOrderHist.Close
        End If
        .dbo_CustOrderHist txtCustomerID
        If .rsdbo_CustOrderHist.RecordCount > 0 Then
            Set txtProductName.DataSource = deNorthwind
            Set txtTotal.DataSource = deNorthwind
            cmdFirst.Enabled = True
            cmdLast.Enabled = True
            cmdPrevious.Enabled = True
            cmdNext.Enabled = True
        Else
            txtProductName.Text = ""
            txtTotal.Text = ""
            cmdFirst.Enabled = False
            cmdLast.Enabled = False
            cmdPrevious.Enabled = False
            cmdNext.Enabled = False
        End If
    End With
End Sub
```

Note the difference between deNorthwindSQL.dbo_CustOrderHist and deNorthwindSQL .rsdbo_CustOrderHist. The former refers to the Command object in the Data Environment hierarchy, and the latter refers to the Recordset based on that Command object. Command objects based on stored procedures can be treated as methods within your Visual Basic code. The arguments to the method, of course, are the parameter values you wish to supply.

Also note the block of code that checks to see whether the Recordset is already open and, if it is, closes it. If you try to recreate an open Recordset, you'll get an error, but you'll also get an error if you try to close an already-closed Recordset. This code block avoids both of those errors.

Using ADO Events in the Data Environment

So far in this chapter, I've exclusively used the Data Environment as a visual designer for ADO Connections and Commands. But there's another level to the Data Environment Designer. Like a form, a Data Environment actually consists of a visual representation plus a class module. In this case, the visual piece goes away at runtime, but the class module remains and gets instantiated whenever a client (such as a form or a Data Report) uses data from the Data Environment. And, like a form, a Data Environment supports events. In fact, there are three sets of events you can use from the Data Environment:

- Data Environment events

- Connection events

- Recordset events

I'll review each of these in turn in the next sections of the chapter.

The frmDEEvents form (shown in Figure 24.21) allows you to experiment with events on a simple form bound to a Data Environment that contains a single command. When you launch the Events sample, the Data Environment begins writing rows to the listview as events occur; thus you can see what's going on and in what order.

FIGURE 24.21:

The Events sample in action

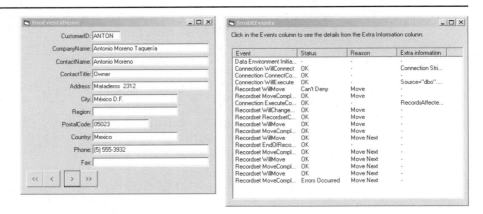

Data Environment Events

The Data Environment itself supports only the two standard class module events, Initialize and Terminate:

```
Private Sub DataEnvironment_Initialize()
Private Sub DataEnvironment_Terminate()
```

The Initialize event is the first event that happens when any client component uses the Data Environment to retrieve data. The Terminate event is the last event that happens when the Data Environment is shut down.

Connection Events

Connection objects in the Data Environment support nine events:

- The connection events WillConnect, ConnectComplete, InfoMessage, and Disconnect

- The execution events WillExecute and ExecuteComplete

- The transaction events BeginTransComplete, CommitTransComplete, and RollBack-TransComplete

Generally, the first connection event is the WillConnect event, which has this signature:

```
Private Sub <ConnectionName>_WillConnect( _
ConnectionString As String, _
UserID As String, _
Password As String, _
Options As Long, _
adStatus As ADODB.EventStatusEnum, _
ByVal pConnection As ADODB.Connection)
```

This event happens when ADO is about to use the OLE DB provider to connect to the data, but before that connection is actually made. The ConnectionString, UserID, Password, and Options arguments are passed straight through from the corresponding properties in the Data Environment. The adStatus argument will be equal to adStatusOK when this event is called. You can set this argument within the body of the event procedure. If you set it to adStatusCancel, the connection will not happen (and the ConnectComplete event will be called with adStatus set to adStatusCancel). If you set it to adStatusUnwantedEvent, your program will not receive any further notifications of WillConnect events on this object during this session. The pConnection argument contains the ADO Connection that's about to be initialized.

TIP   You can set the adStatus argument of *any* Data Environment event procedure to adStatusUnwantedEvent to suppress further firing of that event.

During the connection process, you may receive one or more InfoMessage events:

```
Private Sub <ConnectionName>_InfoMessage( _
ByVal pError As ADODB.Error, _
adStatus As ADODB.EventStatusEnum, _
ByVal pConnection As ADODB.Connection)
```

This event will occur only if the OLE DB provider posts any warnings during the connection process. If it does, the pError argument will be an ADO Error object containing the warning. The adStatus argument will always be set to adStatusOK when this event occurs. You can also get InfoMessage events at other times, depending on the details of the OLE DB provider in use.

The ConnectComplete event occurs when ADO has successfully completed a connection to the underlying data source via OLE DB:

```
Private Sub <ConnectionName>_ConnectComplete( _
ByVal pError As ADODB.Error, _
adStatus As ADODB.EventStatusEnum, _
ByVal pConnection As ADODB.Connection)
```

Here, adStatus will be adStatusOK if all went well, adStatusCancel if the WillConnect event was cancelled, or adStatusErrorsOccurred if something went wrong. In the latter case, pError will be an ADO Error object containing information on what went wrong. The pConnection argument, of course, holds the Connection itself.

The Disconnect event happens when ADO disconnects from the data source:

```
Private Sub <ConnectionName>_Disconnect( _
adStatus As ADODB.EventStatusEnum, _
ByVal pConnection As ADODB.Connection)
```

In this case, adStatus will always be adStatusOK, and the pConnection argument holds the now-closed connection.

The WillExecute event happens whenever a Command object is about to be executed. This occurs most often when you open a Recordset, although you can use Visual Basic code to execute commands that don't return Recordsets. The signature is as follows:

```
Private Sub <ConnectionName>_WillExecute( _
Source As String, _
CursorType As ADODB.CursorTypeEnum, _
LockType As ADODB.LockTypeEnum, _
Options As Long, _
adStatus As ADODB.EventStatusEnum, _
ByVal pCommand As ADODB.Command, _
ByVal pRecordset As ADODB.Recordset, _
ByVal pConnection As ADODB.Connection)
```

The Source argument holds the name of the command, while CursorType, LockType, and Options dictate the type of ADO Recordset that will be opened. If you like, you can alter any of these arguments within the event procedure. If you want to cancel the event (and therefore the Recordset), you can do so by setting adStatus to adCancel. The pCommand, pRecordset, and pConnection arguments are respectively pointers to the ADO Command, Recordset, and Connection objects involved in the operation.

The ExecuteComplete event occurs, of course, after a command has finished executing:

```
Private Sub <ConnectionName>_ExecuteComplete( _
ByVal RecordsAffected As Long, _
ByVal pError As ADODB.Error, _
adStatus As ADODB.EventStatusEnum, _
```

```
ByVal pCommand As ADODB.Command, _
ByVal pRecordset As ADODB.Recordset, _
ByVal pConnection As ADODB.Connection)
```

The RecordsAffected argument specifies how many records the execution changed, if any. If no records are changed (for example, when a Recordset is first opened), this is set to –1. If there was any error, pError will tell you what the error was. The other arguments are the same as for the WillExecute event except, of course, that you can't cancel an ExecuteComplete event.

The BeginTransComplete, CommitTransComplete, and RollbackTransComplete events are called after completion of the corresponding transaction methods:

```
Private Sub <ConnectionName>_BeginTransComplete( _
ByVal TransactionLevel As Long, _
ByVal pError As ADODB.Error, _
adStatus As ADODB.EventStatusEnum, _
ByVal pConnection As ADODB.Connection)
Private Sub <ConnectionName>_CommitTransComplete( _
ByVal pError As ADODB.Error, _
adStatus As ADODB.EventStatusEnum, _
ByVal pConnection As ADODB.Connection)
Private Sub <ConnectionName>_RollbackTransComplete( _
ByVal pError As ADODB.Error, _
adStatus As ADODB.EventStatusEnum, _
ByVal pConnection As ADODB.Connection)
```

These events give you an easy way to check whether transactional processing is going as planned. Each of them sets adStatus to adStatusOK if all is well and adStatusErrorsOccurred if something is wrong. In the latter case, pError points to an ADO Error object with details on the problem. The pConnection argument passes in the Connection that's hosting the transactional operations. The TransactionLevel argument to BeginTransComplete tells you the current nesting depth of transactions.

Recordset Events

Command objects in the Data Environment don't support events directly. However, the ADO Recordsets based on those objects do expose 11 events to the Data Environment Designer:

- The record fetch events FetchComplete and FetchProgress
- The movement events WillMove, MoveComplete, and EndOfRecordset
- The field change events WillChangeField and FieldChangeComplete
- The record change events WillChangeRecord and RecordChangeComplete
- The Recordset change events WillChangeRecordset and RecordsetChangeComplete

The FetchComplete and FetchProgress events are called during lengthy asynchronous record retrievals:

```
Private Sub <RecordsetName>_FetchComplete( _
  ByVal pError As ADODB.Error, _
  adStatus As ADODB.EventStatusEnum, _
  ByVal pRecordset As ADODB.Recordset)
Private Sub <RecordsetName>_FetchProgress( _
  ByVal Progress As Long, _
  ByVal MaxProgress As Long, _
  adStatus As ADODB.EventStatusEnum, _
  ByVal pRecordset As ADODB.Recordset)
```

You won't actually see these two events unless you explicitly open a Recordset asynchronously in code, by setting asynchronous operation in the Open method. If you do this, the FetchProgress event is fired once every time the cache is loaded with records from the data source. The Progress argument tells you how many records have been retrieved, and the MaxProgress argument tells you how many records the command expects to receive when it's done. The FetchComplete method is fired when there is no more data to fetch on an asynchronous connection.

The WillMove and MoveComplete events bracket all movement through the Recordset:

```
Private Sub <RecordsetName>_WillMove( _
  ByVal adReason As ADODB.EventReasonEnum, _
  adStatus As ADODB.EventStatusEnum, _
  ByVal pRecordset As ADODB.Recordset)
Private Sub <RecordsetName>_MoveComplete( _
  ByVal adReason As ADODB.EventReasonEnum, _
  ByVal pError As ADODB.Error, _
  adStatus As ADODB.EventStatusEnum, _
  ByVal pRecordset As ADODB.Recordset)
```

The WillMove event is called before the Recordset is actually repositioned, and the MoveComplete event is called after the new record is the current record. For both events, the adReason argument tells you why the event has been fired. Table 24.3 lists all the possible values of this argument and shows which values can occur during which events. You can cancel the WillMove event but not the MoveComplete event. If the WillMove event can't be cancelled, the adStatus argument will be adStatusCantDeny; otherwise, it will be adStatusOK. If the MoveComplete is successful, it will have an adStatus argument of adStatusOK; otherwise, it will be adStatusErrorsOccurred, and the pError argument will contain an ADO Error object with the details.

TABLE 24.3: ADO EventReasonEnum Values

alue	Reason	WillMove/ MoveComplete	WillChangeRecord/ RecordChangeComplete	WillChangeRecordset/ RecordsetChangeComplete
adRsnAddNew	New record added	No	Yes	No
adRsnClose	Recordset closed	No	No	Yes
adRsnDelete	Record deleted	No	Yes	No
adRsnFirstChange	Any field in the Record-set was changed for the first time	No	Yes	No
adRsnMove	Move to a bookmark	Yes	No	No
adRsnMoveFirst	Move to first record	Yes	No	No
adRsnMoveLast	Move to last record	Yes	No	No
adRsnMoveNext	Move to next record	Yes	No	No
adRsnMovePrevious	Move to previous record	Yes	No	No
adRsnRequery	Requery of the data source	Yes	No	Yes
adRsnResynch	Synchronize a discon-nected Recordset	No	No	Yes
adRsnUndoAddNew	Undo of an Add New	No	Yes	No
adRsnUndoDelete	Undo of a Delete	No	Yes	No
adRsnUndoUpdate	Undo of an update	No	Yes	No
adRsnUpdate	Record updated	No	Yes	No

The EndOfRecordset event is fired when you attempt to move past the current end of the Recordset:

```
Private Sub <RecordsetName>_EndOfRecordset( _
  fMoreData As Boolean, _
  adStatus As ADODB.EventStatusEnum, _
  ByVal pRecordset As ADODB.Recordset)
```

Here, of course, the pRecordset argument is a pointer to the current Recordset, and the adStatus argument will be either adStatusOK or adStatusCantDeny, depending on whether the movement can be cancelled. If you like, you can add more records to the Recordset within this event procedure. If you do this, you must set the fMoreData argument to True.

The WillChangeField and FieldChangeComplete events flank any change to a field within a Recordset:

```
Private Sub <RecordsetName>_WillChangeField( _
  ByVal cFields As Long, _
  ByVal Fields As Variant, _
```

```
  adStatus As ADODB.EventStatusEnum, _
  ByVal pRecordset As ADODB.Recordset)
 Private Sub <RecordsetName>_FieldChangeComplete( _
  ByVal cFields As Long, _
  ByVal Fields As Variant, _
  ByVal pError As ADODB.Error, _
  adStatus As ADODB.EventStatusEnum, _
  ByVal pRecordset As ADODB.Recordset)
```

In both of these events, the Fields argument is an array of ADO Field objects contained in a Variant. The cFields argument tells you how many Field objects are in this array, and the pRecordset argument is a pointer to the Recordset being changed. In the WillChangeField event, the adStatus argument will be adStatusOK or adStatusCantDeny. If it's adStatusOK, you can set it to adCancel to cancel the change and roll back the changes. In the Field-ChangeComplete event, adStatus will be adStatusOK if the change succeeded, or adStatus-ErrorsOccurred if it failed. In the latter case, you can check the pError argument, which points to an ADO Error object, to determine what went wrong. These events fire when you set the Value property of a field, which you do automatically when you change data in a bound control and then move to another control or another record.

The WillChangeRecord and RecordChangeComplete events surround every change to an individual record in the Recordset:

```
 Private Sub <RecordsetName>_WillChangeRecord( _
  ByVal adReason As ADODB.EventReasonEnum, _
  ByVal cRecords As Long, _
  adStatus As ADODB.EventStatusEnum, _
  ByVal pRecordset As ADODB.Recordset)
 Private Sub <RecordsetName>_RecordChangeComplete( _
  ByVal adReason As ADODB.EventReasonEnum, _
  ByVal cRecords As Long, _
  ByVal pError As ADODB.Error, _
  adStatus As ADODB.EventStatusEnum, _
  ByVal pRecordset As ADODB.Recordset)
```

In both of these events, the cRecords argument tells you how many records are being changed (which could be more than one if you're doing a batch update through code, although it will always be one if you're simply navigating through bound records). The pRecordset argument is a pointer to the Recordset being changed. In the WillChangeRecord event, the adStatus argument will be adStatusOK or adStatusCantDeny. If it's adStatusOK, you can set it to adCancel to cancel the change and roll back the changes. In the Record-ChangeComplete event, adStatus will be adStatusOK if the change succeeded, or adStatus-ErrorsOccurred if it failed. In the latter case, you can check the pError argument, which points to an ADO Error object, to determine what went wrong. These events fire when you update a record in the Recordset, usually by moving to another record on a bound form.

The WillChangeRecordset and RecordsetChangeComplete provide before and after notification of changes to the entire Recordset as the result of Open or Requery operations:

```
Private Sub <RecordsetName>_WillChangeRecordset( _
  ByVal adReason As ADODB.EventReasonEnum, _
  adStatus As ADODB.EventStatusEnum, _
  ByVal pRecordset As ADODB.Recordset20)
Private Sub <RecordsetName>_RecordsetChangeComplete( _
  ByVal adReason As ADODB.EventReasonEnum, _
  ByVal pError As ADODB.Error, _
  adStatus As ADODB.EventStatusEnum, _
  ByVal pRecordset As ADODB.Recordset20)
```

The pRecordset argument is a pointer to the Recordset being changed. In the WillChangeRecordset event, the adStatus argument will be adStatusOK or adStatusCantDeny. If it's adStatusOK, you can set it to adCancel to cancel the change and roll back the changes. In the RecordsetChangeComplete event, adStatus will be adStatusOK if the change succeeded, or adStatusErrorsOccurred if it failed. In the latter case, you can check the pError argument, which points to an ADO Error object, to determine what went wrong.

Using Data Reports to Display Data

Data Reports are banded reports (that is, they contain "bands" of information that can be repeated multiple times) that can be bound to data sources, either via the Data Environment or directly through code. In this section, you'll learn how to create and manipulate Data Reports and see how you can use them to create a permanent record of the data you've retrieved via ADO.

Figure 24.22 shows a typical Data Report (the drSalesDetail Data Report from the ADOChapter24 sample project) at runtime. Note that some information is repeated, such as the label that says "OrderID," while other information is unique, such as the ID number of each order. The actual appearance of the Data Report at runtime depends on the data in the data source when the Data Report is displayed, printed, or exported. The "shape" of the Data Report is determined at design time.

Just like forms, Data Reports have a different appearance at design time than they do at runtime. Figure 24.23 shows the same Data Report as Figure 24.22, but this time it's open in the Data Report Designer. As you can see, the report consists of a series of bands, each of which can be repeated one or more times (or even no times at all, depending on the data that the report is attached to).

FIGURE 24.22:

Typical Data Report at runtime

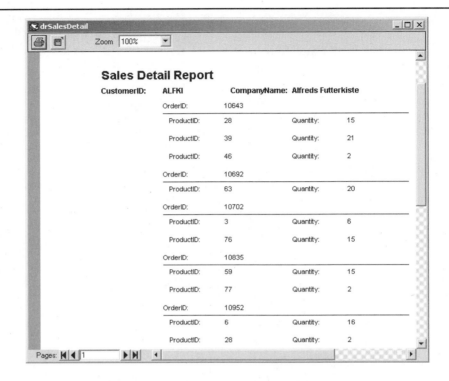

FIGURE 24.23:

The Data Report Designer

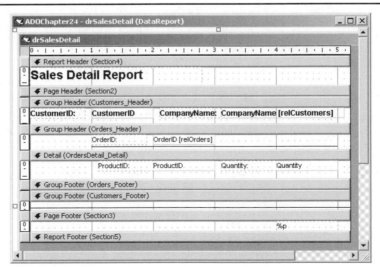

This particular Data Report is based on a hierarchical set of Command objects (Customers, Orders, and Order Details) in a Data Environment that uses the SQL Server Northwind database as its data source. The bands in the Data Report mimic the structure of the relational hierarchy, along with a few extra bands thrown in:

- The Report Header is displayed once at the top of the entire report.
- The Page Header is displayed at the top of each page.
- The Group Header (Customers_Header) is displayed once for each row returned by the relCustomers Command.
- The Group Header (Orders_Header) is displayed once for each row returned by the relOrders Command.
- The Detail (OrderDetails_Detail) is displayed once for each row returned by the relOrderDetails Command. (The Detail band corresponds to the lowest level in the relational hierarchy.)
- The Group Footer (Orders_Footer) is displayed once for each row returned by the Orders Command.
- The Group Footer (Customers_Footer) is displayed once for each row returned by the Customers Command.
- The Page Footer is displayed at the bottom of each page.
- The Report Footer is displayed once at the bottom of the entire report.

Note that some of these bands, such as the Page Header, are empty. Nothing will be displayed for an empty band. You'll also see that the structure is symmetrical, with each Header eventually matched by a corresponding Footer. The most general information is at the top and bottom of the designer; the most specific information (the Detail section) is at the center. The Headers and Footers surround the Detail section like the layers of an onion. The overall structure should be very familiar to users of other reporting products such as Access or Crystal Reports.

Creating Data Reports

Now that you've got some idea what a Data Report looks like, it's time to see how to create one. In this section, you'll see that Data Reports are intimately linked to Data Environments and that you can create controls on a Data Report by dragging and dropping objects from the Data Environment. You can also use a special set of controls (displayed on a reserved tab of the Visual Basic Toolbox) to create controls from scratch. These controls include calculated fields and special controls destined for use in headers and footers.

Using Drag-and-Drop from the Data Environment

The simplest possible Data Report starts with a single Command in a Data Environment. Suppose you have a Data Environment that contains a Command object connected to the Product table in the SQL Server version of the Northwind database. The first step of creating a Data Report to display information retrieved by this Command object is to create the Data Report itself. You can do this by choosing the Project ≻ Add Data Report menu item in Visual Basic, or by choosing the Data Report item on the New Object drop-down toolbar button. Either way, you'll get a blank Data Report, open in the Data Report Designer. By default, it will have five sections:

- Report Header
- Page Header
- Detail
- Page Footer
- Report Footer

There's not much use for a Data Report without data. To connect the Data Report to the data, of course, you use the properties of the Data Report. (You'll need to set these properties directly in the Visual Basic properties window, since Data Reports don't have a property sheet.) Besides naming the Data Report something sensible—such as drProducts, in this case—you need to set two properties to make the data connection:

- The DataSource property should be set to the name of the Data Environment that connects to the data you want to display on this report.

- The DataMember property should be set to the name of the Command object in the Data Environment that contains the top (in this case, only) grouping level for the Data Report.

Once you've set these two properties, you need to refresh the Data Report so that it will display the correct headers and footers. To do this, right-click anywhere in the Data Report Designer and choose Retrieve Structure. Visual Basic will warn you that this will pretty well destroy the existing report and will ask for permission to proceed. If you're just creating the report, it's safe to respond Yes to this warning. This will insert additional Header and Footer sections as necessary and assign standardized names to all the Headers and Footers and the Detail section.

WARNING   For any operation that requires access to the data source (such as refreshing the structure of the Data Report), you'll need to have the Data Environment open in its designer as well.

To continue, you'll need to arrange objects in the Visual Basic design space so that you can see both the Data Report and the Data Environment in their respective designers. Then you can drag either fields or entire Command objects from the Data Environment and drop them on the Data Report. If you drag and drop a field, the Data Report Designer will create a Rpt-TextBox control bound to that field and a RptLabel control with the name of that field to use as a caption. If you drag and drop a Command, the designer will create RptTextBox and Rpt-Label controls for each field in the Command and arrange them vertically on the report. (You'll learn about the RptTextBox and RptLabel controls in the next section.)

Controls within the Data Report Designer can be manipulated just like controls in the Form Designer. That is, you can move and resize them with the mouse, or change their properties in the properties window. (However, the items on the Format menu are grayed out and unavailable when you're working with Data Report controls.) You can even drag controls from section to section. However, there's a limit on dragging controls between sections, as well as on creating controls in the first place: A control can be placed only on a section at or below its place in the relational hierarchy. For example, if you have a hierarchy based on Categories and Products, with Categories as the parent Command, you can place objects from the Categories Command in any section, but objects from the Products Command can be placed only in the Detail section.

WARNING   The Data Report Designer doesn't support multidimensional hierarchies. That is, suppose you have a Data Environment containing a Command based on Orders that has child Commands based on both Employees and Order Details. If you base a Data Report on the Orders Command, only one of its children (the one that is alphabetically first) will be available on the Data Report. The only way to use the other child Command is to create an entirely separate hierarchy that contains only that child Command.

Using the Data Report Toolbox

You can also create controls on a Data Report by using the controls in the Data Report Toolbox. This is a tab in the regular Visual Basic Toolbox that's created the first time you open the Toolbox while a Data Report is open in Design View. Although this tab looks just like any other Toolbox tab, Data Report controls can only be used on Data Reports. You'll find that you can't drag them to other tabs in the Toolbox, and you can't drag controls from other tabs to the Data Report tab. For all practical purposes, the Data Report tab is a completely separate Toolbox that just happens to be displayed in the same window as the regular Toolbox.

The Data Report Toolbox contains seven icons, shown in Figure 24.24. From top to bottom, starting in the left column, these icons represent the following controls:

Pointer   Works just like the Pointer in the regular Toolbox, but only on Data Reports.

RptLabel   Holds static text on a Data Report, and is similar to a regular Label control.

RptTextBox   Holds dynamic, bound text on a Data Report, and is similar to a regular TextBox control.

RptImage   Holds static images on a Data Report, and is similar to a regular Image control.

RptLine   Can be used to draw lines on a Data Report, and is similar to a regular Line control.

RptShape   Can be used to draw circles, squares, ellipses, and rectangles on a Data Report, and is similar to a regular Shape control.

RptFunction   Can be used to create special text boxes displaying summary information on a Data Report. It has no analog in the regular Forms Toolbox. You'll learn more about the RptFunction control later in the chapter.

FIGURE 24.24:

The Data Report Toolbox

The only bound control available in the Data Report Designer is the RptTextBox control. You might think that a RptImage control could display bound data from fields containing image data, but you'd be wrong. If your database contains information that won't display properly in a text box, there's no way to show that information on a Data Report. The best you can do is to show the binary information in the field, which is not usually very helpful.

Creating RptLabel, RptImage, RptLine, and RptShape controls is very similar to creating their Form Designer analogs. The only major difference is that these controls may have somewhat fewer properties. (I'll cover report control properties later in the chapter.) Creating a RptTextBox is the same as creating a regular TextBox control except that you'll need to set the three data properties:

DataMember   Holds the name of the Command object in the Data Environment from which this RptTextBox control's data comes.

DataField   Holds the name of the field in the Command object in the Data Environment from which this RptTextBox control's data comes.

DataFormat   Holds an optional format name for displaying the data with formatting.

The Data Report Designer does its best to help you select the DataField and DataMember properties for a RptTextBox control that you create by hand. If you drop such a control in the top level of a Data Report based on a hierarchy, the DataField property will display a combo box with choices based only on the top Command in the corresponding relational hierarchy. If you select a value for the DataField property in such a case, it will fill in the proper DataMember for you. If you drop a RptTextBox control into a lower section, the DataMember property will also display a combo box letting you choose from any table at or above that level, and the DataField combo box will be adjusted accordingly.

In most cases, unless you have very limited screen real estate, you'll find it more convenient to create bound fields by simple drag-and-drop operations from the Data Environment than by using the Data Report Toolbox.

Using Calculated Fields

Sometimes you'll want to display derived information on a Data Report. For example, the drSalesDetails2 Data Report from the ADOChapter24sample project shows the total of each line in the detail section of the Order. This total is calculated by multiplying the quantity by the unit price for each row in the Order Details table.

In some report designers (such as the one provided with Microsoft Access), you can create such calculated controls directly in the designer. The Data Report Designer, unfortunately, is not sophisticated enough to support this functionality. If you inspect the design of the drSalesDetail2 Data Report, you'll discover that it's based on the Customers2 hierarchy within the deNorthwind Data Environment. At the lowest level of this hierarchy, there's a Command object based on a SQL statement:

```
SELECT OrderID, ProductID,
Quantity * UnitPrice AS LineTotal
FROM [Order Details]
```

In other words, the calculation is embedded directly in the Command, rather than being calculated in any way by the report. This is generally the only way to place calculated fields on a Data Report. However, you can use the RptFunction control to create aggregate calculation in the Data Report Designer. You'll learn more about this technique later in the chapter.

Special Header and Footer Controls

In addition to bound information and static information (such as the label for a field), you can place some special variable controls on a Data Report. Typically, these controls are most useful in Headers and Footers. You can insert these controls by right-clicking in a section and choosing Insert Control, followed by the type of control you wish to insert. Table 24.4 lists all the special controls that are supported by the Data Report Designer.

You can also create these special controls by inserting a RptLabel control and using a code, starting with a percent sign, where you'd like the variable information filled in. These codes are also listed in Table 24.4. To use a percent sign in the caption of a RptLabel control, you must double it to %%.

TABLE 24.4: Special Controls for Data Reports

Control (Menu Choice)	Code
Current Page Number	%p
Total Number of Pages	%P
Current Date (Short Format)	%d
Current Date (Long Format)	%D
Current Time (Short Format)	%t
Current Time (Long Format)	%T
Report Title	%i

Properties on Data Reports

Like just about everything else in Visual Basic, Data Reports and their components have properties that you can set in the Visual Basic properties window or (in some cases) from code. In this section, I'll summarize the properties that are available for customizing Data Reports.

Data Report Properties

Some properties of Data Reports are similar to those of forms. Others are completely new. Here's the complete list of Data Report properties:

Name   Contains the name of the object.

BorderStyle   Can be set to vbBSNone, vbFixedSingle, vbSizable (the default), vbFixed-Double, vbFixedDialog, vbFixedToolWindow, or vbSizableToolWindow. These properties control the type of border shown on the Data Report window when it's displayed in preview mode at runtime.

BottomMargin, LeftMargin, RightMargin, and TopMargin   Specify in twips (the default is 1,440) how much white space should be left around the report when it's printed.

Caption   Specifies the window title for the Data Report when it's displayed in preview mode.

ControlBox, Icon, MaxButton, and MinButton   Set the display of the window widgets when the Data Report is displayed in preview mode.

DataMember   Contains the name of the top Command object used by the report.

DataSource   Contains the name of the Data Environment used by the report.

Enabled   Specifies whether the Data Report should respond to runtime events.

Font   Specifies the default font to be used on the report. This font can be overridden on a section or control basis.

GridX and GridY   Specify the granularity of the control placement grid at design time.

Height, Left, StartupPosition, Top, and Width   Specify the size and location of the window that will display the report at runtime.

MouseIcon and MousePointer   Set a mouse pointer to use when the report is displayed in preview mode at runtime.

Palette and PaletteMode   Control the display of any graphics on the Data Report.

ReportWidth   Specifies the width of every section on the report, in the designer, in twips. (Each section has its own Height property.)

RightToLeft   Controls text display on BiDirectional language systems.

ShowInTaskbar   Is set to True if you'd like the report to have its own button in the Windows Taskbar at runtime.

Tag   Is present, as it is on every other Visual Basic object, to hold arbitrary designer-specified data.

Title   Is used to label the report when it's printed or exported to HTML.

Visible   Controls whether the report can be seen on-screen when it's previewed. You'll probably want to leave this set to its default value of True.

Section Properties

By contrast, sections on Data Reports have very few properties:

Name   Identifies the section. This property is originally assigned by the Data Report Designer when you retrieve the structure for the Data Report, but you can change it if you like.

ForcePageBreak   Tells the designer whether this section should cause any special action when the Data Report is previewed or printed. By default, it's set to rptPageBreakNone. You can also choose rptPageBreakBefore to ensure that this section starts at the top of a new page every time it's processed, rptPageBreakAfter to have this section be the last thing on a page, or rptPageBreakBeforeAndAfter to combine both of these effects.

Height   Controls the vertical distance the section takes up. Of course, you can also adjust this by dragging the report section baselines within the designer.

KeepTogether   Is used to keep important information on the same page. If you set this property to True and the section won't fit on the current page, printing or previewing the Data Report will start a new page at this point.

Visible   Controls whether this section will be displayed at runtime.

Control Properties

For the most part, properties for RptLabel, RptTextBox, RptImage, RptLine, and RptShape controls are exactly the same as for the Label, TextBox, Image, Line, and Shape controls that you're already familiar with. I won't review these basic properties, such as BackColor and RightToLeft, here. But there are a few properties of the RptTextBox control that are unique. You've already seen several of them, but I'll repeat them here for reference:

DataMember   Holds the name of the Command object in the Data Environment from which this RptTextBox control's data comes.

DataField   Holds the name of the field in the Command object in the Data Environment from which this RptTextBox control's data comes.

DataFormat   Holds an optional format name for displaying the data with formatting.

CanGrow   Tells the Data Report whether it can allocate additional space to this control at runtime. If you set this property to True and the data for the control is larger than will fit in the size that was set for the control at design time, the Height property of the control will be increased to hold the additional data.

WARNING   Unlike the report designer in Microsoft Access, the Data Report Designer doesn't implement a CanGrow property on sections. You need only to change the control property to allow this behavior, and the section will grow to fit the control.

Summarizing Data on Data Reports

It's often convenient to have summary data presented on reports. For example, on a sales report, you might want to see both the details of individual sales and the total of all sales for the month. The Data Report Designer allows you to create summary information by using a special control (the RptFunction control) or by using a grouping or aggregate hierarchy within the Data Environment that the report is bound to. In this section, you'll see how to use both of these techniques.

Using the Function Control

The RptFunction control has no exact analog in the regular Visual Basic controls. It looks like a regular text box at runtime, but it has the unique ability to summarize information from the Data Report. Figure 24.25 shows the last page of the drSalesDetails2 Data Report from the ADOChapter24 sample project. The Line Total for each line of the report is based on a calculated field in the SQL statement that the Command object is based on, as you learned earlier in the chapter. However, the Order Total, Customer Total, and Grand Total controls are RptFunction controls. As you can see, these controls give an aggregate sum for information above them in the Data Report.

FIGURE 24.25:

Using the RptFunction control

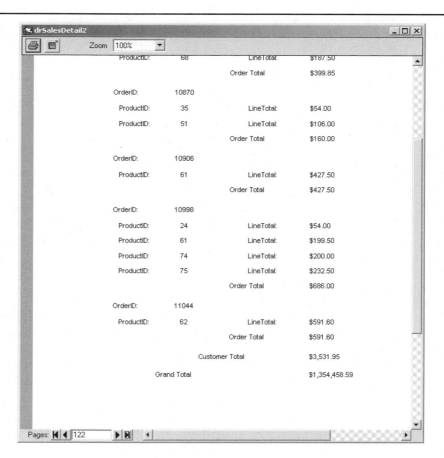

To use the RptFunction control, select it in the Data Report Toolbox and draw it on the Data Report, just as you would any other text box. However, you can place this control only in a Footer section of the report. The Data Report Designer enforces this limitation and won't allow you to place a RptFunction control in a Header or Detail section.

In addition to the DataField, DataMember, and DataFormat properties that it shares with the RptTextbox control, the RptFunction control supports a FunctionType property. You can set this to eight values:

- rptFuncSum (the default) to add values together
- rptFuncAve to average values
- rptFuncMin to choose the smallest value
- rptFuncMax to choose the largest value
- rptFuncRCnt to count the number of rows
- rptFuncVCnt to count the number of non-null distinct values
- rptFuncSDEV to calculate standard deviation
- rptFuncSERR to calculate standard error

Whatever function you choose is applied over the entire scope of the Footer section that contains the control. For example, if you place a RptFunction control in the Orders Footer and set its FunctionType property to rptFuncMax, it will display the maximum value of the field for each order. If you place the identical control in the Report Footer (or copy it from the Orders Footer to the Report Footer), it will display the maximum value from the entire report.

Using Grouping and Aggregate Hierarchies

The Data Report Designer can use grouping and aggregate hierarchies to display grouped information. Figure 24.26 shows a portion of the drGrouping Data Report in the ADO-Chapter24 sample. This particular report is based on the grpProducts command in the deHierarchies Data Environment. This command groups product data by category.

Grouping reports are just beyond the limit of what the Data Report Designer can do for you automatically. In order to create such a report, you need to first create a Data Environment Command object that uses grouping. When you do this, of course, the Data Environment Designer displays the grouping and detail fields separately. For example, if you open the deHierarchies Data Environment, you'll find that there's a Command object named "grpProducts grouped using Category." This object has subfolders labeled "Summary fields in Category" and "Detail fields in grpProducts."

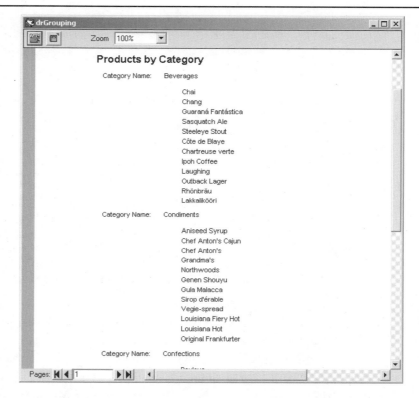

The confusing thing about grouping reports is that none of these choices appears explicitly for the DataMember property of a Data Report. Once you've chosen this Data Environment as the DataSource, you'll find that the choices for DataMember include grpProducts and Category. These are the actual names of the saved Command objects that underlie the grouping hierarchy. For a grouping report, of course, you need to choose the Category command object.

You can complete the grouping report by using the same drag-and-drop actions that you would for any other Data Report. You'll find that the fields from the grouping folder in the Data Environment can be dragged to the Header, Footer, or Detail section, while the fields from the detail folder in the Data Environment can be dragged only to the Detail section on the Data Report.

You can also base a Data Report on an aggregate Command object within the Data Environment Designer. Figure 24.27 shows part of the drAggregate Data Report in the ADOChapter24 sample project.

FIGURE 24.27:

Aggregate Data Report

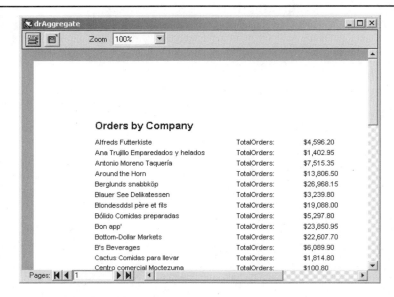

To create such a report, you need to first create a Data Environment containing an aggregate field. This particular report is based on the Command hierarchy that I created earlier in the chapter in the deHierarchies Data Environment. This Command, aggOrders, includes an aggregate field named TotalOrders.

Creating a Data Report including this field is straightforward. You just hook up a blank Data Report to this Command hierarchy using the DataMember property of the Data Report, and drag and drop fields as you always would. You'll find that the aggregate field can be dropped in any section except the Page or Report Headers and Footers.

Aggregate fields and the RptFunction control perform the same task of aggregating some piece of information across an entire section. There are two differences between them:

- Because aggregate fields are precalculated by the Data Environment, they can be placed in Header sections. RptFunction controls, in contrast, can be placed only in Footer sections, since their value isn't known until the entire section has been processed.

- There are differences in the functions available. In particular, aggregate fields can use the Any function to pick a random value, which isn't available to RptFunction controls. On the other hand, RptFunction controls can summarize by Value Count or Standard Error, neither of which is available in an aggregate field.

Printing and Exporting Data Reports

Once you've created a Data Report, what can you do with it? There are four basic operations that you can perform on Data Reports:

- Print Preview
- Print
- Export to Text
- Export to HTML

In this section, I'll cover each of these operations in turn.

Print Preview

To show a Data Report on-screen, you place it into print preview mode at runtime. You do this by calling the Show method of the Data Report:

```
<DataReportName>.Show([Modal], [OwnerForm])
```

The Modal and OwnerForm arguments work the same way for Data Reports as they do for regular Visual Basic forms. That is, by default, Data Reports are not modal, but you may set the Modal argument to vbModal to make them modal instead. By default, the window in which a Data Report is displayed is owned by the desktop. You can also specify that it is owned by a particular Visual Basic form. This has the effect of keeping the report on top of the form.

When you display a Data Report in print preview mode, the toolbar in the Data Report's window contains three controls:

- The Print button, of course, will print the report.
- The Export button allows you to export the report to a number of file formats.
- The Zoom box allows you to select the magnification of the report on-screen. You can set this to 100%, 75%, 50%, 25%, 10%, or Fit, which makes sure the entire report can be seen in the window.

WARNING   Before you can display a Data Report on-screen, you must have a printer installed.

Print

To print a Data Report, you call the report's PrintReport method:

```
<DataReportName>.PrintReport ([ShowDialog As Boolean=False], _
   [Range As PageRangeConstants=rptRangeAllPages], _
   [PageFrom],[PageTo]) As Long
```

The ShowDialog argument controls whether you'd like the report to go straight to the printer or prompt the user for details. If this argument is omitted (the default), the report is printed immediately, on the default printer, and all pages are printed. If you set ShowDialog to True, Visual Basic will display a Print dialog box, allowing the user to choose a non-default printer and select the pages and number of copies to print.

The Range argument can be set to rptRangeAllPages to print the entire report, or rptRangeFromTo to print selected pages. Either way, entire pages are printed, even if only part of the page shows on-screen.

The PageFrom and PageTo arguments let you specify the first and last pages for the print job, if you've chosen rptRangeFromTo as the Range argument.

The PrintReport method returns a unique identifier that can be used for asynchronous event processing. You'll learn about this later in the chapter.

If the user clicks the Print button on a Data Report that's open in print preview mode, the user will always be presented with the Print dialog box.

WARNING   If you use IntelliSense in Visual Basic, you'll also see a PrintForm method in the list of available methods for the Data Report. This shows up only because Data Reports are based on forms. For all practical purposes, you can ignore this method.

Export

Data Reports can be exported programmatically or interactively by the user. In Visual Basic code, you can call the ExportReport method:

```
<DataReportName>.ExportReport([FormatIndexOrKey],[FileName], _
   [Overwrite As Boolean=True], _
   [ShowDialog As Boolean=False], _
   [Range As PageRangeConstants=rptRangeAllPages], _
   [PageFrom],[PageTo]) As Long
```

The FormatIndexOrKey argument specifies one of four built-in export formats: rptFmtHTML for export to HTML, rptFmtUnicodeHTML for export to HTML with the Unicode character set, rptFmtText for export to text, or rptFmtUnicodeText for export to text with the Unicode character set.

The FileName argument specifies the file to be created by the ExportReport method.

The OverWrite argument tells the method whether to overwrite an existing file.

The ShowDialog argument determines whether or not the Export dialog box, seen in Figure 24.28, will be displayed to the user.

The Export dialog box
for a Data Report

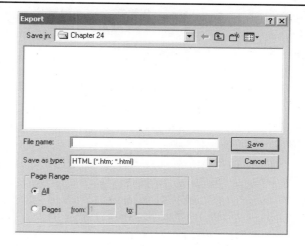

The Range argument can be set to rptRangeAllPages to export the entire report, or rptRangeFromTo to export selected pages. Either way, entire pages are exported, even if only part of the page shows on-screen.

The PageFrom and PageTo arguments let you specify the first and last pages to be exported, if you've chosen rptRangeFromTo as the value for the Range argument.

The Export method returns a unique identifier that can be used for asynchronous event processing. You'll learn about this later in the chapter.

If the user clicks the Export button on a Data Report that's open in print preview mode, the user will always be presented with the Export dialog box.

WARNING   The pages specified to the ExportReport method won't necessarily match the pages seen in the print preview mode, because the ExportReport method uses the exported fonts to calculate page breaks.

Figure 24.29 shows how the drGrouping Data Report from the ADOChapter24 sample project looks when exported to text and HTML formats.

FIGURE 24.29:

Exported Data
Reports

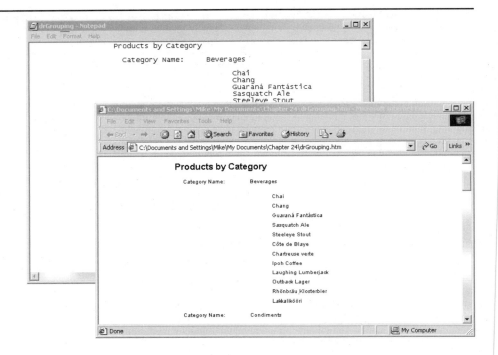

Data Report Events

You've already seen the important methods and properties of Data Reports. To wrap up the coverage of Data Reports, I'll discuss the nine events that Data Report objects support:

- Initialize and Terminate
- Activate and Deactivate
- ProcessingTimeout
- AsyncProgress
- Error
- Resize and QueryClose

The frmDREvents form in the ADOChapter24 sample project, shown in Figure 24.30, will let you experiment with these events. This form instantiates the drSalesDetail3 Data Report; the Data Report contains code in each event procedure that writes information back to this form.

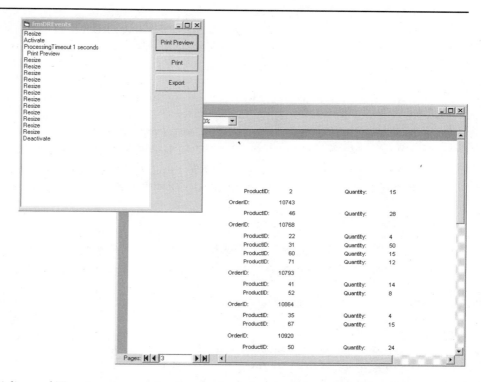

The Initialize and Terminate events are the standard class module events. Because a Data Report consists of a user interface and a class module (just like a form), it supports these events:

```
Private Sub DataReport_Initialize()
Private Sub DataReport_Terminate()
```

The Initialize occurs as soon as the report is created, and the Terminate occurs when the report is closed and all references to it are released.

The Activate and Deactivate events track whether the Data Report is the active window:

```
Private Sub DataReport_Activate()
Private Sub DataReport_Deactivate()
```

The Activate event is fired whenever the Data Report becomes the active window, and the Deactivate event is fired whenever the focus moves to another window.

The ProcessingTimeout event occurs during synchronous processing:

```
Private Sub DataReport_ProcessingTimeout( _
 ByVal Seconds As Long, Cancel As Boolean, _
 ByVal JobType As MSDataReportLib.AsyncTypeConstants, _
 ByVal Cookie As Long)
```

When you use the Show method to display a report on-screen, there are two steps involved in the processing. First, ADO has to process the query from the Data Environment to the data provider. You can't get into the middle of this process from the Data Report; you just have to wait for it to finish. After that, the Data Report has to work out how to display the data on-screen. This process is synchronous—that is, the Show method blocks other Visual Basic code from executing. However, during this synchronous process, the ProcessingTimeout event will be fired approximately once per second. The Seconds argument will tell you how many seconds have elapsed since control returned to the Data Report. If you like, you can set the Cancel argument to True to cancel the remaining processing.

This event also occurs when you are printing or exporting a Data Report. You can check the JobType argument to determine what exactly is going on. JobType will have one of three values:

- rptAsyncPreview if you're in the Show method

- rptAsyncPrint if you're in the Print method, or the user has clicked the Print button

- rptAsyncExport if you're in the Export method, or the user has clicked the Export button

WARNING   Don't get fooled by the constant names. ProcessingTimeout is a synchronous event despite using the rptAsync constants.

The Cookie argument contains the return value from the ExportReport or PrintReport method if one of those methods was used to start the process. You can use this argument to determine which of several concurrent processes triggered this event.

The AsyncProgress event fires about once per second during asynchronous processing:

```
Private Sub DataReport_AsyncProgress( _
  ByVal JobType As MSDataReportLib.AsyncTypeConstants, _
  ByVal Cookie As Long, _
  ByVal PageCompleted As Long, _
  ByVal TotalPages As Long)
```

When you (or your user) print or export a Data Report, there are three steps involved. First, ADO has to process the query from the Data Environment to the data provider. You can't get into the middle of this process from the Data Report; you just have to wait for it to finish. After that, the Data Report has to work out how to display the data on-screen. This process is synchronous. Finally, the Data Report triggers the print or export process. These processes are asynchronous—that is, other Visual Basic code will continue executing while the print or export is proceeding. However, because the AsyncProgress event is triggered about once per second, you can keep track of what's going on.

The JobType and Cookie arguments allow you to track which process triggered the event, just as they do in the ProcessingTimeout event. You can't track the number of seconds that processing has taken (unless you maintain your own timer), but you can use the Page-Completed and TotalPages arguments to tell how far the process has proceeded. Because printing and exporting are actually handled by external libraries, you can't cancel these events.

WARNING Don't count on ProcessingTimeout and AsyncProgress events to happen precisely once per second. If your system is heavily loaded, some of these events might be skipped. In particular, if you're checking for a length of time in the ProcessingTimeout event, be sure to check that the elapsed time is greater than the length you're interested in, rather than precisely equal to that length.

The Error event is triggered whenever an error occurs that's not in Visual Basic code:

```
Private Sub DataReport_Error( _
  ByVal JobType As MSDataReportLib.AsyncTypeConstants, _
  ByVal Cookie As Long, _
  ByVal ErrObj As MSDataReportLib.RptError, _
  ShowError As Boolean)
```

Once again, the JobType and Cookie arguments allow you to determine which process triggered the error. The ErrObj argument contains the details of the error. If you process the error yourself, you'll want to set the ShowError argument to False to suppress the default error display.

WARNING If you're printing or exporting, not every error will trigger this event. For example, if no printer driver is installed, you will receive an Error event. However, if a printer is installed but is out of paper, you won't receive an error. That's because the "out of paper" error belongs to the asynchronous print process, not to Visual Basic itself.

Finally, the Resize and QueryClose events are identical to their counterparts from forms:

```
Private Sub DataReport_Resize()
Private Sub DataReport_QueryClose( _
  Cancel As Integer, CloseMode As Integer)
```

The Resize event is fired whenever the Data Report is in preview mode and the user resizes the window. (This event does *not* fire when the user changes the zoom factor of the Data Report.)

The QueryClose event is fired whenever the Data Report preview window is about to be closed. The CloseMode argument is set to a value that indicates what is closing the window:

- vbFormControlMenu if the user closed the Data Report manually
- vbFormCode if the Data Report is closed from code
- vbAppWindows if the current Windows session is ending
- vbAppTaskManager if the Windows Task Manager is closing the application

If you like, you can attempt to cancel the closing by setting the Cancel argument to True.

Data Consumers

In previous versions of Visual Basic (through Visual Basic 5), you used a data control to provide data and used intrinsic Visual Basic controls (text boxes, combo boxes, and so on) to show data, with data binding providing the connection between the two. But that was all that data binding was good for.

Visual Basic 6 extends the reach of data binding by allowing you to use it programmatically. You can create both data consumers and data sources, and bind one to the other in code. Your own components can play either or both roles in the data binding relationship. In this section, you'll see how easy it is to create a data consumer. Later in the chapter, you'll learn how to create your own data sources as well.

What Is a Data Consumer?

A *data consumer* is any Visual Basic component that can accept data from a data source. In other words, it can be the target of a data binding relationship. Using Visual Basic 6, you can create objects and UserControls that function as data consumers. You do this by setting the DataBindingBehavior property of the class to an appropriate value:

- vbNone (the default) indicates that this class is not a data consumer.

- vbSimpleBound indicates that the class is a *simple binding data consumer.* A simple binding consumer is one that can be bound to a single data field. For example, the intrinsic TextBox control is simple-bound.

- vbComplexBound indicates that the class is a *complex binding data consumer.* A complex binding consumer is one that can be bound to an entire row of data. For example, the Hierarchical FlexGrid control is complex-bound. It might look like the control is bound to an entire Recordset, but that's an illusion caused by it fetching multiple rows to display. Only one row is current at a time.

To use these new properties, you need to add some references to your Visual Basic project. A reference to the Microsoft Data Binding Collection is necessary for simple data binding, and a reference to the Microsoft Data Source Interfaces is necessary for complex data binding. If you choose the Data Project choice when you create a new Visual Basic project, these references are added automatically. If you need to add them by hand, just search for them in the References dialog box available from Project ➤ References.

Data-Aware Classes

You can create a class that's either simple bound or complex bound to data. By setting appropriate properties at runtime, you can then bind an instance of such a class to any data source in your project.

Simple Binding with a Class

The first example is the easiest to understand. If you open the frmSimpleClass form in the ADOChapter24 sample project, you'll find a form with an ADO Data Control and a text box. As you use the navigation buttons on the data control to move through the underlying Recordset (in this case, the Customers table from the SQL Server version of the Northwind database), the text box is continually updated to show the CompanyName field. This could be done just by binding the text box to the ADO Data Control, but it's not. Rather, the text box is displaying information from an instance of the clsSimpleExample class, which is itself bound to the ADO Data Control.

There's not much code in the class itself:

```
Private mstrName As String
Public Property Get Name() As String
    Name = mstrName
End Property
Public Property Let Name(NewName As String)
    mstrName = NewName
End Property
```

As you can see, this is just a class that exposes a single persistent read/write property named Name. The key, though, is something that doesn't show in code: The DataBindingBehavior property for the class is set to vbSimpleBound in the property sheet for the class.

The code behind the form makes use of the BindingCollection object (supplied by the Microsoft Data Binding Collection library):

```
Private mobjBindingCollection As BindingCollection
Private mobjSimpleExample As clsSimpleExample

Private Sub Form_Load()
    ' Create the objects we need
    Set mobjBindingCollection = New BindingCollection
    Set mobjSimpleExample = New clsSimpleExample
    ' Tell the binding collection where to get data
    Set mobjBindingCollection.DataSource = _
     Me!AdodcCustomers
    ' And add a binding
    mobjBindingCollection.Add mobjSimpleExample, _
     "Name", "CompanyName"
End Sub

Private Sub AdodcCustomers_MoveComplete( _
 ByVal adReason As ADODB.EventReasonEnum, _
 ByVal pError As ADODB.Error, _
 adStatus As ADODB.EventStatusEnum, _
 ByVal pRecordset As ADODB.Recordset)
    Me!txtName = mobjSimpleExample.Name
End Sub
```

The BindingCollection object is the mechanism that Visual Basic uses to expose the internals of the data binding process. A BindingCollection object takes information from its DataSource property and supplies that information to all members of its internal collection of Binding objects. To add a new Binding object, you use the Add method of the BindingCollection:

```
BindingCollection.Add(Object As Object, _
    [PropertyName As String], _
    [DataField As String], _
    [DataFormat As IDataFormatDisp],
    [Key As String]) As Binding
```

The Add method takes the following parameters:

Object   Represents any data consumer. In this example, this is an instance of the clsSimpleExample class.

PropertyName   The name of the property on the data consumer that should be bound. In this example, this is the Name property (the only property that clsSimpleExample exposes).

DataField   A field from the DataSource property of the BindingCollection object that you're working with. In this case, it's the CompanyName field.

DataFormat   An optional object that specifies a format for the display of the data.

Key   An optional key into the collection of Bindings. This is most useful if you have a single data source bound to multiple data consumers and wish to work with the properties of an individual consumer.

So, here's how the pieces of this example fit together:

1. When you open the frmSimpleClass form, it creates an instance of the clsSimpleExample class and a new BindingCollection object.

2. The form then specifies the location of its data by setting the DataSource property of the BindingCollection object to the ADO Data Control that's sitting on the form.

3. The class then gets hooked to the other side of the BindingCollection object by using that object's Add method to add a binding.

4. Whenever you navigate to a new record using the ADO Data Control, the control's MoveComplete event fires.

5. In the event procedure for the MoveComplete event, the current value of the Name property of the class is retrieved and displayed in the text box on the form.

WARNING   Neither the intrinsic Visual Basic data control nor the RDO-based Remote data control can be bound programmatically—yet another reason to switch to ADO for data access.

Complex Binding with a Class

A class with complex data binding can bind to an entire Recordset at once. For example, the frmComplexClass form in the ADOChapter24 sample project demonstrates binding an instance of a class to a Recordset delivered by a Command object in a Data Environment.

The code in this case is a bit more complex (no surprise!) than for the simple data binding case. Here's the class module, clsComplexExample:

```
Private WithEvents mrst As ADODB.Recordset

Public Property Get DataSource() As DataSource
    Set DataSource = mrst.DataSource
End Property

Public Property Set DataSource( _
 ByVal NewDataSource As DataSource)
    Set mrst.DataSource = NewDataSource
End Property

Public Property Get DataMember() As DataMember
    DataMember = mrst.DataMember
End Property

Public Property Let DataMember( _
 ByVal NewDataMember As DataMember)
    mrst.DataMember = NewDataMember
End Property

Private Sub Class_Initialize()
    Set mrst = New ADODB.Recordset
End Sub

Public Property Get CurrentRow() As String
    Dim fld As ADODB.Field
    Dim strTemp As String
    For Each fld In mrst.Fields
        strTemp = strTemp & fld.Name & ": "
        If fld.Type = adBinary Then
            strTemp = strTemp & "<Long Binary>" _
            & " "
        Else
            strTemp = strTemp & CStr(fld.Value & _
            "") & " "
        End If
    Next fld
    CurrentRow = strTemp
    Set fld = Nothing
```

```
    End Property

    Public Sub MoveNext()
        mrst.MoveNext
    End Sub

    Public Sub MovePrevious()
        mrst.MovePrevious
    End Sub
```

Classes that implement complex data binding must expose DataMember and DataSource properties, just like any other data consumer that can bind to an entire Recordset (for example, a grid control). The DataMember and DataSource datatypes are provided by the Microsoft Data Source Interfaces type library. Of course, the DataBindingBehavior property of this class is set to vbComplexBound.

This class functions by maintaining an internal, hidden ADO Recordset that will be populated by the data source to which the class instance is bound. When you set the DataMember and DataSource properties (in that order), this Recordset is automatically initialized from the specified data source.

In the case of the frmComplexData sample form, those properties are set when the form is loaded, and they serve to connect the instance of the class to a Data Environment command that draws its data from the SQL Server version of the Northwind database:

```
    Private mobjComplexExample As clsComplexExample
    Private Sub Form_Load()
        Set mobjComplexExample = New clsComplexExample
        With mobjComplexExample
            .DataMember = "cmdCustomers"
            Set .DataSource = deNorthwind
        End With
        txtCurrentRow = mobjComplexExample.CurrentRow
    End Sub
```

The CurrentRow method of the class demonstrates the ability to retrieve data from the Recordset. The MoveNext and MovePrevious methods of the class are thin wrappers around the corresponding Recordset methods.

NOTE   DataMember is a simple datatype, not a class. That is, it doesn't require the Set keyword when you assign a value to it.

Data-Aware UserControls

Although data-aware classes are interesting, you're more likely to want data-aware User-Controls in a real application. The most typical use of bound data is to build up a user interface on a form, and, of course, UserControls are the perfect tool to encapsulate a combination of user interface elements and code. In this section, you'll see how to build UserControls that can bind to a field or a Recordset.

Simple Binding with a UserControl

You might think that simple binding with a UserControl would be as easy as adding a Data-Field property to the UserControl and properly delegating it—but you'd be wrong. The Visual Basic developers chose to hide the details of setting up a DataField property by adding this property to the Extender object, which is used to supply standard properties for all User-Controls (for example, the Top property is an Extender property). What this means to you is that setting up simple binding is a matter of making proper settings in several different places. The good news is that once you learn how to set it up, it works.

The frmSimpleControl form in the ADOChapter24ControlTest sample project demonstrates a simple bound UserControl. You'll find the control itself saved as SimpleControl in the ADOChapter24Controls project (both projects are included in the ADOChapter24Controls project group). In this case, the interface of the control supplies a text box and a tabstrip. The bound data shows up in the text box, which is implemented by the UserControl. Figure 24.31 shows the frmSimpleControl form in action, reading records from the SQL Server version of the Northwind database.

FIGURE 24.31:

Using a simple bound UserControl

TIP   You should open the ADOChapter24Controls project group rather than the individual projects to properly test this code. Alternatively, you can open the ADOChapter24Controls project and compile it before opening the ADOChapter24ControlTest project.

Here are the essential steps for making the constituent text box in the UserControl available for simple data binding:

1. Create a new UserControl and set its DataBindingBehavior property to vbSimpleBound.

2. Place a TextBox control within the UserControl.

3. If you haven't already done so, use the Add-In Manager to load the ActiveX Control Interface Wizard.

4. Using the ActiveX Control Interface Wizard, add a Text property to the UserControl. Map this property to the Text property of the constituent TextBox control.

5. With the UserControl selected, choose Tools ➤ Procedure Attributes. Select the Text procedure and click the Advanced button. Select the check boxes for Property is Data Bound, This Property Binds to DataField, and Property Will Call CanPropertyChange Before Changing. Figure 24.32 shows how this dialog box should look for the property that you want to be bound for the UserControl. Click OK to dismiss the dialog box.

6. Write code to save the value of the Text property whenever it's changed, whether it's changed by setting the property programmatically or by the user typing a new value into the constituent text box:

```
Private Sub Text1_Change()
    Me.Text = Text1.Text
End Sub
Public Property Let Text(ByVal New_Text As String)
    If CanPropertyChange("Text") Then
        Text1.Text() = New_Text
        PropertyChanged "Text"
    End If
End Property
```

FIGURE 24.32:

Setting the Data Binding properties for a UserControl

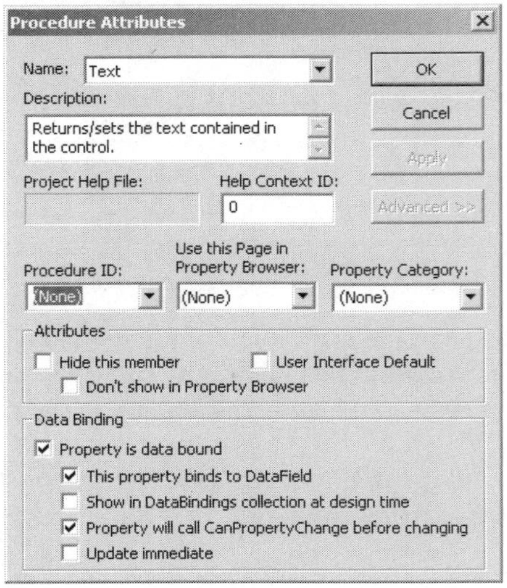

If you've worked with UserControls in the past, you'll know that the PropertyChanged method is used to notify the control's container that a new value for some property needs to be saved. However, that's not quite what's going on here. The Visual Basic development team chose to overload this method, using it for a second purpose: If the property is bound, calling the PropertyChanged method tells the data source that there's changed data ready to write back to the database.

The CanPropertyChange method, in theory, is used to check whether or not the data source is read-only. Although it should return False if the data is read-only, in Visual Basic 6, it always returns True. Fortunately, Visual Basic 6 won't raise an error if you call Property-Changed on a read-only data source. You could leave the check of CanPropertyChange out of your code entirely, but it's insurance for some future version in which it will actually work as advertised.

Multiple Simple Bindings in the Same UserControl

You may also find that you need to bind multiple fields to a single UserControl. This is the case, for example, when you're building a composite control to enforce a uniform user interface for certain data across multiple applications. In this case, you'll need to use a DataBindings collection, but UserControls are set up to let you do this without writing any code.

The frmMultipleControl form demonstrates this technique, using the MultipleControl UserControl. As in the preceding example, the DataBindingBehavior property of the control is set to vbSimpleBound. However, with this control, there are three text boxes on the user interface, each tied to a separate property of the control: CustomerID, CompanyName, and ContactName.

Within the control itself, there's delegation code to handle all three of these properties, as well as to manage the PropertyChanged notifications when someone changes any value:

```
Public Property Let CustomerID(ByVal New_CustomerID As String)
    If CanPropertyChange("CustomerID") Then
        txtCustomerID.Text() = New_CustomerID
        PropertyChanged "CustomerID"
    End If
End Property

Public Property Let CompanyName(ByVal New_CompanyName As String)
    If CanPropertyChange("CompanyName") Then
        txtCompanyName.Text() = New_CompanyName
        PropertyChanged "CompanyName"
    End If
End Property
```

```
Public Property Let ContactName(ByVal New_ContactName As String)
    If CanPropertyChange("ContactName") Then
        txtContactName.Text() = New_ContactName
        PropertyChanged "ContactName"
    End If
End Property

Private Sub txtCompanyName_Change()
    Me.CompanyName = txtCompanyName.Text
End Sub

Private Sub txtContactName_Change()
    Me.ContactName = txtContactName.Text
End Sub

Private Sub txtCustomerID_Change()
    Me.CustomerID = txtCustomerID.Text
End Sub
```

As with the single-field control, you use the Tools ➢ Procedure Attributes menu to set the data binding properties of the control. For each of the three properties, select these check boxes: Property Is Data Bound, Show in DataBindings Collection at Design Time, and Property Will Call CanPropertyChange Before Changing. For one of the properties (it doesn't matter which one), you need to also select the This Property Binds to DataField check box. This will become the default bound property for the control. More importantly, though, Visual Basic won't assign a DataSource property to the control if you miss this step.

By setting the properties to appear in the DataBindings collection at design time, you can avoid having to write any code to populate that collection at runtime. Instead, when you site an instance of the control on a form, you can click the ellipsis button in the control's Data-Bindings property in the properties window to open the Data Bindings dialog box. This dialog box, shown in Figure 24.33, lets you assign data properties to each of the control's bound properties.

The frmMultipleControl form in the ADOChapter24ControlTest sample project uses a Data Environment to retrieve its data from the SQL Server version of the Northwind sample database. You'll find code behind the form that allows the command buttons to navigate through the Recordset returned by the Orders command within this Data Environment:

```
Private Sub cmdFirst_Click()
    deNorthwindSQL.rsCustomers.MoveFirst
End Sub
```

```
Private Sub cmdLast_Click()
    deNorthwindSQL.rsCustomers.MoveLast
End Sub

Private Sub cmdNext_Click()
    With deNorthwindSQL.rsCustomers
        .MoveNext
        If .EOF Then
            .MoveLast
        End If
    End With
End Sub

Private Sub cmdPrevious_Click()
    With deNorthwindSQL.rsCustomers
        .MovePrevious
        If .BOF Then
            .MoveFirst
        End If
    End With
End Sub
```

Note that you don't have to do anything special to synchronize this navigation with the display in the UserControl. Because they're both attached to the same Command within the same Data Environment, the control and the navigation code automatically work with the same Recordset.

FIGURE 24.33:

The Data Bindings dialog box

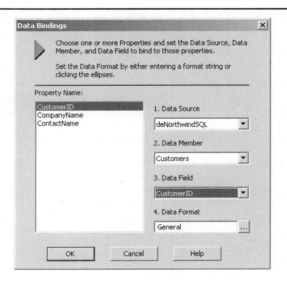

Complex Binding with a UserControl

Of course, you may also want to develop a UserControl that uses complex binding—that is, one that binds to an entire row of data at once. This is surprisingly easy, once you figure out the trick. To create a complex bound UserControl, you need to follow these steps:

1. Create a new UserControl. Set its DataBindingBehavior property to vbComplexBound.

2. Add at least one intrinsic Visual Basic control that can be bound to the UserControl. You don't have to keep this control, but if you don't add it, the next step won't work.

3. Use the ActiveX Control Interface Wizard from the Add-Ins menu to add DataMember and DataSource properties to your new UserControl.

Note the catch mentioned in step 2: If you don't have any bindable constituent controls, the ActiveX Control Interface Wizard won't let you add the DataMember and DataSource properties. You don't need to keep the constituent control after you've added the properties, but it has to be there to begin with.

For such a control to be of any use, obviously, you need to have the DataMember and DataSource properties actually do something. Typically, you use them to initialize an internal ADO Recordset object that will then be bound to whatever external data source you use when you instantiate the UserControl. Figure 24.34 shows the frmComplexControl sample form, which fleshes out this notion a bit, using the ComplexControl UserControl from the ADOChapter24Controls sample project.

FIGURE 24.34:

A UserControl with complex data binding

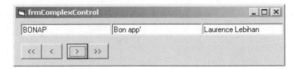

Some of the code within the ComplexControl UserControl may be of interest. First, there's the code that actually does the work of initializing and managing the internal Recordset object:

```
Private WithEvents mrst As ADODB.Recordset

Private Sub UserControl_Initialize()
    Set mrst = New ADODB.Recordset
End Sub

Public Property Get DataMember() As String
    DataMember = mrst.DataMember
End Property

Public Property Let DataMember( _
  ByVal New_DataMember As String)
```

```
    mrst.DataMember = New_DataMember
    PropertyChanged "DataMember"
End Property

Public Property Get DataSource() As DataSource
    Set DataSource = mrst.DataSource
End Property

Public Property Set DataSource( _
 ByVal New_DataSource As DataSource)
    Dim intI As Integer
    Dim intFields As Integer
    Set mrst.DataSource = New_DataSource
    PropertyChanged "DataSource"
    If Text1.Count > 1 Then
        For intI = Text1.Count - 1 To 1 Step -1
            Unload Text1(intI)
        Next intI
    End If
    intFields = mrst.Fields.Count
    If intFields > 0 Then
        Text1(0).Width = ScaleWidth / intFields
        For intI = 1 To intFields - 1
            Load Text1(intI)
            With Text1(intI)
                .Visible = True
                .Top = 0
                .Width = ScaleWidth / intFields
                .Left = .Width * intI
            End With
        Next intI
    End If
End Property
```

Setting the DataMember and DataSource properties is fairly straightforward, except for the extra work that happens in the Property Set procedure for the DataSource property. The UserControl originally contains only a single TextBox control. When the DataSource is set, the control is able to determine how many fields the target Recordset contains and uses this text box as the basis for a control array. This lets the UserControl adapt to any data source.

The UserControl is also designed to proportionately resize all those text boxes so that it can be stretched across a form as appropriate:

```
Private Sub UserControl_Resize()
    Dim intI As Integer
    Dim intBoxes As Integer
    intBoxes = Text1.Count
    For intI = 0 To intBoxes - 1
```

```
        With Text1(intI)
            .Width = ScaleWidth / intBoxes
            .Left = .Width * intI
        End With
    Next intI
End Sub
```

And, of course, the UserControl must get data into the text boxes somehow. Because the internal Recordset variable was declared WithEvents, all of its events are available for the code within the UserControl to work with. The logical place to update the user interface is whenever a new record has been completely fetched. Fortunately, the text box array and the Recordset's Fields collection have the same indexing, which makes the job simpler:

```
Private Sub mrst_MoveComplete( _
  ByVal adReason As ADODB.EventReasonEnum, _
  ByVal pError As ADODB.Error, _
  adStatus As ADODB.EventStatusEnum, _
  ByVal pRecordset As ADODB.Recordset)
    Dim intI As Integer
    On Error Resume Next
    mfLoaded = False
    For intI = 0 To mrst.Fields.Count - 1
        Text1(intI) = mrst.Fields(intI).Value & ""
    Next intI
    mfLoaded = True
End Sub
```

Any changes the user makes through the text boxes have to be written back to the Recordset:

```
Private Sub Text1_Change(Index As Integer)
    If mfLoaded Then
        mrst.Fields(Index) = Text1(Index).Text
    End If
End Sub
```

Finally, in this control, I've provided wrappers around the Move methods of the bound Recordset. This makes it easier to navigate through the Recordset when the data source is a Data Environment (or anything else other than a data control):

```
Public Function MoveFirst() As Variant
    If Not mrst Is Nothing Then
        mrst.MoveFirst
    End If
End Function
Public Function MovePrevious() As Variant
    If Not mrst Is Nothing Then
        If Not mrst.BOF Then
            mrst.MovePrevious
        End If
    End If
```

```
End Function
Public Function MoveNext() As Variant
    If Not mrst Is Nothing Then
        If Not mrst.EOF Then
            mrst.MoveNext
        End If
    End If
End Function
Public Function MoveLast() As Variant
    If Not mrst Is Nothing Then
        mrst.MoveLast
    End If
End Function
```

Because the control is complex bound, there's no need to worry about calling the Recordset's Update method. Visual Basic will automatically take care of that little bit of bookkeeping whenever there are changes ready to be written.

Given all that work in the control, the code behind frmComplexControl is really rather simple (as it should be, since the purpose of a UserControl is to encapsulate user interface and behavior together):

```
Private Sub cmdFirst_Click()
    ComplexControl1.MoveFirst
End Sub

Private Sub cmdLast_Click()
    ComplexControl1.MoveLast
End Sub

Private Sub cmdNext_Click()
    ComplexControl1.MoveNext
End Sub

Private Sub cmdPrevious_Click()
    ComplexControl1.MovePrevious
End Sub

Private Sub Form_Load()
    With ComplexControl1
        .DataMember = "Customers"
        Set .DataSource = deNorthwindSQL
    End With
    deNorthwindSQL.rsCustomers.MoveFirst
End Sub

Private Sub Form_Resize()
    ComplexControl1.Width = Me.Width
End Sub
```

Creating an OLE DB Provider

Throughout this book, I've been using Visual Basic at the downstream end of ADO connections: as the consumer of data supplied by some external data source. But what about the other end of the connection? Well, as it happens, you can create OLE DB data providers in Visual Basic as well. If you're faced with a situation where you have data that you'd like to use in an ADO client application, but no appropriate OLE DB provider, this capability will come in useful.

To build a class that acts as an OLE DB provider, you can use a piece of software called the OLE DB Simple Provider (OSP) Toolkit. This toolkit exists to provide the OLEDBSimple-Provider interface that you must implement to create a simple OLE DB provider. OLEDB-SimpleProvider is a version of the OLE DB interface that contains the basic, most necessary members used by any data consumer. The OSP Toolkit is part of the Microsoft Data Access Components (MDAC) SDK. This SDK is automatically shipped to Microsoft Developer Network (MSDN) members as a part of their annual subscription. However, it's also available for free on the Web (as long as you don't mind a 13-megabyte download) from the Microsoft Universal Data Access site (www.microsoft.com/data).

> **WARNING**   The Visual Basic Help mentions a constant vbOLEDBProvider. This constant doesn't actually exist; it was part of a beta version of Visual Basic 6 that was removed from the product but not from the Help. To create an OLE DB provider with Visual Basic, you *must* use the OSP Toolkit.

When you're installing the MDAC SDK, you can choose which components to install. The only thing you really need for this section of the chapter is the OLE DB Simple Provider Toolkit. Although that toolkit takes up less than 100KB of disk space, you'll still need about 120MB of free space to complete the installation.

Implementing the OLE DB Simple Provider

I could walk you through building all the code for a simple provider from scratch, but there's an easier way. When you install the OLE DB Simple Provider Toolkit, it places a sample Visual Basic project in the OSP\vb subfolder of the install location that you choose. Rather than writing all the code for a simple provider, it's much easier to make a copy of this code and modify it for your own purposes.

I'll demonstrate this strategy in the creation of the Random Number Provider sample application. This OLE DB provider will be used to provide a localized interface for a product. It provides a Recordset containing random numbers to the data consumer. Of course, there are other ways to generate random numbers; this code merely exists to demonstrate the mechanics necessary in constructing a provider.

The provider begins as a new ActiveX DLL project (the ADOChapter24Random project on the companion CD). It contains two multiuse classes, RandDataSource and RandOSP. The first of these has its DataSourceBehavior set to vbDataSource. This will be the class to which you can bind other Visual Basic applications. The project also needs references to three libraries:

- The Microsoft OLE DB Simple Provider 1.5 Library contains the OLEDBSimple-Provider interface definition.

- The Microsoft OLE DB Error Library has error codes for OLE DB operations.

- The Microsoft Data Source Interfaces enable the Visual Basic data source behavior for the project.

Setting the reference to the OLE DB Error Library is trickier than it needs to be. It's possible for a single DLL to contain multiple type libraries, and, in fact, the OLE DB Error Library is the second type library in the oledb32.dll file. Unfortunately, Visual Basic provides no means for you to set a reference to the second type library in a DLL through the user interface. Believe it or not, you'll need to close your project and edit the VBP file in a text editor to do this! You can copy the applicable line from the SampleOSP_VB.vbp file that ships with the OLE DB Simple Provider Toolkit or from the CD's ADOChapter24Random.vbp file. Here's the start of this file:

```
Type=OleDll
Reference=*\G{00020430-0000-0000-C000-000000000046}#2.0#0#
➥ ..\..\WINNT\System32\stdole2.tlb#OLE Automation
Reference=*\G{E0E270C2-C0BE-11D0-8FE4-00A0C90A6341}#1.5#409#
➥ ..\..\WINNT\System32\SIMPDATA.TLB#
➥ Microsoft OLE DB Simple Provider 1.5 Library
Reference=*\G{C8B522D5-5CF3-11CE-ADE5-00AA0044773D}#1.0#0#
➥ ..\..\Program Files\Common Files\System\ole db\
➥ Oledb32.dll\2#Microsoft OLE DB Error Library
Reference=*\G{7C0FFAB0-CD84-11D0-949A-00A0C91110ED}#1.0#0#
➥ ..\..\WINNT\System32\msdatsrc.tlb#Microsoft Data Source Interfaces
Class=MyDataSource; MyDataSource.cls
Class=MyOSPObject; MyOSPObject.cls
Startup="(None)"
```

The boldfaced line above is the one that you'll need to copy to your own Visual Basic project file in order to set this reference. Once you've done this, you can open the Project ➢ References dialog box to confirm that you can use the library.

TIP   Don't worry about fixing the path to the library in your VBP file. Visual Basic will do that when you open the file in Visual Basic.

The next step is to fill in the boilerplate code for the two classes by copying it directly from the code in the SampleOSP_VB project. I copied the entire contents of `MyDataSource.cls` to `RandDataSource.cls` and the entire contents of `MyOSPObject.cls` to `RandOSP.cls`.

WARNING   The sample project from the OLE DB Simple Provider Toolkit doesn't use `Option Explicit`. You should insert this statement at the top of each class in your project. Doing so, unfortunately, will expose several errors in the sample code, which uses variables without declaring them, as well as one place where the Boolean constant False is mistyped as "Flase." It's hard to think of a better demonstration of the worth of Option Explicit!

The next step is to modify the copied code to work with the data you want to provide. The modifications to `RandDataSource.cls` are minimal. This class exists only to pass on the Data-Member to the other class and to return the data that it provides. All I've done in this case is change the name of the property used within the other class to hold the DataMember value, and change the name of the class variable that gets instantiated. Here's the full code for the RandDataSource class:

```
Option Explicit

Private Sub Class_GetDataMember(DataMember As String, _
 Data As Object)

    Dim RN As New RandOSP
    RN.LoadData

    Set Data = RN

End Sub
```

The modifications to RandOSP are somewhat more extensive. First, I created a constant to hold the size of the Recordset, replacing the existing FilePath variable:

```
Const RandCount = 50
```

Next, the LoadData procedure needs to be modified. This is the procedure that fetches (or, in this case, creates) the data you want your provider to provide. It loads it into an array named MyOSPArray for the rest of the code within the class to use. The sample project supplied with the OLE DB Simple Provider Toolkit uses FilePath to specify a text file and then loads the array with semicolon-separated data from that file. The code in the RandOSP class in the sample project creates an array of random numbers instead:

```
Public Sub LoadData()
    Dim intI As Integer

    On Error GoTo ErrorTrap
```

```
    RowCount = RandCount
    ColCount = 1

    ReDim MyOSPArray(0 To RandCount + 1, 1 To 1)
    Randomize Timer

    MyOSPArray(0, 1) = "RandomNumber"
    For intI = 1 To RandCount
        MyOSPArray(intI, 1) = Rnd(1)
    Next intI

    Exit Sub
ErrorTrap:
    Err.Raise (E_FAIL)
End Sub
```

NOTE   Note that the array has as many columns as the Recordset has fields, and as many rows as the number of records plus one. The zeroth row is reserved for field names that you want to present to the data consumer.

The template code from the sample Toolkit project also contains a SaveData sub. This sub is called from the Class_Terminate event to persist changes back to the original disk file. In the case of the RandOSP class, there's no way to persist changes, since the values are hard-coded into the class. But because you might want to modify this code in the future (for example, to save changes to a disk file or the Registry), I've retained an empty SaveData procedure:

```
Public Sub SaveData()
    On Error GoTo ErrorTrap
    Exit Sub
ErrorTrap:
    Err.Raise (E_FAIL)
End Sub
```

The remaining code in the sample Toolkit project is written on the assumption that the data is internally stored in the array; it manipulates the array rather than the original data source. What this means is that I didn't have to make any further modifications to use the code to provide my random data.

The next step is to compile the DLL (this is where you'll need to fix the errors in the Microsoft sample code, if you haven't already done so). Although this registers the DLL's classes on your system, it's not enough to make the DLL recognized as an OLE DB provider. To do this, you need to make a copy of the Sample0SP_VB.reg file from the OLE DB Simple Provider Toolkit. For the ADOChapter24Random sample project, this copy is named

RN.reg. Open the copy and change the descriptive strings and class names to match your project. Here is what's in RN.reg:

```
REGEDIT4

[HKEY_CLASSES_ROOT\ADOChapter24Random]
@="Random Number OLE DB Provider"

[HKEY_CLASSES_ROOT\ADOChapter24Random\CLSID]
@="{C8529C64-0AEB-46ee-9F2E-D61EEF53E909}"
"OLEDB_SERVICES"=dword:00000000

[HKEY_CLASSES_ROOT\CLSID\{C8529C64-0AEB-46ee-9F2E-D61EEF53E909}]
@="ADOChapter24Random"

[HKEY_CLASSES_ROOT\CLSID\
➥ {C8529C64-0AEB-46ee-9F2E-D61EEF53E909}\InprocServer32]
@="c:\\Program Files\\Common Files\\System\\OLE DB\\MSDAOSP.DLL"
"ThreadingModel"="Both"

[HKEY_CLASSES_ROOT\CLSID\{C8529C64-0AEB-46ee-9F2E-D61EEF53E909}\ProgID]
@="ADOChapter24Random"

[HKEY_CLASSES_ROOT\CLSID\{C8529C64-0AEB-46ee-9F2E-D61EEF53E909}\
    VersionIndependentProgID]
@="ADOChapter24Random"

[HKEY_CLASSES_ROOT\CLSID\{C8529C64-0AEB-46ee-9F2E-D61EEF53E909}\OLE DB Provider]
@="Random Number OLE DB Provider"

[HKEY_CLASSES_ROOT\CLSID\{C8529C64-0AEB-46ee-9F2E-D61EEF53E909}\OSP Data Object]
@="ADOChapter24Random.RandDataSource"
```

Note that there's a GUID (globally unique identifier) assigned to the OLE DB provider. In this case, it's C8529C64-0AEB-46ee-9F2E-D61EEF53E909, but you can't just reuse some other provider's GUID. You need to generate a GUID just for your provider. The simplest way to do this is to use the tool GuidGen.exe, which is included on the Visual Basic CD-ROM.

GuidGen (shown in Figure 24.35) is a simple utility. When you need a new unique identifier, run it, select the appropriate format (here, the format used by the Registry), and copy the resulting GUID to the clipboard. Then you can paste it into your code or, as here, your Registry file.

After you've created the Registry file for your provider, run this file on the system where your provider will be used. This will merge the special keys into the Registry to tell the system that your provider really is an OLE DB provider.

FIGURE 24.35:

GuidGen

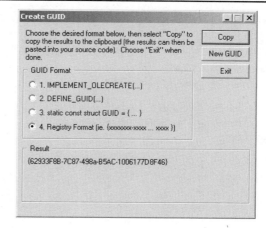

Using the OLE DB Simple Provider

Once you've created your provider, compiled it, and registered it on your system, you're ready to use it to retrieve data. How do you use it? The answer is that it's a bona fide OLE DB provider that you can use in any context where an OLE DB provider is expected.

Figure 24.36 shows the frmRandom form from the ADOChapter24RandomTest sample project. This project uses the random number OLE DB provider that I created to retrieve a Recordset containing random numbers.

FIGURE 24.36:

Testing the random
number provider

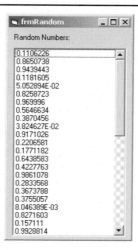

This sample project doesn't need any references to any special libraries. Instead, it does its work just by calling the random number provider. Here's the code that does the work:

```
Private Sub Form_Load()

    Dim cnn As ADODB.Connection
    Dim rst As ADODB.Recordset

    Set cnn = New ADODB.Connection
    cnn.Provider = "ADOChapter24Random"
    cnn.Open

    Set rst = New ADODB.Recordset
    rst.Open "", cnn

    Do Until rst.EOF
        lboRandom.AddItem rst.Fields(0).Value
        rst.MoveNext
    Loop

    ' Clean up
    rst.Close
    Set rst = Nothing
    cnn.Close
    Set cnn = Nothing

End Sub
```

As you can see, the code to use data from the random number provider is quite simple—and the same as the code to use data from any other OLE DB provider! To retrieve the data, the program follows these steps:

1. Open a connection using the random number provider (with the project name under which I chose to compile the provider).

2. Open a Recordset using a blank source (because the random number provider doesn't use any DataMember).

3. Move through the Recordset using the MoveNext method until the EOF property is True, transferring the contents of the first (and only) field in the Recordset to the form's user interface.

Note that all the ADO code, including the use of the Open methods, is identical to code for any other OLE DB provider. Providers compiled with the OSP Toolkit also support the Find method.

If you compile this sample on your computer, you'll find that the random number provider works in other contexts that expect an OLE DB provider. For example, this provider appears in the list of providers available to any Data Link file.

Summary

Visual Basic 6 features tight integration with ADO in a number of ways. Although ADO 2.0 was the current version when Visual Basic 6 was released, all of the ADO features still work fine with more current versions. Here are some of the techniques that you saw in this chapter:

- The use of bound controls to display data from an ADO data source
- The use of the Data Environment to manage ADO Connections, Commands, and Recordsets with a visual interface at design time
- The use of the Data Report as a banded report writer
- The creation of bound classes and controls, including both simple and complex data binding
- The creation of a simple OLE DB provider entirely in Visual Basic

The length of this chapter alone should give you an indication of the importance of ADO in the Visual Basic world! In the next chapter, I'll turn my attention to another client program that is well integrated with ADO, Microsoft Access 2002.

CHAPTER 25

Using ADO from Microsoft Access

- The Client Data Manager

- Binding Access forms to ADO Recordsets

- Shaped Recordsets and Access reports

Microsoft began making serious use of ADO in its desktop database with the release of Access 2000, although the older DAO object library was probably more heavily used by Access developers using that version. In the newer version, Access 2002 (a component of Office XP), ADO is the default data access library—preferred over the older DAO library. In this chapter, I'll examine some of the unique features of the Access/ADO combination, including the use of Access to display arbitrary ADO Recordsets, and the Client Data Manager, a special OLE DB service provider used by Access 2002. I'll also discuss the use of shaped Recordsets as a way to supply data directly to Access reports.

The Client Data Manager

Chapter 2, "Understanding Data Access Architectures," introduced the concept of an OLE DB service provider. A service provider doesn't connect directly to a data source the way that a data provider does. Rather, a service provider takes data from a data provider and transforms it before delivering the data to a client application (or to another service provider). Service providers that you've seen in previous chapters include the data shaping service (which supplies hierarchical Recordsets), the cursor service (which supplies client-side cursors), and the remoting service (which handles access to data providers over the Internet).

Access 2002 introduces a new service provider, the Client Data Manager, sometimes called the CDM. The goal of the Client Data Manager is to bridge the gap between working with Jet data and working with SQL Server data within Microsoft Access. Although Access 2000 included the first version of Access Data Projects (ADPs), which allowed the Access user interface to run directly on the SQL Server database engine, there were a number of problems with the initial implementation of ADPs. Developers discovered that some features they were accustomed to from Access databases (MDBs—the Access user interface atop the Jet database engine) didn't work properly in ADPs. The Client Data Manager is designed to address these deficiencies. Figure 25.1 shows the data access layers used in Access 2002.

TIP   The provider name for the Client Data Manager is Microsoft.Access.OLEDB.10.0.

NOTE   Figure 25.1 doesn't include all the data access components that are available to Access 2002. In particular, the older DAO library is still supported for use with native Jet databases and, through them, other data sources. I'll use only the ADO and OLE DB components in this chapter.

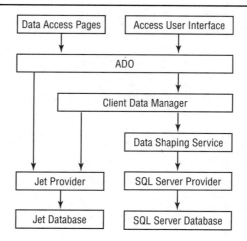

FIGURE 25.1:

Access 2002 data access components

The Client Data Manager offers benefits for the Access developer in these areas:

- Improved update semantics
- Improved auto-lookup
- Stable cursors
- Visible defaults

WARNING You can use the Client Data Manager from applications other than Microsoft Access by creating an appropriate OLE DB connection string. Such use is unsupported by Microsoft and is at your own risk. Before using the Client Data Manager from other applications, you should consider two factors. First, because the Client Data Manager is installed by Access, it's available only on computers where a licensed copy of Access is installed. Second, there are other ways to get some of the functionality of the Client Data Manager. For example, the ADO Data Control in Visual Basic offers some of the same update semantic benefits.

Connection Strings and Properties

Constructing OLE DB connection strings to use the Client Data Manager is similar to constructing connection strings for other service providers. There are three rules to follow:

- Start the string with `Provider=Microsoft.Access.OLEDB.10.0`.
- Specify the underlying data provider with the Data Provider argument.
- Supply any other connection properties that need to be passed to the data provider as additional arguments.

You can transform any OLE DB connection string to a connection string that uses the Client Data Manager by following these steps:

1. Create or retrieve an existing connection string. For example, a connection to a SQL Server database might use this connection string:

```
Provider=SQLOLEDB.1;Data Source=(local);
➥ Integrated Security=SSPI;Initial Catalog = Northwind
```

2. Change the existing Provider keyword to Data Provider:

```
Data Provider=SQLOLEDB.1;Data Source=(local);
➥ Integrated Security=SSPI;Initial Catalog = Northwind
```

3. Add the new Provider to the start of the connection string:

```
Provider=Microsoft.Access.OLEDB.10.0;
➥ Data Provider=SQLOLEDB.1;Data Source=(local);
➥ Integrated Security=SSPI;Initial Catalog = Northwind
```

WARNING   Although you can use the Client Data Manager with any data provider, Microsoft has tested it with only the Jet and SQL Server providers. For any other provider, you should do your own testing until you're satisfied that the combination meets your needs.

If you're working within Access 2002, you'll also find two properties that can be used to retrieve connection strings. Both the Connection property and the AccessConnection property of the Access CurrentProject object return ADO Connection objects. You can use these objects to connect directly to the data source that Access is using in the current database or project. This technique allows you to minimize the performance impact of your code by sharing the existing Connection rather than creating and hooking up a new Connection object.

In an Access project (remember, an Access project is the Access user interface atop the SQL Server database engine), there is no functional difference between the AccessConnection property and the Connection property. Either property will return a Connection that uses the Client Data Manager to retrieve data from the current SQL Server database. You can verify this by retrieving both properties in the Access Immediate Window:

```
?CurrentProject.AccessConnection
Provider=Microsoft.Access.OLEDB.10.0;Persist Security Info=False;
➥ Data Source=(local);Integrated Security=SSPI;
➥ Initial Catalog=Northwind;Data Provider=SQLOLEDB.1
?CurrentProject.Connection
Provider=Microsoft.Access.OLEDB.10.0;Persist Security Info=False;
➥ Data Source=(local);Integrated Security=SSPI;
➥ Initial Catalog=Northwind;Data Provider=SQLOLEDB.1
```

In an Access database (an Access user interface atop the Jet engine), though, there is a difference between the two properties. The Connection property returns a Connection object directly to the Jet OLE DB provider, while the ActiveConnection property returns a Connection object that uses the Client Data Manager. Again, you can verify this in the Immediate Window:

```
?currentproject.Connection
Provider=Microsoft.Jet.OLEDB.4.0;User ID=Admin;
➥ Data Source=C:\ADOChapter25.mdb;Mode=Share Deny None;
➥ Extended Properties="";Jet OLEDB:System database=
➥ C:\PROGRA~1\COMMON~1\System\SYSTEM.MDW;
➥ Jet OLEDB:Registry Path=
➥ SOFTWARE\Microsoft\Office\10.0\Access\Jet\4.0;
➥ Jet OLEDB:Database Password="";Jet OLEDB:Engine Type=5;
➥ Jet OLEDB:Database Locking Mode=1;
➥ Jet OLEDB:Global Partial Bulk Ops=2;
➥ Jet OLEDB:Global Bulk Transactions=1;
➥ Jet OLEDB:New Database Password="";
➥ Jet OLEDB:Create System Database=False;
➥ Jet OLEDB:Encrypt Database=False;
➥ Jet OLEDB:Don't Copy Locale on Compact=False;
➥ Jet OLEDB:Compact Without Replica Repair=False;
➥ Jet OLEDB:SFP=False
?currentproject.AccessConnection
Provider=Microsoft.Access.OLEDB.10.0;Persist Security Info=False;
➥ Data Source=C:\ADOChapter25.mdb;User ID=Admin;
➥ Data Provider=Microsoft.Jet.OLEDB.4.0
```

If you intend to create an ADO Recordset that you can bind directly to an Access form, you should use the AccessConnection property. On the other hand, you must use the Connection property if your code will use any of the following libraries with the returned Connection object:

- ADO Extensions for DDL and Security (ADOX)
- ADO code that requires the Index property or the Seek method
- Jet Replication Objects (JRO)

Code using these libraries will not work with the Client Data Manager.

If you're using the Connection or ActiveConnection property in order to share connections, be sure that you don't accidentally create additional Connection objects in your code. This code snippet demonstrates a common mistake:

```
Dim cnn As New ADODB.Connection
cnn.open CurrentProject.Connection
```

If you run that code, it will retrieve the ConnectionString property of the CurrentProject.Connection object and then use that string to open an additional Connection object. To avoid this problem, you need to use the Set keyword and avoid the Open method entirely:

```
Dim cnn As New ADODB.Connection
Set cnn = CurrentProject.Connection
```

Improved Update Semantics

In Access 2000 projects, it was difficult to update data in a form based on a Recordset created by joining multiple tables. Only the data in the most-many table could be updated, and only if you specified the name of that table in the form's UniqueTable property.

NOTE   The *most-many table* is the one farthest to the "many" side of all the joined tables in a query or other record source. For example, if one customer has many orders, and one order has many order details, then order details is the most-many table of the combined data.

For example, suppose you based a form on this RecordSource:

```
SELECT Customers.CompanyName, Customers.ContactName,
Orders.CustomerID, Orders.OrderID, Orders.OrderDate
FROM Customers INNER JOIN Orders
ON Customers.CustomerID = Orders.CustomerID
```

If you didn't specify a value for the UniqueTable property, data displayed on the form would be read-only. If you did specify "Orders" as the unique table, you could update the Orders .CustomerID and Orders.OrderDate values. (Orders.OrderID could not be updated in any case, being an identity field.) Nothing would make the fields from the Customers table updatable.

In Access 2002, the situation is improved and simplified. If an Access 2002 project contains a form that's based directly on a view or SQL statement, the Client Data Manager will take care of the mechanics of making as many fields as possible updatable. If the form is bound to a Recordset at runtime, the updatability depends on the providers used. If you use the Microsoft.Access.OLEDB.10.0 provider to invoke the Client Data Manager, you'll get an updatable form. If you use only the SQLOLEDB provider, the form will be read-only, even if you specify a value for the UniqueTable property.

Figure 25.2 shows frmUpdate from the ADOChapter25 sample project, which demonstrates runtime Recordset binding and updatability.

NOTE   This sample project is designed to use a copy of the Northwind database stored in a SQL Server on the local computer. If you're using a remote SQL Server, you'll need to choose File ➤ Connection and supply the proper remote server information. You may also have to modify the sample code, substituting the name of your server for "(local)."

FIGURE 25.2:

Updatable Recordset
bound at runtime

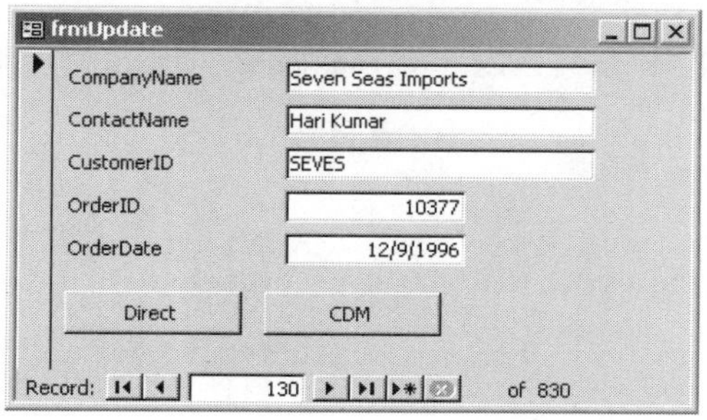

The code behind this form starts by declaring two form-level variables to hold the necessary ADO objects:

```
Dim mcnn As ADODB.Connection
Dim mrst As ADODB.Recordset
```

When the user clicks a button on the user interface, the code connects to the database and retrieves a Recordset, which it then binds to the form's Recordset property. The only difference between the two buttons is that the CDM button uses a connection string with the driver for the Client Data Manager, whereas the Direct button goes directly to the SQL Server OLE DB driver. Listing 25.1 shows the code for both methods.

Listing 25.1:   **Connecting with and without the Client Data Manager**

```
Private Sub cmdCDM_Click()

    If Not mrst Is Nothing Then
        mrst.Close
        Set mrst = Nothing
    End If

    Set mcnn = New ADODB.Connection
    Set mrst = New ADODB.Recordset

    mcnn.Open "Provider=Microsoft.Access.OLEDB.10.0;" & _
      "Data Provider=SQLOLEDB.1;Data Source=(local);" & _
      "Integrated Security=SSPI;Initial Catalog=Northwind;"
    mrst.Open "SELECT Customers.CustomerID AS CID, " & _
      "Customers.CompanyName, Customers.ContactName, " & _
      "Orders.CustomerID, Orders.OrderID, Orders.OrderDate " & _
      "FROM Customers INNER JOIN Orders " & _
      "ON Customers.CustomerID = Orders.CustomerID", mcnn, _
      adOpenKeyset, adLockOptimistic

    Set Me.Recordset = mrst

End Sub
```

```
Private Sub cmdDirect_Click()

    If Not mrst Is Nothing Then
        mrst.Close
        Set mrst = Nothing
    End If

    Set mcnn = New ADODB.Connection
    Set mrst = New ADODB.Recordset

    mcnn.Open "Provider=SQLOLEDB.1;Data Source=(local);" & _
      "Integrated Security=SSPI;Initial Catalog=Northwind;"
    mrst.Open "SELECT Customers.CustomerID AS CID, " & _
      "Customers.CompanyName, Customers.ContactName, " & _
      "Orders.CustomerID, Orders.OrderID, Orders.OrderDate " & _
      "FROM Customers INNER JOIN Orders " & _
      "ON Customers.CustomerID = Orders.CustomerID", mcnn, _
      adOpenKeyset, adLockOptimistic

    Set Me.Recordset = mrst

End Sub
```

If you experiment with this form, you'll discover that you can edit the data if you load it with the CDM button, but not if you load it with the Direct button.

Improved Auto-Lookup

The Client Data Manager also supports immediate auto-lookup in Recordsets. Autolookup is a feature that has long been available with the Jet engine, but not with other database engines. With Autolookup, changes to a foreign key in a Recordset containing a join are automatically reflected in fields from the table containing the corresponding primary key. This keeps all the fields in the current row of the Recordset consistent.

You can see Autolookup in action by using the frmUpdate form. To do so, follow these steps:

1. Open this chapter's sample project.

2. Open the frmUpdate form.

3. Click the CDM button to load data to the form via the Client Data Manager.

4. Change the value of the CustomerID field to ALFKI. At this point, before you tab out of the field, the data displayed on the form is inconsistent, as shown in the upper portion of Figure 25.3. That is, although the CustomerID is ALFKI, the CompanyName and Contact-Name from the VINET customer are still displayed.

5. Tab out of the CustomerID field. Autolookup will take over and fix the values of the CompanyName and ContactName fields so that they are consistent with the new value that you entered for the CustomerID field, as shown in the lower portion of Figure 25.3.

Autolookup in action

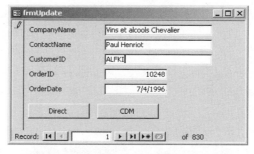

There are four requirements for Autolookup to work:

- You must be using the Client Data Manager.

- The Recordset must include both the primary key and the corresponding foreign key fields.

- One of the key fields must be aliased (assuming that they have the same field name); without aliasing, Access can still display the data but won't be able to update it.

- The foreign key field must be displayed for editing.

Stable Cursors

One of the largest annoyances in using Access projects in Access 2000 was the phenomenon of *unstable cursors*. An unstable cursor is one whose order changes when records are edited. Access 2000 didn't preserve sorts across many operations, leading to much user confusion. For example, the upper portion of Figure 25.4 shows the Customers table from an Access 2000 ADP connected to the Northwind SQL Server database. At this point, the records are sorted by Country, because the user clicked the Country column and selected the Sort Ascending button on the toolbar. The lower portion of Figure 25.4 shows the same table when the user has started entering a new record. Note that simply typing the first field in the new record completely destroys the existing sort order.

Unstable cursor in
Access 2000 ADP

Figure 25.5 shows exactly the same situation in Access 2002. Because Access 2002 uses the
Client Data Manager even when it's displaying data on a datasheet, it's able to preserve the
user's sort order when the user starts to add a new record.

Stable cursor in
Access 2002 ADP

NOTE   Even with the Client Data Manager, new records are added to the end of the Recordset, rather than being sorted to the appropriate position when they're added.

Visible Defaults

In Access 2000, default values from SQL Server tables aren't available on forms in an Access project. The SQL Server OLE DB provider doesn't supply default values by itself when you open a Recordset. It's possible to work around this deficiency in Access 2000 by using the DefaultValue property of the controls on the form. The disadvantage to this workaround, though, is that if the default values are changed on the table, someone will have to edit the form to apply the new default values there as well.

The Client Data Manager in Access 2002 automatically retrieves default values for fields when you open a Recordset and supplies them to the user interface. It does this by executing the undocumented sp_MShelpcolumns stored procedure:

```
EXEC sp_MShelpcolumns N'Products'
```

This stored procedure returns a detailed Recordset with schema information for the desired table, including column datatypes, default values, and much more.

Figure 25.6 shows the frmProducts form in this chapter's sample project. When you scroll to empty records to add new ones to the table, you can see that the form shows the default values for the fields that have defaults. Some fields, such as ProductName, don't have a default value and thus appear as empty.

FIGURE 25.6:

Default values from the Client Data Manager

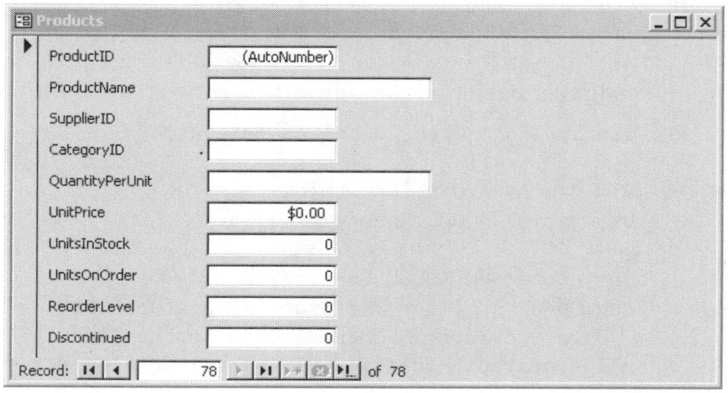

Binding Access Forms to ADO Recordsets

Access 2002 makes it possible to bind arbitrary ADO Recordsets to Access forms—that is, to cause the information from the Recordset to appear on the form, with full use of the navigation, sorting, and filtering tools built into Access. Depending on the Recordset's properties, the data may even be fully editable in Access. In this section, I'll show you how to bind a Recordset to an Access form, and discuss some of the strengths and limitations of this process.

A Simple Binding Example

Figure 25.7 shows the frmSQLCustomers form from this chapter's Access database. This form displays data from the Customers table in the SQL Server version of the Northwind database. The form is bound to the data at runtime.

FIGURE 25.7:

Runtime binding of SQL Server data in Microsoft Access

The code that performs the runtime binding is in the form's Open event:

```
Private Sub Form_Open(Cancel As Integer)

    Dim cnn As ADODB.Connection
    Dim rst As ADODB.Recordset

    Set cnn = New ADODB.Connection
    cnn.Open "Provider=Microsoft.Access.OLEDB.10.0;" & _
      "Data Provider=SQLOLEDB.1;Data Source=(local);" & _
      "Integrated Security=SSPI;Initial Catalog = Northwind"

    Set rst = New ADODB.Recordset
    rst.Open "SELECT * FROM Customers", cnn, _
      adOpenKeyset, adLockOptimistic
```

```
Set Me.Recordset = rst

' Clean up
rst.Close
Set rst = Nothing
cnn.Close
Set cnn = Nothing

End Sub
```

This procedure first uses the Client Data Manager to open a connection to a local instance of SQL Server, as I discussed earlier in the chapter. It then opens an updatable Recordset based on this connection and sets the form's Recordset property to this Recordset. After the Recordset is bound to the form, the Connection and Recordset variables in this procedure are no longer needed, and can be allowed to fall out of scope and close.

If you experiment with this form, you'll discover that you can add, edit, and delete records, just as you can with a traditional Access form that's bound at design time rather than at runtime.

Requirements for Updatable Recordsets

Although you can bind any ADO Recordset to an Access form, Access imposes certain requirements if your goal is to be able to update the Recordset via the form. These requirements are not overly restrictive. As long as you control the parameters with which you open the Recordset, you should be able to meet the Access requirements.

Access supports updatability in runtime-bound forms for four different types of Recordsets:

- SQL Server Recordsets
- Jet Recordsets
- ODBC Recordsets
- Oracle Recordsets

I'll look at each of these Recordset types in turn.

SQL Server Recordsets

In order for a form using a SQL Server Recordset to be updatable, the Recordset must meet one requirement: It must use the Client Data Manager as a service provider for the OLE DB connection.

NOTE   Of course, there are other updatability requirements; for example, the Recordset must not use a read-only cursor. In this section, I'm concerned only with the additional requirements imposed by Access for forms bound to Recordsets at runtime.

Earlier, you saw a simple example of runtime binding of a SQL Server Recordset in an Access database. The code is even simpler in an Access project, because you can reuse the existing connection to the SQL Server database (assuming, that is, that the desired Recordset is within the same database that the project is using for its data storage). Here's an example from frmCustomers in this chapter's sample project:

```
Private Sub Form_Open(Cancel As Integer)

    Dim rst As ADODB.Recordset

    Set rst = New ADODB.Recordset
    rst.Open "SELECT * FROM Customers", _
     CurrentProject.Connection, _
     adOpenKeyset, adLockOptimistic

    Set Me.Recordset = rst

    ' Clean up
    rst.Close
    Set rst = Nothing

End Sub
```

Of course, if the data is in a different SQL Server database than the one used by the current project, you'll have to somehow get a connection to that database. One alternative is to create an independent Connection object and initialize it, just as you saw in the Access database example earlier. Another is to use an ad hoc or permanent linked server to make the other database available from within your back-end database. You can learn more about linked servers in Chapter 20, "ADO and SQL Server."

Jet Recordsets

If you're using data from a Jet database, there are two ways to make a form using a runtime-bound Recordset updatable:

- Use the Client Data Manager with a server-side Recordset.

- Use the Jet OLE DB provider directly with a client-side Recordset.

WARNING   This sample opens a second connection to the database that's currently open. If you've opened the database exclusively, you'll receive a runtime error when you try to open the form.

The ADOChapter25 sample database contains frmJetCustomers with code to illustrate both of these possibilities. (Remember, a database has the extension .mdb, in contrast to an Access project, which has the extension .adp.) This procedure uses the Client Data Manager:

```
Sub UseCDM()

    Dim cnn As ADODB.Connection
    Dim rst As ADODB.Recordset

    Set cnn = New ADODB.Connection
    cnn.Open "Provider=Microsoft.Access.OLEDB.10.0;" & _
     "Data Source=" & CurrentProject.FullName & ";" & _
     "User ID=Admin;Data Provider=Microsoft.Jet.OLEDB.4.0"

    Set rst = New ADODB.Recordset
    rst.CursorLocation = adUseServer
    rst.Open "SELECT * FROM Customers", cnn, _
     adOpenKeyset, adLockOptimistic

    Set Me.Recordset = rst

    ' Clean up
    rst.Close
    Set rst = Nothing

End Sub
```

This routine uses the Jet provider directly:

```
Sub UseDirect()

    Dim cnn As ADODB.Connection
    Dim rst As ADODB.Recordset

    Set cnn = New ADODB.Connection
    cnn.Open "Provider=Microsoft.Jet.OLEDB.4.0;" & _
     "Data Source=" & CurrentProject.FullName

    Set rst = New ADODB.Recordset
    rst.CursorLocation = adUseClient
    rst.Open "SELECT * FROM Customers", cnn, _
     adOpenKeyset, adLockOptimistic

    Set Me.Recordset = rst

    ' Clean up
    rst.Close
    Set rst = Nothing

End Sub
```

Figure 25.8 shows frmJetCustomers in action. The option buttons at the bottom of the form let you switch back and forth from one type of Recordset to the other.

NOTE If you modify the code for the UseDirect procedure to specify adUseServer for the Cursor-Location, you'll discover that the resulting Recordset becomes read-only when bound to the form.

Because this form is opening a separate connection to retrieve records, you need to worry about closing the connection when the form is finished with it. There's code in the Form_Unload event to handle that:

```
Private Sub Form_Unload(Cancel As Integer)

    Dim cnn As ADODB.Connection
    Set cnn = Me.Recordset.ActiveConnection
    cnn.Close
    Set cnn = Nothing

End Sub
```

Without this procedure, you may find yourself locked out of making design changes on the form after it's been open in browse mode.

ODBC Recordsets

If you can retrieve an updatable Recordset from an ODBC data source using the Microsoft OLE DB Provider for ODBC Data Sources, you can update it via runtime binding to an

Access form. The only requirement in this case is that you use a client-side cursor for the Recordset.

In the sample database, the frmODBCCustomers form presents an example of this technique:

```
Private Sub Form_Open(Cancel As Integer)

    Dim cnn As ADODB.Connection
    Dim rst As ADODB.Recordset

    Set cnn = New ADODB.Connection
    cnn.Open "Provider=MSDASQL.1;" & _
     "FileDSN=" & CurrentProject.Path & "\LocalSQL.dsn"

    Set rst = New ADODB.Recordset
    rst.CursorLocation = adUseClient
    rst.Open "SELECT * FROM Customers", cnn, _
     adOpenKeyset, adLockOptimistic

    Set Me.Recordset = rst

    ' Clean up
    rst.Close
    Set rst = Nothing

End Sub
```

`LocalSQL.dsn` is, in this case, an ODBC file DSN that uses the SQL Server ODBC driver to connect to a SQL Server database on the local computer with Windows integrated security. Of course, this is just an example. In a real application, you should use the SQL Server OLE DB driver instead of going through the ODBC driver.

Oracle Recordsets

You can also bind an Access form to an Oracle Recordset at runtime and have the data be updatable. There are two requirements in this case:

- You must be using the Microsoft OLE DB Provider for Oracle (rather than the provider supplied by Oracle).

- You must use a client-side cursor.

The frmOracleEMP form in this chapter's sample database demonstrates this technique. Here's the code to open and bind the Recordset to the form:

```
Private Sub Form_Open(Cancel As Integer)

    Dim cnn As ADODB.Connection
    Dim rst As ADODB.Recordset
```

```
Set cnn = New ADODB.Connection
cnn.Open "Provider=MSDAORA.1;Password=TIGER;User ID=SCOTT;" & _
 "Data Source=sample"

Set rst = New ADODB.Recordset
rst.CursorLocation = adUseClient
rst.Open "SELECT * FROM EMP", cnn, _
 adOpenKeyset, adLockOptimistic

Set Me.Recordset = rst

' Clean up
rst.Close
Set rst = Nothing

End Sub
```

NOTE   This code depends on having an instance of the Oracle sample database registered under the name *sample*. For more details on Oracle naming and on hooking up Oracle databases to ADO, see Chapter 21, "ADO and Oracle."

Oracle tables represent one of the best uses of the runtime Recordset-binding technique. Although Access supports basing the user interface directly on Jet tables (using an Access database) or on SQL Server tables (using an Access project), there's no way to base the Access user interface directly on Oracle. By using runtime binding of Oracle Recordsets to Access forms, you can get something very close to Access that's based directly on Oracle. The alternative for dealing with Oracle data is to use linked Access tables, which work via the ODBC driver for Oracle instead of the OLE DB driver. Because they're based on the ODBC driver, linked tables are slower than direct Recordsets for dealing with Oracle data.

A Flexible Unbound Form

For a more elaborate example of runtime binding of Recordsets to Access 2002 forms, take a look at the frmGeneralDriver form in this chapter's sample database. This form opens a second form, frmGeneral, and lets you set an arbitrary connection string and record source. The resulting Recordset is bound to frmGeneral for display. Figure 25.9 shows this pair of forms in action.

If you change the SQL statement or connection string displayed on frmGeneralDriver and click the Update button, the display on frmGeneral will change to match. This includes changing the labels, rebinding the text boxes, and showing more or fewer text boxes as necessary (up to a limit of 20 displayed fields). Listing 25.2 shows the code that handles these tasks.

FIGURE 25.9:

Displaying arbitrary
SQL Server data

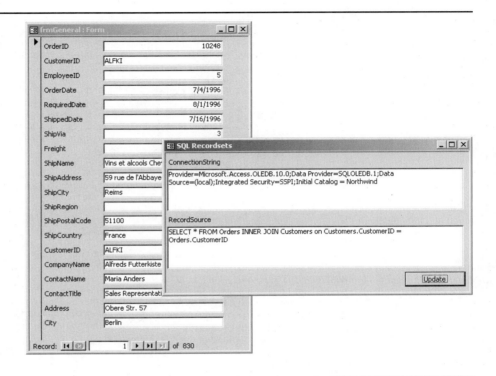

Listing 25.2:   **Updating the User Interface to Match a New Data Source**

```
Private Sub LoadControls()

    ' Update the user interface

    Dim cnn As ADODB.Connection
    Dim rst As ADODB.Recordset
    Dim intI As Integer

    ' Close any previously open connetion
    If Not Me.Recordset Is Nothing Then
        Set cnn = Me.Recordset.ActiveConnection
        cnn.Close
        Set cnn = Nothing
    End If

    ' Open the new connection string
    Set cnn = New ADODB.Connection
    cnn.Open mstrConnection
```

```
' Open the new Recordset
Set rst = New ADODB.Recordset
rst.Open mstrRecordSource, cnn, _
 adOpenKeyset, adLockOptimistic

If rst.Fields.Count <= 20 Then
    For intI = 0 To rst.Fields.Count - 1
        Me.Controls("Label" & CStr(intI)).Caption = _
         rst.Fields(intI).Name
        Me.Controls("Text" & CStr(intI)).ControlSource = _
         rst.Fields(intI).Name
        Me.Controls("Label" & CStr(intI)).Visible = True
        Me.Controls("Text" & CStr(intI)).Visible = True
    Next intI

    For intI = rst.Fields.Count To 19
        Me.Controls("Label" & CStr(intI)).Visible = False
        Me.Controls("Text" & CStr(intI)).Visible = False
    Next intI
Else
    ' If more than 20 fields, show only the first 20
    For intI = 0 To 19
        Me.Controls("Label" & CStr(intI)).Caption = _
         rst.Fields(intI).Name
        Me.Controls("Text" & CStr(intI)).ControlSource = _
         rst.Fields(intI).Name
        Me.Controls("Label" & CStr(intI)).Visible = True
        Me.Controls("Text" & CStr(intI)).Visible = True
    Next intI
End If

Set Me.Recordset = rst

' Clean up
rst.Close
Set rst = Nothing

End Sub
```

Several times already in this chapter, you've seen the code that actually deals with opening the Recordset and assigning it to the form's Recordset property. What's new is the code for handling controls. Access does supply a CreateControl statement, but it works only at design time, not runtime. So rather than dynamically create controls, this example hides and shows existing controls. Figure 25.10 shows frmGeneral in design view. As you can see, it contains 20 labels and 20 text boxes.

At runtime, the code in the LoadControls procedure loops through the fields in the Recordset and looks at the Name property of each field. This property is used as the caption for the label and the ControlSource of the corresponding text box. The code then hides the remaining text boxes and labels by setting their Visible property to False. Note, too, the check to make sure that you're not trying to display too many fields; this is necessary because of the design decision to supply a fixed number of controls on the form.

Controls waiting
to be bound

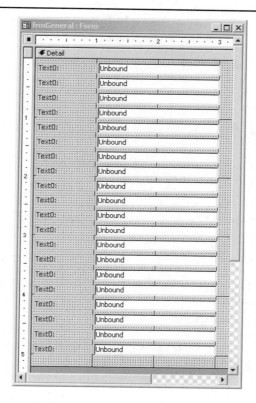

LoadControls is called from several places. First, there's the form's Open event, which sets up an initial connection to the local SQL Server database and opens a Recordset specified by the OpenArgs argument to the OpenForm method:

```
Private Sub Form_Open(Cancel As Integer)

    Dim intI As Integer

    ' Arbitrarily connect to the local SQL Server
    ' database when first opened
    mstrConnection = "Provider=Microsoft.Access.OLEDB.10.0;" & _
      "Data Provider=SQLOLEDB.1;Data Source=(local);" & _
      "Integrated Security=SSPI;Initial Catalog = Northwind"
    mstrRecordSource = Me.OpenArgs & ""
```

```
    If Len(Me.OpenArgs & "") > 0 Then
        LoadControls
    Else
        ' If there's no record source supplied at form open,
        ' hide the controls
        For intI = 0 To 19
            Me.Controls("Label" & CStr(intI)).Visible = False
            Me.Controls("Text" & CStr(intI)).Visible = False
        Next intI
    End If

End Sub
```

Second, the form provides a public method that external callers can use to alter the displayed data:

```
Public Sub ResetData(strConnection As String, _
  strRecordSource As String)

    mstrConnection = strConnection
    mstrRecordSource = strRecordSource
    LoadControls

End Sub
```

The code behind frmGeneralDriver is easy, because all of the hard stuff is encapsulated in frmGeneral. Here it is:

```
Private Sub cmdUpdate_Click()

    Forms!frmGeneral.ResetData txtConnectionString.Value, _
      txtRecordsource.Value

End Sub

Private Sub Form_Load()
    DoCmd.OpenForm "frmGeneral", , , , , , txtRecordsource.Value
End Sub
```

When the user opens frmGeneralDriver, it uses the DoCmd.OpenForm method to open the frmGeneral form with default values. When the user clicks the Update button, it calls the ResetData method of the frmGeneral form to place new data on the user interface.

Shaped Recordsets and Access Reports

Reports in an Access 2002 project also allow you to assign your own Recordset to the report's Recordset property. In this section, I'll dig into this area of Access, which is still a bit rough around the edges.

TIP This feature works only in Access projects; it's not available in Access databases.

A Report's Recordset and Shape

The Recordset property of a report is write-only; you cannot retrieve a report's Recordset into an independent Recordset variable. To see the schema of the Recordset that a report is using, you can retrieve its Shape property. For example, Figure 25.11 shows the rptCustomerOrders report from this chapter's sample project. This report shows customers together with their order dates and order numbers.

FIGURE 25.11:

Customer Orders report

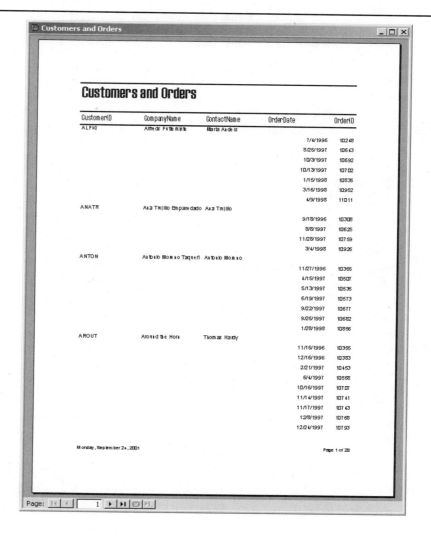

With this report open, you can use the Immediate Window to retrieve the value of
`Reports!rptCustomerOrdersShape.Shape`. If you do so, this is what you'll get (slightly
reformatted here for easier reading):

```
SHAPE (
    SHAPE {
        SELECT "Customers"."CustomerID",
                "Customers"."CompanyName",
                "Customers"."ContactName",
                "Orders"."OrderDate",
                "Orders"."OrderID"
        FROM ("Customers" INNER JOIN "Orders"
        ON "Customers"."CustomerID" ="Orders"."CustomerID")
        } AS rsLevel0
    COMPUTE rsLevel0,
        ANY(rsLevel0.CompanyName) AS __COLRef1,
        ANY(rsLevel0.ContactName) AS __COLRef2 BY CustomerID
    AS __COLRef0
) AS RS_171
```

NOTE   You may see a different alias in place of RS_171 on your computer.

You can see that this SQL statement consists of two nested SHAPE statements. The outer
statement is simple:

```
SHAPE (
    . . .
) AS RS_171
```

All this statement does is assign a name (RS_171) to the overall shaped Recordset. It doesn't
add any new columns of calculations to the result. Access creates a nested SHAPE statement
for each level of grouping on the report, whether there are any calculations at this level or
not. The outermost SHAPE statement would implement any grand total calculations for the
report.

NOTE   For more information on the SHAPE statement, see Chapter 7, "Data Shaping."

The inner SHAPE statement, on the other hand, does perform some calculations. Here
are the steps that it follows:

1. Create a Recordset consisting of the CustomerID, CompanyName, and ContactName
    columns from Customers, and the OrderDate and OrderID columns from Orders. Assign
    this Recordset the alias *rsLevel0*.

2. Create a parent Recordset (ultimately aliased as *__COLRef0*) with the three columns
    __COLRef1, *__ColRef2*, and *rsLevel0* (the latter being a chapter column pointing at the
    child Recordset).

This parent Recordset, together with the child Recordsets for each row, has exactly the "shape" required by the Access report. Figure 25.12 shows this Recordset displayed on a Hierarchical FlexGrid control (this control includes special code to display all levels of a hierarchical Recordset).

FIGURE 25.12:

A hierarchical Recordset

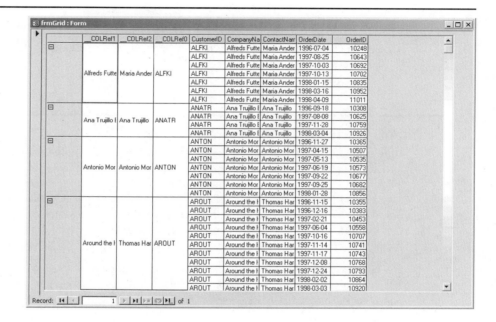

Supplying Your Own Recordset to a Report

WARNING The Recordset property of a report in an Access project is read/write. You can assign your own (properly shaped) Recordset to this property during the report's Open event. The Recordset property of a report in an Access database cannot be retrieved or set. You'll get a runtime error if you attempt these operations in an Access database.

For an example of assigning your own Recordset to a report, take a look at rptSelected-Companies in this chapter's sample project. This report uses an InputBox to prompt the user for a letter and then displays information on customers whose CustomerID starts with that letter. This is all done with code in the report's Open procedure:

```
Dim mrst As ADODB.Recordset

Private Sub Report_Open(Cancel As Integer)
```

```
Dim strCustomerID As String
Dim strShape As String

strCustomerID = InputBox("Enter First Letter for Customer IDs:")
strShape = "SHAPE (SHAPE {SELECT CustomerID, CompanyName " & _
  "FROM Customers WHERE CustomerID LIKE '" & strCustomerID & "%' " & _
  "} AS rsLevel0 COMPUTE rsLevel0) AS RS_306"

Set mrst = CurrentProject.Connection.Execute(strShape)
Set Me.Recordset = mrst

End Sub
```

Why You Should Not Use the Recordset Property

The bad news is that things are seriously broken in the original release of Access 2002. Although assigning a shaped Recordset works for extremely simple reports such as rptSelectedCustomers, the technique breaks down for more complex reports. As an example, take a look at rptCustomerOrdersAssign, which uses the identical technique on a report that draws its data from a view containing two tables (in fact, it's a copy of the original rptCustomerOrders report). If you try to open this report, though, you'll find that Access cannot bind the fields from the Customers table.

The culprit appears to be a bug in Access that adds additional levels of data shaping to the supplied Recordset. The code behind rptCustomerOrdersShapeInput creates a Recordset based on the original SQL statement that was returned by the report's Shape property:

```
SHAPE (
    SHAPE {
        SELECT "Customers"."CustomerID",
               "Customers"."CompanyName",
               "Customers"."ContactName",
               "Orders"."OrderDate",
               "Orders"."OrderID"
        FROM ("Customers" INNER JOIN "Orders"
        ON "Customers"."CustomerID" ="Orders"."CustomerID")
        } AS rsLevel0
    COMPUTE rsLevel0,
        ANY(rsLevel0.CompanyName) AS __COLRef1,
        ANY(rsLevel0.ContactName) AS __COLRef2 BY CustomerID
    AS __COLRef0
) AS RS_171
```

continued on next page

But if you retrieve the Shape property of the report after opening it, you'll find that it has been changed to something like this:

```
SHAPE (
    SHAPE {
        SHAPE (
            SHAPE {SELECT "Customers"."CustomerID", "Customers"."CompanyName",
                "Customers"."ContactName", "Orders"."OrderDate",
                "Orders"."OrderID"
                FROM ("Customers" INNER JOIN "Orders"
                ON "Customers"."CustomerID" = "Orders"."CustomerID")}
                AS rsLevel0
                COMPUTE rsLevel0, ANY(rsLevel0.CompanyName) AS __COLRef1,
                ANY(rsLevel0.ContactName) AS __COLRef2
                BY CustomerID AS __COLRef0
        ) AS RS_171} AS rsLevel0 COMPUTE rsLevel0,
            ANY(rsLevel0.CompanyName) AS __COLRef1,
            ANY(rsLevel0.ContactName) AS __COLRef2
            BY CustomerID AS __COLRef0
    ) AS RS_335
```

I hope that this problem gets fixed by an Office XP service pack. In the meantime, the best workaround is to use the report's RecordSource property if you want to change the data that the report will display at runtime.

As you can see, the Recordset is generated by executing a parameterized SHAPE statement on the current project's connection. I determined the format for this SHAPE statement by first opening the report without any code and retrieving its Shape property via the Immediate Window. Then I altered the SQL to insert the LIKE clause. This changes the records returned by the statement without changing the shape of the resulting Recordset.

Summary

In this chapter, you saw some of the special synergies available between Microsoft Access 2002 and ADO. In particular, you learned about the Client Data Manager, binding disconnected Recordsets to Access forms, and investigating the Shape properties of Access reports. Now it's time to turn to another ADO client from Microsoft Office XP: Excel 2002.

CHAPTER 26

Using ADO from Microsoft Excel

- Connecting data to Excel

- Working with OLAP data in Excel

In this chapter, I'll take a look at the ADO integration in another member of the Microsoft Office XP suite, Microsoft Excel 2002. Excel 2002 builds on the existing Excel tradition of solid access to data by making it easy to use ADO data, either via the user interface or programmatically. I'll look at both means of using data in Excel and then cover Excel's support for multidimensional OLAP data.

Connecting Data to Excel

Excel 2002 features both programmatic and user interface methods for displaying Recordsets on an Excel worksheet. In this section, I'll first review the user interface method and then show how you can use Excel's object model to handle the entire process from code.

Importing External Data

The Excel 2002 user interface enables the user to import external data from a variety of sources. Although the details are largely hidden from the user, this feature uses OLE DB to connect to the data. And although "import" might make you think of a one-time process, imported data can easily be refreshed to show the latest data from the data source at any time.

To display data from an OLE DB data source on an Excel 2002 worksheet, follow these steps:

1. Launch Excel and open a new worksheet.

2. Select Data ➤ Import External Data ➤ Import Data. This will open the Select Data Source dialog box, shown in Figure 26.1. If you explore the Files Of Type list, you'll see that Excel can use data from a variety of data sources, including Microsoft Data Link files, ODBC DSNs, XML files, and others.

FIGURE 26.1:

Selecting a data source for Excel import

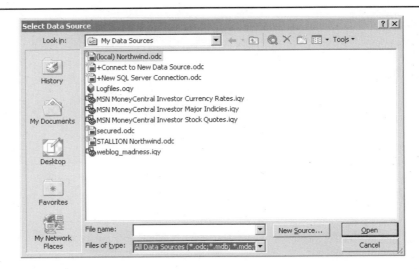

3. For OLE DB data, you can use either a Microsoft Data Link (UDL) file or an Office Database Connection (ODC) file. The Office Database Connection file format is new in Office XP, and it stores more information than does a Microsoft Data Link file. This dialog box offers you several ways to create a new Office Data Link file. You can choose one of the new connection items from the list of data sources, or just click the New Source button. Any of these choices will launch the Data Connection Wizard, shown in Figure 26.2.

4. On the first panel of the Data Connection Wizard, choose the type of data that you wish to use and then click Next. Each choice in the list corresponds to a different OLE DB provider. The Other/Advanced choice will open the Data Link Properties dialog box to let you pick an arbitrary provider. For this example, I'll use the Microsoft SQL Server choice.

5. On the next panel of the Data Connection Wizard, enter the server name and login information. You can use an actual server name here, or the special "(local)" string to indicate a local instance of SQL Server. You can also supply logon credentials (username and password) if you're not using Windows integrated authentication. Click Next to proceed.

6. On the next panel of the wizard, select the database and (optionally) the table that contains the data that you'd like to import. If you don't select a table, you'll be asked to choose one when you insert the data. Click Next to proceed.

7. Finally, assign a filename and optional description for the saved ODC file and then click Finish. This will return you to the Select Data Source dialog box with the new data source selected. Click Open to connect to the data.

8. Excel will display the Import Data dialog box. Choose whether you'd like to place the data on an existing worksheet or a new worksheet, and click OK to finish the process. Your data will appear in Excel.

FIGURE 26.2:

Excel Data Connection Wizard

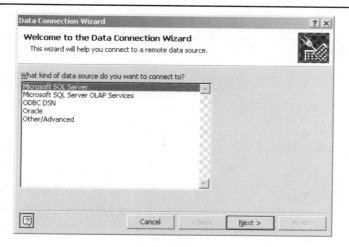

Figure 26.3 shows the result of importing the Customers table from the SQL Server version of Northwind to an Excel worksheet. Excel automatically opens the External Data toolbar when the focus is within an imported data range. Table 26.1 lists the functions that are available from this toolbar.

FIGURE 26.3:

Imported data in Excel

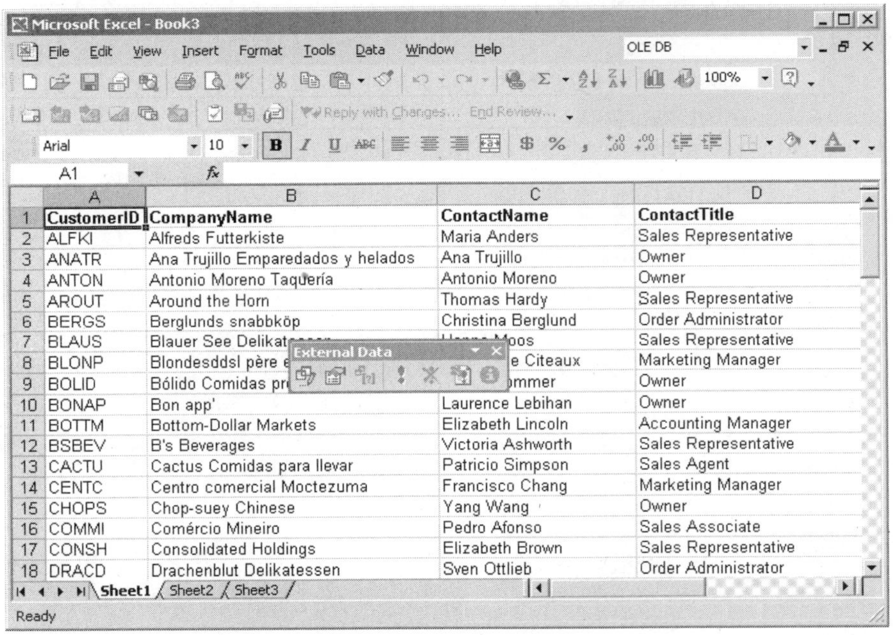

TABLE 26.1: Functions of the External Data Toolbar

Button	Function
Edit Query	Opens the Edit OLE DB Query dialog box, which lets you edit the connection string, command type, and command text for the data range.
Data Range Properties	Opens the External Data Range Properties dialog box, which lets you control some of the interactions of Excel with the data range. For example, you can decide how to handle new rows in the data and whether to show row numbers.
Query Parameters	Lets you specify values for query parameters if the data range is based on a parameterized query.
Refresh Data	Fetches the latest data from the server for the current data range.
Cancel Refresh	Halts refresh activity. This is useful if a refresh is taking a long time.
Refresh All	Refreshes all data ranges on the worksheet.
Refresh Status	Provides information on a refresh in progress.

If you view a saved ODC file with Notepad or another text editor, you'll find contents resembling those in Listing 26.1.

Listing 26.1:   **An ODC File**

```
<html>
<head>
<meta http-equiv=Content-Type content="text/x-ms-odc; charset=utf-8">
<meta name=ProgId content=ODC.Table>
<meta name=SourceType content=OLEDB>
<meta name=Catalog content=Northwind>
<meta name=Schema content=dbo>
<meta name=Table content=Customers>
<xml id=docprops><o:DocumentProperties
  xmlns:o="urn:schemas-microsoft-com:office:office"
  xmlns="http://www.w3.org/TR/REC-html40">
  <o:Description>Customers table from Northwind</o:Description>
  <o:Keywords>Customers Northwind</o:Keywords>
 </o:DocumentProperties>
</xml><xml id=msodc><odc:OfficeDataConnection
  xmlns:odc="urn:schemas-microsoft-com:office:odc"
  xmlns="http://www.w3.org/TR/REC-html40">
  <odc:Connection odc:Type="OLEDB">
   <odc:ConnectionString>Provider=SQLOLEDB.1;
➥ Integrated Security=SSPI;Persist Security Info=True;
➥ Data Source=(local);Use Procedure for Prepare=1;
➥ Auto Translate=True;Packet Size=4096;Workstation ID=SKYROCKET;
➥ Use Encryption for Data=False;
➥ Tag with column collation when possible=False;
➥ Initial Catalog=Northwind</odc:ConnectionString>
   <odc:CommandType>Table</odc:CommandType>
    <odc:CommandText>&quot;Northwind&quot;.&quot;dbo&quot;.&quot;
➥ Customers&quot;</odc:CommandText>
  </odc:Connection>
 </odc:OfficeDataConnection>
</xml>
<style>
<!--
    .ODCDataSource
    {
    behavior: url(dataconn.htc);
    }
-->
</style>

</head>
 <body onload='init()' scroll=no leftmargin=0 topmargin=0
➥ rightmargin=0 style='border: 0px'>
<table style='border: solid 1px threedface; height: 100%;
➥ width: 100%' cellpadding=0 cellspacing=0 width='100%'>
```

```html
   <tr>
     <td id=tdName style='font-family:arial; font-size:medium;
 padding: 3px; background-color: threedface'>
        
     </td>
     <td id=tdTableDropdown style='padding: 3px;
 background-color: threedface; vertical-align: top;
 padding-bottom: 3px'>
        
     </td>
   </tr>
   <tr>
     <td id=tdDesc colspan='2' style='border-bottom: 1px
 threedshadow solid; font-family: Arial; font-size: 1pt;
 padding: 2px; background-color: threedface'>
        
     </td>
   </tr>
   <tr>
     <td colspan='2' style='height: 100%; padding-bottom: 4px;
 border-top: 1px threedhighlight solid;'>
       <div id='pt' style='height: 100%' class='ODCDataSource'></div>
     </td>
   </tr>
 </table>

 <script language='javascript'>

 function init() {
   var sName, sDescription;
   var i, j;

   try {
     sName = unescape(location.href)

     i = sName.lastIndexOf(".")
     if (i>=0) { sName = sName.substring(1, i); }

     i = sName.lastIndexOf("/")
     if (i>=0) { sName = sName.substring(i+1, sName.length); }

     document.title = sName;
     document.getElementById("tdName").innerText = sName;

     sDescription = document.getElementById("docprops").innerHTML;

     i = sDescription.indexOf("escription>")
     if (i>=0) { j = sDescription.indexOf("escription>", i + 11); }
```

```
        if (i>=0 && j >= 0) {
          j = sDescription.lastIndexOf("</", j);

          if (j>=0) {
             sDescription = sDescription.substring(i+11, j);
           if (sDescription != "") {
              document.getElementById("tdDesc").style.fontSize="x-small";
              document.getElementById("tdDesc").innerHTML = sDescription;
              }
            }
          }
        }
     catch(e) {

        }
      }
  </script>

  </body>

  </html>
```

As you can see, ODC files are a mix of HTML, XML, and JavaScript. If all you're concerned about is the data properties, you need only look at the `<xml id=msodc>` section of the document. This section contains XML elements that specify the connection string, command type, and command text that Excel uses to retrieve data.

In fact, that's the only section that Excel itself needs to do its job. This book's companion CD contains a file, `test.odc`, with these contents:

```
<xml id=msodc><odc:OfficeDataConnection
  xmlns:odc="urn:schemas-microsoft-com:office:odc"
  xmlns="http://www.w3.org/TR/REC-html40">
  <odc:Connection odc:Type="OLEDB">
   <odc:ConnectionString>Provider=SQLOLEDB.1;
➥ Integrated Security=SSPI;Persist Security Info=True;
➥ Data Source=(local);Use Procedure for Prepare=1;
➥ Auto Translate=True;Packet Size=4096;Workstation ID=SKYROCKET;
➥ Use Encryption for Data=False;
➥ Tag with column collation when possible=False;
➥ Initial Catalog=Northwind</odc:ConnectionString>
    <odc:CommandType>Table</odc:CommandType>
     <odc:CommandText>&quot;Northwind&quot;.&quot;dbo&quot;.&quot;
➥ Customers&quot;</odc:CommandText>
   </odc:Connection>
  </odc:OfficeDataConnection>
</xml>
```

If you browse to this stripped-down ODC file from the Excel Select Data Source dialog box, you'll discover that it works perfectly well for retrieving data. So, why is all that other stuff in the ODC file that Excel generates? The answer is that the HTML and JavaScript allow Internet Explorer to use the file to retrieve data. You can right-click an ODC file in Windows Explorer and select View In Browser, and Internet Explorer will deliver live data via the Spreadsheet component of the Office Web Components, as shown in Figure 26.4.

FIGURE 26.4:

ODC file open in Internet Explorer

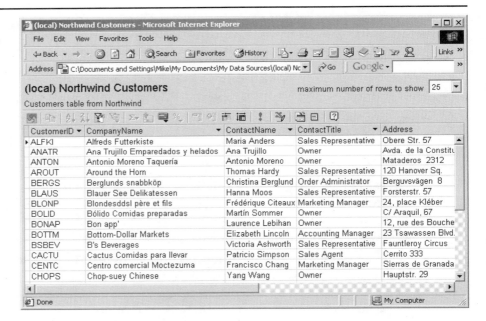

Using the CopyFromRecordset Method

Although the Excel user interface for importing data is excellent, there will, of course, be times when you want to deal instead with data from your own code. As always, writing code offers a level of control and power that cannot be matched by user interface tools.

If you're faced with the task of displaying the contents of a Recordset on a worksheet in Excel, your first impulse may be to write looping code such as that in Listing 26.2.

NOTE   The sample code for this chapter can be found in the ADOChapter26.xls file on this book's companion CD. You'll need to set your Excel security levels to medium to run this code; if you have high security set, you'll be prompted about this when you open the file. Remember to return your security levels to high when you've finished your testing!

Listing 26.2:   **Using a Loop to Display a Recordset**

```vb
Public Sub GetDataLoop()

    Dim cnn As ADODB.Connection
    Dim rst As ADODB.Recordset
    Dim intRow As Integer
    Dim intCol As Integer

    On Error GoTo HandleErr

    Set cnn = New ADODB.Connection
    cnn.Open "Provider=SQLOLEDB;Data Source=(local);" & _
     "Initial Catalog=Northwind;Integrated Security=SSPI"

    Set rst = New ADODB.Recordset
    rst.Open "SELECT * FROM Region, Orders", cnn

    intRow = 1
    Do Until rst.EOF
        For intCol = 1 To rst.Fields.Count
            ActiveSheet.Cells(intRow, intCol) = rst.Fields(intCol - 1).Value
        Next intCol
        rst.MoveNext
        intRow = intRow + 1
    Loop

    ' Clean up
    rst.Close
    Set rst = Nothing
    cnn.Close
    Set cnn = Nothing

ExitHere:
    Exit Sub

HandleErr:
    MsgBox "Error " & Err.Number & ": " & Err.Description, _
     vbOKOnly, "GetDataLoop"
    Resume ExitHere
    Resume

End Sub
```

This code will, of course, work for the desired task. It opens the Recordset, walks through every record, and loops over every field in the record, writing them one by one to the user interface. But Excel offers a better alternative, because the Excel developers recognized that this is a common task that could be optimized by being moved into the Excel object model.

This alternative is the CopyFromRecordset method of the Range object. Listing 26.3 shows the preceding routine rewritten to use the CopyFromRecordset method.

Listing 26.3:   **Using CopyFromRecordset to Display Data**

```
Public Sub GetDataNoLoop()

    Dim cnn As ADODB.Connection
    Dim rst As ADODB.Recordset
    Dim intRow As Integer
    Dim intCol As Integer

    On Error GoTo HandleErr

    Set cnn = New ADODB.Connection
    cnn.Open "Provider=SQLOLEDB;Data Source=(local);" & _
      "Initial Catalog=Northwind;Integrated Security=SSPI"

    Set rst = New ADODB.Recordset
    rst.Open "SELECT * FROM Region, Orders", cnn

    ActiveSheet.Cells(1, 1).CopyFromRecordset rst

    ' Clean up
    rst.Close
    Set rst = Nothing
    cnn.Close
    Set cnn = Nothing

ExitHere:
    Exit Sub

HandleErr:
    MsgBox "Error " & Err.Number & ": " & Err.Description, _
      vbOKOnly, "GetDataNoLoop"
    Resume ExitHere
    Resume

End Sub
```

Not only is the second version of this procedure more precise, it's also faster. On my test machine, the first version took 8 seconds to copy the 3,320 rows of data to the worksheet, and the second version took only 1 second.

The CopyFromRecordset method offers a pair of optional arguments that you can use to limit the amount of data copied:

```
Range.CopyFromRecordset Data [, MaxRows] [, MaxCols]
```

You can use the MaxRows and MaxCols arguments respectively to limit the number of rows and columns that are copied from the Recordset to the worksheet. This won't save you any time in retrieving the data in the first place (the Recordset must already exist before you can call the CopyFromRecordset method), but it will keep you from overwriting other parts of your worksheet with data if you get an unexpectedly large amount back from the data source.

WARNING   The CopyFromRecordset method cannot handle hierarchical Recordsets or OLE Object fields. You'll get a runtime error if you try to use CopyFromRecordset with such data.

Creating a QueryTable Object

Excel also offers the QueryTable object, which encapsulates the entire process of importing data to a worksheet. Here's an example of using this object to import data from a SQL Server data source:

```
Public Sub GetDataQueryTable()

    Dim qtbl As QueryTable

    On Error GoTo HandleErr

    Set qtbl = ActiveSheet.QueryTables.Add( _
      "OLEDB;Provider=SQLOLEDB;Data Source=(local);" & _
      "Initial Catalog=Northwind;Integrated Security=SSPI", _
      ActiveSheet.Cells(1, 1), "SELECT * FROM Region, Orders")
    qtbl.RefreshStyle = xlInsertEntireRows
    qtbl.Refresh True

    ' Clean up
    Set qtbl = Nothing

ExitHere:
    Exit Sub

HandleErr:
    MsgBox "Error " & Err.Number & ": " & Err.Description, _
      vbOKOnly, "GetDataQueryTable"
    Resume ExitHere
    Resume

End Sub
```

Every worksheet in Excel has a QueryTables collection (although this collection is empty until you import data to the worksheet). As you can see in the preceding code, you create a new QueryTable by calling the Add method of this collection:

```
QueryTables.Add(Connection, Destination[, Sql])
```

This method takes three arguments:

- The *Connection* argument specifies the source of the data. This is actually a very flexible argument that allows for data sources other than OLE DB providers. Table 26.2 lists the possible formats for this argument.

- The *Destination* argument is an Excel Range object that specifies the top-left corner of the resulting data range.

- The *Sql* argument is a SQL string to be used to retrieve data from the specified connection. You can omit this argument, in which case you need to specify a SQL string in the Sql property of the QueryTable argument before calling its Refresh method.

TABLE 26.2: QueryTable Connection Argument Formats

Format	Meaning
FINDER;*filename*	Excel-formatted data finder (IQY or OQY) file
ODBC;*connection string*	ODBC connection string
OLEDB;*connection string*	OLE DB connection string
Recordset variable	ADO or DAO Recordset object that should be used as the data source
TEXT;*filename*	Text file containing data
URL;*query*	Excel-formatted web query

Calling the Add method creates the QueryTable object, but it doesn't transfer any data to the worksheet. To transfer data, you need to take two more steps:

1. Set the RefreshStyle property to indicate how the worksheet should behave when new data is inserted. If you set this property to xlInsertDeleteCells, Excel will insert data in partial rows. (For example, if your query is three columns wide, the data in the first three columns of the worksheet will be moved down to accommodate the new data, but data to the right of this will be left in its original position.) If you set this property to xlOverwriteCells, the new data will simply overwrite any existing data. If you set this property to xlInsertEntireRows, Excel will insert full rows to hold the new data, moving everything on the worksheet down regardless of how many columns the query returns.

2. Call the Refresh method of the QueryTable object. The optional BackgroundQuery argument to this method can be set to True to perform the query asynchronously or to False to perform the query synchronously.

The QueryTable object has a rich interface that can be used to manipulate the data after it has been inserted. Table 26.3 lists some of the members of this interface.

TABLE 26.3: Selected QueryTable Interfaces

Name	Type	Meaning
AfterRefresh	Event	Occurs when a refresh completes or is cancelled.
BeforeRefresh	Event	Occurs before any refresh. Note that this event is triggered by calling the Refresh method in code or by user action to refresh the data range.
CancelRefresh	Method	Cancels any refresh currently being performed.
CommandText	Property	SQL or object name for the data being retrieved. Takes precedence over the Sql property.
CommandType	Property	ADO command type for the CommandText property.
Delete	Method	Deletes the QueryTable object.
EnableEditing	Property	If True, the user can edit the data in the data range. If False, the user can refresh but not edit the data.
EnableRefresh	Property	If True, the user can refresh the data. If False, the user cannot refresh the data.
FieldNames	Property	Set to True to use field names as the first row of the data range.
MaintainConnection	Property	Set to True to keep a connection to the data source open. Useful if you plan to refresh the data frequently.
Refresh	Method	Refreshes the data displayed on the worksheet.
Refreshing	Property	True if a background refresh is currently in progress.
RefreshOnFileOpen	Property	Set to True to automatically refresh the data range when the workbook is opened.
RefreshPeriod	Property	Number of minutes between automatic refresh calls.
ResultRange	Property	Returns an Excel Range object for the portion of the worksheet occupied by the data range.
RowNumbers	Property	Set to True to show row numbers as the first column of the data range.
SaveAsODC	Method	Saves an ODC file representing this QueryTable.

Working with OLAP Data in Excel

Excel is also the premiere Office XP client for dealing with OLAP data. The PivotTable Service, which ships as part of Excel, allows you to work with data from Microsoft Analysis Services directly on an Excel worksheet. It also allows you to create and manipulate local data cubes without having an Analysis Services server available. In this section, I'll discuss the architecture of the PivotTable Service and then show you how to use the Cube Wizard in Excel to create new local data cubes.

NOTE   Excel may well be surpassed as an OLAP client in Office by Microsoft Data Analyzer. This product, which just started shipping in late 2001 as this book was being published, is a dedicated business intelligence client program. For more information, see www.`microsoft` `.com/office/dataanalyzer/default.htm`.

Architecture of the PivotTable Service

Figure 26.5 presents the overall architecture of Analysis Services, Microsoft's set of components for dealing with multidimensional data. In this section, I'll focus on the PivotTable Service component of this architecture. Note that all client communication with Analysis Services flows through the PivotTable Service.

FIGURE 26.5:

Analysis Services architecture

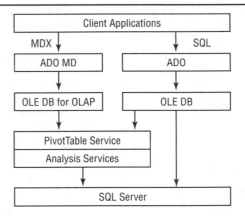

NOTE   For more information on Analysis Services, see Chapter 10, "Analyzing Multidimensional Data with ADO MD."

The PivotTable Service plays a dual role in Microsoft's OLAP architecture. On the one hand, it is a layer of software that every request from a client to an Analysis Services server must pass through. On the other hand, it is an independent, multidimensional engine that contains code to perform many of the tasks that the full version of Analysis Services can perform, although generally with less data and at a slower rate. It's this second role that makes the PivotTable Service interesting in the context of Microsoft Excel. This service is the component that allows Excel to perform multidimensional analysis (for example, the construction of pivot tables on a worksheet) even without the presence of an Analysis Services server.

In this role as a local calculation engine, the PivotTable Service delivers the ability to create, populate, and query *local cubes*. A local cube is the equivalent of an Analysis Services database kept in a disk file. By using the PivotTable Service, client applications such as Excel can perform multidimensional analyses on the contents of a local cube file.

Connecting to Analysis Services

Figure 26.6 shows the connection architecture when using the PivotTable Service with an Analysis Services server. In this case, the PivotTable Service is used to mediate requests and data between Excel and Analysis Services. All communication with the actual data, whether it's stored in ROLAP or MOLAP format, is done by Analysis Services itself (possibly, as in the case of ROLAP data, by using SQL Server to retrieve the actual data).

FIGURE 26.6:

Connecting to an Analysis Services server

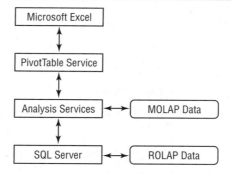

The nature of the connection between the PivotTable Service and Analysis Services depends on whether the two components are running on a single computer. If they are (for example, when you're working directly at the computer running Analysis Services), communication between the two is via a block of shared memory. More often, the PivotTable Service will be installed on a client computer, and Analysis Services will be running on a server computer elsewhere on the network. In this case, communication between the two will be via a network protocol, usually TCP/IP.

Connecting to an OLE DB Provider

When the PivotTable Service is used with a local ROLAP cube (as opposed to a ROLAP cube from an Analysis Services server), it employs the hybrid architecture shown in Figure 26.7.

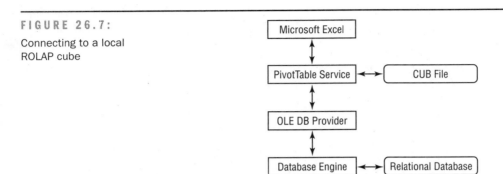

In the case of a local ROLAP cube, the CUB file stores the metadata describing the cube, but not any actual data or aggregations. The data remains in a relational database accessible via OLE DB, and the PivotTable Service makes a connection to the appropriate provider whenever it is asked to return data from the cube.

Compared with local MOLAP cubes, local ROLAP cubes are smaller (because they don't store precalculated aggregations) but slower (because they must connect to the relational database to retrieve data).

Connecting to a Local MOLAP Cube

Finally, Figure 26.8 shows the architecture used when the PivotTable Service retrieves data from a local MOLAP cube.

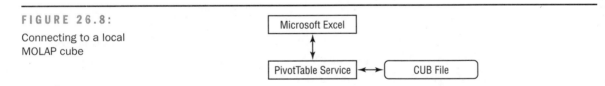

A local MOLAP cube contains the data, metadata, and aggregations necessary to answer MDX queries from the cube. After it has been created and processed, a local MOLAP cube doesn't require any connection to the database containing the data. The PivotTable Service can answer queries directly from the CUB file.

Note that local MOLAP cube files are completely portable. After you've created one, you can move it to another computer and it can still be used by the PivotTable Service, even if the original relational data is unavailable. The drawback, of course, is that all that data has to be stored in the cube file, which can make it very large for a large data set.

Creating and Using Local Cubes

In this section, I'll look at the use of the PivotTable Service to create a local cube file. Such files are useful in situations when you don't have a full Analysis Services server available. For example, any copy of Microsoft Excel 2000 or 2002 can create a local cube file, even if there is no Analysis Services server on your network. I'll show you how to do this by invoking the OLAP Cube Wizard from within Excel.

NOTE   You can also call the OLAP Cube Wizard programmatically. For details about this technique, see Mike Gunderloy and Tim Sneath's *SQL Server Developer's Guide to OLAP with Analysis Services* (Sybex, 2001).

Using the OLAP Cube Wizard

The easiest way to get started with local cubes is to use the OLAP Cube Wizard. This is a component of Microsoft Excel that first shipped as part of Excel 2000. Assuming that you have Office XP installed on your computer, you can create a local cube file by following these steps (this procedure also works with Office 2000, with minor variations in the object names):

1. Launch Excel 2002.

2. Choose Data ➢ Import External Data ➢ New Database Query. The Choose Data Source dialog box opens.

3. Make sure the box for Use the Query Wizard to Create/Edit Queries is checked, choose <New Data Source> on the Databases tab, and click OK.

4. In the Create New Data Source dialog box, name the new data source **Northwind**, select the Microsoft Access Driver, and click Connect. Although this is an ODBC driver, the final cube will use OLE DB; you're just setting up an initial connection to the data here.

5. In the ODBC Microsoft Access Setup dialog box, click the Select button.

6. Navigate to the `c:\Program Files\Microsoft Office\Office10\Samples` folder, and choose `Northwind.mdb`. Click OK.

7. Click OK to dismiss the ODBC Microsoft Access Setup dialog box.

8. In the Create New Data Source dialog box, click OK (do not select a default table).

9. In the Choose Data Source dialog box, make sure the new Northwind data source is selected. Click OK.

10. On the Choose Columns panel of the Query Wizard, select the entire Customers table, the EmployeeID and LastName fields from the Employees table, and the entire Orders table. Click Next.

11. Do not choose any fields to filter by. Click Next.

12. Do not choose any fields to sort by. Click Next.

13. On the Finish panel of the Query Wizard, select Create an OLAP Cube from This Query and then click Finish. This will launch the OLAP Cube Wizard.

14. As with other wizards, the OLAP Cube Wizard opens with a welcome panel. Read this and then click Next.

15. On the Step 1 panel of the OLAP Cube Wizard (see Figure 26.9), select Count Of OrderID and Sum Of Freight as the fields to summarize. Uncheck the other suggested summary fields. Click Next. Although the OLAP Cube Wizard doesn't use the term, these are the measures for your cube.

FIGURE 26.9:

Defining measures in
the OLAP Cube Wizard

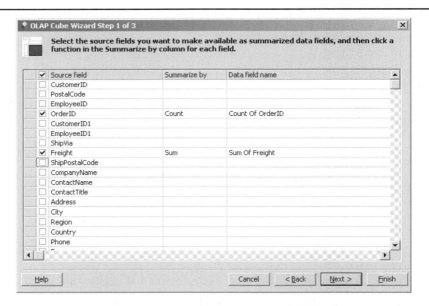

16. On the Step 2 panel of the OLAP Cube Wizard (see Figure 26.10), drag the Region field to the "Drop fields here to create a dimension" node. Then drag and drop City on Region, Address on City, and CompanyName on Address. What you're doing here is building up a dimension, one level at a time. You can right-click the topmost node of a dimension and click Rename to assign a name such as Geography. Drag the OrderDate field to the "Drop fields here" node to create a date hierarchy. Click Next.

17. On the final panel of the OLAP Cube Wizard, select a storage option. The first two options create ROLAP cubes; the third creates a MOLAP cube. Retain the default selection for the storage option, assign a name to the cube file, and then click Finish. You'll also be prompted to save an OQY file, which is Excel's pointer to a cube file.

FIGURE 26.10:

Defining dimensions
in the OLAP Cube
Wizard

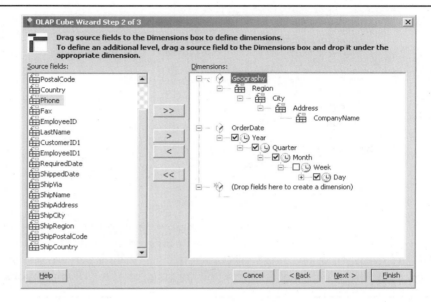

18. You'll be returned to Excel, at Step 3 of the PivotTable and PivotChart Wizard. Click
Finish to create a pivot table based on the cube in the Excel worksheet. By dragging and
dropping the fields from the PivotTable Field List to the worksheet, you can create an
interactive pivot table such as the one shown in Figure 26.11.

Although the interface used by the OLAP Cube Wizard is unique, the concepts that it uses
should be familiar to you from the discussion of OLAP in Chapter 10. The Office designers
chose to hide much of the complexity and terminology of Analysis Services from their users.

Note how thoroughly ADO and OLE DB are hidden from the user in this sequence. This
is an excellent model to follow with your own ADO applications. Ideally, the user should
never know that ADO is there.

Using a Local Cube from Code

A local cube can be used just like a remote cube, once you have connected to it. The cubes
created by the OLAP Cube Wizard use OCWCube as the name of both the catalog and the
cube itself. Thus, you can use code like this to open a cube created with the OLAP Cube
Wizard:

```
Dim cst As ADOMD.Cellset

On Error GoTo HandleErr
```

```
Set cst = New ADOMD.Cellset
cst.ActiveConnection = _
  "Provider=MSOLAP.2;Data Source=" & App.Path & _
  "\Query from Northwind.cub;Initial Catalog=OCWCube"
cst.Source = "SELECT" & vbCrLf & _
  "{[OrderDate]} ON COLUMNS," & vbCrLf & _
  "{[Geography]} ON ROWS" & vbCrLf & _
  "FROM OCWCube"
cst.Open

MsgBox cst.Axes.Count

' Clean up
cst.Close
Set cst = Nothing
```

This code, from the ADOChapter26 sample project, uses the same ADO MD functionality that you saw in Chapter 10. The only difference is that the data source is now the local file Query from Northwind.cub, rather than an Analysis Services server. After you've connected to the local cube, you can use the full range of ADO MD operations with its data.

FIGURE 26.11:

Pivot table based on a local cube file

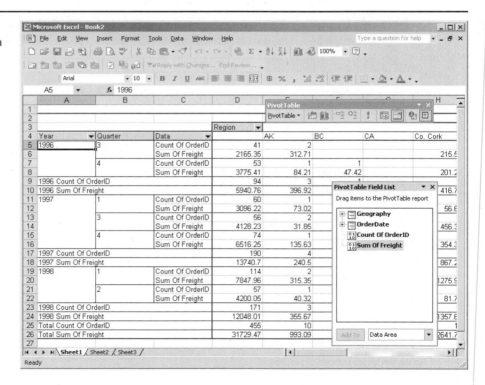

Summary

Microsoft Excel offers deep integration with ADO—so deep, in fact, that there are many parts of the Excel–ADO link that are closed to developers like you. In this chapter, you saw some of the user interface portions of Excel that use ADO to do their job. You also saw some Excel-specific code, including the use of the CopyFromRecordset method and the Query-Table object, that makes working with ADO data inside Excel easy.

In the next chapter, I'll take a look at one more client application. This time, though, it's not an ADO client. Rather, I'll close this section of the book by looking at some of the rapid application development features built into Visual Basic .NET that take advantage of ADO.NET.

CHAPTER 27

Using ADO.NET from Visual Basic .NET

- Using the Server Explorer

- Visual data objects on forms

- Using the Data Form Wizard

- Working with XML schema files

In Part IV of this book, I introduced you to many of the tools available for working with data from within Visual Basic .NET. In this chapter, I'll drill into some of those tools in a bit more depth. As you'd expect from Microsoft's latest rapid development environment, there are many tools designed to make data access faster and easier. These tools won't always generate the exact code that you might write yourself, but they will make working with data much simpler.

Using the Server Explorer

The first tool that you should become familiar with is the Server Explorer. This tool, shown in Figure 27.1, is designed to let you work with server resources of many types, not just data. Table 27.1 lists the resource types that you can manage with Server Explorer.

FIGURE 27.1:

Server Explorer

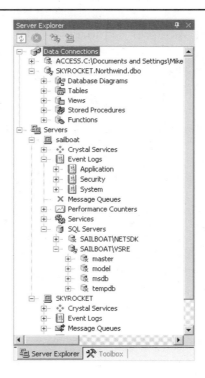

TABLE 27.1: Server Explorer Resource Types

Resource Type	Represents
Data Connection	A connection to a particular database
Crystal Services	Options for Crystal Reports
Event Logs	Windows event logs
Message Queues	Windows message queues
Performance Counters	Windows performance counters
Services	Windows services
SQL Servers	Microsoft SQL Servers

The most important part of Server Explorer for use with ADO.NET is the Data Connections node and its children. In the rest of this section, I'll show you some of the operations that you can perform with these nodes.

NOTE   Microsoft SQL Server databases can also be managed from the SQL Servers section of Server Explorer. The Data Connections section is more flexible, in that it can manage SQL Server databases as well as other types of data.

Adding a Data Connection

Before you can work with the data from a Data Connection, you must create the Data Connection. To do so, follow these steps:

1. Open Server Explorer.

2. Right-click the Data Connections node and then select Add Connection. This will open the Data Link Properties dialog box.

3. Fill in the connection information for your data source. The dialog box will default to using the Microsoft OLE DB Provider for SQL Server, but you can change that on the Provider tab if you like.

4. Click OK to create the Data Connection.

WARNING   Server Explorer doesn't check whether you have used a supported data provider for your Data Connection. Remember, only the SQL Server, Oracle, and Jet providers are supported by .NET directly. Other data providers may work in some circumstances, but you'll need to test their use carefully.

Visual Studio .NET remembers your Data Connections across sessions and projects. Any Data Connection that you've created will appear in Server Explorer in all your projects unless you right-click the Data Connection and choose Delete.

Object Design from Server Explorer

Server Explorer allows you to examine and change the design of objects stored in the data sources that your Data Connections refer to. Which objects you can manipulate depends on the type of database. Table 27.2 sums up the possible design actions.

TABLE 27.2: Server Explorer Capabilities

Database	Object	Edit Data?	Design?	Create New?
Access	Table	Yes	No	No
Access	View	Yes	No	No
Access	Stored Procedure	No	No	No
Oracle	Database Diagram	N/A	Yes	Yes
Oracle	Table	Yes	Yes	Yes
Oracle	Synonym	Yes	No	No
Oracle	View	Yes	Yes	Yes
Oracle	Stored Procedure	Yes	Yes	Yes
Oracle	Function	Yes	Yes	Yes
Oracle	Package Specification	No	Yes	Yes
Oracle	Package Body	No	Yes	Yes
SQL Server	Database Diagram	N/A	Yes	Yes
SQL Server	Table	Yes	Yes	Yes
SQL Server	Synonym	Yes	No	No
SQL Server	View	Yes	Yes	Yes
SQL Server	Stored Procedure	Yes	Yes	Yes
SQL Server	Function	Yes	Yes	Yes

NOTE   For Microsoft Access databases, queries without parameters are considered views, and queries with parameters are considered stored procedures.

For SQL Server and Oracle databases, the .NET designers make it possible to perform a wide variety of design actions. These include, for example:

- Adding columns to a table
- Adding triggers to a table
- Setting keys, indexes, and relationships for a table

- Selecting fields for a view either graphically or by writing SQL statements
- Editing the SQL for stored procedures and functions
- Editing SQL blocks within stored procedures and functions graphically

In addition, Visual Studio .NET supports running SQL Server stored procedures in debug mode, so that you can see their effects one statement at a time. To run a SQL Server stored procedure in debug mode, right-click the stored procedure and select Step Into Procedure.

> **TIP** Stored procedure debugging is automatically available for a SQL Server that's installed on the same computer as Visual Studio .NET. For other servers, you need to run the .NET Remote Components setup on the SQL Server.

Drag-and-Drop from Server Explorer

One of the most useful capabilities of Server Explorer is acting as a drag source for drag-and-drop operations. You can drag and drop database objects from Server Explorer to a Windows Form in the Visual Studio .NET IDE to create visible data objects. Table 27.3 shows the effect of dragging various items from Server Explorer to a Windows Form.

TABLE 27.3: Drag-and-Drop from Server Explorer

Object Dragged	Object Created
Database	OleDbConnection or SqlConnection
Table, View, Synonym, Table Column, or View Column	OleDbDataAdapter or SqlDataAdapter
Stored Procedure or Table-Valued Function	OleDbCommand or SqlCommand
Database Diagram, Package, Stored Procedure Parameter, Stored Procedure Column, Inline Function, or Scalar Function	Not supported

Figure 27.2 shows the appearance of the created objects on a Visual Basic .NET form. This figure also includes a DataSet object; you'll see shortly how to generate a DataSet object in the form designer.

As you might guess from their placement below the form's design surface, these visual data objects are not visible at runtime. At design time, they provide access to instances of their underlying class. For example, the SqlConnection1 object in the designer is a visual representation of an instance of the SqlConnection class. If you view the code behind the form, and expand the "Windows Form Designer generated code" region, you'll find the declaration that Visual Basic .NET created when you dropped the object on the form:

```
Friend WithEvents SqlConnection1 As System.Data.SqlClient.SqlConnection
```

FIGURE 27.2:

Visual data objects in
the form designer

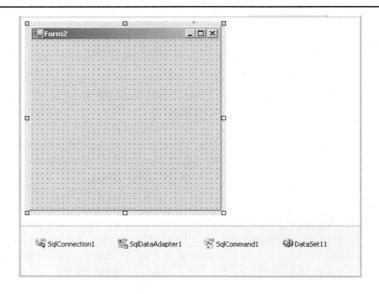

| SqlConnection1 | SqlDataAdapter1 | SqlCommand1 | DataSet11 |

TIP   The Friend keyword makes this object accessible from anywhere in the assembly that contains this code. The WithEvents keyword makes it possible to connect event handlers to this object.

Visual Basic .NET also adds code to the form's InitializeComponent procedure to initialize the objects. Here's the initialization code for a particular Connection object:

```
Me.SqlConnection1 = New System.Data.SqlClient.SqlConnection()

'SqlConnection1

Me.SqlConnection1.ConnectionString = "data source=SKYROCKET;
➡ initial catalog=Northwind;integrated security=SSPI;persist " & _
"security info=False;workstation id=SAILBOAT;packet size=4096"
```

Visual data objects behave like controls in a couple of ways:

- Their properties are accessible through a property sheet as well as through code.

- You can double-click them to open a default event procedure for the object.

I'll explore the features and capabilities of the individual visual data objects in the next section.

Visual Data Objects on Forms

There are five different types of visual data objects:

- Connection (SqlConnection and OleDbConnection)
- Command (SqlCommand and OleDbCommand)
- DataAdapter (SqlDataAdapter and OleDbDataAdapter)
- DataSet
- DataView

The first three of these object types can be created by drag-and-drop from Server Explorer or by drag-and-drop from the Data tab in the Toolbox. The DataSet and DataView objects can be created by drag-and-drop from the Toolbox or by other links and wizards within the Visual Studio .NET IDE.

NOTE   The Connection, Command, and DataAdapter objects have two different implementations, depending on whether the data source uses the System.Data.OleDb namespace or the System.Data.SqlClient namespace.

The Connection Object

If you create a Connection object by dragging from Server Explorer, it will automatically be configured to connect to the server that was the source of the drag operation. If you create a Connection object by dragging from the Toolbox, it will be configured for the type of Connection (OleDbConnection or SqlConnection) but won't be connected to any particular server.

You can control the Connection by modifying the ConnectionString property in the Properties window. If you click this property, Visual Basic .NET will display a drop-down list of choices. You can choose from any appropriate Data Connection that already exists in Server Explorer, or you can select New Connection to display the Data Link Properties dialog box. If you create a new Connection, Visual Basic .NET will create a new Data Connection in Server Explorer, in addition to setting the properties of this Connection object.

Figure 27.3 shows the Properties window for a SqlConnection object. Many of the properties are grayed out and cannot be changed directly. That's because these properties (ConnectionTimeout, Database, and so on) are set as part of the ConnectionString property. Modifying the ConnectionString property automatically modifies these subsidiary properties.

FIGURE 27.3:

Properties for a Sql-
Connection object

When you create a Connection object, Visual Basic .NET inserts code behind the form to
declare and initialize the object, similar to this example:

```
' Code in form declarations section
Friend WithEvents SqlConnection1 As System.Data.SqlClient.SqlConnection

' Code in InitializeComponent()
Me.SqlConnection1 = New System.Data.SqlClient.SqlConnection()
'
'SqlConnection1
'
Me.SqlConnection1.ConnectionString = "data source=SKYROCKET;
➡ initial catalog=Northwind;integrated security=SSPI;persist " & _
"security info=False;workstation id=SAILBOAT;packet size=4096"
```

The Command Object

If you create a Command object by dragging from Server Explorer, it will automatically be
configured to use the object that you dragged (stored procedure or table-valued function) as
its CommandText. In addition, if there is already a Connection object on the form that connects to the server that was the source of the drag operation, the Command object will use
that Connection object for its Connection property. If there is no such object, Visual Basic
.NET will create a new Connection object for the appropriate Data Connection and use the
new Connection object for the Command's Connection property.

If you create a Command object by dragging from the Toolbox, it will be configured for
the type of Command (OleDbCommand or SqlCommand) but won't be initialized to use any
particular source object. In this case, Visual Basic .NET won't create an associated Connection object.

You can edit the Parameters of a Command by clicking the build button in the Parameters property of the Properties window. This opens the Parameters editor, shown in Figure 27.4. From here, you can inspect the existing Parameters, as well as add or delete Parameters.

FIGURE 27.4:

Parameters editor

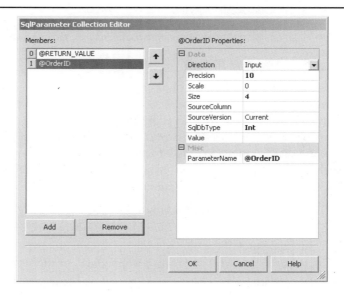

If you add or remove Parameters from a Command, you must remember to edit the source object on the server as well. If the Command's Parameters don't match the source object's Parameters, you'll get a runtime error when trying to use the Command.

When you create a Command object, Visual Basic .NET inserts code behind the form to declare and initialize the object. Here's an example:

```
' Code in form declarations section
Friend WithEvents SqlCommand1 As System.Data.SqlClient.SqlCommand

' Code in InitializeComponent()
Me.SqlCommand2 = New System.Data.SqlClient.SqlCommand()
'
'SqlCommand2
'
Me.SqlCommand2.CommandText = "dbo.[CustOrdersDetail]"
Me.SqlCommand2.CommandType = System.Data.CommandType.StoredProcedure
Me.SqlCommand2.Connection = Me.SqlConnection1
Me.SqlCommand2.Parameters.Add(New
➥ System.Data.SqlClient.SqlParameter("@RETURN_VALUE",
➥ System.Data.SqlDbType.Int, 4,
```

```
➡ System.Data.ParameterDirection.ReturnValue, False, CType(10, Byte),
➡ CType(0, Byte), "", System.Data.DataRowVersion.Current, Nothing))
Me.SqlCommand2.Parameters.Add(New
➡ System.Data.SqlClient.SqlParameter("@OrderID",
➡ System.Data.SqlDbType.Int, 4, System.Data.ParameterDirection.Input,
➡ False, CType(10, Byte), CType(0, Byte), "",
➡ System.Data.DataRowVersion.Current, Nothing))
```

The DataAdapter Object

If you create a DataAdapter object by dragging from Server Explorer, it will automatically be configured to use the object that you dragged (table, view, and so on) as the source for its various Command properties. In addition, if there is already a Connection object on the form that connects to the server that was the source of the drag operation, the DataAdapter object will use that Connection object for the Connection property of the Commands. If there is no such object, Visual Basic .NET will create a new Connection object for the appropriate Data Connection and use the new Connection object for the Connection properties.

If you create a DataAdapter object by dragging from the Toolbox, Visual Basic .NET will launch the Data Adapter Configuration Wizard. This wizard has five panels:

1. The first panel of the wizard explains in general terms the actions that the wizard will perform. Click Next to proceed when you've read this panel.

2. The second panel of the wizard allows you to select or create a Data Connection for the DataAdapter to use. You can select any Data Connection of the appropriate type that already exists in Server Explorer, or click New Connection to create a new Data Connection. When you've selected or created a Data Connection, click Next.

3. The third panel of the wizard offers you three choices for setting up the Commands that will be used by the DataAdapter. You can choose to use SQL statements, to have the wizard create new stored procedures, or to use existing stored procedures. When you've made your choice, click Next.

4. If you choose to use SQL statements or new stored procedures, the fourth panel of the wizard lets you specify the data that will be loaded into the DataAdapter. You can type in a SQL statement, or you can click the Query Builder button to launch the graphical Query Builder. You can also click the Advanced Options button to set further options for the DataAdapter:

   - The *Generate Insert, Update, and Delete Statements* check box controls whether the wizard should generate these additional Commands for the finished DataAdapter. By default, this check box is checked. If you plan to use this DataAdapter to edit data, you should leave this box checked. If you plan to use this DataAdapter only for retrieving data, you can uncheck this box.

- The *Use Optimistic Concurrency* check box controls whether the wizard writes code to detect whether another user has changed a record while you were editing it. By default, this check box is checked. In most cases, you should leave this box checked.

- The *Refresh the DataSet* check box controls whether the wizard writes code to refresh any DataSet based on this DataAdapter after data has been inserted or updated. By default, this check box is checked. If any values in new records are supplied by identity columns or by default values, you should leave this box checked.

If you choose to use existing stored procedures, the fourth panel of the wizard lets you choose the stored procedures to use for the Select, Insert, Update, and Delete Commands of the DataAdapter. When you've made the appropriate choices, click Next.

5. The last panel of the wizard, shown in Figure 27.5, summarizes the actions performed by the wizard. Click Finish to exit the wizard and create the new DataAdapter.

If you create a DataAdapter by dragging an existing object from Server Explorer, Visual Basic .NET writes the code for this DataAdapter without prompting you for any input. In this case, Visual Basic .NET makes these decisions:

- Create SQL statements for Commands.

- Generate Insert, Update, and Delete statements.

- Use optimistic concurrency.

- Refresh the DataSet.

FIGURE 27.5:

Completing the Data Adapter Configuration Wizard

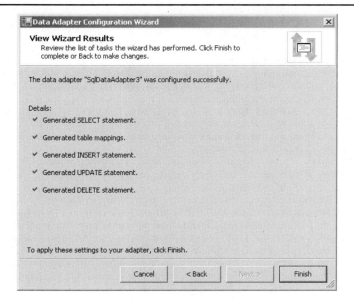

If you want to customize those choices, you'll need to start with a blank DataAdapter object from the Toolbox, instead of dragging from Server Explorer.

The DataAdapter object is complex, and, as you might expect, Visual Basic generates a good deal of code when you create a DataAdapter. For example, Listing 27.1 shows the code generated by dragging a table from a SQL Server Data Connection and dropping it on a form.

Listing 27.1:   **Automatically Generated Code for a DataAdapter**

```
' Code in form declarations section
Friend WithEvents SqlSelectCommand1 As System.Data.SqlClient.SqlCommand
Friend WithEvents SqlInsertCommand1 As System.Data.SqlClient.SqlCommand
Friend WithEvents SqlUpdateCommand1 As System.Data.SqlClient.SqlCommand
Friend WithEvents SqlDeleteCommand1 As System.Data.SqlClient.SqlCommand
Friend WithEvents SqlDataAdapter1 As System.Data.SqlClient.SqlDataAdapter

' Code in InitializeComponent()
Me.SqlSelectCommand1 = New System.Data.SqlClient.SqlCommand()
Me.SqlInsertCommand1 = New System.Data.SqlClient.SqlCommand()
Me.SqlUpdateCommand1 = New System.Data.SqlClient.SqlCommand()
Me.SqlDeleteCommand1 = New System.Data.SqlClient.SqlCommand()
Me.SqlDataAdapter1 = New System.Data.SqlClient.SqlDataAdapter()
'
'SqlSelectCommand1
'
Me.SqlSelectCommand1.CommandText = "SELECT CustomerID, CompanyName,
➥ ContactName, ContactTitle, Address, City, Region," & _
" PostalCode, Country, Phone, Fax FROM Customers"
Me.SqlSelectCommand1.Connection = Me.SqlConnection1
'
'SqlInsertCommand1
'
Me.SqlInsertCommand1.CommandText = "INSERT INTO Customers(CustomerID,
➥ CompanyName, ContactName, ContactTitle, Address" & _
", City, Region, PostalCode, Country, Phone, Fax) VALUES (@CustomerID,
➥ @CompanyNa" & _
"me, @ContactName, @ContactTitle, @Address, @City, @Region,
➥ @PostalCode, @Country" & _
", @Phone, @Fax); SELECT CustomerID, CompanyName, ContactName,
➥ ContactTitle, Addr" & _
"ess, City, Region, PostalCode, Country, Phone, Fax FROM Customers
➥ WHERE (Custome" & _
"rID = @CustomerID)"
Me.SqlInsertCommand1.Connection = Me.SqlConnection1
Me.SqlInsertCommand1.Parameters.Add(New
➥ System.Data.SqlClient.SqlParameter("@CustomerID",
➥ System.Data.SqlDbType.NVarChar, 5, "CustomerID"))
Me.SqlInsertCommand1.Parameters.Add(New
➥ System.Data.SqlClient.SqlParameter("@CompanyName",
➥ System.Data.SqlDbType.NVarChar, 40, "CompanyName"))
```

```
Me.SqlInsertCommand1.Parameters.Add(New
➡ System.Data.SqlClient.SqlParameter("@ContactName",
➡ System.Data.SqlDbType.NVarChar, 30, "ContactName"))
Me.SqlInsertCommand1.Parameters.Add(New
➡ System.Data.SqlClient.SqlParameter("@ContactTitle",
➡ System.Data.SqlDbType.NVarChar, 30, "ContactTitle"))
Me.SqlInsertCommand1.Parameters.Add(New
➡ System.Data.SqlClient.SqlParameter("@Address",
➡ System.Data.SqlDbType.NVarChar, 60, "Address"))
Me.SqlInsertCommand1.Parameters.Add(New
➡ System.Data.SqlClient.SqlParameter("@City",
➡ System.Data.SqlDbType.NVarChar, 15, "City"))
Me.SqlInsertCommand1.Parameters.Add(New
➡ System.Data.SqlClient.SqlParameter("@Region",
➡ System.Data.SqlDbType.NVarChar, 15, "Region"))
Me.SqlInsertCommand1.Parameters.Add(New
➡ System.Data.SqlClient.SqlParameter("@PostalCode",
➡ System.Data.SqlDbType.NVarChar, 10, "PostalCode"))
Me.SqlInsertCommand1.Parameters.Add(New
➡ System.Data.SqlClient.SqlParameter("@Country",
➡ System.Data.SqlDbType.NVarChar, 15, "Country"))
Me.SqlInsertCommand1.Parameters.Add(New
➡ System.Data.SqlClient.SqlParameter("@Phone",
➡ System.Data.SqlDbType.NVarChar, 24, "Phone"))
Me.SqlInsertCommand1.Parameters.Add(New
➡ System.Data.SqlClient.SqlParameter("@Fax",
➡ System.Data.SqlDbType.NVarChar, 24, "Fax"))
'
'SqlUpdateCommand1
'
Me.SqlUpdateCommand1.CommandText = "UPDATE Customers SET CustomerID =
➡ @CustomerID, CompanyName = @CompanyName, Contac" & _
"tName = @ContactName, ContactTitle = @ContactTitle, Address =
➡ @Address, City = @" & _
"City, Region = @Region, PostalCode = @PostalCode, Country = @Country,
➡ Phone = @P" & _
"hone, Fax = @Fax WHERE (CustomerID = @Original_CustomerID) AND
➡ (Address = @Origi" & _
"nal_Address OR @Original_Address IS NULL AND Address IS NULL) AND
➡ (City = @Origi" & _
"nal_City OR @Original_City IS NULL AND City IS NULL) AND (CompanyName
➡ = @Origina" & _
"l_CompanyName) AND (ContactName = @Original_ContactName OR
➡ @Original_ContactName" & _
" IS NULL AND ContactName IS NULL) AND (ContactTitle =
➡ @Original_ContactTitle OR " & _
"@Original_ContactTitle IS NULL AND ContactTitle IS NULL) AND (Country
➡ = @Origina" & _
"l_Country OR @Original_Country IS NULL AND Country IS NULL) AND (Fax =
➡ @Original" & _
"_Fax OR @Original_Fax IS NULL AND Fax IS NULL) AND (Phone =
➡ @Original_Phone OR @" & _
```

```
"Original_Phone IS NULL AND Phone IS NULL) AND (PostalCode =
➥ @Original_PostalCode" & _
" OR @Original_PostalCode IS NULL AND PostalCode IS NULL) AND (Region =
➥ @Original" & _
"_Region OR @Original_Region IS NULL AND Region IS NULL); SELECT
➥ CustomerID, Comp" & _
"anyName, ContactName, ContactTitle, Address, City, Region, PostalCode,
➥ Country, " & _
"Phone, Fax FROM Customers WHERE (CustomerID = @CustomerID)"
Me.SqlUpdateCommand1.Connection = Me.SqlConnection1
Me.SqlUpdateCommand1.Parameters.Add(New
➥ System.Data.SqlClient.SqlParameter("@CustomerID",
➥ System.Data.SqlDbType.NVarChar, 5, "CustomerID"))
Me.SqlUpdateCommand1.Parameters.Add(New
➥ System.Data.SqlClient.SqlParameter("@CompanyName",
➥ System.Data.SqlDbType.NVarChar, 40, "CompanyName"))
Me.SqlUpdateCommand1.Parameters.Add(New
➥ System.Data.SqlClient.SqlParameter("@ContactName",
➥ System.Data.SqlDbType.NVarChar, 30, "ContactName"))
Me.SqlUpdateCommand1.Parameters.Add(New
➥ System.Data.SqlClient.SqlParameter("@ContactTitle",
➥ System.Data.SqlDbType.NVarChar, 30, "ContactTitle"))
Me.SqlUpdateCommand1.Parameters.Add(New
➥ System.Data.SqlClient.SqlParameter("@Address",
➥ System.Data.SqlDbType.NVarChar, 60, "Address"))
Me.SqlUpdateCommand1.Parameters.Add(New
➥ System.Data.SqlClient.SqlParameter("@City",
➥ System.Data.SqlDbType.NVarChar, 15, "City"))
Me.SqlUpdateCommand1.Parameters.Add(New
➥ System.Data.SqlClient.SqlParameter("@Region",
➥ System.Data.SqlDbType.NVarChar, 15, "Region"))
Me.SqlUpdateCommand1.Parameters.Add(New
➥ System.Data.SqlClient.SqlParameter("@PostalCode",
➥ System.Data.SqlDbType.NVarChar, 10, "PostalCode"))
Me.SqlUpdateCommand1.Parameters.Add(New
➥ System.Data.SqlClient.SqlParameter("@Country",
➥ System.Data.SqlDbType.NVarChar, 15, "Country"))
Me.SqlUpdateCommand1.Parameters.Add(New
➥ System.Data.SqlClient.SqlParameter("@Phone",
➥ System.Data.SqlDbType.NVarChar, 24, "Phone"))
Me.SqlUpdateCommand1.Parameters.Add(New
➥ System.Data.SqlClient.SqlParameter("@Fax",
➥ System.Data.SqlDbType.NVarChar, 24, "Fax"))
Me.SqlUpdateCommand1.Parameters.Add(New
➥ System.Data.SqlClient.SqlParameter("@Original_CustomerID",
➥ System.Data.SqlDbType.NVarChar, 5,
➥ System.Data.ParameterDirection.Input, False, CType(0, Byte),
➥ CType(0, Byte), "CustomerID", System.Data.DataRowVersion.Original,
➥ Nothing))
Me.SqlUpdateCommand1.Parameters.Add(New
➥ System.Data.SqlClient.SqlParameter("@Original_Address",
```

```
➥ System.Data.SqlDbType.NVarChar, 60,
➥ System.Data.ParameterDirection.Input, False, CType(0, Byte),
➥ CType(0, Byte), "Address", System.Data.DataRowVersion.Original,
➥ Nothing))
Me.SqlUpdateCommand1.Parameters.Add(New
➥ System.Data.SqlClient.SqlParameter("@Original_City",
➥ System.Data.SqlDbType.NVarChar, 15,
➥ System.Data.ParameterDirection.Input, False, CType(0, Byte),
➥ CType(0, Byte), "City", System.Data.DataRowVersion.Original,
➥ Nothing))
Me.SqlUpdateCommand1.Parameters.Add(New
➥ System.Data.SqlClient.SqlParameter("@Original_CompanyName",
➥ System.Data.SqlDbType.NVarChar, 40,
➥ System.Data.ParameterDirection.Input, False, CType(0, Byte),
➥ CType(0, Byte), "CompanyName", System.Data.DataRowVersion.Original,
➥ Nothing))
Me.SqlUpdateCommand1.Parameters.Add(New
➥ System.Data.SqlClient.SqlParameter("@Original_ContactName",
➥ System.Data.SqlDbType.NVarChar, 30,
➥ System.Data.ParameterDirection.Input, False, CType(0, Byte),
➥ CType(0, Byte), "ContactName", System.Data.DataRowVersion.Original,
➥ Nothing))
Me.SqlUpdateCommand1.Parameters.Add(New
➥ System.Data.SqlClient.SqlParameter("@Original_ContactTitle",
➥ System.Data.SqlDbType.NVarChar, 30,
➥ System.Data.ParameterDirection.Input, False, CType(0, Byte),
➥ CType(0, Byte), "ContactTitle",
➥ System.Data.DataRowVersion.Original, Nothing))
Me.SqlUpdateCommand1.Parameters.Add(New
➥ System.Data.SqlClient.SqlParameter("@Original_Country",
➥ System.Data.SqlDbType.NVarChar, 15,
➥ System.Data.ParameterDirection.Input, False, CType(0, Byte),
➥ CType(0, Byte), "Country", System.Data.DataRowVersion.Original,
➥ Nothing))
Me.SqlUpdateCommand1.Parameters.Add(New
➥ System.Data.SqlClient.SqlParameter("@Original_Fax",
➥ System.Data.SqlDbType.NVarChar, 24,
➥ System.Data.ParameterDirection.Input, False, CType(0, Byte),
➥ CType(0, Byte), "Fax", System.Data.DataRowVersion.Original,
➥ Nothing))
Me.SqlUpdateCommand1.Parameters.Add(New
➥ System.Data.SqlClient.SqlParameter("@Original_Phone",
➥ System.Data.SqlDbType.NVarChar, 24,
➥ System.Data.ParameterDirection.Input, False, CType(0, Byte),
➥ CType(0, Byte), "Phone", System.Data.DataRowVersion.Original,
➥ Nothing))
Me.SqlUpdateCommand1.Parameters.Add(New
➥ System.Data.SqlClient.SqlParameter("@Original_PostalCode",
➥ System.Data.SqlDbType.NVarChar, 10,
➥ System.Data.ParameterDirection.Input, False, CType(0, Byte),
➥ CType(0, Byte), "PostalCode", System.Data.DataRowVersion.Original,
➥ Nothing))
```

```
Me.SqlUpdateCommand1.Parameters.Add(New
➥ System.Data.SqlClient.SqlParameter("@Original_Region",
➥ System.Data.SqlDbType.NVarChar, 15,
➥ System.Data.ParameterDirection.Input, False, CType(0, Byte),
➥ CType(0, Byte), "Region", System.Data.DataRowVersion.Original,
➥ Nothing))
'
'SqlDeleteCommand1
'
Me.SqlDeleteCommand1.CommandText = "DELETE FROM Customers WHERE
➥ (CustomerID = @Original_CustomerID) AND (Address = @O" & _
"riginal_Address OR @Original_Address IS NULL AND Address IS NULL) AND
➥ (City = @O" & _
"riginal_City OR @Original_City IS NULL AND City IS NULL) AND
➥ (CompanyName = @Ori" & _
"ginal_CompanyName) AND (ContactName = @Original_ContactName OR
➥ @Original_Contact" & _
"Name IS NULL AND ContactName IS NULL) AND (ContactTitle =
➥ @Original_ContactTitle" & _
" OR @Original_ContactTitle IS NULL AND ContactTitle IS NULL) AND
➥ (Country = @Ori" & _
"ginal_Country OR @Original_Country IS NULL AND Country IS NULL) AND
➥ (Fax = @Orig" & _
"inal_Fax OR @Original_Fax IS NULL AND Fax IS NULL) AND (Phone =
➥ @Original_Phone " & _
"OR @Original_Phone IS NULL AND Phone IS NULL) AND (PostalCode =
➥ @Original_Postal" & _
"Code OR @Original_PostalCode IS NULL AND PostalCode IS NULL) AND
➥ (Region = @Orig" & _
"inal_Region OR @Original_Region IS NULL AND Region IS NULL)"
Me.SqlDeleteCommand1.Connection = Me.SqlConnection1
Me.SqlDeleteCommand1.Parameters.Add(New
➥ System.Data.SqlClient.SqlParameter("@Original_CustomerID",
➥ System.Data.SqlDbType.NVarChar, 5,
➥ System.Data.ParameterDirection.Input, False, CType(0, Byte),
➥ CType(0, Byte), "CustomerID", System.Data.DataRowVersion.Original,
➥ Nothing))
Me.SqlDeleteCommand1.Parameters.Add(New
➥ System.Data.SqlClient.SqlParameter("@Original_Address",
➥ System.Data.SqlDbType.NVarChar, 60,
➥ System.Data.ParameterDirection.Input, False, CType(0, Byte),
➥ CType(0, Byte), "Address", System.Data.DataRowVersion.Original,
➥ Nothing))
Me.SqlDeleteCommand1.Parameters.Add(New
➥ System.Data.SqlClient.SqlParameter("@Original_City",
➥ System.Data.SqlDbType.NVarChar, 15,
➥ System.Data.ParameterDirection.Input, False, CType(0, Byte),
➥ CType(0, Byte), "City", System.Data.DataRowVersion.Original,
➥ Nothing))
Me.SqlDeleteCommand1.Parameters.Add(New
➥ System.Data.SqlClient.SqlParameter("@Original_CompanyName",
```

```
➡ System.Data.SqlDbType.NVarChar, 40,
➡ System.Data.ParameterDirection.Input, False, CType(0, Byte),
➡ CType(0, Byte), "CompanyName", System.Data.DataRowVersion.Original,
➡ Nothing))
Me.SqlDeleteCommand1.Parameters.Add(New
➡ System.Data.SqlClient.SqlParameter("@Original_ContactName",
➡ System.Data.SqlDbType.NVarChar, 30,
➡ System.Data.ParameterDirection.Input, False, CType(0, Byte),
➡ CType(0, Byte), "ContactName", System.Data.DataRowVersion.Original,
➡ Nothing))
Me.SqlDeleteCommand1.Parameters.Add(New
➡ System.Data.SqlClient.SqlParameter("@Original_ContactTitle",
➡ System.Data.SqlDbType.NVarChar, 30,
➡ System.Data.ParameterDirection.Input, False, CType(0, Byte),
➡ CType(0, Byte), "ContactTitle",
➡ System.Data.DataRowVersion.Original, Nothing))
Me.SqlDeleteCommand1.Parameters.Add(New
➡ System.Data.SqlClient.SqlParameter("@Original_Country",
➡ System.Data.SqlDbType.NVarChar, 15,
➡ System.Data.ParameterDirection.Input, False, CType(0, Byte),
➡ CType(0, Byte), "Country", System.Data.DataRowVersion.Original,
➡ Nothing))
Me.SqlDeleteCommand1.Parameters.Add(New
➡ System.Data.SqlClient.SqlParameter("@Original_Fax",
➡ System.Data.SqlDbType.NVarChar, 24,
➡ System.Data.ParameterDirection.Input, False, CType(0, Byte),
➡ CType(0, Byte), "Fax", System.Data.DataRowVersion.Original,
➡ Nothing))
Me.SqlDeleteCommand1.Parameters.Add(New
➡ System.Data.SqlClient.SqlParameter("@Original_Phone",
➡ System.Data.SqlDbType.NVarChar, 24,
➡ System.Data.ParameterDirection.Input, False, CType(0, Byte),
➡ CType(0, Byte), "Phone", System.Data.DataRowVersion.Original,
➡ Nothing))
Me.SqlDeleteCommand1.Parameters.Add(New
➡ System.Data.SqlClient.SqlParameter("@Original_PostalCode",
➡ System.Data.SqlDbType.NVarChar, 10,
➡ System.Data.ParameterDirection.Input, False, CType(0, Byte),
➡ CType(0, Byte), "PostalCode", System.Data.DataRowVersion.Original,
➡ Nothing))
Me.SqlDeleteCommand1.Parameters.Add(New
➡ System.Data.SqlClient.SqlParameter("@Original_Region",
➡ System.Data.SqlDbType.NVarChar, 15,
➡ System.Data.ParameterDirection.Input, False, CType(0, Byte),
➡ CType(0, Byte), "Region", System.Data.DataRowVersion.Original,
➡ Nothing))
'
'SqlDataAdapter1
'
Me.SqlDataAdapter1.DeleteCommand = Me.SqlDeleteCommand1
Me.SqlDataAdapter1.InsertCommand = Me.SqlInsertCommand1
```

```
Me.SqlDataAdapter1.SelectCommand = Me.SqlSelectCommand1
Me.SqlDataAdapter1.TableMappings.AddRange(New
➡ System.Data.Common.DataTableMapping() {New
➡ System.Data.Common.DataTableMapping("Table", "Customers", New
➡ System.Data.Common.DataColumnMapping() {New
➡ System.Data.Common.DataColumnMapping("CustomerID", "CustomerID"),
➡ New System.Data.Common.DataColumnMapping("CompanyName",
➡ "CompanyName"), New
➡ System.Data.Common.DataColumnMapping("ContactName", "ContactName"),
➡ New System.Data.Common.DataColumnMapping("ContactTitle",
➡ "ContactTitle"), New
➡ System.Data.Common.DataColumnMapping("Address", "Address"), New
➡ System.Data.Common.DataColumnMapping("City", "City"), New
➡ System.Data.Common.DataColumnMapping("Region", "Region"), New
➡ System.Data.Common.DataColumnMapping("PostalCode", "PostalCode"),
➡ New System.Data.Common.DataColumnMapping("Country", "Country"), New
➡ System.Data.Common.DataColumnMapping("Phone", "Phone"), New
➡ System.Data.Common.DataColumnMapping("Fax", "Fax")}})})
Me.SqlDataAdapter1.UpdateCommand = Me.SqlUpdateCommand1
```

The code that Visual Basic .NET writes for you is straightforward but tedious—a perfect job for a wizard. In summary, the code in Listing 27.1 performs these tasks:

1. Declares the DataAdapter object, as well as the Command objects that are needed to configure the DataAdapter object.

2. Sets the Command for the SelectCommand property to select all fields from the desired table.

3. Set the Command for the InsertCommand property to insert a new record into the table. After performing the INSERT, the code executes a SELECT to refresh the DataSet. The InsertCommand has one Parameter for each field in the record.

4. Sets the Command for the UpdateCommand property to update an existing record in the table. The WHERE clause of this command checks every field in the record to be certain that no other user has altered the record after this user read it into the DataSet. After performing the UPDATE, the code executes a SELECT to refresh the DataSet. The UpdateCommand has one Parameter for each field in the record.

5. Sets the Command for the DeleteCommand property to delete an existing record from the table. The WHERE clause of this command checks every field in the record to be certain that no other user has altered the record after this user read it into the DataSet. The DeleteCommand has one Parameter for each field in the record.

6. Sets the Command properties of the DataAdapter to refer to the appropriate Commands.

7. Adds a TableMapping to the DataAdapter to specify the mapping between the source columns in the database and the columns in any DataSet based on this DataAdapter.

In some situations, Visual Basic .NET may be unable to complete all of these steps. For instance, if you create a DataAdapter by dragging a view with a GROUP BY clause to the form, there is no general method available to update the source data of the view. In this case, you'll see a warning such as the one shown in Figure 27.6. If you click OK in this dialog box, Visual Basic .NET will create the DataAdapter but leave the troublesome properties empty. If you click Cancel, no DataAdapter will be created.

FIGURE 27.6:

Problems creating a DataAdapter

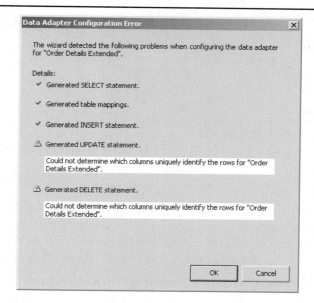

The Properties window provides additional options for managing a DataAdapter object. If you expand any of the Command properties, you can review the properties of the individual Command objects that are attached to the DataAdapter. Clicking the CommandText property of any of these objects will reveal a build button that launches a Query Builder window (similar to the one shown in Figure 27.7) to allow you to easily alter the SQL statement executed by that particular Command.

There are also three hyperlinks that appear beneath the properties list of the Properties window:

- Configure Data Adapter
- Preview Data
- Generate DataSet

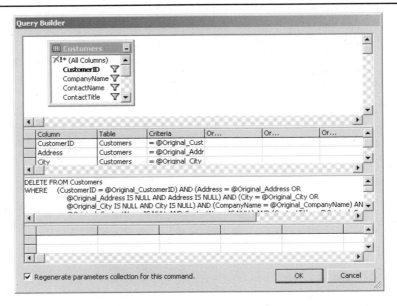

The *Configure Data Adapter* hyperlink launches the Data Adapter Configuration Wizard (this is true whether the original DataAdapter was created with the wizard or not). This wizard is fully re-entrant, so you can use it to alter the properties of a DataAdapter or to just inspect the properties that are already set for the DataAdapter.

The *Preview Data* hyperlink opens the Data Adapter Preview dialog box, shown in Figure 27.8. This dialog box lets you supply values for any Parameters required by the DataAdapter's SelectCommand, and then displays the data that the DataAdapter retrieves from the data source.

WARNING   The Data Adapter Preview dialog box lets you edit the data that it displays, but any changes you make are not saved to the original database.

The *Generate DataSet* hyperlink opens the Generate DataSet dialog box. This dialog box allows you to choose an existing DataSet or to create a new DataSet. If the DataAdapter returns multiple tables, you can also choose which tables to add to the DataSet. A check box (which is checked by default) lets you control whether to create a visual data object for this DataSet.

The DataSet Object

If you create a DataSet by clicking the Generate DataSet link from a DataAdapter, the DataSet will automatically be configured to use the data supplied by the DataAdapter. If you

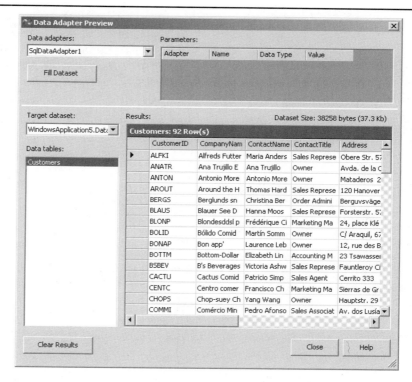

create a DataSet by dragging from the Toolbox, you'll see an Add DataSet dialog box. This dialog box gives you the choice of selecting a DataSet already in your project as the basis for the new DataSet, or creating a new, untyped DataSet to work with.

DataSets generated from a DataAdapter are always strongly typed. That is, they are based on an XSD schema that Visual Basic .NET builds for you, so that you can refer to the tables and columns in the DataSet as properties of their parent objects. If you create a DataSet named DataSet1, for example, Visual Basic .NET will create `DataSet1.xsd` as an XSD schema for that DataSet and then create a DataSet object named DataSet11 based on that schema.

NOTE   For more information on strongly typed DataSets, see Chapter 14, "Using the ADO.NET Objects to Retrieve Data."

Visual Basic .NET generates minimal code to instantiate a DataSet object. Here's an example:

```
' Code in form declarations section
Friend WithEvents DataSet11 As WindowsApplication1.DataSet1

' Code in InitializeComponent()
'
```

```
'DataSet11
'
Me.DataSet11.DataSetName = "DataSet1"
Me.DataSet11.Locale = New System.Globalization.CultureInfo("en-US")
Me.DataSet11.Namespace = "http://www.tempuri.org/DataSet1.xsd"
```

The Properties window for a strongly typed DataSet includes two hyperlinks:

- View Schema

- DataSet Properties

If you click the *View Schema* hyperlink, the XSD file on which the DataSet is based will open in the XSD designer inside Visual Basic .NET.

Clicking the *DataSet Properties* hyperlink opens the DataSet Properties dialog box, shown in Figure 27.9. This dialog box lets you drill down to inspect the properties of the tables and columns within the DataSet, but you can't edit them here. Instead, you'll need to do any editing in the XSD designer.

FIGURE 27.9:

DataSet Properties
dialog box

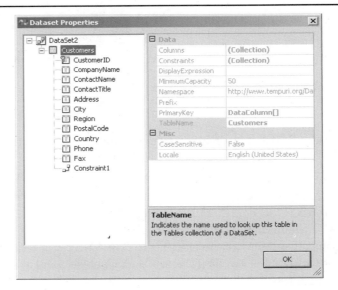

The DataView Object

You can create a DataView object by dragging the DataView control from the Data tab of the Toolbox and dropping it on a form. This is most useful when there is already a DataSet object on the form, because a DataView represents a view into the data contained in a DataSet.

After you create the DataView object, you can select the table from which it will draw data in the Table property in the Properties window. You can choose from any table contained in any DataSet that exists on the form. You can also set other properties to customize the data presented by the DataView. Table 27.4 lists these properties.

TABLE 27.4: DataView Properties

Property	Meaning
AllowDelete	If True, records can be deleted through the DataView.
AllowEdit	If True, records can be edited through the DataView.
AllowNew	If True, records can be added through the DataView.
ApplyDefaultSort	True to sort the data in the DataView.
RowFilter	Supplies a filter expression to limit the data in the DataView. This expression takes the form of a SQL WHERE clause.
Sort	Supplies a sort expression for the data in the DataView. Generally, this will be the name of a column followed by ASC for an ascending sort or DESC for a descending sort.
Table	Name of the table that will supply data for the DataView.

When you create a DataView, Visual Basic .NET creates code for it as in the following example:

```
' Code in form declarations section
Friend WithEvents DataView1 As System.Data.DataView

' Code in InitializeComponent()
'
'DataView1
'
Me.DataView1.Table = Me.DataSet11.Customers
```

At runtime, you can bind a DataView to a control such as a DataGrid to display and edit the data supplied by the DataView.

Creating Edit Forms with Drag-and-Drop

The drag-and-drop operations outlined earlier are almost (but not quite) enough to create a data-editing form. You'll still need to write a few lines of code to perform two tasks. First, you'll need to fill the DataSet with data. Second, you'll need to get that data connected to the user interface. To build a quick data-editing form using these tools, you can follow these steps:

1. Open Visual Studio .NET and create a new Visual Basic .NET Windows application.

2. Select an existing Data Connection in Server Explorer or create a new Data Connection.

3. Drag a table from the Data Connection and drop it on the default Form1 to create a Connection and a DataAdapter.

4. Select the DataAdapter and then click the Generate DataSet hyperlink.

5. Accept the defaults in the Generate DataSet dialog box and then click OK to create DataSet11.

6. Select the DataGrid control in the Toolbox and draw a DataGrid control on the form.

7. Add a Button control to the form, name it **btnSave**, and set its Text property to **Save**.

8. In the code behind the form, add a Form_Load procedure:

```
Private Sub Form1_Load(ByVal sender As Object, _
  ByVal e As System.EventArgs) Handles MyBase.Load
    SqlDataAdapter1.Fill(DataSet11)
    DataGrid1.DataSource = DataSet11.Tables(0)
End Sub
```

9. In the code behind the form, add a btnSave_Click procedure:

```
Private Sub btnSave_Click(ByVal sender As System.Object, _
  ByVal e As System.EventArgs) Handles btnSave.Click
    SqlDataAdapter1.Update(DataSet11)
End Sub
```

That's it! If you run the project, you'll have an editing form for the table you selected that allows updates, inserts, and deletions, and that writes the changes back to the original database when you click the Save button.

Using the Data Form Wizard

Of course, there's a lot more you could do to enhance the simple data-editing form that you just created. For instance, you could do any of the following:

- Add navigation buttons.
- Split the fields up among individually bound controls instead of a grid.
- Make explicit provisions for adding records.
- Alter the form to show multiple tables.

But it turns out that you don't have to write code for any of these operations by hand. Visual Basic .NET includes a flexible Data Form Wizard that can build a variety of bound forms for you without your needing to write any code.

In this section, I'll demonstrate several uses of the Data Form Wizard; then I'll look at the code that it generates and discuss places where you might like to make changes.

Building a Single-Table Data Form

To create a Data Form that draws its data from a single table and allows editing in a Data-Grid control, follow these steps in a Visual Basic .NET project:

1. Select Project ➤ Add Windows Form.

2. In the Add New Item dialog box, select the Data Form Wizard, choose a name for the new form, and click Open.

3. Read the introductory panel of the Data Form Wizard and then click Next.

4. On the Choose a DataSet panel, select the option button to create a new DataSet and assign a name to the new DataSet. I used Customers as the DataSet name in this example. Click Next.

5. On the Choose a Data Connection panel, choose an existing Connection to the SQL Server Northwind database, or create a new Connection to that database by clicking the New Connection button. Click Next.

6. On the Choose Tables or Views panel, shown in Figure 27.10, select the Customers table in the Available Items list and click the > button to move it to the Selected Items list. Click Next.

7. On the Choose Tables and Columns panel, leave all the columns selected in the list and click Next.

FIGURE 27.10:

Choosing tables or views for the Data Form

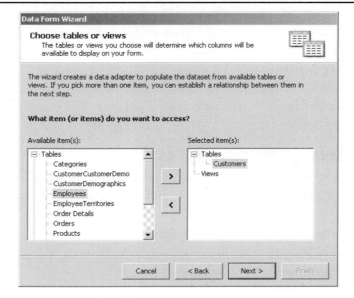

8. On the Choose the Display Style panel, select the All Records in a Grid option. Check the Cancel All check box and then click Finish to create the Data Form.

Figure 27.11 shows the completed Data Form with data loaded.

FIGURE 27.11:

A single-table
Data Form

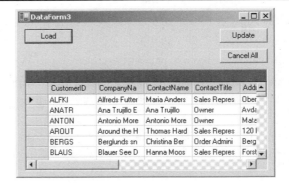

On this form, the Data Form Wizard created three buttons to manage the data:

- The *Load* button loads the data into the DataGrid. The form opens without any data initially loaded. This makes the form faster to load, at the cost of an extra step when you actually want to view the data.

- The *Update* button saves all changes that have been made in the DataGrid back to the SQL Server database.

- The *Cancel All* button cancels all changes since the most recent update and restores the original data to the DataGrid.

With this version of the Data Form, edits can be performed directly in the DataGrid control. You can delete a row by clicking in the left-hand column of the DataGrid and pressing the Delete key. You can add a new row by scrolling to the end of the DataGrid and entering values for the new row there.

Building a Multiple-Table Data Form

For a more complex example, I'll build a Data Form that allows editing the Products and Categories tables together. To build this form, follow these steps in a Visual Basic .NET project:

1. Select Project ➤ Add Windows Form.

2. In the Add New Item dialog box, select the Data Form Wizard, choose a name for the new form, and click Open.

3. Read the introductory panel of the Data Form Wizard and then click Next.

4. On the Choose a DataSet panel, select the option button to create a new DataSet and assign a name to the new DataSet. I used CategoryProducts as the DataSet name in this example. Click Next.

5. On the Choose a Data Connection panel, choose an existing Connection to the SQL Server Northwind database, or create a new Connection to that database by clicking the New Connection button. Click Next.

6. On the Choose Tables or Views panel, select the Categories table in the Available Items list and click the > button to move it to the Selected Items list. Then select the Products table in the Available Items list and click the > button to move it to the Selected Items list. Click Next.

TIP The Data Form Wizard will allow you to choose more than two tables on this panel, but it will display only two tables at most on the final form.

7. On the Create a Relationship between Tables panel, shown in Figure 27.12, name the new relationship **relCategoryProduct**. Select Categories as the parent table and Products as the child table. Select CategoryID as the key in each table. Click the > button to create the relationship. Click Next.

FIGURE 27.12:

Creating a new relationship

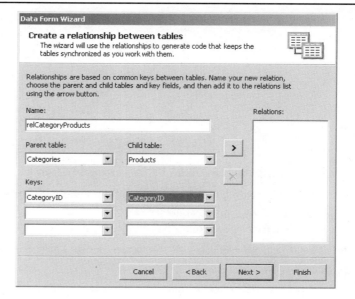

8. On the Choose Tables and Columns panel, select Categories as the master table and Products as the detail table. Leave all the columns selected in the list and click Next.

NOTE   The Data Form Wizard will not let you select a long binary field, such as the Picture field in the Categories table, to display on a form.

9. On the Choose the Display Style panel, select the Single Record in Individual Controls option. Check all the check boxes and then click Finish to create the Data Form.

Figure 27.13 shows the completed Data Form with data loaded.

FIGURE 27.13:

A multiple-table
Data Form

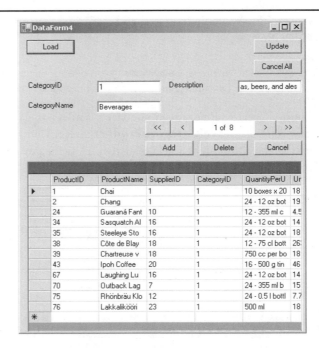

On this form, the Data Form Wizard created 10 buttons to manage the data:

- The *Load* button loads the data into the individual controls and into the DataGrid. The form opens without any data initially loaded. This makes the form faster to load, at the cost of an extra step when you actually want to view the data.

- The *Update* button saves all changes that have been made in the data back to the SQL Server database.

- The *Cancel All* button cancels all changes since the most recent update and restores the original data to the form.

- The << button returns the individual controls to the first category.
- The < button moves the individual controls to the previous category.
- The > button moves the individual controls to the next category.
- The >> button moves the individual controls to the last category.
- The *Add* button adds a new category.
- The *Delete* button deletes the currently displayed category.
- The *Cancel* button cancels any changes to the current category.

With this version of the Data Form, edits to products can be performed directly in the Data-Grid control. You can delete a row by clicking in the left-hand column of the DataGrid and pressing the Delete key. You can add a new row by scrolling to the end of the DataGrid and entering values for the new row there. When you enter a new row, the Data Form automatically fills in the CategoryID that corresponds to the currently displayed category.

Code Generated by the Data Form Wizard

One good use of wizard-generated code, even if you're not going to use it in your application, is learning new techniques. In this section, I'll review the code that the Data Form Wizard generated for the multiple-table form that displays categories and products.

NOTE   I've added some line-continuation characters to the code listings in this section to make them fit more easily on the page. Otherwise, the code is exactly as it was created by the wizard.

The first thing the wizard does, of course, is declare the variables that it will use to access the data:

```
Friend WithEvents OleDbSelectCommand1 As System.Data.OleDb.OleDbCommand
Friend WithEvents OleDbInsertCommand1 As System.Data.OleDb.OleDbCommand
Friend WithEvents OleDbUpdateCommand1 As System.Data.OleDb.OleDbCommand
Friend WithEvents OleDbDeleteCommand1 As System.Data.OleDb.OleDbCommand
Friend WithEvents OleDbSelectCommand2 As System.Data.OleDb.OleDbCommand
Friend WithEvents OleDbInsertCommand2 As System.Data.OleDb.OleDbCommand
Friend WithEvents OleDbUpdateCommand2 As System.Data.OleDb.OleDbCommand
Friend WithEvents OleDbDeleteCommand2 As System.Data.OleDb.OleDbCommand
Friend WithEvents objCategoryProducts As _
  WindowsApplication5.CategoryProducts
Friend WithEvents OleDbConnection1 As System.Data.OleDb.OleDbConnection
Friend WithEvents OleDbDataAdapter1 As System.Data.OleDb.OleDbDataAdapter
Friend WithEvents OleDbDataAdapter2 As System.Data.OleDb.OleDbDataAdapter
```

These variables are declared in the System.Data.OleDb namespace, even though I chose a SQL Server data source. The wizard always uses System.Data.OleDb for its data variables.

This works for a SQL Server data source, even though it's not as well optimized for such a data source as the System.Data.SqlClient namespace (because accessing SQL Server data via System.Data.OleDb requires loading additional layers of drivers to access the data). If you're dealing with SQL Server data and you're sure you won't need to change the type of data source, you should use search and replace to switch all the variables to the System.Data.Sql-Client namespace.

The DataSet that the code uses is declared as an instance of a schema also created by the wizard (in this case, WindowsApplication5.CategoryProducts). This allows the use of strongly typed expressions in dealing with the data.

Because this form displays data from two tables, it uses two DataAdapter objects. But both of those objects draw data from the same OleDbConnection, and both deliver their data to the same DataSet.

The wizard also adds a great deal of code to the form's InitializeComponents procedure, starting with code to instantiate all the objects involved:

```
Me.OleDbSelectCommand1 = New System.Data.OleDb.OleDbCommand()
Me.OleDbInsertCommand1 = New System.Data.OleDb.OleDbCommand()
Me.OleDbUpdateCommand1 = New System.Data.OleDb.OleDbCommand()
Me.OleDbDeleteCommand1 = New System.Data.OleDb.OleDbCommand()
Me.OleDbSelectCommand2 = New System.Data.OleDb.OleDbCommand()
Me.OleDbInsertCommand2 = New System.Data.OleDb.OleDbCommand()
Me.OleDbUpdateCommand2 = New System.Data.OleDb.OleDbCommand()
Me.OleDbDeleteCommand2 = New System.Data.OleDb.OleDbCommand()
Me.objCategoryProducts = New WindowsApplication5.CategoryProducts()
Me.OleDbConnection1 = New System.Data.OleDb.OleDbConnection()
Me.OleDbDataAdapter1 = New System.Data.OleDb.OleDbDataAdapter()
Me.OleDbDataAdapter2 = New System.Data.OleDb.OleDbDataAdapter()
```

The wizard also calls the BeginInit method on both the DataGrid control and the DataSet:

```
CType(Me.objCategoryProducts, System.ComponentModel. _
  ISupportInitialize).BeginInit()
CType(Me.grdProducts, System.ComponentModel. _
  ISupportInitialize).BeginInit()
```

The BeginInit method prevents the object in question from being used until the corresponding EndInit method is called. This prevents the user from interacting with the user interface or the data while they're still being loaded.

The next task for the code is to initialize all the Command objects that are used by the DataAdapter objects. This initialization is similar to the example that you saw in Listing 27.1 earlier in the chapter, so I won't repeat it here. After the Commands have been initialized, the code sets up the DataSet, the OleDbConnection, and the two OleDbDataAdapter objects. Listing 27.2 shows the code that handles these jobs.

Listing 27.2:   **Initializing Components for a Data Form**

```
'objCategoryProducts
'
Me.objCategoryProducts.DataSetName = "CategoryProducts"
Me.objCategoryProducts.Locale = New System.Globalization. _
 CultureInfo("en-US")
Me.objCategoryProducts.Namespace = _
 "http://www.tempuri.org/CategoryProducts.xsd"
'
'OleDbConnection1
'
Me.OleDbConnection1.ConnectionString = "Provider=SQLOLEDB.1;" & _
 "Integrated Security=SSPI;Persist Security Info=False;Initial " & _
 "Catalog=Northwind;Data Source=SKYROCKET;Use Procedure for " & _
 "Prepare=1;Auto Transla" & _
 "te=True;Packet Size=4096;Workstation ID=SAILBOAT;Use " & _
 "Encryption for Data=False;T" & _
 "ag with column collation when possible=False"
'
'OleDbDataAdapter1
'
Me.OleDbDataAdapter1.DeleteCommand = Me.OleDbDeleteCommand1
Me.OleDbDataAdapter1.InsertCommand = Me.OleDbInsertCommand1
Me.OleDbDataAdapter1.SelectCommand = Me.OleDbSelectCommand1
Me.OleDbDataAdapter1.TableMappings.AddRange(New System.Data. _
 Common.DataTableMapping() { _
 New System.Data.Common.DataTableMapping("Table", "Categories", _
 New System.Data.Common.DataColumnMapping() { _
 New System.Data.Common.DataColumnMapping("CategoryID", "CategoryID"), _
 New System.Data.Common.DataColumnMapping( _
 "CategoryName", "CategoryName"), _
 New System.Data.Common.DataColumnMapping( _
 "Description", "Description"), _
 New System.Data.Common.DataColumnMapping("Picture", "Picture")})})
Me.OleDbDataAdapter1.UpdateCommand = Me.OleDbUpdateCommand1
'
'OleDbDataAdapter2
'
Me.OleDbDataAdapter2.DeleteCommand = Me.OleDbDeleteCommand2
Me.OleDbDataAdapter2.InsertCommand = Me.OleDbInsertCommand2
Me.OleDbDataAdapter2.SelectCommand = Me.OleDbSelectCommand2
Me.OleDbDataAdapter2.TableMappings.AddRange( _
 New System.Data.Common.DataTableMapping() { _
 New System.Data.Common.DataTableMapping("Table", "Products", _
 New System.Data.Common.DataColumnMapping() { _
 New System.Data.Common.DataColumnMapping("ProductID", "ProductID"), _
 New System.Data.Common.DataColumnMapping( _
 "ProductName", "ProductName"), _
 New System.Data.Common.DataColumnMapping( _
```

```
    "SupplierID", "SupplierID"), _
    New System.Data.Common.DataColumnMapping( _
    "CategoryID", "CategoryID"), _
    New System.Data.Common.DataColumnMapping( _
    "QuantityPerUnit", "QuantityPerUnit"), _
    New System.Data.Common.DataColumnMapping("UnitPrice", "UnitPrice"), _
    New System.Data.Common.DataColumnMapping( _
    "UnitsInStock", "UnitsInStock"), _
    New System.Data.Common.DataColumnMapping( _
    "UnitsOnOrder", "UnitsOnOrder"), _
    New System.Data.Common.DataColumnMapping( _
    "ReorderLevel", "ReorderLevel"), _
    New System.Data.Common.DataColumnMapping( _
    "Discontinued", "Discontinued")}})
Me.OleDbDataAdapter2.UpdateCommand = Me.OleDbUpdateCommand2
```

The wizard writes code to bind each of the TextBox controls to the corresponding data within the DataSet. Here's the binding code for the editCategoryID control; the code for the other controls is similar:

```
'editCategoryID
'
Me.editCategoryID.DataBindings.Add( _
  New System.Windows.Forms.Binding( _
  "Text", Me.objCategoryProducts, "Categories.CategoryID"))
```

At the end of the initialization code, the form calls the EndInit methods of the DataGrid control and the DataSet object. This makes those objects available for user interaction:

```
CType(Me.objCategoryProducts, System.ComponentModel. _
  ISupportInitialize).EndInit()
CType(Me.grdProducts, System.ComponentModel. _
  ISupportInitialize).EndInit()
```

Most of the code for the controls on the form is pretty straightforward. The code for the Cancel button simply invokes the CancelCurrentEdit method of the DataTable that contains the category data:

```
Private Sub btnCancel_Click(ByVal sender As System.Object, _
  ByVal e As System.EventArgs) Handles btnCancel.Click
    Me.BindingContext(objCategoryProducts, "Categories").CancelCurrentEdit()
    Me.objCategoryProducts_PositionChanged()

End Sub
```

TIP   The btnCancel_Click procedure (and several of the others) doesn't contain any error handling. If you wish to make sure any errors in your application are trapped, you'll want to add Try/ Catch blocks to these procedures.

Similarly, the code for the Delete button is a thin wrapper around the appropriate RemoveAt method:

```
Private Sub btnDelete_Click(ByVal sender As System.Object, _
  ByVal e As System.EventArgs) Handles btnDelete.Click
    If (Me.BindingContext(objCategoryProducts, "Categories"). _
    Count > 0) Then
        Me.BindingContext(objCategoryProducts, "Categories"). _
        RemoveAt(Me.BindingContext(objCategoryProducts, "Categories"). _
        Position)
        Me.objCategoryProducts_PositionChanged()
    End If

End Sub
```

The btnAdd_Click code makes sure that any edit in process is finished and then calls the AddNew method of the DataTable. Note that this bit of code does pass any errors through to the user interface:

```
Private Sub btnAdd_Click(ByVal sender As System.Object, _
  ByVal e As System.EventArgs) Handles btnAdd.Click
    Try
        'Clear out the current edits.
        Me.BindingContext(objCategoryProducts, "Categories"). _
        EndCurrentEdit()
        Me.BindingContext(objCategoryProducts, "Categories").AddNew()
    Catch eEndEdit As System.Exception
        System.Windows.Forms.MessageBox.Show(eEndEdit.Message)
    End Try
    Me.objCategoryProducts_PositionChanged()

End Sub
```

The code for the Update button is just a wrapper around the UpdateDataSet procedure:

```
Private Sub btnUpdate_Click(ByVal sender As System.Object, _
  ByVal e As System.EventArgs) Handles btnUpdate.Click
    Try
        'Attempt to update the data source.
        Me.UpdateDataSet()
    Catch eUpdate As System.Exception
        'Add your error handling code here.
        'Display error message, if any.
        System.Windows.Forms.MessageBox.Show(eUpdate.Message)
    End Try
    Me.objCategoryProducts_PositionChanged()

End Sub
```

The UpdateDataSet procedure is itself written by the wizard. Listing 27.3 shows this procedure, along with the companion UpdateDataSource procedure. Both of these procedures are straightforward. UpdateDataSet extracts any changed rows from the DataSet and passes them to UpdateDataSource, which calls the Update methods of the two DataAdapter objects to make the changes. The wizard-generated code checks twice (once in each of these procedures) to see whether there are any changes. This is a bit wasteful, but possibly useful if you plan to call UpdateDataSource from elsewhere in your code.

Listing 27.3:   The UpdateDataSet and UpdateDataSource Procedures

```
Public Sub UpdateDataSet()
    'Create a new dataset to hold the changes that have been made
    'to the main dataset.
    Dim objDataSetChanges As WindowsApplication5.CategoryProducts = _
    New WindowsApplication5.CategoryProducts()
    'Stop any current edits.
    Me.BindingContext(objCategoryProducts, "Categories").EndCurrentEdit()
    Me.BindingContext(objCategoryProducts, "Products").EndCurrentEdit()
    'Get the changes that have been made to the main dataset.
    objDataSetChanges = CType(objCategoryProducts.GetChanges, _
    WindowsApplication5.CategoryProducts)
    'Check to see if any changes have been made.
    If (Not (objDataSetChanges) Is Nothing) Then
        Try
            'There are changes that need to be made, so attempt
            'to update the data source by
            'calling the update method and passing the dataset
            'and any parameters.
            Me.UpdateDataSource(objDataSetChanges)
            objCategoryProducts.Merge(objDataSetChanges)
            objCategoryProducts.AcceptChanges()
        Catch eUpdate As System.Exception
            'Add your error handling code here.
            Throw eUpdate
        End Try
        'Add your code to check the returned dataset for any
        'errors that may have been
        'pushed into the row object's error.
    End If

End Sub
Public Sub UpdateDataSource(ByVal ChangedRows As _
WindowsApplication5.CategoryProducts)
    Try
        'The data source only needs to be updated
        'if there are changes pending.
        If (Not (ChangedRows) Is Nothing) Then
            'Open the connection.
            Me.OleDbConnection1.Open()
            'Attempt to update the data source.
```

```
            OleDbDataAdapter1.Update(ChangedRows)
            OleDbDataAdapter2.Update(ChangedRows)
        End If
    Catch updateException As System.Exception
        'Add your error handling code here.
        Throw updateException
    Finally
        'Close the connection whether or not the exception was thrown.
        Me.OleDbConnection1.Close()
    End Try

End Sub
```

The Load button calls another wizard-generated procedure named LoadDataSet:

```
Private Sub btnLoad_Click(ByVal sender As System.Object, _
  ByVal e As System.EventArgs) Handles btnLoad.Click
    Try
        'Attempt to load the dataset.
        Me.LoadDataSet()
    Catch eLoad As System.Exception
        'Add your error handling code here.
        'Display error message, if any.
        System.Windows.Forms.MessageBox.Show(eLoad.Message)
    End Try
    Me.objCategoryProducts_PositionChanged()

End Sub
```

LoadDataSet, which is shown in Listing 27.4 (along with the FillDataSet procedure, which it calls), is one of the more interesting pieces of code that the wizard generates. Rather than filling the DataSet used by the form directly, it fills a temporary DataSet and then merges the records from the temporary DataSet to the permanent DataSet. Because the permanent DataSet is empty when this procedure is called the first time, that has the effect of loading all the records to the permanent DataSet. Subsequent calls to LoadDataSet will have the effect of merging any new records or changes that other users have made to the existing records.

Note also that FillDataSet sets the EnforceConstraints property of the DataSet to False before it loads data. This ensures that the calls to the DataAdapter.Fill methods won't fail if they try to load child records before parent records.

Listing 27.4:   The LoadDataSet and FillDataSet Procedures

```
Public Sub LoadDataSet()
    'Create a new dataset to hold the records returned from the
    'call to FillDataSet.
    'A temporary dataset is used because filling
    'the existing dataset would
```

```
        'require the data bindings to be rebound.
        Dim objDataSetTemp As WindowsApplication5.CategoryProducts
        objDataSetTemp = New WindowsApplication5.CategoryProducts()
        Try
            'Attempt to fill the temporary dataset.
            Me.FillDataSet(objDataSetTemp)
        Catch eFillDataSet As System.Exception
            'Add your error handling code here.
            Throw eFillDataSet
        End Try
        Try
            'Empty the old records from the dataset.
            objCategoryProducts.Clear()
            'Merge the records into the main dataset.
            objCategoryProducts.Merge(objDataSetTemp)
        Catch eLoadMerge As System.Exception
            'Add your error handling code here.
            Throw eLoadMerge
        End Try

End Sub
Public Sub FillDataSet(ByVal dataSet As _
  WindowsApplication5.CategoryProducts)
    'Turn off constraint checking before the dataset is filled.
    'This allows the adapters to fill the dataset without concern
    'for dependencies between the tables.
    dataSet.EnforceConstraints = False
    Try
        'Open the connection.
        Me.OleDbConnection1.Open()
        'Attempt to fill the dataset through the OleDbDataAdapter1.
        Me.OleDbDataAdapter1.Fill(dataSet)
        Me.OleDbDataAdapter2.Fill(dataSet)
    Catch fillException As System.Exception
        'Add your error handling code here.
        Throw fillException
    Finally
        'Turn constraint checking back on.
        dataSet.EnforceConstraints = True
        'Close the connection whether or not the exception was thrown.
        Me.OleDbConnection1.Close()
    End Try

End Sub
```

Listing 27.5 shows the code that is used to navigate records in the main part of the form (where the categories are displayed). This code works by manipulating the Position property of the appropriate BindingContextObject. Of course, there's no similar code for the table displayed in the DataGrid, which doesn't require navigation buttons.

⤵ **Listing 27.5:**   **Navigation Code**

```
Private Sub btnNavFirst_Click(ByVal sender As System.Object, _
 ByVal e As System.EventArgs) Handles btnNavFirst.Click
    Me.BindingContext(objCategoryProducts, "Categories").Position = 0
    Me.objCategoryProducts_PositionChanged()

End Sub
Private Sub btnLast_Click(ByVal sender As System.Object, _
 ByVal e As System.EventArgs) Handles btnLast.Click
    Me.BindingContext(objCategoryProducts, "Categories").Position = _
     (Me.objCategoryProducts.Tables("Categories").Rows.Count - 1)
    Me.objCategoryProducts_PositionChanged()

End Sub
Private Sub btnNavPrev_Click(ByVal sender As System.Object, _
 ByVal e As System.EventArgs) Handles btnNavPrev.Click
    Me.BindingContext(objCategoryProducts, "Categories").Position = _
     (Me.BindingContext(objCategoryProducts, "Categories").Position - 1)
    Me.objCategoryProducts_PositionChanged()

End Sub
Private Sub btnNavNext_Click(ByVal sender As System.Object, _
 ByVal e As System.EventArgs) Handles btnNavNext.Click
    Me.BindingContext(objCategoryProducts, "Categories").Position = _
     (Me.BindingContext(objCategoryProducts, "Categories").Position + 1)
    Me.objCategoryProducts_PositionChanged()

End Sub
Private Sub objCategoryProducts_PositionChanged()
    Me.lblNavLocation.Text = (((Me.BindingContext(objCategoryProducts, _
     "Categories").Position + 1).ToString + " of  ") _
     + Me.BindingContext(objCategoryProducts, "Categories"). _
     Count.ToString)

End Sub
```

Finally, the Cancel All button calls the RejectChanges method of the DataSet:

```
Private Sub btnCancelAll_Click(ByVal sender As System.Object, _
 ByVal e As System.EventArgs) Handles btnCancelAll.Click
    Me.objCategoryProducts.RejectChanges()

End Sub
```

Working with XML Schema Files

To conclude this chapter, I'll take a brief look at the tools that are used for editing XML schema (XSD) files. You've seen in earlier chapters that these files are useful in declaring strongly typed DataSets as well as in working with XmlDataDocument objects.

Creating a New Schema

To create a new XML schema file in a Visual Basic .NET project, select Project ➤ Add Component. You then have two choices for inserting a new XML schema file into your project:

- Select the XML schema template to create only an XML schema file.

- Select the DataSet template to create an XML schema file and an associated DataSet class.

In either case, assign a name to the XSD file and then click OK to create the XML schema. If you're working with XML schemas as a way to design DataSet classes, you'll usually want to use the DataSet template. That way, any changes you make to the schema will automatically be reflected in the DataSet class without any manual intervention.

TIP   To see the DataSet class file, you need to click the Show All Files button in the Solution Explorer toolbar.

Visual Basic .NET will open the new XSD file in the designer. The file will initially be open in DataSet view, which is the view that you can use to design the schema graphically. You can use the tabs at the bottom of the designer to switch back and forth between DataSet view and XML view, which lets you edit the raw XML contained in the file.

There are two ways to add new objects to the XSD file: by drag-and-drop from Server Explorer or by drag-and-drop from the Toolbox. I'll cover each of these techniques in turn.

Working with Server Explorer

One way to create objects in the XSD file is to drag them from Server Explorer:

- You can drag a data-containing object (such as a table, view, stored procedure, or table-valued function) from Server Explorer to the XML designer. This will create a complex XML element containing all the fields from the object.

- You can drag multiple data-containing objects from Server Explorer at once by Ctrl+clicking or Shift+clicking to select them in Server Explorer. This will create a complex XML element for each of the objects you select.

- You can drag a container node (such as Tables or Views) from Server Explorer to create complex XML elements for every object in the container.

- You can drag individual columns, either one at a time or by selecting a group of individual columns with Shift+click and Ctrl+click operations. This will create a complex XML element containing constituent elements only for the columns that you dragged.

Working with the Toolbox

Dragging objects from Server Explorer is the fastest way to build up an XML schema if you have a Data Connection to the data that you wish to work with. But sometimes this won't be the case. For example, you may be creating a schema to work with data on a server that doesn't exist at your location, or you may be creating a schema to hold data that your application will generate itself. In these cases, you can use the XML Schema tab of the Toolbox to create schema objects.

To create a new table using the Toolbox, first drag an element from the Toolbox to the XML designer. This will create an empty designer for a complex element, as shown in Figure 27.14. Type a name in the center column to name the table. At this point, you can create columns for the table in several different ways:

- Click in the left-hand column of the designer to select whether to create an attribute or an element. Name the attribute or element in the center column, and select a datatype for it in the right-hand column.

- Right-click in the table and select Add ➤ New Element or Add ➤ New Key. Name the attribute or element in the center column, and select a datatype for it in the right-hand column.

- Drag an element or attribute from the Toolbox and drop it on the new table. Name the attribute or element in the center column, and select a datatype for it in the right-hand column.

- Copy and paste fields from another table in the designer. The easiest way to match the properties of an existing field in a database table is to drag and drop that table from Server Explorer to the XML designer, and then copy and paste the fields in which you're interested to your new table.

FIGURE 27.14:

Designer for a complex element

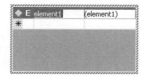

You'll probably also want to create a primary key for the new table. To do this, you can right-click in the table and select Add ➤ New Key, or drag a Key object from the Toolbox and drop it on the table. Either of these actions will open the Edit Key dialog box, shown in Figure 27.15.

Name the key in the Edit Key dialog box and choose the fields that make up the key. To create a primary key, make sure the Nullable check box is unchecked and the DataSet Primary Key check box is checked. Click OK to create the key.

Creating a new key in
the XML designer

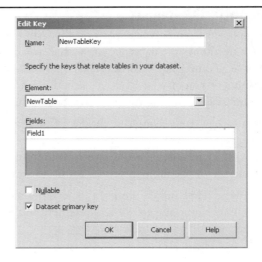

You can also create keys by creating relations between tables, which I'll discuss in the next section. This will automatically create the necessary primary and foreign keys.

Creating Relations

Whether you create tables in your XML schema from Server Explorer or from the Toolbox, the tables will be unrelated to one another. This is true even if there are relations defined between the tables in the original data source.

To add a new relation, right-click in a table and select Add ➤ New Relation, or drag the Relation object from the Toolbox and drop it on a table. Either action will open the Edit Relation dialog box, shown in Figure 27.16.

To create the relation, select the parent and child tables on the form. The Key combo box will offer you a selection of all the keys in the parent table. You should choose that table's primary key here or, if none exists, use the New button to create a new primary key. Then, in the Fields list, select the key fields from both the parent and child tables.

If you check the Create Foreign Key Constraint Only check box, the created key will be used only for limiting the rows that can be entered in the child table; you won't be able to use it to navigate between the parent table and the child table.

The Update Rule, Delete Rule, and Accept/Reject Rule combo boxes let you select rules for cascading referential integrity between the two tables.

When you've filled in the dialog box, click OK to create the relation.

The Generated Code

Figure 27.17 shows an XML schema in DataSet view. This particular schema was created by dragging the Northwind Customers and Orders tables from Server Explorer. I then used the Relation object in the Toolbox to create a relation between the two tables. Listing 27.6 shows this same schema in XML view.

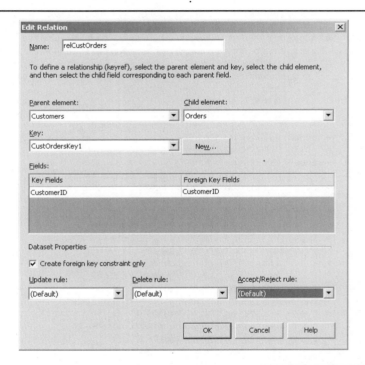

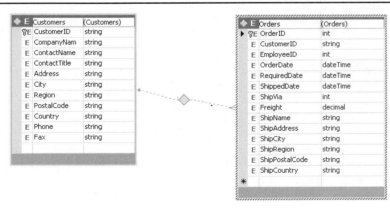

Listing 27.6:   **XML Schema in XML View**

```xml
<?xml version="1.0" encoding="utf-8" ?>
<xs:schema id="CustOrders"
targetNamespace="http://tempuri.org/CustOrders.xsd"
elementFormDefault="qualified" attributeFormDefault="qualified"
xmlns="http://tempuri.org/CustOrders.xsd"
xmlns:mstns="http://tempuri.org/CustOrders.xsd"
xmlns:xs="http://www.w3.org/2001/XMLSchema"
xmlns:msdata="urn:schemas-microsoft-com:xml-msdata">
  <xs:element name="CustOrders" msdata:IsDataSet="true">
    <xs:complexType>
      <xs:choice maxOccurs="unbounded">
        <xs:element name="Customers">
          <xs:complexType>
            <xs:sequence>
              <xs:element name="CustomerID"
 type="xs:string" />
              <xs:element name="CompanyName"
 type="xs:string" />
              <xs:element name="ContactName"
 type="xs:string" minOccurs="0" />
              <xs:element name="ContactTitle"
 type="xs:string" minOccurs="0" />
              <xs:element name="Address"
 type="xs:string" minOccurs="0" />
              <xs:element name="City"
 type="xs:string" minOccurs="0" />
              <xs:element name="Region"
 type="xs:string" minOccurs="0" />
              <xs:element name="PostalCode"
 type="xs:string" minOccurs="0" />
              <xs:element name="Country"
 type="xs:string" minOccurs="0" />
              <xs:element name="Phone"
 type="xs:string" minOccurs="0" />
              <xs:element name="Fax"
 type="xs:string" minOccurs="0" />
            </xs:sequence>
          </xs:complexType>
        </xs:element>
        <xs:element name="Orders">
          <xs:complexType>
            <xs:sequence>
              <xs:element name="OrderID"
 msdata:ReadOnly="true" msdata:AutoIncrement="true" type="xs:int" />
              <xs:element name="CustomerID"
 type="xs:string" minOccurs="0" />
              <xs:element name="EmployeeID"
 type="xs:int" minOccurs="0" />
              <xs:element name="OrderDate"
```

```
➡ type="xs:dateTime" minOccurs="0" />
                <xs:element name="RequiredDate"
➡ type="xs:dateTime" minOccurs="0" />
                <xs:element name="ShippedDate"
➡ type="xs:dateTime" minOccurs="0" />
                <xs:element name="ShipVia"
➡ type="xs:int" minOccurs="0" />
                <xs:element name="Freight"
➡ type="xs:decimal" minOccurs="0" />
                <xs:element name="ShipName"
➡ type="xs:string" minOccurs="0" />
                <xs:element name="ShipAddress"
➡ type="xs:string" minOccurs="0" />
                <xs:element name="ShipCity"
➡ type="xs:string" minOccurs="0" />
                <xs:element name="ShipRegion"
➡ type="xs:string" minOccurs="0" />
                <xs:element name="ShipPostalCode"
➡ type="xs:string" minOccurs="0" />
                <xs:element name="ShipCountry"
➡ type="xs:string" minOccurs="0" />
              </xs:sequence>
            </xs:complexType>
          </xs:element>
        </xs:choice>
      </xs:complexType>
      <xs:unique name="CustOrdersKey1" msdata:PrimaryKey="true">
        <xs:selector xpath=".//mstns:Customers" />
        <xs:field xpath="mstns:CustomerID" />
      </xs:unique>
      <xs:unique name="CustOrdersKey2" msdata:PrimaryKey="true">
        <xs:selector xpath=".//mstns:Orders" />
        <xs:field xpath="mstns:OrderID" />
      </xs:unique>
      <xs:keyref name="relCustOrders" refer="CustOrdersKey1">
        <xs:selector xpath=".//mstns:Orders" />
        <xs:field xpath="mstns:CustomerID" />
      </xs:keyref>
    </xs:element>
</xs:schema>
```

Note that by default, the designer created two temporary namespaces for your XML:

```
targetNamespace="http://tempuri.org/CustOrders.xsd"
xmlns:mstns="http://tempuri.org/CustOrders.xsd"
```

Remember, XML namespaces are supposed to be unique. If you're actually going to ship a component that uses this XML schema, you should rename those namespaces to something unique to your own organization.

The designer also created a matching DataSet class from the schema. Listing 27.7 shows this class. I've added some line continuation characters to make sure the code fits on the printed page.

Listing 27.7:   **DataSet from an XML Schema**

```
' --------------------------------------------------------------------
' <autogenerated>
'     This code was generated by a tool.
'     Runtime Version: 1.0.3215.11
'
'     Changes to this file may cause incorrect behavior and will be
' lost if
'     the code is regenerated.
' </autogenerated>
' --------------------------------------------------------------------

Option Strict Off
Option Explicit On

Imports System
Imports System.Data
Imports System.Runtime.Serialization
Imports System.Xml

<Serializable(), _
 System.ComponentModel.DesignerCategoryAttribute("code"), _
 System.Diagnostics.DebuggerStepThrough()> _
Public Class CustOrders
    Inherits DataSet

    Public Sub New()
        MyBase.New
        Me.InitClass
        Dim schemaChangedHandler As _
          System.ComponentModel.CollectionChangeEventHandler = _
          AddressOf Me.SchemaChanged
        AddHandler Me.Tables.CollectionChanged, schemaChangedHandler
        AddHandler Me.Relations.CollectionChanged, schemaChangedHandler
    End Sub

    Private Sub New(ByVal info As SerializationInfo, _
      ByVal context As StreamingContext)
        MyBase.New
        Dim strSchema As String = CType(info.GetValue( _
          "XmlSchema", GetType(System.String)),String)
        If (Not (strSchema) Is Nothing) Then
            Dim ds As DataSet = New DataSet
            ds.ReadXmlSchema(New XmlTextReader( _
            New System.IO.StringReader(strSchema)))
```

```vb
            Me.DataSetName = ds.DataSetName
            Me.Prefix = ds.Prefix
            Me.Namespace = ds.Namespace
            Me.Locale = ds.Locale
            Me.CaseSensitive = ds.CaseSensitive
            Me.EnforceConstraints = ds.EnforceConstraints
            Me.Merge(ds, false, System.Data.MissingSchemaAction.Add)
            Me.InitVars
        Else
            Me.InitClass
        End If
        Me.GetSerializationData(info, context)
        Dim schemaChangedHandler As _
         System.ComponentModel.CollectionChangeEventHandler = _
         AddressOf Me.SchemaChanged
        AddHandler Me.Tables.CollectionChanged, schemaChangedHandler
        AddHandler Me.Relations.CollectionChanged, schemaChangedHandler
    End Sub

    Public Overrides Function Clone() As DataSet
        Dim cln As CustOrders = CType(MyBase.Clone,CustOrders)
        cln.InitVars
        Return cln
    End Function

    Protected Overrides Function ShouldSerializeTables() As Boolean
        Return false
    End Function

    Protected Overrides Function ShouldSerializeRelations() As Boolean
        Return false
    End Function

    Protected Overrides Sub ReadXmlSerializable( _
     ByVal reader As XmlReader)
        Me.Reset
        Dim ds As DataSet = New DataSet
        ds.ReadXml(reader)
        Me.DataSetName = ds.DataSetName
        Me.Prefix = ds.Prefix
        Me.Namespace = ds.Namespace
        Me.Locale = ds.Locale
        Me.CaseSensitive = ds.CaseSensitive
        Me.EnforceConstraints = ds.EnforceConstraints
        Me.Merge(ds, false, System.Data.MissingSchemaAction.Add)
        Me.InitVars
    End Sub

    Protected Overrides Function GetSchemaSerializable() _
     As System.Xml.Schema.XmlSchema
        Dim stream As System.IO.MemoryStream = _
```

```
            New System.IO.MemoryStream
            Me.WriteXmlSchema(New XmlTextWriter(stream, Nothing))
            stream.Position = 0
            Return System.Xml.Schema.XmlSchema.Read( _
            New XmlTextReader(stream), Nothing)
        End Function

        Friend Sub InitVars()
        End Sub

        Private Sub InitClass()
            Me.DataSetName = "CustOrders"
            Me.Prefix = ""
            Me.Namespace = "http://tempuri.org/CustOrders.xsd"
            Me.Locale = New System.Globalization.CultureInfo("en-US")
            Me.CaseSensitive = false
            Me.EnforceConstraints = true
        End Sub

        Private Sub SchemaChanged(ByVal sender As Object, _
          ByVal e As System.ComponentModel.CollectionChangeEventArgs)
            If (e.Action = _
            System.ComponentModel.CollectionChangeAction.Remove) Then
                Me.InitVars
            End If
        End Sub
    End Class
```

This file declares a class, CustOrders, which inherits from the built-in DataSet class. This inheritance gives the CustOrders class all the interfaces of the DataSet class. In addition, it contains the code necessary to make this a strongly typed DataSet. The key to this is the InitClass procedure, which uses the XML namespace defined in the XSD file to set the Namespace property of the DataSet. The bottom line is that you don't have to worry about writing this code: Design your schema in the XML designer, and the strongly typed DataSet will just work.

Summary

In this chapter, you saw some of the tools that make Visual Basic .NET an attractive development environment. In particular, you saw how to use the Server Explorer to create data-oriented objects in a Visual Basic .NET project, how to use the Data Form Wizard to create bound forms without writing code, and how to use the XML designer to develop XML schemas for your DataSets. With these tools, you should be able to quickly create the data access code that you'll need for many applications.

PART VII

Appendices

APPENDIX A

The ADO Object Model

- The Connection Object

- The Command Object

- The Recordset Object

- The Parameter Object

- The Field Object

- The Record Object

- The Stream Object

- The Error Object

- The Property Object

introduced the ADO object model in Chapter 3, "Using the ADO Objects to Retrieve Data." This object model, shown in Figure A.1, contains objects that implement all the functionality of ADO. This appendix lists all the properties, methods, and events that characterize these objects. For further information about these interfaces, refer to the MDAC SDK, which contains complete documentation on each one.

TIP   You can download the full MDAC SDK from www.microsoft.com/data/download.htm.

FIGURE A.1:
The ADO object model

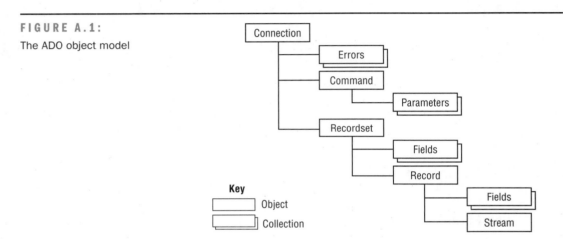

The Connection Object

A Connection object represents a single connection to an OLE DB data source. Table A.1 details the functionality of the Connection object.

TABLE A.1:   Connection Object Details

Name	Type	Description
Attributes	Property	Bitmapped property that indicates whether the data source supports retaining commits and retaining aborts.
BeginTrans	Method	Begins a transaction.
BeginTransComplete	Event	Occurs after a BeginTrans method is completed.
Cancel	Method	Cancels a pending asynchronous Open or Execute method.
Close	Method	Terminates the Connection with the data source.

continued on next page

TABLE A.1 CONTINUED: Connection Object Details

Name	Type	Description
CommandTimeout	Property	Number of seconds to wait for a response from the data provider when using the Execute method.
CommitTrans	Method	Commits a transaction.
CommitTransComplete	Event	Occurs after a CommitTrans method is completed.
ConnectComplete	Event	Occurs when a Connection is successfully connected to a data source, or when an asynchronous Connection attempt is cancelled.
ConnectionString	Property	Data source name or arguments to use for this Connection.
ConnectionTimeout	Property	Number of seconds to wait for a Connection to the data source after executing the Open method.
CursorLocation	Property	Controls whether cursors are created on the client (adUseClient) or the server (adUseServer).
DefaultDatabase	Property	Database that other objects using this Connection will use by default.
Disconnect	Event	Occurs after the Connection is closed.
Errors	Collection	Collection of Error objects.
Execute	Method	Executes a Command on the Connection without creating a Command object.
ExecuteComplete	Event	Occurs after a Command is executed on this Connection.
InfoMessage	Event	Occurs when this Connection receives an informational message from the underlying provider.
IsolationLevel	Property	Constant indicating the isolation level of transactions in this Connection from those in other Connections.
Mode	Property	Set to one of adModeUnknown, adModeRead, adModeWrite, adModeReadWrite, adModeShareDenyRead, adModeShareDenyWrite, adModeShareExclusive, or adModeShareDenyNone to indicate the permissions for this Connection.
Open	Method	Initializes the Connection with the data source.
OpenSchema	Method	Obtains schema information from the provider.
Properties	Collection	The collection of Property objects describing this Connection.
Provider	Property	OLE DB provider used for this Connection.
RollbackTrans	Method	Rolls back a transaction.
RollbackTransComplete	Event	Occurs when a RollbackTrans operation is completed.
State	Property	Constant indicating whether the Connection is open or closed.
Version	Property	Version of ADO.
WillConnect	Event	Occurs just before an attempt to connect to a data source. Can be cancelled.
WillExecute	Event	Occurs just before an attempt to execute a Command on this Connection. Can be cancelled.

The Command Object

A Command object represents a single instruction to an OLE DB data source to produce data. Depending on the back end, this might be a SQL query, a stored procedure, or something else entirely. Table A.2 shows the functionality of the Command object.

TABLE A.2:   Command Object Details

Name	Type	Description
ActiveConnection	Property	Connection object or string on which to execute this Command.
Cancel	Method	Cancels a pending asynchronous Command.
CommandText	Property	Text (SQL statement, stored procedure name, or table name) of the Command.
CommandTimeout	Property	Number of seconds to wait for a response from the data source.
CommandType	Property	One of adCmdText, adCmdTable, adCmdStoredProc, or adCmdUnknown.
CreateParameter	Method	Creates a new Parameter object associated with this Command.
Dialect	Property	A GUID that indicates which SQL dialect should be used by the data source to interpret Command Streams.
Execute	Method	Executes the Command and returns any Recordset(s) it generates.
Name	Property	String identifying this Command object.
NamedParameters	Property	True to pass Parameters to the data source by name; False (the default) to pass Parameters to the data source by position.
Parameters	Collection	The collection of Parameter objects associated with this Command.
Prepared	Property	If set to True, causes the data provider to save a compiled version of the Command on the first execution.
Properties	Collection	The collection of Property objects describing this Command.
State	Property	Constant indicating whether the object is open, closed, executing a Command, or fetching records.

The Recordset Object

A Recordset object represents a set of records retrieved from an OLE DB data provider. Table A.3 lists the methods, properties, and collections supplied by the ADO Recordset object. Remember, not all of these will apply to every Recordset. Which methods and properties are relevant depends on both the Recordset type and the underlying data provider.

TABLE A.3: Recordset Object Details

Name	Type	Description
AbsolutePage	Property	Number of the data page where the current record resides.
AbsolutePosition	Property	Ordinal position of the current record in the Recordset.
ActiveCommand	Property	Command from which this Recordset was created.
ActiveConnection	Property	Connection from which this Recordset was created.
AddNew	Method	Prepares a new record to be added to the Recordset.
BOF	Property	True if you have moved before the beginning of the Recordset.
Bookmark	Property	Unique identifier for the current row of the Recordset.
CacheSize	Property	Number of records that are cached in local memory.
Cancel	Method	Cancels an asynchronous Open method.
CancelBatch	Method	Cancels all pending changes in the Recordset.
CancelUpdate	Method	Throws away an AddNew or Edit without saving changes.
Clone	Method	Produces a second Recordset identical to the current Recordset.
Close	Method	Closes the Recordset.
CompareBookmarks	Method	Determines which of two bookmarks points to an earlier row in the Recordset.
CursorLocation	Property	Constant indicating the location of the cursor used for this Recordset. Can be adUseClient or adUseServer.
CursorType	Property	Constant indicating the type of cursor used for this Recordset. Can be adOpenDynamic, adOpenForwardOnly, adOpenKeyset, or adOpenStatic.
DataMember	Property	Specifies which member of a particular data source to bind this Recordset to when using bound Recordsets.
DataSource	Property	Specifies the data source to use for a bound Recordset.
Delete	Method	Deletes the current record.
EditMode	Property	Enumerated value indicating whether the current record is being edited. Can be adEditNone, adEditInProgress, adEditAdd, or adEditDelete.
EndOfRecordset	Event	Occurs when a MoveNext method fails because there are no more records in the Recordset.
EOF	Property	True if you have moved past the end of the Recordset.
FetchComplete	Event	Occurs when all the records in an asynchronous operation have been fetched.
FetchProgress	Event	Occurs periodically during an asynchronous record retrieval operation.
FieldChangeComplete	Event	Occurs after the value in a Field is changed.
Fields	Collection	Fields collection of the Recordset.
Filter	Property	Allows you to select a subset of the Recordset to work with.

continued on next page

TABLE A.3 CONTINUED: Recordset Object Details

Name	Type	Description
Find	Method	Finds a record matching some criterion.
GetRows	Method	Fills an array with records from a Recordset.
GetString	Method	Returns the Recordset as a delimited string.
Index	Property	Sets the index to use when performing a Seek operation.
LockType	Property	Controls the type of locks placed during editing. Can be adLockReadOnly, adLockPessimistic, adLockOptimistic, or adLockBatchOptimistic.
MarshalOptions	Property	Controls the marshalling of records to the server for a client-side Recordset. Can be adMarshalAll or adMarshalModifiedOnly.
MaxRecords	Property	Maximum number of records to be returned in the Recordset.
Move	Method	Moves to an offset from the current record (you can specify the number of records to move).
MoveComplete	Event	Occurs after the record pointer is repositioned.
MoveFirst	Method	Moves to the first record.
MoveLast	Method	Moves to the last record.
MoveNext	Method	Moves to the next record.
MovePrevious	Method	Moves to the previous record.
NextRecordset	Method	Returns the next Recordset from the current Command object.
Open	Method	Opens a Recordset.
PageCount	Property	Number of data pages in the Recordset.
PageSize	Property	Size of a single data page.
Properties	Collection	Collection of Property objects describing this Recordset.
RecordChangeComplete	Event	Occurs when a change to an entire record has been saved.
RecordCount	Property	Number of records in the Recordset. May return adUnknown (−1) if ADO cannot determine how many records are in the Recordset.
RecordsetChangeComplete	Event	Occurs when all changes to the Recordset have been committed.
Requery	Method	Reruns the original query that created the Recordset.
Resync	Method	Synchronizes the Recordset with the underlying data.
Save	Method	Persists the Recordset to a file.
Seek	Method	Searches for a record using an index. Can only be used on client-side Recordsets, and only if the provider supports this functionality.
Sort	Property	Specifies the Field(s) to sort the Recordset on.
Source	Property	Command or SQL query that's the source of the Recordset.

continued on next page

TABLE A.3 CONTINUED: Recordset Object Details

Name	Type	Description
State	Property	Constant indicating whether the object is open, closed, executing a Command, or fetching records.
Status	Property	Array of values containing the results of batch update operations.
StayInSync	Property	Applies to hierarchical Recordsets only. If True, the child Recordset pointers are automatically updated whenever a parent pointer is changed.
Supports	Method	Operator to determine which operations a Recordset supports.
Update	Method	Saves the changes made during an Edit or AddNew operation.
UpdateBatch	Method	Commits all pending changes on a batch cursor.
WillChangeField	Event	Occurs before a Field object's value is changed.
WillChangeRecord	Event	Occurs before a row is changed.
WillChangeRecordset	Event	Occurs before changes to a Recordset are committed.
WillMove	Event	Occurs before the record pointer is repositioned.

The Parameter Object

A Parameter object represents a single parameter for a Command object. Table A.4 lists the methods, properties, and collection for Parameter objects.

TABLE A.4: Parameter Object Details

Name	Type	Description
AppendChunk	Method	Stores data in a long binary Parameter.
Attributes	Property	Bitmapped set of attributes for the Parameter.
Direction	Property	Indicates whether a Parameter is input, output, both input and output, or a return value from a stored procedure.
Name	Property	Name of the Parameter.
NumericScale	Property	Scale (number of digits to the right of the decimal point) for a numeric Parameter.
Precision	Property	Precision (total number of digits) for a numeric Parameter.
Properties	Collection	The collection of Property objects describing this Parameter.
Size	Property	Maximum length of the data that a Parameter can hold.
Type	Property	Constant indicating the datatype of the Parameter.
Value	Property	Current value of the Parameter.

The Field Object

A Field object represents a single column of data from a Recordset object. Table A.5 shows the methods, properties, and collection available from the Field object.

TABLE A.5: Field Object Details

Name	Type	Description
ActualSize	Property	Size of the data actually stored in the Field.
AppendChunk	Property	Stores a chunk of data in a long binary Field.
Attributes	Property	Bitmapped value indicating some of the characteristics of the Field, including whether it may be updated and whether it is valid for long binary operations.
DataFormat	Property	For a bound Field, represents the DataFormat object that controls formatting for the Field.
DefinedSize	Property	Maximum data the Field can store.
GetChunk	Method	Retrieves a chunk of data from a long binary Field.
Name	Property	Name of the Field.
NumericScale	Property	Scale (number of digits to the right of the decimal point) for a numeric Field.
OriginalValue	Property	Value in the Field before another user changed it.
Precision	Property	Precision (total number of digits) for a numeric Field.
Properties	Collection	Collection of Property objects describing this Field.
Status	Property	Value containing the result of batch update operations.
Type	Property	Constant indicating the datatype of the Field.
UnderlyingValue	Property	Value currently stored in the database for this Field (might have changed since the Field's Value property was set).
Value	Property	Data stored in the Field.

The Record Object

The ADO Record object is designed to represent a row in a Recordset when the underlying OLE DB provider naturally supports a hierarchical data store rather than rows and columns. Table A.6 describes the Record object.

TABLE A.6: Record Object Details

Name	Type	Description
ActiveConnection	Property	The Connection that this Record was retrieved from.
Cancel	Method	Halts execution of an asynchronous operation.
Close	Method	Removes the Connection between this object and the original data source.
CopyRecord	Method	Copies the contents of the Record object to another location.
DeleteRecord	Method	Deletes the contents of the Record.
Fields	Collection	Field objects contained within this Record.
GetChildren	Method	Opens a Recordset containing the subdirectories and files contained below this Record.
Mode	Property	Controls the permissions to this Record. Takes the same values as the Mode property of the Connection object.
MoveRecord	Method	Moves the contents of this Record to another location.
Open	Method	Associates the Record with a data source.
ParentURL	Property	Returns the URL of the folder containing this Record.
Properties	Collection	Collection of Property objects describing this Record.
RecordType	Property	Indicates the type of data represented by this object. Can be adCollectionRecord, adSimpleRecord, or adStructDoc.
Source	Property	Contains the URL or Recordset from which this Record was derived.
State	Property	Contains information on the state of an asynchronous operation. Can be adStateClosed, adStateConnecting, adStateExecuting, adStateFetching, or adStateOpen.

The Stream Object

The Stream object represents binary data. Table A.7 describes the functionality of the Stream object.

TABLE A.7: Stream Object Details

Name	Type	Description
Cancel	Method	Cancels an asynchronous operation.
Charset	Property	Character set to be used when storing this Stream.
Close	Method	Disassociates this object from its data source.
CopyTo	Method	Copies the contents of this Stream to another Stream.

continued on next page

TABLE A.7 CONTINUED: Stream Object Details

Name	Type	Description
EOS	Property	True if the end of the Stream has been reached.
Flush	Method	Writes data from the ADO buffer to the hard drive.
LineSeparator	Property	Specifies the character used to separate logical lines within the Stream.
LoadFromFile	Method	Loads the contents of a local disk file into an open Stream.
Mode	Property	Specifies the permissions of the Stream.
Open	Method	Retrieves data into the Stream.
Position	Property	Location of the current position in the Stream.
Read	Method	Reads data from a binary Stream.
ReadText	Method	Reads data from a text Stream.
SaveToFile	Method	Writes the contents of the Stream to a local disk file.
SetEOS	Method	Sets the end of the Stream.
Size	Property	Number of bytes in the Stream.
SkipLine	Method	Skips a logical line when reading a text Stream.
State	Property	State of a Stream during an asynchronous operation.
Type	Property	Specifies whether the Stream is binary (adTypeBinary) or textual (adTypeText) information.
Write	Method	Writes data to a binary Stream.
WriteText	Method	Writes data to a text Stream.

The Error Object

An Error object represents a single error from a data provider or an error that's internal to ADO. Table A.8 lists the properties of the Error object.

TABLE A.8: Error Object Details

Name	Type	Description
Description	Property	Text of the Error
HelpContext	Property	Help topic for the Error
HelpFile	Property	Help file for the Error
NativeError	Property	Original provider-specific Error number
Number	Property	Error number
Source	Property	Object that raised the Error
SQLState	Property	Original ODBC SQLState constant

The Property Object

The Property object is the building block of the other ADO objects. That is, properties describe the other objects. Table A.9 lists the properties of a Property object.

TABLE A.9: Property Object Details

Name	Type	Description
Attributes	Property	Information about the Property. Can be a combination of adPropNotSupported (not supported by this provider), adPropRequired (must be specified before initializing the data source), adPropOptional, adPropRead (the user can read the Property), and adPropWrite (the user can change the value of the Property).
Name	Property	Name of the Property.
Type	Property	Datatype of the Property.
Value	Property	Current value of the Property.

APPENDIX B

The ADOX Object Model

- The Catalog Object

- The Table Object

- The Column Object

- The Index Object

- The Key Object

- The Group Object

- The User Object

- The Procedure Object

- The View Object

- The Command Object

I introduced the ADOX object model in Chapter 9, "Using ADOX for Data Definition and Security Operations." This object model, shown in Figure B.1, contains objects that implement all the functionality of ADOX. This appendix lists all the properties and methods that characterize these objects. For further information about these interfaces, refer to the MDAC SDK, which contains complete documentation on each one.

> **TIP** You can download the full MDAC SDK from www.microsoft.com/data/download.htm.

FIGURE B.1:
The ADOX object model

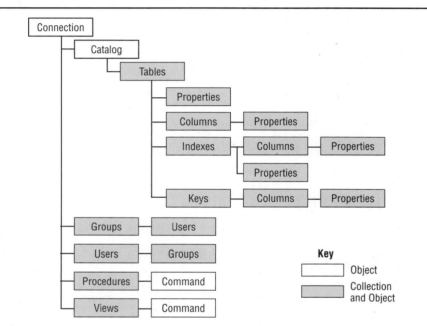

The Catalog Object

The Catalog object represents the schema (design information) of a data source. Table B.1 shows the methods and properties of the Catalog object.

TABLE B.1: Methods and Properties of the Catalog Object

Name	Type	Description
ActiveConnection	Property	ADO Connection through which schema information is to be retrieved.

continued on next page

TABLE B.1 CONTINUED: Methods and Properties of the Catalog Object

Name	Type	Description
Create	Method	Creates a new Catalog.
GetObjectOwner	Method	Determines the database user who owns a particular object.
Groups	Property	Pointer to the Groups collection.
Procedures	Property	Pointer to the Procedures collection.
SetObjectOwner	Method	Specifies the database user to own a particular object.
Tables	Property	Pointer to the Tables collection.
Users	Property	Pointer to the Users collection.
Views	Property	Pointer to the Views collection.

The Table Object

As you might expect, the Table object represents a table in a database. Table B.2 shows the properties of the Table object. The Table object has no methods.

TABLE B.2: Properties of the Table Object

Name	Type	Description
Columns	Property	Pointer to the Columns collection of the Table
DateCreated	Property	Original creation date and time of the Table
DateModified	Property	Date and time of the last design modification to the Table
Indexes	Property	Pointer to the Indexes collection of the Table
Name	Property	Name of the Table
Keys	Property	Pointer to the Keys collection of the Table
ParentCatalog	Property	Pointer to the Catalog containing the Table
Properties	Property	Pointer to the Properties collection of the Table
Type	Property	Type of the Table

The Column Object

The ADOX Column object represents a single column or field in a table, index, or key. Because of its general-purpose nature, not all Column properties apply to all instances of a Column object. For example, the RelatedColumn property is meaningful only for Columns that are part of Key objects. Table B.3 shows the properties of the Column object. The Column object has no methods.

TABLE B.3: Properties of the Column Object

Name	Type	Description
Attributes	Property	Returns the value adColFixed for a fixed-length Column, adColNullable if the Column can contain Null values, or the sum of these two constants for a fixed-length nullable Column.
DefinedSize	Property	Maximum length of the Column.
Name	Property	Name of this Column.
NumericScale	Property	Scale for a numeric Column.
ParentCatalog	Property	Pointer to the Catalog containing the Column.
Precision	Property	Precision for a numeric Column.
Properties	Property	Pointer to the Properties collection of the Column.
RelatedColumn	Property	Related Column if this Column is part of a Key.
SortOrder	Property	Sort order for the Column if this Column is part of an Index.
Type	Property	Datatype of the Column.

Table B.4 shows the possible values for the Type property of a Column object.

TABLE B.4: ADOX Datatypes for Column Objects

Constant	Value	Description
adBigInt	20	8-byte signed integer
adBinary	128	Raw binary data
adBoolean	11	Boolean
adBSTR	8	Null-terminated Unicode character string
adChar	129	Character string
adCurrency	6	Currency, stored with 4 digits to the right of the decimal point
adDate	7	Date/time
adDBDate	133	Date only, with no time value
adDBTime	134	Time only, with no date value
adDBTimeStamp	135	Time stamp
adDecimal	14	Decimal with fixed precision and scale
adDouble	5	Double-precision floating-point number
adError	10	32-bit error code
adFileTime	64	64-bit file time stamp
adGUID	72	Globally unique identifier
adInteger	3	4-byte signed integer
adLongVarBinary	205	Long binary

continued on next page

TABLE B.4 CONTINUED: ADOX Datatypes for Column Objects

Constant	Value	Description
adLongVarChar	201	Long string
adLongWVarChar	203	Long Unicode string
adNumeric	131	Decimal with fixed precision and scale
adSingle	4	Single-precision floating-point number
adSmallInt	2	2-byte signed integer
adTinyInt	16	1-byte signed integer
adUnsignedBigInt	21	8-byte unsigned integer
adUnsignedInt	19	4-byte unsigned integer
adUnsignedSmallInt	18	2-byte unsigned integer
adUnsignedTinyInt	17	1-byte unsigned integer
adUserDefined	132	User-defined datatype (UDT)
adVarBinary	204	Binary
adVarChar	200	String
adVarNumeric	139	Numeric
adVarWChar	202	Null-terminated Unicode character string
adWChar	130	Null-terminated Unicode character string

The Index Object

An ADOX Index object represents an index on a table. Table B.5 shows the properties of the Index object. The Index object has no methods.

TABLE B.5: Properties of the Index Object

Name	Type	Description
Clustered	Property	True if this is a clustered Index
Columns	Property	Pointer to the Columns collection of the Index
IndexNulls	Property	True if records with Nulls in their indexed Fields are indexed
Name	Property	Name of the Index
PrimaryKey	Property	True if the Index is the primary key of the Table
Properties	Property	Pointer to the Properties collection of the Index
Unique	Property	True if values in the Index must be unique

The Key Object

A Key object in ADOX represents a primary, foreign, or unique key on a table. Table B.6 shows the properties of the Key object. The Key object has no methods.

TABLE B.6: Properties of the Key Object

Name	Type	Description
Columns	Property	Pointer to the Columns collection of the Key
DeleteRule	Property	Constant indicating referential integrity rules for deletions
Name	Property	Name of this Key
RelatedTable	Property	Related table for a primary or foreign Key
Type	Property	Constant indicating whether this is a primary, foreign, or unique Key
UpdateRule	Property	Constant indicating referential integrity rules for updates

The Group Object

The ADOX Group object represents a single security group within a Jet database. Table B.7 shows the properties and methods of the Group object.

TABLE B.7: Properties and Methods of the Group Object

Name	Type	Description
GetPermissions	Method	Returns the current permissions of this Group on a database object.
Name	Property	Name of this Group.
ParentCatalog	Property	Pointer to the Catalog containing this Group.
Properties	Property	Collection of provider-defined properties.
SetPermissions	Method	Sets the permissions of this Group on a database object.
Users	Property	Pointer to a collection of Users in this Group.

The User Object

The ADOX User object represents a single user in a Jet database. Table B.8 shows the properties and methods of the User object.

TABLE B.8: Properties and Methods of the User Object

Name	Type	Description
ChangePassword	Method	Changes the password of this User.
GetPermissions	Method	Returns the current permissions of this User on a database object.
Groups	Property	Pointer to a collection of Groups containing this User.
Name	Property	Name of this User.
ParentCatalog	Property	Pointer to the Catalog containing this User.
Properties	Property	Collection of provider-defined properties.
SetPermissions	Method	Sets the permissions of this User on a database object.

The Procedure Object

The Procedure object in ADOX represents a stored procedure. Table B.9 shows the properties of the Procedure object. A Procedure object has no methods.

TABLE B.9: Properties of the Procedure Object

Name	Type	Description
Command	Property	Pointer to an associated Command object
DateCreated	Property	Original creation date and time of this Procedure
DateModified	Property	Last change date and time of this Procedure
Name	Property	Name of this Procedure

The View Object

The View object in ADOX represents a view. Table B.10 shows the properties of the View object. A View object has no methods.

TABLE B.10: Properties of the View Object

Name	Type	Description
Command	Property	Pointer to an associated Command object
DateCreated	Property	Original creation date and time of this View
DateModified	Property	Last change date and time of this View
Name	Property	Name of this View

The Command Object

If you look again at the ADOX object model diagram in Figure B.1, you'll see that the Procedure and View objects have an associated Command object (retrieved via the Command property of the parent object). In fact, this is a standard ADO Command object. The ADOX library doesn't contain its own Command object. You can see the details of the Command object in Table A.2 in Appendix A, "The ADO Object Model."

The ADO MD Object Model

- The Connection Object

- The Catalog Object

- The CubeDef Object

- The Dimension Object

- The Hierarchy Object

- The Level Object

- The Member Object

- The Cellset Object

- The Cell Object

- The Axis Object

- The Position Object

I introduced the ADO MD object model in Chapter 10, "Analyzing Multidimensional Data with ADO MD." This object model, shown in Figure C.1, contains objects that implement all the functionality of ADO MD. This appendix lists all the properties and methods that characterize these objects. For further information about these interfaces, refer to the MDAC SDK, which contains complete documentation on each one.

TIP   You can download the full MDAC SDK from www.microsoft.com/data/download.htm.

FIGURE C.1:

The ADO MD object model

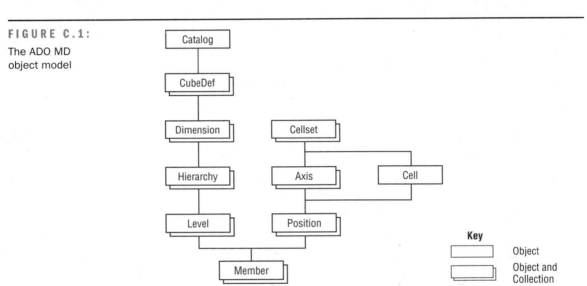

The Connection Object

The Connection object, although not formally a part of the ADO MD library, is essential to using ADO MD. The ADO MD library doesn't contain its own Connection object. You can see the details of the Command object in Table A.1 in Appendix A, "The ADO Object Model."

The Catalog Object

The Catalog object represents the concept of an OLAP database in its entirety, containing all the cubes and their underlying components. Table C.1 details the interface of the Catalog object.

TABLE C.1: Catalog Object Details

Name	Type	Description
ActiveConnection	Property	The connection string used to retrieve the Catalog object
CubeDefs	Collection	A collection containing a CubeDef object for each of the cubes within the OLAP database
Name	Property	The name of the Catalog (i.e., the name of the OLAP database)

The CubeDef Object

The CubeDef object represents the definition of a particular OLAP cube and its underlying dimensions. Table C.2 lists the interface details of the CubeDef object.

TABLE C.2: CubeDef Object Details

Name	Type	Description
Description	Property	Provides a brief description of the OLAP cube as set within OLAP Manager (read-only).
Dimensions	Collection	A collection containing a Dimension object for every dimension within the cube (read-only).
GetSchemaObject	Method	Retrieves a Dimension, Hierarchy, Level, or Member object directly, without the need to navigate through the intervening levels of the object model.
Name	Property	Contains the name of the cube, as used for referencing purposes (read-only).
Properties	Collection	A collection containing an object for each property relating to the cube that has been exposed by the data provider (read-only).

The Dimension Object

The Dimension object contains information about an individual dimension within a cube. Table C.3 shows the properties and collections available within the Dimension object.

TABLE C.3: Dimension Object Details

Name	Type	Description
Description	Property	Provides a description of the Dimension as set within OLAP Manager (read-only).

continued on next page

TABLE C.3 CONTINUED: Dimension Object Details

Name	Type	Description
Hierarchies	Collection	A collection containing a Hierarchy object for every hierarchy within the Dimension (for Dimensions not using hierarchies, this collection contains only a single Hierarchy containing all the levels) (read-only).
Name	Property	Contains the name of the Dimension, as used for referencing purposes (read-only).
Properties	Collection	A collection containing an object for each property relating to the Dimension that has been exposed by the data provider (read-only).
UniqueName	Property	The fully qualified name for a particular Dimension, in the form *[dimension]* (read-only).

The Hierarchy Object

The Hierarchy object contains information for any hierarchies that are stored within the Dimension. Table C.4 lists the properties and collections available within the Hierarchy object.

TABLE C.4: Hierarchy Object Details

Name	Type	Description
Description	Property	Provides a description of the hierarchy as set within OLAP Manager or DSO (read-only).
Levels	Collection	A collection containing a Level object for every level within the Hierarchy (read-only).
Name	Property	Contains the name of the Hierarchy, as used for referencing purposes (read-only).
Properties	Collection	A collection containing an object for each property relating to the Hierarchy that has been exposed by the data provider (read-only).
UniqueName	Property	The fully qualified name for a particular Hierarchy, in the form *[dimension].[hierarchy]* (read-only).

The Level Object

The Level object represents an individual level within a Dimension. Table C.5 shows the properties and collections available for this object.

TABLE C.5: Level Object Details

Name	Type	Description
Caption	Property	A display name for the Level (read-only).
Depth	Property	A value indicating the depth of the Level or the number of Levels between the current Level and the parent Hierarchy (read-only).
Description	Property	Provides a description of the Level as set within OLAP Manager or DSO (read-only).
Members	Collection	A collection containing a Member object for every member within the Level (read-only).
Name	Property	Contains the name of the Level, as used for referencing purposes (read-only).
Properties	Collection	A collection containing an object for each property relating to the Level that has been exposed by the data provider (read-only).
UniqueName	Property	The fully qualified name for a particular Level, in the form *[dimension].[level]* (read-only).

The Member Object

The Member object is the bottom of the hierarchy of schema objects, containing actual information from the underlying database. Table C.6 shows the properties and collections available for the Member object.

TABLE C.6: Member Object Details

Name	Type	Description
Caption	Property	A display name for the Member (read-only).
ChildCount	Property	Returns an estimate of the number of children below this Member (read-only).
Children	Collection	A collection of the Member's children containing a Member object for each child (read-only).
Description	Property	Provides a description of the Member if set within OLAP Manager or DSO (read-only).
DrilledDown	Property	A Boolean value indicating whether there are any child Members of this object; this is faster than using ChildCount to return a number of children (read-only).
LevelDepth	Property	Returns the number of levels between the Member and the root Member (read-only).

continued on next page

TABLE C.6 CONTINUED: Member Object Details

Name	Type	Description
LevelName	Property	Returns the name of the Level to which the Member belongs (read-only).
Name	Property	Contains the name of the Member, as used for referencing purposes (read-only).
Parent	Property	Contains the parent Member, if one exists (read-only).
ParentSameAsPrev	Property	A Boolean value indicating whether the parent of the Member is the same as the Member immediately before it (read-only).
Properties	Collection	A collection containing an object for each property relating to the Member that has been exposed by the data provider (read-only).
Type	Property	A value representing the type of Member (regular, measure, formula, or container), as described in the MemberTypeEnum enumeration (read-only).
UniqueName	Property	The fully qualified name for a particular Member, in the form *[dimension].[hierarchy].[level].[member]* (read-only).

The Cellset Object

In the same way as the ADO object model contains a Recordset object that can be used to store the results of a (relational) SQL query, ADO MD contains an equivalent Cellset object, which can store the results of a multidimensional MDX query. Table C.7 shows the interface of the Cellset object.

TABLE C.7: Cellset Object Details

Name	Type	Description
ActiveConnection	Property	A valid OLE DB connection string or ADO Connection object, against which MDX queries should be executed.
Axes	Collection	A collection containing an Axis object for each of the axes within the result set.
Close	Method	Closes the currently open connection.
FilterAxis	Property	An Axis object containing information about the slicer dimensions used to return this Cellset.
Item	Property	An individual Cell, specified by the index or array.

continued on next page

TABLE C.7 CONTINUED: Cellset Object Details

Name	Type	Description
Open	Method	Opens the Connection and returns a Cellset based on the results of an MDX query against the active Connection.
Properties	Collection	A collection containing an object for each property relating to the Cellset that has been exposed by the data provider (read-only).
Source	Property	Sets the MDX query used to generate the resultant Cellset.
State	Property	Indicates whether the Cellset is open or closed.

The Cell Object

The Cell object represents a single unit of the data contained within the Cellset (and is therefore analogous to the Field object within ADO). Table C.8 shows the properties and collections that can be accessed on the Cell object.

TABLE C.8: Cell Object Details

Name	Type	Description
FormattedValue	Property	Returns a string containing the value in the appropriate format for that value (e.g., "2,187") as defined by the FORMAT_STRING property associated with a Cell.
Ordinal	Property	A number representing the index of the Cell within its parent Cellset (starting with 0).
Positions	Collection	A collection containing the individual positions that together represent the location of the Cell on an axis.
Properties	Collection	A collection of extended properties relating to the Cell; this is populated by the appropriate OLE DB provider.
Value	Property	The value of a Cell in raw, unformatted form (e.g., 2187).

The Axis Object

An Axis object corresponds to an individual axis from an MDX query. Table C.9 shows the interface details of the Axis object.

TABLE C.9: Axis Object Details

Name	Type	Description
DimensionCount	Property	Returns the number of dimensions contained within the Axis.
Name	Property	Returns the name of the Axis, if stored.
Positions	Collection	A collection containing a Position object for each slice or point within the Axis.
Properties	Collection	A collection containing extended properties for the Axis object as exposed by the provider.

The Position Object

You've seen already that an axis contains one or more dimensions and that the corresponding Axis object contains a collection of positions. An individual position is simply a point along the axis. Table C.10 shows the interface details of the Position object.

TABLE C.10: Position Object Details

Name	Type	Description
Members	Collection	A collection containing a Member object for each member contained within the Position
Ordinal	Property	A number representing the index of the Position within the Axis (read-only)

APPENDIX D

The ADO.NET Object Model

- About Data Provider Objects

- The Connection Object

- The Command Object

- The DataReader Object

- The DataAdapter Object

- The DataSet Object

- The DataTable Object

- The DataRelation Object

- The DataRow Object

- The DataColumn Object

- The Constraint Object

- The DataView Object

I introduced the ADO.NET object model in Chapter 14, "Using the ADO.NET Objects to Retrieve Data." This object model, shown in Figure D.1, contains objects that implement all of the functionality of ADO.NET. This appendix lists the members (methods, properties, and events) that characterize the major objects in the ADO.NET object model. For further information about these interfaces, refer to the .NET Framework help file, which contains complete documentation on each one.

FIGURE D.1:

The ADO.NET object model

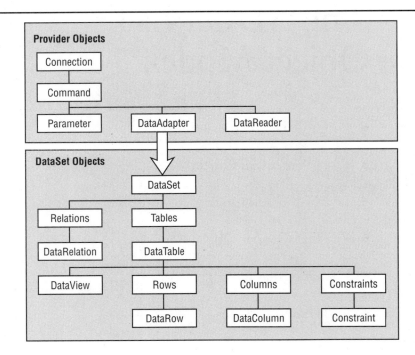

NOTE This appendix doesn't list interface members that are inherited from more general classes within the .NET Framework. For example, every class that inherits from the generic Object class has Dispose, Equals, and GetHashCode methods, which are not covered here. Instead, the tables in this appendix concentrate on the data-access functionality that is unique to the ADO.NET classes.

About Data Provider Objects

Depending on how you look at it, there are either four or twelve main data provider objects. How can this be? The answer is that there are four important types of data provider objects, but each of these objects is implemented within several .NET namespaces. These four objects are as follows:

- Connection
- Command
- DataReader
- DataAdapter

The .NET data provider namespaces are as follows:

- System.Data.OleDb
- System.Data.SqlClient
- System.Data.Odbc

Thus, there are twelve objects to learn about, as shown in Table D.1. But the only major difference between the objects is the data sources with which they work. For example, the OleDbConnection, SqlConnection, and OdbcConnection all implement the same methods and properties. The difference is that they are used with OLE DB data sources, SQL Server data sources, and ODBC data sources, respectively.

TABLE D.1: Core Data Provider Objects

Object	Implementations
Connection	OleDbConnection, SqlConnection, OdbcConnection
Command	OleDbCommand, SqlCommand, OdbcCommand
DataReader	OleDbDataReader, SqlDataReader, OdbcDataReader
DataAdapter	OleDbDataAdapter, SqlDataAdapter, OdbcDataAdapter

In this appendix, I'll refer to the generic object names. There are sometimes minor differences between the implementations of these objects. For example, both the OdbcConnection and the OleDbConnection implement a ReleaseObjectPool method, which is not shared by the SqlConnection object. These differences are covered in the sections on the individual objects.

NOTE Data providers also implement some helper objects, such as the Parameter object, which can be used to supply parameters to a Command object. Like the objects discussed above, these helper objects come in multiple versions.

The Connection Object

The Connection object in ADO.NET, just like its namesake in ADO, represents a single persistent connection to a data source. Table D.2 lists the members of this object.

TABLE D.2: Connection Object Details

Name	Type	Description
BeginTransaction	Method	Starts a new transaction on this Connection.
ChangeDatabase	Method	Switches current databases.
Close	Method	Closes the Connection and returns it to the connection pool.
ConnectionString	Property	Connection string that determines the data source to be used for this Connection.
ConnectionTimeout	Property	Number of seconds to wait before timing out when connecting.
CreateCommand	Method	Returns a new Command object.
Database	Property	Name of the current database open on this Connection.
DataSource	Property	Name of the current server for this Connection.
Driver	Property	ODBC driver in use by this Connection. Applies to OdbcConnection only.
GetOleDbSchemaTable	Method	Returns schema information from the data source. Applies to OleDbConnection only.
InfoMessage	Event	Fires when the server sends an informational message.
Open	Method	Opens the Connection.
PacketSize	Property	Size of network packets (in bytes) used by this Connection. Applies to SqlConnection only.
Provider	Property	OLE DB provider in use by this Connection. Applies to OleDbConnection only.
ReleaseObjectPool	Method	Releases Connections held in the connection pool. Applies to OdbcConnection and OleDbConnection.
ServerVersion	Property	String containing the version number of the server.
State	Property	State of the Connection.
StateChange	Event	Fires when the state of the Connection changes.
WorkstationID	Property	String that identifies the connection client. Applies to SqlConnection only.

The Command Object

The Command object represents a string (such as a SQL statement or a stored procedure name) that can be executed through a Connection. Table D.3 lists the members of the Command object.

TABLE D.3: Command Object Details

Name	Type	Description
Cancel	Method	Cancels execution of the Command.
CommandText	Property	Statement to be executed at the data source.
CommandTimeout	Property	Number of seconds to wait for a Command to execute.
CommandType	Property	An enumeration indicating the type of Command. Possible values are StoredProcedure, TableDirect, and Text. You can also omit this property, and the data provider will determine the appropriate Command type.
Connection	Property	Connection through which this Command will be executed.
CreateParameter	Method	Returns a new Parameter object.
DesignTimeVisible	Property	True if the object should be displayed in the Windows Forms Designer.
CreateParameter	Method	Creates a new Parameter object for the Command.
ExecuteNonQuery	Method	Executes a Command that does not return results.
ExecuteReader	Method	Executes a Command and puts the results in a DataReader object.
ExecuteScalar	Method	Executes a Command and returns the value of the first column of the first row of results. Any other results are discarded.
ExecuteXmlReader	Method	Executes a Command and puts the results in an XmlReader object. Applies to SqlCommand only.
Parameters	Property	Collection of Parameter objects (if any) for this Command.
Prepare	Method	Prepares the Command for faster execution.
ResetCommandTimeout	Method	Resets the CommandTimeout property to its default value.
Transaction	Property	Gets or sets the transaction in which this Command executes.
UpdatedRowSource	Property	Specifies how Command results should be applied to rows being updated.

The DataReader Object

The DataReader gives you a "firehose" set of results based on a Command. You can create a DataReader only from a Command (not by declaring it using the New keyword), and you can only move forward in the data. The DataReader represents the fastest, but least flexible, way to retrieve data in ADO.NET. Table D.4 lists the members of the DataReader object.

TABLE D.4: DataReader Object Details

Name	Type	Description
Close	Method	Closes the DataReader.
Depth	Property	Depth of nesting for the current row of the DataReader.
FieldCount	Property	Number of columns in the current row of the DataReader.
GetBoolean	Method	Gets a Boolean value from the specified column.
GetByte	Method	Gets a byte value from the specified column.
GetBytes	Method	Gets a stream of bytes from the specified column.
GetChar	Method	Gets a character from the specified column.
GetChars	Method	Gets a stream of characters from the specified column.
GetDataTypeName	Method	Gets the name of the source datatype for a column.
GetDateTime	Method	Gets a date/time value from the specified column.
GetDecimal	Method	Gets a decimal value from the specified column.
GetDouble	Method	Gets a double value from the specified column.
GetFieldType	Method	Gets the ADO.NET field type for a column.
GetFloat	Method	Gets a floating-point value from the specified column.
GetGuid	Method	Gets a GUID from the specified column.
GetInt16	Method	Gets a 16-bit integer from the specified column.
GetInt32	Method	Gets a 32-bit integer from the specified column.
GetInt64	Method	Gets a 64-bit integer from the specified column.
GetName	Method	Gets the name of the specified column.
GetOrdinal	Method	Gets the column ordinal, given the column name.
GetSchemaTable	Method	Returns schema information for the DataReader object.
GetSqlBinary	Method	Gets a binary value from the specified column (SqlDataReader only).
GetSqlBoolean	Method	Gets a Boolean value from the specified column (SqlDataReader only).
GetSqlByte	Method	Gets a byte value from the specified column (SqlDataReader only).
GetSqlDateTime	Method	Gets a date/time value from the specified column (SqlDataReader only).
GetSqlDecimal	Method	Gets a decimal value from the specified column (SqlDataReader only).
GetSqlDouble	Method	Gets a double value from the specified column (SqlDataReader only).
GetSqlGuid	Method	Gets a GUID value from the specified column (SqlDataReader only).

continued on next page

TABLE D.4 CONTINUED: DataReader Object Details

Name	Type	Description
GetSqlInt16	Method	Gets a 16-bit integer value from the specified column (SqlDataReader only).
GetSqlInt32	Method	Gets a 32-bit integer value from the specified column (SqlDataReader only).
GetSqlInt64	Method	Gets a 64-bit integer value from the specified column (SqlDataReader only).
GetSqlMoney	Method	Gets a money value from the specified column (SqlDataReader only).
GetSqlSingle	Method	Gets a single value from the specified column (SqlDataReader only).
GetSqlString	Method	Gets a string value from the specified column (SqlDataReader only).
GetSqlValue	Method	Gets a SQL Variant value from the specified column (SqlDataReader only).
GetSqlValues	Method	Gets an entire row of data into an array of SQL Variants (SqlDataReader only).
GetString	Method	Gets a string value from the specified column.
GetTimeSpan	Method	Gets a time value from the specified column.
GetValue	Method	Gets a value from the specified column in its native format.
GetValues	Method	Gets an entire row of data into an array of objects.
IsClosed	Property	A Boolean value that indicates whether the DataReader is closed.
IsDbNull	Method	Indicates whether the specified column contains a Null.
Item	Property	Gets a value from the specified column in its native format.
NextResult	Method	Retrieves the next result set from the Command object.
Read	Method	Loads the next row of data into the DataReader object.
RecordsAffected	Property	Number of rows changed by the DataReader's SQL statement.

The DataAdapter Object

The DataAdapter object provides the essential link between the data provider objects and the DataSet (which I'll discuss in the next section). The DataAdapter is a two-way pipeline between the data as it's stored and the data in a more abstract form that's designed for manipulation. Table D.5 lists the members of the DataAdapter object.

TABLE D.5: DataAdapter Object Details

Name	Type	Description
AcceptChangesDuringFill	Property	If True, all rows in the DataSet are marked as committed when they're added with the Fill method.
ContinueUpdateOnError	Property	If True, updates continue even after updating a single row fails. Not available for OdbcDataAdapter.
DeleteCommand	Property	SQL statement used to delete records from the data source.
Fill	Method	Transfers data from the data source to the DataSet.
FillError	Event	Fires when an error occurs during the Fill method.
FillSchema	Method	Adjusts the schema of the DataSet to match the schema of the data source.
GetFillParameters	Method	Gets any parameters supplied to the SelectCommand.
InsertCommand	Property	SQL statement used to insert records into the data source.
MissingMappingAction	Property	Determines the action to take when there is no matching column for incoming data.
MissingSchemaAction	Property	Determines the action to take when the existing schema does not match incoming data.
RowUpdated	Event	Fired during the Update method just after a row is updated.
RowUpdating	Event	Fired during the Update method just before a row is updated.
SelectCommand	Property	SQL statement used to select records from the data source.
TableMappings	Property	Specifies the mapping between tables in the data source and DataTables in the DataSet.
Update	Method	Transfers data from the DataSet to the data source.
UpdateCommand	Property	SQL statement used to update records in the data source.

The DataSet Object

The DataSet object is a memory-resident representation of data. It's designed to be self-contained and easy to move around between the various components of a .NET application. Table D.6 lists the members of the DataSet object.

TABLE D.6: DataSet Object Details

Name	Type	Description
AcceptChanges	Method	Commits all changes made to the DataSet since it was loaded or since the previous call to AcceptChanges.
BeginInit	Method	Suspends error checking while the DataSet is being initialized.
CaseSensitive	Property	If True, string comparisons within the DataSet are case-sensitive.
Clear	Method	Removes all data in the DataSet.
Clone	Method	Clones the schema of the DataSet.
Copy	Method	Copies both the schema and the data of the DataSet.
DataSetName	Property	Name of the DataSet.
DefaultViewManager	Property	Gets a default DataView for the DataSet.
EndInit	Method	Ends initialization and turns on error checking.
EnforceConstraints	Property	If True, constraints are enforced during updates.
ExtendedProperties	Property	A collection of user-defined string properties.
GetChanges	Method	Gets a DataSet containing only the changed rows from this DataSet.
GetXml	Method	Returns an XML representation of the DataSet.
GetXmlSchema	Method	Returns an XSD schema of the DataSet.
HasChanges	Method	Returns True if the DataSet has changes that have not yet been committed.
HasErrors	Property	Returns True if there are errors in any of the DataRows in the DataSet.
InferXmlSchema	Method	Infers an XML schema for the DataSet.
Locale	Property	Locale to use for string comparisons.
Merge	Method	Merges two DataSets.
MergeFailed	Event	Fires when the Merge method fails.
Namespace	Property	Namespace for this DataSet.
Prefix	Property	XML prefix for this DataSet.
ReadXml	Method	Loads the DataSet from an XML file.
ReadXmlSchema	Method	Loads the DataSet schema from an XSD file.
RejectChanges	Method	Discards all changes made to the DataSet since it was loaded or since the previous call to AcceptChanges.
Relations	Property	The collection of DataRelation objects within the DataSet.
Reset	Property	Returns the DataSet to its original state.
Tables	Property	The collection of DataTable objects within the DataSet.
WriteXml	Method	Writes the DataSet out as XML.
WriteXmlSchema	Method	Writes the DataSet schema out as XSD.

The DataTable Object

As you might guess from the name, the DataTable object represents a single table within a DataSet. A DataSet can contain multiple DataTables. Table D.7 lists the members of the DataTable object.

TABLE D.7: DataTable Object Details

Name	Type	Description
AcceptChanges	Method	Commits all changes to this DataTable since it was loaded or since the last call to AcceptChanges.
BeginInit	Method	Suspends error checking while the DataTable is being initialized.
BeginLoadData	Method	Turns off notifications, index maintenance, and constraint checking while loading data.
CaseSensitive	Property	Returns True if string comparisons within this DataTable are case-sensitive.
ChildRelations	Property	The collection of DataRelation objects that refer to children of this DataTable.
Clear	Method	Clears all data from the DataTable.
Clone	Method	Clones the schema of the DataTable.
ColumnChanged	Event	Fires when the data in any row of a specified column has been changed.
ColumnChanging	Event	Fires when the data in any row of a specified column is about to change.
Columns	Property	The collection of DataColumn objects in this DataTable.
Compute	Method	Computes an expression on a set of rows.
Constraints	Property	The collection of Constraint objects for this table.
Copy	Method	Copies both the schema and the data of the DataTable.
DataSet	Property	The DataSet that contains this DataTable.
DefaultView	Property	The default DataView for this DataTable.
DisplayExpression	Property	Value used to represent this DataTable on the user interface.
EndInit	Method	Ends initialization and turns on error checking.
EndLoadData	Method	Turns on notifications, index maintenance, and constraint checking.
GetChanges	Method	Gets a DataTable containing only the changed rows from this DataTable.
GetErrors	Method	Gets an array of DataRow objects containing errors.
ExtendedProperties	Property	Collection of user-defined string properties.
HasErrors	Property	Returns True if there are errors in any of the DataRows in the DataTable.

continued on next page

TABLE D.7 CONTINUED: DataTable Object Details

Name	Type	Description
ImportRow	Method	Imports a DataRow into this DataTable.
LoadDataRow	Method	Finds and updates a row in this DataTable.
Locale	Property	Locale to use for string comparisons.
MinimumCapacity	Property	Starting size of the DataTable.
Namespace	Property	Namespace for this DataTable.
NewRow	Method	Creates a new, blank row in the DataTable.
ParentRelations	Property	The collection of DataRelation objects that refer to parents of this DataTable.
Prefix	Property	XML prefix for this DataTable.
PrimaryKey	Property	Array of columns that provide the primary key for this DataTable.
RejectChanges	Method	Discards all changes to this DataTable since it was loaded or since the last call to AcceptChanges.
Reset	Method	Returns the DataTable to its original state.
RowChanged	Event	Fires when any data in a DataRow is changed.
RowChanging	Event	Fires when any data in a DataRow is about to change.
RowDeleted	Event	Fires when a row is deleted.
RowDeleting	Event	Fires when a row is about to be deleted.
Rows	Property	The collection of DataRow objects in this DataTable.
Select	Method	Selects an array of DataRow objects meeting specified criteria.
TableName	Property	The name of this DataTable.

WARNING Unlike other object models with which you may be familiar, the ADO.NET object model doesn't necessarily use the same name for a property and the object that it returns. For example, the Rows property of a DataTable returns a DataRowCollection object, which contains a collection of DataRows. In practice, this seldom causes confusion because you're less likely to operate directly on the collection objects.

The DataRelation Object

The DataRelation object represents a relation between two DataTables. Table D.8 lists the members of this object.

TABLE D.8: DataRelation Object Details

Name	Type	Description
ChildColumns	Property	The collection of DataColumn objects that define the child side of the DataRelation.
ChildKeyConstraint	Property	Returns the foreign key constraint for the DataRelation.
ChildTable	Property	Returns the child DataTable for the DataRelation.
DataSet	Property	The DataSet that contains this DataRelation.
ExtendedProperties	Property	The collection of user-defined string properties.
ParentColumns	Property	The collection of DataColumn objects that define the parent side of the DataRelation.
ParentKeyConstraint	Property	Returns the primary key constraint for the DataRelation.
ParentTable	Property	Returns the parent DataTable for the DataRelation.
RelationName	Property	Name of the DataRelation.

The DataRow Object

The DataRow object provides row-by-row access to the data contained in a DataTable. Table D.9 lists the members of the DataRow object.

TABLE D.9: DataRow Object Details

Name	Type	Description
AcceptChanges	Property	Commits changes made to this row since the last time AcceptChanges was called.
BeginEdit	Method	Starts editing the DataRow.
CancelEdit	Method	Discards an edit in progress.
ClearErrors	Method	Clears all errors for the DataRow.
Delete	Method	Deletes the DataRow from its parent DataTable.
EndEdit	Method	Ends an editing session on the DataRow.
GetChildRows	Method	Gets the child rows related to this DataRow.
GetColumnError	Method	Gets the error description for a column.
GetColumnsInError	Method	Gets an array of DataColumns that contain errors.
GetParentRow	Method	Gets the parent row related to this DataRow.
GetParentRows	Method	Gets the parent rows related to this DataRow.
HasErrors	Property	Returns True if the DataRow contains an error.

continued on next page

TABLE D.9 CONTINUED: DataRow Object Details

Name	Type	Description
HasVersion	Method	Checks for the existence of a specified version of the DataRow.
IsNull	Method	Indicates whether a specified column contains a Null.
Item	Property	Returns the data from a particular column of the DataRow.
ItemArray	Property	Returns the data from the entire DataRow as an array.
IsNull	Method	Returns True if a specified column is Null.
RejectChanges	Method	Discards changes made to this row since the last time AcceptChanges was called.
RowError	Property	The error description for the DataRow.
RowState	Property	Returns information on the current state of the DataRow (for example, whether the row has been modified).
SetColumnError	Method	Sets the error description for a column.
SetParentRow	Method	Sets the parent row of this DataRow.
Table	Property	The DataTable that contains this DataRow.

The DataColumn Object

The DataColumn object represents a single column in a DataTable. Table D.10 lists the members of the DataColumn object.

TABLE D.10: DataColumn Object Details

Name	Type	Description
AllowDbNull	Property	Returns True if the DataColumn can contain Nulls.
AutoIncrement	Property	Returns True if the DataColumn automatically assigns new values to new rows.
AutoIncrementSeed	Property	Starting value for an AutoIncrement DataColumn.
AutoIncrementStep	Property	Increment value for an AutoIncrement DataColumn.
Caption	Property	Caption for the DataColumn.
ColumnMapping	Property	Controls the mapping between the DataColumn and the underlying data.
ColumnName	Property	Name of the DataColumn.
DataType	Property	Datatype for the DataColumn.
DefaultValue	Property	Default value for this DataColumn in new rows of the DataTable.

continued on next page

TABLE D.10 CONTINUED: DataColumn Object Details

Name	Type	Description
Expression	Property	Expression used to filter rows or calculate the DataColumn.
MaxLength	Property	Maximum length of a text DataColumn.
Namespace	Property	Namespace for the DataColumn.
Ordinal	Property	Position of the DataColumn in the Columns collection of the parent DataTable.
Prefix	Property	XML prefix for the DataColumn.
ReadOnly	Property	Returns True if the value in the DataColumn cannot be changed after it has been set.
Unique	Property	Returns True if values in the DataColumn must be unique.

The Constraint Object

The Constraint object comes in two varieties. The ForeignKeyConstraint object represents a foreign key, while the UniqueConstraint object represents a unique constraint. Table D.11 lists the members of the Constraint objects.

TABLE D.11: Constraint Object Details

Name	Type	Description
AcceptRejectRule	Property	Constant that specifies cascading commit behavior. Applies to ForeignKeyConstraint only.
Columns	Property	Array of DataColumns that are affected by this Constraint.
DeleteRule	Property	Constant that specifies cascading delete behavior. Applies to ForeignKeyConstraint only.
ConstraintName	Property	Name of the Constraint.
ExtendedProperties	Property	Collection of user-defined string properties.
RelatedColumns	Property	Collection of DataColumns that are the parent of this Constraint. Applies to ForeignKeyConstraint only.
RelatedTable	Property	DataTable that is the parent table of this Constraint. Applies to ForeignKeyConstraint only.
IsPrimaryKey	Property	Returns True if this Constraint represents a primary key. Applies to UniqueConstraint only.
UpdateRule	Property	Constant that specifies cascading update behavior. Applies to ForeignKeyConstraint only.

The DataView Object

The DataView object represents a view of the data contained in a DataTable. Table D.12 lists the members of the DataView object.

TABLE D.12: DataView Object Details

Name	Type	Description
AddNew	Method	Adds a new row to the DataView.
AllowDelete	Property	Returns True if deletions can be performed via this DataView.
AllowEdit	Property	Returns True if updates can be performed via this DataView.
AllowNew	Property	Returns True if new rows can be added via this DataView.
ApplyDefaultSort	Property	Returns True if the DataView is sorted according to its default sort.
BeginInit	Method	Suspends error checking while the DataView is being initialized.
CopyTo	Method	Copies items into an array.
Count	Property	Number of records contained in this DataView.
DataViewManager	Property	The DataViewManager associated with this DataView.
Delete	Method	Deletes a row from the DataView.
EndInit	Method	Ends initialization and turns on error checking.
Find	Method	Searches for a specified row in the DataView.
FindRows	Method	Returns an array of rows matching a filter expression.
GetEnumerator	Method	Gets an enumerator for this DataView.
Item	Property	Returns the data from a particular row of the DataView in a DataRowView object.
ListChanged	Event	Fires when the data in this DataView changes.
RowFilter	Property	Filter expression to limit the data returned in the DataView.
RowStateFilter	Property	Filter to limit the data returned in the DataView by the state of the rows.
Sort	Property	Sorts columns and order for the DataView.
Table	Property	DataTable from which this DataView is derived.

Index

Note to the Reader: Throughout this index **boldfaced** page numbers indicate primary discussions of a topic. *Italicized* page numbers indicate illustrations.

C

O

W

X

TELL US WHAT YOU THINK!

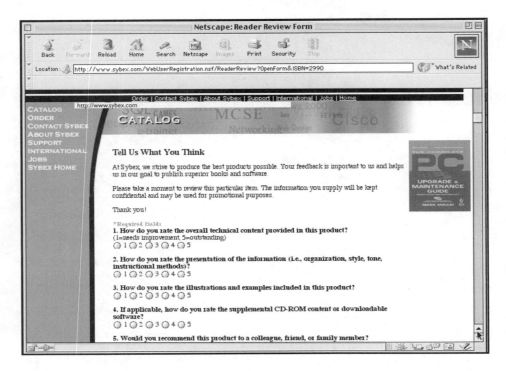

Your feedback is critical to our efforts to provide you with the best books and software on the market. Tell us what you think about the products you've purchased. It's simple:

1. Visit the Sybex website
2. Go to the product page
3. Click on **Submit a Review**
4. Fill out the questionnaire and comments
5. Click **Submit**

With your feedback, we can continue to publish the highest quality computer books and software products that today's busy IT professionals deserve.

www.sybex.com

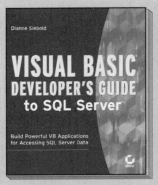

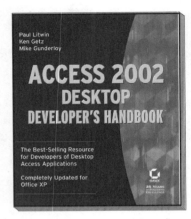
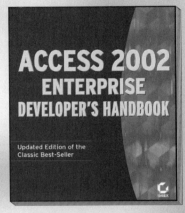